MEDIA MESSAGES

MEDIA MESSAGES

What Film, Television, and Popular Music Teach Us About Race, Class, Gender, and Sexual Orientation

SECOND EDITION

Linda Holtzman

Webster University

Leon Sharpe

Webster University

With the assistance of Joseph Farand Gardner

M.E.Sharpe
Armonk, New York
London, England

Library of Congress Cataloging-in-Publication Data

Holtzman, Linda, 1949–
Media messages: what film, television, and popular music teach us about race, class, gender, and sexual
orientation / by Linda Holtzman and Leon Sharpe; with Joseph Farand Gardner. — Second edition
    p. cm.
Includes bibliographical references and index.
ISBN: 978-0-7656-1756-9 (cloth : alk. paper)—ISBN: 978-0-7656-1757-6 (pbk. : alk. paper)

1. Mass media and race relations—United States. 2. Mass media and sex—United States. 3. Mass media—
Social aspects—United States. 4. Popular culture—United States. 5. Social classes—United States.
6. United States—Social conditions—1980– I. Sharpe, Leon, 1951– II. Gardner, Joseph Farand, 1975–
III. Title.

P94.5.M552U646 2014
302.23—dc23   2013030673

Table of Contents

Special Features and Activities

Preface

This is a book about ideas, histories, theories, ideologies, beliefs, personal experiences, and values. It is academic, and it is deeply personal. It is about stories and the media through which those stories are told, and it is about the messages conveyed through those stories.

We have offered information and perspectives that often go untold in our families, schools, neighborhoods, and places of worship—messages that tend to be invisible on our televisions and in movie theaters and inaudible on our radios and iPods. We have explored the various ways that we all arrive at what we know to be "fact," as well as how we develop deep convictions about human diversity, equality, and oppression. In order to understand this process, we have examined parts of our own stories, and we have encouraged readers to think about their stories as well.

While we have tried to be accurate and fair with this information, we do not claim to be objective—nor do we think that objectivity is possible or desirable. We are addressing emotionally charged and value-laden topics. In this context, claims of objectivity and declarations of truth often lead to oversimplifications and distortions. On the other hand, the explicit and thorough scrutiny of the sources and derivations of our beliefs and values can lead us to deeper and more complex levels of understanding about gender, class, race, sexual orientation, identity, power, and, ultimately, ourselves.

The fabrication of "the other" has caused enormous pain and tragedy throughout history: the death of millions of Africans at sea as they were taken from their homes and brought to the United States to be sold and enslaved; the murder of millions of Jews in the Holocaust; the so-called ethnic cleansing in Bosnia and other nations; the colonization and appropriation of the land and resources of indigenous peoples; the abuse, rape, and trafficking of women; and the ridiculing, bullying, brutalization, and murder of people who are lesbian, gay, bisexual, or transgender.

How is it that individuals who think of themselves as and otherwise appear to be decent people can be convinced that members of a group who are different from them are somehow inferior or even less than human? On the other hand, what motivates other individuals, in the midst of the most violent, repressive, and venomous of times, to rise up and fight such injustice, even at great risk to themselves and their families?

We have asked our students these questions, and as often happens, they have been our best teachers. One student commented, "If we can just get people to look into the eyes of the people they hate, they would see their humanity and the difference would just be difference, not something [that they consider] worthy of violence." Another student wrote, "Humanity is our basic understanding; compartmentalizing people is something that's taught." This student went on to say that he did not fully understand how and why hate and violence could be directed at whole groups due to their race, religion, or sexual orientation. He concluded that he was glad he did not understand or share such a perspective, because "it would be as if I had a hole in my soul."

The possibility of seeing humanity in ourselves and in each other is what interests us. This book is about reflecting on and repairing the "holes in our souls" that have been drilled there by misinformation, biased or incomplete information, and repeated negative messages. It is about examining, revisiting, and, at times, reconstructing the intentional and unintentional lies and partial truths—both explicit and subtle—told by our families, by our peers, and in school, and embedded in situation comedies, reality shows, and other television programs, in popular films, contemporary music, and other media. It is about developing the tools to scrutinize these messages and their sources and examining their impact on our own convictions and values and, ultimately, what we believe to be true.

This book is not about political correctness. It is not about replacing one set of simplistic myths with another. It is about seeing the serious consequences of hate and oppression for those who have been segregated, lynched, ostracized, raped, marginalized, battered, harassed, abused, laughed at, put to death in gas chambers, and bullied. It is about the serious consequences—the "hole in the soul"—that become a part of those who hate and obliterate their ability to embrace the humanity of others. It is about weighing what we have learned in the past in light of what we are learning in the present. And it is about making our own independent choices regarding what to think and believe and how to act in the future.

So many textbooks, academic articles, theological analyses, television programs, films, songs, and authorities in our lives have presented biased information, theories, beliefs, and feelings as if they were facts. Yet, as you will see, much of the information and meaning about diversity and oppression has been socially and politically constructed and contested, and in a continuous state of flux through history and across cultures.

In our in-depth discussions, we have used language that is based on both scholarship and personal experience. We have therefore intentionally described our personal stories in each chapter. We have shared our own observations and perspectives, as well as our academic and media sources, with citations provided according to academic convention. With this information in hand, you can readily evaluate what we say in the same way that we have encouraged you to evaluate other sources of information.

It is our hope that this book will be instructive in illustrating the degree of critical reflection and personal honesty required to be fully aware of how we all collude in perpetuating racism, classism, sexism, and heterosexism in our communities. We have shared stories of our own journeys so you will know that, based on research and lived experience, this is our interpretation of how oppression operates and how destructive it can be. We have also shared our stories because we have learned that the more aware we are of the role each of us plays, consciously and unconsciously, in contributing to that destructiveness, the more effective we can be in interrupting the attitudes and behaviors that cause it.

The time has come for our society to get serious about healing the deep divisions that dehumanize, disempower, and alienate people from one another. We invite you to join us in becoming more knowledgeable, skillful, and intentional about contributing to a world where we recognize and value our differences and our profound human connections.

We are fully present in this book. We hope you will be, too.

Linda Holtzman and Leon Sharpe

Introduction

In 2000, the year that *Media Messages* was first published, the average American household had the television on for seven hours each day and engaged in a combination of active and passive television consumption. By 2012, the average American was actively watching television 33 hours a week, the equivalent of 4.7 hours per day. We also spent another hour per day watching recorded television from TIVOs and more generic DVRs. The biggest changes in American TV viewing were that we doubled the time that we watched recorded television and a full 36 million of us watched recorded TV, movies, and videos on our smartphones, PCs, iPads, and other assorted screens.

The concerns of researchers, parents, educators and others in 2000 focused on how Americans, particularly young adults and adolescents, were spending their leisure time and to what degree it revolved around how much time we spent watching TV, going to the movies, watching prerecorded, rented, or purchased movies at home, and playing video or computer games. By 2012, the question regarding what media we consumed was studied formally and discussed informally using quite different language and parameters.

The term employed most frequently in surveys and interviews inquiring about Americans' use of entertainment media involved how much "screen time" we spent on a daily and weekly basis, which kinds of screens we were using, and what we were doing with those screens. We had network TV, cable, and satellite service, streaming, DVRs, Amazon, Netflix, Hulu, and other movie and rerun rental and subscription options. We had smartphones and computers and tablets as platforms, upon which we watched movies, used Facebook and Twitter, and played classic games such as chess and Scrabble and trendy new Zynga games with friends all over the world.

Despite the overwhelming number of choices we have about how to spend our time and money for bigger and more novel types of home entertainment systems and "screen time," the most watched screen, according to the reliable Nielsen survey, is still the television. We have a world of choices about when and where and how to watch our favorite programs—at 2 o'clock in the morning, on an airplane to South Africa, during a layover in Argentina, or in a tent in rural Missouri. Although Americans are spending six more hours per week recording programs we want to watch on a DVR, most of our leisure time is still spent in front of the most traditional screen for both entertainment and comfort, the television.

So much has changed, yet how we take in, process, and eventually come to understand the messages about human diversity has remained remarkably the same. Most people still choose to watch television according to when they have leisure time available, not by specifically selecting programs of their choice. When we have time to relax, we plop down on the couch, the recliner, or the bed and fiddle with the remote until we find something intriguing, appealing, or tolerable to watch. And despite the multiple types of fictional programs and the fast-growing genre of reality television, we generally are still exposed to a series of homogeneous, consistent messages conveyed during prime-time television regardless of the platform, time of day, network, or program selected.

Even the smartest and most aware television consumers can experience television in two seemingly contradictory ways. On the one hand, most of us know and can articulate the fact that the programs we are watching are fictional. Yet simultaneously and often less than consciously, we believe and internalize the subtle and often subliminal messages we are receiving. This same process occurs as we watch a feature film or listen to popular music.

When most Americans turn on the television in the evening, they want to be entertained, lulled, or simply anesthetized. Following a day of work or studies or simply making our way through the complexities of life's daily challenges, many of us need and desire a break. Prime-time television seems to offer the perfect solution: perhaps mindless fun, perhaps a few laughs, and even the occasional meaty thought to ponder. But as we relax on the couch after a long day, what are the messages we are receiving and what impact do they have on us?

Cultural studies scholar Douglas Kellner says, "Radio, television, film, and other products of the culture industries provide the models of what it means to be male or female, successful or a failure, powerful or powerless. . . . Media culture helps shape the prevalent view of the world and deepest values: it defines what is considered good or bad, positive or negative, moral or evil" (Kellner 1995, 1).

According to media scholar George Gerbner, the late twentieth century marked the beginning of the enormous presence and influence of television in our lives. Television had become the primary storyteller for children, replacing parents, grandparents, and clergy as the most common sources of information and socialization in an otherwise diverse population (Gerbner et al. 1986, 17). Gerbner was well known for his warning that our children are receiving their "stories" and lessons about values and culture and human diversity from people who have something to "sell" rather than people who have something to "tell" (Gerbner 1996, CEM speech).

Other researchers have observed that while television is only one of many things that serve to explain the world, it is "special because its socially constructed version of reality bombards all classes, groups, and ages with the same perspectives at the same time. . . . What makes television unique, however, is its ability to standardize, streamline, amplify, and share common cultural norms with virtually all members of society" (Morgan and Signiorelli 1990, 13).

Throughout *Media Messages*, we will explore accessible methods to analyze the impact of media content as it pertains to four primary social categories: gender, socioeconomic class, race, and sexual orientation identity. We will examine some of the stories, images, and messages of human diversity as they are conveyed on prime-time television, in popular film, and in contemporary music. Although we are writing from a North American perspective, we acknowledge that the audience for U.S. entertainment media extends to countries and cultures throughout the world.

We also acknowledge the increasing impact of social media in our society. Through the expansive growth of video games and social networks, along with the omnipresence of mobile devices with a multitude of apps, media consumption has become much more interactive. Although an in-depth examination of this phenomenon is beyond the scope of this book, we believe that many of the tools and concepts presented here can be directly applied to or readily adapted for use by those who are interested in conducting such a study.

The information and analysis presented in this volume allow the current and future media producer and consumer alike to critically examine entertainment media and decipher what is being portrayed. The contents and interactive exercises in *Media Messages* can be used for academic, professional, and/or personal purposes. We offer the reader a unique combination of historical information, academic theory, research, observation, and analysis. Simultaneously, we offer opportunities for structured reflection that can be used by individuals, small groups, or entire classes to examine personal beliefs, values, and behaviors.

The goal of this combined analytical and introspective approach is to untangle the intricacies of how we have been socialized into forming our beliefs about gender, class, race, and sexual orientation. Together, we will explore the messages we continue to receive from entertainment media in the twenty-first century and how those messages influence what we believe to be true about the various cultural groups to which we belong as well as those groups and individuals we regard as culturally different.

You, the reader, are invited to be a full partner in this endeavor to explore how we see ourselves and others along three parallel paths: (1) the path of *personal experience*, (2) the path of *reconstructing knowledge*, and (3) the path of critical analysis using *entertainment media assessment tools*. Through this exploration, we will seek an understanding of the primary forces that shape who we are and how we think, act, and better recognize the diversity in the world around us. This individual process of recognizing that difference does not necessitate thinking that one group is superior or inferior to another, but rather to acknowledge both our differences *and* our powerful human connections.

The second edition of *Media Messages* is filled with new content, theories, analysis, examples, media activities, personal inventories, and photographs. Among the most exciting changes are the contributions of coauthor Leon Sharpe. He brings a wealth of academic experience and practical knowledge, unique personal observations, and a wisdom that has permeated the content and process of writing this book.

As the authors of the second edition of *Media Messages,* we have spent more time in this edition exploring the various intersections between gender, class, race, and sexual orientation and how people often respond to the multilayered messages they receive from entertainment media. We have introduced the concept of cognitive dissonance as a critical component of how people frequently react to new information that contradicts cherished misinformation we have received from people we love and trust. Cognitive dissonance is the distinctly human psychological or emotional discomfort we all experience when we are presented with evidence that is inconsistent with or even directly challenges attitudes and information we have held to be the "truth." We have asked the reader to consider the phenomenon of cognitive dissonance, both intellectually and experientially.

We invite you to pause periodically in your reading to notice whatever thoughts and emotions you are experiencing as you take in new information that contradicts what you have always believed. If the new information invokes feelings of discomfort, we encourage you to sit with that discomfort. In other words, stop reading, and allow your mind to be contemplative and self-reflective for a few moments. Give your full attention to these uncomfortable emotions. Rather than attempting to ignore your emotions, or brush them aside and continue to read, use them as a signal to delve deeper. The objective is to go beyond your conscious reaction to the information that is being presented and unlock any implicit preconceptions you might be harboring. In the interest of gaining a fuller understanding of the material contained in this text, it is essential for you to seek a fuller understanding of the material residing within your own psyche. As you work your way through the book, we ask you to consider the sources, past and present, of information you have received about human diversity, to evaluate the credibility of the various sources and the information itself, and to make independent decisions about what you *choose* to think and believe.

So many of us are accustomed to living in a binary world in which choices about our understanding and our values regarding human diversity are often presented and internalized as *either* this *or* that. In this limited approach, we often see our range of options as finite: Same-sex marriage is either wrong or right. Men's and women's basic nature is either biologically driven or not.

In this edition, we, the authors, have introduced another way of examining information about human diversity for which we credit our highly respected colleague and friend, Dr. Billie Mayo. This approach opens up infinite possibilities in all of our thinking, our personal experience, and our values and beliefs by approaching human diversity as if *both* this *and* that are possible and can coexist. The *both/and* approach to studying human diversity opens far more doors and windows than the *either/or* approach. Finite ways of understanding diversity help us feel safe in a predictable world with simple explanations. The *both/and* approach allows each of us to embrace more of our humanity and to give free rein to our feelings, experiences, observations, and intellectual knowledge. This enables us to take in new, invigorating, and even liberating information as our views of what is possible expand and we learn about and build relationships with interesting and extraordinary people who are both like us and/or very different from us.

We have added new features to each chapter, including a glossary of key terms and a list of questions that ask you to apply the skills of reflection, summarizing, and analyzing information, theories, concepts, and ideas. In every chapter we provide an opportunity to examine your *experiences* through the use of a variety of personal inventories and activities. Through the exploration of personal experience, together we will examine informal education, information, and incomplete information or misinformation that each of us has received about gender, race, class, and sexual identity and orientation.

Later in each chapter, we will begin to consider the meaning and impact of various forms of popular media, and you will be asked to refer back to your own personal experience as the foundation and context for understanding your relationship to the messages conveyed in entertainment television programs, film, and music. This process will begin to identify what you have learned through your own direct contact and personal experience.

As you do these exercises, you will begin to notice where there are gaps and voids in your experiential learning. For example, if you are white, African American, Latina/Latino, or Asian American, did you grow up without any contact with American Indians? If so, where did you get information or misinformation about American Indians? Most likely, it was through what people told you, what you learned in school, and what you saw and heard in the media.

After exploring and assessing personal experience, a second kind of analysis will be offered that examines more formal sources of correct information and, once again, incomplete information or misinformation concerning gender, race, class, and sexual identity and orientation. This method of investigation involves *reconstructing knowledge* by analyzing explicit information the authors and readers alike have been taught in school and other formal learning organizations.

For example, most U.S. students were taught in school about the Civil War and slavery, but most of us were not taught about slave uprisings and the ongoing resistance movement conducted by African Americans and their white and Native American allies. Why is this information rarely included in high school history books? How has this and other missing information contributed to our beliefs about slavery, the treatment of African Americans, and contemporary racism?

As you review what you have been formally taught, you will be asked to consider the source of your information and beliefs and to place it into the context of reconstructing knowledge. You will not be asked to change your values or convictions. Rather, you are invited to assimilate new information and analyze and reconcile it with what you have been taught in the past. Through this process of evaluating information, we all have the opportunity to reconsider our beliefs and to independently decide whether to reconstruct our own knowledge, let it remain the same, or blend the new information with the old.

After examining personal experience and formal education, the next type of analysis will focus on assessing entertainment media: prime-time television, popular film, and contemporary music. These forms of popular culture are common sources of informal education and socialization that stretch across the United States, forming the media culture in which teachers, students, authors, and readers are all immersed, with or without our consent. While the intent of entertainment media may not be explicitly to educate us, it often fills the voids in our formal and informal learning.

For example, if we did not have any direct contact with Asian Americans as we were growing up, where did we learn about this group? We learned from what people told us, from what we were taught in school, and from media. What we learned in this way may or may not correspond to the actual history and contemporary circumstances of the individuals whose families originally came to the United States from a wide variety of Asian countries and cultures.

Entertainment media (prime-time television, popular film, and contemporary music) are a primary fact of life in most U.S. homes. Much of our sense of personal and group identity, our beliefs about what is "normal," and our understanding of individuals and groups that are different from us is created and/or reinforced by the pervasive entertainment media culture. The ability and the skills to critically observe and analyze these messages and their impact are integral to becoming informed citizens striving for independence in thought, values, and behavior. We will explore many of the theories available for examining popular media culture and its vast impact. In addition, the book offers tools and exercises to assess entertainment media and decode their messages.

For example, most of the families portrayed on prime-time television are heterosexual nuclear families, including a mother, father, and children, and with an income that is at least middle-class or above. What do we learn about what it means to be a "normal" family from these repeated images? How does it affect us whether our family is included or excluded in this media portrait of so-called family normalcy? We will explore these pervasive, consistent, and repeated messages of what it means to be a "normal" family and will determine whether this image reflects and portrays the "dominant culture" in the United States. What messages are inherent in the gradually emerging, but still limited, visibility of single-parent families, extended families, working-class families, families living in poverty, and families with LGBT parents?

This book is divided into six chapters. Chapter 1 establishes the framework and foundation for the essential links between personal experience, reconstructing knowledge, and entertainment media. Key terms that will be used throughout the book are introduced in Chapter 1. Reading Chapter 1 first will help you understand the framework and terms and concepts that are frequently used throughout the book. After that, the book is designed so you may easily read the chapters in any order that you select.

Chapters 2, 3, and 6 are organized around gender, socioeconomic class, and sexual orientation, respectively. Each of these chapters explores the particular issue in our personal experience and how it is described in our formal education and depicted in entertainment media.

Chapters 4 and 5 are both about race. In an effort to explore personal experience, formal education, and entertainment media as they relate to the wide diversity within and between each racial group, including African Americans, Asian Americans, American Indians, Latinos or Hispanics, multiracial Americans, and European Americans, we have divided this mountain of information into two chapters for easier readability.

We have introduced new information in each chapter. Here is a broad sampling:

In Chapter 1, the introductory chapter, we have included new information about media ownership and international conglomeration. We also have addressed the impact on media content and messages when the corporate ownership's central "product" is not media.

In Chapter 2 on gender, we have added extensive information and research about how boys and men are depicted in media and often socialized, encouraged, and taught that in order to be truly masculine they need to be tough, physically and emotionally strong, and powerful. This socialization occurs in much the same way as girls and women continue to learn that to be truly feminine it is essential to be beautiful as defined by the narrowest of media messages, emphasizing thinness, light skin, smooth hair, unblemished skin, and finely chiseled features. We continue to examine how sexism oppresses women institutionally and individually, giving them less access to resources and power than men. We have introduced research that tells us that boys and girls, men and women, regardless of their access to power, all "learn" the limiting and damaging roles and rules of the gender game in order to fit into culturally constructed concepts and images of femininity and masculinity. In addition, we introduce the concept that, while as a group, men and boys are more likely to have access to power, resources, and privilege, both males and females are regularly and deeply hurt by sexism.

There are also interesting new developments when considering actual income along gender lines. Yet in television, despite new images that portray women's work as being outside the home, female characters on TV are still primarily focused on interpersonal relationships more than on work, and male characters are primarily focused on work, with relationships a secondary concern.

In Chapter 3 on socioeconomic class, we examine how the Great Recession of the early twenty-first century and the Occupy movement increased the visibility of class in the United States and significantly altered the way that news media and more and more Americans began discussing a word that has often been taboo in U.S. society: "class." We look closely at prime-time television and popular film and music to see if the profound experiences that many Americans had during the height of the recession and the increased conversations about economic inequality were reflected in the entertainment media that most Americans consumed. We examine messages about the intersection of race and class in popular, award-winning films such as *Blind Side* and independent, award-winning films such as *Precious*.

Chapter 4 focuses on personal experience and reconstructing knowledge about race. We've addressed the American discourse about race in our homes and schools, in our places of business, and in the academy. We introduce information about how and what many Americans have "learned" about race and the less than visible ways we internalize a combination of information and misinformation that eventually hardens into what we "know" to be incontrovertible "truth" and "fact." This process largely influences whether and how we are able to actually see racial inequities, including the nearly invisible mechanisms of white privilege, and where we place blame or credit for who succeeds and who fails in the United States. In Chapter 4, we have provided more information about identity distortion in the form of internalized racism and internalized white superiority. Chapter 4 addresses how individuals have acknowledged and explored white privilege and how new perspectives have contributed to what they previously viewed as strictly individual: personal achievement, success, and failure. Much of the mythology about race is addressed, considered, and dismissed in the discussion of the science and pseudoscience of race.

We also briefly discuss critical race theory and examine the effectiveness of the counternarrative as a tool for challenging the prevailing mental models about racial identity and hierarchy. Demographic information about African Americans, Asian Americans, Native Americans, and Latinas/Latinos is updated in Chapter 4 and compared to the past.

This gives us a better idea of the contemporary reality of racism in the United States and how it impacts where people live and work, our levels of poverty and wealth, and where and whether our children go to school or college.

Chapter 5, following through on the information provided in Chapter 4, is devoted to the portrayal of race in prime-time television, popular film, and contemporary music and the analysis and discussion of the messages media consumers receive and how they affect us. In Chapter 5 we also use a number of photographs to help tell the story about race in a visual manner. By deconstructing the messages in these images, collectively, we can begin to understand what they convey to a vast portion of American media consumers.

In Chapter 6 we identify three sets of social forces that influenced the evolution of mainstream perceptions about sexual orientation in the United States over time. We discuss recent developments in science, law, and public policy regarding people who are lesbian, gay, bisexual, and transgender (LGBT). Additionally, Chapter 6 presents an expanded discussion of language and terminology and updated material on religion and sexual orientation. There is also an examination of the shift in public views of same-sex relationships and the concomitant changes in media depictions of LGBT characters and themes.

Many researchers have maintained that the common messages in entertainment media have a homogenizing or "mainstreaming" effect on the American public. This means that television, film, and music help shape what those of us immersed in this popular culture environment think of as "true" and "normal." Mainstreaming creates and reinforces an invisible set of values that are so firmly entrenched in our culture and belief systems that they seem indisputable to us. These invisible values influence the way we think and act on personal and political levels. We make personal choices, we vote and take political action, and we form public policy based on our values and beliefs. We choose the people we want to date, choose whether and whom we will marry, and choose whether to have children and how to raise them in ways that are deeply and often invisibly influenced by entertainment media. To the extent that these messages, values, and norms are invisible, our choices and actions are automatic, dependent, and less than conscious. The aim of this book is to tease out these messages so that we can see them clearly and make our own conscious, deliberate, and independent choices about our beliefs, values, and behavior when it comes to human diversity.

Together, we will explore content, history, and information about human diversity in the United States through this blend of experience and information. We will also learn how we can extract these invisible messages and look at them directly in order to determine what mixture of fact and fiction we have ingested, internalized, and automatically absorbed into our thoughts, feelings, beliefs, attitudes, and deeds. As we learn more about gender, class, race, and sexual identity and orientation, we will investigate our interactions and experiences with individuals and groups that are the same as us and individuals and groups that are different from us. We will explore and critique what we have been taught about various cultures in school and through religious organizations, and finally, we will decode the messages about diversity in entertainment media.

Through the content and activities in *Media Messages*, we invite you to investigate the meaning, influence, and impact of the information and misinformation that *you* have received and to discover new tools for determining your own values and beliefs and making your own independent life choices. It is that independence and those choices that are central to this book.

BIBLIOGRAPHY

Gerbner, George. 1996. Excerpt from speech at Founding Convention of the Cultural Environment Movement (CEM), St. Louis, Missouri, March 15.

Gerbner, George, Larry Gross, Michael Morgan, and Nancy Signiorelli. 1986. "Living with Television: The Dynamics of the Cultivation Process." In *Perspectives on Media Effects*, ed. Jennings Bryant and Dolf Zillman Lawrence, 17–31. Hillsdale, NJ: Erlbaum.

Kellner, Douglas. 1995. *Media Culture: Cultural Studies, Identity and Politics Between the Modern and the Postmodern*. London: Routledge.

Morgan, Michael, and Nancy Signiorelli, eds. 1990. *Cultivation Analysis: New Directions in Media Effect Research*. Newbury Park, CA: Sage.

MEDIA MESSAGES

1

The Connections

Life, Knowledge, and Media

Once you have learned how to ask questions—relevant and appropriate
and substantial questions—you have learned how to learn, and no one
can keep you from learning whatever you want or need to know.

—Postman and Weingartner

When individuals engage diversity, tension can result from new
information about others that is contrary to the learner's previous
understanding of their identity, the world and the relationship between
the two . . . if we find that the others are not who we thought them
to be, perhaps we are not who we define ourselves to be.

—Institute for Public Media Arts

We learn about the characteristics of the groups we are part of, including our religion, our gender, where we were born and grew up, our race, our socioeconomic class, and our sexual orientation. We also learn about the identity and characteristics of individuals and groups that are different from us. This learning occurs at a time in our childhood when the sources who provide the information are well-meaning people who love us, so the information gets translated as "the truth" in our minds and in our hearts. Invariably, some of the observations we make and the facts we receive are solid and accurate, but other information is based on misunderstanding, misinformation, missing information, bias, and ignorance.

Using this book, together we will explore the variety of information we've observed and received about human diversity. We'll investigate and evaluate the sources of both the accurate information and the misinformation. We'll use some observational, academic, and media skills and tools that will allow us to question this information and these sources and develop our own independent conclusions, our own "truths." We will investigate three major sources of information:

- Personal experience and informal knowledge
- Academic knowledge and formal learning
- Popular media

Each of these sources provides us with rich and varied, often contradictory, and frequently confusing elements of our beliefs and values and "knowledge" about diversity. As you explore the information and perspectives in this book, the tools you learn will help you assess the credibility of the material we present. These tools and strategies will allow you to access some of the highest levels of intelligent pursuit: active exploration and careful consideration of a wide variety of information, skills, and strategies to develop your own independent thinking, values, beliefs, and understanding about human diversity. Our hope is that this book will offer a dynamic approach to learning that will give us all permission to be open to new information, to adjust our thinking, and to grow and change according to our own well-informed internal compass.

Each chapter begins with an inquiry about your personal experience so that you can explore what you were explicitly and implicitly taught, how you were socialized, what you absorbed, what you resisted, and ultimately what you learned to be "true" about gender or class or race or sexual orientation and identity.

PERSONAL EXPERIENCE

Take a journey to your childhood and think about what, if any, holiday your family celebrated in December. Think of the kind of celebration it was. Remember the foods, the smells, the people, the decorations. What was everyone doing? Was there a religious element to the holiday? Was there gift giving? Did the family gather together? Were there songs or prayers? Were there any special family traditions involved? Do you have other significant memories associated with this holiday? Write or tape-record your answers to these questions.

Groups that are predominantly white, middle-class, and Christian often assume that Christmas is *the* December holiday. Often people in such homogeneous groups will preface their answers to the above questions with statements such as "It was your *average* Christmas" or "We ate the *usual* foods" or "The only thing different about my family was we ate duck instead of turkey" or "We were pretty *typical*—nothing exciting."

Yet there are many other possibilities for holidays and celebrations in December. Jews celebrate Chanukah; many African Americans celebrate Kwanzaa; Muslims celebrate Eid al-Adha; and the Winter Solstice is celebrated by many individuals who are part of organized religions and many who are not. During Chanukah, candelabra known as menorahs are lit for eight consecutive days, latkes—potato pancakes—are eaten, and a game is played with a top called a "dreidel." During Kwanzaa a new candle on the kinara is lit each night to represent one of the seven principles: unity, self-determination, collective work and responsibility, cooperative economics, purpose, creativity, and faith (Salzman, Smith, and West 1996, 2475). During Eid al-Adha, families that can afford it often sacrifice a goat or a sheep and share the meat with other families to commemorate the faith of Ibrahim (known as Abraham by Christians and Jews). Since the Muslim and the Jewish calendars are different from the Western calendar, Chanukah and Eid al-Adha do not always fall in the month of December (ReligionFacts 2006). For some faiths, agnostics, or atheists, there may be no traditional December holiday.

If you grew up celebrating Christmas in the United States or another predominantly Christian location in the world, most likely you understood your experience to be the norm. Perhaps you never heard of Chanukah or Kwanzaa or Eid al-Adha until you were much older. Perhaps you still are not completely sure what those holidays are about and why Christmas is not celebrated by everyone. Perhaps you felt sorry for people who did not have Christmas trees. Or perhaps you thought that people who celebrated other, non-Christian holidays were interesting, exotic, odd, or even un-American. As part of the dominant Christian culture in the United States, your early holiday experiences were part of the construct of what you believed to be average and normal and how you understood the "other," or people and groups that were different from you.

If you grew up non-Christian in the United States, you knew, at least for a month or so, what it was like to be different. You heard Christmas music and saw lights and Santa Claus everywhere you went. In stores, schools, and offices, people with the warmest of intentions wished you a "Merry Christmas." Maybe you smiled and nodded politely or maybe you said, "I don't celebrate Christmas." Maybe you went to a school where students sang Christmas carols and you had to decide whether to join in the singing. These examples illustrate the media and cultural saturation of Christmas images and messages and their acceptance as "normal." If you were part of a minority group in a predominantly Christian culture, you learned early on what it was like to be different, to stand outside of the norm, to be the "other."

In fact, there is great variation in how Christians observe Christmas. Some celebrate Christmas as a deeply meaningful religious holiday, while others celebrate it as a secular midwinter holiday of gift giving, food, and festivities.

Your position in this December scenario was a critical element in the establishment of your personal identity and your sense of where you belonged in your neighborhood your school, and in the larger community and culture. Depending on how the adults in your life helped to explain your experience, you may have had a mix of positive, negative, and neutral feelings. But whatever your experience was, it contributed to shaping how you see yourself and people who are different from you.

Exploring how we see ourselves and others is an important first step in understanding human diversity. Later in the chapter we will examine related issues in reconstructing knowledge and entertainment media and make the important connections between your personal experiences and your formal and mediated learning.

Your place as inside or outside the "norm" of the Christmas holiday will contribute to how you regard what you learn in school and the workplace. For example, most public and private schools in the United States are organized around the Christian calendar. School breaks and holidays usually correspond with Christmas and Easter rather than Yom Kippur, Kwanzaa, or Ramadan. This schedule conveys to us that the Christian holidays are "normal," while the other holidays are, at best, for minorities and, at worst, seen as unusual or strange. On a more practical level, Christians generally have time off from school and work to celebrate important holidays, while people of other faiths have to figure out how to accommodate their religious observances. Non-Christians often have to ask, "Should I miss an important test, blow my perfect attendance record, or take a personal leave day to observe my holiday?" Your standpoint in the holiday scenario above also has an enormous impact on how you see the "holiday specials" on television, hear the Christmas music on the radio and in department stores, and feel about the release of December seasonal films. For Christians, these media events may seem like either an overcommercialization of a deeply religious holiday or wonderful examples of holiday spirit. For non-Christians, the media saturation may be disturbing and disorienting. Some non-Christians may feel almost invisible during December. To continue this process of understanding diversity in an experiential context, we invite you to take the multicultural quiz in Personal Inventory 1.1.

After completing the quiz, total your score. The highest possible score is 130 points If you scored 117–130, you have lived in a highly multicultural world. If you scored 104–116 points, your life has been filled with diversity. If you scored 91–103 points, you have been exposed to people who are culturally different from you. If you scored 78–90 points, you have been exposed to some diversity but have primarily lived among people much like you. If you scored below 78 points, you have lived primarily among people who are very much like you in race, religion, sexual orientation, and social and economic class or you have been in the minority among others who were quite similar. And, most importantly, if you did score under 78 points, you are similar to more than 90 percent of the people who have taken this quiz—you have lived in a unicultural world.

What does this all mean? Some people, after taking this quiz, have come to the conscious realization that they have grown up among others who are in fundamental ways very much like them. This simple and unscientific quiz underscores that U.S. society is still largely structured in a way that separates and segregates people who are different from each other. Many people actively and explicitly choose to live among others who are similar to them. Some people make residential choices based on the limits of their income or as a result of discrimination in real estate or lending. Yet, just as often, the choices for diversity continue to be exceedingly limited in this society. People who have lived in communities with great diversity have generally made very deliberate choices to do so, in order to expose themselves and their families to a multicultural world.

If most Americans' experiences are, in fact, unicultural, how do people learn about the nature of *difference*? Young people learn about people and groups that are different from them in several ways: from their families, from their peers, from their religious institutions, from their schools, and from the media.

Through the process of socialization, we grow up learning the values of our culture. The vast majority of us grew up with little diversity, and the values and beliefs we were taught seemed real, central, and "normal." Often we experienced no sense of a pluralist community that included different foods, religious practices, beliefs, or customs. Rather, these invisible norms instilled a sense that our way was the right or only way and that other ways were unusual, weird, abnormal, or wrong.

This exercise is not intended to provoke guilt or to evoke the specter of political correctness. In fact, since most of the United States is quite segregated residentially, particularly by race, ethnicity, income, and religion, the exercise points out that cultural isolation is a common experience shared both by groups in the majority and by groups in the minority.

Personal Inventory 1.1
The Multicultural Quiz

Instructions

Answer each question below to the best of your ability. If you lived in many different places during the time period described, give yourself a score that averages your experiences. Leave blank any experiences (e.g., preschool, religious institution, etc.) that don't pertain to you.

For each answer, score yourself as follows:

1 point: Experience was largely unicultural; most people were of my race, religion, sexual orientation, and income level.

2 points: Experience was largely unicultural, but most people were of a different race, religion, sexual orientation, and income level than I was.

3 points: Experience was largely unicultural, but there were a few people who were different from me in race, religion, sexual orientation, and income level.

4 points: In at least two categories (race, religion, sexual orientation, and income level), there were people present who were different from me.

5 points: In at least three categories, there were people present who were different from me.

Ages 1 to 5
1. The neighborhood where you lived   _____
2. The children with whom you played   _____
3. Your parents' friends   _____
4. The preschool or day care center you attended   _____
5. The religious institution you attended   _____

Ages 6 to 10
6. The neighborhood where you lived   _____
7. The children with whom you played   _____
8. The school you attended   _____
9. Clubs or organizations to which you belonged   _____
10. Religious institution   _____

Ages 11 to 14
11. The neighborhood where you lived   _____
12. Your friends   _____
13. The school you attended   _____
14. Clubs or organizations to which you belonged   _____
15. Religious institution   _____

Personal Inventory 1.1 *(continued)*

Ages 15 to 18
16. The neighborhood where you lived   _____
17. Your friends   _____
18. The school you attended   _____
19. Clubs or organizations to which you belonged _____
20. Religious institution   _____

Ages 19 and over
21. The neighborhood where you lived   _____
22. Your friends   _____
23. The school you attended   _____
24. Clubs or organizations to which you belonged _____
25. Religious institution   _____
26. Your parents' friends   _____

Total score   _____

Source: Presentation by Barbara Love, 1989.

This isolation denies most of us the personal opportunity to be neighbors, friends, peers, or classmates with people who are different from us. This cultural isolation is critical to remember as later in this section we begin to examine what we were taught formally in school and what we have learned about one another from the media. For many of us, the voids and gaps in our personal experience are filled exclusively by formal education and media. These sources of information shape what we "know" and believe regardless of whether they are solid, accurate, and factual or vague, inaccurate, and fictional.

The second experiential exercise in this section, Personal Inventory 1.2, begins the process of developing your autobiography, which can be written in a notebook or recorded in an audio or visual format. The development of autobiographies and their exchange with others from similar and different backgrounds is encouraged over the course of the six chapters of this book. Our sense of individual and cultural identity is integral to how we understand the world we live in and its portrayal in entertainment media.

A closer examination of a few of these questions uncovers some common issues regarding difference, isolation, and the consequences of the type of diversity or lack of diversity we experience as children. Number 4 invites us to report on the treatment of elders in our family and community. Some families and groups are informal in addressing older people and commonly refer to parents' friends, neighbors, friends' parents, and even aunts and uncles by their first names. Other families consider it an essential sign of respect for children to address all elders as "Mr." or "Mrs.," "Ms.," "sir," or "ma'am." Violation of this sign of respect is regarded as an affront and as extraordinarily rude.

Personal Inventory 1.2
Developing an Autobiography: Part One

Instructions

Answer the questions below in as much detail as you can remember. Write or record your responses. There are no right or wrong answers.

1. Describe the neighborhood(s) in which you were raised. Were there houses, apartments, farms? How many generations lived in a single dwelling? Who was at home in your neighborhood on weekdays? On weekends? Describe the roads and the shops. How did neighbors interact? How did children play? What smells, foods, activities, events do you remember from your childhood?
2. What religious institutions were in your neighborhood? Were there churches, temples, synagogues, mosques? What religions did your neighbors and friends observe?
3. How were children treated in your community? How were they disciplined?
4. How were older adults or elders addressed (e.g., first name, sir, ma'am, titles, Mr., Mrs., Ms., etc.), and how were they treated?
5. What were the spoken and unspoken rules about dating, courtship, and marriage? For example, who initiated a date? What were the rules about curfew? Was the young man expected to come to the door and meet the parents of the young woman? Was it acceptable for a young man to honk the horn when he came to pick up the young woman?
6. What were the expectations for your generation regarding education? How many generations of your family have attended college?
7. What holidays did your family celebrate? Describe the rituals, gathering, and food of these celebrations.
8. What music did you grow up listening to among your family and friends? What did you and your family do with your leisure time?

Over the centuries, many African American families have seen their elders treated with disrespect by being called by their first names by very young white children or by being called "boy" or "girl" by children and adults alike. Historically, titles of respect accorded to European Americans were rarely used for African Americans. As a result of this history, some contemporary African American families are emphatic that courtesy titles (Miss, Ms., Mrs., Mr.) be used at all times as a sign of respect and as an important compensatory gesture of courtesy.

Consider a scenario between individuals who have been taught to address elders in very different ways. An African American child, John Harris, and a European American child, Alex Rosen-Fox, become friends in first grade and begin to visit each other's homes to play. John has been explicitly told that all male adults should be addressed as "Mr." and all married women should be addressed as "Mrs." Alex's family has roots in the political and social change movements of the 1960s, and he has been taught to call adults, including his parents, by their first names. His parents believe this informality in language across ages is a symbol of equality and not disrespect. His mother has kept her original, or "maiden," last name and uses the title "Ms." rather than "Mrs."

So when John comes to visit Alex and refers to the adults as Mr. and Mrs. Fox, the adults immediately say, "Call us Larry and Susan," unwittingly putting John in conflict between what his parents have taught him about respect and what other adults are asking him to do. John decides to obey his parents and continues to call Alex's parents Mr. and Mrs. Fox. Correcting him, Susan says that her last name is Rosen and that if he doesn't want to call her by her first name, he should call her Ms. Rosen. John is very confused.

When Alex plays at John's house, he hears the adults call each other by their first names, Renee and Herb, and immediately begins to address them as such. Renee and Herb Harris are disturbed that Alex, who otherwise seems to be a nice little boy, is so disrespectful. They are perplexed by this apparent disrespect and begin to wonder if Alex is calling them by their first names because they are African American and if there is some racial bias among the adults in his family.

Something that on the surface may seem simple can cause two families from different cultures to draw very different conclusions about behavior. If the Harrises understand Alex's background, they will know that he means no disrespect but rather that his family has a different set of traditions, beliefs, and practices regarding the treatment of elders and what constitutes respect. If the Harrises are unaware of this attitude, they may conclude that while Alex is a nice boy, his parents, at best, have not taught him respect and, at worst, are racist. If the Rosen-Foxes understand some of the historical realities for African American families, they will know the significance of courtesy titles and may explain this to their son, Alex, teaching him to respect different histories and cultural traditions. However, if the Rosen-Foxes are unaware of these cultural differences, they may decide that while John is a nice boy, his parents must be old-fashioned and overly formal. They may continue to insist that John call them by their first names or that he call Susan "Ms. Rosen."

Difference in cultural practices, personal histories, or racial history can be spun into many scenarios that can result either in greater understanding of diversity or in harsh judgment and offensive behavior. We bring these experiences and understandings with us as a filter every time we go to school or to church, temple, or mosque; every time we go to a movie, watch television, or listen to music; and every time we meet someone who is different from us.

RECONSTRUCTING KNOWLEDGE

Ronald Takaki describes a personal encounter with a narrowly constructed view of what it means to be American. A taxi driver in Norfolk, Virginia, asked Takaki, a second-generation Japanese American, what country he was from and complimented him on his English. Because Takaki's face was Asian, the driver assumed that he was not American (Takaki 1993, 1). The driver, like many others in U.S. society, had "learned" that the physical appearance of certain people is un-American or foreign. The driver meant no harm. In fact, he thought he was flattering Takaki by complimenting his English.

The driver's comments disclosed what his formal and informal education had taught him about what it means to be American. Takaki says, "What happens . . . when someone with the authority of a teacher describes our society, and you are not in it? Such an experience can be disorienting, a moment of psychic disequilibrium, as if you looked in a mirror and saw nothing" (Takaki 1993, 53). Many groups who have made vital contributions to American society and culture have been excluded from the American curriculum and common knowledge pool. "The result is that what we know—about the experience of both these silenced groups and the dominant culture—is distorted and incomplete" (Andersen and Collins 1995, 1).

Reconstructing knowledge involves another kind of journey through the past in which we examine the explicit information we learned in school and from other formal learning experiences and review it in light of new information. As we assess what we were formally taught and what was omitted in the past, we gain a clearer picture of what we bring to our understanding of people and groups who are different from us. We can begin to ask these questions: Does our formal learning reinforce or contradict what our personal experience has taught us? How do the messages in entertainment media square with this formal and informal learning?

This process requires an openness to questioning what has been learned before, a willingness to assess and incorporate new information, a tolerance for interim confusion, and ultimately the ability to make shifts in how we view the world. Using your developing autobiography as background, reconstructing knowledge invites you to evaluate both your formal and informal education. Each subsequent chapter will include information that is not typically provided in elementary and high school textbooks on the topics of gender, class, race, and sexual orientation. You are never required to change what you think or believe—only to consider new information, to weigh it, and to determine how it fits with what you already "know."

We can begin reconstructing knowledge by looking at a socioeconomic example: the American Dream. What were you taught that this "dream" includes? Were you taught that it could, in fact, be yours someday?

What most Americans are taught in school about the American Dream is that every American, regardless of economic status, race, or family background, can rise to great heights. Historically, it has been the story of the poor *boy* who grows up to be president (of the United States or of Ford Motor Company). The American Dream, a central tenet of American culture, suggests that we all begin on a level playing field and that it is hard work and virtue that determine who succeeds rather than gender, race, ethnicity or economic background. The American Dream focuses on the power and drive of the individual and assumes that American society is classless and that upward mobility is fluid. Regardless of our own personal experience—our race, our economic status, or family background—we are all taught many of these same lessons.

The first step in reconstructing knowledge is to identify these explicit and implicit lessons in our formal learning, to tease out what have been our barely visible assumptions. Have you always just "known" that hard work and virtue would result in upward mobility and success? Has it seemed to you that only "lazy" people fail in this society? Do you believe that most people get what they deserve in their lives?

The next step in reconstructing knowledge is to place these lessons about the American Dream in the context of some newer, perhaps less well-known information that examines economic issues in the United States.

For example, in 2007, New York State paid the highest dollar amount—nearly $16,000 to educate each student in its public schools. The two entities that had the next-highest pupil expenditures were New Jersey and the District of Columbia. By contrast, Utah had the lowest per student expenditure, about $5,600 per pupil, with the states of Idaho and Tennessee right beside it (U.S. Census Bureau 2009).

The disparity between the wealthiest and poorest school districts *within* any given state is equally wide and startling. School districts are supported by property taxes in the district, which means that the communities with the most personal and commercial wealth will also have the public schools with the most money per student.

In 2007, the state of Missouri spent $8,848 per student and was ranked thirty-second in the nation regarding the amount spent by the state per pupil (New America Foundation 2007). Yet one of the wealthiest districts in the state, Ladue, spent more than $22,000 per pupil, while one of the poorest districts, Neosho, spent just over $5,400 per pupil (HomeSurfer.com 2009). It is hard to imagine that the children in Neosho received the same quality of education as the students in Ladue.

Some of the poorest city and rural school districts have lost or are in danger of losing their state accreditation. With poor resources and poor education for some, is it possible for all Americans to begin on a level playing field? Does a child who goes to a school with tattered books, few pencils, and no library have the same life chances as a child who goes to school with the newest textbooks and curriculum, a wealth of supplies, a large library, and computers and DVD players in every classroom?

The process of reconstructing knowledge helps us to understand our relationship to the American Dream. What were you taught about opportunity in the United States? How did your family's economic position affect what you believed to be possible? What, if anything, were you taught in school and at home about race and class disparities in income, education, health care, and housing? What did you believe about who is responsible for poverty or wealth? Were poor people to blame for their lack of resources? Did people of wealth have any responsibility to address inequities in income?

If the American Dream teaches us that virtue, merit, and hard work are the key ingredients in achieving economic and material success, then what does that dream say about people who do not achieve such success? The implied flip side of the classic American Dream is that poor people lack virtue, merit, and the industriousness to succeed. Do you believe that to be true?

Rethinking and reconstructing the American Dream does not mean giving up hope or indulging in cynicism. Challenging the myth means carefully examining and reconsidering what we have been taught about economics and class in the United States and rethinking how opportunity is structured. In much the same way that we have examined the American Dream, you will be invited to reexamine and rethink many issues related to your own experiences, U.S. culture, entertainment media, and the powerful connections between these three topics. Reconstructing knowledge offers you a chance to view familiar terrain, try it on, and see if it still fits. Once again, if our personal lives have not allowed us the opportunity to get to know people and groups that are different from us, something must fill the void. Most often the void is filled with formal education and entertainment media. It is part of our task to determine accuracy, gaps in information, distortion, and misinformation in the lessons we have learned.

In order to examine and evaluate information and knowledge, it will be useful to provide a foundation of terms, language, and theories that can serve as a basis for reconstructing knowledge. This will be the focus of the next section of this chapter. Diversity or multiculturalism is a contested terrain, in which even the overarching categorical terms of diversity, multiculturalism, and anti-oppression are in dispute by experts and practitioners alike. While it is not possible to include every perspective, conflicting theories will be acknowledged as such in order to give the reader every opportunity to evaluate the information provided and to engage in critical and autonomous thinking. Our goal in reconstructing knowledge is not to exchange one set of myths for another but to encourage analytical skills and independence of thought.

THE PROCESS OF SOCIALIZATION

As individuals we develop our sense of personal *identity* from our social interactions with others and the information we receive about ourselves. Our sense of our own biological sex, gender, race, ethnicity, class, and sexual orientation unfolds as our parents, siblings, peers, teachers, and others begin to paint a picture of who we are. For example, when a child is born, parents and grandparents often buy pink outfits for girls and blue for boys, and dolls for girls and footballs for boys. A children's book, *Baby X*, tells the story of an adorable newborn whose parents would not disclose whether "X" was a girl or a boy. Visitors did not know what to say—"Oh, she's so beautiful!" or "Look at his grip!" (Gonzales et al. 1993). This same basic confusion, curiosity, and discomfort is evoked in an old *Saturday Night Live* portrayal of the character "Pat." Like Baby X, Pat's sex is withheld from the audience, and while this gender confusion creates many humorous situations, it also creates social discomfort (Cader 1994, 244). We are accustomed to responding, at least in part, to babies, children, and adults based on conclusions we draw from their sex. From the time of birth, a child is told what it means to be male or female in his or her family and community.

This process is called *socialization*. Socialization is the total set of experiences through which children become clear about norms and expectations and learn how to function as respected and accepted members of a culture. Through socialization, children learn to choose a limited set of behaviors based on these expectations. Children are socialized at both conscious and unconscious levels to internalize the dominant values and norms of their culture and, in so doing, develop a sense of self (Croteau and Hoynes 1997, 18).

There are many theories of how socialization works and how we learn to adapt to our culture. We will explore some of the classic sociological theories as well as newer theories that offer explanations of this phenomenon. Most of these theories include descriptions of the common agents of socialization that strongly influence our cultural adaptation. These agents are the family, the school, the peer group, and the mass media. The peer group and the family correspond with our personal experience and informal learning, and clearly, school is an important source of formal education.

Social Cognitive Theory

One socialization theory that provides a general explanation of human behavior is *social cognitive theory* developed by Albert Bandura (Grusec 1992). According to this theory, we notice some external behavior, we see it rewarded in some way, and after observing it repeatedly we begin to internalize the behavior and mimic it. The key to our decision to copy behaviors, appearance, and even beliefs is the idea of rewards. The rewards may be physical. For example, if you wore your hair like the character Rachel in the situation comedy *Friends*, you may have believed that you, too, would be considered beautiful and men would be strongly attracted to you. The rewards may be concrete or material. If you carry yourself with the confidence and, some might say, arrogance of Donald Trump, you, too, could be a millionaire. And finally, the rewards may be emotional. If you are a "good" little girl or boy and do what adults tell you to do, many people will love you. If the individual copying these behaviors actually receives some of these external rewards for the behavior, the learning will be internalized and repeated. This constitutes social learning.

For example, if a little boy is told repeatedly that big boys do not cry and notices that the men who are admired in his world and on TV never cry when they are sad or hurt, he will begin to consider that behavior as a model for his own. When very young, when his body or feelings are hurt, he will cry. But if he is told that crying is wrong and that "big boys don't cry" or "Batman never cries," or if he simply observes that his tears embarrass or anger his parents, the next time he is hurt, he will try very hard not to cry. If he is successful in holding back the tears, the adults around him might say, "Good boy. You are such a big boy, just like a little man. You are as brave as your favorite superhero on TV." He will enjoy this reward and begin to internalize it as part of the definition of who he is, who boys are, and how men behave. Social learning will have occurred.

In this scenario it is easy to see many other ways in which external events could create different kinds of social learning. For example, adults could have told the little boy that it is good to cry when he is hurt and that it helps release the pain. Or in an example that may seem far-fetched given American socialization, it is possible for adults to tell the little boy that it is manly to cry.

Bandura added media images to social cognitive theory when he observed that people also modeled their behavior after characters who were rewarded for their action in prime-time television and popular film. We obviously do not copy every behavior we see in media or in life. To further explain how social cognitive theory works, Bandura's theory describes two different ways that this modeling occurs. The first is through imitation, in which we directly mimic what we see on television or film. The Hannah Montana haircut, clothes, and makeup are copied zealously by little girls, "tweeners," and young teenagers to the consternation of many parents. The second type of modeling is called identification. In this situation, the copying is less specific than direct imitation. Instead, children or adults see something on television and their response is *related* to what they saw but is not a mirror image of it (Baran 2010, 370). For example, a child or teenager may be exposed to a great deal of television aggression or violence that appears in a realistic manner in programs such as *24* and the various incarnations of *CSI* or *Law and Order* or in far less realistic cartoons. While children are unlikely to use an automatic weapon or an anvil to express aggression, they may still identify with the aggression and select another way to express it, such as hitting or pushing or bullying.

Social cognitive theory is a fairly straightforward way of understanding the socialization process. We see the behavior in life or media, we observe that it is rewarded, we copy it. If we copy the behaviors we see and are rewarded for them, we will repeat them and incorporate them into our own personal repertoire of action.

The Social Self

Another classic socialization theory is George Herbert Mead's analysis of the *social self*. According to Mead, it is our sense of self that differentiates humans from animals. This theory asserts that our identity consists of our self-awareness and self-image, our interaction with others, and our ability to conceive of, understand, and respond to others.

As in social cognitive theory, children begin to mimic behavior of the adults around them as part of their early development of self. But the self continues to develop as our consciousness of our own self and others evolves. Essential to the development of self is our ability to imagine other people's response to us. For example, if we say "Good morning" to someone, we can imagine that person will say "Good morning" in response. If we throw a ball to someone, we can imagine that person catching it and throwing it back. In this way we learn certain rituals of human behavior as well as the norms of interaction.

Another feature of the development of the social self is that the way others think of and respond to us strongly influences our identity and self-image. If, as we grow up, we are told that we are a good friend, then that will contribute to our identity, which will include being a good friend. A negative self-identity can also develop if we are consistently told that we are not smart or that we are unattractive.

One key element of the theory of the social self is the belief that the self continues to evolve throughout our lives as a result of changing circumstances and changing social experiences. A final and hopeful step in this theory is the conviction that as social experiences and society influence us, we too interact with society and other people and can influence and change people, culture, and institutions. This theory views socialization as interactive and regards each individual as potentially powerful (Mead 1995, 63).

Liberation Theory

Liberation theory is a newer theory of socialization that builds on social cognitive and social self theory and adds a political element to it. Liberation theory presumes that individuals from any and every group are born with innate qualities of brilliance and the infinite capacity to be happy and successful. The theory, developed as a construct of reevaluation counseling (also known as RC), maintains that brilliance and the capacity to succeed are *innate*, while misinformation that is oppressive is *learned*. The conclusion of liberation theory is that because this information and behavior are learned, they can also be unlearned (Marcuse).

Liberation theory maintains, as does social self theory, that infants, children, and adults receive messages that shape their sense of identity. When a baby boy is born, he may be dressed in blue and told of all the things that boys can and cannot do. From the time of birth, some parents express disappointment when their new baby, especially a firstborn, is a girl. Many adult women casually report, "I was supposed to be a boy." This early socialization process around sex establishes a set of messages about how boys are supposed to behave and how girls are supposed to behave, and in some instances it assumes male superiority. Once again, according to liberation theory, this information is learned and can, therefore, be unlearned.

Liberation is the process by which we can individually and institutionally observe, recognize, rethink, and interrupt the misinformation and negative messages around us, changing how we see ourselves and others. Engaging in liberation requires an awareness and understanding of the socialization process; the belief that some of the ways we are socialized are limiting and deadening; and the desire, commitment, and deliberate choice to exchange misinformation for accurate information in ways that dismantle oppression and liberate ourselves and other people.

For some people, liberation may be something as simple as interrupting a joke that makes race or gender or ethnicity the offensive brunt of the humor. Others may embark on a self-education process, seeking alternative sources of information to better understand sexual orientation, race, or religion. Some may choose to lead or participate in organizations or movements for liberation and change. Others may introduce policies at work that acknowledge same-sex partnerships and offer health insurance to an employee's life partner. Others may choose to focus on the family level and make a commitment to teach their children about the liberation theory and socialization, and to "unlearn" **prejudice** and **bigotry** on an individual level.

Liberation theory examines the roles of privileged and targeted groups. Members of *privileged groups* have greater access to the resources and power to get what they want in the world because of their membership in a particular group. Individuals in *targeted groups* have less access to privileges, resources, and power to get what they want and need in life because of their membership in a particular group. For example, in the United States, men have traditionally had greater access to positions of power (e.g., senators, chief executive officers, or CEOs, of corporations, presidents of universities) and are therefore considered members of a privileged group. Conversely, women have had less access to positions of power and constitute a targeted group.

Individuals may belong to some privileged groups and some targeted groups. A white, low-income man belongs to two privileged groups by virtue of his race and gender and one targeted group by virtue of his economic class. A wealthy lesbian belongs to two targeted groups by virtue of her gender and sexual orientation and one privileged group by virtue of her economic class.

It is important to note that the designations of "privileged" and "targeted" are based on broad-based information such as the fact that more than 90 percent of CEOs of Fortune 500 corporations are men. This is a clear indication of which *groups* have access to more or less power and privilege. It does not predict the future, however, for individual men and women; rather it suggests the likelihood of access.

According to liberation theory, we learn messages about our identity and place in the world through a thorough and comprehensive socialization process based on our membership in privileged and targeted groups. Central to liberation theory is that in order to "unlearn" biased and missing information about human diversity, we first have to make a commitment to be conscious about it and to convert what may have once been invisible to us to something that is fully visible and subject to change. Liberation theory is an action theory and offers hope for change that is based on individual and/or collective action.

Cultural Competence Theory

Like liberation theory, *cultural competence theory* is based on the premise that society will be better when we understand, respect, and become knowledgeable about each other's cultures. What differentiates this theory is that rather than describing the socialization process itself, it describes a continuum of behavior that characterizes how individuals and institutions may behave and interact with others different from them.

Important to this theory is the understanding that **culture** is the integrated pattern of human behavior that includes the thought, communication, actions, customs, beliefs, values, and institutions of a racial, ethnic, religious, or **social group** (Adams, Bell, and Griffin 1997, 254). "Culture provides the overall framework in which we imagine what we do not encounter directly, and interpret what we do encounter directly. It is the context in which experience becomes consciousness. Culture, then, is a system of stories and other artifacts—increasingly mass-produced—that mediates between existence and consciousness of existence, and thereby contributes to both" (Gerbner 1998b).

Culture can be bisected into *surface* culture and *deep* culture. Think of culture as a tree in which surface culture is the above-ground part of the tree and deep culture is the roots below the surface (see Figure 1.1 on page 18). Surface culture is easily visible in the form of food, clothing, language, music, and dance. When you visit an ethnic festival, you are observing and participating in surface culture. Deep culture reflects less observable values, beliefs, and customs, such as child-rearing practices, rules about courtship and marriage, treatment of elders, and proxemics (the physical distance at which conversation and other interaction feel most comfortable). This image can help us understand that in order to become culturally competent, we need to learn about both the surface and deep culture of groups that are different from us. This learning takes more effort than attending an ethnic festival or reading one book.

Figure 1.1

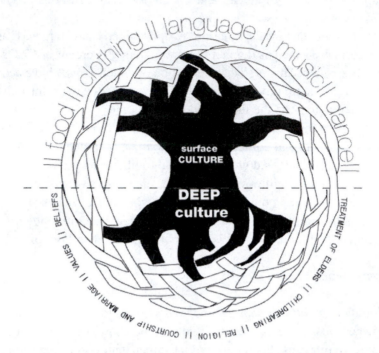

The *cultural competence continuum* (Figure 1.2) helps us identify where we are in this cultural learning process both as individuals and as institutions. Individuals and institutions can be identified according to various points on the continuum.

This continuum is a scale of attitudes and behaviors that describes an individual or a system. As you view the continuum and the points along it, think first of yourself and ask where you belong. Then think of institutions or organizations in which you are involved—for example, a place of employment, a school, a welfare department, or a bank. Ask yourself where the policies of this system fit on the continuum.

On one end of the continuum is *cultural destructiveness*, which is based on the belief that one group is better than another. An individual at this point on the continuum may belong to a white supremacist group or assume that working-class people are ignorant and lazy. A system that is culturally destructive is one in which there are many cultures present, but only one is recognized as legitimate. All other cultures are rejected and regarded as inferior.

For example, in 1620, the Wampanoag Indians in the United States were farmers with a representative political system and a division of labor with workers specializing in arrow making, woodwork, and leather crafts. "However, many colonists in New England disregarded this reality and invented their own representations of Indians. What emerged to justify dispossessing them was the racialization of Indian 'savagery,' Indian heathenism and alleged laziness which came to be viewed as inborn group traits that rendered them naturally incapable of civilization" (Takaki 1993, 37).

Figure 1.2

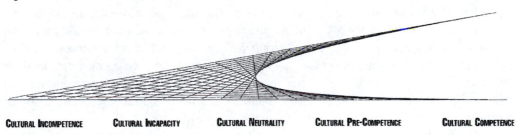

| CULTURAL INCOMPETENCE | CULTURAL INCAPACITY | CULTURAL NEUTRALITY | CULTURAL PRE-COMPETENCE | CULTURAL COMPETENCE |

The midpoint of the continuum is *cultural neutrality*. Those organizations and individuals who are culturally neutral take the stance that there are no differences between groups and all approaches are equally effective for all people. This is perhaps the trickiest point on the continuum, and the word "neutrality" itself is misleading. Many whites have been taught that for people who believe in equality, cultural neutrality is and should be the desired endpoint: a place where everyone is the same and difference does not matter. You may have heard people say, "I do not notice color when I meet a person; I just see a person." Yet for many people of color, racial identity is an important source of pride and self-representation that reflects a shared cultural heritage and a history of struggle and triumph against great odds. While on the surface it may seem noble or benign to ignore or "not see" racial difference, this act of so-called cultural neutrality may render invisible important aspects of a person's racial identity and heritage.

Many groups wish to maintain the food, music, and language of their culture and proudly make them visible for others to see. Cultural neutrality can obliterate these manifestations of heritage and pride. On a deeper level, there are many historically significant events that shape the experiences of a group in ways that contribute to both individual and cultural identity. These may be events that evoke pride, as in the development of the women's movement. These may also be events that evoke pain and perhaps even shame, as in World War II when the U.S. government interned more than 110,000 Japanese American citizens of the United States, treating them as enemies of the state (Hamamoto 1994, 75). Cultural neutrality on an individual level, while often motivated by kindness, requires that people flatten these differences and agree to be the same. However, sameness and equality are very different phenomena.

When cultural neutrality is embedded in a system, it can be quite dangerous. A college or university may decide to treat each entering first-year student exactly the same, a policy that will reflect a commitment to equality and equity. If, in fact, the structural differences in prior public education reflect that schools in poor communities and communities of color tend to have fewer educational resources and lower academic achievement, this so-called color-blind policy may be the *same* for everyone but not *equitable* for everyone. Recognition of these differences and their translation into just policies is challenging and complex.

The issue of cultural neutrality is important to our further discussions of assimilation and diversity. Some immigrant groups, Western Europeans for example, may choose to assimilate for a variety of reasons. After a generation or two, these groups may be fully assimilated if they choose or are forced to give up the language, clothing, and food (surface culture) of their country of origin. As people with white skin, the odds are good that they will become part of the privileged group with respect to race. Other groups, Asians and Africans, for example, may also choose to assimilate and give up elements of their surface culture, but in the United States their skin color makes it impossible for them to fully assimilate into American culture, which defines white skin as the norm. Cultural neutrality ignores the complexity of assimilation and diversity.

Cultural competence is the practice of actively understanding the integrated set of human values and behaviors belonging to a particular group *and* the capacity to function effectively and respectfully in other cultures. The ultimate goal on this continuum is cultural competence in both individuals and institutions. Cultural competence necessitates ongoing self-assessment and learning. Individuals and organizations that are culturally competent pay attention to the dynamics of difference and are committed to the expansion of cultural knowledge. Organizations that are culturally competent review and, when necessary, adapt and change policies and practices with regard to employment, promotion, programming, products, and services.

A *culturally competent individual* is actively committed to understanding other cultures by reading, studying, asking questions, attending cultural events, and interacting. This individual understands the difference between surface and deep culture and does not assume that one interaction bestows expertise. A culturally competent individual is not required to know everything about other cultures but, rather, has an openness and a commitment to learn.

A *culturally competent system or organization* includes a plan to expand and act on cultural knowledge by adapting individual and institutional policies, structure, and services to meet culturally diverse needs and audiences. The employees and students of a culturally competent university would closely resemble the demographics of the surrounding population at every level, from custodial to administrative, from undergraduate students to those seeking a PhD. For example, a public school system in the southwestern United States may develop a culturally competent plan that is bilingual (English and Spanish), studies and displays Mexican and Indian art, and includes Mexican and Indian history and literature as an integral part of the mainstream curriculum. For this school system to fully succeed at cultural competence, there would need to be bicultural and bilingual employees at every level of the organization.

It is possible, and not uncommon, for an individual or organization to be culturally competent in one area and culturally neutral or even destructive in another area. For example, a heterosexual white male may feel knowledgeable and competent regarding women, African Americans, and Asian Americans but have little knowledge and much discomfort regarding Latinos, gays, and lesbians. The concept of cultural competence is not static; it is dynamic. Maintaining cultural competence requires continued openness and commitment to learning and rethinking what has been learned.

Cultural competence differs from the theories presented so far because it applies to both individuals and organizations. As you read through the various definitions, at what point on the continuum did you find yourself with regard to various social groups and cultures? How does that position affect how you see people who are different from you in the world and in the media?

The Fabric of Oppression

The *fabric of oppression* is another theory of socialization that describes the structural arrangement of privilege, resources, and power. This theory is based on a liberal or leftist political understanding of how institutions, systems, and policies can create inequities according to group membership. While liberation theory is based primarily on the individual, the fabric of oppression revolves around organizations and institutions. This theory identifies how the various social groups and cultures that we are part of have an enormous impact on our access to the things we need to achieve our personal, professional, and financial goals in life. Like liberation theory, the fabric of oppression also suggests that each individual has to make choices to either collude with oppression or participate in action for change.

In order to fully understand the fabric of oppression, some basic definitions are essential. These terms will be used in subsequent chapters to examine and rethink issues of gender, race, class, and sexual orientation both in our culture and in the media. Often people use these terms interchangeably, causing some confusion. You will also find these terms in the glossary at the end of this chapter.

Oppression is the structural arrangement by which resources, power, and privileges are organized in a way that creates unequal access to the very things we need to be personally, financially, and professionally successful in life. Oppression is referred to as "structural" because the inequities are not at all random. Rather the resources, power, and privileges that we have access to as individuals depend largely on our membership in social groups.

The fabric of oppression is a systematic phenomenon that creates some groups that are privileged by oppression and other groups that are targeted by it. It is possible to be part of a privileged group and benefit from that system of privileges without ever behaving in a way that is mean, prejudiced, or hateful. Conversely, one can also be part of a targeted group without ever experiencing a hateful act.

For example, a heterosexual, married woman can count on her sexual orientation and position as married to work in her favor and for the benefit of her children as they work their way through life. If she refers to her "husband" when speaking to her children's teachers, they assume that this is a two-parent, heterosexual nuclear family—part of the privileged norm that automatically triggers comfort and respectability. Her lesbian friends with children experience something very different. When one parent is in a conference with a teacher and refers to her partner as "she," she cannot count on the teacher's acceptance or goodwill regarding her family in the same way the heterosexual woman can.

It is important to note that membership in a privileged group does not guarantee wealth, power, and success but rather increases the opportunities for such gains. Similarly, membership in a targeted group does not guarantee failure but implies fewer chances and far more obstacles to overcome. An anecdote attributed to Texas gubernatorial candidate Ann Richards illustrates how this operates. Richards was running for governor of Texas against George W. Bush, who was from a family of great wealth and considerable power. Using a baseball analogy to describe Bush's advantage, Richards said that to this day Bush believes he hit a triple when, in fact, he was born on third base.

Institutionalized oppression refers to the web of organizations and systems that perpetuates unequal access. Institutionalized oppression can be *legal*, overt, and intentionally built into various institutions. For example, before the Nineteenth Amendment was ratified in 1920, women were prohibited from voting, and before the U.S. Supreme Court outlawed the practice in the 1954 *Brown v. Board of Education* ruling, racial segregation was legally protected in American public schools.

Institutionalized oppression can also be *illegal*, covert, and intentional. When something is covert, it is secretive and "undercover" and often poses as something very different from what it really is. For example, a government-funded organization might claim to hire regardless of gender, but rarely interviews women and maintains an all-male workforce; a real estate agency might steer people of different races into neighborhoods where the residents are primarily their same race. These examples violate laws that protect equal rights of women and of people of color.

The third kind of institutionalized oppression is *self-perpetuating* and systemic. This kind of oppression is built deeply into existing structures and is more difficult to identify and change. One example of this type of institutionalized oppression is private colleges and universities that are explicitly committed to race and gender equity, yet whose highest-ranking officials and employees are generally white men. These organizations have not been willing or able to figure out how to put verbal commitment to diversity into meaningful action.

Along with the external lack of access to power, resources, and privilege, members of targeted groups may also experience **internalized oppression**. This phenomenon occurs when individuals from targeted groups receive external misinformation, stereotypes, and negative images about their group and turn the negativity inward. Internalized oppression is never voluntary but rather a result of the targeted group taking in and believing the same misinformation that is conveyed to members of the privileged group.

For example, until the 1960s middle-class men and women were told that women's work was to stay at home, to raise the children, and to cook and clean. As many women in the 1960s began to break out of this singular role and seek meaningful work outside of the home, others condemned them for failing their families and failing to be sufficiently feminine. While this issue was and continues to be politically charged, it is clear that many women believed that to be "real women" they must do women's work as assigned by society. According to the fabric of oppression, a particular woman's difficulty in recognizing the range of options she has, as a woman, is a function of misinformation. If she has internalized the cultural messages of the 1950s, she may believe that the exclusive role of a woman is to take care of her children and her husband and her house. She believes that this is the right place for women and that competing in the workplace with men will diminish her femininity and provide unfair competition to men supporting their families. This piece of internalized oppression poses as the truth for this woman and creates internal barriers that limit her ability to see a wide range of options for her life.

It is important to note that internalized oppression is very different from the process of informed choices nor is it critical of informed choices.

In the example above, the woman could have learned a great deal through the work of the women's movement and even participated in an organization that was dedicated to seeking high-quality child care for working women. She could have come to believe that women whose low family income made work a necessity or who made choices to work were entitled to those choices—the same as men. However, she also wanted to be respected for her choices, to focus her time and her life on raising her children and taking care of the home.

The process by which those in power secure the consent or social submission of those who are not in power is called **hegemony**. Hegemony does not require force but creates social submission through the way that values are taught in religious, educational, and media institutions—through socialization. The structure and values of hegemony are often invisible. For example, until the 1960s, force was rarely needed to convince women to defer to men in financial or business matters. Women and men were socialized to understand their roles and to act them out accordingly.

As you look at Figure 1.3, titled Fabric of Oppression and Social Group Membership, on page 24, think of the upper spaces as representing those groups that are privileged and have greater access to social power, privilege, and resources, and the lower spaces as representing those groups that are targeted by oppression and that have less access to privileges, social power, and resources.

The key word in this process is "access." In considering the issue of ability, people who are physically healthy and able-bodied are considered the privileged group and people who are physically unhealthy or disabled are the targeted group. This does not mean that *all* able-bodied people are wealthy and in positions of great power; nor does it mean the reverse, that *all* people living with disabilities have menial jobs and are subservient. It means that if you examined most institutions, you would be likely to find able-bodied people in the positions that are most highly paid and in positions of power. This is about access, not about predicting who will succeed and who will fail.

As you determine which groups are privileged and which are targeted, it is useful to think about who typically holds the highest positions in major corporations, Congress, state legislatures, universities, and other institutions. In Figure 1.4, Fabric of Oppression—Part 2, on page 25, you will find the completed version of the fabric of oppression with the privileged and targeted groups in each social category clearly identified.

According to the theory of the fabric of oppression, the vast majority of those in power and with access to **social power** in the United States are male, white, physically and mentally able, Christian, part of the owning class, and perceived to be heterosexual. A few of these privileged group descriptions require explanation. *Owning class* refers to those individuals whose wealth is such that they have no financial need to work. The working class consists of people who need to work to survive and are typically two or three paychecks away from poverty. The privileged group, with regard to sexual orienta-

Figure 1.3   **Fabric of Oppression and Social Group Membership**

Source: Adapted from unpublished workshop material created by Joan Olsen.

tion, refers to individuals who are *perceived* to be heterosexual. In this case, the reality of whether individuals personally identify as gay, lesbian, bisexual, or heterosexual is less likely to predict their access to social power than how other people identify them. This perception or appearance affords them access to social power. This does not mean that membership in any one of these groups absolutely guarantees or predicts that an individual will become the president of the United States or the CEO of General Motors. Rather, it describes the group memberships of those who are in positions of power and those who have greater access to it.

The same holds true for individuals who are members of the targeted groups described in the lower spaces of the diagram. The fact that there is *less access* to resources, power, and privilege does not imply that there is *no access*, nor does it forecast inevitable individual disappointment and failure. Rather, it describes the group memberships of those individuals in the contemporary United States who have much less access to positions of power and the **resources and privileges** that come with those positions.

The fabric of oppression further describes the vast majority of those who are targeted by oppression and have less access to social power, resources, and privileges as females;

Figure 1.4   **Fabric of Oppression—Part 2**

GENDER	RACE	CLASS	ABILITY	RELIGION	SEXUAL ORIENTATION
MEN	WHITES	OWNING CLASS	PEOPLE WHO ARE TEMPORARILY ABLE BODIED	CHRISTIANS	PEOPLE WHO ARE PERCEIVED AS HETEROSEXUAL
WOMEN	OTHER RACES	EVERYONE ELSE	PEOPLE LIVING WITH PHYSICAL DISABILITIES	PEOPLE OF OTHER RELIGIONS & BELIEFS	PEOPLE WHO ARE PERCEIVED AS LGBT

Source: Adapted from unpublished material from a workshop by Joan Olsen.

people of color; individuals with physical and/or mental disabilities; individuals who are perceived to be lesbian, gay, bisexual, or transgender (LGBT); non-Christians; and individuals who are middle-class, working-class, or poor.

As you review the completed chart, notice where your various group memberships fit in the categories. Most people find that they have membership in a variety of groups, some privileged and some targeted. Theorists and activists who advocate the fabric of oppression as an accurate description of the unequal organization of resources, privileges, and social power are also generally strong proponents of the need to dismantle all forms of oppression. They concur with Martin Luther King Jr.'s statement, "None of us are free until all of us are free" and Audre Lorde's belief that "There is no hierarchy of oppression."

This theory holds that the pursuit of equity and justice restores wholeness to humanity.

The Cycle of Socialization

The *cycle of socialization* is a theory that describes how we learn the norms of our society by receiving a combination of information and misinformation that is taught to us and reinforced by people, systems, and institutions that we know, love, and trust. These norms are similar to those that appear in Figure 1.1, of surface culture and deep culture. On the surface are the norms such as the ways boys and girls are expected to dress and the food we eat. Below the surface are the norms and values regarding how we treat the elderly in our communities, our religious or spiritual beliefs, the customs of dating, courtship, and marriage, and how we raise our children. They include beliefs, both true and false, about our own race and nationality and those of people who are different from us.

In our childhood or in the "early years," as they are called in the cycle, we receive this mix of solid information, misinformation, biased information, missing information, and stereotypes mostly from our parents and other adults that we trust—often the people who take care of us and love us. We have no reason to doubt what these adults tell us or demonstrate by their own actions; nor do we, as young children, have the skills yet to independently assess the credibility of what we are being told. This time period of our early childhood corresponds with the first circle in Figure 1.5.

The information in the first circle often converts to beliefs that are "installed" in us from this blend of information—sometimes true, sometimes false, some well-intended, and some with malicious intent. Sometimes the trusted adults in our lives are simply passing on what *they* learned to be true and never questioned, challenged, or even pondered.

Unless this information is questioned or challenged by other credible sources in our lives, it will be taken in and pose as "truth." These questions and challenges can occur at any point in the cycle, and while they may initially be confusing, they also offer individuals an opportunity to assess the information and the sources, think critically, and ultimately make independent decisions about what they believe to be true.

The next step in the cycle of socialization (the second circle in Figure 1.5) is our exposure to institutions. If the solid, credible information or the misinformation and stereotypes we received from our families and other trusted adults are consistent with what we learn from these institutions, our beliefs are then reinforced. Our views of human diversity tend to solidify, and we internalize this information, regardless of its credibility and harmless or harmful potential. For example, if our parents, media, faith groups, and schools all convey information that tells us homosexuality is a sin and if we have no information that offers a different way of thinking, we are more likely to believe that the messages equating homosexuality to sin are true.

Figure 1.5

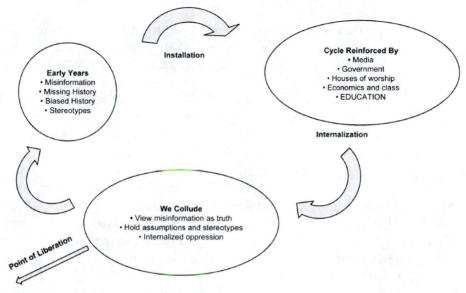

Source: Adapted from unpublished workshop material created by Educational Equity Consultants.

Trusted adults in our family as well as teachers and religious leaders can teach us the skills that prepare us for independence in two major ways. One way is to provide a wide variety of information about the different beliefs and norms that various groups have about a particular issue. For example, there are many ways to raise healthy children; different cultural groups have a wide variety of norms, beliefs, and practices about child rearing. A trusted adult could teach us that as long as parents do no mental or physical harm to their children, we can accept these differences.

Another way that parents and teachers and other trusted adults in our lives can help us cultivate our own independent beliefs is to teach us the skills of respectfully question-ing and challenging the information we've been given. They can model these skills by inviting us to challenge their beliefs or encouraging us to express our own opinions. For example, some middle and high schools have very strict rules about how young people should dress and may send students who don't meet this dress code home to change. This would be a perfect issue to discuss with children to help them develop their own standards and criteria for their beliefs. Adults could ask young people to think about how low-cut a girl's blouse needs to be or how much a boy's pants need to sag before it becomes disrespectful, harmful, or dangerous. They could also ask how much leeway young people should have so that they can express their own individuality through the way they dress.

If any of these institutions or another trusted adult challenges what we have learned in our early years or offers a different perspective, we will get some practice in weighing the credibility of the sources and the information itself. This practice can help us develop the critical thinking skills that can support our conscious and independent decisions about what we choose to believe.

If we don't have the knowledge or tools to independently evaluate what we've heard and learned about human diversity, we are more likely to proceed to the third circle of the cycle of socialization (Figure 1.5) in which we collude. To collude means to actively participate, plot, or conspire in an endeavor. In the "endeavor" of learning about human diversity, we may collude at a more or less conscious level; our intent could be positive, negative, or neutral. But any time and any way we collude, we are passing on the un-evaluated content that we have received about human diversity. This may include some clear and strong information about value differences and/or the biases and stereotypes that we have heard so often that we have internalized them. At this stage, we may view misinformation as truth or hold assumptions and stereotypes as if they were true, letting them harden into bias, prejudice, and **discrimination** toward groups that are different from us. If we internalize the negative assumptions and stereotypes that are perpetuated about our own groups, the result can be pain and difficulty in our own development. If we collude by passing on the biases we've learned as children to the next generation in their early years, the cycle starts all over.

If, at any point in the cycle, the content of what we've been taught is interrupted and questioned or if someone helps us learn the skills of independent thinking, we have the opportunity to notice if we have any confusion and to allow ourselves just to sit with it, to lean into the confusion. Assuming we are strong enough to withstand the discomfort that these contradictions create, then we can embark upon a path of liberation by revaluating the credibility of the information we have received about human diversity.

Here is just one illustration of how the cycle of socialization operates. An American Indian child, Dana, lives in a very loving family, and her parents want her to have a better life than they did. Early in her life they taught her not to speak her tribal language or wear any tribal clothing. Dana's family, with her best interest at heart, tell her that she will fit in better, be accepted more readily, and have a better chance of success if she acts "white." Accordingly, Dana lives in a mostly white neighborhood, attends a Christian church that is predominantly white, and goes to school with white classmates. She attends sporting events where teams have names like "Redskins" and team mascots are depicted as Native Americans in stereotypical fashion. In school, she learns that most of the important people in American history and science have been white. In television and movies, most of the heroes she sees are white. When she does see American Indians in movies and television, they are often portrayed as being violent, alcoholic, backward, and uneducated. Most of the messages from the people and institutions Dana trusts reinforce what her parents told her: that it is better for her if she assimilates into the dominant culture around her. If nothing happens in her life to interrupt this distortion of information, she will pass along these same messages to her own children.

What has she lost in this process, this particular example of the cycle of socialization? First, regardless of Dana's attempts to blend in, she is still American Indian. She has grandparents and other relatives, neighbors, and friends who practice a blend of traditional Indian culture along with the dominant culture. In her young mind, she wonders if that is bad. Her sense of self, identity, authenticity, and self-esteem may be seriously shaken. She may, in fact, internalize oppression and think that, deep down, there must be something wrong with her if it is so terrible to be who she really is. This internalized oppression may reflect itself in many different ways. Dana could become personally withdrawn or depressed. She may express deep prejudice and bigotry toward American Indians as a group, especially those who maintain their original culture. If she is ever in a policy-making position, she may decide that American Indians are not worthy of any special consideration. This same cycle can occur with regard to gender, other races and ethnicities, class, and sexual orientation.

* * *

Most theories regarding oppression mention the media as an institution of socialization. The final and critical piece of the socialization puzzle is an understanding of the role and pervasiveness of entertainment media and how they reinforce or challenge our socialization in U.S. society.

Reconstructing knowledge is an invitation to critical and independent thinking, to intellectual and emotional autonomy. The process invites us to review what we have learned about history and politics and current events and to understand that there is almost always some combination of accurate information, misinformation, and distortion. Reconstructing knowledge asks us not to simply believe everything we are told, even by teachers or parents or the authors of this book, but rather implores us to carefully sift out truth from myth. Our personal experiences in life provide the informal lessons, and school provides the more formal lessons, that we inevitably bring with us every time we turn on a radio or computer, buy a ticket to a movie, or sit at home playing video games or watching television.

ENTERTAINMENT MEDIA

As we have seen, our personal experiences and formal education often create voids and distortions in information about people and groups that are different from us. Studying entertainment media is a third way to examine how these voids and distortions are challenged or reinforced.

Our quest to analyze images of race, gender, class, and sexual orientation in the media constitutes more than a simple appreciation of diversity. It requires inquiry into our own life experiences, exploration and reevaluation of what we have been formally and informally taught about various groups, and an examination of how these messages appear in entertainment media. This section provides a variety of theories and perspectives that assess entertainment media, experience, and knowledge. These theories and tools will be utilized in each chapter to examine the connection between the standing of a particular group and its portrayal in the entertainment media landscape.

We have focused on entertainment media because of the pervasiveness of this dimension of American popular culture through the entire span of our lives. News media have an increasing impact on our view of groups that are different from us as we grow older. However, as we learned through theories of socialization, the messages we receive in early developmental stages have extraordinary influence on how we see the world. From the cradle to the grave, entertainment media in the form of prime-time television, popular music, and popular films offer images that are repeated over and over. Whether we are attending to a traditional TV, a computer, a tablet, a smartphone, a movie, or a concert, we are still receiving the same messages from popular media. These images can either fill in the gaps of our formal and informal learning, reinforce what we have already learned, or challenge previous learning.

In the 1950s and early 1960s, the American family was portrayed in television programs such as *Father Knows Best*, *Leave It to Beaver*, *The Donna Reed Show*, and *Ozzie and Harriet*. In these programs, the family was portrayed as white, middle-class, and Christian, with two heterosexual parents and two or three children. The father worked outside the home and the mother worked in the home; most often the mother wore a dress and sometimes pearls as accessories. In these families, people rarely quarreled or shouted, and wise parents resolved problems in a quick thirty minutes. Sibling conflict ended with a brotherly punch on the arm and a sheepish "Gee, Beav." In the 1950s and 1960s, many people watched these programs and more every week, receiving consistent images and messages about what it meant to be a "normal" American family.

According to our earlier discussion of social cognitive theory, repetition followed by reward becomes internalized learning. Also, according to liberation theory, misinformation gets taken in and internalized both by privileged and targeted groups. The fictional 1950s television family was often projected as the American norm against which all other cultural experiences were to be measured and compared. Even if you lived quite differently because your family was working class or poor, African American or Latino, Jewish or Muslim, subliminally you may have nevertheless come to regard this white upper-middle-class suburban way of life as an ideal to be emulated.

The 1998 film *Pleasantville* offers a critical look at the perfect, simple world portrayed in these early television programs. When two teens get transported into the black-and-white life represented in the TV program *Pleasantville*, they compare the simplicity and predictability of television life to the complexity and unpredictability of their lives in the 1990s. Through a series of conflicts and revelations, the film conveys a strong message about what it means to be human. To be human is to be full of contradictions, to experience a range of often messy feelings, and to face unpredictability. The film clearly prefers this complexity, with all its chaos and pain, to the black-and-white barrenness of the fantasy world of 1950s television.

Television viewers frequently hold contradictory beliefs about what they view on the small screen. On the one hand, we know and can articulate that the program we are watching is fiction, yet on the other hand we often absorb the messages that we are receiving as if they are "the truth" (Jhally and Lewis 1992, 15). This contradiction is key to understanding the impact of entertainment media on consumers. We may say of television, music, or film, "I know it's not real," and yet with heavy consumption of media, the repetition of the images will influence us in spite of our intellectual understanding that it is only make-believe.

This section of the chapter reviews various forms of entertainment assessment theory and offers some accessible, consumer-friendly tools for analyzing media content. These theories and tools provide qualitative, quantitative, and anecdotal methods of assessing the meaning and impact of media content and culture. Current and potential media producers can use these tools to analyze programs they are developing and considering. Media consumers can use these tools to dissect the messages and information they receive from media on a daily basis.

Entertainment assessment, then, is the third component of the three-part analysis system of this book. It is a combination of classic and new theories, approaches, and practical tools to investigate the messages in the media and their impact. By itself it provides us with some interesting analytical possibilities. Combined with our understanding of our personal experiences, informal and formal learning, and reconstructing knowledge, it offers us a comprehensive method of investigation that opens enormous possibilities for critical and independent thinking in all aspects of life.

Entertainment Assessment Theories

Research in entertainment media has grown tremendously in the last half of the twentieth century and the beginning of the twenty-first century. Given the growth in prime-time television, cable television, popular music, film, video games, the Internet, and social media, researchers have an enormous range of media to explore and study. Our focus will be on the industries that produce the media, the messages they contain, and their impact. Some theories offer anecdotal and qualitative means of media analysis, while others construct methods to quantify media messages. Some of the theories claim political neutrality or objectivity, while others begin from a clear and unabashedly political standpoint. The theories and approaches we will consider are selection processes, media literacy, cultural studies, media production and economy theories, the cultural indicators approach, and simple content analysis (characters and themes). We will use these entertainment assessment theories to gain a better understanding of how we interact with entertainment media.

The Processes of Selection

As we investigate our informal and formal experiences and media messages about human diversity, some of the material will seem familiar and consistent with what you have already learned and "know," and that is likely to feel fairly comfortable. At other times, the information not only may be unfamiliar but also may challenge some of your long-held beliefs and values and feel fairly uncomfortable. This discomfort is called **cognitive dissonance**. Cognitive dissonance is the emotional or psychological discomfort that occurs when we receive information that is inconsistent with attitudes and beliefs we have held to be the "truth" (Baran and Davis 2009, 146). According to the theory of selection, this psychological discomfort is often so difficult that many of us seek a way to relieve the tension and return to a more comfortable consistency in our beliefs.

One of the ways people seek a more comfortable position is through *selective exposure*. Through this process, people frequently make choices about how they spend their time and with whom as well as the media they consume. Generally, most of us do our best to expose ourselves to information and messages that are consistent with our preexisting attitudes and beliefs (Baran and Davis 2009, 146). Leon recalls a summer job he had as a teenager working with a pair of school custodians, Mr. Chambers and Mr. Jones. The two of them always listened to the local jazz radio station as they worked. At first, Leon hated the music. He preferred rhythm and blues, pop, Motown, Stax-Volt, anything but the horrible stuff the custodians liked. But outnumbered and powerless, he became a captive audience to this unfamiliar genre. One humid afternoon toward the end of a particularly grueling day of moving furniture and cleaning floors, Leon was sent to the school library to unpack a large shipment of books. As he headed down the hall, he heard the sound of an acoustic bass thumping out the hypnotic rhythms of "A Love Supreme," by John Coltrane. One of the custodians had left his radio in the library. Leon reached for the radio knob so he could switch to one of the R&B stations he liked, but he could not bring himself to do it. There was something so enthralling about what he was hearing that he had to keep listening. It was as though the music was speaking directly to him, calling him by name. For the rest of the afternoon, he worked to the sounds of drums, bass, piano, and saxophone played in ways that he had never heard them played before. When he got home that evening, he lay across his bed tired and a little sore, but instead of falling asleep, he tuned in to the jazz station and listened deep into the night. He continued to listen to it the next day and the day after that. By the end of the summer he had developed what would become a lifelong love of jazz. Leon did not realize it at the time, but in that brief period during his formative years he had gone through an experience that created sufficient *cognitive dissonance* to disrupt his pattern of *selective exposure* and permanently alter his musical interests—expanding his capacity to appreciate a diverse range of musical genres.

Another clear-cut example of selective exposure involves the television news programs people choose to watch. In the age of cable and satellite TV, viewers have an almost endless variety of options for news watching. During the 2008 and 2012 presidential elections, it became increasingly clear that people who were politically conservative leaned in the direction of FOX News and people who were politically liberal or left were much more likely to get their news from MSNBC. The news programs they watched were likely to provide selected information and a spin on big news stories that were compatible with the viewers' political beliefs, allowing media consumers to remain comfortable.

Another one of the selective processes is *selective retention*, in which what we remember the most and the longest are the things that either are consistent with our beliefs or are the most important to us (Baran and Davis 2009, 147). Most of us don't forget breakups of major relationships in our lives, because they were significant to us. However, our brains seem to cooperate with the desire for consistency and allow us to forget things we have read, viewed, or experienced that offer a plausible, reasonable, and credible challenge to our own beliefs.

Selective perception is a strategy we use to reduce the psychological discomfort when our beliefs are challenged. Through this process we actually change the meaning of the information or messages we receive so that they are compatible with our own ideas and convictions. Linda remembers quite clearly an incident of selective perception that occurred when she was teaching second grade in a school in which all the students were black and she was one of three white teachers. One of her seven-year-old students came in from recess crying. After some incoherent words in between tears, Linda pieced together what happened. Wanda said that another little girl had taunted her and teased her by saying that Linda was white and Wanda hit her, starting a fight. Linda said, "Wanda, you know I am white," to which Wanda replied, "No, you're not, Ms. Holtzman. You're not white, you're light." Wanda preferred to think that Linda was a light-skinned African American woman. Wanda really loved her teacher, yet in her short life span most of her experiences with white people and most of the things she had been told about white people were negative or hurtful. Wanda's selective perception was to make a translation in her own mind that allowed her to reconcile her affection for Linda and her distrust of white people—she just changed her teacher's race.

The selective processes can be very powerful, but they are not foolproof or beyond our own conscious will. The extreme discomfort of cognitive dissonance can set off an automatic launch sequence into selective retention, perception, or exposure, or we can try something different when we feel this dissonance. We can pause. We can lean into the discomfort and allow ourselves to feel it. We can recognize that we do not need to make a choice of what to believe right in that moment. This pause can give us the chance to use analytical thinking to evaluate the discomfort and to consider the two sets of information with an open mind and an open heart. This process can move us from an automatic mode toward a process that encourages us to stay awake enough to evaluate the credibility of the contradictory information and to make a solid, independent decision about what we believe.

Cognitive dissonance is a concept and an analytical tool that is used in both human diversity theory and in media theory. If we are not aware of the process of cognitive dissonance, we will not have the consciousness to observe our resistance to new information and ideas, nor will we have the wherewithal to make independent decisions. If we are aware of our psychological discomfort and resistance to new ideas and images of diversity, we are no longer going down the highway on cruise control; we are in much more control in the driver's seat.

Media Literacy

One relatively new approach to analyzing the messages in entertainment media is *media literacy*. Media literacy is an international field of study that involves observing media content, production, and impact as well as the industry itself. According to media literacy scholar Art Silverblatt, media literacy includes five elements:

1. *Awareness of the impact of media* on the individual and society involves educating media students, consumers, and producers to understand the enormous influence of media and to learn independence from its impact on us.
2. *Understanding the process of mass communication* involves learning the ways that messages are sent and received in both interpersonal and mass communication.
3. *Developing strategies to understand and interpret media messages* utilizes detailed analytical questions or keys that revolve around process, context, framework, and production values.
4. *Using media to understand contemporary culture and ourselves* reviews media texts and images to unravel cultural values, beliefs, and attitudes.
5. *Enhanced appreciation and enjoyment of the media* is one of the aims of media literacy that is advanced by the insights that are integral to the process. (Silverblatt 1995, 2–3)

The educational application of media literacy is highly adaptable from elementary through graduate school and in the home as well as in school. Given the pervasiveness of media and their influence on young people, some states have included media literacy as an element of their required public school curriculum. The purpose of teaching the tools of media literacy to students early in their lives is to help them make sense of the maze of media messages they receive and to sift out fiction from fact. This is a relatively new curriculum in the United States, and while it is too early to determine results, there is anecdotal information to suggest that even young children are enthusiastic about playing media detective to uncover hidden messages. For example, children who are glued to video games are intent on winning and are often only semiconscious in the process. Children who learn about the roles of women and the presence of violence in these games may be more aware of the messages in the game, may discuss what they think about these messages, and may at times make different choices.

Media literacy provides a wide array of methods and tools to analyze media texts and serves as an important educational foundation. Media literacy does not take an explicitly political or activist stand. However, even though the methodology is apolitical, what this analysis uncovers can have strong political ramifications.

Cultural Studies

Another approach to understanding the messages conveyed through media is *cultural studies*. Understanding the **ideology** that is present in various forms of entertainment media is an important element of cultural studies. Ideology is "a system of meaning that helps define and explain the world and that makes value judgments about the world" (Croteau and Hoynes 1997, 163). We can examine programs, songs, or films to see how they demonstrate certain kinds of thinking about cultural issues and about the social order of things and people. The ability and tools to discern this ideology are central to the understanding of how cultural studies allow media scholars and consumers to see beyond the surface entertainment value.

The analysis of political economy and production, analysis of media texts (e.g., film, music, television), and understanding of audience reception are the main components of cultural studies. The field of cultural studies examines the content of media within a framework of media ownership by analyzing how ownership and economic self-interest in the industry itself influence decisions about media format, content, and distribution.

Unlike media literacy, cultural studies theorists do not claim political neutrality but rather build their analyses from an explicit political position. One cultural studies scholar, Douglas Kellner, defines the field as a critical endeavor with particular views and values, including criticism of media as they re-create images of dominance, repression, and oppression; a critical perspective of media that advances democracy; and an understanding of the potential that media culture has to advance the interests of oppressed groups (Kellner 1995, 2).

One unique aspect of cultural studies is this forthright claim that it is not neutral. In fact, most theories about media and about diversity, multiculturalism, and oppression are not neutral. Just as individuals bring their personal experiences and values to their understanding of media and human diversity, so do the researchers who study media and develop theories as well as the people who write books such as *Media Messages*. In cultural studies, however, the politics and values are explicit.

Another important contributor to the development of cultural studies, Stuart Hall, defines ideology as "those images, concepts, and premises which provide the frameworks through which we represent, interpret, understand and 'make sense' of some aspect of social existence" (Hall 1995, 18). According to Hall, while individuals may make ideological statements in the media, they are the product of the conditions of socialization and the way the society and culture have formally and informally taught individuals to make sense of the world. Ideology works best when it operates at a less than conscious level—that is, when our socialization has been so thorough that we do not identify our positions as ideology but rather see them as the articulation of "truth." Hall uses the example, "Little boys like playing rough games; little girls, however, are full of sugar and spice." While to some this may seem like a reflection of "truth," according to cultural studies it is largely based on a series of ideological beliefs about the nature of boys and girls (Hall 1995, 19).

Media is an important source of information for introducing, replicating, and reinforcing a society's dominant ideologies, and as cultural studies theorists point out, these ideologies are often invisible to the media consumer. They often simply confirm what the consumer already "knows" to be true.

Television is the most pervasive form of contemporary entertainment media. A popular TV show can reach millions of households and individual viewers. In 2010, CBS's reality program *Undercover Boss* drew 38.6 million viewers, the largest audience for a new series (Hibberd 2010). "One reason why television is considered to be so ideologically charged is that it relies, almost exclusively, on conventional 'realist' forms of image construction that mask the workings of the camera" (Croteau and Hoynes 1997, 180). For example, most of us know from our own experience that problems rarely resolve themselves neatly in a thirty-minute format. But when the characters and plot of a particular TV program closely resemble "real people," the thirty-minute resolutions seem more credible, authentic, and possible to the audience.

Prime-time television (regular programming that occurs Sunday through Friday from 8 P.M. to 11 P.M. eastern standard time), both in the fictional narrative and "reality" formats, tells stories that create a sense of what is normal and acceptable. According to cultural studies, if we can dig beneath the surface of the plot and characters, we can discover if and to what extent the program reinforces the dominant ideology. For example, the *perceived* family "norm" in the United States involves married heterosexual couples with children. Cultural studies proponents suggest that this norm explicitly and implicitly conveys the message that any family outside of this configuration is by definition "other" or abnormal.

To illustrate that, we can examine images of gay and lesbian characters and families on television. Until recently, gay and lesbian couples did not exist in prime-time television. By the 1990s, some programs, such as *Northern Exposure*, *thirtysomething*, and *Roseanne*, featured minor, recurring characters who were gay or lesbian, and in 1996 the program *Ellen* depicted the coming out of its main character, played by Ellen Degeneres. Yet throughout most of prime time, gays and lesbians have remained relatively invisible. By 1998 *Ellen* was off the air. The program's ratings were down and network executives claimed the character was "too gay."

When *Ellen* went off the air, there was an underrepresentation of gay and lesbian characters. This lack of images of gays and lesbians in prime time underscored a central ideology that characterizes the heterosexual couple and family as normal and marginalizes other kinds of couples and families. The way that television orders its realities and tells its stories thus creates a central and dominant ideology with few opportunities for alternate stories to be told.

Despite the combination of economics and bias in the demise of *Ellen*, it paved the way for shows that featured gay characters and gay themes to successfully make their way into mainstream and cable television. One of the most successful programs in this category was *Will and Grace*, on NBC from 1998 to 2006 (Internet Movie Database 2010). Cultural studies analysis raises the question whether the mainstream economic success of *Will and Grace* and other programs with gay characters and themes also means success in the reduction of stereotypes and a shift in the idea of "normalcy" in relationships and in family.

Does *Will and Grace* tell an alternative story? According to cultural studies analyses, the characters of Jack and Will tell two stories. The first and most obvious story is that two gay men are major characters on the program and that while they have very different personalities and expression of their masculinity, they are both gay men who are clearly and proudly "out." However, does the ideology of the program reinforce or challenge dominant culture in which heterosexuality is the norm? According to cultural studies analysis, in the end, *Will and Grace* reinforces the dominant ideology that heterosexual relationships are normal. It does this through the following repetitive portrayal and themes:

Will and Grace (1998–2006): What defines family? Is this a family? [Left to right: Grace (Debra Messing), Will (Eric McCormack), and Jack (Sean Hayes).] *(Source: Courtesy of Getty Images. Copyright © 2012 NBCUniversal, Inc. Used by permission of Getty Images.)*

- Most of the visual images of sexuality are between Grace and her various male romantic partners; we rarely see a parallel kind of physical interaction between two men.
- The consistent and central relationship in the program is between Will and Grace, and although they are not romantically or sexually involved, their relationship mimics a heterosexual marriage.

While this cultural studies interpretation sees an ongoing replay of dominant culture in *Will and Grace*, other cultural studies scholars assert that the existence of gay characters in a mainstream program such as *Will and Grace* offers audiences an opportunity to interpret or "read" the stories in a way that challenges the norms of love, romance, and family.

According to Croteau and Hoynes (1997, 233), media can hold multiple meanings, which in turn offer the raw material for multiple interpretations. This broad scope empowers the audience to create meaning by bringing their formal learning, socialized experience, and critical and independent thinking to their media experience. Audiences can thus interpret or "read" media in three different ways.

The first kind of media reading is the *dominant reading*, in which the media consumer is relatively passive and takes in the content without consciously thinking about or processing the messages. In this case, the consumer almost always takes in the dominant message that was intended by the media producer. A *negotiated reading* of media assumes more active consumers who accept part of the dominant message but also interpret part of the content according to their own experience and preferences. An *oppositional reading* is an active stance in which media consumers consciously interpret the content in a way that fits with their own experience, preferences, and worldview. These three positions depend largely on the experience, knowledge, and critical tools of the audience.

All in the Family, which aired from 1971 to 1983 as one of the all-time most popular television series, illustrates the possibilities of these various forms of interpretation or readings. The creator of this series, Norman Lear, developed the character of Archie Bunker to reflect bigotry and political conservatism and as a symbol of the resistance to the movements for social and political change occurring in the 1960s and 1970s.

So the *dominant* reading, as put forth by the show's producer, would be that Archie Bunker was a conservative bigot; his wife, Edith, a sweet simple soul; and his daughter, Gloria, and son-in-law, Mike, comic but politically correct liberals. What came as a surprise to the show's creators was the phenomenon that a large segment of the television audience agreed with the ideology put forth by Archie Bunker and revised Archie into something of a folk hero—a gruff but lovable character who held on to traditional American values. This would be considered an oppositional reading of the program.

Another central tenet of cultural studies is its foundation in politically radical theories that explain dominance and oppression. Cultural studies scholars use Marxist theories of economics and class to explain media as one of many institutions that control individual freedom via dominant structures and hegemony. This analysis offers a way to understand political and ideological positions and how dominance and resistance to these positions are reflected in the media (Kellner 1995, 56).

What this means is that a program such as *All in the Family* could be analyzed in terms of feminist theories about gender. Through this lens, Archie's wife, Edith, represents the old gender order. Edith defers to Archie, cooks for him, waits on him, and runs back and forth to the kitchen as Archie sits comfortably in his easy chair pontificating about the troubles of the world. Edith is a warm and likable character. Their daughter, Gloria, is a quintessential 1960s woman. She believes that women should be independent and often criticizes her father's demands and expectations of her mother. Yet as a character, Gloria is shrill, sometimes strident, and not nearly as warm or likable as Edith. Based on the contradictions between character likability and political ideology, the audience would be drawn to mixed conclusions about the role of women. While Gloria's political views of gender are presented as palatable, it is ultimately Edith's likability to which the audience is drawn. According to this cultural studies analysis, *All in the Family* would ultimately convey a dominant ideology about gender. This ideology would say that women like Edith, who go out of their way to wait on everyone, particularly their husbands, are the "good women." This is a *negotiated* reading of the program, which uses feminist ideology as a lens.

Cultural studies scholars take an activist position in their outright criticism of the reflection of dominant ideology in media. They position themselves as advocates and

Roseanne (1988–1997) was a widely popular program that featured a white, working-class family, one of first TV programs to do so since the early 1960s [Clockwise: the Connor family: Roseanne (Roseanne Barr), Darlene (Sara Gilbert), Becky (Alicia Goranson), Dan (John Goodman), and DJ (Michael Fishman.] *(Source: Courtesy of Getty Images. Copyright © 1989 by Moviepix. Used by permission of Getty Images.)*

allies of oppressed groups whose alternate stories and ideologies need to be heard (Kellner 1995, 57). This aspect of cultural studies is compatible with liberation theory and the fabric and cycle of oppression in that its goal is transformation of the media and the dismantling of oppression.

Some forms of entertainment media have a history of offering alternative voices and ideologies. One such example is rap music. Some forms of rap and hip-hop music criticize the dominant culture and ideology. "In essence, rap presents an ideological critique from below; it is a musical form that criticizes social institutions from the perspective of those who have comparatively little power in contemporary society" (Croteau and Hoynes 1997, 184–185).

Rehearsal of *Little Mosque on the Prairie* (2007–2012), a popular Canadian sitcom about a diverse Muslim community and a makeshift mosque in Canada. The series never made it to the United States. [Nigerian Muslim character Fatimah (Arlene Duncan), fixes the back of shock jock Fred (Neil Crone).] *(Source: Courtesy of Associated Press. Copyright © 2006 by Associated Press. Used by permission of Associated Press.)*

Cultural studies theorists and activists regard entertainment media as a battleground in which dominant themes and ideologies are challenged by oppositional readings as well as themes and ideologies of resistance. This theory of criticism involves developing an alternative norm as a vantage point for criticism. This norm takes a particular political stand that includes the values of resistance, empowerment, democracy, and freedom used to criticize forms of oppression and domination.

According to cultural studies, what do you think would be the norms of a family as defined by the dominant culture ideology and what would be considered alternatives to this ideology? Think of some of the TV families you grew up with and whether, and to what extent, they met the criteria of the dominant ideology of family in the United States. Then consider whether your own family and others that you know reflect the dominant culture as expressed on prime-time television. How does your family's position vis-à-vis the norms of the dominant culture family affect you? Would the family in *Roseanne* fit the parameters of the dominant culture ideology? What about traditional and non-traditional Muslim families living near and worshipping at a "Little Mosque on the Prairie"?

Analysis of Media Production and Economy

The *analysis of media production and economy* is another set of theories used to examine entertainment media. This analysis is often used in tandem with other methods that ascribe meaning to content. In the last fifty years, there has been increasing concentration of ownership of the media. By 1992 only twenty national and international corporations dominated the mass communications industry. Media integration occurred in these conglomerates in which ownership of production of multiple types of media as well as distribution structures had become increasingly concentrated (Bagdikian 1997, 7). By 2008, the "U.S. media landscape" was "dominated by massive corporations that, through a history of mergers and acquisitions, have concentrated their control over what we see, hear and read. In many cases, these giant companies are vertically integrated, controlling everything from initial production to final distribution." The top seven corporations that own the vast majority of media are Disney, News Corp., Time Warner, Clear Channel, Comcast, Viacom, and CBS (FreePress.net 2013).

Most media consumers are unaware that the many different production companies whose programs they enjoy in a given week may actually all be owned by a single conglomerate. If in one week you see a film from Miramax and a film from Buena Vista, order DVDs from Netflix that were produced by Touchstone and Pixar Animations, watch FOX news or read *TV Guide*, you have actually spent a week as a media consumer of just one source: Disney (FreePress.net 2013).

> When the same corporations expand their control over many different kinds of media, they speak glowingly of providing richer public choices in news and entertainment. But the experience has been that the common control of different media makes those media more alike than ever. Movies become more like television series. Cable, once thought to be a fundamental alternative to programs on commercial television but now under control of companies also in television and other media, is increasingly an imitation of commercial television. (Bagdikian 1997, 9)

Ben Bagdikian, who has conducted important research in this area, does not see this concentration of ownership as a conspiracy. Rather, Bagdikian asserts that the level of wealth, ownership, and experience of individuals who run these conglomerates results in a high degree of shared values. These corporate decision makers become primary shapers of how we see the world and interpret its meaning. Their shared values translate into an ideology that is consistently conveyed in the media. The power to "treat some subjects briefly and obscurely but others repetitively and in depth" is where the power of concentrated ownership is most apparent. And as in social cognitive theory, "continuous repetition and emphasis create high priorities in the public mind and in government" (Bagdikian 1997, 16). Another media theory, known as agenda setting, explains that while media may not always be able to tell us what to think, they do often tell us what to think *about* (Baran and Davis 2009, 278).

Concentration of media ownership makes it difficult for alternate voices to be heard because the bottom-line profit motive affects programming decisions. According to media analyst Todd Gitlin, "one consequence of the profit-driven logic of safety is the general tendency to avoid controversy, even though it might bring high ratings" (Gitlin 1983, 50). This approach makes television, music, and film more formulaic and predictable. It certainly drives the enormous numbers of sequels that we see in films such as *The Mighty Ducks 3*, *Amityville 4*, and *Deathwish 5*. The profit motive also links advertising and music videos so that most "video versions of songs . . . are the result of marketing decisions made by record companies, not the artistic expression of the musicians" (Gitlin 1983, 50).

The motive for profit and the goals of advertisers have an enormous impact on the content of television as well. Sex and violence are used extensively because they are formulaic, are easily produced, and attract a large audience, which in turn sells more products. According to Bagdikian, advertisers kill even successful serious dramas because they remind audiences that their problems cannot be easily solved by "switching to a new deodorant" (Bagdikian 1997, 160). The resulting narrowness of content limits ideas and information that are presented to the American public, thus limiting independence of thought and choice. "If a nation has narrowly controlled information, it will soon have narrowly controlled politics. . . . In the end, no small group, certainly no group with as much uniformity of outlook and as concentrated in power as the current media corporations, can be sufficiently open and flexible to reflect the full richness and variety of society's values and needs" (Bagdikian 1997, 223).

As the consumers of television programming, we focus on the programs and their content as central. The producers and owners of television programming view television's advertising time as central. Most TV is not a public service offering, but a business, a vehicle for profit. For network executives, the shows are often high-visibility couriers that deliver the real moneymakers: the commercials! In 1998, ABC sold thirty-second spots during the final episode of *Seinfeld* for a record $1.7 to $1.8 million each (Haber and Edelson 1998, 11). A thirty-second commercial in the 2009 Superbowl averaged $3 million on NBC (Associated Press 2010).

This relationship between advertisers and program producers affects the content of prime-time television. Networks want advertisers; advertisers want programs with audience demographics that match the products being advertised. From the network point of view, then, it is not surprising that segments of the population who are outside desirable demographic target groups find themselves marginalized or excluded from vast stretches of prime-time TV. If we do not have the necessary discretionary income and the cheerful willingness to spend it, then in strictly financial terms we are not worth courting.

Cultural Indicators Analysis

Another method of analyzing entertainment media is the *cultural indicators approach*, a comprehensive system originated and utilized by the late George Gerbner in his many years of studying and analyzing entertainment television. This approach has three components: institutional process analysis, message system analysis, and cultivation analysis (Gerbner et al. 1986, 22).

Institutional process analysis examines the formation of policies directing media messages. The work of Bagdikian, Gitlin, and Croteau and Hoynes that evaluates the economics of media production fits into this category of analysis. Federal Communications Commission (FCC) regulations and policies, production codes, censorship, ratings, and laws that govern the Internet all are subject to examination in order to further the understanding of media messages. For example, when the technology of television became available, there were many options for how it could have operated as an industry. It could have been primarily government owned and operated, as in England, or it could have been a commercial enterprise, as it ended up being in the United States. Because TV has always been a profit-making endeavor in the United States, we assume this to be a natural attribute of the industry. Its commercial nature has meant that program content is largely dictated by economic forces and desires for profit. But suppose the government, a quasi-governmental agency, or an independent nonprofit organization such as the Public Broadcasting Service operated television. The motivation for programming and the content itself might vary according to whether it was meeting needs for profit, propaganda, or art.

Message system analysis is a quantitative assessment of the content in entertainment television and another component of cultural indicators analysis. The Cultural Indicators Project, founded by Gerbner, annually collects a large sample of prime-time television. The research team uses *content analysis* and develops measurable units that assess and describe characters, themes, and plots. The data are summarized and the messages are analyzed. Content analysis provides information about a single TV program, film, or song or a group of media that forms a "sample" of what's being studied. For example, someone may use content analysis to examine the role of men in television programs in the 1950s as compared with the role of men on TV in the twenty-first century. The results provide a snapshot of the characteristics, personality, employment, appearance, and behavior of men in the sample and also provide information about changes in messages, roles, stereotypes, and relationship to dominant ideology.

Message system analysis is larger in scope than content analysis and refers to the overall messages that tend to be repeated over and over in television, rather than a focus on a particular issue or a particular type of programming. The theory and practice of message system analysis suggests that if we are heavy TV viewers (watching more than fifteen hours per week), the messages we receive from television will be homogeneous across the board and create an effect Gerbner calls "mainstreaming" in which audiences are flooded with the same repetitive messages (Gerbner et al. 1986, 31). In 1997, Gerbner's team examined 1,755 prime-time characters from ABC, CBS, NBC, and FOX, as well as WB and UPN. Here are some of the major findings:

- Poor people are nearly invisible on television.
- African American men are surprisingly overrepresented on television and portrayed as wealthier than their white counterparts. This does not square with current demographics and thus misrepresents the actual situation.

- Children and older adults, particularly women, are grossly underrepresented.
- Women, Latinos, and Asian American characters are significantly underrepresented. (Gerbner 1997, 1)

The third component of the cultural indicators approach is *cultivation analysis*, which assesses audience impact. Cultivation analysis utilizes the content and messages gathered from message system analysis. Depending on the number of hours an individual views television per week, he or she is categorized as a light or heavy viewer. Subsequently, light and heavy television viewers are questioned about their beliefs and worldviews, and a determination is made as to whether their beliefs conform to the overwhelmingly consistent "TV reality." Given the homogeneous and repetitive messages on prime-time television, the exact programs viewed are not particularly relevant to this analysis. For example, Gerbner has repeatedly found that the violence on television is far more extreme and prevalent than in reality. Heavy television viewers, however, tend to believe the "TV reality" over the documented reality of crime statistics or even their own experience (Gerbner et al. 1986, 22). Gerbner's term for this is the "Mean World Syndrome" through which heavy viewers of TV see the world as a more violent and "meaner" place than it is in fact.

During the summer of 1996, Linda took her then nine-year-old son to see the hot film of the season, *Independence Day*. While the critic in Linda found weaknesses and flaws, the consumer in her loved it. Never mind that most of the women still had their blouses tucked in, high heels on, and impeccable lipstick after hours and days of grueling battle—the movie was engaging, visually dazzling, and fun. Everyone got what they paid for—a few hours of entertainment. So why go through the tedious process of analyzing something that is clearly not designed to inform or educate?

Leon experienced a similar moment of inner discord in early 2013 while sitting in a crowded theater watching the movie *Django Unchained*, about a freed slave returning to the South to find his wife. Although, like most of the audience, he found parts of the film entertaining—in a violent, shoot-'em-up, old-fashioned-Western sort of way—he could not help but grow increasingly angry at the historical distortions and gross misrepresentations of the slave experience. It is a part of U.S. history that deserves to be told with much more accuracy, depth, and truthfulness before it is utilized as source material for parody.

The producers of entertainment media are the "storytellers" of the twentieth and twenty-first centuries (Gerbner 1998b, 1). Before the middle of the twentieth century, children heard stories and were taught values primarily from parents, grandparents, members of their extended family, religious institutions, and other trusted adults in their community. The socialization process continued with the "stories" learned in school and from peers. From these sources and stories, children learned what it meant to be male or female, rich or poor, American, right or wrong, and so forth.

After the advent of television, while many families have continued these traditions of conveying their beliefs and values to their children, they now face stiff competition from a little box that lives in their house and can tell their children stories with a flick of the remote. The video game storytellers and the multiple narratives on the Internet join the stories children receive from television. What are these stories, and what impact do they have on children and adults alike? What are the messages conveyed by popular television, film, and music? How are we socialized by the Internet and by the culture built into social media, cell phone communication, texting, or Twitter? Are there consistent messages that children and adults receive from these various forms of entertainment media? What are we learning about what is right and wrong, and what are we learning about people who are different from us?

Realistically, our society has moved beyond the stage where most parents can effectively compete with television, video games, and social media for their children's attention. The challenge now is to make wise and effective use of media programming. Parents, teachers, and other caring adults must become adept at being critical interpreters of the stories, images, and messages to which children are relentlessly exposed. By strategically interacting with their children as their children engage with the media, parents can become more purposefully involved in helping them develop their own media literacy skills.

The theories and methods discussed above provide important background for critical analysis of entertainment media and will be used throughout this book to interpret the meaning of selected samples of popular media. However, some of these methodologies are beyond the scope of what one individual can do in daily life to discern the messages in film, television, and music. In the next section of this chapter, we will look at accessible entertainment assessment tools that are designed with the individual in mind. While these tools do not provide us with the generalized conclusions that media researchers can determine from large samples, they will help students of media, media producers, and consumers of media to think critically about media culture and to recognize and understand its underlying ideology and values.

With these tools we will continue to investigate and compare the stories we heard from our families, from school, and from TV and film, video games, and the Internet.

Entertainment Assessment Tools

Entertainment assessment tools examine how diversity by race, gender, sexual orientation, and socioeconomic class appears and is treated in popular film, prime-time television, and popular music. Although beyond the scope of this book, these tools can also be used to analyze messages in video games, print and electronic news, social media, and so on. With these tools we can investigate trends, patterns, messages, images, and stereotypes. We can compare one program, song, or film to another. Researchers, using larger and more random samples, can determine whether a particular program is unique in the messages it sends or whether it is part of a broader trend that conveys homogeneous content and meaning. Whether the investigation is on a small or large scale, we can begin to unravel some of the explicit and implicit values in media texts and to search for their underlying meaning and ideology.

Character Investigation

Central to the application of entertainment assessment tools to social groups is the under-standing of stereotypes. A **stereotype** is a preconceived and oversimplified generalization about a particular social group. Generalizations are one way that people organize information so that we do not have to rethink everything every day. When we are babies and toddlers, our parents may tell us daily, "Don't touch the stove—it's hot!" Every day is a new day for toddlers who are intrigued by this tempting stove and the meaning of the word "hot." The child who succumbs to temptation and touches the stove learns quickly what that particular meaning of "hot" is and is unlikely to touch the stove again. This is a generalization that works for us.

Another example of generalizations or stereotypes involves hair color. As a young child, you may meet someone with red hair who is very funny. As an elementary school student, you may meet another redhead with an engaging sense of humor. Your mind organizes that information to say that redheads are hilarious: a fairly benign stereotype. But suppose the first two redheads you meet have made a strong impression on you because they are mean or lazy or not so smart. This creates a negative expectation or fear every time you encounter someone with red hair. If these images are also conveyed in the media with any regularity or repetition, you are more likely to believe that they are true.

Stereotypes operate most effectively in entertainment media in three ways. The first is by limited exposure. So, for example, if there are few American Indian characters depicted in film, television, and popular music, the images that are there take on added significance and have a more powerful impact on audiences. The second way stereotypes operate in media is through the range of characters portrayed. If there are a limited number of American Indians in media, it is unlikely that there will be a wide range of different character types. And if one or two character types are consistently repeated, a stereotype will be created or reinforced. If we grow up in a community where there are few American Indians, the media images take on a more significant role—they fill in the gaps in our experience and we often come to believe that these images, messages, and stereotypes are true. If, however, there are Indians who are doctors and construction workers and poets and alcoholics and mystical and educated and uneducated and middle class and unemployed, this wide range of possibilities makes it much less likely for stereotypes to occur and to be taken in as the "truth about American Indians."

Finally, stereotypes work best in media because they are conveyed through simple characters. Complex characters, whether heroes or villains, have many different layers and contradictions. They more closely resemble real people, and their depth and intricacy defy easy categorization. Simple characters generally convey one or two strong elements of their personality or behavior and have little texture, complexity, or depth.

The well-known character Kramer in the TV program *Seinfeld* is a simple character. He is personally eccentric and has quirky physical moves that automatically trigger audience laughter. He is often involved in some moneymaking or relation-building scheme that is so bizarre and outlandish that everyone but Kramer knows it will end in the kind of disaster that causes laughs. The audience gets only small peeks into any complexity in Kramer that would reveal any depth of motivation for his actions or explanation of his character through exploring his childhood or past relationships. Kramer is the clown or jester of the program, with an almost slapstick quality that is similar to other characters of that type. He is basically one-dimensional.

Media Activity 1.1
Detecting Character Stereotypes in Entertainment Media

Instructions

Select three entertainment television programs or films that you have recently seen, or three current popular songs, and answer the following questions:

1. Are there any Asian Americans portrayed in the films, TV programs, or songs?
2. If so, how many Asian Americans are speaking characters? List the names of these characters.
3. For each Asian American character identified, determine the following:
    a. Is the character simple or complex?
    b. Is there a range of simple and complex characters?
    c. Is there a range of different types of characters?
4. Do you detect any patterns in the presence or absence of Asian American characters in your media sample?
5. If there are no Asian Americans in your sample, what does this absence suggest about Asian Americans in the United States in terms of their presence, their importance, or what you and others might know about them?

Meredith Grey of *Grey's Anatomy* is another story. On the surface, Meredith is smart and attractive and has a promising career as a surgeon. She is also damaged or, as she describes herself, "dark and twisty" as a result of abandonment by her father and neglect by her mother. The program develops Meredith's backstory over time to explain some of her fears, contradictions, and skittish behavior with men. The audience also is witness to Meredith's emotional pain in present time as both of her parents continue to hurt her and as she is deceived or disappointed by men. Meredith Grey is a character that is multilayered and complex.

There are several ways to detect *character stereotypes* in a particular media text. The first is to ask simple questions about the social group we are investigating. We will focus on Asian Americans as the social group to investigate for now, but we could also replace this group in the questions below with any other race, ethnic group, gender, sexual orientation, or class. The instructions in Media Activity 1.1 show how this works.

This is a simple tool to use while watching prime-time television. Try it over the course of a week to investigate images of Asian Americans in the prime-time television programs that you normally watch. Determine the actual number of images that appear and ascertain whether the characters are simple, complex, or a mix. Remember, simple characters are one-dimensional and unrealistic. Complex characters are multilayered, perhaps contradictory, and seem like real people. Either simple or complex characters can be heroes or villains. Most likely you will find very few or perhaps no Asian American characters. This provides an important piece of information. If you live in a community with few Asian Americans, where and what will you learn about this group? And if you live in a community with many Asian Americans, what are the implications of the disparity you note between the Asian American population on television and that within your own community?

Another layer of analysis that can be used in character investigation is to distinguish between major and minor characters. Major characters are those without whom the plot makes no sense; they are essential to what unfolds. Minor characters are all other characters with speaking parts. If you look back at the character investigation you conducted, you can distinguish between major and minor characters and see if there are any other patterns. If there are no major characters that are, for example, Asian American or working-class, that provides some messages about the conveyed significance of the group.

As a follow-up to the simple analysis of Asian American characters in Media Activity 1.1, Media Activity 1.2 invites you to observe an evening of prime-time television and count the number of major actors and note their race. This exercise takes us a step further in assessing the depiction of race in prime-time television and to begin to make some sense of the messages these depictions convey. Whether a major character is a "good guy" or a "bad guy," the character's importance in the development of the plot sometimes makes a tacit statement as to the significance of his or her racial identity. When you complete Media Activity 1.2, observe which racial groups are depicted most frequently as major characters in your sample. Which groups are depicted less frequently? What messages about race do you think the characters in your sample convey?

As you conduct these mini research projects, it is important to thoroughly understand that the results suggest some messages and perhaps ideology about the particular programs you have observed. But without a larger sample and more thorough investigation you will not be able to make large-scale generalizations about prime-time television.

You have just conducted your first content analysis in Media Activity 1.2. As described earlier, content analysis is the quantification of information contained in media that allows researchers and consumers alike to identify patterns and meaning in the media studied. Content analysis can only describe and summarize messages. From the messages, meaning can be extracted, but content analysis does not measure influence. In conducting content analysis, it is tempting to assume that powerful or surprising trends in the content will have an equally powerful impact on the audience. This may seem like a logical conclusion; however, while we can speculate that recurring messages may have a particular effect on the audience, it is important to remember that these conclusions cannot be drawn exclusively from the data gathered from content analysis. We will be using content analysis frequently as an important tool to ascertain messages in popular media as we examine the media content of gender, class, race, sexual orientation, and international conflict.

Media Activity 1.3 (page 51) uses content analysis to examine women's physical appearance in another small sample of narrative fiction in prime-time television. You may select three dramas or comedies from prime-time television. As defined earlier, prime-time television is regular programming that occurs Sunday through Friday from 8 P.M. to 11 P.M. eastern standard time. This programming does not include news, infotainment,

Media Activity 1.2
Comparing Character Portrayals in Entertainment Media

Instructions

This time, watch one night of prime-time television from 8 P.M. to 11 P.M. eastern standard time (EST). Limit the programs you observe to narrative and fictional situation comedies and/or dramas. Do not include news, infotainment, reality shows, game shows, or anything else that is nonfiction. Complete the chart below. Examine the major characters in each program (those who are essential to the plot) and indicate their race. Total the number of characters of each race in the sample you viewed and then figure the percentage of each race compared to the total number of characters.

If you'd like to explore this point further, you could use the same chart and observe an evening of prime-time reality programs to determine if there is any difference in how race is depicted in the percentage of major characters in the sample and in the way they are portrayed.

Note: There is space in the chart for five programs. Depending on the number of thirty-minute and one-hour programs in your sample, you will probably have between three and six programs to review.

Analysis of Race of Major Characters in Prime-Time Television

Date of Sample _____ Day of the Week _____

Name of program, network, and date aired	Major characters/ white	Major characters/ black	Major characters/ Latino	Major characters/ Asian	Major characters/ American Indian	Major characters/ mixed race	Major characters/ cannot tell
#1							
#2							
#3							
#4							
#5							
Total/number							
% of U.S. population of each race							

Summarize Your Findings

As you draw some preliminary conclusions from your media sample, it's important to remember that this is a small sample and may not be representative of percentages of race in a larger and more representative sample. Still, this exercise will help you determine what viewers would be exposed to and how it might affect them if they were regular viewers of these programs.

Use the most current U.S. census to determine how the most recent population count in the United States is divided according to race. You can find this information at http://quickfacts.census.gov/qfd/states/00000.html. How do the census percentages compare to the percentages in your sample? In your sample, who is portrayed the most and who is portrayed the least? By percentages alone, which group(s) are portrayed as the most important and the most prevalent? How does this compare to the census percentages? What other observations do you have from this simple study?

sports, variety programs, or special broadcasts. Once again we will be investigating only major characters; those who are essential to one or more of the plot lines We'll define a scene as any time there is a change in the physical setting of the program.

Media Activity 1.3 is called a "codebook" and can be copied so that each of the major female characters can be coded on a separate sheet of paper. The results should then be tallied and added. For example, if you are investigating six major female characters, how many of them are plain, extremely attractive/glamorous, and so on? To take the analysis one step further, you may figure the percentage for each category. Are most of the women average, attractive, or extremely attractive/glamorous? Are most of them thin, average, voluptuous, or overweight? What patterns do you see and what messages do you think are conveyed by the results? To carry this particular content analysis one step further, you could investigate the major and minor male characters and compare the results and perhaps draw some preliminary conclusions from the comparison. There are other kinds of character investigations that will be introduced throughout the text to examine particular social groups and cultures.

Examination of Themes

Still another way to analyze entertainment media is to observe the occurrence of various themes. *Themes* are subjects that are introduced in the media text (music, film, television); they can be minor, significant, or central to the unfolding of the story. For example, themes can involve crime, health and medicine, friendship, or sexual orientation. Analyzing themes is another method of understanding messages and ideologies. The types of themes that occur in popular media convey what is important in society and suggest appropriate values and norms.

To understand how themes convey messages, examine the last few feature films you have seen at the theater or viewed on television, DVD, or video. Using Media Activity 1.4 (page 53), determine which of the themes listed were present in the film and to what degree. Again, you may copy the codebook and apply it to each film investigated.

After completing one form for each film, tally the results and note the following totals:

- How many times did various themes appear as major?
- How many times did various themes appear as significant?
- How many times did various themes appear as minor?
- In how many of the films were various themes nonexistent?
- Which themes were most and least prevalent?

As you review the appearance and relative significance of these themes in films you have seen, you can begin to ascribe meaning to their presence or absence, keeping in mind that without a larger and more random sample you will not be able to make broad generalizations and conclusions. However, you can understand messages in the particular films that you investigate.

Media Activity 1.3
Content Analysis of Women in Prime-Time Television

Instructions

Choose a minimum of three prime-time television programs that offer a fictional narrative. They can be dramas or comedies but cannot be news, movies, infotainment, reality shows, award shows, or any other nonfiction programs. For the purpose of this activity, major characters are defined as those who are essential to the plot and without whom the plot would not make sense.

As you determine the attractiveness of the character, rely on U.S. norms and conventional standards of beauty rather than your personal preferences. Thinking about what is considered to be beautiful in fashion magazines and advertising, as well as in magazines that feature movie stars, will help you determine these criteria. Answer questions #1 through #8 for each of the major female characters.

If you would like to repeat this activity with a sample of reality programs, you could select three of those programs. Ask the same questions and compare the two different sets of results.

And for even more extensive research, you could view the same programs and determine the attractiveness of the major male characters. An interesting research question to ask in this comparison is how attractive female prime-time characters (and by extension actresses) are required to be as compared to male prime-time characters (and by extension actors)? If one gender is required to be more attractive than the other in order to appear in prime-time television, what does this imply about comparative job opportunities in TV acting for men and women?

Name of program _____ Date viewed _____ Day of the week _____

1. Summary of basic plot: _____
2. Number of major characters: _____
3. Number of major male characters: _____
4. Number of major female characters: _____
5. Name of major female character # ___ (fill in the blank giving each character a number):
   _____
6. Is the character: _____
   0 = cannot code; 1 = very thin; 2 = slim; 3 = average weight; 4 = voluptuous;
   5 = overweight; 6 = other (describe) _____
7. Is the character: _____
   0 = cannot code; 1 = blonde; 2 = brunette; 3 = red-haired; 4 = gray-haired; 5 = other
   (describe) _____
8. Is the character: _____
   1 = cannot code; 2 = very unattractive; 3 = plain; 4 = average; 5 = attractive;
   6 = extremely attractive and/or glamorous; 7 = other (describe) _____
   _____

This survey investigates only themes that involve targeted groups, groups that tend to be disempowered in our culture. In a large sample, this kind of research can determine how these groups are treated in film. In our small sample, we can begin to see if these groups appear at all in the films we watch and if they are significant to the development of the plot. If there are never themes regarding physical and mental disability in the films we view, we can draw at least one conclusion: the message conveyed is that issues involving disabilities are nonexistent or unimportant. If there are few or no themes about disabilities in film or television, where do we learn about life's challenges and rewards for people living with disabilities? If our personal experiences do not involve people with disabilities and we are not taught in school about disabilities, the media become an important conveyor of information. As we note the absence of certain themes in entertainment media, we may then begin to question what our source of information is about disabilities or other topics. This questioning increases our independent thinking. We may determine that we have learned a great deal about disabilities from school or our own personal experiences so the absence of media themes makes little difference. We may realize that we have had almost no exposure to the issues facing people with disabilities and decide to learn more. If we are living with a disability, we may feel invisible or be angry that issues and topics that affect us are rarely conveyed in media and are often inaccurate when they do appear.

This exercise assesses themes simply in terms of their occurrence. Themes can also be investigated in more depth to determine underlying ideology in the way that a theme is conveyed. Further analysis can be conducted regarding plot and interactions between characters. These, in combination with the character and theme analyses above, can be used to evaluate messages in various forms of entertainment media.

CHAPTER SUMMARY

This chapter describes a three-part process of how we learn about individuals and groups that are different from us. We learn about diversity from direct experience with our families, our neighbors, our friends, our classmates, and the people who attend our place of worship. This informal kind of learning through exposure to and interaction with different people is called *personal experience*. When there are many groups missing from this direct experience, there are gaps and voids in our informal learning. Some of the gaps and voids may be filled through what we learn about groups that are different from us in our formal education. In the schools we attend, our teachers and textbooks are sources of information. *Reconstructing knowledge* is a method of reviewing this formal education to detect what is accurate and where there are gaps, misinformation, and distortion. This will be used as a basis to consider and evaluate information we may not have learned. Finally, we receive indirect or mediated information from entertainment media in the form of popular film and music and prime-time television. The messages and ideology in media may fill in some of the gaps in our personal experience and formal education, or they may reinforce or challenge what we have learned elsewhere. Entertainment assessment theories and tools provide us with methods to determine, understand, and evaluate the messages we receive as well as their accuracy.

Media Activity 1.4
Analysis of Social Group Themes in Feature Film

Instructions

Themes are subjects, issues, or topics that are present in each film. This particular activity is designed to observe and analyze the presence of themes that suggest human diversity in these films. A theme may be minor or incidental if it appears in one scene of the film or if it is present throughout but not framed as important to the plot or the development of the film. Significant themes are present in more than one scene and are framed in such a way that they make a difference in the plot and development of the film. Finally, a theme is central to the film if a majority of the plot and character interactions revolve around this subject, issue, or topic.

Select a minimum of three feature films that you have recently seen in the theater, on TV, on DVD, or on video. Answer the questions below separately for each film you viewed, using the codes below.

0 = the topic was not present
1 = the topic was present but minor or incidental to the story
2 = the topic was significant to the story
3 = the topic is the outstanding issue or is central to the story

1. Race   _____
2. Ethnicity/nationality   _____
3. Sexual orientation   _____
4. Gender   _____
5. Socioeconomic class   _____
6. Physical or mental disability   _____
7. Religion   _____
8. International cultures   _____
9. Other (please describe) _____ _____

Examples: Suppose you are trying to assess the theme of socioeconomic class in a film. The film is set in a very wealthy, upscale community in the United States, and there are several characters that play a significant role in the film. If the subject of the film or the interactions between the characters are explicitly or implicitly about class, then this theme is present. If some of the characters are portrayed as shallow, materialistic, or judgmental of people who they think are "beneath" them in class, and if other characters are dissatisfied with the values and lifestyle they have been brought up to think of as normal, the theme is present and could be either minor or significant to the story. If one or more of these characters go out in the world to explore different classes or change their lives from being a socialite or a corporate lawyer to becoming a social worker in a low-income community or a legal aid lawyer, then the theme is likely to be either significant or central to the story.

As we employ this process of assessing entertainment media, we can review media messages in the context of what we know about our personal experience and through reconstructing knowledge as we examine what we have been formally taught. This is not an exercise in political correctness but rather an exploration of a multitude of possibilities of how to see and interpret the world. After we consider the many ways available to understand diversity, we may choose to change how we understand difference or we may choose to maintain our original values, beliefs, and perspectives.

As we investigate and assess and perhaps revise what we have learned, we will be building a warehouse of tools. These tools allow us to consciously and independently choose and construct our own identity, beliefs, and values and a deeper understanding of human diversity in our culture.

GLOSSARY OF KEY TERMS

bigotry: The tolerance and prejudice that glorifies one's own group and disparages members of another group. Bigotry can be a thought or belief or it can be expressed through words or actions.

cognitive dissonance: A psychological discomfort that occurs when we receive information that is inconsistent with attitudes and information that we have held to be the "truth."

culture: The integrated pattern of human behavior that includes the thought, communication, actions, customs, beliefs, values, and institutions of a racial, ethnic, religious, or social group.

discrimination: The negative and harmful treatment of other groups that provides an advantage to one's own group. While prejudice is a thought, belief, or feeling, discrimination builds on prejudice and is converted to words or actions.

hegemony: The process by which those in power secure the consent or social submission of those who are not in power. Hegemony does not require force but creates social submission through the way that values get taught in religious, educational, and media institutions—through socialization. The structure and values of hegemony are often invisible.

ideology: A system of meaning that helps define and explain the world and that makes value judgments about the world. Ideologies include sets of beliefs about the way the world is and should be organized and about what values are most important. Ideologies can be based on religious beliefs, political beliefs, or any other set of beliefs that established a structure and hierarchy of priorities and values.

internalized oppression: This phenomenon occurs when individuals who are members of groups that are targeted by oppression receive external misinformation, stereotypes, and negative images about their group and turn them inward. Internalized oppression is never voluntary but rather a result of the targeted group taking in and believing the same misinformation that is conveyed to members of groups that are privileged by oppression. Internalized oppression may trigger prejudiced beliefs or inferiority that is pervasive in the wider culture.

oppression: A structural arrangement through which social groups receive more or less access to resources, privilege, or social power depending on their social standing.

prejudice: An attitude, opinion, or feeling based exclusively on an individual's membership in a particular group. It is not based on any prior knowledge, thought, or reason, and it is not grounded in fact. Prejudice is an internal experience that is often expressed in words and actions through bigotry or discrimination.

resources and privileges: Unearned benefits that accrue to people who belong to social groups with social power. For example, white parents can count on their children learning about Europeans and whites who made significant contributions to U.S. history. People who are perceived as heterosexual are likely to face fewer barriers when they seek employment or housing than those who are perceived as homosexual.

social groups: Groups that share a common social or cultural identity. These groups may be set apart by socially defined boundaries such as race, gender, sexual orientation, age, ethnicity or nationality, ability, or socioeconomic class.

social power: The access to resources that increase one's chances of influencing others and getting what one wants and needs in life. Social power is based on social group standing.

stereotype: A preconceived and oversimplified generalization about a particular social group.

REFLECTION, SUMMARY, AND ANALYSIS

Instructions

The chapter questions invite you to engage in an exercise of reflection, summary, and analysis about key terms, topics, and issues discussed in the chapter. The skills involved in responding to the questions are a combination of summary and analysis.

The *summary* component of the questions requires you to demonstrate your understanding of the terms and concepts in the chapter through the use of describing, explaining, and restating. *Summary* involves primarily answering questions that begin with the word "what."

The *analysis* component of the questions requires you to use your own independent thinking, your own ideas and arguments. *Analysis* requires breaking something—like a concept, theory, or argument—into parts so you can understand and describe how those parts work together to make the whole. Analytic writing goes beyond the obvious to discuss questions of how and why—so ask yourself those questions as you read. Your responses to these kinds of questions will require that you carefully and clearly state your argument, opinion, or "thesis" statement and use evidence from the chapter as well as your own experience or observations to support your thesis statement.

The University of North Carolina's Writing Center website has an excellent two-page handout on analysis and summary (http://writingcenter.unc.edu/handouts /summary-using-it-wisely/).

Study Questions

Describe the following terms and theories about socialization. Choose one of the theories listed below (item 3, 4, or 5) that makes the most sense to you and explain why it seems realistic. Then describe a situation that you have personally experienced or observed that illustrates this theory.

1. Socialization
2. The social self
3. Cultural competence theory
4. The fabric of oppression
5. The cycle of socialization

Briefly describe the following entertainment assessment theories and give one example that illustrates each theory:

6. Media literacy
7. Cultural studies
8. Media production and economy
9. Cultivation analysis
10. Character investigation
11. Examination of themes

Describe the concepts below and discuss how they are relevant to the study of media images and stereotypes.

12. Hegemony
13. Ideology
14. The selection processes

BIBLIOGRAPHY

Adams, Maurianne, Lee Anne Bell, and Pat Griffin, eds. 1997. *Teaching for Diversity and Social Justice: A Sourcebook.* New York: Routledge.

Andersen, Margaret L., and Patricia Hill Collins, eds. 1995. *Race, Class, and Gender: An Anthology*. 2nd ed. Belmont, CA: Wadsworth.

Associated Press. 2010. "Super Bowl Ad Prices Fall; Still Cost Millions." January 11. www.wkyc.com /news/story.aspx?storyid=128625.

Bagdikian, Ben H. 1997. *The Media Monopoly*. 5th ed. Boston: Beacon.

Baran, Stanley J. 2010. *Introduction to Mass Communication: Media Literacy and Culture*. 6th ed. New York: McGraw Hill.

Baran, Stanley J., and Dennis K. Davis. 2009. *Mass Communication Theory: Foundations, Ferment, and Future*. 5th ed. Boston: Wadsworth Cengage Learning.

Cader, Michael, ed. 1994. *Saturday Night Live: The First Twenty Years*. Boston: Houghton Mifflin.

Chesebro, James W. 1987. "Communication, Values, and Popular Television Series: A Four-Year Assessment." In *Television: The Critical View*, 4th ed., ed. Horace Newcomb, 25–37. New York: New York University.

Croteau, David, and William Hoynes. 1997. *Media/Society: Industries, Images, and Audiences*. Thousand Oaks, CA: Pine Forge.

Dines, Gail, and Jean M. Humez, eds. 1995. *Gender, Race and Class in Media*. Thousand Oaks, CA: Sage.

Educational Equity Consultants. 2008. Unpublished workshop material. St. Louis.

FreePress.net. 2013. "Who Owns the Media?" www.freepress.net/ownership/chart.

Gerbner, George. 1996. "Coding Forms, Revised, Fall 1996." Cultural Indicators Project. www.asc .upenn.edu/Gerbner/Archive.aspx?sectionID=152&packageID=68.

———. 1997. "Television Demography: What's Wrong With This Picture?" Unpublished manuscript. www.asc.upenn.edu/gerbner/asset.aspx?assetID=342

———. 1998a. "Casting the American Scene: A Look at the Characters on Prime-Time and Daytime Television from 1994–1997." Screen Actors Guild Report. December. www.sagaftra.org/files/sag /documents/1998castingtheamericanscene.pdf.

———. 1998b. "Why the Cultural Environment Movement?" Unpublished manuscript. www.asc .upenn.edu/gerbner/archive.aspx?sectionID=20

Gerbner, George, Larry Gross, Michael Morgan, and Nancy Signiorelli. 1986. "Living with Television: The Dynamics of the Cultivation Process." In *Perspectives on Media Effects*, ed. Jennings Bryant and Dolf Zillman Lawrence, 17–31. Hillsdale, NJ: Erlbaum.

Gitlin, Todd. 1983. *Inside Prime Time*. New York: Pantheon Books.

Gonzales, Anthony, Bryon Laurie, Brigit McDowell, and Kristin Tymrak. 1993. *Baby X*. Presented as part of the President's Peace Commission program, "Identity in the 90s: Individual, Family and Community." Video.

Grusec, Joan E. 1992. "Social Learning Theory and Developmental Psychology: The Legacies of Robert Sears and Albert Bandura." *Developmental Psychology* 28: 776–786.

Haber, Holly, and Sharon Edelson. 1998. "Retail Ads: Upping the Ante." *Women's Wear Daily*, May 15, 11.

Hall, Stuart. 1995. "The Whites of Their Eyes: Racist Ideologies and the Media." In *Gender, Race, and Class in Media*, ed. Gail Dines and Jean M. Humez, 18–19. Thousand Oaks, CA: Sage.

Hamamoto, Darrell Y. 1994. *Monitored Peril: Asian Americans and the Politics of TV Representation*. Minneapolis: University of Minnesota Press.

Hibberd, James. 2010. "Super Bowl Dethrones 'M*A*S*H,' Sets All-Time Record!" *Hollywood Reporter*, February 8. www.hollywoodreporter.com/blogs/live-feed/super-bowl-dethrones-mash -sets-53083.

Hochschild, Jennifer. 1995. *Facing Up to the American Dream: Race, Class and the Soul of the Nation*. Princeton, NJ: Princeton University Press.

HomeSurfer.com. 2009. Missouri School District Ranking Report. Table. www.homesurfer.com /schoolreports/view/schoolrankreports.cfm?state=MO.

Institute for Public Media Arts. 1997. "(N)ISM Toolkit." Unpublished manuscript.

Internet Movie Database. 2010. "Will & Grace." www.IMDb.com/title/tt0157246/.

Jhally, Sut, and Justin Lewis. 1992. *Enlightened Racism: The Cosby Show, Audiences and the Myth of the American Dream*. Boulder, CO: Westview.

Kellner, Douglas. 1995. *Media Culture: Cultural Studies, Identity and Politics Between the Modern and the Postmodern*. London: Routledge.

Love, Barbara. 1989. Presentation at "Parallels and Intersections" Conference, University of Iowa.

McIntosh, Peggy. 1995. "White Privilege and Male Privilege: A Personal Account of Coming to See Correspondences Through Work in Women's Studies." In *Race, Class and Gender: An Anthology*, ed. Margaret L. Andersen and Patricia Hill Collins, 76–86. Belmont, CA: Wadsworth.

McNeil, Alex. 1996. *Total Television: The Comprehensive Guide to Programming from 1948 to the Present*. 4th ed. New York: Penguin Books.

Mead, George Herbert. 1995. *Mind, Self, and Society from the Standpoint of a Social Behaviorist*. Chicago: University of Chicago Press.

Morgan, Michael, and Nancy Signiorelli, eds. 1990. *Cultivation Analysis: New Directions in Media Effects Research*. Newbury Park, CA: Sage.

New America Foundation. 2007. Federal Education Budget Project. http://febp.newamerica.net /k12/.

Postman, Neil, and Charles Weingartner. 1969. *Teaching as a Subversive Activity*. New York: Delacorte.

ReligionFacts. 2006. "Eid Al-Adha: Festival of the Sacrifice." www.religionfacts.com/islam/holidays /adha.html.

Salzman, Jack, David Lionel Smith, and Cornel West, eds. 1996. *Encyclopedia of African-American Culture and History*. New York: Macmillan Library Reference USA, Simon and Schuster.

Sherover-Marcuse, Ricky. "Liberation Theory: A Working Framework." www.unlearningracism.org /writings.htm.

Silverblatt, Art. 1995. *Media Literacy: Keys to Interpreting Media Messages*. Westport, CT: Praeger.

Takaki, Ronald. 1993. *A Different Mirror: A History of Multicultural America*. Boston: Little, Brown.

U.S. Census Bureau. 2009. "New York Leads in Per-Pupil Public Education Spending at Nearly $16,000," *Census Bureau Reports*. www.census.gov/newsroom/releases/archives/education/cb09-113.html.

Zinn, Howard. 1995. *A People's History of the United States: 1492–Present*. New York: Harper Perennial.

2

Gender

In Pink and Blue and Vivid Color

> To see that all knowledge is a construction and that truth is a mat-
> ter of the context in which it is embedded is to greatly ex-
> pand the possibilities of how to think about anything, even those
> things we consider to be the most elementary and obvious.
>
> —*Field Belenky et al.,* Women's Ways of Knowing

> The ideal situation would be a setting in which success could not be predicted by
> a person's sex, their race, their ethnicity, or their level of income—that people
> would have not only equal access to opportunities but also equal outcomes.
>
> —*AAUW Educational Foundation,* Beyond the "Gender Wars"

PERSONAL EXPERIENCE AND GENDER

As we explore what it means to be male or female, feminine or masculine, we ask you to pay close attention to your reaction to the information. Are you nodding in agreement, are you rejecting various elements, are you confused? In order to resolve any dissonance between past beliefs and "knowledge," and current information, you will need to actively decide what blend you believe to be accurate and true. The first experiential step in exploring what you have come to understand about gender in both your thoughts and your behavior is the "gender journey" in Personal Inventory 2.1 (page 60) on the following page (Orenstein 1994, xii). As you analyze your two journeys as a girl and as a boy, it will begin to be clear that some of your experiences represent your own clear choice, some have been explicitly chosen for you, and some have been subtly suggested to you. Examples of a relatively independent or gender-neutral choice may be the food you eat or the type of music you listen to. Expressions of your gender that were most likely directed by your parents and perhaps the media include the clothes, toys, and room decorations of babyhood and early childhood.

Consider another scenario. After having three boys in a row, Jennifer's parents were thrilled when she was born. Her parents and grandparents, aunts, and uncles lavished her with gifts—lacy pink dresses, tiny pearl necklaces, china tea sets, and delicate dolls. After years of wearing pink dresses and bows as a baby, toddler, and young girl, Jennifer *decided* that this is what girls wear to be feminine and beautiful. She decorated her room

Personal Inventory 2.1
The Gender Journey

Step One: Transport yourself to the time when you were a junior in high school. Picture yourself in one of your classes. Pay attention to where you are sitting and the way you are sitting. Then think about the following questions:

1. What were you wearing and how was your hair styled?
2. What kind of shoes, jewelry, or makeup were you wearing?
3. How was your bedroom at home decorated? What were the colors? What was on the walls?
4. Who were your friends outside of class?
5. What kinds of activities did you participate in outside of school?
6. What clubs or organizations did you belong to?
7. What did you do for fun?

Step Two: Now picture yourself in seventh grade. Again, situate yourself in one of your classes and ask these same questions.

Step Three: Next, imagine yourself in second grade and once again ask the questions above.

Step Four: Finally, take one more step back in time to the day you were born. Imagine the excitement of your family and answer the questions below:

8. Were your parents expecting a boy or a girl?
9. What do you imagine your parents and other relatives might have said when they discovered what sex you were?
10. What kind of clothes and stuffed animals and toys do you think people bought for you?

Step Five: Now pause for a moment. Take a breath. Imagine that same instant of your birth, but this time envision that you were born the opposite sex. With this new identity take a parallel journey forward through time. Visualize yourself, again, at the moment of your birth and ask the same questions through the perspective of your new gender identity. Move through the same experiences and questions from second grade to seventh grade, and finally to your junior year in high school. Ask all of the same questions you asked the first time.

Step Six: When you complete this journey forward through time as the opposite sex, take a moment and write down all of the things that were the same and all of the things that were different depending on what sex you were born as. Were you dressed in pink or blue as a baby? Did you wear dresses or pants to school? Did your friends play baseball, dolls, or both? Did you sit with your legs crossed or wide open? Did you curl or blow-dry your hair or just let it hang after washing? Did your bedroom have pictures of dancers, animals, race cars, or athletes hanging on the walls?

Source: Orenstein (1994).

in lavender and pink and *chose* ruffles on the bedspread with lots of dolls and stuffed animals piled on the bed. By the time she was in high school, her old jewelry box with the musical ballerina was crammed with earrings and necklaces that she sifted through daily to find the right match for her outfit. Her parents and some of her girlfriends commented on how sweet and pretty and feminine she was, and her teachers complimented her on her quiet, well-mannered behavior. By junior high school, boys began calling Jennifer and noticed the same things her friends, teachers, and parents had been telling her for years. While Jennifer may have felt that she was making independent choices, the early choices made for her and the support and reinforcement she received for their continuation constituted a subtle, perhaps unintentional way of leading her to a particular set of characteristics that defined her femininity, her gender identity. The story of Jennifer paints a clear, though somewhat extreme example of how and by whom we are influenced in defining what it means to be a girl or a boy. For most of us, the messages are not always extreme, and when we see most of our friends receiving the same messages, we often conclude that what our parents, societal norms, and the media tell us about being feminine or masculine is really the absolute "truth."

However, boys and girls can also be raised to make their own choices early on. They may be presented with Legos or toy ovens from which to choose. Their rooms may be decorated in yellow or red with gender-neutral pictures on the walls. Girls and boys may also rebel against the gender expression that was chosen for them as young children. A girl might decide that she hates dresses and pink and dolls and prefers trucks and football. A boy may decide he hates sports and mud and prefers dolls and playing house. More frequently, boys and girls make a mix of choices that include the traditionally feminine or masculine toys and clothes and games noted above, some that are traditional for the other sex, and some that are gender-neutral, such as jeans and T-shirts and bike riding and board games. These options have become increasingly acceptable in some subcultures in the United States, but in many communities, even in the twenty-first century, girls who make nontraditional gender choices are called "tomboys" and boys who make nontraditional gender choices are called "sissies."

Later in this chapter, the issues of gender identification and socialization will be systematically explored and analyzed. For now, focus on your own experience as a boy or a girl, working to trace and describe your childhood without judging, defending, or criticizing it. To continue the process of understanding your experience of gender, take the quiz in Personal Inventory 2.2, on page 62. This quiz analyzes a set of elements in your life that serve as indicators of how you were raised to express your "masculinity" or "femininity" and what choices you made in that context.

- If you scored 12–15 points, your gender socialization as a child tended to match the culture's definition of traditionally masculine.
- If you scored 5–8 points, you were socialized to express your gender as traditionally feminine.
- If you scored 9–11 points, your gender socialization as a child tended to be mixed or neutral.

Personal Inventory 2.2

Childhood and Gender Quiz

Instructions

Mark the answers that come closest to matching elements of your life. Don't skip any questions. Select the one answer that comes closest to matching your experience, even if there is only one small part of the response that applies to you. When you have completed the quiz, total your score.

1. Which of the toys or games below were your favorites to play with as a young child?
   a. ___ dolls, paper dolls, tea sets, play kitchen toys (1 point)
   b. ___ Candyland, Chutes and Ladders, Monopoly, Yahtzee, checkers, chess (2 points)
   c. ___ action figures, toy guns, toy cars and trucks, toy tools (3 points)
2. What kind of interactive play with other children was your favorite?
   a. ___ playing dolls, house, hopscotch (1 point)
   b. ___ playing board games, riding bicycles (2 points)
   c. ___ playing softball, football, baseball, play war or forts (3 points)
3. As a young child, what did you want to be when you grew up?
   a. ___ a mother or father, model, teacher, dancer, nurse, secretary (1 point)
   b. ___ a musician, salesperson (2 points)
   c. ___ a firefighter, police officer, truck driver, doctor, lawyer, architect, athlete (3 points)
4. What household chores were you responsible for as a child?
   a. ___ setting or clearing the table, helping with cooking, dusting, washing dishes (1 point)
   b. ___ cleaning bathrooms, sweeping, making your bed, keeping your own room clean (2 points)
   c. ___ taking out the trash, raking leaves, mowing the lawn, shoveling snow (3 points)
5. Which of the statements below comes closest to what you were told (or what you learned by observing) as a child about what you were supposed to do if your body or feelings were hurt?
   a. ___ "Oh, sweetheart, I'm so sorry that happened. Go ahead and cry. I know that hurts." (1 point)
   b. ___ "If you're hurt really badly, go ahead and cry if you have to. But you don't have to make such a big deal out of everything." (2 points)
   c. ___ "Buck up. You're a big boy/girl now. Big boys/girls don't cry. Be a little man/little woman)." (3 points)

The next set of questions is for you to ponder, but not for which you gain points. If as a child, you had a sibling or close cousin or friend of the opposite sex, answer questions 1–5 with that individual in mind. What are the differences and what are the similarities in the two sets of responses? Do you see any patterns for what boys are assigned to do, what they are told to feel, and what they choose versus what girls are assigned to do, what they are told to feel, and what they choose? Were there any other gender differences that you remembered as you were responding to these questions the first time and, again, the second time?

As you examine your score, resist the pull to judge and evaluate your experience. Instead, use these rough indicators as a means to understand what you were told and how you behaved according to standard definitions of masculinity and femininity. Understand that there are no right or wrong answers, but rather descriptions that will serve as a foundation, an underpinning to analyze and reconstruct what you have learned explicitly and implicitly about what it means to be male or female in U.S. society.

Try the preening exercise in Personal Inventory 2.3 (beginning on page 64) to investigate your current experience as a male or female. This is most useful when a group of five or more people of eighteen or older compare their answers and determine if there are any similar patterns that are mostly recorded by men or a parallel set of patterns primarily selected by women.

After answering the questions, compare the total number of products and hours of preparation to the totals of other men and women and see if you detect any patterns. Generally, this activity reveals that there is somewhat of a continuum based on whether you are male or female. People who report spending five hours or more preparing for a special event are principally women. People who jump in and out of the shower, get dressed, and head for the door are most frequently men.

Are these preparations biologically hardwired? Probably not. Does our culture socialize us in such a way that primping and pampering seem more feminine? Probably so. Do the words "primping" and "pampering" themselves convey an ultrafeminine, self-indulgent connotation that subtly mocks so much focus on appearance? And when these words are applied to men for the same reasons, are they even more devastating in their mockery?

Assessing females according to their appearance reflects a social tendency to sexually objectify women by valuing their bodies primarily for the utilization and appreciation of others. There has been significant research that suggests girls are socialized from a very young age to view their physical appearance as having primary significance over other characteristics. There are also strong indicators that the cultural emphasis on thinness combined with a narrow definition of a virtually unattainable type of beauty are contributors to the physical and mental health problems that disproportionately afflict females as they reach adolescence and young adulthood (Szymanski et al. 2011). In a male-dominant society, women are often compelled to collude with this aspect of their own gender oppression to the potential detriment of their self-esteem.

This exercise has some clear implications for traditional masculine and feminine socialization. "[T]o fail at the feminine difference is to appear not to care about men, and to risk the loss of their attention and approval. To be insufficiently feminine is viewed as a failure in core sexual identity" (Brownmiller 1984, 15).

According to a 1995 study conducted by the American Association of University Women (AAUW), girls emerged from their teen years with reduced expectations and less confidence than boys. In fact, this drop in self-esteem was reflected in lowered scores on standardized tests (AAUW 1995, 62). Gender socialization has profound consequences that are emotional and financial and that impact the definitions, expectations, and the experience of success for both men and women.

In the next section of this chapter, the *reconstructing knowledge* approach will be used to build a framework for analysis of the experiences you have reported above.

Personal Inventory 2.3
Gender and the Fine Art of Preening

Instructions

Think of an extremely special and somewhat formal occasion that you are preparing to attend, such as a prom, a dance, or a wedding. Imagine that you are going to this event with someone you have liked for a long time. You want to look and feel exceptionally good. Think of all the items you need and activities you plan to prepare yourself for this event. Mark everything that you would use and do on the list below and add anything else that is not on the list.

PART I

Preparation Activities: Indicate the amount of time in hours that each activity will take, add the amounts, and write the total as a decimal—for example, 2.5 hours. Be sure to include the total time for any activity that you need to do more than once, such as shopping for clothes or going to the florist to order and buy flowers for a special occasion.

shopping for clothes	_____
shopping for shoes	_____
shopping for or borrowing a friend's clothes	_____
renting or buying a tuxedo	_____
buying a tie	_____
ironing	_____
going to the cleaners	_____
going to the hairdresser or barber	_____
taking a bath or shower	_____
shampooing/conditioning hair	_____
taking a bubble bath	_____
curling, straightening, or otherwise fixing hair	_____
shaving	_____
getting car washed and/or detailed	_____
getting manicure and/or pedicure	_____
getting a massage	_____
getting a facial	_____
shopping for cosmetics or hair products	_____
buying a corsage, boutonniere, or bouquet	_____
any other preparation activities	_____

Total preparation time in hours and minutes _____

PART II

Products: Write the number of each product you use; be sure to indicate separate numbers for each product. For example, if you use five different kinds of lotion or eleven different types of eye makeup, write the total number in the blank. Then add the total number of products.

toothpaste	_____
dental floss	_____
mouthwash	_____
deodorant	_____
shampoo	_____
conditioner	_____
hair products (hair gel, spray, mousse, relaxer)	_____
body lotion	_____
face lotion or cream	_____
moisturizer	_____
soap	_____
shower gel	_____
nail polish, nail polish remover, cuticle remover, etc.	_____
perfume, cologne, or aftershave	_____
bubble bath	_____
facial masque or lotion	_____
makeup (include various shades of eye shadow, foundation, highlighter, eyebrow pencil, blush or rouge, lipstick and/or gloss	_____
shave cream	_____
razor, razor cartridges	_____
beard and/or mustache trimmer	_____
any other products you use (list below)	_____

_____

_____

_____

_____

_____

Total number of products _____

RECONSTRUCTING KNOWLEDGE AND GENDER

Gender socialization is a universal experience. Even if parents work very hard to raise their children with gender neutrality, input from grandparents and other adults, peers, religious institutions, schools, and the media provide daily cues and information about what it means to be a boy or a girl. When Linda's daughter was born in 1985, she had almost no hair. Yet the hospital, without Linda's consent, allowed a photographer to tape a pink bow on her bald head and try to sell the photographs to the parents.

Linda's daughter and son were born fifteen months apart and were both in diapers at the same time. It was just at that time, 1987, that plain disposable diapers became unfashionable and difficult to find because major diaper companies began decorating their diapers. There were blue diapers (for boys) with drawings of trucks and cars and baseball bats, and pink diapers (for girls) with pictures of teddy bears and ballerinas. According to the manufacturers, these diapers were designed anatomically to specifically fit boys or girls. Had Linda wanted to switch diapers, she might have reduced stereotypes and increased wetness. There are not many choices under these circumstances.

When Leon's children were young, he consciously steered them toward what he perceived to be "gender-appropriate" activities. He made sure his son had a football or a baseball bat in his hands at all times—sometimes at the same time. He saw to it that his daughter took dance lessons and had plenty of dolls to play with. Fortunately, as they grew older, his children asserted their independence and gravitated to the things that interested them with full confidence in their gendered identities and little concern for their father's warped perceptions. His son did play baseball and football in school, but while working on his teaching degree, he also coached a seventh-grade girls' cheerleading squad. Leon's daughter played with dolls and performed with the pompom team, but she also converted her Barbie dollhouse into a miniature department store and worked with officials at her school to establish a chapter of Future Business Leaders of America.

When it comes to gender, oppression is defined as the structural way that the resources, power, and privileges that individuals need to get what they want in life are organized so that men have greater access to these assets than do women, which means that, in general, men also have greater access to success than do women. By that construct, men are *privileged* by gender oppression and women are *targeted* by gender oppression. This does not predict a successful life for every man and failure for every woman. As we will see, there are many ways that gender inequities hurt both men and women. But practically speaking, this means that historically men have earned more money than women and have held more positions of authority and power than women.

While some things have changed since 1999, much of the structure and dynamics of gender oppression still exists in 2013. Overall, men still make more money than women; the vast majority of CEOs of large corporations, senators, and members of Congress, and all U.S. presidents, to date, have been men. So strictly by the definition of oppression, statistics tell us that men still have greater *access* than women to power, privilege, and resources. But the situation is not that simple, and it probably never was. The big picture painted by statistics and demographics explains the trends and patterns in jobs, income, and positions of power, but it does not explain how class and gender and race intersect to give some men far less access to the whole set of assets that are likely to help them get what they want in life. And these figures do not tell us that while oppression targets women, gender socialization hurts both boys and girls, both men and women. In 1999, when this section about gender was first written, the bulk of the research available was about the institutionalized and socialized oppression of girls and women. By 2013, the research and the gender terrain itself were far more complex.

For example, the big picture of working men and women tells us that in 2008 women earned 79.9 percent as much as men as compared to 1979 when women earned 62.5 percent as much as men (U.S. Bureau of Labor Statistics 2009). This is real progress for women. However, the income gap between men and women of different races differs significantly. White women and Asian American women earn about 78 to 80 percent of what men earn within their own racial groups, while African American women earn 89.4 percent and Latinas earn 89.6 percent *more* than the men within their own racial groups (U.S. Bureau of Labor Statistics 2008). How do we sort this out? Are African American women and Latinas faring better than their white and Asian American sisters? Or is the job discrimination against African American and Latino men so severe that the gap between these men and women of color is widened because the employment picture for men is so grim?

These are complex questions and situations that require some complex thinking. In the late twentieth century, many U.S newspapers and news magazines attempted to simplify the issues of equity and inequity according to sex as so-called gender wars and to reduce these so-called battles to a zero sum game in which the game rules suggest that if boys and men are doing well in terms of academic achievement, careers, income, and so on, then it stands to reason that girls and women are doing poorly and vice versa. In 1999, the *U.S. News and World Report* article "Gender Wars Redux" said that the "educational status of boys, not girls, is the real problem. . . . If we put ideology aside, which gender do we think needs help now?" (Leo 1999, 24). According to the *Arizona Republic*, "For many boys, school has been a punishment, where boy behavior was pathologized and girl behavior was sanctified. In our noble attempt to elevate girls and women, we've denigrated boys and men" (Parker 1998).

Does this mean that over the last fifty years the "gender wars" were waged and that as a result girls and women are winning and boys and men are losing?

Is this making your head spin yet? Are you trying to figure out which side you are on and whether boys or girls are the targets of the most discrimination in school and in the job market?

We invite you to try something as you continue to read this section. Suspend all efforts to draw conclusions about the ultimate winners and losers in the "gender wars." Instead, take in the information and theories and examples and reflect on your own experiences as a boy or as a girl, as a woman or as a man. Notice when information and theories in this section affirm your experience and beliefs and when other information challenges your experience and beliefs. Take in all of the information, contradictions and all, and resist making any final decisions about what you believe to be true. Perhaps it might just be possible that in this case we may all be both winners and losers. It may not be a case of "either/or" but rather a case of "both/and."

This section will shed some light on the subject of gender and recast the tale of "gender wars" into a different story. We will examine:

- Some basic definitions of terms
- A brief summary of gender history
- Demographic information about boys and girls and men and women in employment, income, education, and other factual information
- Various theories about gender and gender socialization
- The real-life ways that gender socialization has affected and often hurt us all

Perhaps we can look at the way the relative success of men and women is cast as a competition, a "war" that has been constructed out of stereotypes, misinformation, missing information, and biased information. And this construct may not necessarily match the reality of the strengths and weaknesses and potential for success for both men and women. And perhaps we could even imagine a different construct in which men and women provide support to each other from their own areas of strength to bolster the areas that challenge their counterparts. Such a new construct, and the reality itself, would include very few permanent "losers," but rather men and women who have not quite "gotten it" yet.

Definitions

Sex is determined biologically. When you are born, the doctor informs your parents that you are a boy or a girl according to your genitals. Later in life, other characteristics that are determined by your sex and hormones are breasts, menstruation, relative hairiness, and to some degree bone and muscle structure. It is important to note that some babies are born with ambiguous genitalia. These families and children have difficult decisions to make and a whole set of issues to face, which will be discussed in Chapter 6.

However, **gender** is something entirely different. Gender is constructed socially, culturally, and psychologically. In fact, many studies have demonstrated that roles of males and females vary in different cultures. Anthropologist Margaret Mead conducted studies of three different tribes in New Guinea and found that in one tribe both sexes behaved in ways that were considered traditionally feminine in the United States: nurturing, passive, peaceful, and deferential. In a second tribe, men and women assumed gender roles that are regarded in the United States as traditional: the men were aggressive hunter-gatherers, with most of their work occurring outside the home and hearth, while the women were peaceful nurturers who took care of the children and worked inside the home. In a third tribe, the roles were reversed and the women played the U.S. version of traditionally masculine roles, while the men assumed traditionally feminine roles (Mead 1935). "What we do know with confidence is that however strong the influence of biology may be, it seldom, if ever, determines behavior. It *influences* behavior in greater or lesser amounts, but it doesn't determine behavior, personality, and so on" (Wood 2011, 20–21).

As you read this section on reconstructing knowledge, reflect on the experiences you explored in the first section of this chapter. As you observe your response to the data and theories discussed in the chapter, note whether you find your own beliefs challenged or reinforced by the material and determine whether there is any connection between your reactions and your own gender socialization, your life experiences as a boy or as a girl coming of age.

Gender and U.S. History

Think carefully about the people in U.S. history you were taught were significant, the ones you were told made key contributions to the development of the United States. Who were they? Linda's list, which comes from her high school years in the mid- to late 1960s, would include John Smith, George Washington, Thomas Jefferson, Benjamin Franklin, Ulysses S. Grant, Robert E. Lee, Abraham Lincoln, John D. Rockefeller, Theodore Roosevelt, Franklin D. Roosevelt, and John F. Kennedy. Leon's list is pretty much the same. The only women both Leon and Linda remember learning about as historical figures were minor players in the textbooks—a pre-Disney Pocahontas and Betsy Ross of American flag fame. Perhaps those of you who are younger have more women on your list, but by and large, our U.S. history books continue to be the story of men's contributions, literally *his* story.

Consider the women described below and their contributions to U.S. history. How many of them have you studied? How many even sound familiar to you? How do you think your perspective on U.S. historical figures and history itself would have been different had you learned about these women and others who have made significant contributions to life in the United States?

In 1539, Francesca Hinestrosa was the first European woman to reach the Americas alive (Rappaport 1990, 6). In 1634, Anne Hutchinson was the first U.S. woman to challenge the unequal status of women. Defying the Puritan clergy, she held meetings that ran against the rules and norms of society. These meetings, held in her home, were attended by men and women together to discuss religious and political ideas contrary to the dominant ones of the times. In 1638 Hutchinson was found guilty of religious and civil slander and improper behavior. As a result, she was excommunicated and banished (Rappaport 1990, 37). It is not commonly known that most women who were brought to the United States as indentured servants and slaves fought for their freedom. "In 1781, in an unusual act of defiance, Elizabeth Freeman protested her enslavement by going to court and arguing that the Massachusetts Bill of Rights had ended slavery. She won her case and her freedom" (Rappaport 1990, 28). These are bits and pieces of U.S. history rarely found in history textbooks.

In the first decades of the nineteenth century, one of the outcomes of the Industrial Revolution was a dramatic change in the gender assignment of work and labor. Tasks that had previously belonged to women were taken over by factories. Ironically, as white middle-class women became revered as mothers, wives, and "ladies," their position in the family became less productive and began to be regarded as inferior. "The world of business, trade, and government was seen as the right place for men, whom society viewed as competitive, aggressive, and materialistic. Women were thought of as gentle, spiritual, and nurturing. The idea of a woman's sphere, separate and different from the man's sphere, was accepted as an eternal truth" (Rappaport 1990, 50). The woman's domestic sphere was not only separate but unequal as well.

Most high school history books address the development and consequences of the Industrial Revolution with little mention of how this phenomenon impacted the organization of labor inside and outside the home and how earning money became more highly valued. More importantly, there is rarely any mention of how the assignment of labor was done along gender lines—with the highly valued *paid labor* in the public sphere assigned to men and the *unpaid and devalued home labor* assigned to women.

The untold stories above are predominantly about white women, particularly white women of the middle class and above. Stories that are even more deeply hidden from accessible and common history are the stories of women of color. While there are many stories of immigration, discrimination, and valor, the story of African American women is a quintessential American story rarely told in general U.S. history books.

"Judged by the evolving nineteenth century ideology of femininity, which emphasized women's roles as nurturing mothers and gentle companions and housekeepers for their husbands, Black women were practically anomalies" (Davis 1981, 5). African women, brought to the United States as slaves, were first valued according to the amount of labor they could do. Contrary to myths established in such films as *Gone With the Wind*, seven out of eight black women were field workers rather than housekeepers or nursemaids (Davis 1981, 5).

One former enslaved black woman described her situation:

> We had ragged huts made out of poles, and some of the cracks chinked up with mud and moss, and some of them wasn't. We didn't have no . . . good beds, just scaffolds nailed up to the wall out of poles and the old ragged bedding throwed on them. That sure was hard sleeping, but even that felt good to our weary bones after them long hard days' work in the field. I tended to the children when I was a little gal and tried to clean house jus' like Old Miss tells me to. Then as soon as I was ten years old, Old Master, he says, "Git this here nigger to that cotton patch." (Watkins and David 1970, 16)

While motherhood was revered in white middle-class society in the nineteenth century, after the abolition of the international slave trade black women were instead valued for their ability to reproduce as many offspring as possible to continue to "supply" free labor in the form of more slaves. The central place that work occupies in many contemporary black women's lives and some of the features of relationships between black women and men were established during slavery. Because black women's labor was measured the same as that of black men, "the economic arrangements of slavery contradicted the hierarchical sexual roles incorporated in the new [post–Industrial Revolution] ideology. Male-female relations within the slave community could not, therefore, conform to the dominant ideological pattern" (Davis 1981, 18).

The tragic irony of slavery for women was that while post–Industrial Revolution white women's work was taken over by factories and their status thus reduced, black women were performing the same work as black men. In the limited domestic life of slaves, the work black women and men performed for themselves was characterized by equality. "Within the confines of their family and community life, therefore, Black people managed to accomplish a magnificent feat. They transformed the negative equality which emanated from the equal oppression they suffered as slaves into a positive quality: the egalitarianism characterizing their social relations" (Davis 1981, 18).

Although resistance to American slavery began with the institution itself, the publication of David Walker's *Appeal* in 1829 and the Nat Turner rebellion in 1831 were significant events in the modern abolition movement (Harding 1981, 101–103). At the same time, strikes in the textile factories by working-class white women in the northeast began, and groups of wealthier white women began fighting for the right to education and careers outside the home. These women used the language of "slavery" to describe their oppression in factories and in marriage, and while the comparison was often exaggerated, the stage was set for the affinity of the first phase of the women's movement and the antislavery movement.

Some of these women began to engage in acts of courage and heroism, important elements of history that are rarely documented in our common education. For example, in 1833 Prudence Crandall, a white teacher in Canterbury, Connecticut, accepted a black girl into her school. She remained steadfast as the parents of the white girls boycotted the school. She ultimately recruited more black girls and eventually operated an all-black school in defiance of the white people of the town (Davis 1981, 34–35).

Sarah and Angelina Grimké were white women born in South Carolina to a slave-holding family. They moved to the North and became outspoken abolitionists and the first to explicitly link women's rights to black rights. "More than any other women in the campaign against slavery, the Grimkés urged the constant inclusion of the issue of women's rights. At the same time they argued that women could never achieve their freedom independently of Black people" (Davis 1981, 44).

While Sojourner Truth's "Ain't I a Woman" speech has attained some recognition and acclaim, few people are aware of this ex-slave's contribution to the fight for freedom of women and slaves. She had to struggle simply for the right to speak at women's conventions: "I know that it feels a kind of hissing and tickling like to see a colored woman get up and tell you about things and Woman's Rights. We have all been thrown down so low that nobody thought we'd ever get up again, but we have been long enough trodden now, we will come up again, and now I am here" (Davis 1981, 59).

Meanwhile, "large numbers of Black women were manifesting their commitment to freedom and equality in ways that were less closely connected with the newly organized women's movement" (Davis 1981, 64). African American women from the North were prominent in the Underground Railroad and took enormous risks to illegally transport slaves to freedom. This work was separate from the newly organized women's movement. There was Jane Lewis from Ohio, who rescued slaves through hundreds of crossings of the Ohio River. There was Frances E.W. Harper, a poet and antislavery lecturer, and there was Charlotte Forten, an important black educator and abolitionist. There was Sarah Remond, who took her antislavery lectures to England and helped dissuade the British from intervening on the side of the Confederacy (Davis 1981, 64).

The Grimkés, Crandall, Sojourner Truth, Lewis, Harper, Forten, and Remond are just a few examples of courageous women, white and black, who took strong antiracist steps to change their own lives and to contribute to changing history. The omission of their stories and historical significance frames what we think of as important historical information and what we think of as tangential or trivial. The women you have just read about made enormous contributions and changes in history, yet they are rarely mentioned in U.S. history. This gap in important information contributes to how boys and girls construct the meaning of the importance of each gender. These voids in the story of America have a subtle but enormous impact on how boys and girls see themselves in the context of history as well as their own relative value.

The Women's Movement and Feminism

> She is dissatisfied with a lot that women of other lands can only dream of. Her discontent is deep, pervasive, and impervious to the superficial remedies which are offered at every hand. . . . From the beginning of time, the female cycle has defined and confined woman's role. As Freud was credited with saying: "Anatomy is destiny." Though no group of women has ever pushed these natural restrictions as far as the American wife, it seems that she still cannot accept them with good grace. A young mother with a beautiful family, charm, talent and brains is apt to dismiss her role apologetically. "What do I do?" you hear her say. "Why, nothing; I'm just a housewife." (Diamond 1960, 60)

There are several interesting elements embedded in this 1960 quote from a *Newsweek* magazine article titled "Young Wives." The first, and most obvious, is that women are identified, even in the title, by their relationship to their husbands. They are young *wives*, not young *women*. A second embedded belief is that a woman's menstrual cycle and her body dictate the kind of person she is to be and the work she is destined to perform. The third is the scorn with which the dissatisfaction of middle-class women is treated, as if to say, "How dare they be unhappy and apologetic when they have so much?" The fourth, and perhaps most subtle, is the acceptance of the "natural restrictions" imposed upon women's lives and the implication that women who reject these restrictions are by extension unnatural. Fifty years later, most of us would find this analysis of women silly or even outrageous. However, it is important to recognize that these statements, which now seem painfully outdated, were regarded by and large as "truth" in the 1950s and 1960s. Women and men who were raised in this time period internalized these "facts" about gender. Part of the process of reconstructing knowledge is to lift these "truths" to a conscious level and analyze them. What are the invisible "truths" about gender that we hold onto today?

It was in 1963 that Betty Friedan first published *The Feminine Mystique*, which began the public challenge to these "natural restrictions" (Friedan 1963). The feminine mystique is the belief that middle-class women with cars and garages, dishwashers and garbage disposals, children and car pools, husbands and products that get the ring out of the collar should be pleased with their lives. Dissatisfied women believed, and few questioned, that either something was wrong with them as individuals or that their lives and marriages were not living up to a well-known and well-accepted ideal. During this period, there was little thinking that perhaps this ideal was a myth. Until the 1950s and 1960s, few women discussed their sense of dissatisfaction. Many believed their unhappiness to be an individual problem or failure rather than a collective or political issue. It was in the late 1950s that women began to communicate with each other about the problem with no name, the dissatisfaction, the lack of fulfillment, the emptiness, the invisibility, the sense of having no identity independent of their husbands or children.

In some ways, the 1950s repeated societal conditions that were similar to those during the period following the Industrial Revolution. New technology meant less housework for middle-class women and more pressure to be the constantly available wife and mom. The division between the private and public spheres, female and male, became increasingly sharp. Women were told that being a wife and mother should be all they needed for fulfillment. For those who were not filled up by those roles, there was often anguish and guilt. By 1962 the "plight of the trapped housewife" was a popular topic in articles and conversation.

Again, middle class-women found their way to political organizations, this time in the form of the civil rights movement of the 1950s and 1960s and the antiwar movement of the 1960s and 1970s. Many of these women were organizing behind the scenes and marching in the streets in these struggles for justice for other groups.

During the 1960s, as the women's movement began to form, some women organized consciousness-raising (CR) groups in which they began speaking to each other about the shortage of good-quality options for child care, about rape and incest, abortion, body image, and the need for greater access to choices in education and work. CR groups differed from therapy sessions in that while part of their intent and outcome was therapeutic, they were organized primarily so that women could begin to understand the collective and political nature of their problems. The CR groups were not led by professionals. Rather, women in the groups shared leadership, avoiding the kind of permanent hierarchy that they believed had elevated men and damaged women. When the topic for a CR session was child care and individual women spoke of their inability to work or go to school because of the few good choices of care available for their children, it became increasingly clear that this was a collective problem, not an individual one, and women began to organize to demand legislation and increased funding for quality child-care centers.

It was from this perspective that a central slogan of the women's movement emerged: "The personal is political." This meant that while women were traditionally programmed to keep their problems to themselves because they were believed to be private and personal, the more they spoke to each other, the more they realized that what had been contained in the woman-occupied private sphere was neither neutral, natural, nor apolitical (Shreve 1989).

Parallel to the development of CR groups and the embryonic women's movement was women's involvement in the burgeoning student group Students for a Democratic Society (SDS). SDS was participating in sit-ins for the rights of black people in the south and organizing demonstrations to protest the Vietnam War. While women were in the thick of this planning and these activities, it was men who occupied the formal leadership positions. And when women demanded that issues of child care and rape awareness and assistance be made a part of the SDS platform, once again they were scorned and told that their problems were trivial compared to race discrimination and the war in Vietnam. Yet this time the scorn did not emanate from the middle-class establishment or sources like *Newsweek* but rather from the political left that was trying to create a more just world.

Women's participation in the consciousness-raising movement, the civil rights movement, the New Left, and the emerging counterculture provided them with important lessons that translated to the women's movement of the 1960s and 1970s. These lessons included nontraditional political experiences, radical ideas about the individual and society, alternative institutions, and an awareness of the discrepancies between egalitarian ideals and sexist practices. While there were radical and liberal branches of the women's movement that wanted society restructured in different ways, the essential feminist ideals were the importance of equality and equity and the need to change the quality and the economics of human relationships and institutions.

Yet by the late 1970s through the present, **feminism** was often regarded as a dirty word, conjuring up images of strident, hairy-legged man-haters. How did this revision and distortion happen? The news media often reported on the women's movement's work to change the norms of social interaction with derision and negativity. For example, women who were part of a guerrilla theater protest at a 1960s Miss America pageant burned stereotypical "feminine" artifacts to symbolize how beauty and cosmetics served as instruments of women's oppression. This event was reported not as the symbolic protest it was, but rather as women scandalously burning their bras. As late as 1970, West Virginia senator Jennings Randolph was quoted by ABC's Howard K. Smith as referring to the women's movement as "a small band of bra-less bubbleheads" (Douglas 1994, 163).

The news media also regularly reported that the women's movement was about women wanting to open their own car doors, light their own cigarettes, and pay for themselves on dates with men. The shift in these norms of interaction between men and women was certainly an element of feminism. But what went largely underreported was the women's movement focus on the fundamental issues of equality in relationships, pay equity, child care, a wider array of choices for women, and women's rights to make decisions about their bodies (Faludi 1991).

Seeking to address the challenges at the intersection of gender, race, and class oppression, many African American and other women of color have embraced *womanism* as a movement that more accurately defines and confronts the complexity of the issues they face. In coining the term *womanist* (Walker 1983, xi–xii), Alice Walker adroitly referenced an African American folk expression that contests the racism and cultural narrowness of some elements of feminism, while simultaneously presenting a universalist vision of liberated womanhood that goes beyond the politics of social protest and summons the full range of human wisdom, emotion, and spiritual power.

Education: What You Know and How You Know It

The snapshots of missing history described above tell us what content was typically missing from our common United States history. They tell us of women who made important contributions in their lives, careers, and their work for equality. This information is a small portion of the story of American women, but it begins to paint a picture of the partial nature of what children learn and do not learn in the formative years of their lives. While the specific content of early history books may not always stick in the minds of young children, the subtle message about the relative importance of men and the relative unimportance of women becomes an essential element of what Peggy Orenstein calls the "hidden curriculum" (Orenstein 1994, 5) and what Julia T. Wood calls "gendered education" (Wood 2011, 206).

> A genuine expansion of academic, professional, social, or personal options for both boys and girls—one hallmark of a truly equitable education—would require substantial changes in cultural perceptions and values. Currently, society tends to overvalue conventional measures of success, such as wealth, power, or professional status, and devalue those associated with conventionally feminine skills or attributes, such as caring for or nurturing others. . . . If we don't start valuing some of the things that women have traditionally been assigned—those roles and the things they've done well—we're never going to get to the point of offering a wide range of choices to men or to women. . . . For both boys and girls, the more traditional their assumptions about what it means to be and how you should behave as a boy or a girl, the [higher the] rates of depression. For girls, adolescent pregnancy tends to be higher, and for boys, belief in coercive behavior in relationship with girls is higher. . . . Holding these very traditional stereotypes about yourself as boy or girl is not healthy. (AAUW Educational Foundation 2001, 14, 27)

We will examine how education contributes to a mix of courses, programs, and degrees that conceal an underground curriculum in which boys and girls learn many of the limiting roles and rules they are supposed to accept to be regarded by mainstream society as appropriately masculine or feminine. As we begin to uncover some of the ways that education socializes us to conform to traditional masculinity and femininity, we can also begin to think creatively about revising the "measures of success."

Young girls are often boisterously androgynous, barreling through their lives with enthusiasm and little regard for sexual stereotyping. Up to the end of the twentieth century, something dramatic happened to girls in early adolescence, including the dropping of IQ scores and the plummeting of math and science grades (AAUW 1995). Simone de Beauvoir says that part of what happened to teenage girls is that they realized that men have power and that the largest part of their own power as girls comes from agreeing to be submissive adored objects. "All girls, from the most servile to the haughtiest, learn in time that to please they must abdicate" (McPhee and Fitzgerald 1979, 17).

By the twenty-first century, things began to shift. According to the AAUW's 2008 report, the education gap between girls and boys was decreasing. Boys still scored higher than girls on achievement tests in math and science, but the gap was getting smaller and smaller. The same was true about girls who continued to outperform boys in reading, but by a much smaller margin. (Corbett et al. 2008, 13). Something was beginning to look very different in some of the manifestations of the gender gap.

AAUW's groundbreaking research of 1995, *How Schools Shortchange Girls*, explained the phenomenon that, across the board, there were minor to major gaps in achievement between girls and boys in school. AAUW's most recent report of 2008, *Where the Girls Are: The Facts About Gender Equity in Education*, tells a much brighter story about closing the gap between girls and boys in academic achievement.

Unfortunately, the story is not a happily-ever-after one for all school-age children. The 2008 report discovered that it is primarily white girls and boys who are making these gains and closing these gaps in academic achievement.

> The report goes beyond gender to look at other factors that influence student achievement—specifically family income level and race/ethnicity—and finds that many girls as well as boys are not acquiring the educational skills needed to succeed in the twenty-first century economy. This report illustrates that while educational trends for both girls and boys are generally positive, disparities by race/ethnicity and family income level exist and are critical to understanding the landscape of education in America today. (Corbett et al. 2008, xi)

Just as it has been demonstrated that boys are not inherently smarter than girls, it is also true that white children are not inherently smarter than children of color. The theories from Chapter 1, including the fabric of oppression and the cycle of socialization, can begin to explain the structural and institutional causes of the persistent gaps in education that affect children of color and low-income children of any race or ethnicity. We'll explore this phenomenon further in Chapters 3 and 5.

For now, it is important to take a moment to notice where you stand in terms of cognitive dissonance and the dizzying and multilayered gaps in education according to gender, according to gender by race and ethnicity, and according to gender when family income is factored into the picture. It is only natural for cognitive dissonance to whisper, "They make this way too complicated. Either you're smart or you're not. Either you work hard in school and do well or you don't work hard and you do poorly." This is your brain telling you to hang on to simple explanations and/or old, familiar beliefs that don't make your brain hurt. If you find that your current or previous beliefs about why children succeed or fail in school are being challenged, allow yourself time to sit with the discomfort and remind yourself that there is no need to draw conclusions and that no one is challenging you to an intellectual duel where the winners take all. Allow yourself the luxury to live with ambiguity and uncertainty for as long as you can tolerate it. If you need an image to hang on to during that time, you can tell yourself that this is a long and complicated case, the jury needs lots of time to deliberate, and for now, the jury is still out.

There are many things we learn in schools in addition to reading, math, and science. Schools are powerful agents of socialization, a central source of learning about gender identity. The organization of education, the information that is taught, and the roles that adult males and females play in the educational hierarchy convey a sense of standards to children about what is normal and who holds power. At the higher levels of education, where status and compensation increase, the numbers of women in teaching positions traditionally decreased. In 1994, these patterns of employment limited the kind of role models available for both boys and girls and became a part of the hidden curriculum in which there are many ways to tell students which sex is more important in the world. In the twenty-first century, these patterns also began to shift.

From elementary school on, the explicit curriculum continues to reinforce the image of men as more important than women. A 1990 study documented pervasive gender stereotypes in elementary school reading primers. While the numbers of male and female characters in primer stories had evened out, males were still represented in two-thirds of the pictures and photographs. In addition, the study demonstrated that the male characters were more likely to be depicted as adventurous risk takers, while the female characters were portrayed as more dependent on males for help (Purcell and Stewart 1990, 177–185).

Over a period of several years, sociology professor Frank Taylor worked with groups of college students to conduct content analyses of male and female images and stereotypes in Dr. Seuss books and in the Berenstain Bears book series, two sets of books that have remained tremendously popular among children over several decades. The team of researchers analyzed language and appearance and clothing and play and found several consistent themes. Their observations of gender themes and messages in these books included the following:

- Boys most often played the important roles in the books; girls were secondary characters.
- Boys were shown as active and strong and imaginative, while girls were often more subdued, passive, with a strong desire to be "pretty."
- Mothers spent much of their time cleaning and cooking and wearing aprons, while fathers worked hard and served as the authority figures. (Taylor 2003, 17)

Taylor put the results of these studies into the context of when and how children learn about gender and when they begin to make sense of what it means to be a boy or a girl:

By age seven, and perhaps as early as age four, children begin to understand gender as a basic component of self. The literature affirms that many masculine and feminine characteristics are not biological at all; they are acquired. Gender schema theory, for instance, suggests that youngsters develop a sense of femaleness and maleness based on gender stereotypes and organize their behavior around them. . . . Children's books may be an important source of gender stereotypes that children use to help organize gendered behavior. (Taylor 2003, 7)

As discussed earlier in the chapter, history books also chronicle primarily male involvement in discoveries, politics, inventions, war, and social change. "Women virtually disappear in historical accounts of our country and the world . . . when education makes women invisible and distorts their experiences by using male standards, social life as a whole is distorted" (Wood 2011, 212).

The academic gaps in achievement, college attendance, graduation, and in teaching careers have begun to close, some slowly and some quite dramatically. Despite these gains, many studies continue to observe that even the most well-meaning teachers are still more likely to recognize and affirm the participation of boys than of girls. Some of the teacher attitudes that have been documented reflect praise and reinforcement for quiet girls while allowing and encouraging more boisterous and aggressive behavior for boys. Despite strong advances for girls and more academic options for both boys and girls, schools continue to contribute to the socialization of boys and girls into traditional gender roles by encouraging boys to be competitive and assertive and girls to build relationships and to be nurturing (AAUW 1995). "People who have learned to use communication to build relationships and collaborate with others find it uncomfortable to compete, to assert themselves over others and to speak in absolute terms that don't invite others to participate. This may explain why many women students in coeducational institutions speak up less often in the classrooms" (Wood 2011, 220).

Child-rearing practices and family dynamics often reinforce the gender socialization that occurs in schools. Leon was watching television at his sister's house one night when the two of them got into a heated argument about the differences in how they had each been raised. Leon's sister contended that their parents had been more permissive with the two boys in the family, allowing them freedom while she was forced to live under much tighter restrictions. Leon agreed but suggested that "it was for her own good because girls need to be protected." Leon has blocked from memory the specifics of what his sister said to him after that. What he does recall is that she obliterated his argument with lightning swiftness and laser-like precision. "Now protect that!" he remembers her saying as she stormed out of the room, leaving him sitting in stunned silence. After a period of thoughtful reflection and soul searching, Leon came to a deeper awareness of the sexist and patriarchal attitudes that were embedded in his statement.

Differences in gender socialization begin to reveal themselves quite early in life. When Linda's son was in first grade and her daughter was in third grade, they briefly played on the same coeducational soccer team. Most of the boys played competitively; winning was their main objective. They were rough and tough and sometimes crashed into each other or hit or got hit hard by a fast-moving errant soccer ball. For the most part, by six and seven years of age, these boys shook off their bumps and bruises and moved back quickly into competitive play. Not so Linda's daughter. During one particular day, she kicked the ball hard and it smacked right into the belly of a little girl from the other team, who cried briefly and after a time-out and consulting with her coach decided to stay in the game. Despite her parents' valiant efforts at socializing their son and daughter in similar ways, Linda's daughter spent the rest of that soccer game running up behind the other little girl and inquiring with a very worried voice and face, "Are you okay? Are you sure you're okay? I'm so, so sorry."

The educational socialization of boys and girls does not end when they complete high school but continues into higher education. A 1994 study indicated that verbal and non-verbal practices by college and university teachers provide more recognition to males than females. Faculty members are more likely to know male students' names, ask more challenging questions of males, and call on male students more often. According to the study, female students' responses are dismissed more often than those of males (Wood 2011, 232).

According to more recent information from Columbia University, "Yet even though women now receive significantly more BAs than men [in public education], they have not achieved equality in the classroom. Today's college classrooms still contain subtle, and not so subtle, gender biases" (Mintz 2013).

The research about gender bias in college classrooms describes trends that favor male students over female students and in some ways demand that female students shed their own socialization and "convert" to models of communication that are more traditionally masculine. The process of this type of conversion requires multiple steps for women in college:

- They would need to be highly aware of how men and women are socialized to communicate and participate in class.
- They would need to fully understand that conforming to certain ways that women are socialized to communicate and participate in class is likely to work against their academic achievement and success.
- Ultimately, they would need to be able to figure out how to change some of their subtle socialization as women, identify the ways that males are socialized to communicate, and make changes in their own styles to conform to the specific types of communication and participation that will strengthen their academic success.

That is a tall order, especially when it is combined with the need to study and learn about the content in each of their classes.

The combination of gender socialization in and out of college contributes to very different attitudes of male and female college students in the classroom. Because of your own unique socialization and personality, you may or may not find yourself in these descriptions. But by and large, studies have found that male students are more boisterous, are more confident, speak longer in class, and often dominate classroom discussions. By contrast, female students are quieter, more hesitant, more indirect, and less assertive. Women in college classrooms are far more likely than men to begin a comment with phrases such as "I guess . . . ," "Don't you think . . . ," "I may be wrong but . . . ," "Well, maybe it's because . . . ," or "I'm not really sure, but it might be . . ." (Mintz 2013). Some of this has begun to change. Linda's personal experience in teaching at a university for twenty-five years is that these behaviors are more common when there are more men than women in the class and change dramatically when women are in the majority in a class. Leon has observed that the women in his classes are increasingly assertive and outspoken, often expressing their opinions more readily than the men. Some things have progressed more slowly, however, such as the gender dynamics that occur when students work on projects in small, coed groups. Also, certain majors, such as audio production, continue to be male-dominated.

So far, we have considered the gendered content of education and the gendered information we receive through the organization of education and teacher behavior. But have you ever thought about *how* you know things? How do you *know* or how did you learn who Christopher Columbus was? How do you *know* what it means to be polite, kind, or courteous? How do you *know* whom to believe when different people give you conflicting information or perspectives? It is not just what we learn but also how we learn it and the way we express it that has relative value. "Nowhere is the pattern of using male experience to define the human experience seen more clearly than in models of intellectual development. The mental processes that are involved in considering the abstract and the impersonal have been labeled 'thinking' and are attributed primarily to men, while those that deal with the personal and interpersonal fall under the rubric of 'emotions' and are largely relegated to women" (Field Belenky et al. 1988, 7).

A 1986 study interviewed 135 women, documenting distinct ways in which people learn or "know" things. Comparing the findings from those interviews with previous research, which had focused primarily on male subjects (Field Belenky et al. 1988, 7), the study found that while there was some gender overlap, particularly in the way that formally educated men and women know things, overall there were distinct patterns of learning that fell along gender lines. According to this study, the kind of knowledge that is most revered in education is **received knowledge**, which comes primarily from outside sources or authorities. Traditionally, this kind of knowing has been largely the domain of men, who have been socialized to believe this is the proper or only way to learn, as well as women who have learned that received knowledge is the way to successfully navigate academia. Those men and women who succeed academically have *mastered* (a gendered word, you may notice) the ability to take in and analyze received knowledge. **Subjective knowledge**, which values personal and internal sources of information, is often regarded as soft and invalid in the academy. Yet, as we have learned, many women are socialized to learn about personal relationships and life experiences in this way (Field Belenky et al. 1988, 54). The authors of the study propose a third way of knowing, **constructed knowledge**, which allows for the blend of information that comes from both inside and outside the self, recognizing both as valid authorities (Field Belenky et al. 1988, 119).

When education is modeled predominantly along the lines of received knowledge, all authority exists outside the self. Paulo Freire refers to this kind of teaching as the banking model, in which the teacher "fills" the student with deposits of information and the student regularly returns the same deposits to the teacher (Freire 1989). When models of learning are used that are predominantly and traditionally male, both boys and girls receive messages about which kind of knowing is superior. If boys and girls are successfully socialized to believe that internal knowledge is inferior, they may be unnecessarily and destructively cut off from an important source of information—themselves.

"To see that all knowledge is a construction and that truth is a matter of the context in which it is embedded is to greatly expand the possibilities of how to think about anything, even those things we consider to be the most elementary and obvious" (Field Belenky et al. 1988, 138). When we learn about our history and our place in it as men and women, when we learn about what it means to be feminine or masculine, we are only receiving knowledge. We are relying on other authorities—parents, school, or the culture at large—to tell us who we are and what we should think. In order to transcend and expand a one-way receipt of knowledge, it is essential to understand that all knowledge and information are limited by perspective, context, experience, and time. *As you read this book, it is important to recognize that even as the authors or "experts" in the field, we cannot tell you what we do not know, have not been told, have not learned, have not experienced, or do not see.*

Gender Disparities in Employment, Income, and Occupational Status

By 1997, the percentage of women working full-time and earning wages had increased from 29 percent in 1967 to 41 percent. By 2010, women and men were neck and neck; 50 percent of men and 50 percent of women were working full-time and earning wages on an annual basis. By 2009, despite severe problems in the economy and rising unemployment, women were earning 76.5 percent of what men earned annually (Weinberg 1998, 1). This was up over 2 percent from 1996. ("Women and the Economy: 25 Years of Progress, But Challenges Remain"; Weinberg 1998, 1). Yet an analysis of the earnings of men and women over the course of the prime fifteen working years of their lives found that women earned only 38 percent of what men earned. The researchers speculated that this was largely due to the reality that women, at many levels of income, employment position, and status, were considered the appropriate person to take extensive leave from work, not only to give birth, but also to be the primary caregiver, to "be there" for the children ("Women and the Economy: 25 Years of Progress, But Challenges Remain" 2010, 33).

While the education gap between men and women continued to close in the twenty-first century, there were still considerable differences in income. According to a study by the AAUW, women with high school diplomas earned 76 percent of men's salaries, while women with doctoral degrees earned 72 percent of men's salaries. Some of this wage gap was due to men and women being paid different amounts for the same work, and some of the gap was due to the kinds of jobs that were considered gender-specific for men or women. According to the AAUW, "As a rule, earnings increase as years of education increase for both men and women. While more education is an effective tool for increasing earnings, it is not an effective tool against the gender pay gap. At every level of academic achievement, women's median earnings, on average, are less than men's median earnings, and in some cases, the gender pay gap is larger at higher levels of education" (AAUW 2013).

Yet while this income gap continued to benefit men, another parallel phenomenon was occurring. For the first time since this information was recorded, a higher percentage of women than men began to earn degrees at every level of higher education.

By 2008 there were 31 million women who were considered heads of household, a status that has become a strong predictor of poverty. The median income of female heads of household was $22,592 as compared to $43,150 for all other households. Almost twice as many families headed by single women were living in poverty as compared to families headed by single men (Cawthorne 2008).

Another indicator of authority and power is the number of top positions held in government and private industry. In 1998, a record fifty-five women were members of the House of Representatives and nine women were senators (Cawthorne 2008). By 2013 those numbers had grown to an all-time record number of women—seventy-seven, or 17.7 percent, in the House of Representatives and twenty, or 20 percent, in the Senate (Center for American Women and Politics 2013). While at first glance this progress is impressive, the thrill is deflated when we face some other important numbers. The ratio of women to men in Congress in 2013 as compared to the same ratio in the U.S. population is still staggeringly disproportionate. In the 2010 census, 50.8 percent of the U.S. population were women and 49.2 percent were men—as close to equal as it gets. Yet in 2013 the comparative percentages in the House and Senate combined were 18.4 percent women and 81.6 percent men. This is another set of facts that can rattle our understanding of gender equity. Yes, there is slow but certain progress, but still it is far from proportionate to the actual population. We encourage you to take a moment to think about these numbers and your own interpretation of what they mean for the progress and success of men and women and in your own life.

Despite this progress for women in government, by December 2013 only 4.2 percent or twenty-one women, were chief executive officers (CEOs) of Fortune 500 companies. When the analysis was expanded to include the top 1,000 companies, the percentage increased only slightly to 4.5 percent or a total of forty-five positions (Catalyst 2013).

Gender Identity and Self-Esteem

In a 1995 report, the AAUW documented sharp differences in self-esteem and scores on standardized tests for boys and girls as they moved through puberty and adolescence.

> Large-scale empirical studies, public-opinion polls, and in-depth clinical studies following individual girls through school all report significant declines in girls' self-esteem and self-confidence as they move from childhood to early adolescence.... A nationwide survey commissioned by the AAUW in 1990 found that on average 69 percent of elementary school boys and 60 percent of elementary school girls reported that they were "happy the way I am"; among high school students the percentages were 46 percent for boys and only 29 percent for girls. (AAUW 1995, 19)

More recently, other studies have examined the status of gender bias and the gap in achievement between boys and girls in schools. While girls made significant progress, Sadker and Zittleman (Sadker et al. 2009, 39) found some troubling patterns of gender bias that affected both boys and girls, but in very different ways:

- Boys lag behind girls in reading for a variety of reasons, one of which is that boys often think that reading is feminine.
- Boys and girls both do well in math and science in elementary school, but by high school girls lag behind boys in these subjects and report less confidence than boys in math and science.
- Girls receive higher grades overall throughout school, but boys tend to outscore girls on high-stakes tests, such as SATs and ACTs, that give them greater access to college and scholarships.
- Teachers call on boys more often than they do girls and give them much more detailed feedback.
- Teachers tend to punish boys more frequently, even when boys and girls have committed the same offense. (Sadker et al. 2009, 39)

One definition of self-esteem is "the individual evaluation of the gap between self-image and ideal self" (Highland Council 2010). Self-esteem is not fixed; we are all constantly engaged in the processes that test, modify, and restructure it. Despite some steps forward for girls in school, they still trail behind boys in the all-important measure of self-esteem. Many studies have found a direct correlation between high self-esteem and success in learning; without strong self-esteem, children will not use their full ability to learn (Highland Council 2010). A less than conscious thought often goes through the minds of children who have little confidence in their ability to succeed in school. It goes something like this: "If I don't try, then the teacher and the other kids will think I'm being disrespectful and bad. They won't know the truth that I am really not very smart." Some children may consider it more desirable to be identified by their teacher and peers as being incorrigible rather than incapable. Obviously, neither of those choices puts the student on a path to school success.

Boys tend to regard themselves as smart when they do well on a test or paper and as unlucky when they do not. By contrast, girls are relieved and think of themselves as lucky when they do well and see failure as evidence of their lack of ability. Teachers often unconsciously reinforce these harmful perceptions (Sadker et al. 2009, 39). These structural and personal types of gender bias can lock both boys and girls into a social and intellectual box with a steep wall that makes it extremely challenging for both groups to stretch the limits of what they are *supposed* to do and decide independently what they *want* to do without the fear of looking "too smart" for girls or "too feminine" for boys.

One final bit of information that adds another layer to the issue of self-esteem involves how women regard their appearance. Linda graduated from high school in 1967. At least ten girls in her graduating class—at least 5 percent of the girls in the class—had had "nose jobs": cosmetic surgery in which their noses were broken and reshaped. Linda remembers visiting them in the hospital and shuddering at the enormously bruised eyes resulting from the break and the huge white bandages on their noses. These girls all began as attractive. Yet with the permission, encouragement, and footing the bill of their parents, they were willing to undergo this ordeal in order to more closely match societal norms. In fact, from 1981 to 1984, the number of women who had elective cosmetic surgery increased by 30 percent (Franck and Brownstone 1993). In 1997, plastic surgeons performed close to 2 million cosmetic procedures to reduce the size of noses, enlarge the size of breasts, and suck the fat out of women's thighs. This figure had gone up 50 percent since 1992, and procedures such as breast augmentation and liposuction had more than tripled (Hamilton and Weingarden 1998, 14). During the year 2010, plastic surgeons performed almost 9.5 million cosmetic procedures, over 1.6 million of which were surgical procedures. Women had almost 8.6 million of these cosmetic procedures, more than 92 percent of the total. The top five surgeries in 2010 were breast augmentation, liposuction, eyelid surgery, abdominoplasty (commonly known as a "tummy tuck"), and breast reduction. It's ironic that the image of the ideal breast size is so precise that women are spending millions of dollars getting their breasts enlarged *and* reduced. Women spend over $4 billion per year on these top five surgeries alone.

Gender Theory

While biology and interpersonal dynamics clearly have an important impact on the development of gender identity, many theorists believe that culture is the most critical determinant. Research and theories in biology, interpersonal relationships, and culture offer various explanations.

Whereas, biological research has made tremendous progress in understanding the brain, efforts to link specific behavioral differences to gender distinctions in brain anatomy are fraught with uncertainty. According to psychologist Ute Habel, who specializes in hormonal influences in brain activation, "Gender differences are strongly influenced by gender stereotypes, socialization and learning, as well as genes and hormones and environmental factors. When we do research, it's very difficult to disentangle the individual contributions of each of those factors; instead, we have to acknowledge and take into account that there is a complex interaction" (Larkin 2013). This is not to say that brain-based gender differences do not exist. Rather, it is important to note that the research in this area has not reached a stage where definitive conclusions can be drawn about how those differences correlate with male/female behavior.

Theories of *interpersonal* relationships and dynamics also explain elements of gender development. These theories focus on the impact that family dynamics and social learning have on personality development and gender identification. According to social cognitive theory, individuals learn to be masculine or feminine based on what they see and observe. In Chapter 1 we discussed social cognitive theory, which explained that if children mimic behavior they are told is appropriate to their gender and receive reinforcement and tangible or intangible rewards, they are likely to continue that behavior (Wood 2011, 37).

Social cognitive theory can also be applied to the impact of media on children, adolescents, and adults. When audiences view negative, positive, or neutral behavior and attitudes on television that are rewarded, they will tend to mimic such behavior. For example, if adolescents view sexual activity on television repeatedly and the activity either is rewarded or lacks consequences, they will be much more likely to imitate this behavior. The rewards can be obvious, such as if a TV character is sexually active and as a result gets the long-desired boyfriend or girlfriend. The rewards can also be subtler, such as the sexually active teen on television who is attractive, popular, and "cool." Equally important to this theory is viewers' tendency to mimic characters' sexual behavior that has no negative consequences. If these characters do not get pregnant, do not acquire sexually transmitted diseases, and do not lose status or popularity, audiences will be more likely to imitate their behavior.

Jean Piaget and Carol Gilligan are major contributors to cognitive development theories contending that children play an active role in the development of their own gender identity. According to these theorists, by age five or six, children begin to see their gender definition as permanent and seek role models to pattern themselves after (Wood 2011, 44–45).

Cultural explanations of gender development include both interpersonal and biological theories and research. According to anthropological studies,

> The more technologically complex and advanced a culture is, the more stratification it creates to divide people by gender, as well as by other factors such as race and class. With technological advancement comes competition, and this lays a foundation for inequality, since some people will have more than others of whatever is valued in a culture. One of the arrangements that capitalism encourages is a division between public and private realms of life and the placement of women in the private or domestic sphere. Because public life is considered more important, this arrangement fosters subordination of women. (Wood 2011, 47)

In other words, according to cultural explanations of gender, traits such as aggressiveness and nurturance exist in both boys and girls. It is in the way the culture fosters and encourages the assignment of these characteristics to males or females that determines which characteristics are acceptable for each gender to cultivate. This reinforcement of traits assigned according to gender is the work of parents, peers, religious institutions, schools, and the media.

Cultural theories regarding gender development are often constructed in a political context and analyzed according to which gender wields more power. This political analysis conforms closely to the fabric of oppression as described in Chapter 1. You may recall the definition of targeted groups as those with less access to resources, privileges, and power. In the United States, according to these definitions, men constitute the dominant group and women constitute the targeted group. This does not mean that all men have great power and wealth, nor does it mean that all women are powerless or impoverished. Rather, this theory addresses structural access to the factors that lead to success. U.S. culture tends to value traits that are considered traditionally masculine and that lead to the kind of success defined as economic wealth and professional status. This is often a less than visible cultural norm.

Parallel to the second-wave women's movement of the 1960s and 1970s was a movement of men who supported feminism and were interested in equity and the liberation of all people. The "men's movement" spawned activism in support of gender equality and became interested in how inequities between men and women and discrimination against women impacted, privileged, and simultaneously and ironically also hurt men. It is important to make the distinction between how *oppression* and *hurt* affect people. Oppression is structural and institutional and affects a whole group or class of people; in the case of gender oppression, the group targeted by oppression is women. It is also true that, regardless of how much access to privilege a group such as men may have, it does not immunize them from the kind of hurt that can result from the limits that occur from their socialization.

An example of gender oppression is the fact that, in 2013, women still earn less money than men do, even in similar jobs and occupations. This oppression occurs systematically and systemically, and, although it does not impact every woman, almost all women have had to work around it or fight it. An example of how men are hurt by the way that gender oppression operates involves how boys and men are socialized to suppress the "soft" emotions of sadness and fear; boys are warned that "big boys don't cry" and learn that boys and men may make fun of them if they expose their tenderness and vulnerability. This conditioning causes many men and boys to practice holding back these emotions, damaging their ability to have close friendships and primary relationships and depriving them of the richness of intimacy. Many women, in turn, are exasperated when the men in their lives do not express their feelings and do not even appear to be fully in touch with those feelings. It is sometimes difficult for women to understand the extent to which men are often socialized to limit themselves to a very narrow range of emotional expression and self-engagement.

An important type of scholarship developed through the activism and academic exploration of the men's movement is typically categorized as "men and masculinity." In general, this organizational and academic side of the men's movement supported radical feminism, the branch of the women's movement that saw the structural inequities and stratification that privileged men and disadvantaged women in personal, professional, social, economic, and political spheres. While, in general, liberal feminists were interested in women getting a "piece of the pie" that men had dominated for so long, radical feminists wanted to change the whole pie and turn it upside down (Wood 2011, 71–72).

As the men's movement provided support to women's equality, men began to examine the ideology and stereotypes of masculinity and coined two terms that have been the subjects of extensive research: masculinity ideology and hegemonic masculinity.

Masculinity ideology is a set of beliefs that embody the traditional cultural definitions of masculinity, of what it means to be a "real man." Like most ideologies, masculinity ideology is sometimes visible, but just as often it is invisible; the individuals and groups who cling most strongly to these beliefs see them not as an ideology but as the truth. Masculinity ideology refers not only to cultural beliefs about masculinity but also to the way these beliefs are structurally embedded in major institutions (education, employment, media, politics, and so on) and internalized by individual men.

To bring this concept from theory to reality, this means that masculinity is often culturally defined in terms of strength, power, aggressiveness, and a tendency to approach problems and problem solving by intellect rather than emotions. This definition is reflected in the way that individual men internalize these ideal male roles as guidelines for their own attitudes and behaviors as the breadwinner, the dominant one in relationships with women, the adult in charge of the household decision making, the protector, and so on. The cycle is complete when both men and women see this "ideal" masculinity reflected in the media and in the male leaders who sit in powerful positions in business, government, and elsewhere.

In contrast, **hegemonic masculinity** "was not assumed to be normal in the statistical sense; only a minority of men might enact it. But it was certainly normative. It embodied the currently most honored way of being a man, it required all other men to position themselves in relation to it, and it ideologically legitimated the global subordination of women to men." And as we learned in Chapter 1, hegemony is not enforced by the police or the military, nor by laws or by violence, but rather by assumptions that this way of being in the world is correct and most people abide by it for that reason. The belief of both men and women in the ideals of men's superiority, dominance, and power in personal and institutional relationships "was achieved by culture, institutions and power" instead of by force (Connell and Messerschmidt 2005, 832).

There are mountains of theories about gender, and there are theories about theories and corollaries about the secondary theories and critiques and metastudies . . . and . . . you get the point. There is one more conceptual approach to gender that provides an interesting framework and also has some practical use as individuals sort out their own gender identity and figure out what they believe to be true about gender and how we are socialized to understand ourselves as men and women. That approach involves examining gender from two different perspectives, fixed and situational. The fixed approach "treats genders as distinct roles that are strongly socialized and make men and women inherently different in all circumstances" (Webster and Rashotte 2009, 325).

According to this more traditional approach, gender traits are "fixed" and unchangeable, which means that men will respond in most or all situations in a way that is practical, task-oriented, rational, and nonemotional. Women, on the other hand, will respond to situations in a way that demonstrates immutable traits that are emotional, social, and personal.

Suppose that a mother and father find out that their adolescent daughter has been skipping school and drinking alcohol with her friends. The fixed-trait model would suggest that the father will respond in a rational, clear-cut, and practical way that does not involve much emotion, personal analysis, or speculation as to why his daughter is doing this. He may calmly say to his wife, "Sandy is clearly breaking the rules—our rules, the school rules, and how we have raised her. We need to let her know right away that this is not acceptable behavior and that we will not tolerate it. She needs to be grounded for one month—both from going out with friends and from talking on the phone unless it involves homework."

The mother, according to the fixed approach to gender traits, will react from a more social, emotional, and personal perspective. She speaks to her husband with a deeply concerned expression, at times marked with tears: "I am really worried about Sandy. This just isn't like her at all. I wonder if she has inherited a genetic trait from your father—alcoholism is supposed to be hereditary. Maybe she is feeling rejected by her old friends and that's the reason she's hanging out with a different crowd. She must be really upset about something to act this way. I agree that we need to stop her behavior, but I'm not sure punishment is the answer. I think she's crying out to us for help. We need to listen to her and let her know we really want to help her and maybe take her to a therapist."

From the perspective of fixed gender traits, the behavior and attitudes of men and women are generally predictable and there is very little room for role differentiation. People who view human behavior from this vantage point, the so-called masculine traits of rationality and task-orientation are always viewed as superior to the so-called feminine traits of emotional, social, and personal concern (Webster and Rashotte 2009). By the way, if this theory is accurate, the father's ideas about punishment would prevail in the scenario above because of his inherent power in the situation.

The newer approach to gender traits views femininity and masculinity as relative, as "situational" and changeable depending both on the gender socialization of the particular man or woman and on the circumstances. From this vantage point, gender role differences emerge from a variety of ways that men and women can be socialized and can be modified by cultural context and by social situations. This variability implies the recognition of an extremely wide range of masculine and feminine traits in different parts of the world. This view of gender still maintains that most cultures view certain traits as intrinsically superior and others as intrinsically inferior, but those traits that are considered superior are not permanently attached to men, nor are the inferior traits permanently attached to women. In fact, "when anyone—male or female—is in a subordinate position, social and expressive behaviors predominate, and when anyone is in a status advantaged position, competition, dominance, and competence are more likely" (Webster and Rashotte 2009, 330).

The situational approach provides a completely different context to understand gender inequities. Not only are gender traits and gender socialization situational, but so is gender inequity. Say a man, Roy, and woman, Dale, meet as they are both waiting in line at a specialty upscale cooking store in Austin, Texas. Their attitudes and behaviors could change each time a different piece of information is introduced. Beginning idle small talk as they wait for the clerk, Dale explains that she is looking for a new kind of springform pan for a cheesecake recipe she is trying out. Still at the small talk level, Roy comments that he likes good New York–style cheesecake with amaretto and a fresh strawberry on top. At this point, Roy assumes that Dale cooks for her family and is knowledgeable about cooking. Dale then replies that she is visiting her family and actually lives in Manhattan, where she is a theater director of a hit show on Broadway and where she regularly visits a nearby deli to get extraordinary New York cheesecake. Dale goes up a notch in Roy's estimation, her status rising from "wife-and-mother" to "successful-smart-woman-with-an-interesting-career." Roy replies that he is buying some new cake pans to make a specialty cake for his niece's wedding. Dale registers a slight interest that Roy is a man who can bake a wedding cake and assumes that he is either a baker by occupation (not nearly as high status as a New York theater director) and/or a man who is comfortable with traditionally feminine activities. Roy then explains that he has found that baking intricate cakes uses some of the same skills he uses as a surgeon, but that he finds baking far more creative and relaxing than removing an appendix. Again, another click and Roy's status increases in Dale's eyes. This scenario, which could go on and on, would have different nuances if the pair worked together as boss and employee or if they were set up on a blind date. Each individual's understanding of the other's relative position and status would also change culturally if one of them was from the United States and the other was from Egypt, Italy, or Brazil, where expectations about gender traits and behaviors may be quite different.

Consequences of the Socialization of Men and Women

The second-wave women's movement of the 1960s and 1970s and the ongoing work of women's rights and feminism have changed many things for women:

- Women's wages have risen as compared to men's.
- A much higher percentage of women receive college degrees, master's degrees, and PhDs.
- Girls' achievement has advanced in subjects such as math and science, in which they previously underachieved.
- Girls and women have made strides in many professions, such as medicine and law, in which they previously fell far behind men.

Despite these important advances in achievement and equity on many levels, some trends remain disturbing in the way they systematically oppress women as a group and hurt and damage them individually:

- Women still hold less than 20 percent of positions in the areas where individuals are likely to wield the most power and earn the most money, including Fortune 500 companies, Congress, and, as of 2014, the presidency.
- Because of the profound impact of the cultural emphasis on physical appearance for women, women spend exorbitant amounts of money on cosmetics and cosmetic surgery to alter their faces and bodies.
- This emphasis on physical appearance affects women in the workplace and in their bank accounts: "workers with 'below average' looks tended to earn about 9 percent less money than workers who were 'above average' in appearance, and those who were 'above average' in appearance made about 5 percent more money than those who were 'average looking.'" (YWCA 2008, 3)

There is a term that is used almost exclusively to describe women and girls, especially in certain interactions with each other: a spiteful and malicious look, a vicious rumor, and a cruel comment to and about each other. This term is "catty." The word on the street is that these petty, malicious, and small-minded attitudes and behaviors are intrinsically female and are why "we can't trust each other." Men and boys, of course, are above all that.

However, the notion that cattiness is somehow an inherently female trait is completely erroneous. The kind of critical, undercutting behavior between women that is called catty is grounded in the way women and girls are socialized, not in their essential, inborn character. According to one study, almost 80 percent of women said they competed with other women over physical appearance and believed that if they "win" the competition, they will somehow be the one to get the husband, the career, and the chance to be the person they want to be. "A major cultural difference in men and women's roles is the emphasis placed on physical appearance. *Women want to be attractive and men want to have attractive partners*, which may result in rivalries with both genders" (YWCA 2008, 7).

As we begin to explore the role that popular media play in the serious consequences of the powerful cultural message that, for females, beauty reigns supreme, we will discover that movies aimed at adolescent girls replay the image of teen girls as superficial, viciously materialistic, obsessed with their own appearance, and driven to be the most beautiful or, at minimum, a part of the beautiful crowd; and that girls, rather than changing into avenging superheroes to save the day, morph into revenging "mean girls" to destroy some other girl's day.

The story for boys and men is parallel in being multifaceted and complex—not a simple case of counting the points, checking with the ref, and announcing whether males or females have won the so-called "gender wars." That is where the similarities of the trends involving males and females end. Reexamining the big picture of gender, it seems clear that men, by and large, still are at the top of the food chain when it comes to institutional, systemic, and individual power. At every level of government and the corporate world, men still hold the positions with the most muscle. Men still have greater access than women to the power, resources, and privileges that are needed to meet their goals in life. Men are still privileged by the structural access to these assets, while women are still targeted by them.

Ironically, despite this access to education, power and authority, and money and positions, boys and men are still hurt and limited in ways that profoundly restrict their access to the understanding and communication of emotions and to the kind of close friendships and intimate relationships that are an integral part of a satisfying life. "Infant research has shown that both boys and girls demonstrate a fundamental capacity and primary desire to establish close, meaningful relationships with other people" (Chu and Tolman 2005, 97). But from that point on, girls are socialized to express emotions and boys are socialized to believe that the only truly masculine emotion is anger. The soft emotions, including sadness and fear, are off base for boys and men. In fact, some recent research shows that adolescent boys and young adult men are no longer motivated primarily by a desire to be superior to or dominate women, but rather are driven by fear of appearing to be feminine, a "sissy," or, worst of all, a "fag."

The limits of socially acceptable emotions that boys and men learn to express are detrimental to them in many ways:

- Overall psychological health is impaired.
- Academic achievement is jeopardized when certain subjects and studying in general are deemed feminine.

- Expression of affection, closeness, and friendship with other boys and men are considered off-limits.
- Emotional intelligence and self-engagement are diminished.

This list reveals what boys and men lose in the potential for personal richness in their lives; it shows what's missing when the "king of hearts" is taken away from the deck. Another element of socialization of boys and men—their social training to feel anger and hostility and to express it both verbally and physically—has significant and very concrete consequences:

- Alarming statistics report increased aggression, bullying, and fighting in school-age boys and acts of rage and violence as they grow older.
- Boys get in more trouble in school and have harsher punishments than girls.
- Boys and men have high levels of incarceration for physical and sexual violence, including sexual assault and rape.
- Boys' and men's socialization toward objectifying women in combination with anger and violence can lead to sexual harassment, domestic abuse, and other behaviors that verbally and physically harm women.

The ramifications of increased male violence are enormous, yet some of the causes of this violence are neither mysterious nor hopeless. "Clinical and empirical research conducted over the past two decades has suggested that the socialization of boys to conform to traditional notions of masculinity such as toughness, aggression, dominance, and the restriction of emotional expression may heighten the potential for boys to engage in violence. This is thought to occur through the emotional socialization process by which boys' sense of vulnerability is discouraged, suppressed, and punished. In contrast to girls, who are generally encouraged to express a broad range of emotions, boys 'have been left in a box'" (Froschl and Sprung 2005, 7). Discouraged from acknowledging and showing feelings of vulnerability and emotional need, "boys organize their inner lives around a 'tyranny of toughness' (Kindlon and Thompson 1999, 54), which predisposes them to increased aggression" (Feder et al. 2007, 387).

Boys and men are positioned to develop traits of traditional masculinity that lead to higher self-esteem and confidence in some areas for which they are rewarded with social acceptance, status, and recognition. Yet ironically and, at times, tragically, adolescent boys who place great value on conforming to conventional norms of masculinity that are unattainable for them not only experience lower self-esteem and all that comes with it, but also often become the targets of bullying, harassment, aggression, and violence from those males who have mastered traditional masculinity (Feder et al. 2007; Hammer and Good 2010).

What if they gave a gender war and nobody came? What if educators and parents universally agreed to teach children to understand that to be men and women does not mean they have to harm themselves or each other? What if we all decided to work to change the messages children receive from parents, schools, and media in a way that allows all children to independently decide how to define themselves without the fear of ridicule or harm? What if we worked with each other as adults to figure out how to teach children to think critically about the messages they receive concerning what it means to be a boy or a girl? What if we learned well enough as adults so that we could teach children that gender messages that limit us or hurt us are probably wrong?

Liberation theory, as applied to gender, presumes that women and men are inherently good and have infinite capacity to be happy and successful in whatever way they each define it. Yet boys and girls are bombarded from birth with messages and misinformation about what it means to be male and what it means to be female. As young boys and girls, we learn these lessons well. Despite all of the ways we are socialized and conditioned to conform to gender norms and rules, liberation theory maintains that the possibility of reaching full potential is innate, while misinformation that is oppressive is learned. Liberation is the group and individual process by which people and institutions can observe, recognize, rethink, and interrupt the negative messages and change how we see ourselves and others.

Therefore, all of the misinformation we receive that narrowly defines masculinity and femininity can be unlearned and replaced with new information and expansive choices about our gender identity and the possibility that our lives, unrestricted by these oppressive rules, can be delightful.

GENDER AND ENTERTAINMENT MEDIA

This next section will guide you as you begin to connect the dots between what you learned through your personal experience, through school and other institutions, and the messages received through entertainment media. Your challenge is to evaluate and integrate new information on gender and reevaluate what you have learned to be true in the past. It will be important to determine whether the messages about gender in entertainment media challenge or reinforce what you have been taught in school and in your life.

Entertainment media are a central source of gender socialization. Consider these differences in the way that men and women were portrayed in television and film in the mid-1990s.

- Women were portrayed in all forms of entertainment media as primarily involved in relationships and men were more often portrayed in the context of their careers.
- Women were portrayed in both television and film as seeking romance 35 percent of the time, while men were portrayed seeking romance only 20 percent of the time.
- Women's appearance was more than twice as likely to elicit comments in television and film than men's appearance.
- Women were shown to groom or preen three times more than men in television and film.
- Across all media, 46 percent of women were portrayed as thin as compared to 16 percent of men. (Signorelli 1997)

By the 2005–2006 prime-time television season, women continued to "inhabit inter-personal roles involved with romance, family and friends," while men were more likely to be seen in roles that involved work. In prime-time television, "the basic social roles assigned to female and male characters by storytellers are tremendously important contributors to the construction and maintenance of gender stereotypes" (Lauzen, Dozier, and Horan 2008, 200–201). The repetition of these stereotypes on television and the tangible or intangible "rewards" that characters receive because they look and act according to these narrow gender rules can have a profound impact on audiences who may see these stereotypes as the truth. If these characters are rewarded on TV, viewers are more likely to imitate them in their own lives (Gerbner 1995; Bandura 2002).

There are several key questions to consider as we analyze media images and their impact on our understanding of gender:

- What images of men and women do prime-time television, feature films, and popular music convey?
- How do media ownership and production affect the images of men and women that we see and hear in these popular media forms?
- What are the underlying messages and ideologies about gender that are represented in the various forms of entertainment media?
- Do the images, ownership, messages, and ideology in entertainment media contribute to the standard socialization of men and women, or do they challenge this status quo?
- What are the connections between these media messages about gender in popular media, our own personal experiences, and some of the theories we have learned about media impact?

These questions will be analyzed in several different ways, including the use of simple content analysis to examine characters and themes, a review of research and analysis about gender in popular media forms as well as media ownership and gender, and finally, an analysis of the particular and overall messages and ideology about gender in entertainment media. The media entertainment tools of content analysis, message system analysis, media literacy, and cultural studies will all be employed to examine these questions.

As you analyze fictional characters and themes in popular film, music, and television, it is critical to keep in mind a fundamental concept about stereotypes. A stereotype organizes information in such a way that it signals repetitive and often negative images based on an individual's membership in a particular group. As you will recall, stereotypes are reinforced in entertainment media by maintaining simplicity. The simpler the character or theme, the more likely it is to be stereotyped. The more complex the characters or themes, the less likely stereotyping will occur and the more likely narrative depth and richness will emerge in a way that defies easy categorization. This method of determining whether a character conveys a stereotype works well with current media material. Yet contrary to what is often intuitive, the fact that the character is complex or simple does not guarantee that the character is a "good guy" or a "bad guy."

Prime-Time Television Content Analysis

It is your turn to conduct a content analysis that will assess gender images on prime-time television when you were a child. Think of yourself from ages four to twelve. Imagine what you did when you got up in the morning, when you came home from school, and during and after dinner. How much television did you watch in the average day? Did you watch television during meals? Record the approximate number of hours of television you watched weekly, and note where and when you watched it. Next, think hard and make a list of your ten favorite television programs during the eight years from four to twelve. You can list cartoons, dramas, comedies, children's programs, and adult programs that were designed to entertain. For the purposes of this exercise, list only programs that had a cohesive narrative and were not variety shows, talk shows, news, or reality programs. This rules out programs such as *Sesame Street*, *MTV*, *American Idol*, *Saturday Night Live*, *The Daily Show*, and *Entertainment Tonight*. As you make your list, think of all of the programs that you begged your parents to allow you to stay up past your bedtime to watch or to watch during dinner. Remember those programs that you loved to watch, discussed with your friends, and even acted out when you were hanging out with your friends (do *Teenage Mutant Ninja Turtles*, *Sabrina, the Teenage Witch*, *Power Rangers*, or *Saved by the Bell* ring any particular bells for you?). When you finish your list, conduct the content analysis outlined in Media Activity 2.1.

After you have completed the questions in the activity, consider the questions below to help you summarize the messages you received from your favorite programs:

- What were the total numbers of males and females in starring roles in the programs you watched as a child?
- Were men or women more numerous in their employment outside of the home?
- Were men or women more likely to work at home or be a homemaker?
- Of those who were employed, were men or women more numerous in lower- or higher-paid positions?
- Were men or women more likely to be victims or heroes?
- Were men or women more likely to be beautiful, fit, and thin?
- Were men or women more responsible for taking care of children?
- Do you observe any patterns by gender in these characteristics and roles?
- Are there some roles in which men are in the clear majority? Which are they?
- Are there some roles in which women are in the clear majority? Which are they?
- What are the characteristics of the roles in which women are the majority?
- What do these numbers signal about who is important in U.S. culture?

To get a larger sample, you can do this exercise with a group or class, ensuring that each program is only listed or analyzed one time.

As you think through the patterns that emerge through this simple content analysis, consider what kind of information was conveyed to you about the appropriate roles, work, and appearance for men and women. Was it about the same, slightly different, or

Media Activity 2.1
Men's and Women's Roles in Prime-Time Television

Instructions

List the television programs that were your favorites as a child. These programs should all be narrative fiction and not news, variety shows (such as *Sesame Street*), infotainment, movies, or specials. Then answer the following questions.

1. Determine how many males and how many females in each program had starring roles. Starring roles are those for which you can bank on the actors making the biggest salaries of the cast. Do not count characters who are on the program regularly but only featured occasionally as a major character. Now total the numbers of men and women in starring roles in all of the programs you listed.

    a. Total number of male characters in starring roles   _____
    b. Total number of female characters in starring roles   _____
    c. Total number of all characters in starring roles   _____

2. Take a closer look at the list of males and females in starring roles and note, by gender, how many of them played the following roles in the programs:

	Males	Females
a. homemakers	_____	_____
b. worked outside home	_____	_____
c. professionals	_____	_____
d. secretaries/clerical workers	_____	_____
e. law enforcement	_____	_____
f. doctors	_____	_____
g. victims/martyrs	_____	_____
h performed deeds or took actions that were heroic	_____	_____
i. took major responsibility for children	_____	_____
Totals	_____	_____

3. Look at the starring roles by gender once again and add up the totals of males and females who exhibited the characteristics of appearance as follows:

	Males	Females
a. average in appearance	_____	_____
b. attractive in appearance	_____	_____
c. glamorous in appearance	_____	_____
d. thin in size	_____	_____
e. average in size	_____	_____
f. overweight	_____	_____
g. physically fit	_____	_____
h. voluptuous or sexy	_____	_____
Totals	_____	_____

significantly different for each sex? If you watched a minimum of ten hours of television per week as a child, the messages about gender that were conveyed by the programs you watched had an impact on you. What were the messages you received about being a boy or a girl, a man or a woman from the entertainment television you watched?

Popular television has an enormous impact on children and teenagers. These programs play a key role in shaping a sense of self, gender identification and roles, and beliefs about what we can do as well as what we want to be and do as both children and adults. The roles and characteristics of men and women on television signal a sense of norms to the audience and can either confirm or challenge what we learn about gender roles and identification at home, in school, and from our peers. In fact, studies by George Gerbner, among others, have indicated that people who watch fifteen hours or more of television weekly tend to believe the "TV reality" over their own experience and observations in the world (Gerbner 1997, 1).

And as we learned in the previous section of this chapter, we are most impressionable and easily influenced by media images when two things occur:

- We are young enough to still be forming our own gender identity and our understanding of what is expected of us as boys and girls, as women and men.
- We are exposed to repetitive images and messages.

From 1965 to 1985, the percentage of male characters on prime-time television was 71 percent and that of female characters was 29 percent. While more women were portrayed as workers by the 1990s, overall women were still underrepresented, held lower status, and were chiefly focused on domestic issues (Elasmar et al. 1999, 21–26). From 1997 to 2006, the split changed significantly, with the percentage of male characters on prime-time at 58 percent and female characters at 42 percent. As prime-time television has become increasingly racially diverse over the last few decades, the gender images by race have been quite different. In prime-time programs with only white characters, the gender breakdown of characters was 52 percent male and 48 percent female. In programs with characters that were predominantly people of color, the split was 48 percent male and 52 percent female, and for programs that were racially diverse, male characters weighed in at 63 percent and female characters at 37 percent (Signorielli 2001, 340). While the reasons are unclear for the varying gender mix on TV according to the racial mix, one thing is certain: depending on what types of shows they watch, audiences are getting very different messages about the relative importance of men and women.

Sally Steenland examined eighty television entertainment programs during the spring 1990 season and found the following:

- Most men and women were portrayed in their twenties and thirties; the presence of female television characters began to decrease at age forty, while the presence of male characters began to decrease at age fifty.
- The most common job for women was clerical.
- The most common job for men was law enforcement.

- The number of female characters depicted as full-time homemakers on television had increased rather than decreased from previous seasons.
- Almost twice as many men as women were portrayed in the workplace.
- Women of color were largely segregated on prime time television, appearing mostly in situation comedies.
- As a rule, men wore more clothes and kept them on longer than women. (Steenland 1995, 180–187)

Despite Steenland's findings that the most common job on television for women was clerical, she also determined that television characters, including women, were likely to have more money than their real-life counterparts. Advertisers seek attractive surroundings for their thirty-second commercials. They want programs featuring affluent characters who can afford to buy their products, and producers of both new and current series need to take that into consideration if they want some longevity.

Approximately 50 percent of the U.S. population are women, but in the mid-1990s only one-third of all characters on prime-time television were women. In children's programming, only 18 percent of all characters were female (Gerbner 1997, 1).

A study of the 2005–2006 season examined the social roles of men and women in prime-time television through a wider lens. This study found that, ten years after Steenland's study, women were still more likely to focus on the interpersonal roles in television, including family and romantic relationships and friendships. Male characters were far more likely to be focused on work roles. The "findings of this study counter popular media reports claiming that well-worn stereotypes of female characters have been supplanted by 'the New Woman' identified as a more progressive type of character. . . . Such reports often rely on high-profile yet anecdotal examples of the fortunes of just a few programs, such as *Grey's Anatomy*, to make their case" (Lauzen, Dozier, and Horan 2008, 211).

The media activities in this section will introduce you to different types of media analyses that will help you decide if and to what degree current gender images and stereotypes have changed on television as well as how accurate and equitable they appear to be.

Television as a Tool of Culture

Television interacts with gender in two critical ways. It reflects cultural values and it serves as a trusted conveyor of information and images (Wood 2011, 231). A 1986 study determined that children who watched television had more stereotyped views of the sexes than children who did not (Kimball 1986, 265–301).

Prime-time television provides girls and women with a series of mixed and confusing messages. For baby boomers, who grew up in the 1950s and 1960s and even 1970s, these jumbled messages looked like this:

> American women today are a bundle of contradictions because much of the media imagery we grew up with was itself filled with mixed messages about what women

should and should not do, what women could and could not be. This was true in the 1960s, and it is true today. The media, of course, urges us to be pliant, cute, sexually available, thin, blond, poreless, wrinkle-free and deferential to men. But it is easy to forget that the media also suggested we could be rebellious, tough, enterprising and shrewd. (Douglas 1994, 9)

While messages of what it meant to be a "real" woman in this era were contradictory for girls and women, boys growing up in this same era received TV messages that were much more straightforward. To be a "real man" meant being strong, tough, the breadwinner whose strength was demonstrated through his physical power, work status, rational thinking, and the absence of any of the more tender emotions.

As we examine the evolution of gender messages on prime-time television from the 1950s through the first decade of the twenty-first century, the messages for girls and women suggest a wider range of choice of what it means to be feminine, while for men, the meaning of masculinity and its confusing and limited choices become far more complicated.

Let us take a walk through some of the trends in gendered images in prime-time television and see what we find. As your read through the following portrayals and shifts in gender representations, think about other programs from that decade that you are aware of or have seen on cable stations and ask yourself if they conform or deviate from a fixed image of men and women for that time period.

The 1951 debut of *I Love Lucy* (1951–1957) featured a woman who, although dizzy and troublesome, was the central character of the program. Producers tried to emulate this success with other programs such as *I Married Joan* (1952–1955) and *My Little Margie* (1952), but few of the copies were successful. The early 1950s to the mid-1960s were filled with situation comedies in which women were housewives and played the supporting role while men were the central characters, the workers, and often the problem solvers. Programs such as *Father Knows Best* (1954–1963), *Leave It to Beaver* (1957–1963), and *The Donna Reed Show* (1958–1966) represent this genre. This television depiction was a good match for what was happening in post–World War II U.S. culture, at least in middle-class white culture. After the war, women were largely taken out of the job market and remained at home while their husbands went back to work. For middle-class white women, the role of homemaker became central to the postwar economy and the ongoing division of the public and private spheres (Lout 1995, 169).

African American women were largely absent from early television except for occasional minor roles as maids and other servants. One exception was an early 1950s program, *Beulah* (1950–1952). The program started out on radio, where the original voice for the title character, Beulah, was provided by a white man. Eventually the radio program hired Hattie McDaniel as the voice of Beulah. McDaniel was the first black actor to win an Academy Award, for her supporting role in the film *Gone with the Wind* (1939). "A refreshing and progressive entertainer, Hattie refused to play Beulah with the hyper-exaggerated dialect typified by Marlin Hurt and Bob Corley who came before her.

Race and gender collide in the stereotypical emasculated roles for boys and men and defeminized roles of slaves and maids for girls and women, played by African American actors in the 1940s and 1950s. This publicity photo for the movie *Belle Starr* (1941) portrays actors Matthew Beard [at left] who played Stymie in *The Little Rascals* (*Our Gang*) from 1930 to 1935 and Louise Beavers [at right] who, along with Ethel Waters and Hattie McDaniel, played the lead role of a housekeeper and cook working for a white family in the TV show *Beulah* (1950–1952). They accepted such roles because these were among the few available to them. (*Source: Courtesy of Getty Images. Copyright © 2011 John D. Kisch/Separate Cinema Archive. Used by permission of Getty Images.*)

McDaniel fought for, and won, a provision in her contract that included script approval to ensure her role would not be a degrading one" (Ingram 2011).

The TV version of Beulah was an overweight, wide-faced woman with an equally wide grin, typically depicted with a head rag, reminiscent of the blatantly racist depiction of Aunt Jemima and the "mammy" stereotype most widely known from the film *Gone with the Wind*. Beulah is a housekeeper for a white family and, as the troublesome cliché goes, "like a member of the family." She genuinely cares for the family, especially the children, and is depicted in a way that suggests her whole life revolves around the white family for whom she works. Beulah is never shown to have a family of her own, nor is she portrayed independently, in her own right, even in the limited conventions of TV drama or comedy of the times. The program *Beulah* is rarely mentioned in analysis of gender in early television, where the term "women's roles in TV" often translates exclusively to white women.

Despite the rigid gender roles on prime-time programs, even the 1950s offered choices, complexities, and ambiguities for some women. Susan Douglas examines the interplay of prime-time television with news coverage in the 1950s and 1960s. Along with *Leave It to Beaver*, there was the news coverage of the civil rights movement, the Nixon–Kennedy debates, and rocket launches. Girls got the impression that to be an *American* was to be tough, individualistic, brave, and smart, while to be a *girl* was to be nurturing and passive (Douglas 1994, 26).

Since girls were both female and American, this meant some confusing choices amid the contradictions. Linda can remember a dilemma of this sort when she was about thirteen years old. Her family had a pool table in the basement, and she became quite proficient at pool, able to clobber most of the boys she played against. But the teen magazines Linda read warned her never to beat a boy at a game because winning was not feminine and because their egos could not take losing. She compromised by beating the boys she considered "just friends" and letting prospective boyfriends win. While Leon cannot remember reading teen magazines in his youth, he did read comic books and collect baseball cards, which provided him with a multitude of superheroes and sports figures to emulate. The messages he received from these male role models were all about winning. The idea of letting schoolmates beat him at a game so they would like him more would have been completely foreign.

By the 1970s there was an increase in TV programs that centered on female characters. Working women were depicted on shows ranging from *Mary Tyler Moore* (1970–1977) to *Rhoda* (1974–1981) to *Charlie's Angels* (1976–1981). By the mid-1970s, beautiful female cops emerged in *Police Woman* (1974–1978) and *Get Christie Love* (1974–1975). By the mid-1970s to early 1980s, more roles for black women emerged in *Good Times* (1974–1979) and *What's Happening!!* (1976–1978). Yet in each of these shows the central black female characters, Florida and Shirley, respectively, played the role of the good-natured "mammy" (Lout 1995), continuing the damaging stereotype present in the 1950s program *Beulah*. As we continue to analyze the images of men and women through these years, it is important to note that when there is progress in the development of more complex characters, they are primarily white women; little or none of the same type of progress occurs for women of color.

Male characters in the 1950s were the fathers in charge (*Father Knows Best*, 1954–1960), the serious dedicated detective (*Dragnet*, 1951–1959), and the charming, cowboy-era gambler (*Maverick*, 1957–1962). These men were primarily simple characters who shared, in varied settings, the common traits of being the knowing, problem-solving man

The cast of *Father Knows Best* poses as and portrays the 1950s ideal family. [Left to right: the Andersons: Bud (Billy Gray), Margaret (Jane Wyatt), Jim (Robert Young), Kathy (Lauren Chapin), and Betty (Elinor Donahue).] *(Source: Courtesy of Getty Images. Copyright © 1956 by Hulton Archive. Used by permission of Getty Images.)*

in charge. And even though the character Bret Maverick was a good-hearted rogue, he always came out on top at the end.

The 1960s men in popular prime-time series were still family men (Rob in *Dick Van Dyke* and Darrin in *Bewitched)* who, while sometimes slightly bungling, were still the ultimate man in charge. The more classic macho types were played for irony and comedy (Fred Flintstone) and for dead-serious drama (Perry Mason).

Although the 1970s featured more female characters in prime-time television, studies reveal that there were more males in evening television than females, more diverse roles were available to males, and female characters appeared less competent than male characters. From 1972 to 1981, only 44 percent of female prime-time characters worked outside the home, as compared to more than 60 percent of women in reality (Steenland 1990).

The CBS series *Cagney & Lacey* (1982–1988) broke some of these conventional portrayals and omissions of women characters on television. This story of two female police officers who solved their own cases without relying on men was the first TV drama to star two women. In the series, Christine Cagney was single with an active sex life, and Mary

The made-for-TV film *Cagney & Lacey* (1981) featured Meg Foster and Tyne Daly in the lead roles. CBS thought they were too "women's lib." *(Source: Courtesy of Getty Images. Copyright © 1982 CBS Photo Archive. Used by permission of Getty Images.)*

Beth Lacey was the primary breadwinner of her family and often shown as the partner to initiate sex with her husband. *Cagney & Lacey* was first made as a TV movie (1981), which received high ratings and moved on to become a series starring Meg Foster as Cagney and Tyne Daley as Lacey. After a few episodes, CBS determined that the women were too tough and aggressive, "too women's lib," and replaced Foster with a softer and more conventionally attractive Sharon Gless: "The quest for the working women's market in the late 1970s and 1980s led to women oriented programs and feminist subject matter in prime time. But . . . when these representations deviated too much from the acceptable conventions of the industry, they were quickly brought back in line" (D'Acci

Cagney & Lacey (1987): In this feminist to feminine makeover, Sharon Gless plays Cagney, and Tyne Daly returns as Lacey. *(Source: Courtesy of Getty Images. Copyright © 1987 CBS Photo Archive. Used by permission of Getty Images.)*

1995, 454–459, 465). Because so many women viewers hungered for alternative female images, they persisted in identifying with Cagney and Lacey as women in nontraditional roles, despite changes to soften the characters and make them more traditionally feminine (D'Acci 1995, 460).

A new image in the 1980s was women as "superwomen." Women who held professional jobs, were raising families, had fun at home, and resolved problems gracefully within thirty to sixty minutes were seen on *Family Ties* (1982–1989) and *The Cosby Show* (1984–1992). There were also increasingly diverse roles available for women in such 1980s programs as *Murder She Wrote* (1984–1996), *Frank's Place* (1987–1988), *Cheers*

(1982–1993), and *Murphy Brown* (1988–1998). "Prior to the late 1980s, men were more likely to interact with other men, whereas women were more likely to interact with men, thus reinforcing the ideas that women compete with one another and prefer to be with men. In the mid-1980s groups of women were shown as friends and family and primary in each others lives, with the role of men as secondary in such programs as *Designing Women* [1986–1993] and *Golden Girls* [1985–1992]" (Lout 1995, 171).

Another 1980s television phenomenon was the meteoric rise of the single dad in programs such as *Full House* (1987–1995), *My Two Dads* (1987–1990), and *Who's the Boss?* (1984–1993). While in the real world, then and now, the vast majority of single parents are women, in TV land of the 1980s, single parents were predominantly men.

In the 1970s and 1980s, men were in starring roles more frequently than women and outnumbered women in their appearance on the small screen. The characters they played were most often involved in action and drama rather than depicting "humor, emotions, and interpersonal relationships." They held higher-status jobs than women did and were far more likely to be lawyers, police officers, ministers, and doctors shown at work rather than at home (Sigoloff 2009, 26).

Soap operas were still another television genre that generally offered a unique perspective on gender. According to British author Christine Geraghty, the structure and characterization in soap operas offered an oppositional point of view with regard to gender. In the first place, daytime soaps were slow paced in the development of action, reflecting some of the drudgery in the lives of housewives. In the second place, these daytime soaps presented female characters as the glue that held the family together. Evening soaps, in particular, often presented strong female characters and addressed issues from a point of view that was sympathetic to women. For example, evening soaps often featured an unusually high number of middle-aged women and women with access to great power. The characters of Alexis and Angelica from *Dynasty* (1981–1989) and *Dallas* (1978–1991) represented atypical television examples of the successful, independent career woman (Geraghty 1991, 43).

Perhaps most importantly, Geraghty provides an analysis of soap operas that reinforces the feminist notion that the personal is political: "Soaps overturn a deeply entrenched value structure which is based on the traditional opposition of masculinity and femininity. . . . Instead, the essence of soaps is the reflection on personal problems and the emphasis is on talk not on action, on slow development rather than the immediate response, on delayed retribution rather than instant effect" (Geraghty 1991, 41). The action in soap operas is strongly rooted in the personal sphere of life.

The 1990s offered a wider array of female characters in continuing programs such as *Murphy Brown* and newer programs such as *Roseanne* (1988–1997) and *Northern Exposure* (1990–1995). But these less traditional female characters continued to be the exception rather than the rule (Lout 1995, 171). The most-watched prime time TV programs in the 1990s were the following:

- *The Arsenio Hall Show*
- *Family Guy*
- *The Simpsons*

- *Buffy the Vampire Slayer*
- *Law and Order: SVU*
- *Saturday Night Live*
- *Friends*
- *South Park*
- *WWE Monday Night Raw*
- *Futurama*
- *Charmed* (TV.com 2013)

These shows offered quite a stew of messages about men and women. There were three adult animated cartoons with disrespectful boys and bumbling dads (*The Simpsons*, *South Park*, and *Family Guy*), two programs with teen girls or young women with power to do good as vampire slayers and witches (*Charmed* and *Buffy the Vampire Slayer*) two programs featuring single, working women who were sexually active with varying degrees of independence from men (*Friends* and *Sex and the City*), and two programs in which murderers and rapists were rounded up by hypermasculine detectives and as-sistant district attorneys, along with smart and beautiful female detectives and underling attorneys who typically showed ample cleavage and/or length of leg (*Law and Order* and *Law and Order: SVU*). When you throw in the two talk or variety type shows (*Arsenio Hall* and *Saturday Night Live*) and round it out with wrestling, and futuristic programs (*WWE Monday Night Raw* and *Futurama*) the message patterns seem wide and varied. On closer look at the roles, characteristics, jobs, and appearance of men and women, we may find more similarities than appear on the surface. Take another look at the television shows we've just named in this paragraph. See if you can identify the gendered message patterns in this diverse array of programs.

In the first decade of the twenty-first century, the most popular narrative television programs were the following.

- *Grey's Anatomy*
- *NCIS*
- *Bones*
- *House*
- *Criminal Minds*
- *Supernatural*
- *The Mentalist*
- *The Secret Life of the American Teenager*
- *The Vampire Diaries*
- *Desperate Housewives* (TV.com 2011)

Table 2.1 (page 106) begins to tell parts of the gender story of these popular programs from the first decade of the new millennium. According to both Glascock (2001) and Lauzen et al. (2008), when there is at least one woman behind the scenes of a television program, serving as creator, writer, or executive producer, something begins to shift in both the characters and the story line: we start to see more women in working situations and more men immersed and active in interpersonal relationships. Two of the programs,

Table 2.1

Top Ten Popular Narrative TV Programs, June 1, 2011

	Network	Creators by gender	Executive producers by gender	Stars (listed in order of IMDb billing)	Highest paid actors in each program*
1. *Grey's Anatomy*	ABC	1 woman	4 men 2 women	Ellen Pompeo Sandra Oh Justin Chambers	Patrick Dempsey: $250,000 Ellen Pompeo: $250,000
2. *NCIS*	CBS	2 men	3 men	Mark Harmon Michael Weatherly Pauly Perrette	Mark Harmon: $375,000 Michael Weatherly: $125,000
3. *Bones*	FOX	1 man	4 men	Emily Deschanel David Boreanaz Michaela Conline	David Boreanaz: $200,000
4. *House*	FOX	1 man	7 men	Hugh Laurie Robert Sean Leonard Lisa Edelstein	Hugh Laurie: $400,000+
5. *Criminal Minds*	CBS	1 man	unavailable	Shemar Moore Matthew Gray Gubler Thomas Gibson	Joe Mantegna: $125,000 Thomas Gibson: $100,000
6. *Supernatural*	CW	1 man	4 men 2 women	Jared Padalecki Jensen Ackles Jim Beaver	Information unavailable.
7. *The Mentalist*	CBS	1 man	2 men	Simon Baker Robin Tunney Tim Kang	Information unavailable.
8. *The Secret Life of the American Teenager*	ABC	1 woman	1 woman	Shaileen Woodley Mark Derwin India Eisley	Shailene Woodley: $40,000
9. *The Vampire Diaries*	CW	1 man 1 woman	2 men	Paul Wesley Ian Somerhalder Nina Dobrey	Ian Somerhalder: $40,000
10. *Desperate Housewives*	ABC	1 man	11 men	Teri Hatcher Felicity Huffman Marcia Cross	Eva Longoria: $200,000

Sources: Internet Movie Database (www.IMDb.com), *TV Guide* and TV.com.
*The term "actors" here is used inclusively for both men and women of the acting profession.

Grey's Anatomy and *The Secret Life of the American Teenager*, were created by women, and three, once again *Grey's Anatomy* and *The Secret Life of the American Teenager* joined by *Supernatural*, included at least one woman in the list of executive producers.

 Grey's Anatomy is an interesting example of the kind of changes that can happen when women are prominently on board behind the scenes. Shonda Rhimes, an African American

Grey's Anatomy successfully presents a variety of complex and diverse gender images. [Left to right in 2005: front row: Dr. Cristina Yang (Sandra Oh); back row: Dr. Richard Webber (James Pickens Jr.), Dr. Miranda Bailey (Chandra Wilson), Dr. Alex Karev (Justin Chambers), Dr. Izzie Stevens (Katherine Heigl), Dr. George O'Malley (T.R. Knight), Dr. Preston Burk (Isaiah Washington), Dr. Meredith Grey (Ellen Pompeo), and Dr. Derek Shepherd (Patrick Dempsey).] *(Source: Courtesy of Getty Images. Copyright © 2005 American Broadcasting Companies, Inc. Used by permission of Getty Images. Photographer/© ABC/Getty Images.)*

woman, is the creator and key executive producer of the program. The ensemble cast was populated with women of various races, temperaments, and character types. A few demonstrated some of the traditional characteristics mixed in with their nontraditional traits. Dr. Lexie Grey is a smart *and* compassionate young doctor, independent *and* feminine and not at all interested in having children at this point in her career. Dr. Callie Torres is a well-respected attending physician, a strong and powerful Latina woman, in a committed relationship with another woman doctor, bisexual, openly interested in sex, *and* longing to have children. Dr. Christina Yang, who demonstrates far less nurturing characteristics, is a brilliant, cutthroat, hypercompetitive surgeon with a tender and fiercely loyal friendship with Dr. Meredith Grey. All of the women who are main characters in the program are depicted primarily at work as doctors at Seattle Grace Hospital and demonstrate a wide range of character traits, competence, authority, and interest in career and/or love. The main male characters in the 2010 season were Alex Karev, Derek Shepherd, Owen Hunt, and Mark Sloan, all of whom were portrayed as "hot" and/or "hunky." Karev is the bad boy who is a sweetheart below the surface; Owen and Derek are both warm, compassionate, sexy, and at the top of their game as attending physicians; and Mark, the handsome, recovering sex maniac, is shown hopelessly in love with Lexie. Owen and Derek are the warm and fuzzy partners in their respective relationships with Christina and Meredith; and Owen, Derek, and Mark are passionately and almost desperately interested in having children—far more interested than their respective partners. Three of the four men are at the highest rank of attending physicians at the hospital; Christina, Meredith, and Lexie are all mid-rank as residents. The two female attending physicians, Miranda Bailey and Callie, are both strong women of color, African American and Latina, respectively, and the hospital chief is an African American man. The cast offers a head-spinning combination of some traditional, but far more nontraditional roles of men and women. Lauzen's and Glascock's research about how one woman in a prominent role behind the scenes can be a game changer for a wide range of gender characteristics for both women and men holds true with this popular program.

Yet although the stars of the show were billed in order as Ellen Pompeo (Meredith), Sandra Oh (Christina), and Justin Chambers (Alex), the highest-paid actors on the set were Patrick Dempsey (Derek) and Ellen Pompeo (Battaglio 2010).

In 2010, *TV Guide* listed the highest-paid actors in television, some of whom appeared in these top ten most popular programs. Six actors—four men and two women—earned $200,000 and above per episode. The others, who earned from $40,000 to $125,000 per episode, were four men and two women (Battaglio 2010).

A content analysis, conducted in 2009, of the six most popular programs of that year—*Grey's Anatomy, NCIS, CSI, House, Criminal Minds*, and *The Mentalist*—explored male occupations and characteristics in order to determine to what degree male depictions corresponded to the traits that are most notably elements of hegemonic masculinity. The male characters were assessed according to their occupational positions relative to power; their character traits such as aggression, sensitivity, and emotional expression; and the types of their interactions with men and women. According to Justin Sigoloff, the male characters in the study represented "the traditional, historical, and heavily stereotyped sense of masculinity." The men in these programs were featured in high-status jobs in medical, religious, legal, and law enforcement professions. The only other significant "work" of male characters in the sample was criminal (Sigoloff 2009).

A large percentage of the men in the study were portrayed with the following characteristics:

- angry
- aggressive
- unemotional
- competitive
- direct
- intelligent
- insensitive to other people's feelings

Violence in these programs was primarily between men. Men were depicted as more aggressive and competitive with each other than with women. Higher-ranking men were more aggressive, competitive, and insensitive than their subordinates. Yet, ironically, these male characters who demonstrated the epitome of the classic male traits that add up to hegemonic masculinity, were respected by men and women characters alike (Sigoloff 2009, 69). Despite some significant changes in both power positions of women characters in television, a wider range of careers and personality traits among female characters, and some interesting and atypical male characters, by and large it appears that male characters continue to demonstrate stereotypical male characteristics *and* are held in high regard. In some of the most watched programs in the first decade of the twenty-first century, the most highly regarded male characters continue to be predominantly tough, aggressive, competitive, and unemotional. The fact that these characters are highly regarded underscores the message that these hypermasculine traits serve as the ideal of masculinity.

A few other notable TV programs from 2000 to 2010 offer some unique and sometimes groundbreaking images of men and women. *Sex and the City* depicted four stunning thirty- and forty-something women who are single through most of the series, professionally successful, and unabashedly sexually active. The women often take the initiative in seeking relationships with men, sexual or otherwise. Some are still searching for true love in addition to or other than true sex and have many ups and downs as they seek and finally fulfill their dreams. The women are the epitome of liberated women in designer clothes and $400 shoes. Some critics refer to the characters as postfeminist examples of the downside of the liberated woman, while others describe the program as an example of the commodification of feminism: beautiful and independent women who are walking advertisements for high-style clothes with price tags far too high for the average woman. However, the relationships of the four women are primary: their loving loyalty to one another is unshakable and most often comes before their relationships with men. Yet by the end of the six-year run of the program, all four women pair up with the perfect man of their dreams.

Men of a Certain Age is another example, however short-lived, that bends the traditional portrayal of men. This program focuses on the lives and relationships of three forty- and fifty-something men who are looking for meaning in their lives. One of the most unusual aspects of this program is the relationship between the three men, who, despite an occasional burst of macho bravado, spend regular time together in a coffee shop talking about their feelings, doubts, and questions about their lives and relationships. Owen (Andre Braugher) is a happily married adult son of a famous basketball star turned successful car dealership owner. Owen is always falling short of his father's success as well as his father's praise. Joe (Ray Romano), the owner of a party supply store, is divorced with two children and is just tentatively beginning to date. Terry is a struggling actor, single, well-known for brief serial relationships, and just beginning to explore the possibility of more stable work and a stable, loving relationship in his life. They all have jobs that provide a paycheck but are not the center of their lives or passion. They each find occasional passion and joy in their lives in ways that do not involve the high drama of police work or the supersuccess of handsome, life-saving doctors. Their age, the way they realistically poke fun at each other, their connection to each other, and the way they love and struggle in relationships with women seem both gritty and real and offer some hope. Added to the interest is that two of the characters are white and one is black, and while race is often present in their conversations and lives, it is not the central focus of the series or the relationships between the men. In all of these ways, the characters and the program offer a unique depiction of middle-aged men.

Prime-Time Television: Employment and Economics

Sally Steenland's study revealed a gender gap in employment in prime-time television production. In 1990, only 15 percent of all producers were women, 25 percent of all writers were women, and 9 percent of directors were women. In addition, two-thirds of entertainment network executives at the vice president level and above were men (Steenland 1990). By the 2009–2010 television season, 27 percent of TV creators, writers, producers, editors, and directors of photography in broadcast television were women (Lauzen 1990, 1). These behind-the-scene numbers show some substantial progress for women. But the most recent U.S. census reveals that the adult male and female population is close to fifty/fifty, which points out that the progress is still far from what could be considered gender equity.

The conglomerate ownership of media described in Chapter 1 and the prevalence of males in charge in entertainment media have tended to proscribe and limit the roles and personality traits of women characters on television. As emphasized by Ben Bagdikian in *The Media Monopoly*, this does not indicate a conspiracy or devious plot. Rather, the level of wealth, ownership, and experience of the individuals who own and run entertainment television results in a high degree of shared values, which are conveyed in programming (Bagdikian 1992, 16). If men dominate the writing, production, and direction of prime-time television, it is likely that their collective life experiences and worldview will be reflected in the characters, themes, and plots

By and large, female characters in prime time are likely to be knee-deep in interpersonal roles that involve romance, family, and friends while male characters are far more likely to be shown primarily in their work roles. But when programs hire one or more women as program creators or writers, these very same programs are more likely to feature both men and women at work (Lauzen et al. 2008). This is ample evidence to demonstrate that increasing the roles of women behind the scenes can change some of the more common gender stereotypes and norms on the little screen. It stands to reason that as the numbers of women working in television increase, gender roles will become more interchangeable, unpredictable, and fluid. Boys and girls, women and men, will be able to breathe more easily as television signals to them that the range of choices of who they can be and what they can do in the world expands. It is not so hard to imagine that if unyieldingly rigid gender roles in media became more pliable and fluid, then there will eventually be more widespread acceptance of diversity in how women and men are expected to dress, talk, work, play, and deal with relationships in real life.

As it emerged in the 1960s and continues today, feminism challenged the conventional place of women by criticizing and proposing to change traditional roles in order to allow women a wider array of life choices. Feminism invites women to question the narrowly defined, exclusive, and prescribed roles as homemaker and primary nurturer, as secretary and waitress, as nurse and teacher. Feminism does not criticize the value of these jobs and roles but rather asks why they offer such low pay and low status and are occupied predominantly by women. Feminism also asks women to consider what they put on and do to their faces and bodies to conform to an image of beauty that is almost universally inaccessible. The men's movement supported these opportunities and changes for women as well as the work and personal options that would expand for men.

"One of the reasons why television is resistant to the messages of feminism, then, is that they [sponsors] view those messages as conflicting with women's desire to consume. Women buy products, it is thought, to please their families and to make themselves more attractive. Feminism, which argues that women should not base their self-image on the approval of others, inhibits women's desire to consume" (Dow 1995, 200). It is critical to remember that in addition to its explicit function to entertain and what we have discovered to be its implicit function to socialize, entertainment television is a vehicle for advertising. It is not in prime-time television's self-interest to promote characters and themes that discourage women from buying products that pay for a program's survival.

Gender Ideology in Entertainment Media

Gender ideology in entertainment media is hegemony—that is, socialization without the use of force—at its subtle best. TV entertainment executives, directors, producers, and advertisers do not participate in hegemony because they are evil. They participate in perpetuating stereotypical images of women and men because those images, and the products and programs they help to sell, generate profits and because profit-driven capital expansion is the world in which they live quite comfortably and from which they derive tremendous benefits.

But the most compelling aspect of this hegemony is that while we are often aware of being amused, enlightened, or pacified by popular media, we are far less likely to be aware of the less than visible messages that the media convey about what it means to be masculine or feminine, a real man or a real woman. This is the classic way that hegemony works: we are so accustomed to seeing traditional gender roles both in and out of media that we become accustomed to them and they seem normal and right to us. We often take on the roles as our own without even thinking about them and just as frequently pass them on to the next generation. Even without actually seeing or being able to articulate these hegemonic structures, limits, and barriers, many of us still manage to conform to their rules.

One way to examine the operation of hegemony and to make the invisible visible is to use a simple content analysis in a small sample of prime-time television to understand how it works. Chapter 1 describes ideology as "a system of meaning that helps define and explain the world and that makes value judgments about the world" (Croteau and Hoynes

Table 2.2

Traditional Gender Ideology

Male traits of the traditional ideology	*Female traits of the traditional ideology*
Rough and tumble	Sweet
Athletic	Pretty
Tough	Tender
High-status job	Low-status job
Supports the family financially	Supports the family emotionally
In charge at work	In charge at home
Active	Sensitive
Adventurous	Supportive
Powerful	Nurturing
Strong	Patient
Unemotional	Emotional
Confident	Dependent
Rational	Irrational
Competent	Helpless

1997, 163). Ideology in entertainment media works best when it operates at a less than conscious and less than visible level and is applied to aspects of the social order that are considered the norm and rarely questioned. Some examples of long-standing male and female traits of traditional ideology about gender are listed in Table 2.2.

We have learned through the information about gender socialization that we accept, through parents, peers, education, media, religious and/or spiritual groups, and other institutions, stereotypes that are sometimes visible and sometimes far more subtle. How can we identify these traits in prime-time television, tease them out so they become visible and consciously recognized, so we can determine what gender ideology is operating?

Does gender ideology in media still conform to the traditional list, or are there any indications that it is changing?

Complete Media Activity 2.2 (beginning on page 114) for a better understanding of how gender ideology operates in contemporary prime-time television. If more than half of the characters you listed primarily display the traditional traits, the program is likely to reflect a traditional, dominant, or hegemonic gender ideology. If more than half of the characters primarily display the nontraditional traits, the program most likely offers a different gender ideology, which can be called nontraditional, alternative, or counterhegemonic. If more than half of the characters combine the traditional and nontraditional traits, it is most likely that the program conveys a mixed gender ideology or an ideology in transition. While the small sample of prime-time programs is not large enough to be fully representative, it does help tease out the often invisible gender framework that exists on prime-time television.

From your sample, what do you conclude about the way that gender within the TV family is represented? Do you see any consistent or repeated patterns in the programs you reviewed? Is there a framework or a somewhat uniform story that is being told about men and women in the family? Is there a norm that is repeated about the configuration of the family? What were some of the recurring images in the TV programs from your younger years (refer to your responses in Media Activity 2.1, if necessary)? Can you identify some of the messages you received during that time about what it meant to be feminine and what it meant to be masculine?

As you uncover and understand these messages about the gender roles on prime-time television, you can begin to make your own independent judgments about whether and to what extent television serves as a force to socialize boys and girls, and men and women, to play their assigned roles in the family and society and to adhere to the dominant ideology regarding gender.

Film

Not surprisingly, the history of the depiction of women in film often runs parallel to the history of women's treatment in U.S. society. In the early 1900s, industrialization produced leisure time for a certain group of women, mostly middle-class white women. This leisure time was characterized by a split into public and private spheres of labor for those in the middle classes and above. By and large, women were assigned to the private sphere to care for children, hearth, and home, while men were assigned the higher-status and higher-paid public sphere of the business world of work. During this time, it was an important societal norm for women of the middle class and above to be traditionally feminine and run a smooth household. Yet there were also women in the labor force in 1900. Eighteen percent of the working population was female. Working-class women were employed in sweatshops and factories forty-eight to sixty hours per week and earned $3 to $6 per week. "The birth of the movies coincided with—and hastened—the genesis of modern woman" (Rosen 1973, 19, 23).

The sweetheart of the early 1900s film was Mary Pickford. Her specialty was the winsome waif, the sweet ragamuffin who appealed to Victorian audiences. During the 1920s, several genres of film developed that portrayed women in clear and concrete roles. There was the continuation of the good girl as originated by Mary Pickford. There was the flapper, who was in danger of becoming a bad girl, and there was the chorus girl, often portrayed by Gloria Swanson or Joan Crawford (Rosen 1973, 99).

At the end of 1941, the Japanese bombed Pearl Harbor and the United States officially entered World War II. Women entered the workforce with a bang. The previous call to middle-class femininity, which involved holding down the home front, switched to a call for patriotic women to support their men at war by going to work. With men off to war, the movie audience changed and for the first time there was a preponderance of films that were dubbed "women's pictures." Some of these films, such as *Spellbound* (1945) and *Mildred Pierce* (1945), explored women's lives and emotions and careers, while others, such as the Katharine Hepburn/Spencer Tracy classics *Adam's Rib* (1949) and *Woman of the Year* (1942), explored a new version of a woman who could be simultaneously feminine and independent (Rosen 1973, 190).

Media Activity 2.2
Gender Ideology in Prime-Time Television

Instructions

Select three current prime-time television programs that are narrative fiction and family-based. For the purposes of this activity, families are defined as two or more people living together who are related by blood, marriage, or adoption or who clearly self-identify as a family. By this definition, a heterosexual or same-sex couple who live together without being married and have one or more children by a previous relationship would be considered a family. According to this definition, it does not matter how traditional the family structure is or how functional or dysfunctional a family is.

Write the title of each program and the names of the major male and female characters in each program. (Major characters are those who are essential to the plot of the episode.) Place the letter M by each male character's name and the letter F by each female character's name.

Title of Each TV Program in the Sample
Program 1 title_____
Program 2 title_____
Program 3 title_____

Major Characters in Each of the three Programs

Program 1	Program 2	Program 3
_____	_____	_____
_____	_____	_____
_____	_____	_____
_____	_____	_____
_____	_____	_____

After the war ended, if Hollywood had "built on its image of the career woman, films might have become a more positive force in shaping the role of women in years to come. But as the men returned home from the war, box office—and social—demands changed. Slowly heroines moved into the background, becoming less aggressive or incapable of working out their own fates" (Rosen 1973, 201). By the late 1940s more than 3 million women had resigned or been fired from their wartime jobs (Douglas 1994, 47). And film, rather than reflecting this phenomenal change in the roles of men and women, reverted to women's role as playful, as love object, or as steadfast companion. *The Best Years of Our Lives*, starring Fredric March and Myrna Loy, was a powerful portrayal of men coming home from war with all their joy, agony, and ambivalence. However, the film, which won the Academy Award for Best Picture in 1947, demonstrated no parallel transition or difficulty for women, but rather depicted the "good woman" as remaining constant throughout and after the war, lovingly, patiently, and unambiguously supporting the struggles and erratic moods and behavior of her man.

Place a check (√) beside each male character's name (adults and children) for every characteristic he exhibits that is listed in the Male Traits column of the table below.

Place an X beside each male character's name (adults and children) for every characteristic he exhibits that is listed in the Female Traits column of the table below.

Place a check (√) beside each female character's name (adults and children) for every characteristic she exhibits that is listed in the Female Traits column of the table below.

Place an X beside each female character's name (adults and children) for every characteristic she exhibits that is listed in the Male Traits column of the table below.

Male Traits of the Traditional Ideology	*Female Traits of the Traditional Ideology*
Rough and tumble	Sweet
Athletic	Pretty
Tough	Tender
High-status job	Low-status job
Supports the family financially	Supports the family emotionally
In charge at work	In charge at home
Active	Sensitive
Adventurous	Supportive
Powerful	Nurturing
Strong	Patient
Unemotional	Emotional
Confident	Dependent
Rational	Irrational
Competent	Helpless

Over the years, film has inaccurately reflected working women. In 1930, more than one-third of U.S. films reviewed by the *New York Times* featured working women in the leading female role. In 1975, just over one-fourth of these films featured working women. "Compare this decline in Hollywood representations with the extraordinary growth in the percentage of actual adult women who work, from less than 20 percent in 1930 to 56 percent in 1975" (Galerstein 1989, xviii).

During the 1950s, 75 percent of women were married by the time they were nineteen (Rosen 1973, 245). During this Eisenhower era, there were signs of conformity in suburbia contrasted by the development of the Beat Generation and the seeds of the civil rights and women's movements. During this period, there were few representations of powerful, independent, or career-minded women in film. Women were catching their men in *How to Marry a Millionaire* (1953) and *Seven Brides for Seven Brothers* (1954). They were preparing for marriage in *Father of the Bride* (1950) and *High Society* (1956). They were discontented wives and hopeful lovers in *From Here to Eternity* (1953). Many films, such as *Twelve Angry Men* (1957) and *Mister Roberts* (1965), featured no women at all. There were the lovelorn and perky women in rock and roll–influenced films such as *April Love* (1957), *Tammy and the Bachelor* (1957), and *Gidget* (1959). By the late 1950s, Doris Day had emerged as the symbol of the struggle of the virginal woman (in which virginity was the winner) in *Pillow Talk* (1959) and *That Touch of Mink* (1962) (Rosen 1973, 205–305). By contrast, the 1950s was also the decade of Marilyn Monroe as the ultimate sex symbol.

In 1962 Helen Gurley Brown wrote *Sex and the Single Girl*, which advised women on romance and sex for its own sake; birth control pills began to be widely prescribed. In 1963 Betty Friedan wrote *The Feminine Mystique*, which analyzed the dissatisfaction of the trapped middle-class housewife. Yet the early 1960s were dominated by films such as those in the James Bond series, which treated women as sex objects and made intelligent women invisible. Barbra Streisand dominated the roles of strong women that were available in films such as *Funny Girl* (1968) and *What's Up, Doc?* (1972) (Lout 1995, 226).

By 1964, Beatlemania was in full swing. The youth and drug culture and the beginning of more open sexuality emerged in Haight Ashbury, college dormitories, and concerts. Yet the mid-1960s film industry chose to depict teenage angst with such films as *Beach Party* (1963), *Bikini Beach* (1964), and *Muscle Beach Party* (1964). "The most astonishing aspect of Hollywood in the mid-1960s was its total inability to reflect the tapestry of youth culture—and perhaps its unwillingness to do so. During these years of turmoil, the industry opted out of making meaningful contributions in interpreting the role of the new young woman" (Rosen 1973, 317). Instead we got *Mary Poppins* (1964), *My Fair Lady* (1964), and *The Sound of Music* (1965). All were period pieces—the lead characters were all women: an ideal nanny with magic powers, a street urchin turned lady through the will of a man, and a nun struggling with her own identity.

By the late 1960s, the youth culture began to be explored as Hollywood's awareness of the market potential of the youth audience was awakened with the popularity of *The Graduate* in 1967. In 1969, films such as *Easy Rider*, *Midnight Cowboy*, and *Alice's Restaurant* focused attention on the emerging alternative youth culture. Yet few of these youth films depicted strong women or reflected the struggle with identity, role, and sexuality that young women were facing.

While the early 1970s continued by and large to lock women into stereotypical roles, there were some breakthrough films. In *An Unmarried Woman* (1978), a married woman who had steadfastly played her part as wife by the rules of the time is discarded by her husband for another woman. The film conveys her struggles with traditional roles, career, and love and her emotionally rocky path to establish her independent identity. Other strong female characters were depicted by Jane Fonda in *Klute* (1971), *Julia* (1977), and *The China Syndrome* (1979). *Diary of a Mad Housewife* (1970) depicted one of the most horrible manifestations of the feminine mystique, the trapped middle-class housewife. *The Turning Point* (1977) provided a complex portrait of two strong women who were dancers—one chose a dance career and the other chose to raise a family. The film resisted the temptation to oversimplify the lives of these two women and deliver a moral message about which direction—career or family—is the correct choice. Sally Field played a complex working-class woman who becomes a hero in the film *Norma Rae* (1979).

Next to some of these films about strong and often nontraditional women, the 1972 film *The Godfather* stands out as distinctly different. Not only did the film win critical acclaim and multiple awards, but it was and continues to be, an iconic image of hyper-masculinity for generations of boys and men. Even in the twenty-first century, viewing this film still is considered by some as a type of rite of passage, observing the actions of "real men."

The top box office films in the 1980s were the following:

- *E.T.: The Extraterrestrial*
- *Return of the Jedi*
- *The Empire Strikes Back*
- *Raiders of the Lost Ark*
- *Ghostbusters*
- *Indiana Jones and the Last Crusade*
- *Indiana Jones and the Temple of Doom*
- *Beverly Hills Cop*
- *Back to the Future* (Internet Movie Database 1999)

Other than the fact that Harrison Ford appears in five of these films, what do these popular films convey about gender? (A moment's indulgence in film trivia discloses that Ford also was cast as the school principal in a sixth film, *E.T.*, but received no credit for this role because the scene was deleted from the final production.) Of the nine films, eight were categorized as either action or adventure. In all of these action and adventure films, male actors received top billing, and only Karen Allen in *Raiders of the Lost Ark* and Kate Capshaw in *Indiana Jones and the Temple of Doom* received as high as second billing. Despite her higher billing, Allen played the role of a shrill female victim clad in a long white dress and heels who shrieked as Harrison Ford's Indiana Jones saved her from snakes and Nazis. All eight of the action films were dominated by male characters and actors. *Ghostbusters*, the one film that was typed as a comedy, was also overwhelmingly male.

The top money-making films in the 1990s were the following:

- *Jurassic Park*
- *Independence Day*
- *The Lion King*
- *Forrest Gump*
- *Terminator 2: Judgment Day*
- *Ghost*
- *Twister*
- *Titanic*
- *Pretty Woman*
- *Mrs. Doubtfire*
- *Men in Black*
- *Saving Private Ryan*

In *The Godfather* (1972), Marlon Brando stars as Don Vito Corleone in this iconic film of hypermasculinity. [At left: Bonasera (Salvatore Corsitto); center back: Santino "Sonny" Corleone (James Caan).] *(Source: Courtesy of Getty Images. Copyright © 2006 Getty Images. Used by permission of Getty Images.)*

- *Armageddon*
- *The Fugitive*
- *Toy Story* (Internet Movie Database 1999)

These hits reflect more diversity in genre than the 1980s films. Fifty-five percent of the films were action or adventure, 15 percent were children's animation, 15 percent were comedies, and 15 percent were romance. It was only in *Twister* that a woman, Helen Hunt, received top billing. Women received second billing in *Terminator 2: Judgment Day* (Linda Hamilton as a human action figure), *Forrest Gump* (Robin Wright as Gump's misguided, on-again, off-again girlfriend), *Mrs. Doubtfire* (Sally Field as the uptight, shrill ex-wife), *Titanic* (Kate Winslet as the rich young woman who falls in love with a poor, handsome artist), and *Pretty Woman* (Julia Roberts as the prostitute with a big heart and a great flare for classy clothes). Male characters dominated a full 76 percent of these films.

The few major female characters in these popular 1980s and 1990s films were frequently simple, one-dimensional objects of romance or foils for the main character, who, with one exception, was always male. Most of these films depicted important relationships or conflicts between men. A few depicted romance and romantic conflict between men and women, but none of these box office hits portrayed women's relationships. This view of the top money-making films tells us not only who was making the big money and what the messages were, but also that these were the repeated messages about gender that the vast majority of viewers were seeing and internalizing.

The top money-making films rarely overlap with the films that are listed by critics as the top 100 films or with those that receive the Academy Awards Best Picture recognition. Some of these critically acclaimed films feature major female characters who defy simplification and stereotypes. Academy Award winners such as *Ordinary People* (1980), *Out of Africa* (1985), *Driving Miss Daisy* (1989), *The Silence of the Lambs* (1991), and *The English Patient* (1996) portrayed women who were strong, obstinate, and mysterious, and were filled with the complexity and contradictions that occur in real people. But these characters were the exception. Among the eighteen films awarded Best Picture by the Academy from 1980 to 1987, ten were dominated by male characters. The 1995 film *Waiting to Exhale*, based on the book by Terry McMillan, was one of the first mainstream popular films to feature an ensemble cast of African American women. While the characters were depicted as only marginally complex, there was diversity among them.

It is important to note that there were some groundbreaking roles for women in the 1980s and 1990s; some won Academy Awards and some did not. It is equally important to notice that few of the movies featuring complex female characters made it into the top box office hits. The significance of the relatively low ticket sales for these films is that the vast majority of moviegoers continued to regularly view traditional and often stereotypical images of women.

In 1999, Children Now published the results of a comprehensive study about "media's messages about masculinity and their impact on boys" (Children Now 1999, 4). Investigating messages in television, movies, and video games, the organization found some common results, both in the messages about boys and men and masculinity and in how they seem to impact boys. It concluded that the dominant trends in the media's portrayal of men reinforce and support social attitudes that link masculinity to power, dominance, and control. The findings indicated the top problem-solving strategies used by male characters in media, in order of frequency:

- Initiative, leadership
- Offering advice/support, talking about feelings
- Deception/lying
- Risk-taking
- Aggression with weapons
- Aggression without weapons
- Noncompliance/defiance/rebellion
- Dominance
- Verbal aggression
- Helping

Forty-five percent of male characters in the study used initiative and leadership to resolve problems. It's interesting to note that the second most commonly used strategy, used by almost one-third of the male characters, was offering advice and support and talking about feelings. These top two strategies work against type of the hypermasculine characteristics of power, dominance, and control, offering a chink in the stereotype of male armor. They offer some alternatives to traditional definitions of what it means to be masculine, at least when it comes to solving problems. However, the next four strategies of lying, risk-taking, and aggression—either with or without weapons—are used by one out of five male characters. Furthermore, depictions of young adult and adolescent males indicate that in media they solve their problems using antisocial behaviors and sexual behaviors (Children Now 1999, 15–17). It is likely that boys and adolescents would be far more prone to identify with characters closer to their age, adolescents and young adults. If we apply Bandura's social cognitive theory to the impact of these images on boys and adolescents, there's a high probability that the antisocial and sexual behaviors of these characters would be the most likely problem-solving behaviors that young male viewers would imitate in a desire to be cool and acceptably masculine.

In the documentary *Tough Guise: Violence, Media, and the Crisis in Masculinity*, Jackson Katz asserts that the media, film in particular, normalize male violence as a "natural" feature of masculinity (Jhally 1999). Media Activity 2.3, beginning on page 122, invites you to examine the most popular films of the first decade of the twenty-first century to determine the presence and prevalence of some of these stereotypical traits of masculinity and the type of problem-solving strategies used by male characters. The top ten box office hits, in order of popularity, from 2000 to 2010 were as follows:

- *Avatar*
- *The Dark Knight*
- *Shrek 2*
- *Pirates of the Caribbean: Dean Man's Chest*
- *Spider-Man*
- *Transformers: Revenge of the Fallen*
- *Star Wars: Episode III, Revenge of the Sith*
- *The Lord of the Rings: The Return of the King*
- *Spider-Man 2*
- *The Passion of the Christ* (Dirks 2013)

After completing Media Activity 2.3, ask yourself the following questions: What were some of the message patterns about boys, men, and masculinity that you observed in the films that you viewed? Since these were the most viewed films in the first decade of the twenty-first century, what kind of impact do you think these messages may have had on boys and men? What about the impact on girls and women? Think about Bandura's theory of social cognition in which people, children especially, are most likely to imitate those characters who are admirable, likable, and/or rewarded for their traits and behaviors in either tangible or intangible ways.

It is interesting to note that audiences may have seen many of these characters at least once before since six of these movies are sequels. And according to George Gerbner's cultivation theory, the repetition of similar characters, characteristics, images, and themes is likely to have a strong impact on media consumers.

Roles for women in film have expanded and changed since the early twentieth century, when waifs and chorus girls, virgins and "whores" dominated the scene. Yet male characters are still featured most prominently in movies that are box office hits, underscoring messages learned in school and in life about which gender is most interesting and most important. It also means that male actors have access to the highest income.

To determine some of the contemporary gender messages in high-earning films for the year in which you are reading this, conduct your own research. You can find the highest-grossing films of the year through Internet Movie Database (www.IMDb.com) and design your own set of questions using some or all of the questions from Media Activities 2.1, 2.2, and 2.3. Feel free to add other questions that will help you draw some preliminary conclusions about the gender messages that the vast number of moviegoers for this year are seeing and, perhaps, internalizing.

After you conduct your own research, summarize the data in raw numbers and percentages and ask and answer some of the following questions: What different genres were represented in your sample? What were the total numbers of male and female actors that received first, second, and third billing? What was the percentage of males and females in each of the billing categories? What were the total numbers of males and females in the combination of all three billing categories? What were the percentages of male and female characters represented in the totals? Overall, do men or women seem to dominate the money-making films of the year you investigated, or is their representation fairly even? What messages do these films convey about the relative significance of men and women?

Recent studies have revealed a few more trends about gender images in late twentieth- and early twenty-first-century popular films. One is a growing trend for female characters to be socially aggressive (which does not necessarily involve physical contact), most notably in films depicting teenage girls and aimed at adolescent audiences. One study observed that while teenage boys could also be socially aggressive, girls tended to be rewarded for their personal aggressiveness (aggression directed at a specific individual) far more than boys in films. Meanwhile and once more, back to Bandura's social cognitive theory. When characters are rewarded for their behavior and these behaviors are repeated frequently in many films and perhaps other forms of media, people are far more likely to imitate these behaviors. This study concluded that "viewing teen movies is associated with negative stereotypes about female friendships and gender roles" (Behm-Morawitz and Mastro 2008, 131). These negative stereotypes include "girls are catty and vicious," "girls can't be trusted," and "I'd much rather be friends with a boy than a girl. They aren't as mean." As you consider whether you believe that these statements about girls are true, think about whether these are inherent and natural characteristics of girls or if girls have been socialized to display social aggression with each other—at least in part, because the messages in film and other media encourage them to be the most beautiful, the thinnest, and the most successful with men and as a result set girls against each other in often vicious competition.

Media Activity 2.3
Images of Masculinity in Popular Film

Instructions

The instructions for this activity suggest using the top ten box office hits from 2000 to 2010. You can feel free to adjust the sample of films that you use for the top ten box office hits of the most recent completed year. The important thing is to be sure to use the box office hits, because this will provide information about images of masculinity in films that have been viewed by the largest number of people and may have the strongest impact. You can use filmsite.org to find box office hits of any particular year or decade.

If you are working with a group, each person can view one to three of the films and answer the questions below; then the group can compile the answers to examine the results.

If you are working as an individual, the largest number of films you view will yield the most representative results. However, a minimum of three films will provide some preliminary indications of what film audiences learned about masculinity in the first decade of the twenty-first century.

Here are the top ten box office hits in order of popularity for 2000 to 2010 (Dirks 2013):

- *Avatar*
- *The Dark Knight*
- *Shrek 2*
- *Pirates of the Caribbean: Dead Man's Chest*
- *Spider-Man*
- *Transformers: Revenge of the Fallen*
- *Star Wars: Episode III, Revenge of the Sith*
- *The Lord of the Rings: The Return of the King*
- *Spider-Man 2*
- *The Passion of the Christ*

1. For each of the films that you have seen, use Internet Movie Database (www.IMDb .com) to identify the three top-billed male characters in the film and list them below.

Film title	First-billed character	Second-billed character	Third-billed character
1. *Avatar*	_____	_____	_____
2. *The Dark Knight*	_____	_____	_____
3. *Shrek 2*	_____	_____	_____
4. *Pirates of the Caribbean: Dead Man's Chest*	_____	_____	_____
5. *Spider-Man*	_____	_____	_____
6. *Transformers: Revenge of the Fallen*	_____	_____	_____
7. *Star Wars: Episode III, Revenge of the Sith*	_____	_____	_____
8. *The Lord of the Rings: The Return of the King*	_____	_____	_____
9. *Spider-Man 2*	_____	_____	_____
10. *The Passion of the Christ*	_____	_____	_____

2. For each character you listed in question #1, indicate which characteristics describe his personality and behavior best. Check as many of these characteristics as apply to the character. You will need to make a copy of the chart below for each character you examine. You will notice that each of the films is numbered in the chart in question #1. This will save you time in writing out some of the lengthy titles!

Film # ____ Name of character	Traditional/stereotypical male traits	Nontraditional/nonstereotypical male traits
_____	Unemotional	Emotional
_____	Aggressive	Nonaggressive
_____	Violent	Nonviolent
_____	Strong	Weak
_____	High-status job/position	Low-status job/position
_____	Active	Passive
_____	Brave	Cowardly
_____	Insensitive to others	Sensitive to others
_____	Athletic	Unathletic
_____	Independent	Dependent
_____	Rational	Irrational
_____	Confident	Lacking confidence

Total # of traits checked in each column

When you complete tallying and totaling the characteristics in the films you have viewed, total the numbers of all of the traditional/stereotypical male characteristics and total the numbers of all of the nontraditional/nonstereotypical male characteristics. Then figure the percentages of the total number of each of these types of characteristics. Was one of the columns of characteristics far more prominent than the other or were they fairly close together? What do you think the messages are about masculine characteristics in this group of films? If you want to examine these features more closely, you can divide the characters into "good guys" and "bad guys," the characters most likely to be admired by the audience and the characters least likely to be admired. According to the research on this issue, the characteristics of the good guys are the characteristics that the boys and adolescent males in the audience will most likely want to emulate.

3. Next, check off all the problem-solving approaches that each of these characters uses in the film. You will need to make a copy of the chart below for each character that you examine.

Film # ____ Name of character	Traditional/stereotypical male problem- solving strategies	Nontraditional/nonstereotypical male problem- solving strategies
_____	Initiative, leadership	Offering advice/support, talking about feelings
_____	Deception/lying	Helping
_____	Risk-taking	Asking for help/advice
_____	Aggression with weapons	Affection/nurturance
_____	Aggression without weapons	Facilitating peaceful compromise
_____	Noncompliance/defiance/ rebellion	Compliance
_____	Dominance	Submissiveness

Media Activity 2.3 *(continued)*

When you complete tallying and totaling the problem-solving strategies of the characters in the films you have viewed, total the numbers of all of the traditional/stereotypical male strategies and total the numbers of all of the nontraditional/nonstereotypical male strategies. Then figure the percentages of the total number of each of these types of strategies. Was one of the columns of strategies far more prominent than the other or were they fairly close together? What do you think are the messages about masculine problem-solving strategies in this group of films? If you want to examine these features more closely, you can divide the characters into "good guys" and "bad guys," the characters most likely to be admired by the audience and the characters least likely to be admired. The problem-solving strategies of the good guys are the strategies that boys and adolescent males in the audience will most likely want to emulate.

4. When you combine the results from #2 and # 3, what are your thoughts about the messages and message patterns about masculinity that were conveyed through these box-office hits? What do they convey about the rules and norms of what it means to be a man, what it means to be masculine? What do you think the take-away messages might be for boys and adolescent males in the audiences that viewed these films in the theaters and at home on DVD? What were some striking examples of the characteristics and problem-solving strategies in these films?

There are also recent studies about gender images in G-rated films. These movies may have more far-reaching impact than those that adults see in the theaters, since parents often buy the DVDs of children's favorite movies and children watch them over and over and over. Bandura's social cognitive theory is beginning to sound like a mantra for audience impact: as you probably have memorized by now, the combination of character behavior that is rewarded with repetition of the same images and/or repeated viewing often results in audiences imitating the characteristics or behavior. So what are the gender images in G-rated films? What impact do they have on children?

Stacy Smith and her research team at the University of Southern California examined 101 of the G-rated top box office hits from 1990 to 2005 and found that the depictions of boys and girls, men and women remained largely stagnant over this period (Smith et al. 2010, 774). Males repeatedly outnumbered females by a ratio of 2.5 to 1 through these fifteen years. Females were more often than males depicted as young, smart, good, and beautiful. They were also more likely to play traditional roles than males. Female characters were more often depicted as parents and depicted more frequently than males as involved in committed romantic relationships. Men were shown working far more than women and were much more likely to be in the military. "Exposure to such distorted 'reel' world images may be having detrimental effects on youths' gender-role socialization" (Smith et al. 2010, 783, 774).

Repeated viewing of these movies can influence children to see females as "invisible" or believe that stories about girls and women are not important enough to tell. For boys, the social learning may be positive in the sense that they see male images as prevalent and male stories as important. But, ultimately, both boys and girls who view these traditional depictions are likely to have limited ideas of what is real and true about men and women emblazoned in their brains, hearts, and beliefs. For girls, this may mean a negative hit to their self-esteem and sense of strength and empowerment. For both boys and girls, the status quo, the traditional gender hegemony—the largely invisible sense of the right order of anything involving gender—remains stagnant (Smith et al. 2010, 783).

While the images in R-rated films and some PG-13 films were beginning to show some diversity in roles and characteristics and choices for women, children were continuing to see replays of the same traditional gender stereotypes in repackaged color, superanimation, and special effects.

Gender and Popular Music

Popular music has traditionally featured romance as its central theme, with lyrics sung by both men and women proclaiming the joy of love and the agony of its loss. In the 1930s and 1940s, Frank Sinatra, Ella Fitzgerald, and others rhapsodized and idealized love and romance in melodic ballads. In the 1950s, when rock and roll began, the popular music scene exploded, however, and control of the industry and reflection of gender in the music became more highly contested.

In the 1950s, the emergence of the first "girl groups" began with the Shirelles' top ten song, "Will You Still Love Me Tomorrow?" Written by Carole King, this was the first song by a group of women to make it to the top ten (Lout 1995, 321).

> The most important thing about this music and the reason it spoke to us so powerfully, was that it gave voice to all the warring selves inside us struggling blindly and with a crushing sense of insecurity, to force something resembling a coherent identity. Even though the girl groups were produced and managed by men, it was in their music that the contradictory messages about female sexuality and rebelliousness were most poignantly and authentically expressed. (Douglas 1994, 87)

These groups sang about dependence on men, rebellion, sexuality, resistance, and compliance.

More than film or television, these songs of the 1950s reflected the struggle and upheaval in the changing lives and roles of young men and women. The lyrics of "I Will Follow Him," sung by Little Peggy March, demonstrate the traditional compliant girl who goes to the ends of the earth for the man she loves. "Sweet Talkin' Guy" by the Chiffons conveys the sexual pull of a smooth talker and the struggle of the girl to sort out love and sex. By the mid-1960s, the "girl singer" replaced the "girl group" and more women entered the musical scene, singing a wide range of songs with a variety of gender representations. By and large, these soloists and groups depicted "girls" with a single purpose—finding and keeping their true love.

Before continuing the analysis of the next round of female singers, we should note the language used to describe the women who sang popular songs in the 1950s and 1960s. Male singers were called "singers" or "rock and roll groups" or "recording artists," but female singers were called "girl groups" or "girl singers." This language difference is significant in two ways. First, the terms for men are generic and assume that male singers are the norm; second, the term for females is the diminutive, childlike "girl." This is the beginning of the era when people struggling to find inclusive, gender-neutral language used terms such as "lady mailman" instead of the contemporary gender-neutral "mail carrier."

From 1963 to 1965, a total of sixty-nine songs made it to the number one spot on the popular music chart. Of these songs, only fifteen were recorded by women. One of them was the 1963 hit "He's So Fine" by the Chiffons, in which the woman sings lyrics such as "If I were a queen and he asked me to leave my throne, I'd do anything that he asked, anything to make him my own. 'Cause he's so fine." In the classic 1964 Mary Wells hit "My Guy," the singer praises her guy and notes all the things she would pass by for him. The 1965 Supremes song "Stop in the Name of Love" begs the man to stop seeing another woman for sex and to stay with his woman for real love.

In the mid-1960s, Lulu sang "To Sir with Love," while Leslie Gore poured out her heart with such romantic sorrows and triumphs as "It's My Party" and "It's Judy's Turn to Cry." Yet in "You Don't Own Me," Gore deviates from the schoolgirl dependence on her guy to declare independence and her unwillingness to change for him. Then there were Tina Turner belting out strong songs full of female lust and desire and Aretha Franklin insisting on "Respect." Despite this distinction, their songs and styles shared a strength and an assertion of their rights and needs vis-à-vis men.

By the mid-1960s, the so-called "British invasion" by the Beatles and their many clones dominated the U.S. music scene and white female soloists lost much of their audience. During this time, the only American music with a substantial audience was Motown, which included a second wave of "girl groups," including the Supremes, Martha and the Vandellas, and the Marvelettes. While not as conventionally popular as the others, another female phenomenon hit the music scene of the 1960s and that was political folk music as sung by artists such as Joni Mitchell, Judy Collins, and Joan Baez (Lout 1995, 322). These women sang of peace and the environment as well as love and romance. But there were still few images of strong independent girls and women, or women struggling with their own gender identities in a rapidly shifting society.

"Music is perhaps one of the most powerful tools for the conveyance of ideas and emotions. It is also a great vehicle for propaganda. Lyrics in music reinforce a culture's values. Rock music, as part of the youth culture, always sent out strong messages, picked up by listeners, consciously or unconsciously. Embedded with the messages are female and male portrayals" (Lout 1995, 324). And it appears that both the singers and the lyrics reinforced traditional expectations of the roles of males and females in U.S. society.

By the 1970s, rock was a central component of the cultural revolution and most rock bands were male. Tina Turner and Janis Joplin were early exceptions, followed soon by female musicians, such as Bonnie Raitt, Joan Armatrading, and Joan Jett, who began to play electric instruments. A study conducted from 1970 to 1979 revealed that fewer than twelve of more than 260 prominent musical acts featured individual women or women in a band.

> Females growing up in the 1960s and 1970s were offered narrow roles to emulate. As teenagers, they listened to chirpies, love-crazed girl groups, folk madonnas, or sexy black singers. When rock became popular, teenage girls could be "groovy chicks" or "uptight." In general, women's roles in rock music were prescribed by men and handed to women to fulfill. Real problems (being different, peer pressure, abuse, homosexuality) were rarely discussed. Yet, there was little room for growth or diversity. (Lout 1995, 325)

Janis Ian's song "Society's Child" was a notable exception, telling the poignant and politically charged story of a girl's family's rejection of her interracial relationship.

By the 1980s, the number of female bands had increased and 1981 ushered in a new era—music television or MTV. In the early days of television broadcast, producers saw audiences as largely homogeneous and undifferentiated. As cable developed the idea of capturing a narrower audience with buying power, the television industry began to make programming decisions based on the results of demographic research and its potential to attract sponsors. Fred Silverman at NBC made broadcast history by perfecting this concept, using market research to determine program content. This research said that young adults aged eighteen to twenty-nine, mostly female, were the main buyers of television goods. Bob Pittman followed this marketing strategy to create an audience of buyers for MTV (Lewis 1990, 17).

MTV's target audience was twelve- to thirty-four-year-olds, whom Pittman defined as a cultural group that grew up on two dominant forms of media: television and rock and roll. The goal of MTV was to combine these two entertainment phenomena. MTV established another strategy that began as a financial consideration and ultimately dictated programmatic decisions. Pittman decided to replicate the standard radio format, which utilized free demos on the air, by using free video demos promoted by the companies that produced them. "What had begun as a practical approach to securing cheap (free) programming within the parameters of MTV's concept ended up being a factor that determined MTV's program content. By getting record companies to supply videos, MTV ensured that the videos would look like advertisements for record companies" (Lewis 1990, 21, 24).

Before the advent of MTV, the musical and ideological foundations of rock music and popular music had been quite different. Some musicians, audiences, and music critics saw pop music as "bubblegum" and formulaic while viewing rock as the "people's" music—more complex and cutting-edge in both music and lyrics. Before MTV, hard rock had taken a more anticommercial stance—which MTV turned upside down (Lewis 1990, 28–35).

The commercially driven MTV became a central cultural phenomenon for U.S. adolescents, and its depiction of gender had a strong impact. Teenagers developed their own fashion and style based on popular music videos. Girls assumed the style of Madonna—exposed underwear and blonde hair with dark roots—in the 1980s, and in the 1990s young boys wore the scarves and goggles of 'N Sync or the sagging pants and exposed underwear of rap and hip-hop artists. These trends exemplified the extent to which music videos and other media content continued to contribute to the gender socialization of youth.

Adolescence has assumed an important role in U.S. culture as a life phase in which young people are given permission, or take the chance without permission, to explore sexuality and rebel against authority. Yet in the past, this was a largely masculine tradition in American culture in which the construct of femininity restricted how girls participated in this rebellion and exploration (Lewis 1990, 28–35). "Adolescence and masculinity are united ideologically to support a social system of male privilege. . . . Toward this end, boys learn to feel comfortable in public space, adjust to competitive pressures, network with their male peers, build a familial support system, and to prepare for risk-taking in future work endeavors. However, the social authorization given to such practices is directed specifically to boys, and does not extend as fully to girls" (Lewis 1990, 35). The videos in MTV "were united by a central focus on articulating adolescence within the context of male-adolescent experience and sexual desire" (Lewis 1990, 35, 53).

A 1987 study of MTV music videos found that men were more likely to be aggressive, violent, or dominant, while women were more likely to wear revealing clothing, show affection, and pursue sex (Seidman 1992, 209). By 1989, the increasing presence of female singers seemed to have changed those numbers. In 63 percent of videos depicting female or mostly female groups, women were treated the same way as men (Lout 1995, 335).

The careers of Tina Turner, Cyndi Lauper, and Madonna represent the contradictions in MTV gender ideology and the opportunities for women to succeed. These women exerted some creative control over their music and its production, and their careers and personal stories offered inspiration and served as role models to adolescent girls. While Turner's and Madonna's images were hard and sexual, their lives told a different story of rising above abuse and dependence and creating and controlling their own music and images. "The emergence of female-adolescent discourse on MTV is important politically because it has provided a vehicle for girls to speak about their experiences as female adolescents. But it is also important because it has expanded the reconsideration of gender inequality to include adolescence, thus beginning the much needed work of acknowledging the fact that oppressed women begin their lives as oppressed girls" (Lewis 1990, 234).

As in other forms of entertainment media and popular culture, the impact of popular music is measured primarily through repetitive images. To understand the role of women, men, and romance in popular music, it is critical to determine if there is any range, diversity, and complexity in the images or if these images of men, women, and romance reinforce the dominant ideology of gender in the United States.

What are some images of love, romance, and sex in popular music as conveyed in lyrics, music videos, and CD covers? What kind of gender roles do these images of love, romance, and sex convey? In what ways do these images reinforce or challenge conventional gender ideology?

It is useful to examine what constitutes dominant ideology in the interaction of gender with love, sex, and romance. First, despite some real movement toward the acceptance of same-sex relationships, the dominant ideology of U.S. culture positions heterosexual individuals, couples, and relationships as normal. The second aspect of a traditional ideology involves the roles played by men and women in heterosexual romance. The conventional role of men in romance and sex is that of the initiator or the aggressor, the one most interested in sex, the detached partner, the one least interested in romance. The conventional role of women is that of the pursued, uninterested in or torn about sex, the involved partner, the one engrossed in romance. The dominant ideology involves a dramatization of love as intense, highly romanticized, and/or tragic as opposed to a relationship of intermittent and perhaps more moderate passion, conversation, conflict, and resolution. Of course, one could easily argue that song lyrics depicting moderation and mundane conversation would not ignite the audience or record sales. But given the impact that popular music has on its young listeners, it is critical to understand the messages that are being offered.

Much of the finger pointing about demeaning and derogatory images of women has centered on rap and hip-hop music. According to some studies by both men and women, a substantial impetus for diminishing women comes from the corporate culture of the music industry. These "issues of concern include the ever-increasing global reach of the U.S. music industry—a multi-billion dollar business that markets music as a profitable entity while simultaneously inculcating worldwide audiences with dominant ideologies of race, class, gender, sexuality, and nationality" (Hobson and Bartlow 2007). Another study suggests that rap artists are frequently pressured by the decision makers in the music industry to abandon the origin of rap and hip-hop in its criticism and rejection of racism and other elements of the dominant culture in favor of content and lyrics that are primarily aimed to sell records. Music producers encourage rap and hip-hop artists to be "hard-core," to use provocative language, images, and lyrics that emphasize and exaggerate sexual exploitation, violence, denigration of women, and material wealth (Weitzer and Kubrin 2009). Hip-hop historian Kevin Powell explains it like this: "This privileging of hegemonic masculinity and negative depiction of women is driven by an interest in selling records" (quoted in Rhym 1997).

Examining images of women in other musical genres helps us place rap in a larger context and determine whether it has been singled out for its misogyny. A 1999 study found that in 57 percent of rock music videos, traditional, stereotypical images of women emphasized women's physical appearance and showed women as dependent on men (Alexander 1999). Country music was also found to put a negative spin on women, with two-thirds of the videos in a 1999 study deemed to devalue women (Andsager and Roe 1999).

The issue of demeaning and stereotyped images of women seems to cut across various genres of popular music. Rap and hip-hop use more explicit sexual language, degrading slang that often describes women as "bitches" and "hoes" and uses offensive words for genitalia. Weitzer and Kubrin suggest that three major social forces influence these derisive and often obscene descriptions of women in rap and hip-hop: (1) the larger issues of gender that are pervasive in popular media and the general culture, (2) the values and demands of the music industry, and (3) what the writers refer to as "neighborhood conditions."

The larger issues regarding gender are framed in terms of hegemonic masculine ideology, which suggests that in order to be a "real" man, a man must demonstrate his domination over women. Rap and hip-hop are a special case of these deep cultural expectations for men. Rappers who are aiming for success with a major label have additional pressures. Even if they wanted to convey a less traditional masculinity and a more respectful attitude toward women, they would be unlikely to find support for that approach in the mainstream music industry. These corporate giants have found a formula for success in rap music that involves hypermasculinity, hypersexuality, frequent use of the profane rap idiom, and thorough disdain for and objectification of women (Weitzer and Kubrin 2009).

The third area of influence on the content of the lyrics about men, women, sex, and violence in rap is located at the intersection of racism and sexism. "Poor, marginalized Black males have historically faced obstacles to asserting their masculinity, and they continue to be denied access to conventional institutional avenues through which masculinity may be established . . . music historically served as a medium that provided Black men with an alternative resource for asserting their masculinity" (Weitzer and Kubrin 2009). The roots of African American rap and hip-hop are in storytelling about and protest against poverty and racism, using the rhythms and language of the street. Profanity, sex, and violence were frequently used to make a point about the way that racism weighs on a group of black men with few options. While some rap and hip-hop on independent labels still maintain allegiance to these roots, much of it has been hijacked by three "isms": racism, sexism, and commercialism.

THE COMPLEXITY OF GENDER TARGETING

One of the fundamental lessons in the study of diversity and oppression that focuses on one issue, such as gender, is its complexity, which often meanders and bumps into other places where discrimination and oppression sit (such as race or class or sexual orientation). While it is essential to criticize the degrading images of women and the violence against women in certain types of music, it is equally essential to understand the way the music is positioned in terms of the violence and degradation of racism and poverty—not as an excuse but as a compassionate understanding that allows room for authentic change. The poet Audre Lorde said:

> I was born Black, and a woman. I am trying to become the strongest person I can become to live the life I have been given and to help effect change toward a liveable future for this earth and for my children. As a Black, lesbian, feminist, socialist, poet, mother of two including one boy and a member of an interracial couple, I usually find myself part of some group in which the majority defines me as deviant, difficult, inferior or just plain "wrong." From my membership in all of these groups I have learned that oppression and the intolerance of difference come in all shapes and sexes and colors and sexualities; and that among those of us who share the goals of liberation and a workable future for our children, there can be no hierarchies of oppression. I have learned that sexism and heterosexism both arise from the same source as racism. (Lorde 1983)

Lorde says that we cannot afford to choose which discrimination to fight or say that one is worse or a higher priority than another: "I must battle these forces of discrimination wherever they appear to destroy me. And when they appear to destroy me, it will not be long before they appear to destroy you."

GENDER DIVERSITY AND SOCIAL POWER

As we have seen, by virtue of their lack of authority and power, and income much lower than men's, and less access to privileges and resources that would allow them to get what they want in life, women are still on the targeted end of structural oppression. Women are still largely defined and valued by their attractiveness and their slenderness; women who are deemed unattractive get fewer and lower-paying jobs. Women's self-esteem is still so tied to physical attractiveness that it often leads to dangerous eating disorders and high-priced cosmetic surgery. Yet women have made enormous progress in their presence and success in undergraduate and graduate education, and there are significant changes and wider ranges in how women are depicted in media. While traditional femininity is still prescribed as soft, noncompetitive, and nurturing to the exclusion of strong or professional, what it means to be a woman is far more diverse and expansive than it was even ten years ago. The picture has changed significantly in many directions for women. But lest we become too prone to look through the proverbial rose-colored glasses, it's important to remember that women are still far more likely to live in poverty than are men.

According to a late twentieth-century study by Children Now, "today's boys navigate a perilous path toward manhood. Even if he is raised in a healthy, loving environment, a boy must sort out powerful societal messages that limit and restrict the definition of masculinity—the definition of who he should become. . . . Serious or subtle, the media's role in defining manhood is significant" (Children Now 1999, 21). The study found the following key messages about men conveyed to children in the videos, music, television programs, and movies they watched the most:

- Men are leaders and problem solvers, funny, successful, confident, and athletic.
- Men are focused on sex.
- Men rarely cry.
- Men are not sensitive.
- Men are violent.
- Boys and men are angry.
- Men work in high-status jobs and women take care of the home front. (Children Now 1999, 3)

When we connect the dots between these messages about men and what we learn from our personal experiences and how we are socialized to understand the cultural expectations of what it means to be a man, it becomes increasingly clear that not only are individual boys and men hurt and limited by the ideals of hypermasculinity, but our larger society is damaged by the spillover of aggression, violence, and the suppression of emotions. And lest we focus on the way men are individually limited and hurt by the way they are socialized, it is important to remember that in terms of structural oppression, men are still on the privileged side of things. Men have more access to the power, privileges, and resources they need to get what they want in the world. Men have far more positions at the higher levels of government, education, and business, and men earn far more money in any given year and over a lifetime than women.

Yet with gender, as with the other social categories we will be discussing in this book, privilege is least visible to the privileged. For instance, while conducting a workshop at an academic conference, Leon called for a ten-minute break. After making a quick trip to the restroom and refilling his coffee cup, Leon returned to the podium and waited for participants to finish their break. When twenty minutes had passed and many people were still not back, he walked into the corridor to see what was going on. He immediately realized his mistake. Several female participants were still waiting in line to get into the ladies' room. In allowing only ten minutes for a break, Leon had failed to take into account that many buildings, especially those designed by men, do not have adequate restroom facilities for women. It simply had not occurred to him to make the break longer because, as a male, he usually did not have to think about such things.

In 1989, when Linda's daughter was four years old, she took her first dance class with seven or eight other little girls. The dance teacher chose the music, choreographed the dance steps, and designed costumes for their first recital. The girls and the parents were very excited and exuberant, but when Linda learned what the selected song was, her heart sank. It was "Chapel of Love" by the Dixiecups. The chorus goes like this:

> Going to the chapel and I'm gonna get married,
> Going to the chapel and I'm gonna get married,
> Going to the chapel and I'm gonna get married,
> Going to the chapel of love.

The lyrics were traditionally romantic and centered on marriage. The costumes were white leotards with silver sparkles and headbands with gauzy material made to look like wedding veils. All the other mothers were cooing over the cuteness of the music, the dance, and the costumes. Linda knew this event by itself would not damage or finish off the socialization of these girls permanently. But this was only one event of many that would teach them that cuteness, relationships to men, and being a bride were at the core of what it meant to be a girl and were considered good practice for becoming a woman. However, her own gender socialization got in the way of intervening. She thought that if she protested the content, no matter how politely, she would be viewed as a curmudgeon at best and a spoiler at worst. Socialized as she was to be a woman who was polite, easy to get along with, and pleasing to others, she chose not to raise these concerns.

But the more that individuals understand how all these events in the lives of children add up to limit their ultimate choices and independence, the more people and institutions will have the wherewithal to intervene and interrupt. Schools can examine the policies and practices that primarily value received knowledge and reinforce the boisterousness and quietness in both boys and girls. They can change the curriculum to include more information about the roles women have played in history and science. Parents can offer more choices to boys and girls early in their lives so they can decide whether to play with dolls or trucks or both; parents can encourage all children to develop strong character, intellect, rational thinking, and integrity *and* to be open about their feelings and vulnerabilities. Institutions can analyze employment and salaries according to gender and promote changes that are more equitable. Individuals can read more about gender history and socialization and can find ways to interrupt gender oppression when they see it. Film, television, and music can portray girls and women and boys and men as complex characters with a range of personalities and roles in life.

Parents, schools, and media can become better informed of the disservice we are doing to the larger society and to the well-being of individual boys and men by teaching them that in order to be "real men" they need to be tough, competitive, aggressive, and unemotional and to downplay their more tender and vulnerable sides.

CHAPTER SUMMARY

The connections between personal experience, formal knowledge, and entertainment media are key to an understanding of U.S. gender socialization in general and your own gender experience and expression in particular. This chapter guides you through the discovery of what you were taught formally and informally about what it means to be male or female in this society. We are born a particular sex and taught how to be a particular gender. The concepts of dominant, alternative, and mixed gender ideology are fundamental to the understanding of what we were taught about gender and what other ways of being male and female are available. Entertainment media in the forms of popular music, film, and television are central tools of socialization and send strong messages about what it means to be a boy or a girl, a man or a woman. Entertainment assessment tools are a means to uncover these messages and to determine whether a particular song, film, TV program, or an entire genre reinforces or challenges dominant gender ideology. The ability to understand how our personal gender values and behavior are formed is the foundation to making independent choices about how and who we want to be.

GLOSSARY OF KEY TERMS

constructed knowledge: A blend of knowledge that comes from external authorities combined with internal authority derived from intuition and instinct and is a synthesis of many experiences and much information.

feminism: The movement, set of beliefs, and commitment to economic, political, and social equity for women. Historically, the two main branches of feminism have been liberal feminism and radical feminism. Liberal feminists believe that the most important goal is that women have access to their fair share of the economic, political, and social pie. Radical feminists believe that the American "pie" is structurally inadequate and needs to be restructured so that gender equity is fundamental rather than piecemeal and incremental.

gender: Gender is the expression of what it means to be male or female, masculine or feminine, and is largely grounded in cultural norms that define what it means to be a "real man" or a "real woman." Gender thus differs from one's biological sex, which is determined by one's genitalia as well as secondary identifiers such as differences in muscle structure, body hair, speaking voice range, and so on.

hegemonic masculinity: Hegemonic masculinity positions men as correctly and properly superior, dominant, and powerful and positions women as "naturally" subordinate to men. The use of the term "hegemonic" indicates that these rules of masculinity are not imposed by law or by force but rather conveyed by the often invisible process of socialization by family, peers, schools, religious institutions, and media. Hegemony suggests that the least powerful group—in this case, women—consent to play their assigned role, sometimes eagerly, sometimes passively, sometimes without critical awareness, and sometimes with quiet or feigned acquiescence.

masculinity ideology: A set of beliefs that suggests the ideal norms for individual men and for men's positions in society. This ideology frequently asserts that men, by nature and by their skills, are naturally suited for dominant and powerful positions as the family breadwinner and decision maker and as the person in authority in business and government. When masculinity ideology and hegemonic masculinity are firmly in place, they are regarded not as a perspective, a theory, or a set of beliefs, but rather as "the truth."

received knowledge: This type of knowledge derived from external sources, such as parents, teachers, and clergy, that are perceived as authorities on a particular subject.

sex: Sex is determined biologically by the genitalia with which a child is born.

subjective knowledge: Subjective knowledge relies on internal knowing that may be in the form of original ideas, intuition, instinct, and/or observations and feelings from personal experiences.

womanism: A term coined by writer Alice Walker to define the unique challenges that face black women and other women of color at the intersections of sexism, racism, and classism. Womanism seeks to expand and deepen the movement to confront the multiple layers of female oppression, while simultaneously celebrating women's individual and collective triumphs over that oppression.

REFLECTION, SUMMARY, AND ANALYSIS

Instructions

Answer these questions using a blend of summary and analysis and thoroughly support your opinions and arguments with information from Chapter 2.

The *summary* component of the questions requires you to demonstrate your understanding of the terms and concepts in the textbook through the use of describing, explaining, and restating. This includes using your own words to paraphrase the materials in the textbook as well as using an occasional direct quote. Any direct quote requires quotation marks and the use of a simple internal citation at the end of the quote in the form of parentheses, the author's last name, and the page number that will look like this: (Holtzman 38). *Summary* involves primarily answering questions that begin with "what."

The *analysis* component of the questions requires you to use your own independent thinking, your own ideas and arguments that are often combined with existing positions on controversial issues. *Analysis* requires breaking something—like a concept, theory, or argument—into parts so you and your reader can understand and describe how those parts work together to make the whole. Analytic writing goes beyond the obvious to discuss questions of how and why—so ask yourself those questions as you read. Your responses to these kinds of questions will require that you carefully and clearly state your argument, opinion, or "thesis" statement that states your position, using evidence from the text, other sources, and your own observations as support. You may also include your own personal experiences in the analysis insofar as they are relevant and support your thesis statement and are not generalized in such a way as to suggest that your experiences are universal.

The University of North Carolina's Writing Center website has an excellent two-page handout on analysis and summary (http://writingcenter.unc.edu/handouts/summary-using-it-wisely/).

Study Questions

1. What is the difference between an individual's sex and an individual's gender?
2. How are people in the United States socialized to understand gender roles and expectations?
3. How does gender oppression affect men and women differently?
4. How does gender oppression target women and hurt men? What is the difference between being "targeted" and being "hurt" by gender oppression?
5. What are some of the financial consequences of gender?
6. What are some of the patterns in how prime-time television portrays men and women? What range of gender expression have you seen on television? What

are some common gender stereotypes you have observed? What are some examples of characters in prime-time TV that are different from the norm and are not stereotypes? Be sure to give specific examples from television programs to support your answers.

7. What are some of the ways that emphasis on rigid and largely unattainable standards of beauty and size affects girls and women socially, politically, and economically? How has that ideal of beauty and the pressure it places on girls and women affected your life?

8. Boys and men receive a lot of pressure to suppress their softer emotions and behaviors such as sadness, crying, tenderness, and vulnerability. Often the only acceptable emotion for "real" men is anger. How do these kinds of expectations of what it means to be masculine affect and limit boys and men? How have these limitations for the ideal man and the pressure they place on men and boys affected your life?

BIBLIOGRAPHY

Alexander, Susan. 1999. "The Gender Role Paradox in Youth Culture: An Analysis of Women in Music Videos." *Michigan Sociological Review* 13, 46–64.

American Association of University Women (AAUW). 1995. *How Schools Shortchange Girls: The AAUW Report*. New York: Marlowe.

American Association of University Women (AAUW) Educational Foundation. 2001. *Beyond the "Gender Wars": A Conversation about Girls, Boys and Education*. Washington, DC. AAUW. www.aauw.org/files/2013/02/Beyond-the-Gender-Wars-A-Conversation-about-Girls-Boys-and-Education.pdf.

———. 2013. *The Simple Truth About the Gender Pay Gap*. Washington, DC: AAUW.

Andsager, Julie, and Kimberly Roe. 1999. "Country Music Video in the Country's Year of the Woman." *Journal of Communication* 49: 69–82. *http://onlinelibrary.wiley.com/doi/10.1111/j.1460-2466.1999.tb02782.x/abstract*.

Bagdikian, Ben H. 1992. *The Media Monopoly*. Boston: Beacon Press.

Bandura, Albert. 2002. "Social Cognitive Theory Of Mass Communication." In *Media Effects: Advances in Theory and Research*, 2nd ed., ed. Jennings Bryant and Dolf Zillmann, 121–153. Mahwah, NJ: Lawrence Erlbaum Publishers.

Battaglio, Stephen. 2010. "Who Are TV's Top Earners?" *TV Guide*, August 10.

Behm-Morawitz, Elizabeth, and Dana E. Mastro. 2008. "Mean Girls? The Influence of Gender Portrayals in Teen Movies on Emerging Adults' Gender-Based Attitudes and Beliefs." *Journalism and Mass Communication Quarterly* 85, no 1: 131–146.

Brownmiller, Susan. 1984. *Femininity*. New York: Ballantine Books.

Catalyst. December 2013. "Women CEOs of the Fortune 1000." www.catalyst.org/knowledge/women-ceos-fortune-1000.

Cawthorne, Alexandra. 2008. "The Straight Facts on Women in Poverty," Center for American Progress, October 8. Washington, DC.

Center for American Women and Politics. 2013. "Women in Elective Office 2013." Eagleton Institute of Politics, Rutgers University, New Brunswick, NJ.

Children Now. 1999. *Boys to Men: Entertainment Media: Messages About Masculinity*. Oakland, CA: Children Now. www.childrennow.org/uploads/documents/boys_to_men_entertainment_1999.pdf.

Chu, Michelle V. Porche, and Deborah L. Tolman. 2005. "The Adolescent Masculinity Ideology in Relationships Scale: Development and Validation of a New Measure for Boys." *Men and Masculinities*.

Connell, R.W. 1987. *Gender and Power: Society, the Person, and Sexual Politics*. Stanford, CA: Stanford University Press.

Connell, R.W., and James W. Messerschmidt. 2005. "Hegemonic Masculinity: Rethinking the Concept." *Gender & Society*, 829–859.

Corbett, Christianne, Catherine Hill, and Andresse St. Rose. 2008. *Where the Girls Are: The Facts About Gender Equity in Education*. Washington, DC, American Association of University Women (AAUW).

Croteau, David, and William Hoynes. 1997. *Media/Society: Industries, Images, and Audiences*. Thousand Oaks, CA: Pine Forge Press.

D'Acci, Julie. 1995. "Defining Women: The Case of Cagney and Lacey." In *Gender, Race and Class in Media: A Text Reader*, ed. Gail Dines and Jean M. Humez, 454–459. Thousand Oaks, CA: Sage.

Davis, Angela Y. 1981. *Women, Race, and Class*. New York: Random House.

Diamond, Edwin. 1960. "Young Wives." *Newsweek*, March 7, 57–60.

Dirks, Tim. 2013. "All-Time Box Office Top 100." AMC Filmsite. www.filmsite.org/boxoffice.html.

Douglas, Susan. 1994. *Where the Girls Are: Growing Up Female with the Mass Media*. New York: Times Books.

Dow, Bonnie J. 1995. "Prime-Time Feminism: Entertainment and Women's Progress." In *Women and Media: Content/Careers/Criticism*, ed. Cynthia Lout, 200. Belmont, CA: Wadsworth.

Elasmar, Michael, Kazumi Hasegawa, and Mary Brain. 1999. "The Portrayal of Women in U.S. Prime Time Television." *Journal of Broadcasting and Electronic Media* 3 (Winter): 20–26.

Faludi, Susan. 1991. *Backlash: The Undeclared War Against American Women*. New York: Putnam.

Feder, June, Ronald F. Levant, and James Dean. 2007. "Boys and Violence: A Gender-Informed Analysis." *Professional Psychology: Research and Practice* 38, 385–391.

Field Belenky, Mary, Blythe McVicker Clinchy, Nancy Rule Goldberger, and Jill Mattuck Tarule. 1988. *Women's Ways of Knowing: The Development of Self, Voice, and Mind*. New York: Basic Books.

Franck, Irene, and David Brownstone. 1993. *The Women's Desk Reference*. New York: Viking Penguin.

Freire, Paulo. 1989. *Pedagogy of the Oppressed*. New York: Continuum.

Friedan, Betty. 1963. *The Feminine Mystique*. New York: Dell.

Froschl, Merle, and Barbara Sprung. 2005. "Raising and Educating Healthy Boys: A Report on the Growing Crisis in Boys' Education." Educational Equity Center Academy for Educational Development. New York.

Galerstein, Carolyn L. 1989. *Working Women on the Hollywood Screen: A Filmography*. New York: Garland.

Geraghty, Christine. 1991. *Women and Soap Opera: A Study of Prime Time Soaps*. Cambridge, UK: Polity Press.

Gerbner, George. 1995. "Casting and Fate: Women and Minorities on Television Drama, Game Shows, and News." In *Communication Culture Community*, ed. Ed Hollander, Paul Rutten, and Coen van der Linden, 125–135. Omslagontwerp: Ineke de Groen Publisher.

———. 1997. "Television Demography: What's Wrong with This Picture?" Unpublished manuscript.

Gilligan, Carol. 1993. "Joining the Resistance: Psychology, Politics, and Women." In *Beyond Silenced Voices: Class, Race, and Gender in the United States Schools*, ed. Lois Weis and Michelle Fine. Albany: State University of New York Press.

Glascock, Jack. 2001. "Gender Roles on Prime-Time Network Television: Demographics and Behaviors." *Journal of Broadcasting and Electronic Media* 656–669.

Gregory, Mollie. 2002. *Women Who Run the Show*. New York: St. Martin's Press.

Hamilton, Kendall, and Julie Weingarden. 1998. "Lifts, Lasers, and Liposuctions: The Cosmetic Surgery Boom." *Newsweek*, June 15, 14.

Hammer, Joseph H., and Glen E. Good. 2010. "Positive Psychology: An Empirical Examination of Beneficial Aspects of Endorsement of Masculine Norms." *American Psychological Journal*, 303–318.

Harding, Vincent. 1981. *There Is a River: The Black Struggle for Freedom in America*. New York: Harcourt Brace Jovanovich.

Highland Council (UK). 2010. "Self-Esteem." Highland Learning and Teaching Toolkit. www .highlandschools-virtualib.org.uk/ltt/whole_learner/esteem.htm.

Hobson, Janell, and Diane Bartlow. 2007. "Introduction: Representin': Women, Hip-Hop, and Popular Music." *Meridians: Feminism, Race, Transnationalism* 8, 1: 1–14.

Ingram, Billy. 2011. "The Beulah Show." www.tvparty.com/50beulah.html.

Jhally, Sut, dir. 1999. *Tough Guise: Violence, Media, and the Crisis in Masculinity*. Video. Northampton, MA: Media Education Foundation.

Kimball, M. 1986. "Television and Sex-Role Attitudes." In *The Impact of Television: A Natural Experiment in Three Communities*, ed. Tannis M. Williams, 265–301. Orlando, FL: Academic Press.

Kindlon, Dan, and Michael Thompson. August 1999. *Raising Cain: Protecting the Emotional Life of Boys*. Random House.

Larkin, Marilyn. 2013. "Can Brain Biology Explain Why Men and Women Think and Act Differently?" Elsevierconnect. www.elsevier.com/connect/can-brain-biology-explain-why-men-and-women -think-and-act-differently.

Lauze, Martha M. 2010. *Boxed-In: Employment of Behind-the-Scenes Women in the 2009–10 Prime Time Season*. San Diego, CA: Center for the Study of Women in Television and Film, San Diego State University.

Lauzen, Martha M., David M. Dozier, and Nora Horan. 2008. "Constructing Gender Stereotypes Through Social Roles in Prime-Time Television." *Journal of Broadcasting and Electronic Media* (June): 200–214.

Leo. John. 1999. "Gender Wars Redux." *U.S. News and World Report*, February 22, 24.

Lewin, Tamar. 1998. "How Boys Lost Out to Girl Power." *New York Times*, December 13, 3.

Lewis, Lisa A. 1990. *Gender Politics and MTV: Voicing the Difference*. Philadelphia: Temple University Press.

Lorde, Audre. 1983. "There Is No Hierarchy of Oppressions." *Interracial Books for Children Bulletin* 14, no. 3–4.

Lout, Cynthia. 1995. *Women and Media: Content/Careers/Criticism*. Belmont, CA: Wadsworth.

McPhee, Carol, and Ann Fitzgerald. 1979. *Voices of Rebels, Reformers, and Visionaries*. New York: Thomas Y. Crowell.

Mead, Margaret. 1935. *Sex and Temperament in Three Primitive Societies*. New York: Dell.

Merskin, Debra. 2006. "Three Faces of Eva: Perpetuation of Hot Latina Stereotypes in *Desperate Housewives*." Paper presented at the annual meeting of the Association for Education in Journalism and Mass Communication, San Francisco, August.

Mintz, Stephen. 2013. "A Handbook for Teaching Fellows." Graduate School of Arts and Sciences Teaching Center, Columbia University. New York. http://teachingcenter.wikischolars.columbia.edu /Teaching+Center+handouts+archive.

Orenstein, Peggy. 1994. *Schoolgirls: Young Women, Self-Esteem, and the Confidence Gap*. New York: Doubleday.

Parker. Kathleen. 1998. "While Boosting Girls, Educational System Holds Boys Back." *Arizona Republic*, December 9.

Pipher, Mary. 1994. *Reviving Ophelia: Saving the Selves of Adolescent Girls*. New York: Putnam.

Purcell, Piper, and Lara Stewart. 1990. "Dick and Jane in 1989." *Sex Roles: A Journal of Research* 22: 177–185.

Rappaport, Doreen. 1990. *American Women: Their Lives in Their Words*. New York: HarperCollins.

Rhym, Darren. 1997. "'Here's for the Bitches': An Analysis of Gangsta Rap and Misogyny." *Womanist Theory and Research* 2: 1–14.

Ries, Paula, and Anne J. Stone, eds. 1992. *The American Woman: 1992–93: A Status Report*. New York: W.W. Norton.

Rosen, Marjorie. 1973. *Popcorn Venus: Women, Movies and the American Dream*. New York: Coward, McCann, and Geoghegan.

Sadker, David, Myra Sadker, and Karen R. Zittleman. 2009. *Still Failing at Fairness: How Gender Bias Cheats Girls and Boys in School and What We Can Do About It.* New York: Scribner.

Seidman, Stephen A. 1992. "An Investigation of Sex-Role Stereotyping in Music Videos." *Journal of Broadcasting and Electronic Media* 36, no. 2: 209–216.

Shreve, Anita. 1989. *Women Together, Women Alone: The Legacy of the Consciousness Raising Movement.* New York: Viking.

Signorelli, Nancy. 1997. "A Content Analysis: Reflections of Girls in the Media." The Kaiser Family Foundation and Children Now.

———. 2001. "Race and Sex in Prime Time: A Look at Occupations and Occupational Prestige." *Mass Communication and Society,* 332–352.

Sigoloff, Justin. 2009. "Hegemonic Masculinity and Representations of Men on Television." Master's thesis, Webster University, St. Louis, MO.

Smith, Stacy L., Katherine M. Pieper, Amy Granados, and Marc Choueiti. 2010. "Assessing Gender-Related Portrayals in Top-Grossing G-Rated Films." *Sex Roles* 62, no. 11–12: 774–786.

Steenland, Sally. 1990. "Women and Television in the Eighties." *Television Quarterly* 24, no. 3 (Summer).

———. 1995. "Content Analysis of the Image of Women on Television." In *Women and Media: Content/ Careers/Criticism,* ed. Cynthia Lout, 180–187. Belmont, CA: Wadsworth.

Taylor, Frank. 2003. "Content Analysis and Gender Stereotypes in Children's Books." *Teaching Sociology* 31, no. 3: 300–311.

TV.com. 2013. "Most Popular TV Programs." www.tv.com/shows/decade/1990s/

U.S. Bureau of Labor Statistics. 2008. Highlights of Women's Earnings in 2005. "Table 12: Median Usual Weekly Earnings of Full-Time Wage and Salary Workers in Current Dollars by Sex and Age, 1979–2007." Annual Averages 2007. www.bls.gov/cps/cpswom2005.pdf.

———. 2009. Current Population Survey. "Median Weekly Earnings of Full-Time Wage and Salary Workers by Detailed Occupation and Sex." Annual Averages. www.bls.gov/cps/cpswom2009.pdf.

U.S. Census Bureau. 1995. *Statistical Abstract of the United States.* 115th ed. Washington, DC: U.S. Government Printing Office.

Walker, Alice. 1983. *In Search of Our Mothers' Gardens: Womanist Prose.* Orlando, FL: Harcourt Books.

Watkins, Mel, and Jay David, eds. 1970. *To Be a Black Woman: Portraits in Fact and Fiction.* New York: William Morrow.

Watts, Randolph H., Jr., and DiAnne L. Borders. 2005. "Boys' Perceptions of the Male Role: Understanding Gender Role Conflict in Adolescent Males." *Journal of Men's Studies,* 267–280.

Webster, Murray, Jr., and Lisa Slattery Rashotte. 2009. "Fixed Roles and Situated Actions." In *Sex Roles: A Journal of Research* 61: 325–337.

Weinberg, Daniel H. 1998. "Press Briefing on *Measuring 50 Years of Economic Change.*" Washington, DC: U.S. Census Bureau, September 29.

Weitzer, Ronald, and Charis E. Kubrin. 2009. "Misogyny in Rap Music: A Content Analysis of Prevalence and Meanings." *Men and Masculinities* 12, no. 1 (October): 3–29.

"Women and the Economy 2010: 25 Years of Progress But Challenges Remain, A Report by the Joint Economic Committee Representative Carolyn B. Maloney, Chair Senator Charles E. Schumer, Vice Chair August 2010." *Invest in Women, Invest in America: A Comprehensive Review of Women in the U.S. Economy.* Prepared by the Majority Staff of the Joint Economic Committee of Congress, December 2010.

Wood, Julia T. 2011. *Gendered Lives: Communication, Gender, and Culture.* Belmont, CA: Wadsworth.

Young Women's Christian Association (YWCA). 2008. *Beauty at Any Cost: The Consequences of America's Beauty Obsession on Women and Girls.* Washington, DC: YWCA USA. www.ywca.org /atf/cf/%7B711d5519-9e3c-4362-b753-ad138b5d352c%7D/BEAUTY-AT-ANY-COST.PDF.

3

Is the United States a Classless Society?

As a result of the class you are born into and raised in, class is your understanding of the world and where you fit in; it's composed of ideas, behavior, attitudes, values, and language; class is how you think, feel, act, look, dress, talk, move, walk; class is what stores you shop at, restaurants you eat in; class is the schools you attend, the education you attain; class is the very jobs you will work at throughout your adult life.

—Donna Langston

In the absence of real contact or communication, stereotypes march on unchallenged; prejudices easily substitute for knowledge.

—Barbara Ehrenreich

PERSONAL EXPERIENCE AND CLASS

Many people who grew up in the United States were taught that it was a "classless" society and that distinct classes and castes were characteristic of England and India and feudalism. In this chapter we will examine and reconstruct this information and our beliefs. To begin the exploration of your personal experience and social and economic **class**, answer the questions in Personal Inventory 3.1. Scores range from negative 15 to 18. If you scored between 16 and 18 points, chances are you and your family lived a life of wealth or even extreme wealth. If you scored between –13 and –15, you and your family most likely experienced constant or occasional economic circumstances that caused extreme difficulties. If you scored between –12 and +15 points, your family was somewhere in the vast working or middle class. What thoughts did you have as you were answering the questions? What memories did the questions evoke? Were you surprised to discover where you and your family fit in the economic scheme of things?

The exercise you have just completed is designed to help you examine the economics of your family and to guide you in thinking about how your family's economic status may impact your sense of self, your worldview, and your opportunities in life. According to your comfort level, we encourage you to invite others to do this exercise and to compare your score, experiences, and memories with those of classmates, family members, and friends. Then,

Personal Inventory 3.1
The Level Playing Field

Instructions

Answer the questions below based on your personal experience. There are no right or wrong answers.

1. If you were raised in a two-parent family, score 1 point _____
2. If you had your own car as a teenager, add 1 point _____
3. If you had a phone in your room as a teenager, add 1 point _____
4. If you had a separate telephone line as a teenager, add 1 point _____
5. If you had to work out of economic necessity as a teenager, subtract 1 point _____
6. If your family ever experienced economic difficulty, setback, or crisis, subtract 1 point _____
7. If due to finances you ever had to forgo camp or extracurricular activities that your friends participated in, subtract 1 point _____
8. If your parents are paying for or paid for your entire college education, add 1 point _____
9. If you receive or received need-based financial aid for college, subtract 1 point _____
10. If you had all the clothes you wanted as a teenager, add 1 point _____
11. If your family frequently had dinner at restaurants (other than fast food), add 1 point _____
12. If your family had a children's library of fifty or more books, add 1 point _____
13. If your family had an adult library of fifty or more books, add 1 point _____
14. If your family went on regular vacations, add 1 point _____
15. If your family took you to museums, libraries, or other enrichment activities, add 1 point _____
16. If either of your parents completed college, add 1 point _____
17. If you ever needed to or currently need to rely on public transportation to get around, subtract 1 point _____
18. If either of your parents did not complete high school, subtract 1 point _____
19. If there was a period of time in which either of your parents was involuntarily unemployed, subtract 1 point _____
20. If, as a child, you often wore hand-me-down clothes because of necessity, subtract 1 point _____
21. If your family shopped primarily at discount stores because of necessity, subtract 1 point _____
22. f either of your parents worked as a domestic worker, laborer, or service worker, subtract 1 point _____
23. If one or more of your parents or grandparents were immigrants to the United States, subtract 1 point _____
24. If your family owned their own home, add 1 point _____
25. If your family rented an apartment or home, subtract 1 point _____

Personal Inventory 3.1 *(continued)*

26. If your family had major credit cards, add 1 point   _____
27. If you are the first generation of your family to attend college,
    subtract 1 point   _____
28. If supermarkets, cleaners, drug stores, and other amenities were easily
    accessible in your neighborhood, add 1 point   _____
29. If you attended private school for elementary, middle, or high school,
    add 1 point   _____
30. If you lived in a high-crime neighborhood, subtract 1 point   _____
31. If your family did not have a checking or savings account, subtract 1 point   _____

Add all of your "add 1" points and subtract all of your "subtract 1" points
for a total   _____

Source: Based on an unpublished manuscript and workshop exercise by Joan Olsen (1995).

---

through discussion with others who have completed the exercise or through the continuation of your autobiographical journal, answer the questions in Personal Inventory 3.2.

Open discussion of income is often considered impolite in the United States. In fact, it is quite common for children to be unaware of their parents' income and to be chastised if they inquire. While unspoken rules and norms may make it difficult to get precise answers to these questions, we encourage you to probe when you can and estimate if you need to. As you consider your score on the Personal Inventory 3.1 as well as your answers to the autobiographical questions in Personal Inventory 3.2, where do you think you and your family sit economically? Are you above, below, or in the middle of most Americans?

"Class" is a word that is rarely used in American households or schools and is therefore difficult for us to conceptualize concretely. In fact, we are often told that the United States is a "classless" society. But *class*—the understanding of our socioeconomic place and life chances—is exactly what we are addressing here. Later in the chapter, we will examine various sociological and economic definitions of class. For now, we will explore and analyze personal and family experiences that have been driven by family income. Personal Inventory 3.3 (page 144) provides a quiz to assess your family's expectations and assumptions and their connection to social and economic class. Sometimes these expectations are spoken and sometimes they are unspoken, but nevertheless they are remarkably present.

You are invited to begin to sort out how these experiences have influenced your values, beliefs, and behavior. As you review your responses to these statements, be sure to distinguish between family *expectations* and family *goals*, *dreams*, or *hopes* for the future. How did your family's income and/or wealth contribute to these expectations? How did the history of generations of your family's income and/or wealth contribute to these expectations? Examine those statements that accurately describe your family's ex-

Personal Inventory 3.2
Autobiography on Class

Instructions

Answer the questions below in writing or tape-record your answers to explore your experiences with socioeconomic class.

If you don't know some of the answers, talk to family members in your parents' or grandparents' generation to try to find more information. If it's difficult to find this information about your family, you can investigate this in a few other ways. Ask the most open and knowledgeable person in your family to discuss why the information is unavailable or inaccessible. If that doesn't answer your questions, continue reading Chapter 3 and see if you can find answers based on some of the information in the chapter about economics and class.

1. As you were growing up, how did you dress? Where did you shop? What kind of restaurants did you frequent? How did your family's income affect these choices?
2. What kinds of social or athletic activities did your family most frequently participate in (e.g., bowling, golf, tennis, going to the symphony, going to movies, watching television, playing cards)? How did your family's income affect these choices?
3. Describe the neighborhood(s) in which you grew up. Were there houses, apartments, or both? Were the streets and sidewalks well maintained? Were supermarkets easily accessible? What would you say the average income level was for most of the people in your neighborhood? What kinds of jobs did people have? Did many young people go to college? How did your family's income affect the choices of where you lived, what kind of jobs you had, whether to go college, and the range of colleges you considered?
4. How many generations ago did your family come to the United States? Did they come voluntarily or as slaves, indentured servants, or refugees, or were they part of a conquered people (e.g., American Indians)? How many generations back can you identify the kinds of jobs your grandparents and parents had? Were the jobs and income similar or different from generation to generation? Did the income from generation to generation go up, go down, or stay the same?

pectations. Do you think these expectations are characteristic of people with low income, middle income, or high income?

As you investigate your own family's socioeconomic position and class and look at those of others, it is fairly easy to see that there is great wealth in the United States just as there is dire poverty and a middle ground of income. It is also plain to see that the higher the income, the higher the access to better education, health care, housing, travel, employment, and all the other factors that heighten opportunities for success. While we may all see the same things around us, our own class position and experiences deeply influence how we interpret the distribution of wealth and opportunity. Key to this interpretation is our understanding of the "American Dream."

Personal Inventory 3.3
Class and Values Quiz

Instructions

Read each of the items below that describe a range of activities, goals, and norms of various families and groups. Circle the response that most closely matches the expectations your family had for their circumstances and your future as you were growing up. Mark "a" if the statement reflects an accurate account of your family's expectation in life. Mark "b" if your family expected more from life than the statement reveals. Mark "c" if your family expected less from life than the statement reveals, and mark "d" if the statement was never even a consideration in your family. There are no "right" or "wrong" answers. This exercise is an opportunity to tease out some of the invisible norms and expectations in your family and their relationship to socioeconomic class and your life.

Possible Responses for Each Statement

a. accurate expectation
b. expected more
c. expected less
d. not even a consideration

Statements

1. Getting by _____
2. Making a moderate living _____
3. Making a good living _____
4. Gaining social status or prominence _____
5. Working out psychological issues through therapy _____
6. Community service _____
7. Saving money _____
8. Making your money work for you _____
9. Getting a high school degree _____
10. Getting a college degree _____
11. Getting an advanced or professional degree _____
12. Learning a trade _____
13. Being an entrepreneur _____
14. Owning a home _____
15. Going to private school _____
16. Being a professional _____

Source: Based on material from Adams, Bell, and Griffin (1997).

Take a look at four definitions of the **American Dream** as described below.

Definition 1: "What I want to see above all is that this country remains a country where someone can always get rich. That's the one thing we have and that must be preserved" (Hochschild 1995, x).

Definition 2: "[The American Dream] simply states that the playing field is level, that although everyone may not start with the same income and wealth, everyone has the same chance to reach the top of the income hierarchy because a person's class background does not limit a person's chances of economic success . . . this belief is a significant framework within which we think about our society. Although everyone knows and accepts that there is no equality of income, it is also accepted that there is equality of opportunity" (Jhally and Lewis 1992, 89).

Definition 3: "The American dream that we were all raised on is a simple but powerful one—if you work hard and play by the rules you should be given a chance to go as far as your God-given ability will take you" (Hochschild 1995, 18).

Definition 4: "By the American dream, I mean not merely the right to get rich, but rather the promise that all Americans have a reasonable chance to achieve success as they define it—material or otherwise—through their own efforts, and to attain virtue and fulfillment through success" (Hochschild 1995, 32).

Now, for each definition, ask yourself these questions:

1. Does this make sense to you? Do you believe this to be true?
2. Has this been true for you? For your family? For how many generations has this definition been accurate or inaccurate for your family?
3. From your observations, do you believe most Americans regard the American Dream in this way?
4. In the late twentieth and early twenty-first centuries, what do you think prospective immigrants to the United States from India, Bosnia, Mexico, Israel, Vietnam, Palestine, Nigeria, and other countries may have believed to be true about their new home as they made the decision of whether to immigrate to the United States?

Later in the chapter, we will discuss the meaning and significance of the American Dream, both currently and throughout American history. But for now, examine—do not criticize or evaluate—what you have come to believe about the American Dream and how it flavors your hopes and visions and beliefs about your own life chances and the life chances for other Americans.

The definitions of the American Dream above come from a variety of sources and perspectives. Definitions 2 and 4 are reflections by scholars, definition 1 was proclaimed by President Ronald Reagan in 1983, and definition three by President Bill Clinton in

1993. The fact that at least two recent U.S. presidents have incorporated the American Dream into their rhetoric is an indication of the pervasiveness of this concept. Definition 4 is the only one that truly deviates from the original concept of the American Dream, which states that no matter where we begin, if we are virtuous and work hard, we have a chance to go as far up the corporate, government, and/or income level as we want. The implication of the classic American Dream concept is that there are no significant barriers to the dream and that we all are, in fact, on a level playing field.

In 2003, President George W. Bush signed the American Dream Downpayment Act, which authorized up to $200 million annually to help low-income, first-time home owners with down payments and closing costs to buy a home, one of the basic criteria to indicate arrival to American Dreamland (U.S. Department of Housing and Urban Development 2012). As Bush signed this act into law, he said, "The dream of homeownership should be attainable for every hard-working American. That's what we want. And this act of Congress I'm going to sign, the regulations that I hope are finalized soon will help thousands of families fulfill the dream. And so now it is my honor, right here . . . to sign the American Dream Downpayment Act." Four years later, 2007 became the year that officially marked the beginning of the Great Recession, the worst economic downturn in the United States since the Great Depression. Ten days after his inauguration in 2008, in the midst of "the plight of Americans hit by the faltering economy," President Barack Obama said, "It's like the American Dream in reverse." In 2010, a poll conducted by ABC News and Yahoo reported that 43 percent of those Americans surveyed thought that "the American Dream is a thing of the past" and though it was true at one time, it no longer is. The poll indicated that only half of the country still believed that the American Dream was anything close to a reality (Debusmann 2010). Later in this chapter we'll examine the purpose the American Dream has served over time to offer Americans hope or the myth of hope, depending both on your perspective and on your family's experience with money, hope, and the dream. You will be invited to take a close look at your personal and family experience and history with money and the idea of "class" in the context of the collective U.S. experience and history of money and class.

This is just a beginning of understanding our personal experience of class and how our relative position and economic privilege impacts our values, beliefs, and behavior. Class identity differs significantly from racial and gender identity. From very early ages, most of us knew whether we were male or female, African American, European American, Asian American, Native American, Latino, or multiracial. While our life experiences dictate how we perceive gender and racial identities, the identities themselves were generally clearly expressed to us. It is different with class identity. It is rare that Grandpa takes a tot on his knee and says, "Now, Johnny, you know we're working-class and have been for many generations, and that's something you can be proud of," or "Susie, you will inherit great wealth some day. Our family is owning-class and that means that you have more money, clothes, and better education and health care than most Americans."

Because our income determines where we can afford to live, Americans usually settle in communities surrounded by other families of their same means and class. These communities seem "normal" to us. In fact, many adults report that during their childhood they did not know they were "poor" because everybody else they knew was just like them. On the other side of the economic spectrum, many people who were raised with great wealth are often unaware of how rare that is and have a difficult time understanding their life experiences as "privilege." The purpose of this chapter is to help make sense of the concept of class and the American Dream, its reflection in entertainment media, and the way these ideas and messages influence our lives. Much of the literature on socioeconomic class is highly politicized and characterized by strong convictions. As the reader, it will be your task to sort out how your own personal experiences of class have shaped you and how you see the world. You will also be invited to take in new information, and it will be your challenge to think critically about this new information and ultimately make independent decisions about what you choose to believe.

RECONSTRUCTING KNOWLEDGE AND CLASS

According to the theory known as the fabric of oppression, class is defined as the structural arrangement by which income and wealth are distributed unevenly through various layers of society. "Class is about money and it is about more than money. As a result of the class you are born into and raised in, class is your understanding of the world and where you fit in, it's composed of ideas, behavior, attitudes, values, and language; class is how you think, feel, act, look, dress, talk, move, walk; class is what stores you shop at, restaurants you eat in; class is the schools you attend, the education you attain; class is the very jobs you will work at throughout your adult life" (Langston 1995, 101–102). Some sociologists define class as "the relative location of a person or group within a larger society, based on wealth, power, prestige, or other valued resources" (Kendall 1999, 73). Other sociologists define class according to category of occupation. Some economists define class by income and economic status, while others define it by ownership, power, and control (Adams, Bell, and Griffin 1997, 233).

This means that the people with the greatest wealth typically have high-quality education and health care, luxurious homes, and access to extravagant clothes and vacations. The families and individuals at the upper reaches of wealth are likely to have access to the power, privilege, and resources that allow them to get what they want in life. On the other side of the spectrum are people living in the kind of poverty that severely limits their life options. They often live in substandard housing and frequently have to choose between paying for heat or for groceries. Families of four are considered below the poverty line by the U.S. government if they have an income below $20,350. This means they often live in high-crime neighborhoods and their children generally attend schools that are low on books, pencils, and computers and high on class size. Individuals and families at this income level frequently rely on public transportation and rarely have the opportunity to go on vacation or purchase a car that's never been owned by another person. As we address definitions and statistics about class, it's important to remember these stark realities of poverty and what income disparity looks and feels like in real life.

One effective working definition of class is "a relative social ranking based on income, wealth, status, and/or power" (Adams, Bell, and Griffin 1997, 233). In plain language, this means that class involves more than the simple factual information about the amount of money we have earned or inherited; it involves assumptions about our success or failure as a human being and brisk judgments about our character and worth, financially and personally. **Classism**, then, is a set of individual and institutional beliefs, systems, and practices that assign value to people according to their economic ranking and creates an economic inequality affording economic privilege to some while targeting others for oppression.

Because class is discussed so little in the United States, its definitions and measurement and our own class identity are often unclear. At the top of the distribution of wealth is a tiny percentage of people—the owning class—who own and control an enormous amount of resources and wealth. At the bottom of the income and wealth distribution are people who have extremely low incomes or none at all, commonly labeled as "poor." But the lines between poor, working-class, and middle-class people are blurred. Some say that anyone who is not owning-class is working-class. Others say that distinctions in income and household net worth mark the difference in the remaining classes. Still others say that it is the difference in the nature of work; the degree of autonomy, physical labor, and danger of work; and the degree of control over one's labor that distinguishes the middle class from the working class (Zandy 1995, 9).

In the fall of 2011, in the wake of the Great Recession, a grassroots group called Occupy Wall Street staged protests and demonstrations about economic inequities and began to talk about and stimulate a new personal and public debate about the relationship between socioeconomic class and the role of government. One of the things Occupy members talked about was the vast difference between the income and status of the very wealthy as compared with everyone else. They based one of their primary slogans on the information that 1 percent of households in the United States own somewhere between 30 and 40 percent of all privately held wealth (Gautney 2011). The Occupy Wall Street slogan was "We are the 99%!"

Class has historically been disguised, nearly invisible, and a challenging concept to grasp and attribute common meaning to.

History books and school courses have been designed primarily by people who are middle-class and above, and information in these sources has typically been presented from this perspective. Yet class difference and class struggle have been integral to the combination of stories that constitute American history. Some of this struggle has been violent, and its telling contradicts the simpler stories and myths of the United States as a class-free and economically mobile society. "Part of the problem of visibility is a problem of knowledge—how knowledge is constructed, layer after layer, generation after generation. Working-class people have not had much to say about how school knowledge is constructed" (Zandy 1995, 13).

A study of high school textbooks reveals that there is virtually no information about class inequalities or structural barriers to class mobility. Rather, most high school textbooks focus on the openness of opportunity and the fluid nature of social mobility. Yet social class is arguably one of the most important predictors of accessibility to resources and to success in U.S. society. Consider these facts:

- Affluent expectant mothers are more likely to get good prenatal care than poor and working-class mothers, who often see a doctor for the first time in the last month of their pregnancies.
- Wealthy suburban schools spend two to three times more money per student than poor urban and rural schools.
- Poor children often attend classes that are more than 50 percent larger than the classes attended by wealthier children.
- Wealthy high school students are more likely to take courses to prepare them for the Scholastic Aptitude Test (SAT); social class is a strong predictor of SAT scores.
- Social class is the strongest predictor of both the rate of college attendance and the type of college attended.
- Wealthier people have longer life expectancies than poor and working-class people. (Loewen 1995, 204–205)

The lack of information about the structural barriers of social class has clear consequences. Without an understanding of how opportunities for people in the United States have been organized according to income and social standing, many people, both rich and poor, come to blame the poor for being poor and credit the rich for being rich. When working-class people come to understand issues of social class, they often find this information liberating: "to understand is to pardon, for working-class children to understand how stratification works is to pardon themselves and their families" (Loewen 1995, 207). When wealthier students come to understand issues of social class, they are less likely to blame the victims for their circumstances or to see their own lucrative net worth as a reflection of their net worth as a person.

As you consider the low visibility of class in U.S. society, recall how hegemony works by securing the consent of those who are not in power—not by force, but through socialization of values that get taught at home, in school, and through the media. Hegemony is typically neither conspiratorial nor visible. For countless new immigrants as well as for families who have been in the United States for many generations, belief in the American Dream has been virtually synonymous with the belief in democracy and freedom. Many of us feel that if we identify and recognize a class system in the United States, we are challenging and questioning the very fiber of democracy. It may even seem unpatriotic to consider the possibility of the existence of an American class system based on the accident of birth rather than on merit, virtue, and hard work.

As in the discussion of gender in Chapter 2, there is little disagreement that males and females exist, possessing different biological and character traits. While theories diverge as to which character traits are biological and which are socialized according to culture, most of us share a common recognition of the existence of men and women. This shared recognition does not exist regarding the concept of class.

As discussed in Chapter 1, the term "cognitive dissonance" refers to the emotional or psychological discomfort we feel when we receive information that challenges or is inconsistent with attitudes and information that we have held to be the "truth" (Baran and Davis 2009, 146). According to selection theories, this psychological discomfort can be so intense that we seek a way to relieve the tension and return to a more comfortable consistency with our own beliefs. Pause for a moment now and throughout the chapter to pay attention to your own thoughts and feelings in response to the information about social and economic class. If you feel discomfort, allow yourself to lean into it for a while without attempting to resolve the questions, conflict, or uneasiness that you experience as you absorb challenging new information. Stay with the discomfort for as long as you can tolerate it and until you can think clearly about the sources and credibility of your original information and the sources and credibility of the information in this chapter. Ultimately, what you choose to believe is entirely your decision—the goal is to make it an active and conscious process.

As you take the journey through your own personal experience and begin to reconstruct formal knowledge, notice when you experience resistance to and disagreement with some of the theories, concepts, and information introduced. When you notice such resistance, ask yourself what relationship this has to your own class background. As you study gender, class, and race, it is important to remember that a primary objective of this book is to encourage independent thinking on these difficult and controversial issues. You are never required to change your beliefs about any topic. You are invited and encouraged, however, to take the journey whether it leads you to a different place of understanding or takes you back to where you began. The journey of reconstructing knowledge regarding class will include studying moments of American history in relation to class; the status of employment, wealth, and income in the contemporary United States; and analysis of the American Dream.

The word "history" encompasses the word "story"; history is a collection of stories that constitute what we are taught in school and learn to call U.S. history. The stories you are about to read have been culled from primary sources and scholarly works of historians, sociologists, and economists. These stories of U.S. history are *not* among those included in most high school textbooks or curricula.

EARLY U.S. HISTORY

"What has replaced the earlier happy picture of pervasive fluidity is not a grim picture but a mixed one. In many new communities in colonial America, opportunities for poor men were far better than in England—but not everywhere. Seventeenth-century Salem's rich had 'considerable wealth' to start with" (Pessen 1974, 2). A study of more than 1,000 Massachusetts immigrants in 1637 indicated that their economic fate in America was largely determined by their social and economic status upon arrival. Yet there were those who benefited from "shipboard mobility," improving their economic status simply by coming to the New World. Between 1637 and 1676, the population of Maryland grew from 200 to 20,000, and by 1676 "class was settled and to achieve upward mobility meant moving south or west" (Pessen 1974, 3). It is important to note that virtually everyone in this group of people was European American, white, and male.

During the seventeenth century, more than half of all English immigrants were indentured servants whose passage to America was typically paid for by private companies. These new Americans were then compelled to work for five to ten years for these companies to repay their passage. In Virginia, more than two-thirds of these indentured servants died before their contracts were repaid (Adams, Bell, and Griffin 1997, 259). In Maryland, over 40 percent of indentured servants died during that period. For those white, European men who survived, there were many opportunities to move upward in economic and social status.

A study of the mobility of indentured servants in Maryland indicated that many of these young men worked ten to fourteen hours a day, six days a week, and went on to become small planters on leased land. Less than 10 percent of the survivors went on to be prominent in politics by virtue of education or marriage (Menard 1974, 20–27). "It seems probable that Maryland continued to offer ambitious immigrants without capital a good prospect of advancement throughout the 1640s and 1650s. But there is evidence to suggest that opportunities declined sharply after 1660" (Menard 1974, 28).

So while most of us learned that early U.S. history was characterized by vast opportunity for advancement and economic mobility, these studies indicate that in at least some areas of the United States, the chances for upward mobility dropped sharply as early as the seventeenth century in colonial America. These chances, slim though they were, were available only to white men. Women of any race and men who were African American or American Indian had little political recourse to change or improve the economic status or economic prospects of their lives (Adams, Bell, and Griffin 1997, 259).

There were several main avenues to create wealth in eighteenth- and nineteenth-century America. The first route to wealth was through slavery, through which enslaved individuals were bought and sold and forced to work in the same way as farm equipment and farm animals. The business of buying and selling human beings and free labor was the source of this wealth. Likewise, landowners, mortgage holders, and factory owners accumulated wealth on the backs of other humans through immigrant labor, in the form of indentured servitude or by paying immigrant workers an amount that barely constituted subsistence wages. In this scenario, new immigrants were virtual slaves in the form of share-croppers, tenant farmers, and factory workers whose free or cheap labor accumulated wealth for their employers. The final path to wealth during this time period was through land grabs, often won in violent battle, capturing profitable land from American Indians, French settlers, and Mexican residents (Adams, Bell, and Griffin 1997, 259).

Typically, these capital-producing strategies placed enormous wealth in the hands of a few, gave some income boost to those in the middle, and created poverty for the vast numbers of Americans.

There were some organized groups and movements that resisted this accumulation of wealth in the hands of the few. The antirent movement from the 1830s through the early 1850s in New York organized tenants to reduce the power of landowners. The populist movement of the 1880s and 1890s organized farmers in the South and West to work together to protect their land rights.

Yet despite these efforts to seek economic equity and protection, difficult and rigid economic distinctions existed in early America. The United States lacked the European history of feudalism and formally defined class hierarchy and structure, but separations between the economic classes were often impermeable and opportunities for mobility were bleak. European observers such as Alexis de Tocqueville commented on the vast differences between the Old World and New World class structure and hierarchy and interpreted these as the indicators of an egalitarian society. But even as de Tocqueville and others were writing glowingly about opportunities for mobility, the early United States was becoming increasingly stratified. "It was the children and grandchildren of the colonial elite who alone were able to brush off the financial panics of 1819, 1837, and 1839, and who had the necessary capital to participate in the great financial, commercial, and entrepreneurial ventures that beckoned. . . . The evidence indicates that the typical man was a farmer or artisan of little or no property and with modest to bleak prospects. The man on the make was a man who to a large extent was already made" (Main 1974, 57).

By the mid-1800s, 95 percent of New York City's 100 wealthiest individuals had been born into families of wealth or high status and occupation. "The age of egalitarianism appears to have been an age of increasing social rigidity" (Pessen 1974, 114).

The early industrial era (1860–1900) was an era of big business that marked the completion of the railroad network and the rise of giant corporations. During this time, most U.S. citizens still lived in small towns or rural communities. In the early days of manufacturing, some of the men who rose to success in industry may have depended on the skills and knowledge they gained from working in the field (Gutman 1974, 125). A study of working-class upward mobility during the mid-1800s examined 287 people in one town and revealed, "The contrast between the literal claims of the rags-to-riches mythology and the actual social experiences of these families thus appears glaring: a few dozen farmers, small shopkeepers, and clerks, a large body of home-owning families unable to escape a grinding regimen of manual labor; this was the sum of social mobility achieved by Newburyport's unskilled laborers by 1880" (Thernstrom 1974, 163).

Throughout the nineteenth century, only 2 percent of U.S. industrialists rose from the ranks of the working class. Yet most high school textbooks focus on the legendary exceptions, such as Joseph Pulitzer and Andrew Carnegie. "By concentrating on the inspiring exceptions, textbooks present immigrant history as another heartening confirmation of America as the land of unparalleled opportunity" (Loewen 1995, 209).

THE TWENTIETH CENTURY

By 1913, forty-four U.S. families had income of over $50 million a year while most adult workers earned $10 to $20 per week. By 1933, more than one-fourth of the labor force was unemployed (Adams, Bell, and Griffin 1997, 260). How did these vast gaps and changes come about?

World War I had multiple effects on class mobility and the norms for national values. During the war, President Woodrow Wilson called on U.S. citizens to express their patriotism by making personal economic sacrifices to support a larger and more important cause—freedom and democracy. In light of twenty-first-century cultural norms regarding women's employment and independence, some of these sacrifices may seem strange. But in the early twentieth century, most middle-class American women were accustomed to minding the home front while their brothers, fathers, and husbands went to work outside the home. During World War I, when their husbands were fighting overseas, many of these women worked to financially support their families, worked for pay in factories, or volunteered with organizations supporting the war effort. President Wilson encouraged people to show their patriotism through conserving food and buying "Liberty Bonds" to financially support the war. Most U.S. citizens made these sacrifices quite willingly but in the prosperity of the postwar 1920s were ready to return to a self-centered norm characterized by individualism, materialism, and hedonism (McElvaine 1993, 10).

The 1920s were prosperous times for the owning class and for the working and middle classes as well. The late-nineteenth-century values of thrift and savings were replaced by a consumer ethic that encouraged self-indulgence. For the first time, massive advertising was used to convince working-class and middle-class people to use credit and the installment plan to buy products that they could not otherwise afford. The United States was becoming increasingly industrialized and urbanized. In the past, most people lived in relatively small, rural communities in which their survival was more dependent on the family, the farm, and the community than on the job. With the rapid rise in industry and the move to the cities, an increasing number of people were in positions that were dependent on their jobs in industry, which were in turn dependent on market forces (McElvaine 1993, 17).

While workers seemed prosperous on the surface, a deeper analysis disclosed that in 1929, Americans' workweek was longer than that of any other industrial country and workers had no protection against unemployment. The United States, China, and India were the only countries that continued to allow children to work at night (McElvaine 1993, 222).

Economist Adam Smith's concept of laissez-faire—allowing market forces to evolve "naturally" of their own accord—was often applied to the nineteenth-century U.S. economy, in which there were many competing small private businesses and enterprises. Laissez-faire was based on the belief that the market was characterized by a **level playing field** between these businesses, thus making competition fair. With the assumption of fairness and equality at its core, the economic wins and losses of a laissez-faire economy were set in what was believed to be a context of morality.

Despite the flaws in the analysis of the equal starting point of businesses in a preindustrial United States, Smith's concept applied even less in the 1920s. By the end of the 1920s, two-thirds of industrial wealth in the United States went from individual ownership to publicly financed corporations. By 1929, 200 corporations controlled almost half of U.S. industry and roughly 2,000 men dominated U.S. economic life (McElvaine 1993, 37).

Another by-product of World War I was a fanatical rise in patriotism and the valuing of everything American. The sense of who was the "other" was on the rise, as was membership in the Ku Klux Klan and hate crimes directed at Jews, blacks, immigrants, and Catholics (McElvaine 1993, 12).

Concurrent with these changes in business, industry, culture, and the economy, President Calvin Coolidge and his cabinet believed that catering to big business and promoting production would mean continued prosperity for everyone. Business leaders instituted a form of welfare capitalism in which they devised programs to keep the workers happy as a way of increasing productivity. These production incentives included Americanization programs and citizenship classes for immigrants. These industries saw their contribution to immigrant socialization and assimilation as part of their service to the workers. Giving up the language, clothing, food, and culture of one's country of origin was considered a positive step toward becoming a U.S. citizen.

Coolidge's secretary of the Treasury, Andrew Mellon, was explicit about his goals for government to serve the interests of the wealthy. In an outright, public style that would be poor form in the twenty-first century, Mellon said that his major goal was to reduce the tax burden on the rich and shift it to poor and working-class people. In 1926, he initiated legislation that was ultimately passed by Congress in which a person with $1 million in income went from paying $600,000 to $200,000 in taxes. Between 1921 and 1929, $3.5 billion was granted to corporations and friends of the Republican Party. Along with other cabinet members, Mellon devised another tax shift scheme that did not materialize during the Coolidge years, but nevertheless reflects some of the thinking of the owning class. This strategy was to repeal Prohibition, make beer legal, and tax it heavily. Mellon's thinking was that since beer was the workingman's drink, this tactic would significantly shift the burden of taxes in still another way (McElvaine 1993, 23).

For the economy to remain stable, the supply of goods had to equal the demand. During this time, productivity was increasing at a faster rate than worker income, and the supply was exceeding the demand. This wide gap meant that to maintain economic stability, new ways to increase demand were necessary. Working families needed to continue to buy on credit and wealthy families needed to continue to consume luxury items and invest at ever increasing rates to keep up with the increased productivity.

The Great Depression

There were few government regulations and controls on big business, and in this un-restricted culture, the number of mergers, the valuation of real estate, and the amount of stock speculation continued to climb. This speculation meant that buyers and sellers continued to jack up stock market and real estate prices with the idea that they would get out before prices sank. "Once a sizable number of important investors decided the boom had ended, it had ended. It had all been built on expectations of rising prices. As soon as those expectations were reversed, the market had to fail" (McElvaine 1993, 47).

But the stock market crash did not of its own accord necessitate a massive economic **depression**. According to many economists and historians, the causes of the Great Depression were complex and multiple, and one of its main causes was the unequal distribution of wealth, which led to overconsumption and the instigation of stock speculation. The stock market crash and the Depression began in 1929 and ended on December 7, 1941, when the Japanese bombed Pearl Harbor.

The **gross national product (GNP)** adds together the value of all of the goods and services produced in the United States, plus the income earned by U.S. citizens living abroad, then subtracts the income earned by non-U.S. citizens living in the United States.

The GNP is considered an important indicator of the relative health of the U.S. economy (InvestorWords.com 2011).

From 1929 to 1933, the gross national product dropped by 29 percent and consumer spending dropped by 18 percent. Construction and investment fell a whopping 78 percent and 98 percent respectively. Unemployment rose from 3.2 percent to 24.9 percent. The American Dream had turned into the American nightmare. "Glad to believe themselves responsible for whatever success they had enjoyed in the twenties, many 'ordinary' people found themselves during the early Depression in a position similar to that of businessmen and Republicans. Having taken credit for the good, they had little choice but to accept responsibility for the bad" (McElvaine 1993, 75).

Job discrimination became increasingly serious for African Americans and women. Among African Americans, unemployment was close to 50 percent. Jobs that had previously been held by blacks and viewed as "negro occupations," such as elevator operators, bellhops, street cleaners, and so forth, were claimed by many whites. The legacy of slavery and the post-slavery laws continued to perpetuate racial inequities in the United States. The dominant thinking of the times was a result of the semi-visible hegemonic forces that led to the protracted erroneous and deeply damaging belief that whites were superior and as a result "naturally" more deserving of resources and opportunities than blacks. The upshot was that these beliefs in white superiority hardened into individual actions and institutional policies to ensure that no black person should be working while white men were still out of work. A group of whites in Atlanta adopted the slogan, "No Jobs for Niggers Until Every White Man Has a Job." The number of reported lynchings increased from eight in 1932 to twenty-eight in 1935. Black workers who were primarily tenant farmers during the Depression had an average annual income of less than $200 (McElvaine 1993, 187).

A parallel public perception was that women were taking jobs from men who needed to support their families. In fact, most working women were also attempting to support their families and had jobs that had been considered traditionally women's domain, such as domestic and clerical work. Interestingly, throughout the Depression these jobs continued to be considered women's jobs and were neither desired nor filled by men (McElvaine 1993, 183).

The government sanctioned gender employment discrimination with public works programs that paid men $5 and women $3 a week. The 1935 passage of the Social Security Act under Roosevelt's New Deal was significant in its protection of older adults, people with disabilities, and the unemployed and poor people—it was also significant in that it excluded protection for many job categories such as farm and domestic work, which tended to be the domain of blacks and/or women (McElvaine 1993, 256).

By late 1941, when Pearl Harbor was bombed and the United States entered World War II, the economic cycle had turned again. Spending and investment in the defense industry boosted the economy back to prosperity. The U.S. public was once again asked to make sacrifices in the name of patriotism during the war. And by the 1950s, with World War II and a decade of economic depression behind them, Americans were eager to return to materialism and prosperity. This prosperity became available to many in the

1950s. Many Americans also wanted a return to the traditional family roles when men worked outside the home for wages and women worked inside the home for the family. This established order, which had been upset by both the Depression and the war, was restored along with the postwar prosperity. While prosperity lasted for some for a while, the return to the traditional roles of men and women turned out to be only very temporary. As described in Chapter 2, the burgeoning women's movement began in the 1950s and 1960s. It ushered in the expansion of women's choices, allowing for increased employment out of the home, increased economic and personal independence, and the possibility of an identity outside of or in addition to wife and mother. These events and changes turned traditional gender roles upside down.

Historically, Americans' values have often been dictated by their class interests. It is in the interest of the owning class to be individualistic and acquisitive and to run business in a way that is amoral, rather than moral or immoral. It is in the interest of the working class to be individualistic, as well, but in a different way from the wealthy. The working class tends to measure policies and actions according to their impact on individual human beings rather than their effect on production or profit. The middle class has been pulled either in one direction to be in accord with the interests of the owning class, or in another direction to be in accord with the interests of the working class in a way that corresponds to specific historical economic circumstances.

During the Great Depression, middle-class interests and values were aligned with the working class and the poor, and in the 1920s and 1950s with the wealthier classes. "The interplay between the egoistical, amoral individualism of the owning class and the ethical individualism of most workers is essential to understanding many facets of U.S. history" (McElvaine 1993, 201). But owning-class values have often been parlayed in the form of the American Dream and have pushed working-class and middle-class people to consume more, borrow more, and use more credit. This somewhat invisible logic goes something like this for working- and middle-class people: "Someday I will have the real possibility of economic success. For now, while I am waiting for this success, I can borrow and use credit to have the material things I want and that way others will see me as successful."

Post–World War II

The 1950s and 1960s in the United States were characterized by a booming economy and a sudden burst in opportunities for social mobility. "The U.S. came out of World War II with the only intact industrial economy in the world. Tremendous economic growth from exports to the rest of the world created a large middle class and stable working class. Skilled and/or unionized working-class people began to own homes and have pensions; the children and grandchildren of poor immigrants and African Americans went to college in large numbers and populated the new sprawling middle-class suburbs" (Adams, Bell, and Griffin 1997, 260).

This boom represents a time in U.S. history when class lines became more permeable. While structural boundaries, by virtue of race and gender, still prohibited many people from moving upward from the poor and working classes, many low-income white Americans were able to move into the growing middle class. Unemployment was relatively low, businesses were growing, and the G.I. Bill offered unprecedented educational and home-buying opportunities for World War II veterans.

This was the "bootstrap" period in the United States in which postwar economic growth and opportunities created and structured by the government temporarily removed some of the hardened barriers to class mobility. While many of the people who achieved economic success worked hard to earn it, it was the combination of this hard work and the structural changes in society that provided a shift in life chances. Through a combination of personal experience, the absence of information, and the presence of myth, many Americans began to understand this period of growth, individual success, and some class mobility exclusively as the result of individual industriousness and merit. By this interpretation, those worthy and virtuous individuals pulled themselves up by their own bootstraps to achieve class mobility and some measure of economic success. The logical counterpart to this interpretation of the 1950s and 1960s is that those who did not succeed lacked virtue and industriousness and the willingness to use their own bootstraps. By this argument, their economic failure was exclusively a personal failure. As we begin to analyze the myth and reality of the American Dream, we will look at economic success and the dream in terms of both individual effort and structured opportunities and barriers.

Indicators of Class in the United States in the Mid- to Late Twentieth Century

The 1970s through the 1990s were a time of deindustrialization characterized by the loss of manufacturing growth and jobs. This shift threatened the relative prosperity that the working class gained in the 1950s and 1960s. From 1979 to 1984, 11.5 million Americans lost their jobs due to plant shutdowns or the closing of related industries. More than 60 percent of these workers were able to find other jobs. But half of these new jobs were at lower pay. Beginning in 1979, a highly inflated housing market made it difficult for middle-class families to afford to buy homes (Hochschild 1995, 107).

During the 1980s, under Ronald Reagan's presidency, two significant changes affected poor, working poor, and working-class Americans. The first change was in the tax structure, which, as in Coolidge's presidency, shifted benefits to the wealthy. In addition, massive changes in the federal budget increased military spending and simultaneously made huge cuts in domestic spending and programs that had previously benefited low-income families and children.

From 1979 to 1984, the working poor, who earned under $20,000 for a family of four, constituted 40 percent of the population over the age of fourteen. In the 1980s, the after-tax median income was $20,000—not enough to support the kind of lifestyle typically attributed to the middle class (U.S. Census Bureau 1990). Two cars, annual vacations, regular dinners at restaurants, and other middle-class indicators increasingly became the domain of higher-income families. Real wages, corrected for inflation, fell more than 11 percent from 1972 to 1986 (Adams, Bell, and Griffin 1997, 260).

In 1982, a study measured the average wealth of U.S. families, defined as assets or inherited resources that were distinct from income or money earned. The study revealed that the lowest 20 percent of Americans were in debt for an average of $14,000, which meant that their "wealth" was in the negative column. On the other hand, the top 20 percent of Americans had an average wealth that ranged from $243,000 to $12,482,000 (Mishel and Bernstein 1993, 79). The disparity between the top and bottom 20 percent was staggering. Below are just some of the economic realities that characterized U.S. society in the latter half of the twentieth-century:

- From 1977 to 1988, the average income of the poorest U.S. families decreased while that of the highest 20 percent increased.
- By 1990, chief executive officers of U.S. manufacturing corporations were paid 120 times more than the average worker (Phillips 1990, 28).
- By 1992, the poorest 20 percent of Americans earned an average family income of $8,130, while the wealthiest 20 percent earned an average range of $65,700 to $676,000 (U.S. Census Bureau 1992).
- By the late 1990s, the most accurate predictor of one's income was the occupation of one's father (DeLone 1979, 74). This points to some stagnancy in income mobility from generation to generation.

While these factors of income and wealth are devastating simply on the face of the information, there were further consequences for low-income people and significant numbers of people of color in the United States:

- In 1992, 32.1 people per 1,000 were victims of violent crime. For low-income blacks, this number was 60.1 per 1,000 and for low-income whites it was 44.7 per 1,000. Higher-income blacks were victims of violent crime at a rate of 35.0 per 1,000, while the number for well-off whites was 20.7 per 1,000 (Hochschild 1995, 37).
- In 1994, 37 million Americans were without health care coverage and an equal number were underinsured (Barlett and Steele 1992, 29).
- In 1994, poor people and people of color were more likely to live near toxic waste sites than were whites and others of middle incomes and above (Bullard 1993, 33).

As you consider the information in this section of the chapter, think back to your own personal experiences regarding class. As you recall your own family's income and assets, place yourself in the demographic scenario above. Did your economic position as a child impact how you understand, resist, or accept this information today? If your family was relatively wealthy, was it difficult to believe, both as a child and now, that so many Americans had such low income? If your family was poor or working-class when you were younger, do you find any comfort as you read about and begin to understand the structural ways this was determined? If your family was middle-income when you were a child, where do you find yourself, then and now, in these various scenarios?

This may be a good time to take a "cognitive dissonance" pause and check in with yourself to see if you are experiencing any resistance to any of this information. What information seems familiar, what information seems reasonable, what information seems unreasonable and challenges beliefs that you may not have even known were there? Reflect on your own class background and think about these questions, both from your understanding as a child as well as your current understanding of your family's financial circumstances and status. Did you believe then and do you believe now that your family "deserved" whatever income, wealth, or poverty they had? Did they work hard and earn their fortune or was your past and current belief that they were "lazy" or "unambitious" and as a result deserved their economic difficulties? Alternatively, did you believe then or now that the fact of whether your family was wealthy, poor, or somewhere in between was an arbitrary and capricious stroke of good luck or misfortune?

As we continue to consider the American Dream, it is the process of examining our own life experiences regarding income and class and reconstructing knowledge that will help you understand your relationship to the American Dream. What were you taught about opportunity in the United States? How did your family's economic position impact what you believed to be possible? What were you taught in school and at home about disparity in the United States in income, education, health care, employment, and housing? What did you believe about responsibility for poverty or wealth? Were poor people to blame for their lack of resources? Were wealthy people to be credited for their economic status?

THE TWENTY-FIRST CENTURY

Causes of the Great Recession

The National Bureau of Economic Research (NBER) sets the standards for the definition of a **recession** as well as marking the magnitude, depth, and official beginnings and ends of these times of economic hardship. NBER determined that what is now known as "The Great Recession" began in December 2007 and ended in June 2009, nineteen months of a "significant decline in [the] economic activity [that] spread across the country" (NBER 2013).

According to NBER, a recession lasts for at least three months and an economic depression is a more severe recession in which the increase in unemployment and the drop in gross domestic product are deeper, wider, and last longer than a recession (NBER 2013). The **gross domestic product (GDP)** is one of the primary indicators economists use as a dipstick to gauge the health of the country's economy. The GDP is the size of the economy, the total price tag of everything that is produced in the United States, from eggs to fertilizer to deodorant to Cadillacs to diapers to the T-shirt you are wearing right now (Investopedia 2009).

According to the Pew Research Center, "more than half (55 percent) of all adults in the labor force say that since the Great Recession began . . . they have suffered a spell of unemployment, a cut in pay, a reduction in hours or have been involuntary part-time workers" (Pew Research Center 2010, i). Chances are better than fifty-fifty that if you are a U.S. resident reading this sometime between 2012 and 2050, you or your family were affected in some way by the Great Recession of 2007–2009.

For many of us, reading about the complexities of the economy and terms such as "gross domestic product," "subprime loans," and "quintiles" causes us to back off or shut down because the topic is too difficult, too much work to understand. The result can be that while we know whether our immediate circle of family and friends are thriving or suffering from the economy, we often have limited information, misinformation, and biased information about why some Americans have abundant wealth and resources while others live in scarcity. Translating the language of "economicese" into plain English, this section will explore some of the causes, characteristics, and consequences of the Great Recession and how it has affected different social, economic, racial, and ethnic groups in the United States.

According to economists and sociologists alike, the United States was on the verge of a fall long before the crash of the Great Recession (Treas 2010; Waddan 2010). Then,

> in the Fall of 2008, the shifting foundations of inequality . . . became a social, political, and economic earthquake of enormous magnitude. . . . The Big One, a global economic meltdown, had finally arrived. We were riveted by the most serious economic calamity of our lifetimes—a worldwide economic pandemic, financial institutions in seeming free fall, and the crushed dreams of millions of Americans. As the crisis passed, the outlines of an explanation of these frightening developments began to emerge, but it offered little comfort to the many individuals and families who were the casualties of this economic debacle. (Treas 2010, 3)

Who is blamed for the Great Recession depends on who is doing the probing—someone with a politically left or liberal perspective or someone with a politically right or conservative perspective. "The Right's critique blames the crisis mainly on government, which, it is alleged, encouraged risk taking in two ways": protecting large investors against losses and keeping interest rates too low. "From the Left, the explanation is greed, deregulation, misaligned pay incentives, and a mindless devotion to 'free markets' and 'efficient markets' theory. The result, it is said by many on the Left, was an orgy of risk taking, unrestrained either by self-imposed prudence or sensible government oversight" (Samuelson 2011).

The U.S. government appointed a ten-member commission, the Financial Crisis Inquiry Commission (FCIC), to investigate the causes of the financial crisis between 2007 and 2010. According to the commission's findings, reported in January 2011,

> the crisis was avoidable and was caused by: widespread failures in financial regulation, including the Federal Reserve's failure to stem the tide of toxic mortgages; dramatic breakdowns in corporate governance, including too many financial firms acting recklessly and taking on too much risk; an explosive mix of excessive borrowing and risk by households and Wall Street that put the financial system on a collision course with crisis; key policy makers ill-prepared for the crisis, lacking a full understanding of the financial system they oversaw; and systemic breaches in accountability and ethics at all levels. (FCIC 2011)

One of the most common and damaging ways that analysts and media translate complex economic situations into simpler terms and explanations is by "blaming the victim." This approach reduces an extraordinary, multilayered series of events like the Great Recession into something easier to understand, manageable in sound bites. Blaming the victim can also serve another purpose—to relieve us of the kind of psychological discomfort that can be created when we try to wrap our brains around multiple and sometimes contradictory explanations that require us to think in ways that reject simple black-and-white, either/or thinking and challenge us to think in nuances and to consider that "both/and" may be true. "According to this perspective [blaming the victim], we deflect attention from the real—usually structural—causes of misery by pinning responsibility on those individuals who suffer the problem" (Treas 2010, 4).

Such an overly simplistic and frequently inaccurate explanation allows us to see problems from a personalized vantage point in which the players are the "good guys" and the "bad guys." Once we figure out (or more likely are told) who the bad guys are, then the picture comes into focus and our psychological discomfort caused by the complexities and contradictions of multiple causes is relieved. Cognitive dissonance experienced, cognitive dissonance vanquished. We know what to think, we know how to feel, and most likely our new clarity helps us know how to vote.

Here is one example of how "blaming the victim" operated in the early stages of the Great Recession, with a nudge from print and broadcast news media. In 2008, major U.S. automakers were on the verge of bankruptcy and there were efforts in Congress to authorize billions of dollars to bail out these corporate heavy hitters. The reasons for these financial meltdowns were complicated and multidimensional, involving the economic free-fall still in motion, decisions by auto company CEOs, and government policies such as tax structures and the like. A full explanation of this grave situation affecting the auto industry, workers, and the United States as a whole is beyond the scope of this book. However, in 2008, the *Wall Street Journal*, a reputable business newspaper, suggested that the impending disaster for the auto industry was the result of unfair wage demands of auto workers. When a $14 billion emergency bailout for U.S. automakers collapsed in the Senate in December 2008, CBS News reported that the United Auto Workers (UAW, the union representing auto workers) was to blame for not accepting Republican demands for wage cuts. The role of the UAW in the auto industry crisis was debatable, as was the role of corporate owners and the U.S. government. There were and continue to be competing ideas, perspectives, and viewpoints about this volatile situation. As a reputable news source, CBS has solid credibility with viewers. The simple and one-sided viewpoint that CBS provided in this news story posed as the truth for the majority of viewers who don't have the time or inclination to actively pursue multiple news sources. "This explanation is far easier to understand than the intricate details of the interdependence of the auto industry and the policies, economics, and tax structure of the U.S. government. It also ignores factual information that could easily contradict blaming the auto workers who, through the UAW, had agreed to cut new workers' wages by 50 percent" (Treas 2010, 4–5).

Parallel to the economic crash in the Great Depression of the 1930s, the Great Recession in the first decade of the twenty-first century was caused by systemic and systematic factors. Identifying these causes requires a much broader analysis than the close-up view that blames auto workers for industry failure or individual homeowners for the downfall of the housing market, housing prices, and foreclosures. While the causes of the Great Recession are still being argued, three of the chief suspects are as follows.

- *Consumer Culture.* Much as in the Great Depression, American's consumer culture encouraged overspending and overborrowing through the use of credit cards in partnership with media advertising and entertainment media that bombarded us with messages of what we "need" to feel good, clean, pretty, thin, trendy, popular, and successful. "Offering easy credit during periods of economic stress and uncertainty masks social and economic crises within the privacy of Americans' suburban castles" (Manning 2000).
- *Housing Market and Mortgages.* Housing sales had soared in the years preceding the Great Recession. This was due in part to the use of what are called "subprime" loans or mortgages to finance the purchase of homes by people who had credit problems or who could not otherwise afford to buy a house. When people buy houses, they have to qualify for a loan or mortgage by having credit (AKA "good credit") that demonstrates that they pay their bills, owe only a reasonable amount of debt, and have a sufficient income to purchase the home. If their credit is problematic, they may be rejected for a standard loan or mortgage. However, they still may be able to qualify for loans with far higher interest rates as an alternative to the normal interest rate or "prime" loans. **Subprime loans and mortgages** have high interest and high risk. Despite these risks, these high-risk financial deals offered eager, but financially stressed and stretched, prospective home buyers a seductive opportunity to purchase homes they couldn't afford. These high-risk housing loans contributed to the soaring of the housing market in the years before the recession. This extreme peak in housing loans, construction, and sales is known as the **housing bubble**.
- *The Bursting of the Housing Bubble.* In 2007, the so-called housing bubble began to burst when people were unable to keep up with these high-interest, high-mortgage payments and loan losses rose to epidemic proportions. This, along with other companion financial failures, led to housing foreclosures, a severe decline in housing sales and construction, and a loss of construction and related jobs. And the housing market, which was a virtual house of cards, came tumbling down. One of the repercussions of this disaster in the housing industry was the largest bankruptcy in U.S. history. In 2008, Lehman Brothers, the fourth-largest investment banking business in the United States, went belly-up.

Two other more contested causes of the Great Recession were the Federal Reserve's policy of keeping interest rates extremely low and the lack of sufficient financial regulation to prevent an unsupervised stock market from running amok.

Despite the complex economic and political forces that led to the Great Recession, mainstream politicians and media sources often provided simple sound bite explanations that frequently reduced the story to a cautionary tale of heroes and villains. "We Americans turn every major crisis into a morality tale in which the good guys and the bad guys are identified and praised or vilified accordingly. There is a political, journalistic, and intellectual imperative to find out who caused the crisis, who can be blamed, and who can be indicted (either in legal courts or the court of public opinion) and, if found guilty, be jailed or publicly humbled. The great economic and financial crisis that began in 2007 has been no exception" (Samuelson 2011).

According to Robert J. Samuelson, the explanation for the Great Recession is both more "innocent" and more "disturbing" than the blame scenario. This explanation acknowledges "financial excesses, economic miscalculations and crimes" as contributors to the economic disaster, but explains it in a broader context that steps outside of simple blame. Accordingly, there were twenty-five years of economic good times preceding the Great Recession: a "boom" time that homeowners, bankers, investors, economists, and even scholars became accustomed to and came to believe would be permanent. "Their heady assumptions fostered a get-rich-quick climate in which wishful thinking, exploitation, and illegality flourished. People took shortcuts and thought they would get away with them." There was an assumption that modern economic theories, beliefs, and practices would protect us from the vagaries and unpredictability of the business cycle. Nobody, therefore, was prepared for the inevitable downturn and the "bust" time of the economy (Samuelson 2011).

Continuing this account, Samuelson writes:

> In a more honest telling of the story, avaricious Wall Street types, fumbling government regulators, and clueless economists become supporting players in a larger tragedy that is not mainly of their making. If you ask who did make it, the most honest answer is: We all did. Put differently, the widely shared quest for ever-improving prosperity contributed to the conditions that led to the financial and economic collapse. Our economic technocrats as well as our politicians and the general public constantly strive for expansions that last longer, unemployment that falls lower, economic growth that increases faster. Americans crave booms, which bring on busts. That is the unspoken contradiction. (Samuelson 2011)

A Snapshot of the Consequences of the Great Recession

Since the Great Depression of 1929–1941, there have been thirteen recessions, but none has had a more "punishing combination of length, breadth, and depth" than the Great Recession of 2007–2009 (Pew Research Center 2010). This section will examine some of the ways American families, businesses, culture, and expectations were hit by this most recent and most damaging recession.

By all accounts, the years before the Great Recession appeared to be years of relative and widespread prosperity; at least this is what the news media widely reported. A closer look reveals that, even before the recession, there were some extreme disparities in income according to race, class, ethnicity, or social group. The gap between the experiences of the very rich and the very poor was widening and the middle seemed to be falling out of the middle class.

"The period of economic growth that began in November 2001and lasted through 2007 marked the first time on record that poverty and the incomes of typical working-age households worsened despite six years of economic growth. Since the mid-1970s, there has been widening income and wealth inequality. The official poverty rate rose from 11.7 percent in 2001 to 12.5 percent in 2007. The number of families living in households with an income of below 125 percent of the poverty line also increased, from 16.1 to 17 percent" (Waddan 2010, 246).

"Unemployment rates rose faster for African Americans and Latinos than for whites while homeownership rates fell faster. Trends for poverty rates, health insurance coverage, and retirement savings also show widening gaps by race and ethnicity throughout the recession and recovery after 2007" (Weller et al. 2011). According to the data, communities of color sank deeper into the economic hole than whites during the Great Recession. That disparity was compounded by other serious problems for communities of color before, during, and after the recession; people of color were blocked from many economic opportunities by structural barriers that denied access to the same opportunities as whites in both good times and bad times (Weller et al. 2011). These structural barriers include those predictable patterns in employment, housing, and other economic indicators, caused by government laws or government or corporate policies and practices, that consistently place whites and some Asian ethnicities at the high end of job and housing opportunities and African Americans and Latinos at the low end.

As we look at some of the aggregate information about housing, employment, and health care during the Great Recession, it is important to remember that this information combines the experiences of all racial groups; it is a composite picture. And although every racial group has been deeply affected by the Great Recession, African Americans and Latinos have consistently experienced more losses in jobs and housing, with the only consistent gains in the depth of the poverty in these communities.

The High Cost of Being Poor

"Turns out that being poor is expensive." Everything from a loaf of bread to a mortgage costs more in the poorest sections of most cities than in the poshest sections. In Los Angeles, a short-term loan in Compton (one of the poorest neighborhoods) is likely to have an interest rate thirty-five times higher than the rate for the average credit card in California (Katz and Fellowes 2005, 1). It is logical to think (and hope) that people with the lowest incomes would live in communities with the lowest housing and food costs and with better access to inexpensive public transportation. Yet the trends in much of the United States are just the opposite. In this section we will take a look at some key statistics about the high cost of being poor, followed by some of the life challenges of low-income families. Finally, we will investigate if, and to what extent, there are structural explanations for poverty. Our investigation of possible structural reasons for poverty will include government policies, living costs, unregulated economic exploitation of low-income people, and the so-called safety net, a set of government programs established to protect the most vulnerable among us.

The 2009 federal poverty guidelines suggest that a family of four is considered "poor" if their income is at or below $22,050. Here are some of the facts of life for many of these families:

- *Checking Accounts*. Twenty-three percent of families with income less than $30,000 live without checking accounts, while only 6 percent of families with income above $30,000 go without checking accounts. Without checking accounts, families often must pay many of their household bills with money orders. Without a checking account, a money order costs roughly $5.00. If a family pays their rent, electricity, gas, cable, car payment, health insurance, and phone bill with money orders, they are paying an extra $35 per month (Shtauber 2013, 1).
- *Payday Loans*. Payday loans are high-interest loans that are the only recourse for many low-income families when an unusual medical expense, car repair, or emergency causes them to run out of money days or weeks before the next payday. These loans charge an average $15.50 fee for every $100 borrowed. So to borrow $300 for seven days, the effective annual interest rate would be 806 percent (Shtauber 2013, 11).
- *SAT Tests and Income*. College-bound high school seniors from the highest economic groups score higher on the SAT tests than those from the lowest economic groups. In 2009, students with family income of less than $10,000 nationally scored an average of 427 points out of 600 points on the Critical Reading portion of the test as compared to students with family income of more than $100,000, who scored an average of 544 points (Rampel 2009).
- *Car Prices*. Car prices end up being higher for low-income individuals and families. They are charged an extra $50 to $500 more in car prices plus extra percentage points for auto loans that can amount to over $1,000 more for every year of the loan when compared to families and individuals who are middle-income and above (Katz and Fellowes 2005, 7).
- *Home Loans*. In 2011, homeowners with incomes of less than $30,000 paid interest rates on home loans as high as almost 7 percent, while homeowners with incomes of over $120,000 paid a rate of 5.5 percent (Progressive Economics 2011).
- *Health Insurance*. Only about 24 percent of people who make less than $25,000 per year have health insurance (Progressive Economics 2011).
- *Life Expectancy*. Life expectancy for the lowest socioeconomic group is 4.5 years less than the life expectancy for the highest socioeconomic group (Manchester and Topoleski 2008).

In addition, in 2008, "14.6 million people struggle[d] to put enough food on the table. More than 49 million Americans—including 16.7 million children—live[d] in these households and nearly one in four children was at risk for hunger. For African Americans and Latinos, the ratio of children at risk for hunger was even higher, one in three"

(Nord, Andrews, and Carlson 2009). In 2006, low-income families were already paying a higher percentage of their income on food than were families above the poverty line. The average U.S. family spends a little over 12 percent of their income on food, while families with income under $10,000 spend 17.6 percent of their income on food (U.S. Bureau of Labor Statistics 2010).

Numbers and percentages give us a sense of the big picture and its proportions for low-income people in the United States, but they do not necessarily tell us about the real stories, the blood, sweat, and tears of real people. John Scalzi describes some experiences of real people who are called "poor":

- Being poor is having to keep buying $800 cars because they are what you can afford, and then having the cars break down on you because there is not an $800 car in American that is worth a damn.
- Being poor is six dollars short on the utility bill and no way to close the gap.
- Being poor is thinking that earning $8 an hour is a really good deal.
- Being poor is going to the restroom before you get in the school lunch line so your friends will be ahead of you and will not hear you say "I get free lunch" when you get to the cashier.
- Being poor is making lunch for your kid when a cockroach skitters over the bread and you look to see if your kid saw it.
- Being poor is not taking the job because you cannot find someone you trust to watch your kids.
- Being poor is knowing you work as hard as anyone, anywhere.
- Being poor is people surprised to discover you are not actually lazy.
- Being poor is crying when you drop the mac and cheese on the floor. (Scalzi 2005)

While these statements about what it means to be poor are clearly not applicable to every low-income person, they provide a palpable description of some of the real-life details of the excruciating impact of poverty.

As noted above, the U.S. government considers a family of four as living in poverty if their income is at or below $20,050. The National Center for Children in Poverty (NCCP) has calculated what the basic costs are for various family configurations in several U.S. cities. For example, in Boston in 2013, a single-parent family with one school-age and one pre-school-age child would need all the budget items in Table 3.1. These are the most basic living costs such as food, housing, and medical expenses. There is nothing budgeted for clothes or school supplies or school activities. This parent will often have to say "no" to her children for school fund-raisers, field trips, and other common school and child care activities or be late with rent or short on food.

It is clear to see that in Boston this family's very basic expenses of almost $46,000 total more than twice as much as the official U.S. poverty level for a family of four! Imagine that you were head of this household and had to make the money decisions. What would you cut to make ends meet, and what would you do to try and earn more money? If you

Table 3.1

Basic Budget Needs for a Family of Four, 2008*

	URBAN New York, NY	URBAN Houston, TX	SUBURBAN Aurora, IL	RURAL Decatur County, IA
Rent & utilities	$15,816	$10,224	$11,328	$ 6,324
Food	$7,878	$7,878	$7,878	$7,878
Child care	$20,684	$15,422	$18,798	$11,682
Health insurance	$2,609	$2,834	$2,265	$2,436
Transportation	$1,824	$4,808	$4,808	$6,288
Out-of-pocket medical	$732	$732	$732	$732
Other necessities	$6,397	$4,887	$5,185	$3,834
Payroll taxes	$5,113	$3,873	$4,437	$3,270
Income taxes (including credits)	$5,787	−$34	$2,572	$304
Total	$66,840	$50,624	$57,998	$42,748
% of 2008 Federal Poverty Level	315%	239%	274%	202%

*Basic budget needs for a family of four in urban, suburban, and rural locales are based on a two-parent family with one preschool-age and one school-age child; results are based on the assumptions that the children are in child care centers or schools while their parents work and that the school-age child is in after school care. It is also assumed that the parents have employer-based health care insurance, that in New York they rely on public transportation, and that in the other three locales they rely on private transportation.

Source: National Center for Children in Poverty's (NCCP's) Basic Needs Budget Calculator.

could find a part-time job or contract work that would help pay the bills, who would take care of your children? The NCCP website (www.nccp.org/tools/frs/budget.php) (NCCP 2013) provides a Basic Needs Budget Calculator that can help you find what the basic budget costs are for different size families in various cities in the United States. Think about your current income or family income and the costs that you have in the categories listed. List other items that you or your family pay for regularly, such as car expenses (loan payments, insurance, gas, repairs), clothing, birthday and holiday gifts, athletic gear, and so on. How far would this budget go to meet the financial expenses of your life?

Ultimately, is there anyone to praise or blame for our relative wealth or poverty? If we were never able to obtain a college degree because of our parent's income and circumstances and worked hard at a job in retail, labor, or service, landing in our mid-forties with a mid-forties salary in a lower management position, how do we account for that? Is it making the best of the hand we were dealt, barely able to meet our family of four's basic needs in urban Boston? Could we have achieved that law or medical degree along with a shot at a six-figure salary if only we had worked harder or smarter? Or . . . should we look deeper into some of the less than visible structural or policy reasons that our income probabilities had almost predictable upper limits? What if university education was inexpensive or even free, as it is in some countries? What if government financial aid for higher education was a higher priority that allowed every young person who was admitted to college access to the necessary financial resources without going into six-figure debt? Are our life chances and choices determined and limited by our own choices and actions, by governmental policy and practices, by the situation determined by the accident of our births, or by some combination?

We will look deeper into some of those questions as we explore the American Dream in the next section. For now, let us take a look at the structural possibilities and examine just a few of the laws, policies, programs, and practices that seem so normal to us that we barely see them.

A 2004 report by the American Political Science Association analyzed the increasing income disparities in the United States and determined that some of the responsibility for these extreme highs and lows of income could be attributed to conscious public policy (Hacker et al. 2004, 4). One example of the type of public policy that affected income was the tax cut of 2001 "when 36 per cent of the cuts accrued to the richest 1 per cent of Americans—a share almost identical to that received by the bottom 80 per cent"; this "would seem to provide a clear example of policy exacerbating the rise in income inequality" (Waddan 2010, 246). The complex, frequently inaccessible language used to analyze economics and taxes causes many of us to tune out as it muffles the harsh reality that, in many instances, government programs and policies contribute to the extremes of poverty and the real consequences for real people.

Another example of government policies that contribute to class inequities involves the funding of education. Much of the funding for public education comes from local property tax, the amount of tax that homeowners and businesses pay based on the value of a home or any other property (other real estate, cars, etc.) that they own. The result of this policy is that the school districts with the wealthiest residents also have the greatest economic resources, which result in the highest educational benefits for the students. "This can often mean that children that live in low-income communities with the highest needs go to schools with the least resources, the least qualified teachers, and substandard school facilities. For example, in Illinois, two school districts with vastly different incomes resulted in enormous disparities in per pupil expenditures and in the quality of education" (Federal Education Budget Project 2013). In the 2007–2008 school year, the New Trier Township High School District in Illinois spent $21,137 per student in contrast to the Central Unit School District, also in Illinois, which spent $6,728 per pupil. In fact, even within school districts the resources are often distributed in a way that is grossly uneven. "A large portion of the disparity is related to the allocation of teachers. Higher paid, more experienced teachers tend to be congregated in lower needs schools, while less experienced teachers end up in high needs schools" (Federal Education Budget Project 2013). It is ironic that the government policies that fund public education end up penalizing the poorest neighborhoods with the poorest education, seriously decreasing the options for children of low-income families and reinforcing the kind of poverty that tends to persist from generation to generation.

Through the uneven funding of schools, students in each state and throughout the country receive uneven public education, which can affect their ability to do well on high-stakes tests such as the SAT, ACT, and GRE, which are a necessity for admission to most colleges and graduate programs and for money merit scholarship. The ability to pay for and to be admitted to a college and graduate or professional school, in turn, deeply affects students' ability to achieve their personal and professional goals as well as their ultimate earning power.

The way that public education is funded is often taken for granted, especially by those of us who landed in the schools with the most resources. Property tax structure and its marriage to school funding are a function of the laws and public policies of most states in the United States, but that is not the only way to fund education. Unless we have studied the funding of education and alternate ways to fund schools, the status quo may seem to be just one more unfortunate reality. But suppose for a moment that just a slight change was made in the way schools were funded. Suppose public education still relied on personal property tax as the primary source of school funding, but instead of being collected and distributed school district by school district, it was collected at the state level and divided by the total number of students in public schools throughout the state. The result would be an amount to be spent per pupil throughout the whole state—that is, the expenditure for education for each student in the state would be equal. How would the potential for quality education and future opportunities shift if this one change meant that every school district and every student in a given state had equal funding and resources? And if there were still enormous differences in pupil expenditures between the wealthiest states and the poorest states, suppose the personal property taxes were collected by the federal government and divided equally among all the school districts in the country. To the degree that policy could correct the economic disparity, all students would thus have access to the same educational resources.

The examples of policies and practices in public education funding and income inequities are just two issues of economic disparity in the United States that have structural causes. As you consider what you know and don't know about the disparity in opportunities triggered by the vast inequities in income, think about how different policies could create more equitable situations. We invite you to also think about your own situation, depending on if you grew up in the United States or elsewhere. Think about the general types of jobs that people in your community held, their income, and the property they owned or rented. Think about whether there were thriving shopping areas and businesses and perhaps even one or more corporate headquarters that paid a high level of property taxes or, by contrast, if there were just a few struggling businesses. Perhaps where you lived, the kinds of income, individual homes, and businesses were somewhere in between.

Then begin to connect the dots between the high, low, or moderate property taxes that were a significant part of funding the school district where you lived and the kind of facilities and resources in the public schools in your community. Were the school buildings in good shape? Were there state-of-the-art facilities for computers, science labs, video, and other technology? Did the classrooms have modern desks that were in good repair and the right size for the students? Were books and academic media resources current and in good shape and were there enough of these resources for all students? Were there strong advanced placement courses and in-school resources as well as tutoring for strengthening academic achievement? Were there opportunities for a wide variety of extracurricular activity and volunteering or community service for students? Was there an inviting school library that had a wide selection of books that were attractive to you and other students? Were the athletic fields and equipment adequate and the coaching staff well qualified and strong? Were there college counselors, workshops, and materials to help students with their college choices, applications, and financial aid questions and applications? Were there adults in the schools (teachers, administrators, college counselors, custodial staff) that took an interest in the students and their future and encouraged and helped them to clarify and reach their goals? The questions could go on and on. Ultimately, connect the dots between the following:

- the public policy that makes property tax a primary funding source for public schools in the United States
- the level of individual, small business, and/or corporate property ownership in the neighborhood where you lived from kindergarten through high school
- any academic, athletic, extracurricular, instructional, or other opportunities that helped you succeed or excel in certain areas

Finally, connect the dots between these factors stemming from the amount of property tax that supported your school district and your ability to attend the kind of college you wanted and pursue your academic and career goals and dreams.

If you went to school outside the United States, you can still engage in this process, first by determining the primary financial support of public schools in your country. However that funding is distributed economically is the public policy in education and its connection to your life and education that you will be investigating. Perhaps there was a big division between public and private education where you grew up, so people with resources or access to scholarships invariably received a better quality of education and life chances through private schools. As you trace education back to how it was funded in your country, you can then ask yourself the rest of the questions above, connecting the dots throughout the process.

Try these examples of income and educational funding on for size; think about the credibility of the information you have received in the past as well as the credibility of the information you have just read. Notice if there is any conflict in the different types of information you have received and if you are experiencing any discomfort as a result. See if you can banish this discomfort, this cognitive dissonance, just long enough to give yourself time to think it through and make some independent decisions about what you choose to believe about the existence of economic class disparities and some of the public policies and practices that influence family income, educational opportunities and resources, and individual life chances.

The American Dream

Recall your earlier personal exploration of your beliefs and experiences with the American Dream, the promise and the belief in the level playing field, and the conviction that there is equal opportunity for all Americans. This dream includes the ability to move ahead, to move up, to succeed. The four elements of the traditional, classic understanding of the American Dream are as follows:

1. The belief that everyone can participate equally and can always start over.
2. The belief that it is reasonable to anticipate success.
3. The belief that success is a result of individual characteristics and actions that are under one's control.
4. The belief that success is associated with virtue and merit. (Hochschild 1995, 3–30)

"Recent historical studies of popular thought demonstrate that the 'rags-to-riches' myth and variations on it have been a central theme of the American Dream from the seventeenth century to the present" (Pessen 1974, xi). The Horatio Alger stories of the late nineteenth century were an integral part of the development of the American Dream. Alger wrote fictional accounts of young boys and men with low to no education or income who rose to great heights in industry and politics by their individual determination, hard work, and merit. "The hundreds of novels that seemed to fly off Alger's pen popularized as never before the rags-to-riches theme. Many contemporaries mistook fiction for fact" (Pessen 1974, 124). A modest American Dream might involve an aspiration to middle income or slightly above, a secure job, a "nice" house and car, and an annual vacation; the implication of the "real" American Dream is that anyone who demonstrates the character traits of merit, virtue, ambition, drive, and hard work can become president of the United States or of General Motors.

The rags-to-riches stories used to teach the American Dream focus on individuals and their potential and possibilities for success. On the practical side, the dream requires a relatively high income to begin with in order to have access to opportunities. These privileges include access to books, health care, education (both public and private), high-paying jobs, travel, cultural events and institutions, and the resources and wherewithal to do more than simply financially survive in the world. The dream also ignores structural barriers to success. In fact, working-class white people and most people of color face systemic obstacles in employment, housing, education, health care, and so on by virtue of their income and race—despite their individual effort or merit or even their intelligence.

The U.S. history outlined in this chapter indicates critical times in both the early seventeenth and mid-twentieth centuries when there were structural openings for upward mobility created by economic conditions and/or government-constructed opportunities for pursuing and attaining the American Dream. While these opportunities were certainly impacted by individual industriousness, there were still gender and race barriers that locked out other individuals regardless of their hard work and merit. Women and people of color were systematically excluded from Depression-era job programs and post–World War II programs that made low down payments and low-interest mortgages readily available to white men and white families. Further, during other times in U.S. history, such as the late 1660s and the early twentieth century, class barriers were hard and virtually impermeable, so that chances for mobility were bleak and for most people the American Dream was just that—a dream.

Our history teaches us that while there have been times when opportunity is available and hard work and virtue pay off for some, there are many more times when it is the rare individual who is able to pierce the barriers of gender, race, and class and attain the American Dream. One purpose of the American Dream is to give us hope, yet one outcome of belief in the American Dream is that the structural barriers that keep many of us from moving ahead are rendered invisible. If the American Dream is made up of half-truths and myths, what does this mean for Americans as individuals and as a society? The large and often invisible gaps in the American Dream translate into a very different reality: a sense of individual failure and self-blame for those who do not achieve it. The translation goes something like this: "If the American Dream is a real promise for all of us and I don't see the big picture of who benefits from it and who is excluded, then if I fail to reach my dream, it is my fault. Something is wrong with me—I'm a loser."

If we review the American Dream and its four elements, we can begin to see the parts of each that inform, the parts that misinform and distort, and then we can form some sort of analysis of the dream and rethink and reconstruct its place in our lives and society.

Despite all of the structural barriers to success and the myth of the application of the American Dream, some individuals in the United States do burst through the barriers to enormous economic success and recognition. Are these individuals the exceptions that prove the rule or are they the exception that is used to support the myth of the American Dream? As you ponder this question, it is important to factor in your own class position and experience, the U.S. history you have learned in school, and the brief history you have read in this chapter to weed out information from misinformation, distortion from truth. The answers are not always simple or easy or consistent.

If the American Dream has served to sustain many immigrants and people with hard lives through four centuries of U.S. history and has also served to cruelly deceive many into false hope, what are the alternatives? Is it possible to offer hope with a more complex and realistic set of beliefs attached to it? Consider the following summaries of the four tenets of the traditional American Dream and the alternatives posed.

1. "The American Dream has historically been available largely to white men from the middle classes and above."

   Others have found success, but the obstacles have been much greater for most women, men of color, and poor and working-class men and women. As you work toward your dream, it is important to understand that your starting point has a strong impact on the barriers to achieving the American Dream.

2. "Your starting point and standing point by virtue of race, gender, sexual orientation, and circumstances of income and disability have an enormous effect on how much economic success you can reasonably anticipate exclusively through your own individual effort."

   While it is important to hang on to your dream and hopes, it is also important to learn the history of opportunity and success for the groups you belong to and learn how groups have worked together to widen opportunities. As you learn about the efforts of labor unions and civil rights and other social justice groups to create change, you may gain a better understanding of the connection between individual success or failure, structural obstacles, and mobilization for change.

3. "Your economic success depends on a combination of your own individual efforts, the economy, the openness of society to the group or groups to which you belong, and the history of movements for change."

   While your actions, training, skills, hard work, and attitude are critical to walking through the doors of success, it is important to understand that opening those doors is not always exclusively within your individual control and power.

4. "Finally, your virtue and merit are dependent on your values and beliefs and how you choose to lead your life to match these ethics."

   You can choose how you want to define "virtue and merit" and whether you want to be measured according to the heights you attain in your field, by the money and objects you accumulate, by the kind of person you choose to be, or by some combination.

There is a delicate balance required in weighing individual responsibility, the current status of class mobility, and the role of structural bias and discrimination when it comes to being accepted by certain types of colleges and universities, entering particular career paths, and climbing to the top of the ladder in our chosen field. When we face disappointment or failure as we aim for the American Dream, it is easy to blame ourselves, thinking "I really blew it. No wonder they didn't (accept me, hire me, promote me)," or to blame the college or business or human resources office that turned us away. An understanding of the history of the facts and myths of the American Dream can help us have a better grasp of our own professional and economic successes and failure by asking and answering these questions:

- What part is my responsibility? What can I do to change and grow or gain additional skills to be better qualified to reach my goals?
- What's the history of this industry in hiring or promoting people of various races, genders, and socioeconomic classes? Do the leaders evaluate potential employees and their class by examining their connections to the "right" schools, country clubs, sororities or fraternities, and family background?
- Is it possible that any equal employment or antidiscrimination laws have been broken by this college or industry's patterns of hiring and promoting? If so, do I want to find a way to work with other individuals or with organizations that challenge this type of discrimination?

The goals of the classic American Dream are based on status, position, and material wealth. Your goals may or may not match the equation that says that success equals wealth and prestigious positions. Your goals may be to teach in the isolated rural area of your childhood, or you may have a deep passion to be a painter or a novelist, regardless of whether you achieve great material wealth or fame. You may want to combine or modify some of the goals of the American Dream in conjunction with your own. Based on your values and your goals, you have the right to revise either version of the American Dream in a way that matches your sense of the connection between your hopes and goals, on one hand, and a realistic understanding of the potential barriers, on the other. As you assess your own class position and experiences and the history of economic class and mobility in the United States, you can draw your own conclusions about the availability of the American Dream.

From Invisible to Visible: Class and the "Occupy" Movement

> In the 1990s, economists began producing a string of studies documenting rising income inequality in the United States. . . . But the idea did not take a central place on the national stage until the fall of 2011, when it was championed by a diffuse group of activists who began a protest called Occupy Wall Street. Their demonstrations were aimed at corporate greed, the corrosive power of major banks and multinational corporations and, especially, income inequality in America. (Strutz 2013, 16)

The Occupy Wall Street movement literally hit the streets in September 2011. Like many of the social justice movements of the 1960s, Occupy was conceived as a leaderless group that operated on a consensus basis. The initial founders of the movement were determined to design an internal structure and decision-making process that reflected their external goals of economic equity expressed in a simple and powerful point of unity, "'The one thing we all have in common is that we are the 99 percent that will no longer tolerate the greed and corruption of the 1 percent,' an obvious reference to the well-known, yet still appalling, statistic that the top 1 percent of households in the United States own somewhere between 30 to 40 percent of all privately held wealth" (Gautney 2011).

The Occupy Wall Street movement began protesting against the inequities in U.S. income and wealth using Wall Street as both a symbol and the reality of corporate greed and corruption. Through the fall of 2011, the movement spread to locales around the country, with each locale responsible for its own concrete agenda. All the groups were committed to toppling the 99 percent/1 percent distribution of wealth and to a structure and decision-making process designed "to avoid replicating the authoritarian structures of the institutions they are opposing. This is part of what differentiates them from the Tea Party" (Gautney 2011). The "Tea Party" had its start as an early twenty-first-century grassroots group with a strongly conservative social and political agenda, and it successfully helped win some conservative seats in Congress. The Occupy movement never intended to become part of a political party or to enter directly into electoral politics. Its goals and strategies involved direct action through protests, demonstrations, and tent cities to raise awareness about economic inequities and put pressure on the powers that be to make changes.

"The Occupy movement has influenced the national dialogue about economic equality, with the word 'occupy' itself becoming part of the public lexicon. In his third State of the

Union address, President Barack Obama issued a populist call for income equality that echoed the movement's message" (Barr 2012). And on a lighter note, some pizza parlors began serving an item on the menu called "occu-pie" (Gautney 2011). Beyond substantive and symbolic changes in language, political rhetoric, and a new name for pizza, the Occupy movement pulled off some concrete accomplishments.

In 2009, New York State passed the so-called millionaire's tax, a temporary measure to increase taxes for wealthy New Yorkers (despite its nickname, the tax affected individuals whose income was over $200,000) that was scheduled to expire at the end of 2011. The Occupy movement in Albany, New York, supported extending it; Governor Andrew Cuomo opposed the extension. Even with New York State facing an enormous budget deficit and some polls showing that New Yorkers were in favor of extending the tax by a ratio of two to one, Cuomo was adamant about letting the tax expire (Rose 2011). The Albany group "occupied" a city-owned park and began to refer to Cuomo as "Gov. 1%" in reference to his opposition to the millionaire's tax, not to mention the financial support for his election campaign from wealthy corporate executives. The Occupy movement's actions called attention to the inequity of a tax break given to millionaires at the same time that budget cuts would deeply affect low- and middle-income New Yorkers. Ultimately, statewide social justice groups in New York state credited the Occupy movement for making the difference. "In a surprise move, Cuomo reversed his position on the millionaire tax in December to avoid further cuts to schools and health care. Part of the $2 billion in revenue went to a modest but rare income tax cut of $200 to $400 for most middle class families. Cuomo refers to the millionaire tax as the biggest tax cut for the middle class in decades" (Barr 2012).

An even bigger surprise has been credited to the Occupy movement by journalists, activists, and researchers who have worked for decades to create interest, open discussion and debate, and active change regarding class and economic inequities in the United States. After a few months of demonstrations throughout the country, Occupy managed to capture the interest of the news media, not only making the discussion of class public, but also bringing the reality of class inequities in the United States out of the proverbial closet. In October 2011, news coverage of Occupy was 6 percent of the news generated in the United States, and by the middle of November it soared to 14 percent (Schmidt 2012). The news stories were not simply reporting Occupy activities and goals; many of them were reporting information about income and tax inequities, the real struggles to survive of real people, the impact of government and corporate policies and practice—and encouraging public discussion and debate about a topic that had long been underground.

Much of the Occupy direct action dwindled in the early winter months of 2012, accompanied by a drop to below 1 percent of the nation's news coverage by January (Schmidt 2012). By 2013, the large protests that Occupy organized and the high level of news coverage had dwindled. Whatever the future of Occupy, in the first five or six months that it appeared on the scene, the increased public debate about class was notable. The visibility of socioeconomic class and the debate about wealth, poverty, and government responsibility soared in mainstream and independent news sources and as a significant element of the 2012 presidential primaries. From September 2011 through April 2012, diverse news sources, including FOX News, CNN, *The New York Times*, National Public Radio, *The Huffington Post*, and *Mother Jones* reported on class and inequities with headlines such as "Income Inequality" and "It's the Inequality, Stupid." Studies that analyzed the causes and effects of economic inequity as well as the reactions of the American public were conducted and published respectively by the Congressional Budget Office and the Pew Research Center (CBO 2011; Kochhar et al. 2011). Their findings were not simply relegated to dusty libraries and academic journals, but found their way to local and national newspapers, radio stations, and television. Another significant result of the peak activities of the Occupy movement emerged: the word "class," as in socioeconomic class, became far less of a taboo in the American lexicon.

A December 2011 poll by the Pew Research Center stated that 48 percent of Americans agreed with the concerns raised by Occupy, although only 29 percent approved of the way the protests were being conducted. "The public is overwhelmingly critical of the fairness of the economic system. Most (77 percent) agree that there is too much power in the hands of a few rich people and corporations. And while a majority of Americans (58 percent) still say that 'most people who want to get ahead can make it if they are willing to work hard,' this is lower than at any point since the question was first asked in 1994." According to this poll, fewer Americans than ever continue to believe one of the main tenets of the American Dream that honest, hard work will result in the payoff of real economic success. However, despite these significant changes in opinion, 58 percent of Americans do not think that the United States is divided into the "Haves" and "Have-nots," as opposed to 38 percent who do think the country is divided that way (Pew Research Center 2010).

The 2011 report of the nonpartisan Congressional Budget Office (CBO), titled *Trends in the Distribution of Household Income Between 1979 and 2007*, confirmed that income inequality had grown in the United States:

- The top 1 percent of earners more than doubled their share of the nation's income over the previous three decades.
- Since the 1970s, government policies and programs have increasingly done less to reduce this uneven distribution of income.
- Federal benefit payments are doing less to even out the distribution of income, because an increased percentage of benefits, such as Social Security, are directed to a population such as older Americans, regardless of their income.
- From 1979 to 2007, with figures adjusted for inflation, the after-tax income of the 1 percent with the highest income increased by 275 percent, while the average after-tax income of the poorest fifth of the population increased by only 18 percent. For the three-fifths of the population considered in the middle class, after-tax income increased by only 40 percent. (CBO 2011)

The *New York Times* noted, "Among the factors cited as contributing to the rapid growth of income at the top were the structure of executive compensation; the increasing size of the financial services industry; and the growing role of capital gains, which go disproportionately to higher-income households" (Lowrey 2012).

In the next section of the chapter, we consider how entertainment media reflect social and economic class; what messages about class are conveyed through characters, themes, plots, and lyrics; and how popular media may reinforce or challenge some of the myths about socioeconomic class in the United States. As we examine entertainment media, it is important to keep making the connections between your own life experiences and your understanding of concepts, theories, and history about class.

ENTERTAINMENT MEDIA AND CLASS

Although some people raised in the United States are aware of class divisions, others have had little exposure to information, analysis, and understanding about social and economic class. Their personal experiences and formal education have taught them that there are no class divisions or class barriers in the United States. The concept of class is associated with other countries, other cultures, other societies, and the concept of a U.S. class system seems out of reach. In short, to some of us, class is invisible.

In the first two sections of this chapter, we have examined personal experience and have reconstructed knowledge in a way that explains some theories of the existence of class in the United States and how it operates. In this section we will take a close look at entertainment media's depiction of class and the messages that we, the media audience and consumers, receive. We will explore several questions about the relationship of entertainment media and class:

- How do television, film, and popular music depict characters in various occupations and different levels of income?
- What kinds of themes and messages about social and economic status are conveyed in popular media?
- How do the media images of occupation, income, and status compare to U.S. demographic realities regarding occupation, income, and status?
- How do media ownership and control and the organization of entertainment media impact the depiction of class?

These issues will be analyzed in several different ways:

- simple content analysis of class depiction in popular media to analyze characters and themes
- review of research about entertainment media and class
- analysis of the media industry itself, if and how the way it is structured and whom it employs reflect class within the industry, and if and how the industry's class structure may influence the messages about class in the media
- the overall messages conveyed about class and their impact on audiences

Content analysis, message system analysis, media literacy, and cultural studies will be the main entertainment assessment theories and tools used to examine these issues.

As we investigate fictional characters and themes in popular film, television, and music, it is important to keep in mind the ways that entertainment media serve to socialize us and reinforce cultural beliefs and norms. As we tease out images and messages about class, we will often be going against the grain of what we have been explicitly taught and what we have internalized as fact and truth. When our analysis is over, it will be your task to turn on the cognitive dissonance meter and determine if and how to integrate this new information into what you already "know."

Prime-Time Television and Class

It is your turn again. Use the content analysis in Media Activity 3.1 to observe some of the ways in which class is conveyed in prime-time television. When you have completed it, follow the step-by-step procedure and total the data you have collected and calculate the percentages. When you complete the content analysis, ask the following questions:

- Do most of the characters hold high-status occupations, low-status occupations, or middle-status occupations?
- Are there more than 50 percent of the characters in any one of these status categories?
- Do most of the major characters have low income or no income, middle income, or upper income?

If most of the characters are in low-status occupations with low incomes, the characters can be characterized largely as working-class. If most of the characters are in mid-level occupations with middle income, they can be characterized as largely middle-class. If most of the characters have high-status occupations and high incomes, they can be characterized as largely upper-income or owning-class. What messages do you think your sample conveys about economic status and class? To investigate further, you can ask the question: To what degree does this class depiction reinforce or challenge the classic American Dream? If you are interested in examining even further, you can ask questions about appearance, personality, integrity, intelligence, and other characteristics and whether the character is overall characterized as a "good guy" or a "bad guy." You can then see if any of these characteristics correlate with the person's income level and socioeconomic class and determine what, if any, messages are being conveyed.

In Chapter 1, we discussed the way that entertainment television is organized. To recap, television scripts in the United States turn into television programs in a way that is primarily based on financial considerations. Focus groups and other studies are often used to determine the potential popularity of a new TV program. If the program is popular, it will sell more commercial time; the higher the program is rated by the Nielsen consumer surveys, the more the network can charge for commercials. As network television has evolved, its financial success has been based on competing first with the film industry, then VCRs, then cable, then the Internet, then DVRs, and so on. As a result, it has become an increasingly competitive commercial venture.

Media Activity 3.1

**Content Analysis of Characters' Occupation
and Income in Prime-Time Television**

Instructions

Step One: Choose a minimum of three current fictional narrative television programs. These programs can be dramas or comedies. Complete the items below about major characters by selecting the response that most closely resembles the character you are analyzing. Major characters are those characters without whom the plot would make little or no sense.

   The larger the sample of prime-time television reviewed, the more revealing the results will be. You may either choose a larger sample for your individual analysis or work with a class or a group to review more programs. If you work with a group, be sure that no television program is analyzed twice and that the sample is comprised of currently aired programs. You will need to copy the codebook below to have enough copies for each program that you view and record.

Step Two: When you are done recording, respond to all of the items in the codebook below, for each major character in the programs you've viewed.

Step Three: When you have finished tallying all of the major characters of all the television programs in your sample, add the totals of all of the characters you have coded in each of the categories. For example, how many of the characters are unemployed? How many are in the category of clerical workers, technicians, salespersons, and craftsworkers? And so on.

Step Four: Then add together the following:

Occupation:
For poor/low income and working-class: add together A and B
For middle class/income: add together C and D (D being upper middle class)
For upper income or owning class: E only
Uncategorized: add together F and G

Income:
Income definitions for the purposes of this activity:
   Poor or low income is defined as a character's income that is clearly and observably insufficient to support one or more basic needs, including safe housing, and sufficient food, clothing, transportation, etc. The individual may be involuntarily unemployed or "underemployed," working in a low-pay job with few or no benefits.
   An individual is defined as *working class* if he or she works in a steady job with moderate income, which may be sufficient to meet the most basic housing, health, and clothing

Media Activity 3.1 *(continued)*

needs or may fall slightly short of adequate. According to this definition, individuals who are working class have little power or control over their work life, which often translates into having limited or no control over their life choices.

Upper income or owning class is defined as a character's income and/or wealth and position in life that clearly and observably allows a standard of living with expensive housing and private education, expensive clothing, cars, vacations, and the resources to have access to many other privileges and benefits. These individuals may have earned and/or inherited their wealth and are characterized by clear and observable choices of whether or not to work. Their wealth allows them the option not to work, and they have far more power and control over their lives and life choices than do people with other income levels. Their positions and/or wealth often mean that they have some power or control over other people's lives as well.

Middle class or middle income is defined as those individuals whose observable income, employment, housing, education level, and so on fall somewhere between working class and owning class. While this category is often broken down into upper middle class, lower middle class, etc., in general, these individuals have income that is anywhere from adequate to more than adequate to meet basic needs. By employment position and/or income, they may have access to resources that can buy them some of life's privileges and some level of control over their life choices. Middle-class individuals are generally characterized as having worked hard to earn whatever income they have and the limited opportunities this earning power can purchase.

For poor/low income and working-class: add together A and B
For middle class/income: add together C and D (D being upper middle class)
For upper income or owning class: E only
Uncategorized: add together F and G

Step Five: Finally, figure the percentages for each of the categories in Step Four to determine the socioeconomic class and income of each of the major characters.

Name of program _____
Date originally aired   _____
Day of the week _____
Time _____
Network _____/_____

Major Character #1 Name _____

1. *Occupation:*
    a.   unemployed
    b.   clerical worker, technician, salesperson, craftsworker   _____
    c.   store or shop owner, low-ranking professional (nurse, police officer,
         teacher, social worker), middle manager, independent farm owner   _____

Media Activity 3.1 *(continued)*

    d. business executive, upper manager, high-ranking professional
       (lawyer, doctor, architect) _____

    e. owner of major business or corporation, inherited wealth, mega-star
       athlete, entertainer, or other extremely wealthy celebrity _____

    f. unknown _____

    g. other (please indicate) _____ _____

2. *Income:*
    a. clearly very poor or no income _____
    b. clearly low income, struggling to make ends meet _____
    c. clearly middle income, not wealthy but comfortable _____
    d. upper middle income, comfortable plus some luxury _____
    e. wealth or high income, supporting a luxurious lifestyle _____
    f. unknown _____
    g. other (please indicate) _____ _____

Major Character #2 Name _____

3. *Occupation:*
    a. unemployed _____
    b. clerical worker, technician, salesperson, craftsworker _____
    c. store or shop owner, low-ranking professional (nurse, police officer,
       teacher, social worker), middle manager, independent farm owner _____
    d. business executive, upper manager, high-ranking professional
       (lawyer, doctor, architect) _____
    e. owner of major business or corporation, inherited wealth, mega-star
       athlete, entertainer, or other extremely wealthy celebrity _____
    f. unknown _____
    g. other (please indicate) _____ _____

4. *Income:*
    a. very poor or no income _____
    b. low income, struggling to make ends meet _____
    c. middle income, not wealthy but comfortable _____
    d. upper middle income, comfortable plus some luxury _____
    e. wealth or high income, supporting a luxurious lifestyle _____
    f. unknown _____
    g. other (please indicate) _____ _____

Major Character #3 Name _____

5. *Occupation:*
    a. unemployed _____

Media Activity 3.1 *(continued)*

   b. clerical worker, technician, salesperson, craftsworker   _____

   c. store or shop owner, low-ranking professional (nurse, police officer, teacher, social worker), middle manager, independent farm owner   _____

   d. business executive, upper manager, high-ranking professional (lawyer, doctor, architect)   _____

   e. owner of major business or corporation, inherited wealth, mega-star athlete, entertainer, or other extremely wealthy celebrity   _____

   f. unknown   _____

   g. other (please indicate) _____   _____

6. *Income:*

   a. clearly very poor or no income   _____

   b. clearly low income, struggling to make ends meet   _____

   c. clearly middle income, not wealthy but comfortable   _____

   d. upper middle income, comfortable plus some luxury   _____

   e. wealth or high income, supporting a luxurious lifestyle   _____

   f. unknown   _____

   g. other (please indicate) _____   _____

Major Character #4 Name _____

7. *Occupation:*

   a. unemployed   _____

   b. clerical worker, technician, salesperson, craftsworker   _____

   c. store or shop owner, low-ranking professional (nurse, police officer, teacher, social worker), middle manager, independent farm owner   _____

   d. business executive, upper manager, high-ranking professional (lawyer, doctor, architect)   _____

   e. owner of major business or corporation, inherited wealth, mega-star athlete, entertainer, or other extremely wealthy celebrity   _____

   f. unknown   _____

   g. other (please indicate) _____   _____

8. *Income:*

   a. clearly very poor or no income   _____

   b. clearly low income, struggling to make ends meet   _____

   c. clearly middle income, not wealthy but comfortable   _____

   d. upper middle income, comfortable plus some luxury   _____

   e. wealth or high income, supporting a luxurious lifestyle   _____

   f. unknown   _____

   g. other (please indicate) _____   _____

Advertising has a growing influence on network television scripts, content, plots, and characters; scriptwriters often anticipate this influence as they develop and tweak scripts that they hope to sell. Advertisers and network executives make their decisions based on a combination of the quality of the script, the targeted audience, their interest in the script, and what types of programs are most likely to sell the products promoted in commercials. The pressure for ratings of the program and higher rates that can be charged for commercial time absorbs a large part of this equation (Alper 2005).

Early commercial television featured prime-time programs that included both working-class and middle-class characters and families. In the 1950s and early 1960s, these programs often portrayed the American Dream as the pursuit of a better life. Working-class male and female characters in programs such as *I Remember Mama*, *The Goldbergs*, and *The Life of Riley* were frequently depicted as hardworking people striving to provide a better life for their children. By the late twentieth century, successful achievement of the American Dream on prime-time television meant living a robust consumer lifestyle and landing squarely in the middle or upper class. This period was characterized by fewer depictions of working-class people, more standard stereotypes, and an inevitable suggestion that to be stuck in the working class was the equivalent of failure. Some of the most frequent stereotypes of late twentieth- and early twenty-first-century working-class TV characters were lack of intelligence and bad taste, which often meant big hair, unfashionable clothes, white bread, sleeveless undershirts, and low-rent beer.

Richard Butsch analyzed 262 family-based situation comedies from 1946 to 1990. This study revealed that 11 percent of the heads of households were blue-collar, clerical, or service workers—plainly working-class—and that 70 percent of the heads of households were clearly middle-class (Butsch 1992). Several years later, Butsch analyzed the same information for family-based situation comedies through the 2003–2004 television season. According to Butsch, "'Plus ca change, plus c'est la meme chose'" (the more things change, the more they stay the same). While there have been variations and exceptions, the stock character of the unintelligent, ineffectual, even buffoonish working-class man has persisted as the dominant image. "In the prime-time tapestry, he is contrasted with consistently competent working-class wives and children and manly middle-class fathers—a composite image in which working-class men are demasculinized and their class status justified" (Butsch 2003).

In comparison, Butsch found clear changes in the representation of middle-class characters. In the early years of television, middle-class adults in sitcoms were portrayed as nearly perfect and virtually always white. Both men and women were perfect parents, while the men were also excellent providers, fair disciplinarians, rational, and, with the possible exception of Ozzie Nelson, smart and competent. The women were generally pretty (though often bland), impeccably dressed, impeccable housekeepers, warm, loving, nurturing, and, with the exception of Lucy, deferential to their husbands. Over the years, the depictions of middle-class adults and parents "progressively broadened to include a wide range of characters and situations" (Butsch 2003). The range of middle-class adult characters from silly and foolish to smart, sophisticated, and successful, from simple characters to complex characters, means that TV viewers are not locked into repetitive middle-class stereotypes. As we discussed in Chapter 1, generally when a particular group, in this case middle-class characters, is portrayed abundantly in entertainment media, the characters' personalities, jobs, physical appearance, and so on are more varied and diverse. The more diversity there is within the group portrayed, the less likely that narrow images and stereotypes will be conveyed. And the fewer the stereotypes, the less they are internalized by the television audience and the less they end up posing as the "truth" about a group. In this sequence of the development of characters and their influence on the thoughts of the audience, middle-class white characters have been largely protected from damaging stereotypes.

The contrast of the simple, consistent, and persistent images of working-class adults means that these images and stereotypes have endured over time and are more likely to be embedded in the memories and beliefs of those of us who are heavy television viewers. Unless we are extremely conscious of the possibility that these working-class portrayals are stereotypes, they will follow the same sequence from the TV to the audience but with a different result. The stereotypes of working-class characters often pose as the truth in the way that we think of these men and women.

In 1992, professionals constituted only 15 percent of the U.S. workforce, but on television, 44.5 percent of the families were headed by professionals (Butsch 1992, 387). Another study of the 1992–1993 television season demonstrated that 25 percent of all characters were in lower-status occupations. These characters served "neutral plot functions" and were "usually relegated to the sidelines of the story." The researchers found that doctors, lawyers, and other people holding executive or professional jobs populate prime-time television at a significantly higher level than in real life (Lichter, Lichter, and Rothman 1994, 186).

In order to understand this phenomenon of overrepresentation of the wealthy and underrepresentation of the working class and poor, we will take a journey through the years of prime-time television's portrayal of economic class and examine the characters, the depiction of the American Dream, and other economic themes, and analyze the impact of the industry's organization and economy on these messages.

In the early 1950s, working-class people in some situation comedies continued traditions begun in radio. These characters were primarily defined by their ethnicity: *I Remember Mama* (1949–1956) featured the family of a Norwegian carpenter; *The Life of Riley* (1949–1950), an Irish American airplane riveter and his wife and children; and *The Goldbergs* (1949–1954), a Jewish tailor and his family. But even the Goldbergs moved to the suburbs and began to buy appliances on credit (Marc 1997, 105). "As these shows came to the end of their long production runs in the late 1950s, blue-collar ethnic families virtually disappeared from prime time. The only remaining working-class characters were often servants who were typically treated as honorary members of bourgeois families such as Hazel, Grindl, and Mr. French of *Family Affair*. From the mid-1950s until the end of the 1960s, domestic situation comedy narrative was thoroughly dominated by professional, college-educated WASPs [white Anglo-Saxon Protestants]" (Marc 1997, 147).

The suburban families in situation comedies of the 1950s and 1960s, such as *The Adventures of Ozzie and Harriet* (1954–1960), *Father Knows Best* (1954–1960), *Leave It*

The Honeymooners (1955): Bus driver Ralph Cramden and sewer worker Ed Norton constantly scheme (and fail) to hit the financial jackpot and escape lives limited by their meager incomes. Yet Cramden and Norton always wind up back on the economic margins. [Left to right: Jackie Gleason as Ralph Cramden; Art Carney as Ed Norton, Audrey Meadows as Alice Cramden; and Joyce Randolph as Trixie Norton.] *(Source: Courtesy of Getty Images. Copyright © 1955 CBS Worldwide, Inc. Used by permission of Getty Images.)*

to Beaver (1957–1963), and *My Three Sons* (1960–1972), all demonstrated clear signs of being middle-class. They were "upscale, socially conservative, politically inactive, and essentially kind to one another and their neighbors" (Himmelstein 1994, 122).

Far more rare, urban situation comedies of the same period, including such classics as *The Honeymooners* (1955–1956) and *I Love Lucy* (1951–1957), were distinct from their suburban counterparts. The standard suburban situation comedies of the 1950s and 1960s involved middle- to upper-middle-class families in suburban homes; the characters and plot were centered around a nuclear family with a stay-at-home wife, a working dad, and a few children. Popular programs such as *Leave It to Beaver* and *The Donna Reed Show* followed this formula. In contrast, both *The Honeymooners* and *I Love Lucy* were set in urban areas in apartments, and even after Lucy and Ricky had a son, "Little Ricky," the action and character development rarely revolved around family life.

In addition to the talented actors and solid comic writing on *The Honeymooners*, one of its main distinctions was that it was one of the few remaining popular prime-time programs that revolved around struggling, working-class lives. *The Honeymooners'* main characters—Ralph Kramden, bus driver, and Ed Norton, sewer worker—were clearly urban, working-class characters. They were constantly coming up with preposterous schemes that would get them out of the sewer and the bus to a better life. Of all the urban comedies listed above, *The Honeymooners* was the only one whose characters seemed destined to live on meager incomes in extremely spare and cheaply furnished apartments, with no realistic hope for upward mobility. With this one exception, the vast majority of the urban comedies from the 1950s to the 1970s reinforced the same class themes as their suburban middle-class counterparts.

"Whether mildly cynical or bordering on euphoria, at the core of all these comedic works is the myth of eternal progress." From the Cuban-born, New York City nightclub owner and singer and his ditzy wife scheming to get into show business in *I Love Lucy* to the PhD-level psychologist Bob Hartley of *The Bob Newhart Show* to the dry-cleaning entrepreneur and social climber George Jefferson of *The Jeffersons*, "the social construct of the good life is manifest in these works—an urban American vision framed by the achievements of commerce and the ideology of equal opportunity" (Himmelstein 1994, 135). These examples of early prime-time television represent strong reinforcement of the American Dream.

You will recall that ideology is a constructed belief system that explains a version of reality. Television conveys the dominant cultural ideology through the establishment of myths. "Myths occur primarily through the telling of stories that serve to underscore understandings of power, about the fundamental order of things which work against any alternative understandings or ideologies" (Himmelstein 1994, 5). The establishment of the "myth" of equal opportunity disguises and camouflages the reality of the economic inequities present in U.S. society.

The research regarding television's role in the creation and perpetuation of myth and ideology is steeped in the tradition of cultural studies, which takes an explicit liberal or left political perspective. These theories criticize entertainment media because popular film and television almost always reinforce the dominant culture and leave little room for alternative ideologies. While other researchers challenge the observations of cultural studies analysts, they still maintain that "television has transcended its role as mere entertainment to become a potent force shaping everyday life" and that "the most innocuous sitcom carries messages about how our society works and how its citizens should behave" (Lichter, Lichter, and Rothman 1994, 12).

Norman Lear's *All in the Family* (1971–1979) brought the Bunkers, a white working-class family of unknown ethnicity, into the living rooms of America. As we learned in Chapter 1, Lear's character Archie Bunker was intended to reflect the resistance to the movements for social change in the 1960s and 1970s. Archie was clearly a bigot—he disliked people of color and "ethnic" people; he was against "women's lib" and any other movement for liberation. According to researcher Richard Butsch, while Archie Bunker stood with Ralph Kramden, Fred Flintstone, and Homer Simpson as a "white male working-class buffoon" (Butsch 1995, 403), many audiences read him differently.

To liberal audiences, Archie was just what Norman Lear intended—a symbol of the barriers to movements for equality. To more conservative and some working-class audi-

Good Times (1974–1979) depicted the Evans family's life in public housing, with son J.J. as the series clown. Was the series realism with humor thrown in? Or was it filled with race and class stereotypes and blatant misinformation about the "fun of poverty"? [Left to right: the Evans Family: James (John Amos), Florida (Esther Rolle), J.J. (Jimmy Walker), and Michael (Ralph Carter), and neighbor Willona Woods (Ja'Net DuBois).] *(Source: Courtesy of Getty Images. Copyright © 2005 CBS Worldwide, Inc. Used by permission of Getty Images.)*

ences, Archie was neither a buffoon nor a bigot, but a hero of the working class. "Archie's animus is mitigated by the fact that he is the sole breadwinner in a house of four adults, a relevant reminder to any high-minded, middle-class viewers who may be watching that a contempt for hardhatism does not change the fact that workers like Archie are the people who make civilization and culture possible" (Marc 1997, 151).

According to many researchers, *The Cosby Show* (1984–1992) marked a critical shift in how prime-time television portrayed class and the relationship between class and the American Dream. One team of researchers conducted an extensive study of the content, audience impact, and ideology of *The Cosby Show*. The research team, Lewis and Jhally, used content analysis, focus groups, and a cultural studies approach to analyze the phenomenon of this successful series. As you read and assess the conclusions of their study, you may bristle at the criticism of such a popular, entertaining, and highly regarded television series. It will be interesting to take into account that Bill and Camille Cosby funded and supported this critical research.

Different economic classes had very different readings of *The Cosby Show*. Middle- and upper-middle-class viewers, whether white or black, saw the show as being about people like them. Working- and lower-middle-class viewers read the program as universal and classless—about people not like them, by wealth or status, but still struggling to balance work, marriage, and raising children. Both groups interpreted *The Cosby Show* as evidence that anyone in the United States could make it economically (Jhally and Lewis 1992, 28–29).

The intent of the creators of *The Cosby Show* was to convey a positive image of a successful African American family. But like *All in the Family* before it, there was an unanticipated audience impact:

> Television envisages class not as a series of barriers but as a series of hurdles that can be overcome. That view promotes the idea of the American dream. Although the American dream was not invented for television, television appears to nourish and sustain it. We see countless examples of people making it, but few examples of people (apart from the lazy, deviant, or generally undeserving) prevented from making it. This makes it easy for us to think of the individual enterprise that defines the American dream as the organizing principle of the social structure—and difficult for us to conceive or articulate the idea of inequality of opportunity. (Jhally and Lewis 1992, 73)

According to this study, *The Cosby Show* was significant in that it marked a time in which television began to portray few, if any, barriers to the American Dream—particularly for African Americans. The ease of economic success depicted has had an impact on audiences.

The researchers concluded that *The Cosby Show* conveyed an unintended and unanticipated conservative ideology. This conservative ideology says that neither class nor race is a barrier to personal and economic success in the United States. If people work hard and are virtuous, like the fictitious Huxtables, success is theirs. The politically conservative message, according to Jhally and Lewis, is that since achievement and success are based on individual merit and hard work, there is no need for compensatory funds or programs that address structural barriers to success. In concrete terms, the researchers found that, by and large, white audiences concluded that if a fictional family like the Huxtables could be so successful in a multiracial world, racism must not be such a problem anymore and affirmative action was an unnecessary program that favored blacks over whites in hiring, acceptance to college, and so on. By contrast, a large portion of the African American audience members in the study took the following message from *The Cosby Show*: Failure is an individual responsibility; structural racial barriers that have been a problem to blacks in the past have been seriously weakened and blacks need to take responsibility for their own successes and failures and not blame them on racism. The one major message of *The Cosby Show* that white and black audiences shared was the idea that the civil rights movement had "won" and that programs such as affirmative action, intended to level the playing field to correct past racial bias, were a crutch and no longer necessary (Jhally and Lewis 1992).

The Cosby Show was groundbreaking in both its success and its portrayal of an upper-income African American family. Its audience impact was significant for two reasons.

First, its enormous viewing audience demonstrated the potentially wide appeal of African American characters and themes. Second, since, during the time that *The Cosby Show* was on the air, African American characters and programs were so rare, there was little range in characters' income and success. Thus, the Huxtables took on a supercharged meaning in conveying the "black experience" and its possibilities. If *The Cosby Show* had run alongside five other television series with African American families from different income levels, its significance and impact would have been less dramatic and audience members of all races would have seen a variety of ways in which the balance of individual responsibility and racial bias operated in the lives of African Americans.

While there are distinct patterns that portray Americans as middle-class and above on prime-time television, there are notable exceptions. Programs such as *Laverne and Shirley* (1981–1983), *Roseanne* (1988–1997), *The Simpsons* (1989–), *Married with Children* (1987–1997), and *The King of Queens* (1998–2007) portrayed working-class families as the centerpiece of the program and have been successful. We'll assess a few of these series to examine patterns and images that conveyed messages about class.

Laverne and Shirley was distinct from the standard middle-class sitcom formula. The main characters were working-class, single, and female. The two women worked in a factory and struggled to survive economically. These facts alone distinguished the program from most situation comedies. But what set *Laverne and Shirley* apart from the rest most clearly was that they talked about, bemoaned, and joked about being working-class and their conversations rang true: "The Fonz [a popular character in the 1974–1984 TV series, *Happy Days*], Laverne, and Shirley are different [from previous portrayals of the working class]. They have their self-mockeries, but these are leavening features, not the point. They are aware of class and of how it functions in their lives. And they can summon values, which, though not reserved exclusively to their own class, seem securely rooted in a sense of class experience" (Sklar 1980, 16).

Both *The Simpsons* and *Married with Children* clearly feature working-class families who regularly lament their lack of money; they also share many parallels in reinforcing working-class stereotypes. The children in both series are irreverent and often disrespectful to their parents. Neither Marge Simpson nor Peg Bundy works outside the home. Both Homer Simpson and Al Bundy play the role of the buffoon. "In most middle-class series, there is no buffoon. More typically, both parents are wise and work cooperatively to raise their children in practically perfect families, as in *Father Knows Best*, *The Brady Bunch*, and *The Bill Cosby Show*. In the few middle-class series featuring a buffoon, it is the dizzy wife, such as Lucy. The professional/managerial husband is the sensible, mature, partner—thus inverting gender status in working-class but not middle-class" (Butsch 1992, 404). The working-class characters in these series do little to challenge the dominant ideology and the myth of the American Dream. Homer and Al are foolish and dumb, lacking the initiative and virtue that are prerequisites to the American Dream. The audience does not expect them to succeed, and because they are not particularly admirable people, we believe they get what they deserve.

Roseanne was an interesting departure from the stereotypical or invisible ways that working-class people have been portrayed on prime-time television. Even the set of *Rose-*

anne was carefully constructed with furniture ordered from the Sears catalog, inexpensive knickknacks, and clutter that seemed familiar to many working families. The creators of *Roseanne*, including Roseanne Barr herself, insisted on authenticity in the appearance of the set, the characters, and the plot. All of these creative decisions in *Roseanne* marked a deviation from the conventional formulas of family-based situation comedies before it (Mayerle 1994, 102).

> Although its blue-collar setting is not shared by all of its viewers, the problems of surviving in post-Reagan America (e.g., with a mortgage, three children, two wage-earners, and employment problems) has a broad appeal. . . . Roseanne and Dan Conner, as well as others with whom they interact in the series, experience feelings of anxiety and depression in their lives, but they do not have the time or desire to really dwell on them. Their response is not to become more introspective, but to go bowling on a Friday night, to share a six-pack of beer with friends while pretending to fix the truck, to go to the mall even though they cannot afford to buy anything.

Roseanne thus flies in the face of the pop culture establishment by its irreverent and candid putdowns, as well as in the face of the series' sponsors, most of whose products the Conner family cannot afford to buy (Mayerle 1994, 113).

While it is clear that Roseanne is the main character in the show, her husband, Dan, is an unusual male working-class character. Dan has many business failures and is constantly struggling along with Roseanne to support their family. As a couple, they fight, laugh, make love, and playfully tease and torment each other with sarcastic humor. Dan and Roseanne work together, and as a man Dan is portrayed as neither a failure nor a buffoon.

Given the successful long run of *Roseanne*, an obvious question is why this program was so unique. Why hasn't it been copied like so many other television series? These questions can be analyzed by exploring three contributing factors: the role of the network, the organization of decision making, and the culture of the creative team (Butsch 1992, 405).

According to one study, *Roseanne* "provided its audience with critical humor to challenge hegemonic representations of class and gender" (Senzani 2010, 229). Programs of the 1990s were still bound and contained by the rules of the game according to the TV goddess of advertising. But sitcoms such as *Roseanne*, *Married with Children*, and *The Simpsons* used satire, creativity, and good writing to build an audience that essentially paid for commercial time. This earned these programs the right to challenge "the sanitized, middle-class shows of the 80s" (Senzani 2010, 233). While on one level Homer Simpson and Al Bundy carried on the stereotype of the working-class man as buffoon, on another level their characters served as caricatures, satirizing images of class.

Roseanne used biting humor as well as instances of class consciousness to expose and challenge the hegemony of class and offer a different image of what it would mean to be a smart, sassy, irreverent, and successful working woman. Earlier in the chapter, we revisited the concept of hegemony as a process that works by securing the consent of those who are not in power—not by force but through socialization of values that get taught at home, in school, and through the media. Hegemony is typically neither conspiratorial nor visible. One of the chief ways to examine what we have been socialized to believe is true through hegemony is to make those values, those "truths," visible. But without a magic wand, how do we convert the invisible into something we can see, examine, and reflect upon in order to make our own independent decisions about what is true?

Some episodes of *Roseanne* used smart writing and humor as the magic "anti-hegemony" wand to expose alternate ways of seeing class and, in particular, working-class people. In one episode, Roseanne and other working-class women are employed at a plastics factory when a new boss begins to increase production quotas to an impossible level. Roseanne makes a deal with "the devil." In exchange for lower quotas, she agrees to an attitude adjustment of showing more respect and cordiality to the boss and encourages her coworkers to do the same. Roseanne carries her end of the bargain, but the boss double-crosses her and raises the quotas again. Roseanne's response to the raised quotas is to raise hell: after giving a fiery speech about fairness and equity, she leads a walkout of the women working in the factory. This episode was a powerful example of how the program and character stayed true to the framework of humor and sarcasm while simultaneously demonstrating how working-class women have historically been restrained through threatening their livelihood and ability to support their families and offering a model of how these same women can work collectively to change their circumstances. In the episode, class and gender images intersect, and the audience sees different possibilities of what it looks like to be courageous, empowered, and still funny as women who are part of the working class.

Grace Under Fire (1993–1998) was another comedy centered on a working-class family. This time the situation involved a divorced, southern, single woman, a recovering alcoholic, raising her three children while working as the only woman in an oil refinery. Sounds like a lot of laughs, doesn't it? The economic success of *Roseanne* paved the way for ABC to envision the success of this program, using humor, smart writing, and good comic actors combined with serious societal issues such as alcoholism, spousal abuse, on-the-job sexual harassment, and the economic challenges of a working-class family relying on one salary.

The ironic humor and the impeccable timing of stand-up comic Brett Butler, who plays Grace, are used for laughs that mock the odd encounters of her life and often have no political or economic observations or bite to them. When Grace reports to her friends about her umpteenth weird blind date, she describes him as a guy who "wore a little metal hat that prevented Ted Koppel from controlling his thoughts" (O'Connor 1993, 2). Encounters with her friends, next-door neighbor Naomi and local pharmacist Russell, often take place over a cup of coffee in Grace's kitchen in between helping kids with homework and trouble-shooting stolen bicycles, hurt feelings, and trouble at school. Despite an abundance of challenges, the situations in *Grace Under Fire* undermine another insidious stereotype of working-class families as ignorant and dysfunctional. Grace is well read, enjoys classical music, and is part of a family-like community who listen to each other and care for each other without becoming syrupy and sentimental. They are also crabby with each other and verbally snipe at each other when they are tired.

Is this setting in *Grace Under Fire* (1993–1998) a living room, playroom, orderly chaos, or chaotic order? For Grace, "having it all" means living on the edge of personal and financial independence, being rid of an alcoholic husband, embracing good friends, and having the strength to be willing not to shrink herself in order to be with a man. [Left to right: the Kelly family: Jean, the ex-mother-in-law (Peggy Rea), Libby (Kaitlin Cullum), Grace (Brett Butler), and baby Patrick (Dylan and Cole Sprouse).] *(Source: Courtesy of Getty Images. Copyright © 2009 American Broadcasting Companies, Inc. Used by permission of Getty Images. Photographer/© ABC/Getty Images.)*

Some of the one-liners and situations in *Grace Under Fire* underscore the challenges of working-class life, by teasing them out of invisibility along the same lines as *Roseanne*. When Grace is stopped for speeding, the police officer informs her that he is giving her a ticket, to which Grace replies, "Ticket? I can't even afford the car. Just shoot me and get it over with" (O'Connor 1993, 2). Lines like this emphasize that Grace's family and millions of others like hers, with no financial reserves or family backup, can be one speeding ticket away from poverty.

The King of Queens (1998–2007) was chronologically the last of the trilogy of the three most popular situation comedies that revolved around working-class families in the late twentieth and early twenty-first centuries. The messages it conveyed about class were quite different from those of *Roseanne* and *Grace Under Fire*. The characters Roseanne Conner and Grace Kelly were ripe with a blend of comic quips, dialogue, and situations that sweetened some of the bitterness of the serious topics the programs took on and the questions and criticism they raised about class inequities. By contrast, the character Doug Heffernan (Kevin James) was described by TV critics as "the Pillsbury Doughboy" and "an Average Joe." The success of the program itself was attributed to dialogue that reviewers described as funny, brisk, unpretentious, and perceptive (Fretts 1998; Heffernan 2007). Doug is a deliveryman for a company similar to UPS and his wife, Carrie, is a secretary at a law firm. Doug is happy watching sports on TV, eating, and drinking beer, which often conflicts with Carrie's desires to do things that are more cultured or at least appear to be so. What *The King of Queens* had in common with *Roseanne* and *Grace Under Fire* was a seasoned and likable stand-up comic and writers who knew funny. The messages of *The King of Queens* do not address the serious problems and challenges of working-class life and it is arguable whether the messages counter old stereotypes of the working class. Doug is often the brunt of humor in the program thanks to silly antics he employs to get away with doing something that he wants to do but that is frowned upon by Carrie. In this pattern, Doug is portrayed as a lovable buffoon, more childish than harmful.

The cost of producing prime-time television has become exorbitant, and only large corporations can afford this kind of production. The competition between the networks for ratings and advertising dollars is steep. Advertisers want prime time to feature characters that are likely to buy their products. The need to please advertisers and the competition between networks contribute to the push to minimize risks, which in turn drives content decisions and the hiring of creative personnel. All of this often pushes decision makers to stick with safe formulaic characters, plots, and themes and with creative personnel that have proven track records. "This proven talent then self-censor their work on the basis of a product image their previous experience tells them the networks will tolerate; creating an imaginary feedback loop between producers and network executives" (Butsch 1992, 406).

This analysis echoes that of highly regarded media analyst Ben Bagdikian, that there is no evil television conspiracy set up to ignore and stereotype working-class people, but rather a combination of several factors that add up to this result:

- Most of the people who create prime-time television are middle class and above.
- There is great competition between networks for advertising dollars.
- Advertisers want programs and characters that will promote the products they want to sell.
- Creative talent needs to comply with these demands in order to work.

These factors add up to a prime-time television industry and culture that will occasionally create a *Laverne and Shirley* or *Roseanne*, but largely sticks with the safer formulas that have worked over the years.

Popular Film

It is your turn again. For Chapter 3, we have condensed multiple media activities with other information into a comprehensive analysis of one film, as shown in the study questions for the chapter. This time you will need to take a trip to the local video store, the local Redbox, or Netflix or other websites to rent or download the 2005 film *Cinderella Man*, directed by Ron Howard and starring Russell Crowe, Renée Zellweger, and Paul

Giamatti. As you view the film, keep in mind the study questions at the end of this chapter, and answer them at the end of the film. The chapter questions are different from those in Chapters 1 and 2 in that they combine the analysis of the depiction of class in the film with some of the other important issues raised about social and economic class.

Cinderella Man preceded the official start of the Great Recession by almost two years. Critics and audiences generally regarded the film as entertaining and inspiring rather than as a cautionary tale. If it had been made a few years later, it might have struck a different collective national nerve and reverberated with significantly different meaning. Absent this context, *Cinderella Man* was a solid box office hit, grossing over $61 million and ranking forty-second in the top 100 box office hits for 2005 (Box Office Mojo 2005). Russell Crowe received nominations for Best Actor for the Golden Globe and Screen Actors Guild awards, and Paul Giamatti was nominated for Best Supporting Actor for the Academy Awards, Golden Globes, and Screen Actors Guild, winning the last-named award (Internet Movie Database 2005).

Set in the 1920s, *Cinderella Man* is based on the true story of boxer Jim Braddock (played by Crowe), who lives with his family in an upper-middle-class home in New Jersey. The camera takes us on a brief tour of the Braddock home and family, showing that everything and everyone is more than comfortable and only slightly short of plush. These brief opening scenes show clearly that this family is connected by their lighthearted approach to life and by their deep love for one another. As the film opens, Braddock, known as "The Bulldog of Bergen," has had a string of boxing victories and seems destined to make it to the top. But the year is 1929. In the same year that the stock market crash signals the beginning of the Great Depression and devastates the country, Braddock injures his hand, devastating his boxing career and causing a severe crash in the family's circumstances. Boxing is a business, and since bad boxing is bad business, the boxing commission revokes Braddock's license, effectively revoking his ability to earn even a meager income for his family.

Fifteen minutes into the film finds Braddock, his wife, Mae (played by Zellweger), and their three children living in a grim, cold, one-room basement apartment where food and rent money are scarce. Braddock joins hundreds of other men in their daily trek to the dock, to stand in a mob of desperate workers seeking a day's work and a day's wages. On the occasions that Braddock is one of the chosen few, he must carefully conceal his injured hand to avoid losing the little work he has.

According to film critic Roger Ebert, the film conveys far more than the messages in even the best boxing movies. Instead, the film reflects the human face of the individual and collective decline of a family into poverty and despair. The Braddocks' desperate situation "seems to weigh most heavily on the oldest son, Jay (Connor Price), who fears above all being sent away to live with 'rich' relatives. . . . He steals a sausage from the butcher shop, is caught, and then, in a scene typical of Braddock's gentle wisdom, is not punished by his father, but talked to, softly and earnestly, because his father instinctively knows why his son stole the sausage and that the kid's daring was almost noble" (Ebert 2005). As things get worse financially, Mae Braddock is forced to send the children to live temporarily with her sister. Swallowing his remaining pride, Braddock signs the family up for government relief and visits the members of the boxing commission, who are still living the high life, literally begging them for money so that he can bring his children home. Despite his brutal and often violent profession, Braddock is consistently portrayed as strong, peaceful, hardworking, and honest: the quintessential good man, filled with the kind of merit and virtue that Jennifer Hochschild describes as integral to success in the classic American Dream (Hochschild 1995).

Braddock is given the proverbial second chance at the American Dream when his manager finds him a single fight, which Braddock miraculously wins. This leads to the last leg of the family trip from riches to rags and back up again as Braddock wins fight after fight. When asked by reporters what inspires him, Braddock replies that he is "fighting for milk." He vividly remembers the looks on the faces of his hungry children and is determined that they will never have to look that way again. The Braddocks' embodiment of the American Dream earns Braddock the nickname "Cinderella Man," for the hope he represents to people still suffering through the Depression.

The fact that the film is based on a true story calls into question whether Braddock's Cinderella story, the epitome of the American Dream, serves as a symbol of what can happen to anyone in the United States if they follow the rules of the dream or if it is the exceptional story that brings false hope to the public. In the Chapter 3 study questions, you will be challenged to consider whether stories like this reflect realistic hope or create a myth that can eventually be devastating to people who do not make it.

Cinderella Man was a financially successful film that was accompanied by a modest share of prestigious nominations and awards along with solid reviews. As you view the film and complete the Chapter 3 study questions, we invite you to think about what messages this film sends to its wide audience. As we see Braddock's virtue and hard work in the film leading him to climb back up the ladder of financial success, the film introduces us to hundreds of nameless people who have been devastated by the Depression. Is their virtue or hard work somehow inferior to Braddock's? How does the film portray the classic American Dream as described by Hochschild? What messages does the audience receive about class and the American Dream? The credibility and hope of the American Dream looks very different to people depending on their economic position and their experience regarding whether hard work and virtue really do inevitably result in financial success. Think about the American Dream as portrayed in *Cinderella Man* as if you are looking through various lenses. To what degree does the American Dream seem like myth or reality depending on whether the lens is that of the Braddock family's realization of the American Dream, the perspective of those minor characters in the film and in reality who barely survived the Depression, and your own family's economic ups and/or downs. Where do you stand on whether the classic American Dream is a reality or a myth? How might the *Cinderella Man* story affect viewers who in the wake of the 2007–2009 recession are still struggling with unemployment in a tough economy, minus the Braddock happy ending? How might this story affect wealthy viewers who may have been socialized to believe that poverty is invariably the result of a lack of virtue and the presence of laziness?

Have the messages about class in *Cinderella Man* been consistent in popular films throughout motion picture history? Do these messages accurately reflect some of the truths about class mobility, inequities, and access to high-quality education and jobs with high status and high pay? How does the portrayal of socioeconomic class in film intersect with our own personal and family histories of where we worked, where we lived, and where we went to school?

Reflection on these questions and others, then, is our next task—to see, understand, and study a variety of film images about class. There are many critical analyses in the form of articles and books on the depiction of gender and race and sexual orientation in film, but very few on the portrayal of class in film. To see and understand some of the patterns, trends, and exceptions in this depiction, we will examine some key films that contain central images of class. We will examine trends over the last fifty-plus years and review mainstream box office draws as well as independently produced, less financially successful films about class. Most of these are available for rental or downloading at your local video store, Redbox, or services such as Netflix, so that you can read the analysis, see the film, and decide for yourself what you believe the messages about class to be.

A Brief History of Class in Feature Films

In the nineteenth century, many North Americans viewed themselves as workers or part of the working class. How did this class identity change and what role did film play in this shift?

In early twentieth-century silent films, class was a central theme. In 1910, 26 million people, or 30 percent of the U.S. population, went to the movies each week (Ross 1998, 11). At that point in history, popular film had not yet evolved to the strictly fictional, narrative entertainment format that we became accustomed to by the 1930s. Rather, many early silent films were unabashedly political, often explicitly setting out to persuade audiences to think in a particular way. The low cost of producing films made it possible for many different organizations to express their political positions through this new medium.

According to the *National Review*, a conservative weekly magazine, "Movies are the leading art form of our popular culture, with a unique ability to move and enlighten a mass audience" (Warren 1994, 53). The article, titled "The 100 Best Conservative Movies," touts the 1930s and 1940s as promoting important U.S. ideals such as "God and country, tradition and family, freedom and resistance to tyranny, individual achievement and the American Dream," commending these "movies that celebrate the creativity of business achievement, [and] depict the evils of Communism and collectivism." According to the *National Review*, these U.S. ideals were derailed in the 1970s in the "nihilistic themes and chaotic styles" of counterculture films such as *Midnight Cowboy* and *Easy Rider*. These traditional ideals then made a comeback in the late 1970s as the *Star Wars* trilogy once again portrayed the triumph of good over evil as the individual overcame great and even cosmic odds (Warren 1994, 53).

While critics on the left disagree with the politics of the *National Review*, they are in agreement about the power of visual images in film. Many popular films on labor and class presented the subjects negatively, but less mainstream films have shown them in a more balanced manner. "Yet, because we live in a culture that receives so much of its information (and ultimately derives so many of its opinions) from visual media, it is especially important to see, to understand and to study a variety of media images" (Zaniello 1996, 19).

Historically, film audiences in the early twentieth century were largely working-class and had access to hundreds of silent films about strikes and union organizing. "Social realism and political commentary are not the hallmarks of the modern movie industry. Yet there was a time when entertainment and political engagement did not seem incompatible, and when movies and Hollywood were not synonymous in the minds of most Americans. The movie industry began as a small-scale business with small Spartan theaters spread throughout the country and production facilities centered largely in New York, Philadelphia, and Chicago" (Ross 1998, 5).

The composition of the audience and the content of films changed after World War I for two key reasons. First, government authorities feared that radical ideas on the screen might trigger radical activities among workers. These concerns lead to a movement for censorship to keep strike films and other films that featured worker exploitation off the screen. The second major factor in the shift in film content and audience was that elaborate, ornate, and expensive movie palaces were constructed after the war, the price of admission went up, and the audience became largely middle-class. The content of films began to shift from class exploitation to "fantasies of love and harmony among the classes" (Ross 1998, 13, 18).

By the early 1920s, a small group of entrepreneurs transformed film production into a well-financed studio system with which the small-scale producers could not compete. This new system was now based more squarely on building audience and profit. Its new target audience was the middle class, a group with a larger disposable income than the working class. The newer, larger-scale producers made a judgment that more money could be made if the content of films was less controversial and addressed more marketable topics such as "the delights of the new consumer society" (Ross 1998, 11). From 1920 to 1929, romance and fantasy films outnumbered labor films 308 to 67. "Dreams of wealth, mobility, respect, and luxury could all be found on the screen, but love between the classes remained the cornerstone of these films. All problems, both personal and societal, could be solved through love; and true love was strong enough to break down any class barriers. After all, class was an artificial construct, love was real" (Ross 1998, 199). Thus, class conflict virtually disappeared from the big screen.

Despite this fundamental shift in Hollywood film production, the films during the Depression in the 1930s were mixed:

> Although the era is known for glossy entertainment that aimed to keep filmgoers' minds off their economic troubles, it also produced a number of films directly addressing the Depression and its consequences. Within four years of the country's economic collapse, for example, the studios released such pictures as "I am a Fugitive from a Chain Gang," with its imagery of out-of-work veterans forced to steal for a living; "Wild Boys of the Road," in which a group of teens become hobos; "American Madness," an early Frank Capra movie featuring a run on a bank; and

"Gold Diggers of 1933" and its unforgettable "Remember My Forgotten Man" number, which includes a scene of former American doughboys [soldiers who served in World War I] standing in a breadline. (Beale 2010)

Yet the overall transformation of the film industry from an enterprise that supported small businesses with a wide array of agendas and political standpoints to a studio system whose main purpose was to entertain and be commercially successful was complete by the 1930s. This shift had an enormous impact on how class was portrayed in film. Much of popular film has continued to praise the American work ethic and the American Dream while by and large depicting working-class people and their organizations as invisible, lazy, and/or worthy of serious or humorous pity or contempt.

Since films began to talk and the Hollywood system began to prevail, there have been two dominant class themes in popular film. The first of these themes is that of cross-class romance in which true love conquers all. This is depicted in films such as *Pretty Woman* (1990), starring Julia Roberts and Richard Gere, in which a successful but hardened executive undergoes a humanizing transformation as he falls in love with a poor but good-hearted prostitute who teaches him how to love and gets the happy ending she longs for and a lot of expensive clothes in the process. *Pretty Woman* reached an enormous audience as the number four box office hit of 1990 with a domestic take-home profit of more than $178 million. While it would be fair to say that most audiences would not take home the literal message that beautiful prostitutes will end up with the handsome corporate bad guy turned prince, the film does reinforce a common message about relationships that travel across the proverbial tracks . . . *love does conquer all*. It is up to you to determine if this message is a myth that creates unrealistic expectations or if it is one of many credible and plausible outcomes of cross-class relationships.

The second prevalent theme supports the American Dream by the portrayal of the industrious individual's successful struggle against difficult odds to achieve financial and personal success. The message embedded in this theme is that a good person faces no insurmountable structural barriers to success. This underscores one of the primary myths of the American Dream—that virtue and hard work are central to an individual's success and that neither unemployment, structural poverty, hiring discrimination, nor a recession can get in the way of this extraordinary individual. Of course, the flip side of this myth is that financial failure and failure to advance in the workplace are a result of the individual's lack of virtue and/or hard work.

The blockbuster hit *Working Girl*, starring Harrison Ford, Melanie Griffith, Sigourney Weaver, Joan Cusack, and Alec Baldwin, was number eleven on the list of box office hits of 1988. Here was another Cinderella story, this time revolving around Tess (Melanie Griffith), a woman (or "girl" as the title suggests) struggling to succeed in her career and her personal life who moves from a verbally abusive, cheating, working-class boyfriend and a secretarial job to a high-powered career and an upper-middle-class, supportive, enlightened boyfriend. The working-class boyfriend, Mick (Alec Baldwin), buys her Frederick's of Hollywood underwear for gifts while the economically successful Jack (Harrison Ford) buys her a leather briefcase for her first nonclerical job. The audience is also delivered an evil, successful career woman, Catherine (Sigourney Weaver), who demonstrates just what bad things happen to women when they climb all over people to make it in the business world. Of course, there are several gratuitous, audience-pleasing scenes with the working girl herself, Melanie Griffith, in her underwear. On one level, *Working Girl* is a light romantic comedy. But on another level it provides an important, yet largely invisible commentary about class.

The working-class characters of Mick and Cyn (Tess's friend, played by Joan Cusack) are depicted as simple. Cyn is comically sympathetic, somewhat streetwise, and as a friend to Tess believes it is her duty to warn her of the dangers of moving up in the world. She tells her that romance with Jack is a fantasy and encourages her to go back to the abusive Mick. Cyn, like the other "girls" in the steno pool, has big hair teased as high as it will stretch, short tight skirts, heavy eye makeup, and an even heavier Brooklyn accent peppered with colorful slang and incorrect grammar.

Mick reads auto-racing magazines in bed, cheats on Tess in her own bedroom, curses at her, and expects her to continue to make him the center of her life. Neither Cyn nor Mick is portrayed as particularly intelligent or successful. While we, the audience, are coaxed to laugh with and sometimes at Cyn and snarl at Mick, we also are steered to find their working-class lives difficult at best and pathetic at worst. The ultimate sign of their miserable status in life is a comical, but disdainful portrayal of their total ignorance of the symbols and joys of middle-class life. In one scene in a working-class bar where Cyn's engagement is being celebrated, Tess arrives late wearing elegantly tailored work clothes she has "borrowed" from her boss. Mick comments on how good she looks: "What, d'ja [did you] have to go to traffic court?"

Tess, determined to make it in the corporate world, gets rid of her big hair and makeup and exchanges her wardrobe for clothes she temporarily steals from her boss. She attends business school at night and takes voice lessons to rid herself of the remaining external and most visible signs of her class background. Some of Tess's strategies to get ahead are ethically questionable and potentially illegal, yet the audience is invited to like Tess, to approve of her strategic moves, to forgive her for her unscrupulous trespasses, and to root for her success. We are encouraged to understand that the deck is stacked against success for someone like Tess and to acknowledge that the only way for her to get ahead is to break the rules.

By the end of the film, the secretaries and the audience are celebrating Tess's achievement of the American Dream. Her hard work and her necessary, but forgivable deceit have bought her what appears to be a well-deserved slice of the American Dream and proved to the rest of us that individuals with the drive to succeed can escape the working class. On the side, we receive the subtle message that losers like Cyn and Mick deserve to remain in the tedious working class because they fall short of the intelligence, industriousness, and merit needed to move up in the world and lack even the basic awareness of how deficient their lives truly are.

As we have reconstructed what we were taught about class through formal and informal means, it becomes increasingly clear that many, if not most of us raised in the United States have understood or misunderstood that we live in a classless society. This broad

The Best Years of Our Lives (1946) marks the transition of three men from different backgrounds from World War II to home. The challenges they face in returning to civilian life are in direct proportion to their social and economic class. [Here, Sergeant Al Stephenson (Fredric March) looks into the mirror and compares his before-war photo to his after-war visage.] (*Source: Courtesy of Getty Images. Copyright © 2012 Getty Images. Used by permission of Getty Images.*)

understanding of American self-identity as largely middle-class is a twentieth-century phenomenon. While films such as *Working Girl* and *Pretty Woman*, in the late twentieth century, and *Cinderella Man*, in the early twenty-first century, are the norm, these messages about class were not always prevalent in film.

As of 2012, of the 100 films that were rated by Box Office Mojo as the top all-time box office hits in the United States, seven films, or 7 percent, had major themes explicitly involving social and economic class. These films were *Gone with the Wind* (#1, 1939), *Love Story* (#34, 1970), *My Fair Lady* (#54, 1964), *West Side Story* (#66, 1961), *Rocky* (#72, 1976), *The Best Years of Our Lives* (#73, 1946), and *Aladdin* (#87, 1992) (Box Office Mojo 2012).

How do these films rate according to the two themes about class—cross-class romance and the American Dream? Four of these films (*Gone with the Wind, Love Story, My Fair Lady, Aladdin*) tell the story of love across the classes, one has a major theme that involves the American Dream (*Rocky*), and two have themes that address class with somewhat more complexity (*West Side Story*) or with a wide range of characters and deep complexity of characters and themes (*The Best Years of Our Lives*). Five of these seven heavy hitters at the box office also won the Academy Award for best picture. The only two that did not were *Aladdin* and *Love Story*.

The Best Years of Our Lives tells a story of profound complexity with a wide range of both simple and complex characters. Starring Fredric March, Myrna Loy, Dana Andrews, and Teresa Wright, the film follows the lives of three men from three different economic classes as they return from active service in World War II. It does not flinch from the difficult issues of reentry for these men, including the impact of economic class and the competition for jobs. Fred Derry (Dana Andrews) is a working-class man who had left a civilian job as a soda jerk to become a wartime pilot. This enlistment mobility increases Fred's status from being just a guy who works in a soda fountain to a dashing young man in a leather bomber jacket with a newfound air of adventure and glamour and stature that lasts until the day he comes home. When he returns, the only job he can land is the same job as a soda jerk—in the same place he worked before the war. Fred finds his only work option both demeaning and demoralizing. This film does not push a strong political agenda; it nevertheless drives home the message that the availability of opportunities and resources is not equal and that class weighs heavily on Fred's prospects and options, even after he has risked his life for his country.

Gone with the Wind tells a personal story, set in the historical context of the Civil War, of the financial, material, and class losses of a southern white woman, Scarlett O'Hara (Vivien Leigh), and her family. Scarlett's determination, hard work, and scheming pay off as she finds ways to build back her family's money, rebuild the family home, and at the same time demonstrate one tenet of the American Dream—that one can always start over and be successful again even when personal integrity and merit are replaced by conniving and deceit.

In *Love Story*, an owning-class Harvard student, Oliver (Ryan O'Neal), falls in love with and marries a brilliant but poor Radcliffe student, Jenny (Ali MacGraw). After their marriage, his family disowns him because they believe he has married beneath his class. But Oliver's parents return to supporting him when Jenny becomes ill and eventually dies. This film is clearly in the category of love-conquers-all (except for death, of course) and sentimental films; its tagline was "Love means never having to say you're sorry."

Professor Henry Higgins is challenged by Colonel Pickering to transform some poor unfortunate "girl" into a lady. Higgins picks Eliza Doolittle, a crude flower girl with a coarse, unrefined Cockney accent, and whisks her away from all of what he deems her "bad influences" to stay at his home and work on changing her accent, manners, and appearance. And of course, he is so successful that he eventually falls in love with her. The film? *My Fair Lady*, based on George Bernard Shaw's play *Pygmalion*. Love conquers all once more.

Even in the animated Disney film *Aladdin*, we are treated to near-tragic love between royalty and a commoner. Aladdin, a poor boy who is a thief with integrity, falls in love with Princess Jasmine, the daughter of the sultan. Aladdin first poses as a prince, and after many mishaps and adventures, Jasmine, of course, discovers she loves Aladdin despite his deception and his status that is not worthy of a princess.

West Side Story is a twentieth-century, musical *Romeo and Juliet* in which the lovers are separated not by class but by nationality. Tony was born in the United States, and Maria was born in Puerto Rico. Their respective cultures and bigoted families and peers are what separate them, although both groups live side by side in poverty in New York City, and both Tony and Maria's brother are ultimately killed because of the hatred between the two groups. While the lyrical nature of the film removes it from gritty reality, part of its message is that these warring gangs have more in common than they understand. What divides them is their ethnicity. But what should unite them is their class, as both groups struggle to survive the streets and poverty and discrimination. Even though *West Side Story* offers a different look at class than the other five films, it is important to recognize that the characters are simply drawn, much of the interaction is musical, and the concluding message about class is a reach.

In the 1976 film *Rocky*, Rocky Balboa (played by Sylvester Stallone) is a struggling, low-wage bill collector and small-time boxer who longs to make it to the big time (in boxing, not in bill collecting). Rocky goes from being a "nobody" to a "somebody" in a simple rags-to-riches tale in which the American Dream comes true.

Of these seven films about class, three are musicals, five are dramas, two are comedies; one is an animated film geared toward children, and only in *The Best Years of Our Lives* would any of the characters be considered complex. These are the films that Americans have rushed to see over the last seventy-five years, and if both the political left and political right are correct, these are the films that have left an indelible mark on audiences.

As discussed in Chapter 1, images and stereotypes of groups and concepts can be investigated in several ways. The first is to determine the availability of images. The fact that only seven of the 100 box office hits feature themes about class demonstrates that themes addressing class are rarely available to moviegoing audiences. A second investigative strategy is to determine whether the characters and themes are simple or complex. We have seen that of the seven films featuring class, only one addresses class thematically with any level of complexity, and only one has characters with any complexity. This simplicity tends to support the perpetuation of stereotypes. A third strategy of analysis looks for repetition of similar characters and themes. With little range or complexity in the seven films, the themes regarding romance across classes and the achievement of the American Dream become the core messages conveyed to film audiences.

The National Bureau of Economic Research (NBER) determined that the Great Recession began in December 2007 and ended in June 2009, nineteen months of a "significant decline in [the] economic activity spread across the country" (NBER 2013). Table 3.2 displays the top ten box office hits of each year from 2007 to 2011 and indicates which films include a significant theme regarding socioeconomic class. Of the fifty films in the five-year period surrounding the official years of the recession, only three (6 percent) registered observable content about class. By contrast, 80 percent of the films in this group (forty films, including two of the films about class) were sequels or an original with upcoming sequels in development.

The three films with themes involving socioeconomic class were *Alvin and the Chipmunks* (2007, rated PG), *The Blind Side* (2009, rated PG-13), and *Despicable*

Table 3.2

Major Themes About Class in Twenty-First-Century Box Office Hits, 2007–2011

Top Ten Films	2007	2008	2009	2010	2011
#1	Spider-Man 3	The Dark Knight	Avatar[1]	Toy Story 3	Harry Potter and the Deathly Hallows Part 2
#2	Shrek the 3rd	Iron Man	Transformers: Revenge of the Fallen	Alice in Wonderland	Transformers: Dark of the Moon
#3	Transformers	Indiana Jones and the Kingdom of the Crystal Skull	Harry Potter and the Half Blood Prince	Iron Man 2	The Twilight Saga: Breaking Dawn Part 1
#4	Pirates of the Caribbean: At World's End	Hancock[2]	The Twilight Saga: New Moon	The Twilight Saga: Eclipse	The Hangover Part II
#5	Harry Potter and the Order of the Phoenix	WALL-E	Up	Harry Potter and the Deathly Hallows Part 1	Pirates of the Caribbean: On Stranger Tides
#6	I Am Legend	Kung Fu Panda	The Hangover	Inception	Fast Five[3]
#7	The Bourne Identity	Twilight	Star Trek	Despicable Me[4]	Mission Impossible: Ghost Protocol
#8	National Treasure: Book of Secrets	Madagascar: Escape 2 Africa	The Blind Side	Shrek Forever After	Cars 2
#9	Alvin and the Chipmunks	Quantum of Solace	Alvin and the Chipmunks: The Squeakquel	How to Train Your Dragon[5]	Sherlock Holmes: A Game of Shadows
#10	300	Dr. Seuss' Horton Hears a Who	Sherlock Holmes	Tangled	Thor: The Dark World[6]

Films highlighted in light gray are part of a series or sequel.
Films highlighted in dark gray have major themes involving socioeconomic class.

1. The sequel to *Avatar* is scheduled for release in 2016 (Avatar2-movie.com).
2. The sequel of *Hancock* is listed as "currently in development" (Internet Movie Database, www.IMDb.com).
3. *Fast Five* is a sequel to the *Fast and Furious* series of films; *Fast and Furious 6* was released in 2013; the next sequel is expected in 2015 (www.thefastandthefurious.com).
4. The sequel to *Despicable Me* was released in 2013 (Despicableme.com).
5. The sequel of *How to Train Your Dragon* is due for release in 2014 (Internet Movie Database, www.IMDb.com).
6. The sequel to *Thor: The Dark World* was released in 2013 (http://marvel.com/thor).

Me (2010, rated PG). *Despicable Me* and *Alvin and the Chipmunks* are both animated films aimed at an audience of young children. In *Alvin*, struggling songwriter Dave Seville discovers the singing talent of the pesky chipmunks; they join forces and go straight to the top of the pop music charts. This is the American Dream on the accelerated track delivered to preschoolers. There is, however, a moral caveat to this simple tale. When the evil, unscrupulous music executive connives to break up Dave and the Chipmunks and exploit the talent of the "boys," the foursome discover that they really value their relationships above the financial abundance and superficial glamour that surround them.

Despicable Me also involves exploitation, but this story shows the transformation from evil to goodness. Supervillain Gru sets out to borrow money from the bank and is turned down because the bank believes he is getting too old. His pride wounded, Gru decides to literally steal the moon to prove he still has what it takes. In the process, Gru adopts three orphaned little girls to use them in his scheme. But *Despicable Me* is a PG film, so of course Gru sheds his evil ways and discovers that he truly loves the girls, so they all settle into happily-ever-after family life.

Of these three films about class, *The Blind Side* is the only one intended for an adult audience. The messages about socioeconomic class in *The Blind Side* take on added significance because, in the five years surrounding the recession, this is the film about class that more U.S. adults saw than any other, particularly after Sandra Bullock won the Best Actress Academy Award for her role as Leigh Anne Tuohy. Understanding the messages in this film—what is said and what is not said—can provide us with powerful insight into what much of the audience may believe is true.

Thematically, *The Blind Side*'s focus is more visibly about race than class. Although the messages about class are often below the surface, they are nevertheless quite powerful. In some ways, much like *Despicable Me*, *The Blind Side* is another "orphan" story. It's based on a true story about wealthy white southerners, under the matriarchal leadership of Leigh Anne Tuohy (Sandra Bullock), who take in a homeless black teenager, Michael Oher, after they see him walking alone on a cold winter night, wearing nothing but shorts and a T-shirt. The Tuohys discover that Michael is a transfer student at their children's high school. After the requisite mishaps, miscommunication, and mistrust, the Tuohys welcome Michael as part of their family and Michael finds his niche in the family with relative ease.

A big guy, Michael is a natural for the high school football team, and Leigh Anne is an avid football fan. Michael's silence in the film is often conveyed in a way that suggests that he is mentally slow, but Leigh Anne seems to know just what he is thinking and just what he needs. Marching up to the football coach, mid-practice, she tells him exactly how he should coach Michael. She boldly informs the coach that Michael needs to think of the quarterback as his family (meaning the Tuohy family, of course) and that his job is to protect and defend the quarterback as he would protect and defend the Tuohys. And, of course, this strategy works.

On the surface, *The Blind Side* is a story of how love and kindness can transcend the challenges of race and class difference. However, "it never strays from the surface, parading a series of kind acts . . . but never delving into the ramifications of [the family's] actions or exploring more complicated socioeconomic and racial issues" (Puig 2009). Michael is the only major character in the film who is black or low-income, and he is rendered in a way that is simple and one-dimensional. As we noted in Chapter 1, there are two essential elements that contribute to stereotyping. One is that the character is very simple and one-dimensional, and the second is that there are very few characters from the same group. As the audience, we know little about Michael's "story" and are left to wonder how it is possible that Michael received a scholarship to the Tuohy children's private Christian school while simultaneously being left homeless, to wander in the cold wearing summer clothes.

Michael is a poor (in the multiple terms of the word), homeless boy, son of a crack addict, and the Tuohys, Leigh Ann in particular, teach him all about the kindness, generosity, and love of a wealthy white family that has another "blind side," in addition to the film title's football reference. Either they simply do not "see" race or class differences or these differences do not matter to them or, more likely, they are so passionate about wanting to be good people and to see Michael's goodness and their equality that they choose to ignore the racial and class differences. In our discussion of the cultural competence continuum in Chapter 1, we addressed the midpoint of the continuum, which is called cultural neutrality or cultural blindness. Many of us were raised to think that the highest form of treating everyone equally is not to notice difference. In Michael's case, the Tuohys generally ignored Michael's race, his original family's economic background, and his mother's drug addiction. No matter how well-meaning the Tuohys may be in not "seeing" Michael's difference, this kind of "cultural blindness" often results in an individual feeling invisible in a way that ignores all of his personal struggles against the forces of racism and other forms of inhumanity. These struggles are often integral to a person's identity, strength, and ultimate achievements in the face of powerful obstacles.

In order for *The Blind Side* to move beyond simple sentimentality and one-dimensional messages with no more complexity than those in *Alvin and the Chipmunks*, the audience needs to see the straightforward, unconditional love and generosity of the Tuohy family along with the challenges and complexities as they all learn about their powerful human connections as well as the profound ways their lives have been different because one of them is black, poor, and homeless and the others are white, wealthy, and have occupied positions of privilege by virtue of the skin color and financial advantages that occurred by accident of birth.

As a popular form of art, movies have the potential to teach us about the human condition, including the way that economic inequalities operate and the often confusing way that race and economic inequalities intersect. For just a few hours, film lets us into the lives of characters who can teach us about the ugliness and violence of bias and the range of possibilities that we as humans have to let the bias fester and grow and also to find ways to make deep human connections in the midst of painful inequities and perhaps to wobble uncertainly between the two. But during the Great Recession, from 2007 to 2011, few of the current popular films offered the kind of complex characters or themes that would help audiences understand the deep unemployment and economic losses happening in the country during that time. The largest movie-going audiences were rarely, if ever, exposed to the complexities of class and poverty in general or to the economic reality of many Americans during the Great Recession.

It is interesting to note that in all three films, there was only one direct nod to the recession: a slice of dry humor tossed out to the adults in the audience of *Despicable Me*. When Gru is seeking a loan from a bank called the "Bank of Evil," a sign reveals to the audience that the name was "Formerly Lehman Brothers."

Although the recession officially ended in 2009, as late as the spring of 2012, the comeback of the economy was slow and sluggish and the official unemployment rate was still 8.3 percent as compared to the peak 2010 unemployment rate of 10.2 percent (U.S Department of Labor 2012; Goodman and Mance 2011). And "as far as Hollywood is concerned, the economic downturn is not multiplex material. More than two years into the worst financial meltdown since the Great Depression, filmmakers have essentially ignored the stories of average Americans who have been downsized or lost their homes in the collapse of the housing bubble. Instead, when the crisis is addressed, the focus has been on the masters of the fiscal universe, those venal yet somehow glamorous folks who caused the crisis—like the subjects of Oliver Stone's 'Wall Street: Money Never Sleeps'" (Beale 2010).

The 2010 film *Wall Street: Money Never Sleeps*, directed by Oliver Stone and starring Michael Douglas as Gordon Gekko, is the sequel to the 1987 *Wall Street*. According to Roger Ebert, the original *Wall Street*

> was a wake-up call about the financial train wreck the Street was headed for. Had we only listened. Or perhaps we listened too well, and Gordon ("Greed Is Good") Gekko became the role model for a generation of amoral financial pirates who put hundreds of millions into their pockets while bankrupting their firms and bringing the economy to its knees. As "Wall Street: Money Never Sleeps" begins, Gekko has been able to cool his heels for many of the intervening years in a federal prison, which is the film's biggest fantasy; the thieves who plundered the financial system are still mostly in power, and congressional zealots resist efforts to regulate the system. (Ebert 2010)

After Gekko's prison release, he launches a tour of his book *Is Greed Good?* and simultaneously launches two other endeavors: a financial plot to seek revenge against his Wall Street nemesis and a scheme to reunite with his estranged daughter that involves temporarily stealing money from her. Of course, the film itself was launched in 2010 in the aftermath of real Wall Street excesses and greed that left real people homeless and jobless.

Ebert concludes, "I wish it [the film *Wall Street: Money Never Sleeps*] had been angrier. I wish it had been outraged. Maybe Stone's instincts are correct, and American audiences aren't ready for that. They have not had enough of Greed" (Ebert 2010). Ebert seems to reflect some of the same sentiment of many people in the United States who were angry enough to become involved in Occupy Wall Street and its offshoots, while others were angry enough to hold Congress accountable and become involved in the perpetual U.S. political "revolution" to "throw the bastards out."

In any case, there are at least two things about Hollywood and its relationship to the Great Recession that remain puzzling. One is that there were so few box office hits produced that in any direct way addressed class issues, poverty, or the controversies of the recession. The second is that the films we did see involved such characters as chipmunks, animated good versus evil where the villain turns into a hero, and oversimplified good will triumphing over the complexities of poverty and racism. And finally, among the popular films that involved themes about class, there was at least one film that directly addressed the greed involved in triggering the recession by asking the question "Is greed good?" But then it proceeded to answer this question ambiguously.

Other important U.S. films have featured themes of class and working-class characters with greater complexity and range, however, and while they have rarely been box office hits, several of them have been nominated for and won Academy Awards. In some ways, the 2010 film *Company Men*, starring Ben Affleck, Chris Cooper, and Tommy Lee Jones, is the flip side of *Wall Street: Money Never Sleeps*. The film is set in a similar cutthroat corporate environment where ambition and greed seem to rule. However, instead of following the corroded character of its leaders, *Company Men* follows the devastating impact of sudden downsizing on corporate executives who have lived by the treacherous adage "You are what you do" (Holden 2010).

The loss of Porsches and mansions by these families is clearly a far cry from the impact of downsizing on people who have lived from paycheck to paycheck. Nevertheless, *Company Men* offers a complex view of the powerful men who were part of the unscrupulous groups, individuals, and institutions that triggered the recession, as well as men with integrity who may have benefited from the financial schemes, but ultimately lost everything. The complexity of the three main characters gives those of us who did not have the view of the economic downfall from on high an opportunity to see the sights from a different angle than sheer, unadulterated greed. However, despite a strong *New York Times* review, *Company Men* took in a box office gross of just under $4.5 million, outdone by *Wall Street: Money Never Sleeps*, which had a box office take of roughly $52.5 million and an audience more than ten times as large (Box Office Mojo 2010).

Two other interesting films that were released during the five years that surrounded the recession were unflinching in their depiction of the stark worlds of rural poverty and urban life on the edge of poverty. *The Fighter*, both literally and figuratively a heavy hitter, grossed over $93 million, qualifying it as a 2010 box office hit (Box Office Mojo 2010). It was also a critical favorite, with multiple Academy Award nominations (including Best Picture) and wins for Best Supporting Actor (Christian Bale) and Best Supporting Actress (Melissa Leo). The film is based on the actual story of boxer Mickey Ward (Mark Wahlberg) in the stark, working-class town of Lowell, Massachusetts. But unlike *Cinderella Man*, *The Fighter* does not pay homage to a simple depiction of the American Dream. Instead, the film is a powerful character story of Mickey, the brother who succeeds in boxing, and Dicky (Christian Bale), the brother who almost succeeds in the world of boxing but instead gets lost in the world of hard drugs. The characters are mostly complex, as is the toughness of Lowell's working-class trap where drugs and corruption are seductive and integrity does not always pay off. Yet in very different ways, the audience is witness to the phenomenon of "both/and" in which the reality of being just a few feet away from poverty and its pull toward hopelessness and defeat is balanced with a very different kind of victory of the human spirit demonstrated by both Mickey and Dicky.

Winter's Bone, which made roughly $6.3 million at the box office, depicted the struggle of life in the rural Missouri Ozarks, where the corruption and brutality of the country, weather, and people are palpable. Most of the adult characters in the film are already broken and defeated by mental illness, drugs, violence, or isolation. Ree Dolly (Jennifer Lawrence) is a seventeen-year-old girl whose father is in prison and whose mother's mental illness is so severe that she requires far more care than she can possibly provide for Ree and her younger brother and sister. Ree is the responsible one, making sure the family has food and other basic necessities. *Winter's Bone* manages to escape saccharine sentimentality as Ree cares for her mother, demonstrating tenderness and understanding beyond her years, and offers nurturance, protection, and playfulness to her brother and sister.

Ree becomes fiercely determined when her father posts their house for bail and then skips bail. Unless Ree locates her father within the next forty-eight hours, her family will lose the house. Much of the film is a study in the possibilities of how the human spirit can rise above the brutality of people who are supposed to love them and the daily grinding brutality of poverty. *Winter's Bone* is also a cautionary tale about the dangers of broken humanity. The film received rave reviews, as did Jennifer Lawrence and John Hawkes, who played her uncle. The film was nominated for an Academy Award, as were Lawrence and Hawkes, respectively, for Best Actress and Best Supporting Actor.

But *Winter's Bone*'s box office draw and audience were only slightly larger than that of *Company Men*. A larger audience might have taken in multiple messages that contradicted the stereotypes of rural poverty and the media's frequent focus on poverty in black and Latino communities. A larger audience might have seen the complexity of people in this film: the range from cruel to kind, from harsh to loving, from simple-minded to keenly intelligent, and an ambiguous mix of these characteristics. The film could have teased out many less than visible beliefs about rural people and poverty and would have challenged us to a confrontation with our own cognitive dissonance. Despite the excellent writing and acting of *Winter's Bone* and the relentless depiction of the potential for both human cruelty and kindness, and despite the film's clear-eyed, important, and rarely depicted portrayal of white, rural poverty, it did not draw a mass audience. As a result, the more popular, less complex, and more clichéd messages of a film like *The Blind Side* reached millions more people than those of *Winter's Bone*.

Throughout film history, there have frequently been award-winning films that, despite the highest awards and acclaim, still did not make it as box office hits. Award winners in the past such as *Midnight Cowboy* (1969), *The Deerhunter* (1978), and the classics *On the Waterfront* (1954) and *A Streetcar Named Desire* (1951) offer an alternative look at class. The critically acclaimed *Norma Rae* (1979), the controversial *Blue Collar* (1978), and the independently produced *Matewan* (1987) present an even more in-depth view of working-class life and labor unions. Brief descriptions of these films demonstrate the possibilities for feature films to examine serious subjects without serving as propaganda for the unions, as early silent films did, or promoting the dual myths of the American Dream and love-conquers-all. We urge you to watch these interesting, compelling films, along with *The Fighter, Winter's Bone*, and *Company Men*, and view their messages about class for yourself.

A Streetcar Named Desire, originally a play by Tennessee Williams, was released as a film in 1951. Among its many themes was one of class. Stella (Kim Hunter) and her sister Blanche (Vivien Leigh) were raised in a wealthy, elite family in the South, a family that lost their fortune but worked hard to maintain the semblance of their stature. Blanche derided Stella for marrying beneath her by choosing the working-class, Polish Stanley Kowalski (Marlon Brando). Amid Stanley's drinking and physical abuse of Stella is the presence of a powerful lust and a sweet tenderness between the couple. However, the film rarely follows the love-conquers-all theme. If anything, *A Streetcar Named Desire* depicts the American Dream gone sour. As much as Blanche wishes to pretend that nothing has changed while she schemes to rebuild her fortune, she is not able to start over and find financial success once again.

On the Waterfront is the story of Terry Malloy (Marlon Brando) and his stand against racketeering and mob connections in the longshoremen's union. The film takes a hard look at how this corruption exploits the workingmen in the union. In spite of promises, bribes, and direct threats of violence, Malloy stands up to his brother, to the union, and, by extension, to evil in the world. He says to Edie (Eva Marie Saint), "They always said I was a bum. I ain't a bum, Edie." The film is a complexity of messages. The labor union represents corruption and evil, and Terry represents integrity and morality. Terry Malloy is a multilayered character who defies easy stereotypes of working-class men.

Another level of complexity in the film involves its director, Elia Kazan. Kazan had originally refused to testify before the House Un-American Activities Committee (HUAC), but in the middle of the 1952 filming of *On the Waterfront* he changed his mind. He gave names of fellow communists, causing shock and betrayal among friends and fans. At that time in U.S. history, turning friends, colleagues, or even enemies over to HUAC and accusing them of being communists often meant that they would face long-term, if not permanent unemployment in the film industry. Some film critics said that *On the Waterfront* was an attempt on the part of director Kazan and writer Budd Schulberg to use Terry Malloy to exonerate themselves. The film was listed as one of the top 100 conservative films by the *National Review* (Koehler 1999, 98) because of this parallel story about HUAC's anticommunist witch hunt and its implied criticism of people in the film industry who appeared to lean to the left politically.

In the Academy Award–winning *Midnight Cowboy* (1969), the young Texan Joe Buck (Jon Voight) is a handsome, uneducated dishwasher who naively heads to New York City to become rich by prostituting himself to wealthy older women. When a series of encounters fails, the disillusioned and broke Buck meets Ratso Rizzo (Dustin Hoffman), a down-on-his-luck hustler. The *National Review* described *Midnight Cowboy* as an example of the "nihilism and chaotic styles of the 1970s that rejects the ideals of Western civilization" (Warren 1994, 1). Certainly, the film is a dark, grim view of life among the underclasses in New York City. But in many ways it offers a view of the complexity and humanity of the characters that more privileged folks find invisible in large urban areas.

Rizzo and Buck start out simply using each other to expand their respective hustles, but they end up forming a bond, a friendship that eventually finds Joe Buck nurturing a fatally ill Ratso Rizzo. It is not a happy story about the poverty that is depicted in this slice of life—but it sends a message about the reality of its grimness and of the possibilities of human kindness amid darkness.

The 1978 film *Blue Collar* offers both complex themes and characters that revolve around class and race. The film is set in working-class Detroit, and most of the action takes place inside an auto factory. The three main characters (played by Harvey Keitel, Yaphet Kotto, and Richard Pryor) are workers in the factory, good friends who are portrayed as basically good guys. But they are not perfect. They all drink and do drugs occasionally, two of them cheat on their wives, and the third is an ex-convict. They are all struggling to survive financially, and the two family men are shown to love their wives and children. None of these three characters can easily be confined to a standard stereotype. Their friendship bonds are strong and they cross racial boundaries. While all three men do things that are illegal and that audiences may view as immoral, the audience is, nevertheless, pulling for them to overcome the corruption they discover in their union.

Some critics have chided the film for portraying and stereotyping the thinly disguised United Auto Workers union as financially corrupt and lacking commitment to workers' rights; this is a fair criticism. But the film's unflinching look at the struggles of the working poor to fight the IRS and the union and pay for dental work for their children paints an important and multitextured picture. Each of the three men faces the seductive pull of corruption in different ways. One is destroyed by it, one succumbs to it and takes a job offer from the union as a payoff, and the third discloses the details of the corruption to the FBI. Ultimately, *Blue Collar* analyzes power, its impact, and its staggering ability to divide people.

Norma Rae is still another portrait of the working class and organized labor. In this film, organized labor is the hero, management is the villain, and the workers are caught in between. The main character, Norma Rae (Sally Field), works in a textile factory in Alabama. She is a single mother, a woman with fire and ardor who is imperfect and complex. Outraged by the treatment of the workers and the conditions of the factories, she passionately teams up with a labor organizer, Reuben (Ron Leibman), sent from New York to unionize the workers. It is the film's resistance to glamorizing the lead characters, the factory workers, or working-class life that sets it apart from other films about class. The film also resists the cheap shot of creating a relationship in which Norma Rae and Reuben might fall in love, whisking her away from her hard life. While Norma Rae, the character, and *Norma Rae*, the film, convey hope, there is no zealous or unquestioned portrayal of the American Dream or even a hint that love conquers all.

Finally, the 1987 *Matewan*, directed by independent filmmaker John Sayles, tells another story of organized labor, workers, poverty, class, and race. This time the scene is the West Virginia coal mines, the struggle to unionize, and union busting. There is integrity and corruption everywhere—in management, in workers, and in the union itself. There is the hint of love and attraction, but it never emerges as a central theme nor does it suggest that somehow romance will solve the problems of workers owned by the company or the violence that emerges when the black and white workers join forces to unionize. "Swathed in the trappings and pioneer themes of such classic models as *The Godfather* and *Once Upon a Time in America*, it tells of a different American dream—of the unemployed and exploited" (Howe 1987, 1).

Entertainment film is a powerful force. It can reflect the realities or illusions of class, it can reinforce our beliefs and myths, and it can challenge us to question the invisibility of class in the United States. As we have seen, images of class are few in popular film, and their absence reinforces the notion of a classless society. The tools to tease out hidden themes and messages of class and to analyze the meaning in a character's class are critical to independent judgments about any particular film. But these tools play a far more important role: they give us the information and resources that allow us to determine the influence of entertainment media on our values and understanding about class and, if we so choose, to rethink and reconstruct our beliefs.

Music and Class

In the 1962 Top 40 song "Patches," singer Dickey Lee plaintively describes the broken-down house where his love Patches lives in an "old shanty town." The narrator lives on the "right" side of town and painfully sings of his parents' refusal to let him marry Patches because they say she will bring him disgrace. Learning that Patches has killed herself, the narrator ends the song with "It may not be right, but I'll join you tonight. Patches, I'm coming to you" (Lyrics.com 2012).

In the case of this song, love does not conquer all for these young lovers. Their economic differences and the class prejudices of the boy's parents keep them apart, and they decide to die rather than live without each other. While this song may be extreme and melodramatic in its ending, it indicates how the messages about class in music often differ from those in popular film and prime-time television. Though class is not prevalent in all forms of contemporary music, it plays a significant role both in the definition of musical genres and in the expression of divisions by class. Contemporary music does not typically reflect class invisibility, the American Dream, or the love-conquers-all themes we found in prime-time television and popular film.

In this section, we will look at the intersection of class with targeted music audiences and analyze the presence of class themes in contemporary popular music. We will consider late twentieth- and early twenty-first-century music as "contemporary" and will focus on music that has either been generated from the United States or has made a mark on U.S. culture by virtue of its popularity or impact.

Audience Segmentation Through Radio and the Internet

Popular music is distributed through a number of formats, and one of the common features is audience segmentation. Whether you listen to or buy your music on the radio, through the Internet, or through what is still anachronistically called a "record store," the music is divided according to genre. If you're in the mood for "oldies" from the 1960s, you can Google them on the Internet or your smartphone, find them on YouTube, push the button on the radio for the oldies station, or buy an album or a single song from iTunes. In fact, most smartphones have applications allowing you to respond to several songs that are automatically selected for you and indicate whether or not you like the song, the artist, or the genre; the "app" will then build you a custom-made, personalized radio station featuring the types of songs you like. By 2012, audience segmentation had moved from being primarily organized according to musical genre combined with demographics to include the capability of segmenting an audience down as narrowly as to the tastes of one person.

This type of media targeting, combined with the fact that recording a song is generally cheaper than producing a TV show or film, allows musicians to take risks and music producers to select themes, musical styles, and the style of the recording artists based on information from focus groups and audience studies.

By the early twenty-first century, anyone with a computer could record a song and upload it on YouTube, Facebook, and any number of free musical websites. This music can range from the most amateurish a cappella song to a professionally produced, multi-track recording with multiple voices and instruments. New and hot musicians have been "discovered" in these spots that are a far cry from the more formally organized and often regimented venues that are customary in the recording industry. In the traditional type of recording, contemporary music is typically distributed first through popular radio stations, which are formatted according to their listening audience. As recently as 2012, radio was still the primary distributor of newly released contemporary, commercial music and was still a major entry point for artists who are interested in earning their living through music. Other standard forms for the promotion and distribution of recorded music are music videos and concerts.

By 2012, the standard music radio formats, which overlapped with the categories in record stores, included classical, easy listening, Top 40, hip-hop/rap, rhythm and blues (R&B), jazz, country, rock, oldies, and alternative. Rap and hip-hop also frequently cross over to both Top 40 and R&B stations. The segmentation of radio audiences typically occurs according to some combination of age, race, and class. Older listeners, for example, tend to be the dominant audience for classical, oldies, and easy listening while younger audiences listen to R&B, Top 40, rock, and alternative stations.

The segmentation of radio audiences according to race intersects with class and age as well. "Many stations reflect a class style, with some stations wooing urban contemporary listeners with jazz, soul, and traditional R&B while other stations woo black youth with hip-hop influenced R&B and rap music" (Dates and Barlow 1990). Country stations draw a broad white audience with significant working-class representation.

Musical audiences change and evolve, as does the music that is considered "crossover." LeAnn Rimes songs are played on country stations and Top 40. Puff Daddy's (Sean "Puffy" Combs's) songs are played on R&B stations and Top 40. The audience for rap has evolved from primarily young, working-class African American males to middle-class white teens and young men (Samuels 1991, 24). Yet while the class divisions may often be muddy, the segmentation of radio's listening audiences more often corresponds to economic distinctions than those audiences for prime-time television and popular film. Perhaps for this reason, since the mid- to late twentieth century, some musical genres address themes of class more directly and frequently than film or television. This section will examine themes of class in popular music and how they have evolved and changed through the early twenty-first century.

Musical Genres

It is in the musical genres of rap and country that the most explicit themes of class can be found in the lyrics. "Rap and country lyrics implicate underclass reality. . . . Though both genres are based on somewhat different social realities, they both share a rhetoric of violence. Analyses of press coverage of country and rap have found that while the genres share a tendency toward machismo, they are not treated the same way by the press" (Croteau and Hoynes 1997, 227). "When rapper Ice Cube says, 'Let the suburbs see a nigga invasion,' many whites interpret that as an incitement to violence. But when Johnny Cash sings, 'Shot a man in Reno/just to watch him die,' the public taps its feet and hums" (Noe 1995, 20).

Socialization about race often leads to the kind of misunderstanding or overt racism that clearly plays a key role in the different ways the news media react to expressions of violence in rap and in country music. We will explore this further in Chapter 5. For now, it is interesting to note that by the early twenty-first century two very different musical genres had emerged as the primary musical categories that focus on class. Although Top 40, rock, and alternative music have far fewer songs that are reflective of class, they nevertheless share similar themes with rap and country songs. These themes do not generally support the dominant ideology of the American Dream, the invisibility of class, or love conquering all. Rather they focus on the anguish of poverty, violence and poverty, love that cannot overcome the barriers of class differences, political analyses of power and poverty, and the star power, fame, flashy clothes, and fortune that come with striking it rich in the music industry. However, from 2007 to 2012, in the years surrounding the Great Recession of the twenty-first century, there were striking changes in these musical themes about class.

Popular Music

Examine the music charts that reflect the top popular songs of today. You can find these charts online at *Billboard* Hot 100 (www.billboard.com/charts/hot-100). If you would like to hear some of these songs, you will find that many music stores still allow customers to listen to music at the store. Do you find much explicit mention of economic class in contemporary popular music? Like the top box office hits in film and successful prime-time television, there are few examples of popular music that rhapsodize about or criticize economic divisions. But while these numbers are small, from 1955 to 1995 the messages in popular music were distinctly different from those in film and television.

A study that examined themes about class in Top 40 songs during the years 1955, 1965, 1975, 1985, and 1995 revealed some interesting messages and trends (Holtzman 1998). As you recall, stereotypes of class were prevalent in prime-time television and film partially because there were so few themes about class in these popular forms of entertainment. This same phenomenon holds true for popular music.

There were 1,095 songs that made it to the Top 40 lists of the five years in the study (Lyrics.com 2012). Of these songs only forty-one, or 4 percent, had themes or characters that explicitly involved economics or class. As stereotypes work, this means that the messages in these few songs take on a hypersignificance, especially if the same themes are repeated over and over. This same type of phenomenon held true for popular music in the early twenty-first century.

Despite the low occurrence of class themes, the study demonstrated that the themes and their messages that did exist from 1955 to 1995 were surprisingly distinct from those in the other forms of popular entertainment media. In popular film and television, the themes of class largely reflected the belief in the American Dream and the idea that love conquers all, by and large underscoring the dominant ideology. In the 1,000-plus Top 40 songs, the themes were far more diverse.

The 1955 songs about class are strikingly different from each other. "Band of Gold" and "My Boy Flat-Top" are love songs with lyrics such as "Don't want the world to have and hold, For fame is not my line. Just want a little band of gold to prove that you are mine." "The Shifting, Whispering Sand" is a sort of mystical story of how the sands reveal the truth of the life of a miner. "Sixteen Tons" is the only one of these 1955 songs about class to tell the story of a poor man's destiny tied to his physical labor and lack of hope for financial success. The lyrics of the chorus repeat the theme of hard labor, deep debt, and the hopelessness of the cycle, characterized by the line "I owe my soul to the company store" (Lyrics.com 2012).

By 1965, a few patterns about ideology in popular music begin to emerge. Sixty percent of the songs that had themes about class involved the dominant ideology of the American Dream or love conquering all. But all of these songs also had some themes that challenged the dominant ideology by criticizing class or economic disparity, bemoaning the personal sorrows caused by money, or describing complex stories or characters impacted by class. These themes challenging the established order of things were not so surprising in the 1960s, when issues of equity of gender, race, and sexual orientation and movements protesting social injustice were prevalent. Of the thirteen hits in 1965 that involved class, there were three Bob Dylan songs and two Roger Miller songs, as well as an assortment by Barbra Streisand, Sam Cooke, Sonny and Cher, and Billy Joe Royal.

Some of the songs that reflected love-conquers-all theme were "Hang On, Sloopy" by the McCoys, "I Got You Babe" by Sonny and Cher, and "Down in the Boondocks" by Billy Joe Royal. In "Hang On, Sloopy," the male narrator sings of his love for "Sloopy," who, like Patches before her, lives on the wrong side of town. But this time, the narrator defies the people who try to put her down and says, "Sloopy, I don't care what your daddy do, 'cause you know, Sloopy girl, I'm in love with you" because their love will conquer all (Lyrics.com 2012). "Down in the Boondocks" reiterates the same theme, but this time the male narrator is the person who lives on the wrong side, and he bemoans the reality that his love cannot survive since he is the boy from the boondocks (Lyrics.com 2012).

Roger Miller's songs, which have more of a country than pop sound, each tell a story of a man; in "King of the Road" he is a traveler or vagabond, and in "Kansas City Star" he announces the local cartoons on television. In both of these songs, the man is happy with his status and the implication is that he has chosen his life with no implied criticism of the economic system (Lyrics.com 2012).

An interesting song from 1965, silly and somewhat bizarre by today's standards, was "May the Bird of Paradise Fly Up Your Nose," sung by Little Jimmy Dickens. While this song was clearly designed to be humorous, the humor was based on class distinctions made visible in the song. The narrator is a middle- or upper-middle-class man who has interactions with taxi drivers, so-called beggars, and laundry men. His insensitivity to these individuals from the working class causes them to wish him misfortune, albeit with silly curses. When he gives a penny to the "beggar man," the beggar mutters that he hopes that a bird of paradise flies up the narrator's nose, an elephant steps on his toes, and his wife has runs in her hose (Lyrics.com 2012). This certainly does not represent serious social criticism, but even these inane lyrics make class differences visible.

Other songs from 1965, more explicitly critical of the dominant culture, were regarded at the time as protest songs. Bob Dylan had three Top 40 songs during this year, including "Like a Rolling Stone," "Subterranean Homesick Blues," and "Positively Fourth Street." While these songs are distinct, their similarity is that they tell complex stories about individuals and their fall from high to low places or they explore the grimness of poverty and despair (Lyrics.com 2012).

In 1975, the numbers shifted dramatically. Only 21 percent of the songs about class were about the American Dream and none revolved around love conquering all. All of the other songs challenged, criticized, or expressed sorrow about poverty or the emptiness of economic wealth. Interestingly, the three songs that expressed hope in the American Dream or pride in one's status were all country-style songs by either Glen Campbell or John Denver. Campbell's "Rhinestone Cowboy" is the story of a man who is down on his luck; even though he has had to make compromises, he is certain he will make it to the top (Lyrics.com 2012).

The other eleven top hits that featured themes about class varied greatly in content and style. There are songs that are clearly of the protest or social criticism genre by Bob Dylan, Joni Mitchell, Simon and Garfunkel, Janis Ian, and Bruce Springsteen. But there are also songs performed by more standard pop or rock or R&B or country singers that criticize or lament economic disparity. These are songs by such diverse artists as Harold Melvin and the Blue Notes, David Bowie, the Marshall Tucker Band, Chicago, and Neil Sedaka. Chicago's hit "Harry Truman" invokes the spirit of this former president in saving the United States from the corruption of materialism and corporate power (Lyrics.com 2012).

Harold Melvin criticizes the president in "Bad Luck" as he sings about reading the newspaper, "Guess what I saw, huh? Saw the president of the United States, huh. The man said he was gonna give it up. He's giving us high hopes. But he still turned around and left all us poor folks behind" (Lyrics.com 2012). Janis Ian sings of the plight of homely, unpopular girls in "At Seventeen" and ties the success of the beauty queens to their "rich relations" and guarantee of marrying into wealth. Springsteen's "Born to Run" uses rock to explicitly criticize the American Dream. In the first line of the song he refers to the runaway American Dream (Lyrics.com 2012).

By 1985, there were only four songs with themes about class, and none of these had lyrics that supported the dominant ideology. These songs were sung by Madonna, Bruce Springsteen, Tina Turner, and Dire Straits. Madonna's and Turner's songs, "Material Girl" and "Private Dancer," respectively, were snapshots of particular women who do whatever they need to do to make money, including offering sexual favors or prostitution. The Dire Straits song, "Money for Nothing," is the flip side of these last two. While "Material Girl" and "Private Dancer" express a cynicism about material success, "Money for Nothing" speaks of the cynicism of economic failure and the easy road of the musicians who make it on MTV. Springsteen's "Glory Days" speaks of the loss in happiness for some and the decline in prosperity for others. He sings of his father's layoff from the Ford plant and his inability to find work because everyone said he was too old (Lyrics.com 2012).

In 1995, there were 142 songs that made it to number one on the pop charts throughout the year. Of these hits, six directly addressed class or economics. It is interesting to note that four of these songs were rap, one was rhythm and blues, and one could be considered alternative or pop.

"Gangsta's Paradise" bemoans how poverty, racism, and street violence lock young African American men into lives of hopelessness. "I'm living life do or die, what can I say. I'm 23 never will I live to see 24 the way things is going I don't know" (Lyrics.com 2012). The song offers something of a political analysis of how power and economics and the lack of role models and education keep young African American men trapped in a "gangsta's paradise" (Lyrics.com 2012).

"This Is How We Do It" is about "making it" in two ways. Montell Jordan speaks in the first person, using his first name, about how he has made it out of South Central L.A. with his music and his big money. But he still "makes it" sexually the same way they do in the old neighborhood—the "'hood." At first glance, the song seems to be about the American Dream and how money and success can take someone away from poverty and distress. But Jordan is clear that his roots are still in South Central (Lyrics.com 2012).

Songs of political, economic, and personal protest and criticism that challenged the dominant ideology *and* made it to the top of the charts were nowhere to be found in the top ten songs from the *Billboard* Hot 100 in the early twenty-first century—despite the fact that the United States was in the midst of the deepest recession since the Depression.

As we have noted, some of the tools to assess entertainment media revolve around the prevalence of various characters and themes, the range of images and messages, and the repetition of these messages. Messages about class do not prevail in hit songs from the year 1995. However, of the songs that do address class, 83 percent question the dominant culture, the meaning of class divisions, and the human consequences of poverty.

From the 1950s through the 1990s, lyrics that included class in Top 40 hits were less than 5 percent of the songs in the study. But those images were not cookie-cutter replicas of each other. They offered the kind of range and diversity in themes that defy stereotypes and make economic distinctions visible. Perhaps this is because the audience demographics of Top 40 music reveal much younger listeners than those of film or prime-time television. Or perhaps music creators and producers can take more risks because it is cheaper to produce one song or CD than it is to produce a film or TV series. In any case, this time period was a small but mighty example of the possibilities of the expression of diverse themes coupled with the economic success of the media.

The total percentage of themes about class in the 1955–1995 study was 4 percent, with a significant number of these themes offering serious challenges to the dominant ideology about class. By contrast, 36 percent of songs in a 2007–2011 study (Holtzman 2012) involved themes about class. However, the themes in the popular music of the early twenty-first century were quite different from those in the mid- to late twentieth century. There were very few songs that criticized the economic inequities of the recession or challenged some of the strong beliefs that characterized the prevailing ideology about class as a kind of "we all get what we deserve" mentality. And surprisingly, there were no songs that lamented love across class lines nor celebrated the idea that love conquers all (Holtzman 1998, 2012). Table 3.3 on page 218 provides the details of this study of class depiction during the five years that included and surrounded the Great Recession.

The international magazine *Billboard* is one of the oldest, most popular, and most credible trade magazines in the music world. One of the major and most notable tools in its musical arsenal is the collection, maintenance, and distribution of charts that report the popularity of music. The two most well-known *Billboard* charts are the *Billboard* Hot 100, which ranks the top 100 songs regardless of musical genre, and the *Billboard* 200, which charts the top albums. *Billboard* has been producing music popularity charts since 1940 and in 1958 published its first Hot 100 chart.

The songs that constituted the earliest Hot 100 charts were determined by a formula that tracked the song's play-time on the radio, on jukeboxes, and in sales of "singles." As the music industry changed over the years, *Billboard* shifted its Hot 100 calculation method to incorporate the rapid changes in how music is produced, distributed, and listened to by audiences. Jukeboxes have come and gone, and the single recording has come and gone and come back again in the form of ninety-nine-cent online purchases from iTunes and other Internet sources. Digital recordings, Internet streaming, and other similar changes not only set the old-fashioned records spinning in a different direction, but also sent *Billboard*'s methods for tracking music popularity into frequent tailspins, followed by policy changes to accurately reflect the popularity of contemporary music.

Billboard finally found a way to escort the Hot 100 chart into the twenty-first century. By 2005, *Billboard* joined forces with the Nielsen Corporation, the industry standard-bearer for tracking the popularity of TV programs, to use Nielsen's Soundscan program, which tracks digital songs. By 2005, the *Billboard* formula for assessing the popularity of musical singles, regardless of genre, included a combination of radio airplay, record sales, and digital songs. By 2007, *Billboard* added to its formula two more methods of tracking music popularity: streamed and on-demand music (Trust 2013).

A study was conducted to examine the presence of socioeconomic themes in the lyrics

Table 3.3

Themes About Class in *Billboard* Hot 100 Songs, 2007–2011

Year	Total number of themes about class per year	Themes						
		Support the American Dream	Love conquers all	Personal sorrow about money	Criticism of economic disparity	Poverty	Wealth	Recession
		Number (%)	Number (%)	Number (%)	Number (%)	Number (%)	Number (%)	Number (%)
2007	6	0	0	3 (50%)	0	0	2 (33%)	1 (17%)
2008	1	0	0	0	0	0	1 (100%)	0
2009	3	0	0	0	0	0	3 (100%)	0
2010	4	0	0	1 (25%)	1 (25%)	1 (25%)	1 (25%)	0
2011	4	1 (25%)	0	1 (25%)	1 (25%)	0	1 (25%)	0
Total number and percentage per theme	18 (4%)	1 (.2%)	0	5 (1%)	2 (.4%)	1 (.2%)	8 (2%)	1 (.2%)

of the top ten musical hits on *Billboard*'s annual Hot 100 charts for the years 2007 to 2011 (Holtzman 2012). These years coincide with the years that the Great Recession officially began through two years after it officially ended, when unemployment, housing foreclosures, and housing starts were beginning to turn around. We have already seen that the recession-triggered economic plight of high unemployment and record housing foreclosures of working-class and middle-class families barely registered in box office film hits.

Thirty-six percent of the fifty songs that were analyzed from 2007 to 2011 included minor to major themes about money or socioeconomic class. Another 4 percent of these songs involved brief mention of money or class. This is roughly six times the number of popular songs with lyrics about class in the 1955–1995 study discussed above. A surface look at this substantial increase would lead to an assumption that there was a growing trend for music to address class both more frequently, more directly, and more profoundly than TV or film. But this assumption would be wrong. The songs from the 1955–1995 study showed a diversity in the themes about class and indicated a substantial presence of themes that challenged the dominant ideology that love conquers all in matters of class and that virtue and hard work alone can lead to the American Dream of economic success. In the comparable study of songs in the early twenty-first century, there were no songs with themes claiming that love conquers all nor were there any songs proclaiming or criticizing the validity of the American Dream.

Let us take a closer look at these numbers and percentages and the lyrics of some of the songs to get a better idea of whether this sharp increase in the inclusion of class reflects something about the artists' response to the recession or an increased awareness about class issues. The themes that were examined in these songs included the American Dream; the idea that love conquers all; personal sorrow about money; criticism of economic disparity; poverty; wealth; and the recession. The themes that were most prevalent in these songs involved wealth. Eight of the songs included anything from a brief mention of wealth to a major theme about wealth. Five of these songs, all by male singers, involved the connection between money and sex—either to "buy" sex with money or to use money and the indicators of wealth (cars, clothes, cash, sunglasses, etc.) as the main attraction of sexual seduction. One of these songs, "Buy U a Drank" by T-Pain, was number five on the chart for 2007. Its lyrics include "Find me in the gray Cadillac / Let's talk money" (Lyrics.com 2012).

The number 6 *Billboard* Hot 100 song for 2010 was "Airplanes," sung by B.o.B and written by Bruno Mars. This song was very different from most of the other songs about wealth and in fact combined the facts about a successful career that brought wealth with a lament about the negative way money changes things. Alluding to the title of "Airplanes," the narrator wishes that airplanes were shooting stars so he could make a wish, which would be "Somebody take me back to the days / Before this was a job" (Lyrics.com 2012).

Only one song, the 2007 "Umbrella" by Rihanna and Jay Z, made even the briefest and thinnest of references to the recession: "Let it rain, I hydroplane in the bank, coming down with the Dow Jones." In the 2007 song "Glamorous," Fergie sings about the opulent, fashionable, trendy life she leads, hints at the superficiality and emptiness of life in the "fast lane," and directly asserts that "the [music] industry is cold." Fergie's lyrics,

B.o.B.'s "Airplane," and some X-rated lyrics from Ceelo Green's 2011 song "Forget You" are the only three songs out of the fifty in the study that asserted any mild to strong criticism of economic disparity (Lyrics.com 2012).

In the five-year period surrounding the recession, nearly half of the songs about class revolved around wealth in a way that rhapsodized about materialism or cynically and crassly equated wealth with the ability to buy everything you could possibly want in life, which in the eight songs in this category was mostly sex. By contrast, none of the fifty songs from this time period included the theme of love conquers all, in which, despite the opposition of family and friends, love between people on opposite sides of the tracks can overcome any obstacles. On the one hand, very few songs in this time period reinforced the classic media myths about class, including love conquering all and the American Dream. On the other hand, in a time period in which, "in addition to income inequality, some studies have shown declines in social mobility in the United States—where the idea that anyone could rise from humble roots was always a big part of the American dream," only three songs even mentioned economic disparity (Khan 2012).

Many of the most popular recession-era films were all about action and romance and still perpetuated some of the myths about socioeconomic class in the form of the American Dream and the idea that love-conquers-all, while by contrast the popular music from that period mostly addressed class in the form of money insofar as it can buy sex, devoid of love. The main thing that popular film and popular music had in common was that they almost completely avoided topics related to the biggest recession since the Great Depression. During the recession, the most important messages in two of the most influential forms of popular media were nonmessages. Themes in both film and music regarding the individuals and families struggling to survive in an economy characterized by record unemployment and housing foreclosures were missing in action.

There are at least two different ways to interpret this avoidance. On the one hand, perhaps this evasion meets the needs of audiences who are struggling daily to make ends meet and do not want to watch and listen to those same struggles when they pay to see a movie or to buy a CD. On the other hand, at their best, popular media can serve as an art form that helps people understand the big picture, see the reflection of their biggest triumphs, failures, and tragedies, or feel compassion for the triumphs, failures, and tragedies of people different from them. People may see musical or dramatic representations of the structural failures of the economy, the experiences and facts that point to Wall Street as bearing the responsibility for the recession, which may help them understand that the loss of their jobs or their homes was not always a result of their singular personal failure. Good popular art, as in *Winter's Bone*, can also let audiences see the possibility of goodness and integrity and hope in the darkest of times.

CHAPTER SUMMARY

Many of us were taught through formal education and personal experience that the United States is a classless society in which the American Dream of economic success is available to all those who work hard and demonstrate virtue. Through much of the last half of the twentieth century, most of us learned little about the history of labor and the history of structural barriers to economic success. In our informal education, many of us were also taught that it is impolite to discuss money or income or economic status. Most prime-time television and film reinforced these themes about economic class, social mobility, and the possibilities for economic success. For the most part, popular music does not address themes of class. But in the few hit songs that do, the audience is invited to think critically about the existence of economic divisions and how they hurt individuals and groups in the United States. In the early part of the twenty-first century, the messages in film and prime-time television continued this pattern of frequency and content. The messages in music were somewhat different, reflecting some of the personal results of skewed values and the corruption of great wealth. These lyrics were cast not as criticism, but often as a recounting of the material things and empty sex that this money could buy. In the years surrounding the Great Recession, there was little reflection in popular media of the personal impact of massive job loss, housing foreclosures, or other material and emotional consequences of financial loss.

Much of the information in this chapter is different from what we have been taught and from what most of us have learned. As you read it, you may have found yourself resistant to the material or may have had difficulty reconciling it to what you already "know." This is part of the process of reconstructing knowledge. It is your work to weigh what you learned in the past against the material that challenges it in this chapter, rethinking your perspective on economic class and drawing your own independent conclusions.

GLOSSARY OF KEY TERMS

American Dream: The traditional American Dream includes the promise and the belief that there is a level playing field and equal opportunity for all Americans. This dream includes the ability to move ahead, to move up, and to succeed by increasing one's income, wealth, and status. One of the key elements of the classic American Dream is the belief that economic and professional success is based exclusively on individual effort, virtue, and merit and that the actions to reach the highest levels are under each individual's control. By inference, the American Dream teaches that if people succeed, they get the credit, and if they fail, they get the blame; unequal opportunities simply do not factor into the equation.

class: A relative social ranking based on income, wealth, status, and/or power.

classism: A set of individual and institutional beliefs, systems, and practices that assigns value to people according to their ranking by income, wealth, status, and/or power and creates an economic inequality affording economic privilege to some while targeting others for oppression.

depression: Economists disagree on the definition of a depression and how it differs from a recession. The National Bureau of Economic Research (NBER) is officially responsible for defining as well as declaring the official beginning and ending of both depressions and recessions. NBER uses two criteria to distinguish a depression: either the gross domestic product (GDP) must have declined by more than 10 percent or the decline must have lasted for more than one year. The Great Depression of the 1930s met both of these criteria.

gross domestic product (GDP): One of the primary indicators economists use as a dipstick to gauge the health of the country's economy. The GDP is the size of the economy—the total price tag of everything that is produced in the United States.

gross national product (GNP): The value of what is produced by the country's residents or businesses whether in the United States or abroad.

housing bubble: When housing loans and mortgages are based on high risk and high-interest loans, the housing industry soars and sometimes peaks, but is based on a fragile foundation. When people are unable to keep up with these high-interest loans, mortgage and loan losses can reach epidemic proportions. When this occurs, the "bubble" can burst and is often accompanied by other financial failures, including housing foreclosures, severe declines in housing sales and construction, and a loss of construction and related jobs.

level playing field: The classic American belief that there is equal opportunity for everyone in the United States to potentially achieve the same economic, academic, and professional success regardless of one's race, gender, ethnicity, or the income of one's family. The concept of the level playing field ignores or discounts any differences in background that may provide advantages that help some individuals or groups to succeed and disadvantages for other individuals or groups that stand in the way of their success.

recession: The National Bureau of Economic Research (NBER) defines the official start of a recession following two quarters in which there is a decline of the gross domestic product.

subprime loans and mortgages: High-interest and high-risk lending practices in the housing industry were often the only option for the eager but financially stressed and stretched prospective home buyer. These nontraditional alternatives were often the only home loans available to people with poor credit or other financial problems and as a result were seductive opportunities despite the risk.

REFLECTION, SUMMARY, AND ANALYSIS

Instructions

The chapter questions invite you to engage in an exercise of reflection, summary, and analysis about key terms, topics, and issues discussed in the chapter. The skills involved in responding to the questions are a combination of summary and analysis. The *summary* component of the questions requires you to demonstrate your understanding of the terms and concepts in the chapter through the use of describing, explaining, and restating. *Summary* involves primarily answering questions that begin with "what."

The *analysis* component of the questions requires you to use your own independent thinking, your own ideas and arguments. *Analysis* requires breaking something— like a concept, theory, or argument—into parts so you can understand and describe how those parts work together to make the whole. Analytic writing goes beyond the obvious to discuss questions of how and why—so ask yourself those questions as you read. Your responses to these kinds of questions will require that you carefully and clearly state your argument, opinion, or "thesis" statement and use evidence from the chapter as well as your own experience and observations to support your thesis or view.

The University of North Carolina's Writing Center website has an excellent two-page handout on analysis and summary (http://writingcenter.unc.edu/handouts/summary-using-it-wisely/).

Please type and double-space your paper using 12-point font. *The length of your paper is not important as long as you carefully follow the instructions!* A successful paper will use evidence and examples from the film and the text. You can get additional information about the film at the Internet Movie Database website at www.IMDb .com. When you use the text and any other sources, please use internal citations according to the directions of your instructor.

Study Questions

1. Describe your overall observations, thoughts, and feelings about *Cinderella Man*.
2. Using the information from this chapter, describe Jennifer Hochschild's definitions and the four elements of the American Dream. What are some time periods in American history when the American Dream seemed possible and realistic? What were other examples in American history when the American Dream seemed inaccessible to most people? To answer these last two questions, think about the fabric of oppression discussed in Chapter 1 and

Figure 1.4 that indicates which groups are privileged by oppression and which groups are targeted by oppression. In the history of the United States, which of these groups experienced the American Dream as very difficult or nearly impossible to attain?

3. In the film *Cinderella Man*, what kind of character is James Braddock Jr.? Is he simple or complex? Is he generally portrayed as likable? Describe how he and his family move back and forth between different socioeconomic classes. Were you rooting for him to win the various boxing matches he enters?

4. Describe the depiction of the American Dream, as defined in question 2 above, for Braddock and his family in the film. How is this depiction the same for most other characters in the film? How is it different?

5. How likely or unlikely is the American Dream depicted in the film? What does Braddock have to do to reach the American Dream (as defined by Hochschild)? How does he conform or not conform to Hochschild's four elements of the American Dream?

6. If most popular U.S. media conveyed a steady diet of messages similar to those in *Cinderella Man*, what are audiences most likely to believe about socioeconomic class and the American Dream?

7. Describe the fabric of oppression as it relates to class. Which groups are privileged and which groups are targeted in the context of class? Using information for as far back as you can find, describe your family's initial experience in the United States according to one of the categories below. If your heritage involves more than one of these categories, respond separately for each of the categories that applies and explain which one was most likely to match the way your family was treated. Use the guidelines below to help you answer this question.

8. Describe any privilege and/or barriers related to socioeconomic class and the fabric of oppression that your family had in the past three generations (your generation, your parents' generation, and your grandparents' generation).

9. Describe the meaning of the term "cognitive dissonance." Were your experiences and beliefs generally compatible with the information about class, the history of class in the United States, and the ideas and concepts about class that were introduced in this chapter? In the course of your reading of Chapter 3 did you find any ideas or concepts that were completely out of line with what you believe? Did you experience any cognitive dissonance in response to any of the information in this chapter or in response to this assignment? If you experienced a gap between your own beliefs and experiences and the information in the chapter, were you able to sit with that ambiguity for a while without immediately needing to get clarity and decide what was true and what was not? Describe any experience of cognitive dissonance you experienced in response to information in this chapter. Did you make a decision about how to resolve the dissonance based on your emotions, thoughts, or a combination of the two? Were you able to make a deliberate and conscious decision to be open to information that challenged your beliefs?

Guidelines for Question 7

If question 7 is difficult for you to answer, you can ask a member of your family who is most knowledgeable about your family's history, use information from Chapter 3 or Chapter 5, and/or use library or Internet sources to find specific or general information that is applicable to your family history. If, after these attempts, you still cannot find much information about your family, use what you have learned from family historians and your other research to address the factors that may have prevented you from obtaining this information.

If your family lived on land that was conquered by the United States (this may apply to you if your family heritage is part or fully Native American or Mexican):

- From what you know about your family history, did the immigrants in your family come to the United States through their own free choice or were they refugees?
- When would your family have been eligible for U.S. citizenship? If you do not know the answer to this question, do a little Internet digging to find out what year people of your heritage were allowed to become U.S. citizens.
- Were there any barriers that your family might have faced that would have prevented them from having full access to jobs, housing, public education, and so on? Consider issues such as ethnicity, skin color or race, and gender.
- Is there any kind of bias your family may have encountered that would have hindered their success in business or a profession and limited their ability to earn money?

If your family members were taken away from their home and brought to the United States for the purpose of slavery (this may apply to you if all or part of your heritage is African):

- How long was your family enslaved—that is, working without pay, probably living in nearly uninhabitable conditions, liable to be torn apart as a family by being bought and sold, and legally prohibited from learning to read?
- At what time in history was your family "freed" and allowed to live outside of enslavement?
- At what time in history was your family eligible for citizenship?
- At what time in history did your family have equal rights to housing, education, employment, and voting?

Answer if the questions below if you, your parents, grandparents or other ancestors immigrated to the United States:

- Approximately what year or decade did they arrive and from what country?
- From what you know from your family and from history, would your family have been welcomed to the United States when they arrived?

- Were they eligible for citizenship when they arrived? If you do not know the answer to this question, do a little Internet digging to find out.
- Were there any barriers that your family might have faced that would prevent them from having full access to jobs, housing, public education, and so on? Consider issues such as ethnicity, skin color or race, and gender.
- Is there any kind of bias your family may have encountered that would have hindered their success in business or a profession and limited their ability to earn money?

BIBLIOGRAPHY

Adams, Maurianne, Lee Anne Bell, and Pat Griffin, eds. 1997. *Teaching for Diversity and Social Justice: A Sourcebook*. New York: Routledge.

Alper, Loretta, dir. 2005. *Class Dismissed: How TV Frames the Working Class*. DVD. Northampton, MA: Media Education Foundation.

Avatar2. 2012. "Avatar 2 News," Movies.com, March 12. www.movies.com.

Baran, Stanley J., and Dennis K. Davis. 2009. *Mass Communication Theory: Foundations, Ferment, and Future*. Boston: Wadsworth Cengage Learning.

Barlett, Donald L., and James B. Steele. 1992. *America: What Went Wrong?* Kansas City, MO: Andrews and McMeel.

Barr, Meghan. 2012. "Occupy Wall Street: 6 Months Later, What Has Occupy Protest Movement Achieved?" *Huffington Post*, March 16.

Beale, Lewis. 2010. "Recession-Themed Films? Not at the Multiplex." *Los Angeles Times*, November 7.

Box Office Mojo. 2005. "2005 Domestic Grosses." http://boxofficemojo.com.

———. 2010. "2010 Domestic Grosses." http://boxofficemojo.com.

———. 2012. "All-Time Top Box Office Hits." http://boxofficemojo.com.

Bullard, R., ed. 1993. *Confronting Environmental Racism*. Boston: South End Press.

Bush, George W. 2003. "Remarks on Signing the American Dream Downpayment Act." December 16. In *The American Presidency Project*, by Gerhard Peters and John T. Woolley. www.presidency. ucsb.edu/ws/?pid=64935.

Butsch, Richard. 1992. "Class and Gender in Four Decades of Television Situation Comedy." *Critical Studies in Mass Communications* 9, no. 4 (December): 387–406.

———. 1995. "Ralph, Fred, Archie, and Homer: Why Television Keeps Recreating the White Male Working-Class Buffoon." In *Gender, Race, and Class in Media*, ed. Gail Dines and Jean M. Humez, 403. Thousand Oaks, CA: Sage.

———. 2003. "A Half Century of Class and Gender in American TV Domestic Sitcoms." *Cercles: Revue Pluridisciplinaire Du Monde Anglophone* 8: 16–34.

Cauthen, Nancy K., and Sarah Fass. 2008. "Measuring Poverty in the United States." Fact sheet, June. New York: National Center for Children in Poverty. www.nccp.org/publications/pdf/text_825.pdf.

Congressional Budget Office (CBO). 2011. "Trends in the Distribution of Household Income Between 1979 and 2007." Washington, DC, October. www.cbo.gov/sites/default/files/cbofiles/attachments /10-25-HouseholdIncome.pdf.

Croteau, David, and William Hoynes. 1997. *Media/Society: Industries, Images, and Audiences*. Thousand Oaks, CA: Pine Forge Press.

Dates, Jannette L., and William Barlow, eds. 1990. *Split Image: African Americans and the Mass Media*. Washington, DC: Howard University Press.

Debusmann, Bernd. 2010. "Obama and the American Dream in Reverse." *Reuters*, September 24. http://blogs.reuters.com/great-debate/2010/09/24/obama-and-the-american-dream-in-reverse/.

DeLone, Richard D. 1979. *Small Futures: Children, Inequality, and the Limits of Liberal Reform*. New York: Harcourt Brace Jovanovich.

Despicable Me. 2010. http://despicableme.com/.

Ebert, Roger. 2005. "Review: *Cinderella Man*." *Chicago Sun-Times*, June 2. www.rogerebert.com/reviews/cinderella-man-2005.

———. 2010. "Review: *Wall Street: Money Never Sleeps*." *Chicago Sun Times*, September 22. www.rogerebert.com/reviews/wall-street-money-never-sleeps-2010.

Ehrenreich, Barbara. 1995. "The Silenced Majority: Why the Average Working Person Has Disappeared from American Media and Culture." In *Gender, Race, and Class in Media*, ed. Gail Dines and Jean M. Humez, 41. Thousand Oaks, CA: Sage.

Financial Crisis Inquiry Commission (FCIC). 2011. Press Release, January 27.

Federal Education Budget Project. 2013. "Background and Analysis: School Finance—Federal, State, and Local K-12 School Finance Overview." New America Foundation, June. http://febp.newamerica.net/background-analysis/school-finance.

Franich, Darren. 2011. "Who Should Direct 'Thor 2'?" PopWatch, EW.com, July 1. http://popwatch.ew.com/2011/07/01/thor-sequel-director/.

Fretts, Bruce. 1998. "All About the King of Queens." *Entertainment Weekly*, December 11.

Gautney, Heather. 2011. "What Is Occupy Wall Street? The History of Leaderless Movements." *Washington Post*, October 10.

Goodman, Christopher, and Stephen M. Mance. 2011. "Employment Loss and 2007–09 Recession: An Overview." *Monthly Labor Review* 134, no. 4 (April): 53–59.

Gutman, Herbert G. 1974. "The Social Backgrounds of Entrepreneurs in Paterson, New Jersey." In *Three Centuries of Social Mobility in America*, ed. Edward Pessen. Lexington, MA: Heath.

Hacker, Jacob, Suzanne Mettler, Dianne Pinderhughes, and Theda Skocpol. 2004. "Inequality and Public Policy." Report by the Task Force on Inequality and American Democracy of the American Political Science Association.

Heffernan, Virginia. 2007. "Hey! Never Underestimate the Average Joe." *New York Times*, January 3.

Hernandez, Donald J. 2011. "Declining Fortunes of Children in Middle-Class Families: Economic Inequality and Child Well-Being in the 21st Century." Foundation for Child Development, Child and Youth Well-Being Index (CWI) Policy Brief, January. New York: Foundation for Child Development. http://fcd-us.org/sites/default/files/2011%20Declining%20Fortunes_0.pdf.

Himmelstein, Hal. 1994. *Television Myth and the American Mind*. Westport, CT: Praeger.

Hochschild, Jennifer L. 1995. *Facing Up to the American Dream: Race, Class, and the Soul of the Nation*. Princeton: Princeton University Press.

Holden, Stephen. 2010. "Perils of the Corporate Ladder: It Hurts When You Fall." *New York Times*, December 9.

Holtzman, Linda. 1998. Unpublished content analysis of class in popular music, 1955–1995.

———. 2012. Unpublished content analysis of "*Billboard* Hot 100," 2007–2012.

Howe, Desson. 1987. "'Matewan' (PG-13)." *Washington Post*, October 16.

Internet Movie Database. 1999–2000. www.us.IMDb.com.

Investopedia staff. 2009. "What is GDP and why is it so important?" February 26. www.investopedia.com.

InvestorWords.com. 2011. "Definition: GNP." www.investorwords.com/2186/GNP.html.

James, Caryn. 1995. "Dysfunction Wears Out Its Welcome." *New York Times*, December 3.

Jhally, Sut, and Justin Lewis. 1992. *Enlightened Racism: The Cosby Show, Audience, and the Myth of the American Dream*. Boulder, CO: Westview Press.

Katz, Bruce and Matthew Fellowes. 2005. "The Price is Wrong: Getting the Market Right for Working Families in Philadelphia." Brookings Institution Metropolitan Policy Program, April.

Kendall, Diana. 1999. *Sociology in Our Times*. Belmont, CA: Wadsworth.

Khan, Shabaz. 2012. "Income Inequality." Inequality Separates and Destroys Society: A Current Event Connection. http://shahbazkhaninequality.weebly.com/a-current-event-connection.html.

Kochhar, Rakesh, Richard Fry, and Paul Taylor. 2011. "Wealth Gaps Rise to Record Highs Between Whites, Blacks, Hispanics, Twenty-to-One," Pew Research, Social and Demographic Trends. www.pewsocialtrends.org/2011/07/26/wealth-gaps-rise-to-record-highs-between-whites-blacks -hispanics/.

Koehler, Robert. 1999. "Kazan's HUAC Testimony a Permanent Black Mark." *Variety*, March.

Lahr, John. 2000. *Show and Tell: New Yorker Profiles*. Woodstock, NY: Overlook Press.

Langston, Donna. 1995. "Tired of Playing Monopoly?" In *Race, Class, and Gender*, ed. Margaret L. Andersen and Patricia Hill Collins, 101–102. Belmont, CA: Wadsworth.

Lichter, Robert S., Linda S. Lichter, and Stanley Rothman. 1994. *Prime Time: How TV Portrays American Culture*. Washington, DC: Regnery.

Loewen, James W. 1995. *Lies My Teacher Told Me: Everything Your American History Textbook Got Wrong*. New York: Touchstone.

Lowrey, Annie. 2012. "Income Inequality May Take Toll on Growth," *New York Times*, October 18.

Lyrics.com. 2012. www.lyrics.com.

Main, Jackson T. 1974. "Social Mobility in Revolutionary America." In *Three Centuries of Social Mobility in America*, ed. Edward Pessen. Lexington, MA: Heath.

Manchester, Joyce, and Julie Topolesk. 2008. "Growing Disparities in Life Expectancy." Congressional Budget Office, April.

Manning, Robert D. 2000. *Credit Card Nation*. New York: Basic Books.

Marc, David. 1997. *Comic Visions: Television Comedy and American Culture*. Malden, MA: Blackwell.

Mayerle, Judine. 1994. "Roseanne—How Did You Get Inside My House? A Case Study of a Hit Blue-Collar Situation Comedy." In *Television: The Critical View*, 5th ed., ed. Horace Newcomb, 102–113. New York: Oxford University Press.

McElvaine, Robert S. 1993. *The Great Depression*. New York: Times Books.

Menard, Russell. 1974. "The Social Mobility of Indentured Servants." In *Three Centuries of Social Mobility in America*, ed. Edward Pessen, 20–28. Lexington, MA: Heath.

Mishel, Lawrence R., and Jared Bernstein, eds. 1993. *The State of Working America*. Armonk, NY: M.E. Sharpe.

National Bureau of Economic Research (NBER). 2013. http://www.nber.org.

National Center for Children in Poverty (NCCP). 2013. "Basic Needs Budget Calculator." www.nccp.org/tools/frs/budget.php.

Noe, Denise. 1995. "Parallel Worlds: The Surprising Similarities and Differences in Country-and-Western and Rap." *Humanist* 55: 20–23.

Nord, Mark, Margaret Andrews, and Steven Carlson. 2009. "Table 1: Households and Individuals by Food Security Status of Household, 1998–2008" and "Table 1B: Households with Children, and Children, by Food Security Status of Household, 1998–2008." In *Household Food Security in the United States, 2008*, 6–7. Washington, DC: U.S. Department of Agriculture. www.ers.usda.gov /publications/err-economic-research-report/err83.aspx#.UadCq9LYf9g.

O'Connor, John J. 1993. "Review: Finally, Mother Knows Best." *New York Times*, September 29.

Olsen, Joan. 1995. "The Horatio Alger Exercise." Unpublished manuscript.

Pessen, Edward, ed. 1974. *Three Centuries of Social Mobility in America*. Lexington, MA: Heath.

Pew Research Center. 2010. *A Balance Sheet at 30 Months: How the Great Recession Has Changed Life in America*. A Social and Demographic Trends Report, June 30. Washington, DC: Pew Research Center. www.pewsocialtrends.org/files/2010/11/759.

Phillips, Kevin. 1990. *The Politics of Rich and Poor*. New York: Harper.

Puig, Claudia. 2009. "Strong Acting Can't Outrun Shallow Tale in 'The Blind Side,'" *USA Today*, November 20.

Rampel, Catherine. 2009. "SAT Scores and Family Income." *New York Times*, August 27.

Rose, Joel. 2011. "New York Wrestles over Extending Millionaire's Tax." National Public Radio, Morning Edition, October 28. www.npr.org/2011/10/28/141771136/new-york-wrestles-over-extending -millionaires-tax.

Ross, Steven J. 1998. *Working-Class Hollywood*. Princeton, NJ: Princeton University Press.

Samuels, David. 1991. "The Rap on Rap: 'Black Music' That Isn't Either." *New Republic* 205: 24–29.

Samuelson, Robert J. 2011. "Rethinking the Great Recession." *The Wilson Quarterly* (Winter). Woodrow Wilson International Center for Scholars.

Scalzi. John. 2005. "Being Poor," September 3. http://whatever.scalzi.com/2005/09/03/being-poor.

Schmidt, Michael S. 2012. "Less Visible Occupy Movement Looks for Staying Power," *New York Times*, March 31.

Senzani. Alessandra. 2010. "Class and gender as a laughing matter? The case of *Roseanne*." *Humor: International Journal of Humor Research* 23, no 2 (May): 229–253.

Shtauber, Assaf A. 2013. "The Effects of Access to Mainstream Financial Services on the Poor: Evidence from Data on Recipients of Financial Education." Russell Sage Foundation Working Paper, June.

Sklar, Robert. 1980. *Prime-Time America: Life On and Behind the Television Screen*. New York: Oxford University Press.

Strutz, Tilman. 2013. *The Fading American Dream: The Occupy Movement as a Response to Economic Inequality in the American Society*. Munich, Germany: GRIN Verlag Publishing.

Takaki, Ronald. 1993. *A Different Mirror: A History of Multicultural America*. Boston: Little, Brown.

Taskforce on Inequality and American Democracy. 2004. American Political Science Association. https://www.apsanet.org/content_2471.cfm.

Thernstrom, Stephan. 1974. "Working-Class Upward Mobility in Newburyport." In *Three Centuries of Social Mobility in America*, ed. Edward Pessen. Lexington, MA: Heath.

Treas, Judith. 2010. "The Great American Recession: Sociological Insights on Blame and Pain." *Sociological Perspectives* 53, no. 1 (Spring): 3–17.

Trust, Gary. 2013. "Ask *Billboard*: How Does the Hot 100 Work?" *Billboard*, September 29. www.billboard.com/articles/columns/chart-beat/5740625/ask-billboard-how-does-the-hot-100-work.

U.S. Bureau of Labor Statistics. 2010. *Consumer Expenditure Survey, 2006–2007*. Washington, DC: U.S. Department of Labor. Report 1021, July. www.bls.gov/cex/twoyear/200607/csxtwoyr.pdf.

———. 2013. "Databases, Tables and Calculators by Subject," U.S. Department of Labor. http://data.bls.gov/timeseries/LNS14000000.

U.S. Census Bureau. 1990. *Statistical Abstract of the United States*. Washington, DC: U.S. Government Printing Office.

———. 1992. *Statistical Abstract of the United States*. Washington, DC: U.S. Government Printing Office.

U.S. Department of Housing and Urban Development. 2012. American Dream Downpayment Initiative. http://portal.hud.gov/hudportal/HUD?src=/program_offices/comm_planning/affordablehousing/programs/home/addi.

Vannean, Reeve, and Lynn Weber Cannon. 1987. *The American Perception of Class*. Philadelphia: Temple University Press.

Waddan, Alex. 2010. "The US Safety Net, Inequality and the Great Recession." *Journal of Poverty and Social Justice*, 243–254.

Warren, Spencer. 1994. "The 100 Best Conservative Movies." *National Review* 46, no. 20 (October): 53.

Weller, Christian, Jaryn Fields, and Folayemi Agbede. 2011. "The State of Communities of Color in the U.S. Economy." Center for American Progress, January 21. www.americanprogress.org/issues/economy/report/2011/01/21/8881/the-state-of-communities-of-color-in-the-u-s-economy/.

Wolff, Edward. 1995. *Top Heavy: The Study of Increasing Inequality of Wealth in America*. New York: The Twentieth Century Fund Press.

Zandy, Janet. 1995. "Decloaking Class: Why Class Identity and Consciousness Count." *Race, Gender, and Class* 4, no. 1: 9–13.

Zaniello, Tom. 1996. *Working Stiffs, Union Maids, Reds, and Riffraff: An Organized Guide to Films About Labor*. Ithaca, NY: ILR Press.

4

Racing in America

Fact or Fiction?

> Being the other means feeling different. It means being outside the
> game, outside the circle, outside the set. It means being on the edges,
> on the margins, on the periphery. Otherness means feeling excluded,
> closed out, precluded, even disdained and scorned. It produces a sense
> of isolation, of apartness, of disconnectedness, of alienation.
>
> —*Arturo Madrid*

> Was your ethnic or cultural group ever considered not white? When
> they arrived in the United States, what did members of your family
> have to do to be accepted as white? What did they have to give up?
>
> —*Paul Kivel*

> We are trapped in history and history is trapped in us.
>
> —*James Baldwin*

In Chapter 1 you took a multicultural quiz that asked you to examine your experiences in the context of race, religion, sexual orientation, and economic and social class. This time, the questions in Personal Inventory 4.1 will ask you to focus exclusively on race.

Once you have completed the inventory, tally your score. If you scored 6–11 points on this quiz, you, like the majority of U.S. residents, lived in a very racially isolated world as you were growing up. You have been around people who are primarily your race and have had limited contact with people who are racially different from you.

If you scored 12–17 points, you have had some contact with people who are racially different from you. Perhaps you went to school or belonged to clubs with young people of other races. Your regular, daily contact with people of other races was still quite limited.

If you scored 18–23 points, you have had contact with a few racial groups that are different from your own racial group. If you are Asian American, perhaps you went to school with other students who were Latino or African American but had limited contact with American Indians or European Americans.

If you scored 24–30 points, you have had a rare experience living in the United States. You have had extensive contact and interaction with people of many other races where you lived, in school, and socially.

Personal Inventory 4.1
Racing in America

Instructions

Answer the questions below with the response that comes closest to your experience. If you have moved frequently, answer the questions based on your combined experiences. Determine in each instance whether you were in the racial majority or minority. Score 1 point for answers "a," "b," "c," "d," or "e." Score 2 points for "f," 3 points for "g," 4 points for "h," and 5 points for "i."

1. Describe the racial composition of the neighborhood in which you grew up:
   a. mostly European American (white) _____
   b. mostly African American _____
   c. mostly Asian American/Pacific Islander _____
   d. mostly Latino _____
   e. mostly American Indian _____
   f. a strong mix of 2 of the groups listed in a–e _____
   g. a strong mix of 3 of the groups listed in a–e _____
   h. a strong mix of 4 of the groups listed in a–e _____
   i. a strong mix of 5 of the groups listed in a–e _____
2. Describe the racial composition of your friends from grade school through high school:
   a. mostly European American (white) _____
   b. mostly African American _____
   c. mostly Asian American/Pacific Islander _____
   d. mostly Latino _____
   e. mostly American Indian _____
   f. a strong mix of 2 of the groups listed in a–e _____
   g. a strong mix of 3 of the groups listed in a–e _____
   h. a strong mix of 4 of the groups listed in a–e _____
   i. a strong mix of 5 of the groups listed in a–e _____
3. Describe the racial composition of your parents' friends:
   a. mostly European American (white) _____
   b. mostly African American _____
   c. mostly Asian American/Pacific Islander _____
   d. mostly Latino _____
   e. mostly American Indian _____
   f. a strong mix of 2 of the groups listed in a–e _____
   g. a strong mix of 3 of the groups listed in a–e _____
   h. a strong mix of 4 of the groups listed in a–e _____
   i. a strong mix of 5 of the groups listed in a–e _____

Personal Inventory 4.1 *(continued)*

4. Describe the racial composition of the school(s) you attended:
    a. mostly European American (white) _____
    b. mostly African American _____
    c. mostly Asian American/Pacific Islander _____
    d. mostly Latino _____
    e. mostly American Indian _____
    f. a strong mix of 2 of the groups listed in a–e _____
    g. a strong mix of 3 of the groups listed in a–e _____
    h. a strong mix of 4 of the groups listed in a–e _____
    i. a strong mix of 5 of the groups listed in a–e _____
5. Describe the racial composition of the religious institution you attended:
    a. mostly European American (white) _____
    b. mostly African American _____
    c. mostly Asian American/Pacific Islander _____
    d. mostly Latino _____
    e. mostly American Indian _____
    f. a strong mix of 2 of the groups listed in a–e _____
    g. a strong mix of 3 of the groups listed in a–e _____
    h. a strong mix of 4 of the groups listed in a–e _____
    i. a strong mix of 5 of the groups listed in a–e _____
6. Describe the racial composition of the extracurricular activities in which you participated (clubs, athletics, dance, bowling, debate, etc.):
    a. mostly European American (white) _____
    b. mostly African American _____
    c. mostly Asian American/Pacific Islander _____
    d. mostly Latino _____
    e. mostly American Indian _____
    f. a strong mix of 2 of the groups listed in a–e _____
    g. a strong mix of 3 of the groups listed in a–e _____
    h. a strong mix of 4 of the groups listed in a–e _____
    i. a strong mix of 5 of the groups listed in a–e _____

Total score _____

Most of us who have grown up in the United States will score 15 points or under on this quiz. Despite laws and programs regarding school desegregation and open housing, most U.S. neighborhoods and schools are still racially isolated. Even those communities that have been intentional in their goals to be multiracial are still limited.

In the previous exercise, you investigated your exposure to racial groups that are different from yours. In the next exercise, in Personal Inventory 4.2, you will begin to consider what you were told about race. The answers to the eight questions in the inventory will vary greatly across urban, rural, and suburban communities. Your responses may also vary according to your age, the region where you grew up, and the beliefs and values of

Personal Inventory 4.2
Sticks and Stones

Instructions

Answer the questions below in written or oral form to add to your developing autobiography. Exchange your experiences and comments with another person. If you grew up hearing or experiencing hateful things about your race or other races, this exercise may be difficult for you. But if you continue to probe deeply, then you will gain an enormous amount of insight, about your socialization and informal learning regarding race.

1. What did your parents tell you about your race? What words did they use to describe your race? What did your parents tell you about other racial groups? What words did they use to describe other races?
2. What did your grandparents and other extended family tell you about your race? What words did they use to describe your race? What did they tell you about other racial groups? What words did they use to describe other races?
3. Was there ever a time that any of your family members engaged in conflict with each other or people outside of the family regarding race? Describe the situation.
4. What did your friends and classmates say about your race? What kinds of things did they say about racial groups that were different from theirs? What words did they use to describe various racial groups?
5. Did you ever see your friends engage in any conflict regarding race? Describe the situation.
6. Have you ever made a derogatory remark about your race or the race of other people? Have you ever called people a racial name either to their face or behind their backs?
7. Have you ever engaged in any conflict regarding race? Describe the situation.
8. How do you feel about the race you are? What are you most proud of about your race? What is most difficult about being the race you are?

your family and friends. Most significantly, your answers will be influenced by whether your racial group is regarded as the dominant group in the United States (white) or your group has been targeted by racism in the United States (Latino, Asian American, African American, American Indian, multiracial, and so forth).

In an inner-ring suburb of St. Louis called University City, the population of the community is approximately 50 percent European American and 40 percent African American, with only small percentages of other racial groups. The public school population is closer to 90 percent African American. Those black and white children who do go to the public schools have the opportunity to interact with each other, but they have virtually no opportunity to come into contact with young people who are American Indian, Asian American, or Latino. Despite their parents' efforts to live in a racially mixed community, their experiences are still limited.

Reading is a private and often anonymous experience. Unless the author is famous, the readers generally do not know the author's race or ethnicity. And certainly, your race, as the reader, is not known to the author nor are you always conscious of your race and ethnicity as you read fiction and nonfiction, newspapers and magazines. We will change that tradition for this chapter. As coauthors of this book, we will begin by sharing a little bit about who we are and briefly exploring how our lived experiences have been influenced on multiple levels by our racial identities. Then we will invite you, the reader, to do the same.

LINDA'S STORY

My name is Linda Holtzman. I am a white, Jewish woman. Three of my four grandparents were Russian Jews who immigrated to the United States during the first decade of the twentieth century. My fourth grandparent was born in the United States of Russian Jewish immigrant parents. My grandparents' primary language was Yiddish, a combination of Hebrew and German. They spoke little Russian since that was the official language of the land and Jews were not welcome in Russia at that time. Jewish families were targeted by violent pogroms that destroyed their small villages and few possessions.

I do not know the details of what happened to my particular family. I do know that Jews in Russia could only live in certain areas and practice certain jobs and professions. I know that they were generally poor. I know that my grandparents wanted to come to "America," where they could be free to practice their religion and support their families. I know that when they moved to St. Louis, they lived in Russian Jewish enclaves where many people spoke Yiddish and lit candles on Friday night for Shabbes (the Jewish Sabbath, which begins on Friday at sundown and ends on Saturday at sundown) and cooked brisket and rolled meat and cabbage and knishes. They lived in places where they did not feel different from their neighbors.

I know that my paternal grandfather had a small retail store called Holtzman Furniture, Clothing and Appliances in a poor neighborhood in which his customers were primarily African American. As a young girl, I remember "collecting" with my uncle, who would visit customers' homes to secure their monthly payments. My uncle was very nice to the customers, but I noticed that he changed his accent to match theirs when he went to collect. Twenty years later, my first job out of college was teaching elementary school in an African American community. One day, one of my students came running into the classroom and said to me with great excitement, "Miss Holtzman, Miss Holtzman, I found your name on my couch!"

Many of the Jewish families I knew hired someone to clean their houses every week. They were generally personally kind to the people who cleaned their houses, who were always African American women. The employers called these cleaners by their first names and spoke of them to other Jews as "the girl" or "the *schvartze*," which in Yiddish means "black." The women who cleaned earned hourly or daily wages and generally did not receive benefits or health insurance.

My parents were born in the United States and learned English as their first language and today know only a few expressions of Yiddish. My mother can cook some of the traditional Jewish foods, and I can too. I have my grandmother's silver candlesticks, which I light on Shabbes with my family. But I do not know Yiddish, and I do not know in what town in Russia my family lived. I do not know what kind of work they did nor the exact circumstances under which they left Russia. My grandparents never said anything to me about Russia, and there were no records, only a few photos left after they died. In their heavily accented English they were determined to be American and were proud at how American their children and grandchildren were.

My parents, like many second-generation white Americans, pursued the American Dream. My father fought as a U.S. soldier in World War II and was one of the first soldiers present when Allied forces liberated the German concentration camp at Buchenwald. A strong memory from my childhood was my father's story of having captured a German SS guard. My father was holding the German soldier as a prisoner at gunpoint and said to him in German, "I am a Jew," and the man turned and spit into my father's face. Equally strong are the memories my father told my brothers and me about anti-Semitism in the U.S. Army and other soldiers who taunted and tortured him because he was a Jew. He came home from the war to help my grandfather with his small retail business. Neither my parents nor any of my aunts and uncles went to college. They all carved out middle-class incomes through retail businesses they owned or in which they were employed. My mom stayed home to raise the kids. We lived in a middle-class white suburb in a house with a lawn and a two-car garage. There were no people of color in my neighborhood. There was one African American girl in my high school graduating class.

When I was five years old, I remember that while I was walking to kindergarten, a little girl who had just moved in up the street hid behind a tree and threw rocks at me and called me "kike" and "sheeny." I did not know what those words meant, but they sounded mean and hurt my feelings and I told my parents. The girl's father was in the military. My dad told me that he had her father transferred to Okinawa. My dad was in the furniture business with his father at the time and did not have the power to do such a thing. But I believed him and felt protected. When I was in high school, dozens of Jewish girls and a handful of Jewish boys had cosmetic surgery on their noses to "improve their appearance." Now that our families lived in neighborhoods that were both Jewish and Christian, we looked and seemed more different. They wanted to look more like their friends and neighbors.

My teachers, doctors, and neighbors were white, and a few were Jewish. The store clerks and managers were almost all white and Christian. There was one African American woman named Nan who was a clerk at the drugstore near our house. All of the elected officials were white, and none of them were Jewish. The people who owned the big companies around us were white and Christian. The people who owned one of the regional department store chains were Jewish. The milkman was white and Christian. The soda deliveryman was white and Jewish. The man who delivered the dry cleaning was Indian. The African American adults I saw in my community cleaned houses and did yard work or hauled trash or bought what was called "low-end" furniture from Holtzman Furniture. Today, I think of myself as white and Jewish, not Russian American. While I choose to live in a multiracial, multiethnic community and do antiracist work, I am also a product of my story, my history, and my racial legacy. My family's journey to the United States is a story both of being the "other" as Jews and of becoming "white" in America.

LEON'S STORY

My name is Leon Sharpe. I am an African American man. I grew up in a working-class neighborhood in North St. Louis. I am named after my father, who was also born in St. Louis. He was one of six siblings raised by a widowed mother in an area of the city called Mill Creek Valley, a community that has long since been demolished in the name of urban renewal. My father's mother came to St. Louis from Kentucky in 1904 to visit the World's Fair with her sisters. She apparently liked what she saw and never went back home. She eventually married my father's father, who had migrated to St. Louis from Natchez, Mississippi, along with several siblings. He died when my dad was still a toddler. For as long as I can remember, my father's family has gathered at least twice a year to remember, to celebrate, to reunite, and to honor those who came before us.

My mother's family roots are also in the South. Every summer, when I was very young, she would take me and my brother and sister by train from St. Louis to Tupelo, Mississippi, the town where she was born and spent her childhood. She called it "going home." We loved it there. My grandmother, "Big mama," often cooked a big breakfast in the morning—grits and eggs and hot biscuits with fig preserves made from the fruit of the tree behind her house. We spent most of our time outdoors. We would play tag, catch grasshoppers in a jar, chase the neighbor's chickens, and shoot at squirrels with our slingshots and BB guns. Mississippi was where I first experienced drinking well-water from a gourd, eating dinner at lunchtime, eating supper at night, and reading signs that said, "White only." Sometimes, in the after-supper gloaming, we would chase fireflies while all the grown-ups sat around telling stories and listening to the radio on Big mama's front porch. One summer, after we returned home to St. Louis from Tupelo, my mother, father, brother, sister, and I moved from the two-family flat near the Greater Ville area to a house in another neighborhood. It had a nice front porch like the one at Big mama's house down south.

Over the years, our house in St. Louis became a gathering place and way station for my entire extended family. Relatives, distant and close, would stop by en route from Mississippi to Chicago or Kansas City or California. Occasionally, an uncle, aunt, or cousin would move in with us for a spell or a season or some other indeterminate span of time. This usually occurred when people were between jobs or relocating or going through some other form of turbulence in their lives. My brother and sister and I never questioned the presence of these kinfolks and nobody ever bothered to explain. One day they would just be there, melding swiftly into the household flow, and then after a time, just as mysteriously as they had appeared, they would be gone. This always happened so smoothly, and with so little disturbance or fanfare, that it seemed like a natural part of everyday life.

During the holiday season, or whenever a child was born or someone got married or someone died, our house was the place where everybody gathered. There was always something cooking and there was always some kind of gossip or whispered intrigue about goings-on around the city or back home in Mississippi. One summer, my grandmother came to visit us in St. Louis. Big mama was kind and loving but she was not someone to be messed with. She expected children to be God-fearing and to always mind their elders. When we did something wrong, she would whip us with a switch from the nearest tree. The summer Big mama came to visit was even busier with relatives in and out of the house than usual. Just as we had for countless summers before, the children played while the grownups sat on my mother's front porch and told stories all evening long.

I had fallen in love with baseball by then and did not hang around home very much in the daytime anymore, but I was around enough after the sun went down to catch bits and snatches of some of the stories they told: my uncles leaving Mississippi to serve in World War II; my mother and her sister coming to St. Louis during the war to work at the small arms plant and being hassled by a belligerent foreman; my cousin standing up to a gas station owner on a back road near Memphis who would not let his sister use the bathroom and tried to make her pee in a jar; another cousin coming to St. Louis and being attacked during a riot in Fairgrounds Park. Some of their stories seemed painful and scary to my childhood ears, but more often than not, the tales were told and received with laughter. It was as though there was some secret, coded language that you had to know to get the joke. I did not realize it at the time, but although I was only half paying attention, I was learning the language even then. What I know now is that the stories I was hearing were migration tales—tales of adversity and overcoming—one family's slice of a much bigger story of how, during the course of a couple of generations, a large portion of the black population of this country relocated from the rural South to the urban North. At the end of that summer, Big mama died of pancreatic cancer and was lovingly, peacefully laid to rest. The porch tales continued for many years afterward. Eventually, I came to understand the code.

Not long ago, my cousin discovered a 1923 photo of my maternal great-grandparents, Henry Clay Mosely and Annie Eliza Mosely, sitting in front of their home in Mississippi on their fiftieth wedding anniversary. They were surrounded by their eight grown children. Two things came to mind as I looked at the picture. First, I realized that they were both born in slavery yet managed, triumphantly, to acquire a home and raise a family. Also, it occurred to me that I may never be able to go any deeper into the roots of my family tree because documentation of my family origins probably no longer exists. Lacking specific knowledge of the identity of most of my ancestors, I must discern the stories of their struggles and triumphs through the available narratives of their contemporaries. Over the years, I have acquired a renewed appreciation for the efforts of black folks to remain connected with one another across vast distances; educate themselves during slavery and its aftermath; procure food, clothing, books, and medical supplies with meager resources; build homes and schools and churches and communities under the harshest conditions; and advance the material conditions of their lives in defiance of violent opposition. Documented history sheds light on only a small fraction of the individuals involved in the African American movement to resist racial oppression. Yet I draw power from the knowledge that my blood ancestors, though faceless and unnamed, stand somewhere in the shadows of that light. Their messages of self-determination speak to me as clearly as if they were standing beside me, laughing, telling stories, and whispering words of warmth and encouragement in my ear.

MEETING AT THE CROSSROADS:
HOW OUR STORIES CONVERGE

In reading the passages above, it should be clear that the systemic and institutional intersections within each of our lifelines were explicitly influenced by race. It is quite conceivable and, in fact, highly likely that a white Jewish woman, raised in an inner-ring suburb, and an African American man, raised in a racially segregated neighborhood of the same city, would never have even met. Nevertheless, we did meet through our work in anti-oppression and social justice education and through our shared interest in history, culture, and the media. As we came to know each other, we discovered that there was much to be learned through exploring the differences, similarities, and fascinating parallels of our experiences. These kinds of discoveries only come about through genuine dialogue. To bring richness and depth to this kind of cross-cultural interaction and to fully understand the racing of America, it is essential that all of us, regardless of color, agree to engage in honest and continuous examination of ourselves and the ways in which we have been conditioned to think about race in our own lives.

Now it is your turn. Write or record your story and exchange it with at least one other person. As you discuss your stories, ask each other questions and let more details and greater understanding emerge. If you do not know the answers to some of the questions, talk to family members or dig around in scrapbooks, photo albums, or other formal or informal family archives. If you still cannot find the answers to some of the questions, think and write about how your family's race or ethnicity may have contributed to the gaps and voids. For example, given the anti-Semitism in Russia, Linda's grandparents were forced to leave at a time of great danger to them and brought almost nothing with them. Their strong desire to be American and the cultural imperative for **assimilation** meant they talked very little about the "old country," and as a child, it never occurred to her to ask questions. Like many African Americans, Leon has found it difficult to trace his early ancestors. His great-grandparents in Mississippi were most likely born into slavery, but his family has little information about those who came before them, who they were or what they were like.

Consider the questions in Personal Inventory 4.3 as you develop your racial and ethnic autobiography. This autobiographical exploration is intended to dig deeply into each of our personal and family histories regarding race and ethnicity, to delve into what we know of our racial history, and to document our experiences regarding race. Our individual family stories about race are all unique and help define our sense of racial identity. Finding our place in this anthology of stories is critical to understanding the larger story of race in the United States and elsewhere. If you are a Jewish American, you may know the experience of being both other and white in this country. If you are American Indian, you may know how many generations of your family had their land taken by whites, lived on government-controlled, poverty-stricken reservations, or were forced to give up their native language at Indian boarding schools. If you are Irish American, you may know that your grandparents faced signs in New York that said "No Dogs and No Irish" and that their generation was considered nonwhite. You also probably know that by the second and third and fourth generation, your Irish American family had the same job

Personal Inventory 4.3
Autobiography on Race and Ethnicity

1. How many generations has your family been in the United States? If you and/or your family do not live in or only recently arrived in the United States, then respond to these questions in a manner relevant to your reality.
2. What continent and/or country did your ancestors come from?
3. Under what circumstances did your ancestors come to the United States? Were they voluntary immigrants, were they refugees, or were they forced to come as slaves? Were your ancestors part of a group or country that was conquered by the United States, such as American Indians or Mexicans?
4. Were your ancestors welcomed when they arrived in the United States? What race were they considered to be? (If your family was Irish, Jewish, German, Polish, or Finnish and arrived in the United States sometime before the early twentieth century, they were most likely considered nonwhite). If your ancestors were indigenous to this continent, were they treated with friendliness or hostility by the European colonizers?
5. Were there any restrictions as to where your ancestors could live or work when they or others of their same nationality or ethnic background arrived in the United States?
6. What do you know of your ancestors' customs and culture? Discuss what you know of their food, clothing, language, beliefs, and religion. How many of these customs and cultural practices do you and your contemporary family still know about and practice?
7. What kind of work did your ancestors do? Were they laborers, merchants, professionals? What was the race and ethnicity of the people they worked for, their supervisors or bosses, or of the people who worked for them? Did the kind of work they did change and improve through subsequent generations or did it remain basically the same?
8. Was your family able to improve their economic situation over the generations since they first came to the United States? What racial or ethnic factors fostered this improvement or acted as barriers to this improvement?
9. Did your ancestors and subsequent generations live in neighborhoods with primarily one race and ethnicity, or were these neighborhoods racially and ethnically mixed? Did they live in these neighborhoods by choice?
10. How were your ancestors and subsequent generations treated by people who were racially and ethnically different from them? Did that change over time, and if so, in what way?
11. What race and ethnicity were the adults you knew growing up? Think of teachers, doctors, lawyers, store clerks, laborers, and service people. What was the race and ethnicity of people who owned the businesses and stores in your community? What about the elected officials?
12. What experiences involving race or ethnic discrimination did you have or observe as you were growing up? How were you or your parents involved in these experiences? Were you and your family the target or agent of racial or ethnic discrimination? Or perhaps, were you and your family both the target and the agent?
13. How connected do you feel to your family's country of origin today? Is the connection strong, blurry, or nonexistent? Does your own sense of identity include your race, ethnicity, and family background? How much are you aware of the history, culture, customs, and traditions of your ancestors? Are these a strong part of how you see yourself and your interactions with others today?

and housing opportunities as other white people in the United States. If you are Mexican American, you may know that in 1847 what was now Texas belonged to Mexico and that Mexico declared slavery illegal and stopped immigration of people from the United States. You may not know that thousands of U.S. citizens moved into Texas as "illegal aliens," fought a war that "annexed" Texas as part of the United States, and then made it increasingly difficult for your ancestors to get work that was anything above the most menial. If you are Chinese American, you may know that when the Chinese first came to the United States during the gold rush and began working on the railroads, only men were allowed to enter the country, and Chinese families were torn apart out of financial necessity. And if you are African American, you may know that even after slavery was over, those Europeans who immigrated to the United States after the Civil War benefited from the discrimination your ancestors endured. These European immigrants were hired in the factories that would not hire your grandparents and lived in the neighborhoods that would not rent to your families. We will explore the details of these historical facts later in the chapter. For now, we can begin to see how each of our stories is a thread that intertwines with all the other stories and that the threads together weave an intricate American tapestry of race that is complex, interdependent, and interwoven with discrimination and assimilation.

As you reflect upon your personal experiences with race, you may experience a wide range of emotions. Race in this country is a highly charged topic, loaded with strong beliefs, opinions, and feelings. Uncovering old memories and family history may also uncover strong emotions. We encourage you to continue to write about your thoughts and experiences and to talk to others in your community who are thinking about race or teaching or conducting training about race. As you examine your own experiences regarding race, there are two central questions for reflection. First, where is your place in the **racialized** history and atmosphere of this country? In other words, how has your particular story formed your views on race? Second, what is the informal learning that you have gained from your experiences about race, and how has this learning shaped your opinions and feelings about race?

Our stories have shaped us and have formed a unique and particular frame to the window from which we see the world of race, ethnicity, and discrimination. People of other races and histories have frames and windows that are remarkably different. As we each look out our particular racial window, what we see is also different from what others see. Recognizing and acknowledging this difference is the first step toward a larger, broader, and deeper understanding of race in America. As you read this chapter, some of it may challenge what you have been taught and some of it may reinforce your beliefs about race. It will be important to track your reactions to the information in the context of your own experiences and personal history about race.

THE AMERICAN RACIAL DISCOURSE: THEN AND NOW

Since August 2000, when the first edition of this book was published, the U.S. racial dialogue has shifted in many ways yet in many ways has remained the same. Headline national and global events have had a huge influence on the way Americans speak of race:

- The tragic 2001 attack on the Pentagon and the World Trade Center led to the U.S. invasions of Iraq and Afghanistan, and a considerable amount of racial and ethnic profiling in the name of national security.
- Most immigrants coming to the United States in the early twenty-first century arrived from Mexico, the Philippines, India, and China, representing a striking contrast to the trends seen in the early to mid-twentieth century, when most immigrants came from European countries.
- The death and devastation in New Orleans and across a wide swath of the Gulf Coast brought about by Hurricane Katrina in 2005 provided the nation with a gruesome demonstration of the horrific impact a natural disaster can have at the intersection of race and class.
- The election of President Barack Obama in 2008 gave the United States its first African American president yet did little to alter America's entrenched racial antagonisms.

As this section is being written, the national news media are encountering multiple layers of complex racial dynamics in covering the killing of Trayvon Martin, an unarmed black teenager, by George Zimmerman, a white/Hispanic neighborhood watch captain in Sanford, Florida, who was subsequently acquitted. The highly charged racial dialogue over this incident has been expanded and amplified, incidentally, by myriad postings on social networks such as YouTube, Facebook, and Twitter—none of which existed when the first edition of this book was released in the year 2000.

Despite the persistence of racial polarization and conflict in U.S. society, the potential exists, perhaps now as never before, for Americans to dismantle some of the personal beliefs, interpersonal hostilities, and institutional practices that have held **racism** in place. It will be helpful to begin by seeking a deeper awareness of our own implicit and explicit thoughts about race. Our family backgrounds, our cultural frames of reference, our biases, our communication styles, and our identities within various social categories are all part of a varied array of qualities that come together to shape each of us into singular and unique individuals. Our individual and social group identities influence how we think about ourselves in relation to people who are racially different.

The way we are socialized, beginning early in life, has an effect on our interactions with and attitudes toward others in ways that are both conscious and unconscious. As discussed in Chapter 1, we are also influenced by the way our society is structured and by the historical and systemic forces that determine our level of access to opportunity, power, and privilege within the existing social order. The more conscious we are of the racialized nature of those societal forces and the extent to which they influence our lives, the more adept we can become at forming healthy relationships with one another across racial lines and building working communities based on shared power and mutual respect.

RECONSTRUCTING KNOWLEDGE AND RACE

In Personal Inventory 4.3, you reflected on your own experiences with race. You answered questions about your racial identity and your family's racial history. You examined how what you learned informally about race has shaped you and your worldview. What exactly does race mean? The answer to that question has shifted over the years. In 1848, California debated the status of Chinese and Mexican residents and decided that the Mexicans would be considered white and the Chinese would have the same status as African Americans (Kivel 1996, 18). In 1860, three races were acknowledged in the United States: whites, blacks, and mulattoes (who had one black and one white parent). By 1890, these three races had been joined by five more: quadroons (three white grandparents and one black grandparent), octoroons (seven white great-grandparents and one black great-grandparent), Chinese, Japanese, and American Indians. In the 1930s and 1940s in Germany, the two races acknowledged were Aryan and Jewish. Up to the mid-twentieth century, many American schoolchildren were taught a "biological" explanation of race. This description said that the three races were Caucasoid, Negroid, and Mongoloid, based on skin color, skull size, and other physiological characteristics.

The U.S. Census Bureau gathers and organizes race data in accordance with standards set forth by the Office of Management and Budget (OMB). Most recently, OMB has designated five racial categories: white, black or African American, American Indian or Alaska Native, Asian, and Native Hawaiian or other Pacific islander. As of 1997, OMB has allowed people to report more than one race on their census form. People who identify their origin as Hispanic, Latino, or Spanish may be of any race.

The 2010 census indicated that the U.S. population consisted of 196.9 million whites (63.7 percent), 50.7 million Hispanics or Latinos of any race (16.3 percent), 37.9 million blacks (12.3 percent), 14.5 million Asians (4.7 percent), .5 million Native Hawaiians or Pacific Islanders (0.2 percent), and 2.8 million American Indians and Alaska Natives (.07 percent). The overall U.S. population growth from 2000 to 2010 was 9.7 percent. The rate of growth varied widely according to race; Latino growth was 43 percent, Asian growth was 42.9 percent, American Indian and Alaska Native growth was 37 percent, Native Hawaiian and Pacific Islander growth was 35.4 percent, black growth was 11 percent, and white growth was 1.7 percent.

Theories and Constructs of Race

The shifting meaning of race throughout U.S. history provides important clues to its definition. It is not biological, nor is it based primarily on skin color. It is not necessarily based on ethnicity nor is it based on country of origin. Rather, race is constructed socially, culturally, politically, and economically. "Various racial categories have been created or changed to meet the emerging economic and social needs of white United States culture. Racial categories artificially emphasize the relatively small external physical differences among people and leave room for the creation of false notions of mental, emotional, and intellectual differences as well" (Adams, Bell, and Griffin 1997, 83).

While race itself is fiction, the consequences of racism are a historical and contemporary fact of American life. "Racism is based on the concept of whiteness—an identity concept invented and enforced by power and violence. Whiteness is a constantly shifting boundary separating those who are entitled to have certain privileges from those whose exploitation and vulnerability to violence is justified by their not being white" (Kivel 1996, 17). The historical mutability of race is significant because of how it has been used as a marker of group identity and a means of access to privilege in this country and elsewhere. The possession of whiteness represents a valued status that confers upon its owners a set of exclusive citizenship rights (Lipsitz 1998).

The centrality of race in our society is one of the core tenets of **critical race theory (CRT)**. CRT emerged originally in the 1980s as an outgrowth of critical legal studies (Crenshaw et al. 1995; Delgado and Stefancic 2001; Taylor, Gillborn, and Ladson-Billings 2009). Over the years, CRT has expanded to other disciplines such as education. Its ideas and methodologies have also been applied in other areas of focus such as LatCrit, AsianCrit, TribalCrit, FemCrit, and QueerCrit. One of the key concepts of critical race theory is that racism is a core component of the systems and structures of power in our nation. Racial inequity is so deeply embedded in our institutional practices, so integral to our interpersonal relationships and individual attitudes, so inextricably woven into the warp and woof of everyday life, that it has become a permanent feature of the American experience. Therefore, racism, in all its manifestations, must be continuously critiqued and challenged.

Not surprisingly, foundational elements of racial inequity often go unexamined, under-analyzed, or misrepresented by the mainstream media: "Specific media frames select out limited aspects of an issue in order to make it salient for mass communication, a selectivity usually promoting a narrow reading of that issue. . . . A particular frame structures the thinking process and shapes what people see or do not see, in important societal settings" (Feagin 2009, 27). A 2007 study of print media coverage of racial disparities in health care, education, early child development, and employment determined that because racism is framed, for the most part, as being rooted in interpersonal relationships between individuals or among groups of individuals, the systemic nature of race-based power dynamics is rarely reported. In examining the explanatory frames of 140 news articles published by major outlets in eight metropolitan areas nationwide, the study found that articles

> provided clear and unambiguous accounts of how racism can exist in a number of institutions and were easy for a wide audience to identify as racist. However, the dominance of such stories reinforces the notion that racism is primarily about in-dividual actions rather than embedded in social structures. Furthermore, overt and blatant acts of racism were framed as aberrant occurrences that were unfortunate, but did not effectively challenge the perception that the United States has largely transcended its racial past. (O'Neil 2009)

The mischaracterization of contemporary racial oppression as interpersonal and epi-sodic gets in the way of our ability to come to grips with its fundamental nature, which is structural and systemic. Young people today have grown up and come of age during an era when *legally sanctioned* racial segregation of public facilities appears to be a thing of the past. Overt acts of racial violence, although they still occur, are less common than they were prior to the civil rights era. Youth of color and their white counterparts form friendships and interact socially across racial lines more freely today than at any other time in America's past. Yet despite the popular notion that we now live in a "postracial" society, racial injustice continues to thrive in the United States. Glaring racial disparities continue to exist in education, employment, healthcare, housing, bank lending policies, the criminal justice and penal system, household income, household net worth, and a host of other areas. Thus, what has been referred to as America's "pathology of denial" about race (Leary 2006) impedes our ability to develop systemic solutions that will lead to the dismantling of the racialized institutional foundations of our country. It prevents us from devising strategies that are structurally transformative.

The Social and Psychological Impact of Race

The continuous racial targeting of people of color and the privileging of whites, along with misinformation about race passed along from one generation to the next and reinforced through the media, has imbued people of all races with a distorted sense of personal and group identity. Not surprisingly, given the centuries of racial stereotyping and negative messaging directed at people of color, research indicates that a majority of white Americans continue to have strong feelings of racial bias (Banaji and Greenwald 2013, 169–188; Greenwald and Krieger 2006). Many white people in the United States are socialized to regard their race as representing not only the majority group but also the societal norm—the cultural standard and benchmark for what it means to be American. According to one writer, "For many white people, the idea that we have racial identities is difficult to come to terms with. We usually see ourselves simply as people. Whiteness, by virtue of its status as the dominant social position, is unmarked. It is relatively easy for white persons to go through life never thinking about their own racial identity. Whiteness functions as the normative ideal against which other people are categorized and judged" (Kaufman 2001).

This illusory standard of a white societal norm reinforces the notion that people of color are not merely different but also deficient. Studies indicate that, despite a decline in overt expressions of racial bigotry, a large percentage of white Americans continue to consciously or unconsciously regard white identity as positive and black identity as negative (Schmidt and Nosek 2010). The unconscious belief among whites in the superiority of their own racial group relative to blacks and other people of color is a form of *implicit bias*—learned social stereotypes that are sometimes triggered automatically in individuals without their awareness (Greenwald and Banaji 1995). There is evidence to indicate that implicit racial bias exists in children as young as six years old and endures through adulthood (Baron and Banaji 2006). Implicit bias has the capacity to influence people's judgments in regard to how they think about and treat individuals who are racially different from them even when they openly express non-prejudicial views; "to characterize the nature of an individual's prejudice correctly, one must consider both explicit racial attitudes as well as implicit, automatic biases" (Son Hing et al. 2008).

The espousing of racial openness and egalitarianism while simultaneously harboring negative racial attitudes is prevalent in contemporary society. The acting out of biased beliefs through jokes, slurs, and other racial actions and commentary is less likely to occur openly in what sociologist Joe R. Feagin refers to as the *frontstage* of public, professional, and mixed-race gatherings where a diverse range of people is present. Yet such behaviors occur quite frequently in *backstage* settings among friends and close acquaintances where whites with negative feelings toward people of color can comfortably express their beliefs without fear of being judged or marginalized socially (Feagin 2009, 184). A study analyzing more than 600 personal journals from college students throughout the nation revealed thousands of instances of racially bigoted behavior such as name-calling, inappropriate racial humor, and references to stereotypes. Although often characterized as innocent fun, such actions reinforce racial polarization and antagonism (Feagin 2009, 185–190).

In addition, the toleration of duplicitous frontstage/backstage behavior contributes to the perpetuation of an American societal norm that enables schools, employers, public service providers, real estate brokers, law enforcement agencies, and a host of other institutions to publicly embrace equal opportunity policies while privately engaging in practices that deny equal access and fair treatment to members of racially targeted groups. While many white individuals are overtly racist, millions of others benefit from institutionally sanctioned racial privilege in ways that are often invisible to them. When Linda wrote earlier of her personal story, she discussed the anti-Semitism her grandparents faced in Russia and as new immigrants to the United States. But because they and their descendants would ultimately be considered white, they were allowed to find work and housing and education from which African Americans and Japanese Americans were prohibited. Without ever initiating or participating in one overtly hateful act, they benefited from racism.

Misinformation about race and identity also contributes adversely to the socialization of people of color in the United States. The myth of racial inferiority and superiority has been upheld not only by physical violence and discriminatory policies but also by the psychological violence conveyed through the stereotyping and racist messaging to which people of color, beginning early in childhood, are continuously exposed. In the interest of dominant-group hegemony, false notions of a race-based hierarchy are promulgated relentlessly through virtually every mainstream institution in our society. "Oppressed people come to embody in their very being the negations imposed on them and thus, in the reproduction of their lives, harbor a tendency to contribute to the perpetuation of their own oppression" (Outlaw 2005, 14).

People of color in America have always had to wage a battle against **internalized racism,** a condition that can cause an individual to assume self-deprecating attitudes and engage in self-destructive behaviors that reflect the traumatizing effects of racial targeting. When people are regularly subjected to the physical and psychological abuse of overt and covert racial oppression, they sometimes respond by re-enacting that abuse on themselves and other members of their racial group. When Leon wrote earlier about the stories he heard his adult family members telling with such vividness and ironic humor, he was speaking of the unremitting conversations of self-empowerment and cultural affirmation that many African Americans draw upon as a source of healing strength and collective power to counteract the insidious impact of internalized racism. Such stories have been as much a part of the black resistance movement in American history as any civil rights march, economic boycott, or slave uprising.

Internalized racism, which is always involuntary, is a direct by-product of historical and ongoing racial targeting. It works in many ways. For instance, social psychologist Claude M. Steele has advanced the theory of *stereotype threat* to explain the extent to which a person's performance can be detrimentally affected by the psychological triggering of negative stereotypes assigned to one's social group identity (Steele and Aronson 1995; Steele 1997; Steele 2010). Laura Padilla has written about the manner in which many Latinos accept the negative stereotypes directed at their own group and thus question the qualifications of other Latinos who are successful. She refers to this phenomenon as *envidia* or intragroup jealousy and regards it as a clear example of how behaviors resulting from internalized racism can sabotage communities of color (Padilla 2001). Social researcher Dr. Joy DeGruy (formerly Leary) posits the concept of intergenerational trauma resulting from what she has termed *post-traumatic slave syndrome*, a consequence of multigenerational oppression of Africans and their descendants resulting from centuries of chattel slavery followed by decades of institutionalized racism that continues to inflict emotional injury (Leary 2006). In a similar vein, social worker Maria Yellow Horse Brave Heart, through her research and clinical work examining manifestations of intergenerational trauma among Native Americans, has focused on diagnosing and treating what she identifies as *historical unresolved grief* (Brave Heart 2000). Internalized racism among people of color and implicit racial bias among whites are unhealthy psychosocial reactions to the toxic power of racial targeting. Because of their detrimental effects, they must be actively addressed and rigorously interrupted whenever possible. Nevertheless, the injury they cause can only be fully healed as racism in our society is eliminated.

The Science and Pseudoscience of Race

Is race a scientifically verifiable concept? Does racial difference actually exist among human beings? According to biologists, a race is a distinct evolutionary lineage within a species that is sharply defined by measurable genetic differences. Genetic differences between populations are necessary but not sufficient to define race (Templeton 2002). Obviously, differences exist between populations within the human species. Members of what we regard as different racial groups have visibly diverse physical characteristics (skin color, hair texture, facial features). Thus, the question becomes, do diverse human populations exhibit sufficient differences at the genetic level to constitute a scientific basis for establishing the existence of separate races within our species?

A segment of the 2003 documentary, *Race: The Power of Illusion*, depicts a multiethnic group of students meeting with a DNA expert. They compare their skin colors, submit blood and DNA samples, and then discuss their thoughts as to which of their classmates share the closest genetic similarity with them. Most, if not all, of them assume that the students within their own "racial" group will be the closest to them genetically. When their DNA is analyzed, the students are surprised to learn that their assumptions are wrong. The white students do not share the same genetic traits with one another, nor do the African American, Latino, or Asian students. In fact, what they all discover is that, according to the scientific evidence upon which the film is based, there is just as much genetic variation among people of the same so-called "race" as there is among people across racial populations (Gould 1981, 323; Lewontin 1970; Templeton 2002). Differences indeed exist among humans, but they are not racial.

Skin color, the most common visual cue that most of us use as a determinant of race, does not reflect extreme genetic difference, nor does it reflect a distinct evolutionary history. Diversity of skin color merely indicates the geographical adaptation of various populations as they migrated out of equatorial Africa and moved further north to regions where ultraviolet rays from the sun were less concentrated. Overexposure to certain UV rays can destroy folic acid in the body, thus having a detrimental effect on reproduction. In tropical regions, humans evolved with darker skin and large stores of melanin, which protects the body from the harmful effects of solar radiation. On the other hand, insufficient exposure to UV rays can impede the body's ability to produce vitamin D, thus preventing the absorption of calcium by the intestines. As some human populations migrated north and south into the temperate regions, their bodies gradually adapted by developing lighter skin complexions and the ability to tan so as to make optimum use of the available ultraviolet light. Difference in skin color among humans is nothing more than an indicator of the areas of the world to which one's ancestors migrated (Jablonski and Chaplin 2000; 2003). In short, there are no available data to support racial classifications or any form of social hierarchy based on racial or ethnic group membership (Cartmill 1998, 653).

So does that completely answer our question? Is race merely an optical illusion—a trick of the sun? No, it is much more complex than that. Lani Guinier writes, "If we think in categories and think about race only in one category, we conflate many different spheres of racial meaning. We fail to specify if we mean biological race, political race, historical race, or cultural race. We simplify race as a fixed category from which many people want to escape" (Guinier and Torres 2002, 4). Despite the scientific refutation of racial taxonomy as a legitimate means for biologically differentiating and categorizing diverse populations within the human species, it continues to endure as a reality in the social realm. "That race is a social construct rather than a biological fact does not minimize its impact on our lives . . . racial distinctions have powerful social meaning with profound real-world consequences" (Croteau and Hoynes 1997, 138). Most people in our society have a sense of themselves as possessing a racial identity and belonging to a racial group. Various official forms and surveys continue to have checkboxes for designating one's race. Most people harbor conscious and unconscious stereotypes and biases about other racial groups in comparison with their own. People still laugh at racial humor, people still spout racial slurs, and those racial slurs still have the capacity to sting and enrage. People still live in racially segregated communities. People are still denied jobs and promotions because of race. People are still discriminated against economically, incarcerated disproportionately, and educated less effectively because of race. People still attack and kill people because of race.

Stories and Counterstories: Decoding the Master Script

The identity and relationship dynamics of race are so pervasive in our lives today that it feels as though current notions of race have existed since the beginning of historical time. Yet that is far from true. Prior to the fifteenth century, the idea of racial divisions among humans was of minimal significance and had little impact on people's interactions with one another (Vaughan 1995). The early European aggression and hostility toward the indigenous people of Africa, Asia, and the Americas was driven by economic interests and justified primarily by a belief in the right of Christian nations such as Spain, Portugal, Great Britain, and the Netherlands to conquer any civilization and claim any land that was not under the sovereign domain of Christians.

Erecting a social construct with the epic staying power, counterrational robustness, and destructive force that has been exhibited by "race" over the centuries was not a brief or simple process. Our present-day concept of race is based on false ideas, myths, and fabrications that accumulated over the centuries to form a grand, sweeping story or **meta-narrative** to justify the exploitation of entire populations of human beings and the appropriation of their labor, land, natural resources, cultural artifacts, and intellectual property. The social construction of the American meta-narrative—the master script on race and racial hierarchy—has been formulated and upheld through an elaborate system of dehumanizing **schemas**. These racial schemas are mental models created through the telling and retelling of stories that reinforce the idea of a racial hierarchy with the white race at the top, other races beneath, and the black race at the very bottom. Such stories have been utilized to frame our history from a perspective that upholds the language, logic, and worldview of the dominant group and suppresses the language, logic, and worldviews of those who have been targeted for racial oppression.

Throughout our history, there have been an untold number of assaults on the humanness of people of color in the interest of white hegemony. These assaults prime, activate, and reinforce racial schemas and uphold the meta-narrative. They range from the creation of stereotypes and the passage of oppressive laws to the wholesale enslavement, colonization, and genocide of entire populations. In addition to attacks on life, land, and liberty, Africans, Asians, Latinos, Native Americans, and Pacific Islanders have been subject to relentless assaults on their linguistic and cultural traditions, their communal and kinship bonds, their ancestral ties, and their spiritual beliefs.

We have learned that many of the stories we have been told about race are demonstrably false. Yet if those stories go uncontested, we will accept them as truth because of the way we have been socialized. One of the strategies for challenging these stories is through the development of counterstories that refute the assumptions upon which the original stories are based. A counterstory (also referred to as a counternarrative) is a tool utilized by critical race theorists as a means of contesting the race meta-narrative. Counterstories reframe the dehumanizing schemas by revealing additional facts, examining the same facts from different perspectives, personalizing the experiences of the targeted, humanizing the voices of the oppressed, and critically analyzing the misinformation that the dominant group has heretofore represented as unimpeachable.

Let us turn our attention now to an example of how a critical counternarrative can be used to challenge a dehumanizing schema. One of the prevailing beliefs about America's past is that the indigenous people of the Western Hemisphere were primitive, uncivilized, and underdeveloped, with little or no understanding of science and technology prior to the arrival of Europeans from more sophisticated and advanced civilizations. This is a schema—a pattern of thinking that influences the way we organize and simplify our knowledge of the world around us. Let us call it the "primitive people" schema. This schema about American Indians has been repeated in various versions so often over the years that many people accept it as historical fact even though it is just a story—a story told by one group about another. The false beliefs based on this schema can be activated in our minds by a variety of stereotypical words or images, such as "redskins" or "tomahawks," which have become embedded in our popular culture. The schema is dehumanizing because it perpetuates the myth that American Indians were simple people of inferior culture and intelligence. Moreover, this "primitive people" schema contributes to the global meta-narrative of racial hierarchy by implying that, despite the brutality suffered at the hands of whites, the Indians were better off because they had the opportunity to be exposed to more "civilized" people with superior science and technology.

In reality, the notion of Native American technology as limited is grounded in Eurocentric cultural assumptions and misconceptions. If we can acknowledge that simple fact, then we can begin to craft a counternarrative that gets us closer to the truth. Native American science and technology appear to have been highly developed within the context of the Native American social, cultural, and ecological worldview. Conversely, given what we know of the adverse environmental impact that some European technology has had on the North American continent and the rest of the planet, it seems neither appropriate nor accurate to regard European technology as particularly advanced or superior. From the vantage point of twenty-first-century hindsight, the early encounters between the people of the Americas and the people of Europe could more accurately be described as the interrupted development of the technologies of one civilization in service to the overdevelopment of the technologies of another. In other words, it was a missed opportunity for mutually constructive technological synergy. Had the prevailing paradigm of the time been one of cultural reciprocity rather than cultural conquest, it is conceivable that, today, earth-dwellers of all cultures—and all species, for that matter—might be the grateful beneficiaries of the best of both technological frameworks.

STORIES OF RACE, RACISM, AND RESISTANCE IN THE UNITED STATES

The telling of personal stories can be liberating. We can suddenly remember something wonderful that happened in our childhood and the telling of it can bring great joy. We can uncover a painful memory or family secret and the telling of it can bring healing and emotional recovery. As we share these memories with other people, we often find common connections that bind us with understanding and compassion. The same process occurs in the telling of our collective stories, the stories of a nation. These stories too can be liberating and healing and can forge connections between disparate groups. Many of us were taught that history is factual, objective, and indisputable. History is what we read in textbooks and what we were told by teachers about what happened in the past and how things came to be the way they are. We base our knowledge of equality and fairness in the United States on the "stories" we learned. However, many important stories were omitted from our education. Some of these stories will be retold here. Some may challenge your concept of the United States as a nation of justice and equality. Some may make you angry. Some may trigger disbelief. But there is much to be learned by studying the hard facts of conflict, oppression, and violence spurred by race and racism. One extremely significant aspect of American history that has often been omitted or obfuscated, for instance, is the ongoing struggle of all people of color and their white allies to resist racial subordination. We can learn from the parts of our history that remind us of how average people and leaders repeatedly resisted racism, expressed their sense of agency, and laid claim to their rights of citizenship and self-determination. We can learn that neither race nor racism are "natural" but rather they are the result of historical conditions.

As we learned in the first chapter, misinformation is the foundation of oppression. When applied to race, it has meant that during various times in our history, U.S. citizens who considered themselves white have operated from the misinformation that people of color are inferior to them. Some individual white people have been cruel, hateful, and at times violent to people of color. This is *individual racism*, in which the source and the impact are from one person to another. Yet, as you will see, there have been official policies and laws and practices in the United States that have eliminated and discriminated against whole groups of people.

As you learn about the Indian removal policy, the "separate but equal doctrine" of education, the "annexation" of Texas, and the internment of Japanese Americans, you will be learning about *institutional racism*, in which public and private entities have built race discrimination into the very fiber of their existence. Individual racism and institutional racism are always based on the misinformation that one group is superior to another. The instances described above are examples of *overt racism*, in which the hatred and discrimination are outright and on the surface. Name-calling and personal violence are examples of individual acts of overt racism. Examples of overt institutionalized racism are the Jim Crow laws (segregation of public and private facilities) and the practice of red-lining (refusing to offer mortgages or insurance to whole communities of color).

However, racism can also operate on a less blatant, more covert level. It is important to note that the results of *covert racism* are often as discriminatory as those of overt racism. Observe large public and private employers (e.g., corporations, hospitals, and universities) in your community. Do their workforces reflect the racial composition of your community? Are there any or many people of color in upper management positions? Central to the understanding of racism in the United States is the understanding of how power operates on an individual and institutional level. It is the power to name, define, and describe race in textbooks and the census, to make laws, declare war, enforce discrimination, deny education or housing, to hurt and kill that is on the surface or just below the surface in racism.

When we understand our history, we can change the impact of racism. To understand how the construct of race and the practice of racism have evolved is to use history as a means of empowerment. As long as we understand only part of our history, we are prone to perpetuate racial myths and to act upon them as if they are true. Within the following stories and counterstories are people of all races who took small and mighty stands against racism, changing their lives and making a dent in history—moving it closer to the ideals of liberty, justice, and equality. With full information, we have the foundation, the tools, and the options to make changes both in our own actions and in those of our nation. Since this is not exclusively a history book, and there are only a few selected stories in this section, the focus is primarily on the stories that have been left out of traditional American history. The citations and references will point you to more complete historical accounts of the many faces of race in the United States.

American Indians

According to 2010 census data, 22 percent of American Indians lived on reservations, more than 50 percent lived in urban areas, and the rest lived in rural areas. The 2010 U.S. median income was $50,046, and the median income for American Indians was $35,062. Twenty-eight percent of American Indians lived below the poverty line in 2010 as compared to 15.3 percent of the entire American population. Thirteen percent of the American Indian population had earned four-year college degrees compared with 28 percent of the overall U.S. population holding bachelor's degrees during this same year (Norris, Vines, and Hoeffel 2012). What is it in the history of the United States that caused this disparity and these economic and educational difficulties for American Indians? The information in this section will provide some insight into contemporary conditions for American Indians.

It is believed that approximately 30,000 years ago, the people who came to be known as American Indians first entered the New World from Siberia by crossing the Bering Strait (a land mass at the time) into Alaska and Canada, then gradually dispersing southward and eastward over thousands of years until the end of the ice age (Menchaca 2001). Deep in American Indian culture is the belief that extended family and kinship bonds are extremely important. Traditionally, American Indians have considered group needs more important than individual needs and have incorporated communal decision making and sharing as an integral part of life. There is also a traditional and often spiritual belief that all living things are connected and should be treated with care and respect (Tatum 1997, 143–144).

Europeans, on the other hand, placed an emphasis on individualism, materialism, and the acquisition and private ownership of land. In the fifteenth century, Columbus wrote of his encounters with the indigenous people whom he called Indians because he thought he had reached India:

> They . . . brought us parrots and balls of cotton and spears and many other things, which they exchanged for the glass beads and hawks' bells. They willingly traded

everything they owned. . . . They were well-built, with good bodies and handsome features. . . . They do not bear arms, and do not know them, for I showed them a sword; they took it by the edge and cut themselves out of ignorance. They have no iron. Their spears are made of cane. . . . They would make fine servants. . . . With fifty men we could subjugate them all and make them do whatever we want. (Zinn 1995, 1)

In 1607, the English established a settlement at Jamestown, Virginia, and encountered the Powhatan Indians. In a relatively short time, the 8,000 Powhatan Indians were cut down to less than a thousand (Brown 1970, 2). In 1620, the European colonialists we now refer to as Pilgrims encountered the Wampanoag Indians, a farming community with a representative political system and a specialized system of labor. The Wampanoags helped the Pilgrims through the winter by giving them food and teaching them how to cultivate the land. "However, many colonists in New England disregarded this reality and invented their own representations of Indians. What emerged to justify dispossessing them was the racialization of Indian 'savagery,' Indian heathenism and alleged laziness that came to be viewed as inborn group traits that rendered them naturally incapable of civilization" (Takaki 1993, 37).

The impact of the European incursion was devastating to the American Indians. More than three centuries after Columbus arrived and two centuries after the English colonists first landed in the United States, the friendly Taino Indians that greeted Columbus had been obliterated; the Wampanoag, the Chesapeake, the Chicahominy, and the Potomac of the great Powhatan confederacy had vanished; and thirteen other eastern and southern tribes had been scattered with many of their populations significantly decimated (Brown 1970, 7).

When young people conduct research about American Indians, they often begin with Google, or they utilize some other web search engine. One popular site, *International World History Project*, offers the following information for these student papers: "Because of European colonization of North and South America since 1500, Native Americans have been greatly reduced in numbers and largely displaced," and "Native Americans belong to the American Indian geographic race. Characteristics include medium skin pigmentation, straight black hair, sparse body hair, and a very low frequency of male pattern balding. In addition to a marked absence of blood type B and the Rh-negative blood type among Native Americans, several other characteristics of their blood types set them apart from the Mongoloid peoples, with whom they were sometimes classed in the past" (Guisepi 2007).

Notice certain words employed in this brief description of American Indians. The terms "greatly reduced in numbers" and "displaced" make the history of bloodshed seem clean and antiseptic. That the "reduction" and "displacement" are attributed to "colonization" reiterates the theme of the "necessary price to pay for our progress" (Zinn 1995, 8). The notion that American Indians belong to the "Indian geographic race" that was sometimes confused with "Mongoloid peoples" presumes a geographic, physical, and biological construct of race. Anthropologists have rejected the notion of Caucasian, Negroid, and

Mongoloid races. Nowhere in this description is there any mention of how the so-called race of the Indians was constructed by the European colonists to justify taking their land and killing off their people. There is no mention of how setting a group of people apart as "the other" and naming them as a race that has historically been portrayed as savage, brutal, and ignorant might be connected to colonization, reduction, and displacement.

An eighth-grade social studies textbook probes more deeply into this history. It says that the Indians were here before Columbus, and they fought many bloody wars to protect their land but were eventually pushed west into land that was not conducive to their way of life. Ultimately, however, the text ignores the weight of history and puts the responsibility of contemporary poverty and poor education squarely on the shoulders of American Indians by stating, "Many Native Americans realize that to prepare themselves for the future, they must overcome the handicaps of poverty and lack of education" (Davis and Fernlund 1996, 8). It is interesting to note that this text is a civics book that addresses the Constitution and other laws of the land, yet there is no mention of the way that laws were used by the U.S. government for what was called "Indian removal."

In 1829, Andrew Jackson, called "Sharp Knife" by the Indians, came to office and proposed a massive program of Indian removal in which all Indians were to be moved west of the Mississippi (Brown 1970, 5). The policy of Indian removal, in fact, cleared the land from the Appalachians and the Mississippi for growing cotton in the South and grains in the North, expanding the U.S. boundaries, and building railroads and new cities. In 1838, 17,000 Cherokees were rounded up into stockades and sent on foot from Georgia to "resettle" in Oklahoma. During this march, known as the "Trail of Tears," about 4,000 Cherokees died. The purchase of Florida was not simply a land deal. In Florida, this "purchase" meant that Andrew Jackson ordered the burning of Seminole villages in which whole communities were killed. Yet President Jackson is depicted in high school and elementary school textbooks as a "frontiersman, soldier, democrat, man of the people—not Jackson the slaveholder, land speculator, executioner of dissident soldiers, exterminator of Indians" (Zinn 1995, 124–146). In 1820, 120,000 American Indians lived east of the Mississippi; by 1844, fewer than 30,000 remained (Zinn 1995, 124).

As one example of the many acts of Indian resistance, the Florida Seminoles refused to be relocated. Under Chief Osceola and joined by hundreds of black people who had freed themselves from enslavement, they launched a guerrilla campaign known as the Seminole War against Jackson's troops. Chief Osceola was eventually captured, but the Seminoles continued to battle the United States. Although some Seminole groups finally agreed to relocate, a large number of them, joined by African Americans, remained in Florida and continued to fight. The Seminoles never signed a peace treaty with the United States. This resistance and the Indian–African American alliance are little known in U.S. history (Segrest 1994, 201).

Many other U.S. policies and laws contributed to the fate of American Indians. The reservation system was invented in the 1870s by James Amasa Walker, who had visited Indian communities once and learned everything he knew from reading James Fenimore Cooper's novel *The Last of the Mohicans*. Walker believed that the reservation system would give Indians the support they needed to make the transition of being removed from their land and their livelihood of hunting and farming. Walker believed that the Indians were like children who needed structure and discipline to succeed, and he strongly advocated assimilation (Takaki 1993, 231–232).

The U.S. government signed many treaties with various Indian tribes. The Treaty of 1851, with the Cheyenne, Arapaho, Sioux, Crow, and other tribes, permitted European Americans to establish roads and military posts across Indian territories. Within ten years, wagon trains, stagecoaches, forts, Pony Express riders, and telegraph wires had been driven through Indian territories. This invasion was exacerbated by the 1858 gold rush in which thousands of white miners dug for gold on Indian land (Brown 1970, 68). The Treaty of 1868 guaranteed the Indians absolute and undisturbed use of the Great Sioux Reservation. This agreement could be changed only if three-fourths of the adult males on the reservation agreed. However, in 1861 Congress had established the U.S. Territory of Dakota for the use of European Americans. This land was virtually the same as the reservation. The treaty therefore became the source of major dispute and conflict between the Sioux and the U.S. government at two critical times in our history.

The 1887 Dawes Allotment Act was another move toward Indian assimilation. This piece of legislation was based on the belief that the Indians had been shortchanged by the reservation system, which displaced them onto nonproductive land. The stated intent of the Dawes Act was to convert American Indians from their nomadic ways to become individual landowners. It broke up reservations, alloted land to some Indian families for twenty-five years, and granted them citizenship if they would give up their tribal ways and become "civilized." The Dawes Act also authorized the federal government to seek tribal consent to sell some of the land to whites. This move to individual ownership destroyed a Native Amerian tradition of generosity and sharing for the common good. It was a sacred tradition that people could not own land. Indians had no experience of the white economy and had enormous difficulty adjusting to this new system. "Most of those who tried to adjust to the new system were sooner or later relieved of their land" (Matthiessen 1983, 18). Concurrent with the passage of the Dawes Act was another piece of legislation that granted the right of way to railroads through six Indian reservations. By 1891, Indian land was reduced by 17.4 million acres. This process continued in 1902 when a new law was passed stating that all land that had been allotted to the Indians could be sold when the original owner died (Takaki 1993, 231–232).

By the late 1800s, the Lakota (Sioux) were legally forced to assimilate into white culture. They were told that they would be jailed if they continued their traditional spiritual ceremonies. They were forbidden to wear Indian clothing or engage in Indian crafts; their language was discouraged (Matthiessen 1983, 21). From 1890 to 1930, many Indian children were forcibly taken to boarding schools where their hair was cut, their language and traditions were forbidden, and they were socialized into white American culture (Segrest 1994, 222).

It was not until 1924 that Congress gave full citizenship to American Indians (Segrest 1994, 222). The 1934 Indian Reorganization Act rescinded the allotment program and gave Indians the right to vote to maintain communal land. It also gave power for economic planning to tribal councils, which established leadership that would ultimately cooperate with corporate and government efforts to gain rights to profitable mining on Indian land (Segrest 1994, 223).

Two stories dramatically illustrate the complexities of the past and the present and of conflict and bloodshed and resistance. Ironically, both of these events occurred on the Pine Ridge Reservation at Wounded Knee in South Dakota. These stories are not isolated Indian stories; rather, they are an integral component of American history. In 1883, Sitting Bull was a strong, independent leader of the Sioux who had been jailed in Canada for many years. At this point, most Indians were well aware that the U.S. government had told many lies to encourage the Sioux to give up their land. U.S. officials were concerned that the release of Sitting Bull could give rise to armed resistance and conflict between the Sioux and U.S. forces and as a result attempted to marginalize him at every opportunity. But in 1883, the Northern Pacific Railroad celebrated its completion by inviting President Benjamin Harrison to a ceremony and asking Sitting Bull to welcome the president. The old Indian wrote a flowery speech that was reviewed by his interpreter. However, when it came time to deliver the speech, Sitting Bull said instead, "I hate all the white people. You are thieves and liars. You have taken away our land and made us outcasts." Since Sitting Bull knew that the interpreter was the only one who could understand him, he smiled and bowed and paused for applause as he spoke (Brown 1970, 426–427).

This act of resistance came just a few short years before Sitting Bull was killed by U.S. troops on the Pine Ridge Reservation. Two weeks later, on the morning of December 29, 1890, U.S. Calvary troops massacred almost 300 Lakota Sioux Indians at Wounded Knee Creek in southwestern South Dakota. Many of those murdered were women and children. A bizarre series of events led to this massacre. Earlier that same year, Kicking Bear came to the Sioux to tell of Wovoka, who had started the religion of the Ghost Dance. The religion was a combination of Christianity and Indian tradition. The belief was that Jesus Christ would return to earth as an Indian and that all dead Indians would live again and all whites would disappear or die. When the Ghost Dance spread to almost every reservation, the U.S. Army adopted an official policy to stop it (Brown 1970, 431–435). Indian Bureau agent James McLaughlin wired Washington to send military forces to arrest the Ghost Dancers. It was in the violence that ensued during this arrest that Sitting Bull was killed. The others who were arrested were taken to a camp called Wounded Knee near a frozen creek. There were 120 Indian men and 230 women and children and 500 soldiers. The Indians were ordered to give up their weapons, which they did. But some of the Indians began to resume dancing the Ghost Dance, and the soldiers began to fire. Some of the Indians were killed or wounded by gunfire; some of the wounded froze to death. At the end, some 300 Indians and 25 soldiers were dead (Takaki 1993, 228). This was the last nineteenth-century battle between the U.S. Army and American Indians.

Some eighty years later, in the 1970s, another drama unfolded at Wounded Knee Creek on the Pine Ridge Reservation. After the repeal of the land allotment of the Dawes Act, the Bureau of Indian Affairs (BIA) established tribal councils that were largely beholden to the BIA. On Pine Ridge, the tribal council families were mostly biracial (Indian and white) Christians whose administrations were often filled with nepotism and corruption (Matthiessen 1983, 46). Many of these tribal leaders had been assimilated through the process of boarding schools, land allotment, subsequent land deals, and generations of Indian culture being subject to either punishment or ostracism. Dick Wilson was tribal president on the Pine Ridge Reservation during the 1970s. Wilson was a heavy drinker who gave tribal jobs to his family and outfitted and armed a special tribal force, "Guardians of the Oglala Nation," known as GOONs (Matthiessen 1983, 62–63).

Parallel to the development of the tribal councils was the development of another Indian organization, the American Indian Movement (AIM). It is important to understand the context of AIM's evolution. During the 1960s and 1970s, there were many liberation movements working for individual and collective human rights and equality—for example, the civil rights movement, the women's rights movement, the antiwar (Vietnam) movement, and the student rights movement. There was much conflict between these political and social movements on the left that called for drastic change and those on the right that resisted these changes.

It was in this climate of change and conflict that AIM developed its cultural and political agenda. AIM leaders observed the poverty and dependence of both reservation and city Indians and analyzed the historical reasons for this. AIM became a civil rights organization that focused on jobs, housing, and education and received funding from President Lyndon Johnson's War on Poverty program. AIM advocated the principle of Indian sovereignty and reclaimed the identity of Indians as warriors. The atmosphere on many reservations and for many city Indians was one of crime and danger; some AIM members saw this as war and began to carry arms (Matthiessen 1983, 36). In addition to the delivery of social service programs, AIM began to plan and carry out political demonstrations. In 1970 the group occupied Alcatraz to publicize the lack of education, jobs, and housing for Indians. In 1972, AIM participated in the Trail of Broken Treaties march in Washington, DC, in an effort to improve U.S.-Indian relations.

The U.S. government saw AIM as a threat and took two actions. First, the FBI classified AIM as an extremist organization. Counterintelligence tactics of monitoring and disrupting AIM were carried out through COINTELPRO (the FBI's counterintelligence program). The second government action was to withdraw funding from AIM's programs for education, housing, and employment because of the group's political positions and strategies (Matthiessen 1983, 38–46).

In the meantime, there were developments on the Pine Ridge Reservation. The BIA Indian police began to receive training in paramilitary tactics. In 1972, a young Indian from Pine Ridge, Raymond Yellow Thunder, was killed by two white men who were charged only with second-degree manslaughter. AIM leaders went to Pine Ridge to organize the people and were able to secure more serious charges against the killers and to have the police chief fired. This earned AIM great respect among the Pine Ridge traditionalists. The U.S. military and the FBI began to provide what appeared to be unusual support for the tribal council and police. Later, it emerged that valuable uranium had been found on the reservation and the government was protecting these interests. In 1973, another young Indian on the Pine Ridge Reservation was killed by a white man, who was subsequently charged with involuntary manslaughter. This time 200 AIM supporters arrived, and the police beat the young man's mother, claiming she had shouted obscenities at them. Police used tear gas on the demonstrating AIM members, who then overturned police cars and set an abandoned building on fire. This was the first outbreak of violence between Indians and white authorities since the massacre at Wounded Knee in 1890 (Matthiessen 1983, 64).

As a symbolic act, AIM took over the trading post at Wounded Knee, which was soon surrounded by FBI and BIA police. "For seventy-one days, a few hundred men, women, and children—supplied by volunteer airlifts and by sympathizers who slipped in and out during the night—had challenged a large paramilitary force abetted by hundreds of short-haired vigilantes, red and white, who were eager to wipe out the 'long-hair trouble-makers.'" Through the course of the occupation there were outbursts of gunfire on both sides; two Indians were killed, and a U.S. marshal was seriously wounded (Matthiessen 1983, 81).

When the siege ended, there was an agreement for AIM leaders to turn themselves in to authorities and for U.S.-Indian negotiations to proceed about two major issues. The first was a commitment to review the 1868 treaty that was to have protected the Pine Ridge Reservation. The government agreed to work with AIM to determine if there were violations of the treaty and to correct any that existed. The government also made a second commitment to investigate the corruption of the BIA and tribal councils. In the end, more than 100 Indians who participated in the occupation were indicted, and neither of these issues was agreed upon nor were the issues that AIM was protesting discussed with the government (Matthiessen 1983, 85).

The nineteenth-century conflict at Wounded Knee was an overwhelming demonstration of U.S. power in which hundreds of unarmed Indians were killed because of the perceived threat represented by the Ghost Dance. In 1890, the Indians willingly gave up their arms and danced the Ghost Dance as a nonviolent symbol of their spiritual beliefs and of resistance. In the twentieth-century conflict at Wounded Knee, AIM and its supporters recognized the combined power of the U.S. forces and their supporters in the tribal council. They saw the corruption in the laws that took land from the Pine Ridge Indians and saw that the tribal council and its supporters had been co-opted to see their self-interest aligned with the U.S. military and FBI. They looked at Indian history and they saw the conditions under which most reservation and city Indians lived and they chose to be warriors. The circumstances that had plagued American Indians for hundreds of years were present again in the twentieth century at Wounded Knee. This time the ore was uranium instead of gold, the military was the U.S. Army, and the FBI was involved rather than the cavalry. And it was the militant AIM that resisted the government rather than the Ghost Dancers. One AIM supporter who was inside the trading post spoke of the night she saw her nephew killed by sniper fire: "I remember back on days when they had unarmed our ancestors, killed them and let them freeze to death; there was no mercy for our children, there was no mercy for women. That's the very first thing that had come to my mind during that firefight" (Matthiessen 1983, 81).

As you reflect on these pieces of history, remember that this is not *Indian* history, but *U.S.* history. We are not condoning any of the violence that occurred, but rather retelling stories that have often been omitted from the history books. How much of this history have you learned as a student? Does this information confirm or contradict what you have already learned? Where were your ancestors and family in 1890 and 1973? What is the history of the land you live on now? Was it transferred from communal Indian guardianship to private ownership? Did you learn about this transfer when you studied your state's history? Who were you taught to see as the "good guys" in the historical violence between Indians and U.S. forces? How does your best independent thinking reconcile what you have learned (or not learned) in the past with the information you have just read?

African Americans

Anyone who has taken social studies or American history classes in the United States knows something about slavery. Most of the texts and lessons from these classes tell us how wrong slavery was and how it ended with the Civil War. Many of us were taught that Abraham Lincoln was a quintessential American hero who ended slavery with the Emancipation Proclamation. A few passages from *The International World History Project* and a sixth-grade social studies textbook illustrate the kind of information that students often receive about slavery. These passages are standard for much of American education. On closer examination, we can find important values and messages encoded by what they directly say, what they imply, and what they omit:

Passage 1: "American blacks are largely the descendants of slaves, people who were brought from African homelands by force to work for whites in the New World" (Lynch 2007).

Message 1: The passage acknowledges that slavery was a negative part of American history; however, it implies that black Americans have no history prior to their enslavement in the Americas. Moreover, the statement minimizes the violence of slavery, the dehumanization of a whole group of people, and the painful separation and destruction of families both in Africa and in the United States. It also completely omits the millions of Africans who died horrible deaths at sea in the Middle Passage from Africa to the United States. The way this passage is written, and presumably the way it is read and understood, as a simple declaration of "fact" allows the reader to glide easily over the sentence and the horrors and legacy of this part of our history.

Passage 2: "Black slaves played a major, though unwilling and generally unrewarded, role in laying the economic foundation of the United States, especially in the South" (Lynch 2007).

Message 2: According to the encyclopedia, African Americans were not willing slaves but they were sometimes rewarded for their work. The message here is that their biggest reward was the satisfaction of the knowledge of essential contributions to the development of the U.S. economy. There is no mention of the legacy of enslavement, work without compensation, frequent brutal treatment, and life without freedom. There is no indication that these two hundred years have had an impact on contemporary African Americans and their access to the rewards of the contemporary U.S. economy.

Passage 3: A sixth-grade social studies text says that enslaved Africans were one group of immigrants that did not come to America by choice. This textbook says that by 1808, when importing slaves became illegal, about 700,000 Africans had been brought to America against their will. "Individuals suffered terribly, but as a group they managed to persevere and contribute greatly to the nation" (Bednarz et al. 1997, 660).

Message 3: While the text acknowledges the suffering of slaves, the overriding message is the same as message 2: survival and contribution. What has it meant for African Americans to "persevere" in the United States and how have 200 years of the work and "contributions" of slaves measured up to the rewards of groups that immigrated voluntarily?

Passage 4: In a section of the sixth-grade text called "Upholding Our Rights," the focus is on the civil rights provided for in the Constitution for all people. This section indicates that blacks suffered discrimination even 100 years after the Civil War. However, it goes on to say that in the historic case of *Brown v. Board of Education* (in which it was decided that "separate but equal" in education was unconstitutional), the Supreme Court ruled against discrimination. "The civil rights movement of the 1950s and 1960s assured African Americans the rights they were guaranteed under the Constitution" (Bednarz et al. 1997, 663).

Message 4: The message of this excerpt from the text follows logically from the first three messages. Slavery was bad and its legacy continued even after slavery, but *Brown v. Board of Education* and the civil rights movement fixed all of that, and now everything is equal and fine. If you believe this message, you have learned that the injustices of slavery, segregation, and discrimination were fortunately resolved and ended by the Supreme Court and the civil rights movement. Without additional information that supplements and contradicts these glib statements, that is exactly what many Americans believe.

Young students who read these passages and others like them can conclude that slavery was a horrible chapter in U.S. history. But they can also feel relieved at its outcome and be spared disillusion with U.S. justice if they can be led to conclude that not only was slavery eventually abolished, but African Americans were given their rightful entitlements to equality and justice. What are the logical conclusions of thinking and policy that can be drawn from these messages? According to this line of thinking, all's well that ends well. For many people who receive these messages without intervening experiences or contradicting information, there is a progression that leads to certain conclusions. These conclusions, grounded in partial and distorted information, assert that it is time for blacks to stop complaining about the consequences of slavery and racism and take charge of their lives. This leads to thinking that any failure of African Americans is a failure of individuals, not a failure of racist history, laws, policies, or institutions. This thinking leads to policies that are based on the belief that the playing field is level and there is no longer any necessity for laws or resources to assist African Americans or compensate for past injustices. This logic says that the past is past—it is time for all Americans to move on. Perhaps you have heard someone say something like this. Or perhaps you have had thoughts like these or believe policies that seek to remedy racial injustice are no longer necessary. Of course, you are entitled to your own thoughts and politics. What is critical in the assessment of your thoughts and politics about slavery and its relationship to the contemporary situation of African Americans is the availability of informational resources to allow you to arrive at conclusions after careful consideration of history and conditions that may have been omitted from your education.

As you read this section, trace the sources of your thoughts and beliefs and political perspective and join them with your personal experiences with African Americans or as an African American. Carefully observe your thoughts and experience as you take the next journey into American history. "To engage in a serious discussion of race—we need to begin with the flaws of American society rooted in historic inequalities and longstanding cultural stereotypes" (West 1995, 557). Volumes have been written about slavery in the United States, its impact, and its legacies in the contemporary circumstances of African Americans. This comprehensiveness is beyond the scope of this book. This next section will examine some of the conditions of the slave trade, the impact of slavery on the family, and the legacy of slavery for all Americans.

African Civilization and the European Slave Trade

In any discussion of African Americans, it is important to acknowledge the history of African people prior to the European slave trade. Scholarship in a variety of disciplines over the past several decades has established the African continent as the birthplace of humanity and the cradle of human civilization. Africa, the second largest continent on the planet, is the historical site of a multitude of diverse societies, both ancient and modern, and a vast array of ethnic groups. Most of the people enslaved by the Europeans and transported to the Americas came from west central Africa. Places of origin included Senegambia, Sierra Leone, the Windward Coast, the Gold Coast, the Bight of Benin, and the Bight of Biafra (Eltis 2001). Black people in the Americas are descendants of the Fulani, Ibo, Hausa, Yoroba, Wolof, Mandika, Kongo, Akan, Ewe, Mende, Temne, and other African peoples who were enslaved, imprisoned, taken by ship to the Western Hemisphere, and violently forced to work for generations in one of the most brutal and dehumanizing systems of chattel servitude the world has ever known.

When Africans were captured or purchased as slaves, they were pulled from their families and communities and catapulted into intolerable situations.

> The marches to the coast, sometimes for 1,000 miles, with people shackled around the neck, under whip and gun, were death marches, in which two of every five people did not survive. On the coast they were imprisoned in slave pens located in armed fortresses such as those at Cape Coast in Ghana and on Goree Island in present-day Senegal until they were picked and sold. . . . Then they were packed aboard the slave ships, in spaces not much bigger than coffins, chained together in the dark, wet slime on the ship's bottom, choking in the stench of their own excrement. (Zinn 1995, 28)

One of three Africans died aboard these ships, but according to the slave traders, there was still profit to be made. By 1800, 10 to 15 million Africans had been kidnapped and uprooted from their homes and families and transported to North and South America for the purposes of slavery. While this number of enslaved people is staggering, it is important to remember that it represents only the one-third of Africans who survived the journey on foot to the coasts of Africa and the sea voyage known as the Middle Passage. "It is roughly estimated that Africa lost 50 million human beings to death and slavery in those centuries we call the beginning of modern Western civilization, at the hands of slave traders and plantation owners in Western Europe and America, the countries deemed the most advanced in the world" (Zinn 1995, 29).

How could a country that was considered so advanced take the lead in so insidious a trade that profited from the sale of and indifference to human life? How could a country that was founded by people seeking a life free of religious persecution participate in slavery? How could herding, transporting, selling, and owning human beings for profit possibly be explained? Such inhumanity cannot have a reasonable explanation that could cause us to say, "Oh yes, now I understand, that's fine." However, understanding what could lead an entire group of people to enslave another entire group of people can give us enormous insight into the strange workings of racism.

The Europeans and European Americans who were involved in the slave trade as ship captains and crew, high-ranking officials in the trading companies, plantation owners, and small farmers had two things in common. They understood their race as white and as the epitome of humanity, and they understood people with different color skin (American Indians, Africans) as either inferior humans or subhuman. "When these Englishmen met Africans for the first time, one of the most fair-skinned people on the globe came into contact with one of the darkest, a difference reinforced by the existing dichotomy between dark and light in British culture. It led the English to see the Africans as both 'black' and 'heathen' and to link them immediately with barbarity, animalistic behavior and the devil" (Segrest 1994, 191). Once they made this leap to dehumanize an entire group of people and to see them as fundamentally different, this peculiar and insidious logic could and did lead to the human horror of slavery. Once the steps are taken to see other humans as inferior, all of the potential for racism and subsequent dehumanization and violence becomes possible.

Sometimes Americans ask why it is necessary to study in depth the most horrible and inhuman chapters of our history. There are many reasons for this endeavor. One reason is the intrinsic value of knowing the truth, no matter how grim. Another reason is to analyze and understand the faulty premises that such inhumane logic is based on so that it can never happen again. Still another reason is to see the ways in which constructing groups as the "other"—even through jokes or offhanded comments—can build step by step and brick by brick into monumental and destructive hate that becomes violent racism.

As discussed earlier in the chapter, racism is built on the erroneous assumption that skin color and other physical characteristics can make one group of people superior to another group of people. As we can see in the institution of slavery, racism can be grounded both in individual hatred and in a collective belief in superiority/inferiority that can be institutionalized for hundreds of years. The institutionalized racism that was slavery became embedded in commerce, education, housing, labor, the family, and religion, affecting the distribution of power, privilege, land, and material goods for over 200 years. Throughout much of the time that African Americans were enslaved, it was illegal for slaves to learn to read. The institutionalization of slavery impacted the rights to basic human freedom, independence, and privacy.

For 200 years, slavery captured the bodies and the minds of African Americans. As slavery continued from generation to generation, the memories of freedom in Africa grew dim and distant. Nevertheless, African Americans managed to preserve core elements of West African culture despite unspeakably brutal efforts to divest them of those elements and obliterate their sense of themselves as cultural beings. Among the unifying components of a burgeoning African American cultural identity was a cosmology that generated a profound sense of ancestral connection, kinship, and community. According to Evan Zuesse, "the deep structures of African spirituality survived even though they assumed many different expressive forms" (quoted in Paris 1995).

It was this sacred thread of oneness that has connected people of African heritage, consciously and unconsciously, not only spatially across a vast continent and throughout the **diaspora** but also temporally, backward and forward across the arc of human history. The defiant protection and passing on of valued cultural traditions were one of the essential processes by which Africans in the Americas preserved and reproduced their collective identity and sense of humanness.

In the mid-1600s, the plight of enslaved black workers and white indentured servants posed an opportunity for a common cause. In fact, there was evidence of the beginning of alliances along the lines of forced labor and across the color line. In 1661, Virginia passed a law that increased the years of labor for any white indentured servant who collaborated with or ran away with any enslaved black person (Zinn 1995, 39). In 1676, Bacon's Rebellion occurred, which was an uprising of enslaved Africans and white indentured servants and unemployed workers. To preclude any further alliance across racial lines, colonial rulers began conferring on all European settlers rights that had previously been the exclusive domain of the English (Segrest 1994, 195). In 1680, the Virginia legislature permitted whites to abuse blacks physically with impunity (Takaki 1993, 67).

Ultimately, the hierarchy of slavery evolved in such a way that wealthy plantation owners hired poor white men to serve as overseers of enslaved blacks. While poor southern whites were clearly distinct from enslaved southern blacks in their freedom and right to their own labor, their conditions of housing, food, and income were often similar and the potential for alliance based on class existed. But as long as poor whites could be socialized to see blacks as subhuman and to participate in the lower and middle rungs of overseeing slavery, the opportunities for alliance against a common oppressor were virtually nonexistent.

The Enslaved Family

One way to understand the impact of slavery is take a closer look at how the family was configured structurally and what effect this had on the lives and relationships of people who were enslaved. As we consider this information, it is important to remember that the central feature of slavery was that an entire group of people was legally regarded as property. Under this system, there was no acknowledgement that black plantation workers had a right to form families. Laws and social customs protected white American families. There was no such legal protection for black American families.

As early as 1619, the London Company made provisions for young, single, white women to go to America to become the wives of white colonizers. At this point in history, women's labor was still considered essential to the family's survival. The nuclear family served as both a source of emotional support and a unit of labor and economics. In their settling of the "New World," white colonists were encouraged to arrive together and stay together as families (Dill 1995, 237–241). As we learned in Chapter 2, the Industrial Revolution created a split between public and private labor in which, by and large, men worked outside the home and women were in charge of the domestic sphere. While this represents an important historical moment in the continued erosion of the rights of women, the nuclear family was still protected by law and by tradition. In fact, white families in the United States were sacrosanct. "Thus, in its founding, American society initiated legal, economic, and social practices designed to promote the growth of family life among European colonists. The reception colonial families found in the United States contrasts sharply with the lack of attention given to the families of racial-ethnics" (Dill 1995, 241).

As also discussed in Chapter 2, one of the ironies of slavery was that it was not affected by the public/private labor division that so deeply influenced the work of men and women and thus family life for whites. There were few distinctions between the work of black men and black women during slavery. This carried over into the limited domestic life, in which work was shared and rarely distributed along gender lines (Davis 1981, 18). Forced labor was always at the center of slavery and black families during slavery. But when the international slave trade was prohibited in 1807, the only way to increase the number of enslaved workers was to increase the number of offspring. Thus, another essential form of labor for black women became their reproductive labor. For people who were enslaved, reproduction was not like that of wealthy whites, whose purpose was primarily to create their own family and heirs. Nor was it similar to child-bearing in poor white families, who sometimes desired more children so they could increase their family's labor production and income. Rather, as with other aspects of their lives, enslaved men and women had no control over the creation of their own families. Reproduction was encouraged and insisted upon by plantation owners to retain legally protected access to unpaid laborers. This system produced high profits for white families at the expense of the black families they forcibly held as property (Dill 1995, 237–241).

While there were marriages between men and women who were enslaved, the organization and maintenance of the black family was subject to the legal control of the white plantation owner. Thirty-two percent of African American marriages under slavery were disrupted by the sale of one of the spouses or their children (Dill 1995, 246). The following is an eyewitness account of a coffle of enslaved people departing the plantation from which they have been sold.

The "gang" of slaves was arranged in traveling order, all being on foot except the children that were too young to walk and too old to be carried in arms. These latter were put into a wagon. But mothers with infants had to carry them in their arms; and their blood often stained the whip when, from exhaustion, they lagged behind. When the order was given to march, it was always on such occasions accompanied by the command, which the slaves were made to understand before they left the "pen," to "strike up lively," which means that that they must begin a song. Oh! what heartbreaks there are in these rude and simple songs! The purpose of the trader in having them sung is to prevent among the crowd of negroes who usually gather on such occasions, any expression of sorrow for those who are being torn away from them; but the negroes, who have very little hope of ever seeing those again who are dearer to them than life, and who are weeping and wailing over the separation, often turn the song thus demanded of them into a farewell dirge. (Blassingame 1977)

African kinship practices, which extended central familial bonds beyond the nuclear family, became critical for the survival of families during slavery (Dill 1995, 246). This did not originate as a response to slavery nor did it end with emancipation. **Fictive kinship** networks in the African American community hark back to West African traditions and continue to the present day (Chatters, Taylor, and Jayakody 1994).

Another irony of the family in slavery involves the gender norms that white society established during and after the Industrial Revolution. By these norms, the "good" man was the breadwinner and the "good" woman guarded the hearth. While clearly this system and its standards were based on female subordination, it provided white men with the rewards and resources of a patriarchal society. These privileges involved respect, access to jobs, access to political and economic power, and so forth. None of this entitlement to respect or resources for white men was afforded to black men. The black man in slavery was not the breadwinner. In fact, the slave owners emphasized the mother-child relationship because it was the main source of labor (Dill 1995, 242). Within this context, the near egalitarian work relationship between black men and women was extraordinary. Yet ironically, according to what was valued by white society at the time, it was another example of the degradation of the enslaved. "In addition to the lack of authority and economic authority experienced by the husband-father in the slave family, use of the rape of women slaves as a weapon of terror and control further undermined the integrity of the slave family" (Dill 1995, 242). The "one-drop" rule established that any person with any percentage of black "blood" would be considered black and part of the "subordinate race." "This practice allowed plantation masters to have sexual access to Black women without jeopardizing the inheritance of the children of their white wives" (Segrest 1994, 193). A pattern of occasional preferential treatment of children fathered by white slaveholders also contributed to varied treatment of enslaved African Americans according to skin tone, which created psychological wounds and intraracial frictions that persist even in contemporary times. This is one example of *intergenerational trauma* that was discussed earlier in the chapter. The social valuation and devaluation of people in accordance with the relative darkness or lightness of their skin continues among African Americans and other populations of color.

Enslaved Africans were pulled violently from their homes and torn from their families. Their familial ties were not legally recognized. There were no laws that held white slave-holders accountable for cruel and unusual punishment of the black people who worked for them. Slaveholders could beat, torture, maim, and even murder their workers with impunity. There were no legal protections for black women and girls who were raped or coerced into allowing white men to use and abuse them sexually. Nor was there any legal recourse available to a slave mother to compel a white man who fathered her children to be accountable for the children's well-being. There was no legal obstacle to keep a slave-holder from separating an enslaved black family and selling its members individually to different buyers for economic or punitive purposes. These were the circumstances under which African Americans lived for over 200 years. Yet even under these harsh conditions, black people managed to resist dehumanization, organize daring escapes, stage planta-tion rebellions, establish loving families, maintain a sense of community, and pass on a cherished cultural legacy that has endured to the present day.

Contemporary Conditions for African Americans

In what way and to what degree does the legacy of slavery impact the contemporary lives of African Americans? After slavery, southern black labor revolved primarily around sharecropping and debt peonage. For the most part, blacks were shut out of labor unions, which were the source of the best working-class jobs. Supreme Court rulings between 1873 and 1893 culminated with *Plessy v. Ferguson*, which established the separate but equal rule, the foundation of racial segregation in public schools. Racist violence escalated between 1882 and 1930, during which time there were 2,060 documented lynchings of blacks (Segrest 1994, 208–209). "By the turn of the century, the South was in the throes of a resurgent white supremacy" (Segrest 1994, 210). Southern legislators enacted seg-regation laws, prohibitive poll taxes for black voters, and other measures that ushered in the era of Jim Crow, when life for blacks was separate but anything but equal. There are many indices in which the disparity between blacks and whites continues to be wide. These include housing, employment, health care, income, and education. Tracing some of the developments and consequences in education will provide one example of the legacies of slavery.

It is commonly taught in schools and widely known that the 1954 Supreme Court de-cision *Brown v. Board of Education* legally ended the law of separate but equal schools that was established in *Plessy v. Ferguson*. The belief embedded in the *Brown* decision was that black children's education had not been equal to that received by white children and that integration in the schools was an essential step to remedy inferior education. Although *Brown v. Board of Education* was a symbolic and material victory in the fight for equal citizenship for all Americans, it also led to setbacks and distortions in the ongo-ing process of social and cultural capital formation within and on behalf of the African American communities. Many of these distortions were the outgrowth of ill-conceived ethnocentric notions on the part of mainstream policy makers, which led to damaging misfires in attempts to implement the Brown rulings. During the first thirty years following the *Brown* ruling, the cumulative effects of hostility, subterfuge, and violent resistance to integrated schools on the part of some white institutions, the half-hearted efforts of others, and the well-intentioned but poorly executed efforts of still others did serious damage to the black movement for educational equity (Ogletree 2004).

According to one study, school desegregation has merely diminished isolation. Two-thirds of all African American students attend schools that are predominantly attended by students of color, particularly in isolated urban districts and areas with high concentrations of poverty. De facto racial isolation remains strong in U.S. schools and when combined with poverty continues to produce inferior educational opportunities for African Americans and other children of color. Even in more integrated schools, in many instances children are segregated through tracking at the classroom level (Mickelson and Smith 1995, 291). In the district where Linda's children attend school, the racial population in the middle school is approximately 85 percent black and 15 percent white. When Linda's daughter was in eighth grade, she was a student in a gifted reading program and an advanced math program. In the advanced math program there was one African American student and fourteen white students, and in the gifted reading program there were five African American students and twelve white students. The percentage of white students in these advanced classes has been consistently more than five times their percentage of the student population.

As court-ordered desegregation has receded over the past decade, many schools and school districts have resegregated. Since most U.S. neighborhoods continue to be racially segregated, most neighborhood schools continue to be segregated as well. Studies demonstrate that white residents will stay in a neighborhood and some new white residents may move in if the black population does not exceed 8 percent of the neighborhood. But when the black population reaches 10 to 20 percent, the white population begins to move—even if the black residents have the same economic and social standing as the white residents (Hacker 1992, 37–38). Those African Americans who attend college find that their earning potential is still affected by their race. Black men and women who attend one to three years of college earn $825 to white men and women's $1,000. Black men with college degrees end up just a few dollars ahead of white men with high school diplomas (Hacker 1992, 96). Despite the lingering racial inequities in U.S. education, the African American community still supports public education. Seventy-six percent of blacks (as compared to 57 percent of whites) are likely to support increased government spending on schools (Feagin and Sikes 1994, 80). Black voters generally support school tax increases even when the black population's income is lower than that of the white population and will be more deeply impacted by tax hikes.

Discrimination and differential treatment by race often intersect with class issues. As we have noted, most schools whose populations are predominantly students of color are in low-income areas. These schools have lower tax bases and fewer resources. But what of middle-class black children in middle-class neighborhoods and schools? While they tend to fare better than their lower-income counterparts, several studies show that black children in desegregated schools are more likely to be punished than white students and treated differently by white authorities.

> At the heart of what Gunnar Myrdal called "the American dilemma" is the contradiction between white American ideals and the reality of discriminatory actions. Black children often learn about this contradiction at an early age. In desegregated schools black children are taught "The Star-Spangled Banner" and Pledge of Allegiance along with white children, and they read many stories about freedom, liberty, and justice. But degrading experiences with whites in the same schools doubtless raise serious questions about the meaning of these ideals. (Feagin and Sikes 1994, 91)

These same messages that are learned by African American children are also learned by white and Latino and Asian American and American Indian children. Differential treatment according to race contradicts the history lessons children learn about democracy and the American values of justice and equality. These contradictions are devastating to the psyches of children. Despite what young people may learn in the classroom about American justice and racial equality, if the treatment by the school does not reflect equality, the primary lesson learned is one of confusion, disappointment, cynicism, and/or hypocrisy.

How does this educational picture fit together with the legacies of slavery? As noted above, it was illegal for slaves to learn to read. Enslaved children did not have the same right to public education as white children. Many people defied this law. Communities of black people in the United States employed numerous covert strategies to acquire literacy for themselves and their children even under slavery. After emancipation, one of the first things free African Americans began to do was raise the money to hire teachers and set up schools in their communities (Williams 2005, 7–66). Nevertheless, there were 200 years of the denial of formal education for African Americans. That period was followed by another sixty to eighty years of legal segregation in housing and education.

The policy of school segregation was based on what white legislators and judges and parents thought was in the interest of white children with little consideration for black children and their families. These laws were undergirded by the misguided assumption that whites are superior to blacks and therefore the two groups should not be schooled together. We have now had several decades of court-ordered school desegregation, yet the data show that the law in action has not eliminated school segregation nor has it eliminated the race-based disparities in educational outcomes.

Our ability to understand how racism operates in education is central to moving toward a democratic society in which equality of access, opportunity, and outcomes is substantive, not mythical and illusive. The legacy of slavery and segregation has created a system of education characterized by institutional racism. No superintendent or principal or teacher need take overtly racist action or make an openly racist remark in order to perpetuate this system. Our history has taught us that it will require resistance and organization to make substantive changes and reverse this lingering legacy. The reality of over 200 years of denial of education followed by so-called separate but equal education followed by fifty years of mostly ineffective court-ordered desegregation has led to structural inequalities built into U.S. educational history for almost 400 years. This does not mean individuals do not bear responsibility for studying hard in school. But it does mean that in the big picture of race in education there are institutional and historical reasons for differences in outcomes.

It is true that many of us learned about *Plessy v. Ferguson* and *Brown v. Board of Education*, but that is often where the information we received in school on this subject stopped. Many of us learned that *Brown* and the civil rights movement "fixed" racism in the schools and that we now have a level playing field racially. As you consider what you learned in school and came to believe about this nation's history of educating African Americans, think about the kind of social policies those beliefs would lead you to support in the present day. If you believe that schools equally educate all students, how would you evaluate racial differences in academic achievement? If you believe that all is now equal, would you be for or against affirmative action? Would you be for or against educational programs that assist black children in public schools or black students in college? Would you call these programs preferential treatment or reparation?

Now consider the information you have just read about the current consequences of unequal education for African Americans and the continued inequality. Given this information, do you believe that this country provides a level playing field for African Americans? If you do not believe that, what policies would you support? Would you be for or against affirmative action? Would you be for or against programs that assist black children in public schools or black students in college? Would you call these programs preferential treatment?

If you are African American, recall your own educational experiences from prekindergarten through secondary school. What challenges did you face? How did you overcome those challenges? Who helped you along the way and who hindered you? What messages did you receive about your ability to succeed? Did all of your teachers expect and demand the best from you? What role did your parents and extended family play in your education? What role did your peers play in influencing your attitudes about education?

To oversimplify slavery and its legacies is a disservice to students, a way of ensuring continuing distortions and misinformation about racism. If we do not know what happened and why, if we do not know what some people of all races did to try to end slavery and racism, and if we do not know what impact slavery and racism have today, then our beliefs and decisions will be based on a wobbly foundation built from partial truths. As James Loewen notes,

> To function adequately in civic life in our troubled times, students must learn what causes racism. Although it is a complicated historical issue, racism in the Western world stems primarily from two related historical processes: taking land from and destroying indigenous people and enslaving Africans to work that land. To teach this relationship, textbooks would have to show students the dynamic interplay between slavery as a socioeconomic system and racism as an idea system. (Loewen 1995, 143)

We have examined some of the historical legacies of institutional racism with regard to education. We could do parallel historical reviews and analyses of housing, employment, health care, and more. Ultimately, as you weigh what you have learned in the past and the information in this section, it will be your thoughtful and independent decision as to how you will make sense of it all and determine your own understanding and beliefs.

Latinas/Latinos or Hispanics

The 2010 U.S. Census Bureau questionnaire lists fifteen racial categories, places to write in specific races not listed on the form, variations of Hispanic/Latino/Spanish identity, and the names of specific enlisted tribes for American Indians. The sidebars on page 271 and, later in this chapter, on page 287 display the exact questions on race and ethnicity from the 2010 census. This census was only the second census in U.S. history in which Latinos were permitted to self-identify as both a race and an ethnicity.

Technically, the United States defines the term "Hispanic" as an ethnicity rather than a race, but the experience of Latino groups in the United States is more consistent with racial groups that have been treated differently from whites and are often characterized as the "other." The history of Latinos in the United States is often inaccessible and invisible. Taken as a whole, Latinos are the nation's largest and fastest-growing ethnic group. While each immigrant group has a distinct history with and in the United States, there are some commonalities. Researchers have found that Latino Americans tend to be more family-oriented than white Americans, as demonstrated by emotional and material support provided by the family, a sense of obligation to support one's family, and the central role of the family (rather than peers) as a reference point. As an example of this difference, white U.S. teens in one study cited independence and personal accomplishment as the main reasons to seek achievement in school, while Latino teens said that their main reason to succeed academically was to be able to support their families. This kind of research into cultural norms has significant policy implications, particularly in public education. A program created for Latino students in a large urban high school used a simulated family setting to develop a sense of collective academic responsibility and as a result significantly reduced the dropout rate and increased the college attendance rate among the Latino population (Tatum 1997, 137–138).

Another shared issue among Latinos is that of a common first or second language, Spanish. This, too, has public policy implications. In the Southwest and in other regions of the United States where there are large Latino populations, bilingual education has become a lightning rod for issues ranging from English ethnocentrism to cultural pride for Spanish-speaking communities. The conservative backlash involves efforts to dismantle bilingual education, based on the rationale that to refuse to assimilate to English is un-American. Anti-Spanish language laws represent an assault on Latino culture. Studies have indicated that language is an integral component of a child's developing identity. If Spanish is a child's first language and it is rejected in school and in the larger English-speaking community, the rejection can seriously damage a child's positive self-identity. In fact, it has been demonstrated that the more proficient children are in their original language, the more likely they are to develop English-language proficiency.

Students who are encouraged to maintain their Spanish are able to maintain close family ties through their shared use of language and their parents feel more comfortable with the school environment, increasing the likelihood of parental involvement at school . . . bilingual language alone cannot completely reverse the history of school failure that Latino students have experienced. But it does challenge the alienating and emotionally disruptive idea that native language and culture need to be forgotten in order to be successful. (Tatum 1997, 143)

This kind of information has enormous meaning for the development of policies that affect Latino communities.

There are many examples of the exclusion of Latino culture and history in U.S. history. Orlando, Florida, is a multiracial community that works to embrace and celebrate its diverse populations—white, black, Native American, Latino, and Asian American; however, that has not always been the case. A 1970's court-mandated diversity curriculum omitted any reference to history or issues facing Asian Americans or Latinos. A history of central Florida published by the Orlando Historical Society and the daily newspaper in Orlando made no mention of Asian or Latino immigrants or their contribution to or treatment by the community.

Some civics and history texts include the history of Spanish-speaking peoples in the United States, but the accounts are often distorted. The sixth-grade textbook *We the People Discover Our Heritage* includes a section regarding new immigrants and one mention of Latinos: "Some immigrants traveled from Mexico for economic opportunity and to escape political unrest there" (Bednarz et al. 1997, 661). An eighth-grade civics textbook makes little reference to Latinos. It discusses U.S. expansion into Spanish-speaking territory: "As our nation expanded in the 1800s, it added areas that had been settled mostly by Spaniards, and later by people from Mexico, then a Spanish colony. The inhabitants of these regions—the present-day states of Florida, Louisiana, Texas, Arizona, New Mexico and California—became American citizens." The same text also refers to recent immigrants from Spanish-speaking countries in the following way: "Fleeing revolutions and political persecution at home, they have come seeking better jobs and lives for themselves and their families" (Davis and Fernlund 1996, 11).

Assuming that this information is somewhat standard for social studies textbooks, let us examine what we have been told and what we may have learned. The first piece of information is that regions that are currently part of the United States were once Spanish or Mexican. The passages from these texts imply that there was a smooth transition in which the Spanish or Mexicans became American citizens. We also are told that many Mexicans and other Spanish-speaking immigrants have continued to come to the United States to seek a better life than they had in their countries of origin. We are told of no historical or cultural distinctions between different Latino groups. Since we receive no further information, it is implicit that this search for a better life has been successful.

What has been omitted from these brief passages? What significant elements of history are overlooked? Review the questions listed below the sidebar on the facing page to see what you have been taught about Latinos in U.S. history.

2010 U.S. Census: Question Number 5

This is question number five of the official U.S. Census Bureau Questionnaire of 2010. While other questions provided options of self-identifying by race as African American, Asian American or Pacific Islander, white, and other more specific ethnicities, number five was the only question available for people with any identity or family origin that is Hispanic, Latino, Spanish, mixed, or another specific way that they identify with a particular country or region of origin. Individuals were given three choices as to how to self-identify their ethnicity: Hispanic, Latino, or Spanish origin. As the fastest growing "minority," the distinction of this information becomes increasingly important in monitoring equal employment opportunities.

The current thinking about race and ethnicity in 2010 that lies behind this question is that the identity of Hispanic, Latino, or Spanish origin is an *ethnicity* rather than a *race* and that theoretically individuals who answer question number five will also answer number six. What do people do if they identify their race as Hispanic, Latino, or Spanish or if they identify as multiracial with their Latin identity as one part of that?

5. Is this person of Hispanic, Latino, or Spanish origin?

☐ No, not of Hispanic, Latino, or Spanish origin

☐ Yes, Mexican, Mexican Am., Chicano

☐ Yes, Puerto Rican

☐ Yes, Cuban

☐ Yes, another Hispanic, Latino, or Spanish Origin – *Print origin, for example, Argentinean, Colombian, Dominican, Nicaraguan, Salvadoran, Spaniard, and so on.* ↘

Source: Population Reference Bureau.

- Under what circumstances were the Spanish or Mexican territories (now the states of Florida, Louisiana, Texas, Arizona, New Mexico, and California) annexed? Were there treaties, sales, compromises, wars, violence?
- What are the largest Latino populations in the United States? How are their histories of immigration, acceptance, and/or discrimination similar or different?
- What laws have affected the citizenship and treatment of Latinos in the United States?
- What are the current conditions in education, employment, housing, and health care for Latinos in the United States?

As we begin to consider the answers to some of these questions, think about what you have been taught, what has been omitted, and what partial truths or distortions you may have learned. Consider that the information omitted is not simply a reflection of incomplete education but rather an element in the socialization process. If you are Latino or live in an area with a substantial Latino community, you may have some additional information about Latino history and culture. However, if, like me, you grew up in a place with a very small Latino population, these tidbits of history taught in school (with some media information thrown in here or there) may be your only source of information.

Mexican Americans or Chicanos

"The nation's Latino barrios reflect a history of conquest, immigration, and a struggle to maintain cultural identity" (Moore and Pinderhughes 1995, 227). Cherie Moraga, a woman who identifies as Chicana (Mexican American), tells the personal story of how her family conveyed to her how much better it is to be light-skinned than dark-skinned in order to succeed in the United States: 'To her [Moraga's mother], on a basic economic level, being Chicana was perceived to mean being 'less.' It was through my mother's desire to protect her children from poverty and illiteracy that we became 'anglocized'; the more effectively we could pass in the white world, the better guaranteed our future" (Moraga 1995, 60). This is another potent example of racial targeting and internalization. U.S. discrimination, legal barriers, physical attacks, and psychological assaults have been so relentless that some Latinos decided that the only way to survive was to deny or conceal their ethnicity and attempt to pass as white.

What was it in her personal experience or cultural history that would prod Moraga's mother to deny her heritage and encourage her children to identify as white? How have Mexican Americans and other Latino groups fared in the United States?

The 2010 census reports that there were 50.7 million Latinos in the United States, 16.3 percent of the total population. Of the total Latino population, based on information gathered in 2008, 69 percent were Mexican, 9 percent Puerto Rican, 3.4 percent Cuban, 3.4 percent Salvadoran, 2.8 percent Dominican, and the remainder from Central and South America and other Spanish-speaking countries. We will examine some of the hidden history and contemporary conditions for Mexican Americans, Cuban Americans, and Puerto Ricans in order to broaden the base of what we understand as U.S. history.

It is important to recognize that the United States did not annex Texas from Mexico by signing on a dotted line or by exchanging handshakes with Mexican officials. It was not simply a land deal. It involved war and the loss of Mexican and U.S. lives. The connections between the annexation of Texas and slavery are little known, yet are profound elements of our history. In 1830, the Mexican government made slavery illegal and prohibited U.S. immigration into Mexico. Americans living in the Texas part of Mexico were slave owners and furious at these new Mexican laws. Americans continued to illegally cross into Mexican Texas until by 1835 their numbers were 20,000 compared to 4,000 Mexicans (Takaki 1993, 173–174). There is a certain irony in this information since by the twentieth century the issue of illegal immigration from Mexico to the United States had become quite controversial.

In 1846, Congress declared war on Mexico by using some border conflicts as justification. Many congressmen had already determined that war with Mexico would be necessary in order to take over Texas. The Mexican War (1846–1848) was "again driven chiefly by Southern planters wanting to push the borders of the nearest free land farther from the slave states" (Loewen 1995, 150–151). While a majority in Congress voted for this declaration of war, there were strong, clear voices for peace. These peace activists believed that the annexation of Texas was oppressive in two ways: first, in the killing of Mexicans for land, and second, in that the attempted annexation of Texas was an effort to extend slavery. Author Henry David Thoreau and abolitionist Frederick Douglass refused to pay taxes to support the war. Horace Greeley, publisher and editor of the *New York Tribune*, wrote, "Who believes that a score of victories over Mexico, the 'annexation' of half her provinces, will give us more Liberty, a purer Morality, a more prosperous industry, than we now have?" (Zinn 1995, 154–157). The U.S. victory and the treaty that followed the war allowed thousands of Mexicans to remain in what became part of the United States. Initially, Mexicans were allowed to vote in both California and Texas. By the 1890s in Texas, the legislature instituted a poll tax to disenfranchise Mexicans as well as blacks (Takaki 1993, 178–179).

Many of us were taught about the philosophy of Manifest Destiny. We learned that the United States was "destined" to expand from east to west in North America and as far north and south as it could. Manifest Destiny had an enormous impact on the communities and people, primarily Mexicans and Indians, who already lived where the United States was intending or "destined" to go. "The doctrine of 'manifest destiny' embraced a belief in American Anglo-Saxon superiority—the expansion of Jefferson's homogeneous republic and Franklin's American of the 'the lovely white,' . . . Mexicans within this border were alienated, forced into becoming aliens in land that was once theirs, moving from being landholders to laborers" (Takaki 1993, 176). Manifest Destiny was a clear example of institutional racism in which official policies and practices were based on the misinformed belief of white superiority. Subsequent migration laws for Mexicans to the United States were dependent on the vacillating U.S. need for cheap labor.

While the 1848 Treaty of Guadalupe provided citizenship for Mexican Americans in the Southwest, it also displaced them from their land and forced them into a colonized labor force. The work that Mexican Americans found on the railroads and in the mines separated families both because of the nature of the work and the deaths that the work caused. For these reasons, the number of female-headed households and the labor of women and children increased dramatically in the Mexican American community.

In the early 1900s, many young Mexican laborers came to the United States to escape economic hardship in their homeland. By 1918, 70 percent of Mexican Americans in Los Angeles were unskilled blue-collar workers locked into the same low-paying jobs from generation to generation. The conditions in California and Texas prompted many Mexicans to move to the Midwest and to eastern cities, where they worked in factories. In these new industrial locations, many Mexicans were recruited for factory work in order to drive the cost of labor down. Still others migrated to follow the crops, housed in migrant camps in wretched conditions (Takaki 1993, 324).

> Racial etiquette defined proper demeanor and behavior for Mexicans. In the presence of Anglos, they were expected to assume "a deferential body posture and respectful voice tone." They knew that public buildings were considered "Anglo territory," and they were permitted to shop in the Anglo business section of town only on Saturdays. They could patronize Anglo cafes, but only the counter and carry-out service. Schools were segregated. In Texas the schools were explicitly designed to keep Mexicans in their place as laborers. A Texas superintendent said, "You have doubtless heard that ignorance is bliss; it seems that is so when one has to transplant onions. . . . If a man has very much sense or education either, he is not going to stick to this kind of work. So you see, it is up to the white population to keep the Mexican on his knees in an onion patch." (Takaki 1993, 326)

In the 1900s, the large influx of Mexican immigrants to the United States created a racist backlash. The *New York Times* and the president of Harvard were among those pushing for Mexican exclusion from the United States. The American Federation of Labor joined this movement because the union leadership believed that the influx of Mexicans was forcing wages into a downward spiral. Ultimately, 400,000 Mexicans were sent back to Mexico (Takaki 1993, 343). The history of conquest, colonization, and relegation to second-class citizenry has had far-reaching consequences for Mexican Americans. The Spanish language was important to Mexican American culture, but by 1880 there was enormous pressure for English-only public schools (Dill 1995, 249). By the late twentieth century, only 45 percent of Mexican Americans aged twenty-five or older had completed high school, and 26 percent lived below the federal poverty line (Tatum 1997, 134).

These are just a few stories of Mexican Americans and U.S. history. These stories examine the way in which the United States conquered Mexican territory and took control of the conquered people through war. Contemporary problems for Mexican Americans, including high levels of poverty and marginal employment, are based on structural and institutional discrimination that evolved from the bloody Mexican War in which the United States conquered and acquired part of Mexico more than 160 years ago. The few sentences we learn in our history classes omit the devastating impact of Manifest Destiny, the 1846 war, the treatment of a conquered people, and subsequent policies on the lives of real people. Most of us never learn that the impetus for the Mexican War was intimately linked to slavery.

Let us take a second look at one of the quotes from a U.S. history book: "As our nation expanded in the 1800s, it added areas that had been settled mostly by Spaniards, and later by people from Mexico, then a Spanish colony. The inhabitants of these regions—the present-day states of Florida, Louisiana, Texas, Arizona, New Mexico and California—became American citizens." This quote literally whitewashes the long-lasting consequences triggered by our nation's "expansion" and gives the students who read this the impression that all was and is well in the transition from Mexican territory and citizenship to U.S.

territory and citizenship. As a student, it is easy to glide over these words in a textbook. The passage reads as if the issue is about land and property—not about real people. It makes this so-called expansion seem natural and good and right. We are not guided to question this part of history or to look at the role that slavery played in the Mexican War or to consider the human costs of the patriotically depicted policy of Manifest Destiny. There are hidden lessons for all of us when history involving conquest and racism is depicted as progress that is almost organic in its development.

Likewise, it is important to be aware of the steadfast resistance of Mexican-Americans to the discrimination and oppression they encountered. Josefina Fierro de Bright, who moved to California from Mexico as a child, was a determined activist who organized and led a movement to fight unfair labor practices in California and the Southwest. In 1938, she became the first president of El Congreso de Pueblo de Habla Española. Cesar Chavez co-founded the United Farm Workers union with Dolores Huerta in 1966 and spent his life fighting for the rights of immigrant farm workers. Alberto Baltazar Urista authored the "Epic Poem of Aztlán" (1969), a unique piece of counter-storytelling, based on Aztec oral histories of the ancient presence of the indigenous people of Mexico and what is now the American Southwest. The poem helped to inspire and mobilize the Chicano movement for civil rights (Menchaca 2001, 29–34). Important Chicano activist groups included the Alianza Federal de Pueblos Libres (Federal Alliance of Free City States), the Crusade for Justice, and the Brown Berets (Menchaca 2001, 30). The ongoing resistance to racial oppression on the part of people of color tends to be a part of history that is systematically distorted, obscured, or erased.

The misinformation and oversimplification that passes as history reinforces the subtle way that hegemony works to perpetuate a system that we are taught to believe is based solely on individual merit. Without a critical understanding of this part of our history, whether we are Latino or any other race, we will believe that economic success and academic achievement are based exclusively on our own hard work. We will also believe the obverse—that poverty and lower academic achievement are exclusively the results of our own failure. This thinking has profound effects on our sense of self, our beliefs about who is smart and successful and who is not, and on policies created by the government and businesses.

> How people think about the past is an important part of their consciousness. If members of the elite come to think that their privilege was historically justified and earned, it will be hard to persuade them to yield opportunity to others. If members of deprived groups come to think that their deprivation is their own fault, then there will be no need to use force or violence to keep them in their places. (Zinn 1995, 187)

Puerto Ricans

Puerto Rican immigration began in 1898 when the United States took possession of both Puerto Rico and Cuba during the Spanish-American War. Puerto Rico became a commonwealth of the United States in 1952, and thereafter Puerto Ricans were automatically citizens of the United States, not by choice but by conquest. The U.S. takeover of Puerto Rico had major consequences for the island. "As a result of the U.S. invasion, the island's economy was transformed from a diversified, subsistence economy which emphasized tobacco, cattle, coffee, and sugar, to a one-crop sugar economy, of which more than 60 percent was controlled by absentee U.S. owners" (Moore and Pinderhughes 1995, 228). Another consequence of Puerto Rico's status as a U.S. territory was the U.S. insistence on replacing Spanish with English in Puerto Rican schools. This policy, similar to the English-only policy in the newly conquered Mexican territories, was actively opposed by Puerto Rican students and teachers. In 1917, Congress passed the Jones Act, which required citizenship and military service for Puerto Ricans but denied them the right to vote in national elections. In 1951, Puerto Ricans voted to become a commonwealth, which gave them more independence and control in the schools and restored Spanish as the language of instruction (Tatum 1997, 134–135).

From 1900 to 1945, the first wave of Puerto Rican immigration to the mainland was largely to New York. The second wave, from 1946 to 1964, found Puerto Ricans settling in other U.S. cities. What both waves of immigration had in common was a concentration of Puerto Ricans in low-skilled and low-paid jobs in urban areas. Currently, Puerto Ricans have the largest proportion of households living below the U.S. poverty level (24 percent). The median household income for Puerto Ricans is 31 percent lower than the median income of U.S. households overall. Among Puerto Rican adults (25 and over), 25 percent have not received a high school diploma (U.S. Census Bureau, American Community Survey 2010).

Cuban Americans

The pattern of Cuban immigration to the United States was different from that of Mexican and Puerto Rican immigration. While the United States fought wars to annex Mexico and colonize Puerto Rico, Cuba became independent in 1902. The first wave of Cuban immigration to the United States occurred during the first days of Fidel Castro's revolution in 1959. These immigrants were predominantly white or light complexioned, educated, wealthy professionals and business people who settled in Florida and New York and were welcomed by the U.S. government as political refugees.

The second wave of Cuban immigrants, who came to the United States within a few months of the Castro revolution, were middle-income professionals and skilled workers. They, too, received U.S. government welcome and support.

But the third wave of Cuban immigrants was significantly different from the first two groups. They arrived beginning in 1980, having lived much of their lives in postcapitalist Cuba. As a group, they were darker-skinned than earlier groups, less educated, and lower-income (Tatum 1997, 136). This group was not embraced by the U.S. government in the same way as the first two waves of Cuban immigrants. Cuban Americans have the highest family income of all Latino groups, with a median income that is $5,000 higher. Only 18 percent of Cubans are living below poverty level, a much lower level than Mexican and Puerto Rican Americans (Pew Research Center 2012).

As you examine these brief histories of various Latino groups, recall the questions you were asked to consider at the outset. As you consider that the current overall poverty rate for Latinos is 28 percent, do you find historical and structural reasons for these problems? Finally, as you reach for your own independent thinking and conclusions on the impact of war, conquest, language, and discrimination on Latinos, how do you now regard what you have been taught about this component of American history and culture?

Asian Americans

In the documentary film *Skin Deep*, a multiracial group of college students are brought together to discuss their experiences, beliefs, socialization, and hurt involving race. In one segment of the film, students meet in racial affiliation groups in which they discuss their experiences of discrimination among themselves and then proceed to share with the entire group what it is like to be the race they are. The report out of the Asian group was powerful. These students discussed the personal pressure they felt regarding the stereotype of Asians as the "model minority" in the United States. They stood together holding hands and said that they wanted their peers to remember how many different countries they were from—China, Japan, Vietnam, India, Thailand, the Philippines, Sri Lanka, and so forth. One young man said that in elementary school he had had a crush on a little girl who was white. She wrote in his yearbook that he was nice for an "ugly person." This same young man, whose name was Khan, told his peers, "I want you to remember my name" (Reid 1995).

As these students poignantly ask us to remember, Asian Americans come from many places and have many different histories, cultures, and experiences in the United States. The U.S. government includes in its definitions of "Asian" people from East Asia (e.g., Chinese, Japanese, Korean), from Southeast Asia (e.g., Vietnamese, Laotian, Burmese), from South Asia (e.g., Indian, Pakistani, Nepali), from West Asia (Iranian, Afghani, Turkish), and from the Middle East (e.g., Iraqi, Jordanian, Palestinian). The largest Asian American groups in the United States in 2010 were Chinese (3.1 million), Asian Indian (2.8 million), Filipino (2.6 million), Vietnamese (1.5 million), Korean (1.4 million), and Japanese (760,000).

For now, our focus will be primarily on the immigration, history, and treatment of the Chinese, the Japanese, and the more recent immigrants, the Vietnamese. With the passage of the 1965 Immigration Act, the flow of Asian immigrants increased to make Asians the fastest-growing ethnic group in the United States. As the distinctions in these cultures and histories become increasingly clear, it will be important to keep in mind the myth of Asians as the so-called model minority, which cuts across various immigrant groups and labels all Asians as the same. Despite its perceived positive nature, the "model minority" is still a stereotype.

While various Asian immigrant groups have had distinct experiences as they have come to the United States, there are some common features as well. At least three U.S. policies and attitudes have affected most Asian immigrants. First, the United States has typically been ambivalent about Asian labor. This ambivalence has been reflected in U.S.

immigration policy as well as discrimination against Asian immigrants. "The simultaneous necessity and undesirability of Asian immigrant labor is a crucial political economic contradiction that informs much of the past and present experience of Asians in the United States" (Hamamoto 1994, 1).

Second, early Asian immigrant groups of the nineteenth century, Chinese and Japanese in particular, were targeted as the "yellow peril." Chinese immigrants were charged with being debased and clannish, while Japanese immigrants were seen as loyal to the emperor of Japan, thus disloyal to the United States. Ironically, the third common experience has been the ambivalence in the late twentieth century of being held up as the minority group that has "made it" and achieved the American Dream.

As you will see below, there are vast distinctions between the immigration experiences and economic success of various Asian groups. While census data report that Asian American families have higher median family incomes than any other family group, significant information is often overlooked in this aggregate statistic. Asian Americans have more adults contributing to household income than whites, for example. This statistic also breaks down according to specific countries of origin and immigration experiences. Larger percentages of Vietnamese Americans, Laotians, and Cambodians live in poverty. While the overall Asian American high school completion rate is higher than the national average, it is lower for Southeast Asians (Tatum 1997, 161). Yet the concept of the model minority is monolithic. This myth has often been used as "proof" that there is no racism in the United States and that some groups just have what it takes to succeed and others do not. This fallacy not only ignores the different immigration experiences of Asians but blatantly denies the distinction between and legacies of people who immigrated to the United States voluntarily (Chinese, Japanese), people who came as refugees (Vietnamese, Thai), people who were enslaved (Africans), and people who were invaded and colonized (American Indians, Mexicans). To begin to unravel some of this history and explore the various myths and omissions about Asian Americans, we will examine some of the stories of Chinese Americans, Vietnamese Americans, and Japanese Americans. As we explore these immigration experiences, it is important to remember that this is not Asian history but U.S. history.

Chinese Americans

In the 1860s, a Chinese laborer could earn $3 to $5 a month in China and $30 a month in California working on the railroad or in the gold mines. Chinese men came to the United States of their own accord, borrowing money from brokers to cover their transportation. Race discrimination began to be widespread against the Chinese, often forcing them out of the employment they came for and into self-employment. Many Chinese laborers found a niche in the development of laundries. This trade was learned not in China but in the United States as a survival mechanism in a needed service with a low overhead (Takaki 1993, 193–202).

In 1854, a Chinese man was murdered and the suspect was white. In the initial trial, the court convicted the suspect on the basis of testimony by two Chinese witnesses. The conviction was later overturned when a higher court determined that no one who was nonwhite would be allowed to testify against a white person (Takaki 1993, 229). By 1882, Congress passed a law that prohibited further Chinese immigration and prohibited any current Chinese citizens from becoming American citizens. Asian Americans are often stereotyped as passive, but during this period of history many Chinese immigrants fought for their civil rights in court (Takaki 1993, 206).

In previous sections of this book regarding African Americans, American Indians, and Latinos, we analyzed the impact of U.S. laws and informal treatment on the development and disruption of families. Both Chinese culture and American policy made it almost impossible for Chinese women or families to come to America. The Page Law of 1875 restricted the number of female Chinese immigrants, and in 1882 the Chinese Exclusion Law created a total ban. It was not until the late 1960s that miscegenation laws prohibiting the marriage of Chinese Americans and European Americans were lifted. Most Chinese men fully intended to earn enough money in the United States to return to China to re-unite with and support their families in their home villages. In the meantime, the lack of Chinese women created a culture of Chinese bachelors, which in turn created a culture of prostitutes and a double life for these laborers. It was a century after Chinese immigration began that children began to be born to these immigrants (Dill 1995, 247–248). And it was not until 1952 that the McCarran-Walter Act finally made it legal for Asians to become citizens (Segrest 1994, 222–223).

European Americans used the concept of Manifest Destiny as justification for U.S. aggression and violence. It was widely believed that these white Americans were pre-ordained to be the trailblazers and the beneficiaries of westward expansion. This idea not only devastated the lives of American Indians and Mexicans, but also obscured the role played by Asian immigrants in the building of the United States (Hamamoto 1994, 32). For example, railroad work in the mid-nineteenth century was accomplished largely through Chinese labor and ingenuity. Although 90 percent of all workers on the Central Pacific Railroad were Chinese, famous historic photographs of the completion of the transcontinental railroad show no sign of Asian participation (Hamamoto 1994, 48).

The eighth-grade textbook *Discovering Our Democracy* speaks of the diversity of Asian groups and states that it was the early economic success of these groups that instigated laws excluding further immigration (Davis and Fernlund 1996, 12). There is no mention of the disruption of the Chinese family, the internment of Japanese American citizens during World War II, or the orphans created by the Vietnam War. There is no mention of racial discrimination. If you read this textbook or others much like it, the passages about Asians would allow you to think Asians faced no problems other than a brief period of limited immigration. If your experience with Asian Americans was limited, it would al-low you to believe the myth of the model minority. Most of us have had little exposure in our formal education to any knowledge of the way that opportunities and barriers have been constructed for different immigrant and racial groups.

The representation of Chinese and other Asian Americans as a so-called model minority is an insulting reinforcement to the American meta-narrative on race and racial hierarchy. "By focusing on the achievements of one minority in relation to another, our attention is diverted from larger institutional and historical factors which influence a group's success" (Woo 1995, 224). While the achievements of many Asian Americans have been formidable, stories of their successes are often used as a rationale for not supporting programs for African Americans, Latinos, American Indians, or even other Asian Americans. The argument goes something like this: if Asian Americans can be successful, then other groups just have to work harder and not depend on government handouts. This logic ignores how racism has operated in the United States and the way it has dictated who will have opportunities and who will have limited life chances. The myth of the model minority is based on the assumptions of the level playing field and the American Dream, which tell us that only individual effort and merit count when it comes to success. This fiction discounts the widely varied experiences of voluntary and forced immigration, as well as the legacies of slavery and conquest.

Japanese Americans

As was the case with the Chinese, Japanese immigrants came to the United States in search of economic opportunity. Japanese began arriving during the 1890s when severe economic hardship in Japan resulted in massive immigration both to Hawaii and the continental United States. Unlike their Chinese counterparts, 35 percent of Japanese immigrants were women, which resulted in more Japanese Americans than Chinese Americans (Takaki 1993, 246). Japanese immigrants were able to find work as farmers, shopkeepers, railroad laborers, and cannery workers. Their initial labor and economic success triggered a backlash in the United States. By 1908, many states began to prohibit Japanese immigrants from owning or leasing land. In 1922, the Supreme Court ruled that Japanese immigrants could not become naturalized citizens (Takaki 1993, 267).

As the country of Japan emerged as an enemy during World War II, Japanese Americans, many of whom were American citizens whose families had been in the United States for several generations, became suspect of treason by the government and many European Americans. In 1942, Japanese Americans were declared enemy aliens. Ultimately, more than 10,000 people were evacuated from their homes to internment camps. In a tragic irony, 33,000 Japanese Americans served in the United States armed forces during World War II, and at least 600 men were killed (Takaki 1993, 382–383). Even J. Edgar Hoover, director of the FBI, insisted that mass evacuation of Japanese Americans was not necessary for national security and referred to such measures as hysterical. Despite Hoover's recommendations and other government reports that described the loyalty of Japanese American citizens to the United States, General John L. DeWitt of the Western Defense command pursued his plan of mass action. This was fueled by West Coast news media, which described Japanese Americans as spies and vipers, an image pushed by so-called patriotic organizations that were thoroughly anti-Japanese.

The move for mass evacuation operated in a context of "racism and war hysteria. The Japanese Americans on the West Coast were extremely vulnerable. They were not needed as laborers in the mainstream economy and many white farmers viewed Japanese farmers as competitors" (Takaki 1993, 381–382). Despite Hoover's belief that it was unnecessary and Secretary of War Henry L. Stimson's belief that it was unconstitutional, President Franklin D. Roosevelt issued an executive order to place all Japanese Americans into internment camps.

The evacuees were taken to assembly centers, which were crowded, dirty racetracks, stockyards, and fairgrounds in which hundreds and sometimes thousands of people were crowded into single buildings. After a brief stay in these assembly centers, they were herded into trains and sent to ten different internment camps. Whole families lived in one room inside large barracks that most closely resembled a military base or prison. Each family was issued one electric light, army cots, and one blanket per person (Takaki 1993, 383).

Informal surveys of American high school students reveal that well over 50 percent of these students are unaware of the internment of U.S citizens of Japanese descent, a deep violation of human rights. It is rare to find a middle school or high school American history textbook that describes this part of our history. Human rights organizations and, at various times, U.S. government leaders have put pressure on Germany to include teaching about the Holocaust when young people study German history. The purpose is not to create national shame, but rather to provide a more honest, accurate, and complete depiction of historical events. This same principle has rarely been applied by the United States in the United States. It is true that there was no grand plan to kill Japanese Americans, an important distinction between the planned annihilation of Jews by the Nazis and the internment of Japanese Americans by the U.S. government. However, as we have learned, the more we are socialized to fear people who are different from us, the more it becomes acceptable to see them as "other," to hate them, and ultimately to treat them as if they are less than human.

It is important to note that although the United States was also at war with Germany and Italy, neither German Americans nor Italian Americans were rounded up, taken from their homes, and thrown into internment camps. Why were Japanese Americans treated differently from Italian or German Americans? Why was it determined that the risk of treason was so high among Japanese Americans that it was necessary to violate their human and civil rights? The answers revolve around what it takes to become white and what it means to be white in the United States. The descendants of German and Italian immigrants of the early twentieth century had assimilated. They were European and their appearance was white. They had become part of the group that was understood to be mainstream American and as such were not considered a threat to national security.

In Chapter 1 we described the encounter of historian Ronald Takaki, an American citizen whose grandparents emigrated to the U.S. from Japan, with a taxi driver who complimented him on his English because he saw Takaki's Asian face as a sign that he was not American. What are the steps that we take to dehumanize people who are different from each other? How do individuals, families, groups, and entire countries move from making well-meaning comments like the cab driver's to rounding up Japanese American citizens to protect other citizens from them to seeing Jews, as the Nazis did, as subhuman and so dangerous that they must be annihilated?

Japanese immigrants had great hopes of being considered both Japanese and American, but continued to be viewed as strangers. While other immigrants from European countries could assimilate through changing language, clothing, and customs, this was not an available option for Japanese immigrants no matter how many generations they had been in the United States. For Japanese Americans, changing their names or adopting American culture still would not change the fact that in the United States it was their race that marked them as the "other."

Southeast Asians

The newer Asian immigrants—Vietnamese, Laotians, and Cambodians—differ substantially from earlier Asian immigrant groups. They were refugees from Southeast Asia who, as a group, were largely poor, young, and uneducated. These groups have had some economic success, yet by and large they have not lived up to the myth of the model minority (Hamamoto 1994, 168). As of the first decade of the twenty-first century, these trends began changing for the better. Vietnamese families living below the poverty line account for 12 percent. The median income of a Vietnamese family of four is $59,000 a year. Approximately 65 percent of Vietnamese are homeowners, and the number of businesses owned by Vietnamese people has increased by 56 percent since 2002.

The Vietnam War had a devastating impact on Vietnam, Laos, and Cambodia. One million South Vietnamese soldiers and an equal number of Viet Cong and North Vietnam regular soldiers were killed. Civilian deaths are estimated at 3.5 million. In fact, more bombs were dropped on Vietnam than on all of Europe during World War II. By 1975, when South Vietnam fell, the war had created 200,000 prostitutes, 879,000 orphans, 181,000 disabled persons, and 1 million widows. The war transformed the country from a prosperous and self-sufficient agricultural region into an impoverished nation no longer able to independently support its people (Hamamoto 1994, 26).

By 1980, immigration from Southeast Asia to the United States had swelled, increasing the U.S. population to 245,025 Vietnamese, 52,887 Laotians, and 16,044 Cambodians. These newer immigrants brought with them the very real trauma and economic and emotional fallout from a devastating war (Hamamoto 1994, 26).

Those of us who lived through the Vietnam War era may recall that it was the first war that was actually televised. Daily body counts were a regular part of newscasts and newspaper articles. It was a war of great controversy debated between prowar "hawks" and antiwar "doves." It was a war of massive protests by several generations of Americans who walked picket lines and participated in local and national marches in efforts to stop it. President Lyndon B. Johnson decided not to run for reelection in large part because of the massive opposition to his Vietnam policies.

The role of the United States in this war that happened so far away from U.S. soil remains controversial. But though the war ravaged Vietnam and its people and though almost forty years have passed since the war ended, few history books give it much attention. While visual images of the horrors of this war abound, few are found in U.S. textbooks. Rather, the visual images depict soldiers on patrol or the damage done by the violence of the "other side" (Loewen 1995, 247). According to author, editor, and former high school teacher Bill Bigelow, "Textbooks resist telling students that the U.S. government consistently lied about the war, preferring more genteel language" (Bigelow 2013).

This small and narrow depiction of the Vietnam War has many implications for future U.S. policy with regard to Third World countries. But for our purposes of examining the impact of this lack of information on race in the United States, it means that American students who became the classmates of Vietnamese refugees had no context for understanding what their lives may have been like in Vietnam and what they may have lost in both human and material terms. For generations born after the end of the Vietnam War, there was little connection to be made between the U.S. policies that continued the war and the Vietnamese who became the newest Americans.

The first wave of Vietnamese immigrants saw an opportunity in developing manicure and pedicure businesses, commonly known as "nail shops." These shops have thrived. Linda has visited several of these shops as a customer and observed that a significant element of their success is service that anticipates and serves the needs and comfort of the customer. She noticed one common and disturbing feature of this extraordinary customer service in parts of the country as far from each other as Wilton, Connecticut; St. Louis, Missouri; and Oakland, California: in each of these shops, many of the nail technicians changed their names from their original Vietnamese names to American names such as Caroline, Nancy, Lucy, and Anna. As Linda got to know some of these women, they began to share personal information and were eager to talk about their lives in Vietnam and their journeys to the United States. When she asked why they changed their names, they invariably replied something to the effect of, "American women have a hard time pronouncing our names. We want to make them comfortable, so we change our names." When Linda asked, "Would you prefer me to call you by your Vietnamese name or your American name?" the women invariably answered, with delight, "My Vietnamese name." We wonder how this assimilation for the purposes of accommodating other Americans will impact the generations to come and their sense of their own identity.

Multiracial Americans

In a 1908 article, "The Tragedy of the Mulatto," Ray Stannard Baker writes of a meeting he attended at which 1,200 "colored" people were present:

> A prominent white man gave a brief address in which he urged the Negroes present to accept with humility the limitations imposed upon them by their heredity, that they were Negroes and that therefore they should accept with grace the place of inferiority. Now as I looked out over that audience, which included the best class of colored people in Atlanta, I could not help asking myself: "What is this blood he is appealing to, anyway?" For I saw comparatively few men and women who could really be called Negroes at all. Some were so light as to be indistinguishable from Caucasians. (Baker 1908, 586)

Baker challenges the standard racist claim of white superiority by challenging the fluid, mutable, and often indistinguishable color line. He discusses the historical relationships primarily between white slaveholders and black women who were slaves. Even in 1908, with the limits of Baker's understanding of the human costs of slavery and racism, he is able to see some of the impact of the rape and sexual abuse of enslaved female African Americans by white slaveholders : "If there was ever a human tragedy in this world it is the tragedy of the Negro girl" (Baker 1908, 589).

He also details the post–Civil War practice by some white men of having two families, one white and one black, and notes the range in these relationships. Some wealthy white men took care of their second families, sending their biracial children to the finest colleges that would admit them. Some of these interracial families were characterized by deep human emotion and connection. But Baker is quick to point out,

> No legal marriage existed between the races in slavery times and yet there was a widespread mixture of blood. Having concubines was a common practice: A mulatto was worth more in cash than a black man. The great body of Mulattoes now in the country traces their origin to such relationships. And such practices of slavery days no more ceased instantly with a paper Emancipation Proclamation than many other customs and habits that had grown up out of centuries of slave relationships. It is a slow process, working out of slavery, both for white men and black. (Baker 1908, 582)

Despite the dominance of racism of the early twentieth century and the assumption of white supremacy, the author of this article ponders why there is such a fuss about race given that so many people designated as "Negro" are, in fact, racially mixed. "Nothing, indeed," he writes, "is more difficult to define than this curious physical color line in the individual human being" (Baker 1908, 582).

But the line did exist and, until 1960, the "one-drop rule" applied to defining race. A person with any African heritage was defined as Negro or black in the U.S. census from 1920 until 1960. "Though it is estimated that 75–90 percent of Black Americans have White ancestors, and about 25 percent have Native American ancestry, the widespread use of the one-drop rule meant that children with one Black parent, regardless of appearance, were classified as Black. The choice of biracial identity was not a viable option" (Tatum 1997, 170). This meant, of course, that multiracial children were subjected to the same segregation, inferior schools, and other forms of racism as African American children.

This changed in 1960, when the heads of U.S. households were permitted to indicate the race of the family. Still, there was no box to check for biracial or multiracial identity. In 1908, miscegenation laws that made interracial marriage illegal still existed in all of the southern states as well as Arizona, California, Colorado, Delaware, Idaho, Indiana, Missouri, Nebraska, Oklahoma, Oregon, and Utah. It was not until 1967 that the Supreme Court overturned the last laws prohibiting interracial marriage (Tatum 1997, 168). Since that time, interracial births to families with one parent that is white and one parent that is African American, Asian American, or American Indian have more than tripled. But despite legal progress and the development of healthy multiracial families and children, the multiracial legacy from slavery has not completely disappeared.

Parents generally teach their children during their preschool years how to identify themselves racially. When a biracial child is assumed to be white, teachers and classmates often feel shock and curiosity when the darker-skinned parent comes to school. Sometimes, the relationship of the adult to the child is questioned. Some children in this situation experience prejudice when their classmates see the darker-skinned parent. The same shock and prejudice does not occur as frequently when a black-appearing biracial child's white parent arrives on the scene (Tatum 1997, 180–181). While young children may not be able to articulate their feelings at this point, they notice the reactions of children and adults in their world and may feel confusion, discomfort, anger, or sadness. These reactions and their parents' ability to help make sense of them influence the way children experience their multiracial identity.

Census data suggest that some of the past stigma associated with complex racial identity is diminishing. The number of children in the United States who identify themselves as multiracial has increased almost 50 percent, to 4.2 million, since 2000. The number of people of all ages who identify themselves as both white and black soared by 134 percent since 2000 to 1.8 million people. Nationwide, 9 million people, comprising 2.9 percent of the population, chose more than one race on the last census. This represents a change of more than 30 percent since the last census. Of the 57 possible racial combinations on the census, approximately 20 percent of those who identified themselves as biracial chose black and white, and more than 19 percent chose white and "some other race." Asian and white and American Indian and white were the third and fourth most common choices. Those four groups accounted for three-fourths of the U.S. mixed-race population (Jones and Bullock 2012).

Most of the research, interest, and controversy over interracial marriage and biracial and multiracial children has been directed to relationships between whites and blacks, followed by whites and individuals from other communities of color. There has been little research conducted about the interracial children of two different races of color, primarily because these relationships and children do not threaten or blur the lines of whiteness (Tatum 1997, 168). In fact, there has been little research in general regarding the experiences of multiracial children and adults. One of the few studies is a doctoral dissertation by Charmaine Wijeyesinghe, who studied the racial self-identification of black and white biracial adults and the factors affecting their choice of how to name or identify themselves by race. Wijeyesinghe concluded that the factors that affect the process and outcome of self-identification include biological heritage, sociohistorical context of the society, early socialization, culture, ethnic identity and heritage, spirituality, physical appearance, and individual awareness of "self" in relation to race and racism (Wijeyesinghe 1998, 91).

When biracial people experience consistency between their identities and how others respond to them, there is little conflict or serious problem about their racial identity. Tension and conflict occur, however, when discrepancies exist. For example, if a black-white biracial child is assigned "blackness" by the parents and the child appears to be African American, other people in their daily lives will not challenge the child when she says that she is black. However, if a biracial child appears white and is assigned "blackness" by the parents, he is likely to experience discrepancies in the form of questions, curiosity, gossip, and challenges often accompanied by rudeness when he announces that he is black. "While it is clear that biracial children can grow up happy and healthy, it is also clear that particular challenges associated with a biracial identity must be negotiated. One such challenge is embodied in the frequently asked question: 'What are you?'—Biracial individuals challenge the rigid boundaries between black and white" (Tatum 1997, 175).

Closely related to the question of "What are you?" is the question "How much?" This refers to the concept of *blood quantum* (Downing, Nichols, and Webster 2005, 32). The notion of trying to measure what percentage of one's blood is derived from a particular racial group seems almost laughable, yet it has had serious implications throughout American history. Identifiers such as "mulatto," "quadroon," and "octoroon" are blood quantum terms that have been used to enforce a hierarchy of color among African Americans. Native Americans are faced with legal issues centered on blood quantum that pertain to "tribal sovereignty, distribution of economic resources, access to social service programs, and health care" (Downing, Nichols, and Webster 2005, 32).

In addition to blood quantum, certain other aspects of the interracial experience have been identified as hot buttons. These include interracial dating and marriage, adoption and child-rearing, alienation, and passing (Downing, Nichols, and Webster 2005, 23–31). "Passing" is the practice used by some people of color with extremely light skin whose skin color allows them to live in the world as if they were white. Sometimes this is the choice of the individual, other times the result of pressure from parents or grandparents who want their children to have better chances in life. Either way, the purpose of "passing" is to gain greater access to the privileges, resources, and power of whites. This practice is controversial in the African American community since, in addition to choosing to live as white for the opportunities it offers, individuals are also at some level rejecting their black identity and history and often separating themselves from their families. Deciding to pass can create a lifetime of anguish that moves from the background to the foreground depending on the situation and deeply impacts both the individuals making the decision and their families.

Beginning in 2000, the U.S. Census Bureau allowed individuals to declare more than one racial identity. There was considerable controversy and debate as to the ramifications of such a change. Once again, the evolving racial categories and the controversy regarding multiracial identification in the census pointed out the artificial construction of race. The categories of male and female have not changed over the years, nor have the categories of age. But racial categories in this country are in a continuous state of flux. The frenzy has died down now that people were allowed to self-identify as multiracial in both the 2000 census and the 2010 census without the nation experiencing any catastrophic outcomes (see the sidebar on the facing page). Nevertheless, this controversy over the census and the unprecedented demands that political opponents have made for the birth certificate of biracial U.S. president Barack Obama since his election in 2008 have combined to highlight another fact of life for multiracial people that is embedded in the operation of racism as usual. Regardless of whether individuals "choose" their identity to be biracial, multiracial, white, black, Asian, or "none of your business," most likely they will be treated as members of the race that their physical appearance most closely resembles.

Race Questions on the 2010 Census

Question number 6 of the U.S. Census Questionnaire of 2010 allowed people to identify their race by choosing among 15 options and also offered various opportunities for write-ins. The 2010 census was only the second census (the other in 2000) to allow individuals to designate more than one race and self-identify as biracial or multiracial. Recalling the constantly changing race choices on previous census questionnaires, in 2010 people whose family originated in Spain or Central or South America would check the box for number 5, *ethnicity*, and people who identified as Asian American or Pacific Islander whose family of origin was Hmong, Laotian, Thai, Pakistani, Cambodian, Fijian, Tongan, and so on would check a box for number 6, *race*.

To what degree are these changes, like others in the past, a sincere attempt to be more accurate and accessible to the wide range of how people in the United States self-identify according to race and ethnicity, and to what degree are these changes political in the sense of the impact the census has on eligibility for government services and political elections?

6. What is this person's race? Mark ✖ on one or more boxes

- ☐ White
- ☐ Black, African Amer., or Negro
- ☐ American Indian or Alaskan Native — *Print name of enrolled or principled tribe* ➶

[_____]

- ☐ Asian Indian   ☐ Japanese   ☐ Native Hawaiian
- ☐ Chinese   ☐ Korean   ☐ Guamanian or Chamorro
- ☐ Filipino   ☐ Vietnamese   ☐ Samoan
- ☐ Other Asian — *Print race for example, Hmong, Laotian, Thai, Pakistani, Cambodian, and so on.* ➶   ☐ Other Pacific Islander — *Print race, for example, Fijian, Tongan, and so on.* ➶

[_____]

- ☐ Some other race — *Print race.* ➶

[_____]

Source: Population Reference Bureau.

European Americans or Whites

The irony of the socialization of white or European Americans is that it is so thorough and comprehensive that it is often invisible, particularly to whites, and requires great efforts to make it visible. "Whites are taught to think of their lives as morally neutral, normative, and average, and also ideal, so that when we work to benefit others, this is seen as work that will allow 'them' to be more like 'us'" (McIntosh 1988, 82–83). Understanding the history of European Americans and their participation in racism is not the same as white guilt. In fact, guilt is fairly useless in this process of understanding race and often acts as a barrier to reconstructing knowledge and arriving at independent conclusions and making decisions about individual and social change. Understanding the history of racism, the role of white people, and structural **white privilege** is critical not simply for eliminating racism for people of color but for the humanizing of white people as well. It is important for those who are white to understand and embrace two concepts simultaneously: the impact of white privilege and the possibilities of white liberation. As we learned about liberation theory in the first chapter, it became clear that according to these concepts, "We are born without racist attitudes, values or beliefs. Though we are born into social identity groups, we have no information about ourselves or about others. It is through the socialization process that we acquire the sets of attitudes, values, and beliefs that support racism" (Wijeyesinghe, Griffin, and Love 1997, 91).

Racism is dehumanizing for people of color who have been the targets of hundreds of years of violence and discrimination. And racism is also dehumanizing for those whites who have participated in overtly racist acts, for those whites who have actively taken a stand against racism, and for all whites who, despite their best actions and intentions, continue to benefit from racism.

We will also examine the concepts of white supremacy and **internalized white supremacy** as another construct of understanding racism. As we examine the role of European immigrants and white Americans in the U.S. history of racism, we will trace how various groups become "white" in the United States, white-skin privilege, the fallacy of white supremacy and its impact, and the benefits that have accrued to whites. This history will be different from the stories you have just read. Most of the history and social studies texts and curricula that we have been exposed to in the United States have predominantly featured the stories of white Americans. In fact, in most cases, the word "American" in history books has an implicit assumption of whiteness. These stories that have become the sum of standard U.S. history do not need repeating. Rather, as with the rest of the stories of race in this section, it is the inaccessible, the invisible, the out-of-reach counterstories that we will explore.

Before you begin reading this section, pause and consider experiences, thoughts, and feelings that may collide as you take in new information, especially if that information challenges some things you have believed to be true for a long time. Take another look at what you wrote about your experiences in the personal inventories. How frequently and to what extent have you lived near, gone to school with, socialized with, and worked with people whose races are different from yours? What were you told and what did you hear the adults in your life—parents and other family members, teachers, clergy, and others you respected and loved—say about people and races that were different from yours? What did you learn about the racialized history of your family in coming to the United States or in being part of a group whose land was conquered by the United States or whose ancestors were brutally taken from their homes and enslaved in the United States?

Consider the thoughts and feelings you had when you wrote your responses in the personal inventories in this chapter as well as the thoughts and feelings you have now as you begin to read a section about becoming white in America, about white privilege and internalized white supremacy. Are you interested and open to learn about some U.S. history and some constructs and theories you've never been exposed to before? Are you feeling a sense of relief that some of the material you read validates your experience as a person of color or a white ally to people of color or as a white antiracist? Are you anxious or angry at the thought that whites may be blamed for everything that is attributed to racism in the United States?

Whatever your thoughts and feelings as you approach this material, we encourage you to keep a few things in mind. First, remember the concept of cognitive dissonance—that is, the discomfort we feel when we receive information that is inconsistent with information and beliefs that we have learned in the past and that we have understood for a long time as facts or "truth." Understand that while this new information may challenge what you learned in the past, you are never required to change your mind about what is real and what is true.

You are, however, invited to take in the new information and concepts and to stay as open-minded as you can. Determine if the new information seems plausible to you. Consider the sources of your previous information and the present information and which seems credible. Sit with any confusion, conflict, or feelings that you are experiencing in response to new information.

Then continue the process of making independent decisions about what you believe or where you are in the process of forming and re-forming your beliefs. There are many options to consider and we will suggest a few of them to jump-start the process. You may decide that none of the new material is credible enough to stand up to the information that you have always known to be true and that there is no reason to make any changes in your thinking. You may decide that you are reading the material as something separate from what you believe or think and that you will learn what is necessary for the course, but that will be the extent of the time and energy you will put into it. You may find that some of the material that challenges previous information may be confusing, some seems very credible, and some seems too extreme to make sense according to your own thoughts about race. You may find that the information is highly compatible with your own sense of what is true and real about racism and that you are excited to learn solid theories and facts to support your beliefs.

Any and all of these conscious processes of investigating information about race and racism and your own beliefs are acceptable.

Becoming White in America

When students begin the process of exploring their identity in written autobiographies, we ask them to write about their race and their racial and ethnic history and background. Many white students describe their national origin instead (if they know it). For race they offer generic, non-racial descriptions of themselves such as "boring" or "normal." They do not really give much thought to race as a self-identifier that they share with all other white people. Their tendency is to think of racial identity as a means of describing or defining members of other groups. For many white people, and particularly those who have lived in communities that are predominantly white, whiteness is an unexamined norm. "Because they represent the societal norm, whites can easily reach adulthood without thinking much about their racial group" (Tatum 1997, 93). But according to psychologists Janet Helm and Beverly Daniel Tatum, in a race-conscious society racial identity has psychological implications for whites as well as for people of color. The cost of the kind of individual racism that is characterized by hateful and even violent thoughts, words, and actions is the reduction of one's own humanness, what one student referred to as a "hole in the soul."

For those whites who have never participated in a hateful racial act and have never considered their whiteness, there are also costs. These costs sometimes involve fear of people of color, circumscribed or nonexistent relationships with people of color, and sometimes feelings of guilt and shame. "While the task of people of color is to resist negative societal messages and develop an empowered sense of self in the face of a racist society, . . . the task for whites is to develop a positive white identity based in reality, not on assumed superiority. In order to do that each person must become aware of his or her whiteness, accept it as personally and socially significant and learn to feel good about it, not in the sense of a Klan member's 'white pride,' but in the context of a commitment to a just society" (Tatum 1997, 94).

Without this consciousness of one's own whiteness, there is a tendency for many well-meaning European Americans to generalize from their own experience to other racial groups. Most students are taught in school that we live in a just society that has corrected racism with the Civil War and the civil rights movement. For whites who have not experienced **racial discrimination** directed at them and have neither learned nor observed the ways in which people of color continue to be targeted by racism, this teaching of a just society and a level playing field makes sense. Basically good people who would never consciously participate in a hateful act toward a person of color thus see themselves as free of prejudice. This attitude can result in a more subtle form of racism called **aversive racism**, in which there is simultaneously and somewhat ironically a belief in an egalitarian society and an internalization of racial biases and stereotypes. Decent European Americans who have unwittingly been socialized into both of these beliefs may make friendship or dating or housing or hiring decisions with aversive racism at the root of these choices (Tatum 1997, 118).

How do European immigrants become "white" in the United States? An examination of the experiences of Russian and German Jewish immigrants and Irish immigrants serves to illustrate this process of assimilation into the so-called melting pot. The experience of

Jewish immigrants was both the same as and different from that of other European groups. First, there is power in naming. While Christian immigrants from Germany or Russia were named "Germans" or "Russians," Jews from these same countries were named "Jews" or "German Jews" or "Russian Jews." In this naming there are two things implicit. The first is that being Christian is the norm and that Jews deviated from that norm. Second, while Jews would eventually be considered white in the United States, they were simultaneously considered foreign or "other." Unlike Chinese and Japanese immigrants of the nineteenth and early twentieth century, Jews did not arrive in the United States with plans to return to their homelands. Anti-Semitism was already virulent in Europe, and Jews were often prohibited from owning land or participating in certain jobs or professions. Pogroms in Russia, in which officials massacred Jews and burned their towns, were commonplace. "At the end of the nineteenth century, Jews were being allowed into the white working class in the United States, at the same time they were being cast as the most reviled racial Other in Europe" (Segrest 1994, 216).

Part of the immigration experience of Jews in America was coming to Ellis Island in New York and standing by as immigration officials changed their names because they could not pronounce or write them. Later, some Jews changed and anglicized their names themselves so as not to be so easily identified as Jewish and easily targeted for discrimination. So while anti-Semitism continued in the United States, there were contradictions in official and unofficial treatment of Jews according to whether or not they were considered white. The availability of educational opportunity for Jews and the Jewish cultural emphasis on education meant that by the 1920s, many Jews in New York were entering college. The Jewish population at Harvard reached 20 percent (Takaki 1993, 288–301). "But the increasing presence of Jewish students at Harvard provoked a backlash. In 1923, a writer for *The Nation* complained that the upwardly mobile Jew sent 'his children to college a generation or two sooner than other stocks,' and that consequently there were 'in fact more dirty Jews and tactless Jews in college than dirty and tactless Italians, Armenians, or Slovaks" (Takaki 1993, 302). Jews have clearly and strongly benefited from white privilege in the United States and have simultaneously been targeted by anti-Semitism. In the last half of the twentieth century and the beginning decades of the twenty-first century, Jews have had high access to good housing, health care, employment, and education. But white supremacists often refer to the Jewish conspiracy in banking and media and target Jews for violence along with African Americans.

The nineteenth-century potato famine in Ireland triggered the immigration of millions of unskilled laborers to the United States. These immigrants worked primarily in the construction of railroads and roads and lived in substandard housing. In fact, the Irish laborers were initially compared unfavorably to the Chinese who were engaged in similar work. "The Irish were imaged as apelike and 'a race of savages,' at the same level of intelligence of blacks. Pursuing the 'lower' rather than the 'higher' pleasures, seeking 'vicious excitement' and 'gratification merely animal'" (Takaki 1993, 150). The Irish immigrants were criticized as lazy and as drinkers and gamblers. Signs in New York City barred Irish and blacks from employment and housing.

Yet by the late twentieth century, Irish Americans were considered white and many had dropped the Irish part from their identity. How did this happen for this group of immigrants when it failed to happen for other voluntary and involuntary immigrant groups? Like many other European immigrants, the Irish quickly figured out that in order to be white in America, it was necessary to separate oneself from all that is black. As Irish Americans began to compete with blacks for jobs, they often manipulated the racism they found for their own self-interest. They emphasized their whiteness. A powerful way to transform their own identity from Irish to American was to attack blacks. Thus, blacks, as the "other," served to facilitate the assimilation of Irish immigrants. By the early 1900s, Irish women had gone from being maids to becoming schoolteachers, and many Irish men had become prominent in the building trades and the labor movement. It is important to note that even those Irish immigrants who were never slave owners or those who arrived after the Civil War still benefited from antiblack racism.

Other European immigrant groups learned these same lessons. If your skin was white, you could choose to give up your foreign accent, culture, food, customs, and beliefs and then in a generation or two you could receive all the benefits of being white in America. These benefits, including income and access to education, health care, housing, and personal safety, were and continue to be very real, but the trade-offs were also real. Thorough assimilation meant being cut off from one's heritage and left feeling rootless, detached, homogenized. Becoming white was dehumanizing for many European immigrants because proof of one's whiteness was demonstrated by competition, hatred, and even violence toward African Americans, Asian Americans, Indians, and Latinos.

"The 'melting pot' was a popular way of describing the assimilation process of European immigrants to the United States in the late 1800s and early 1900s. Proponents of the model held that immigrants who came to the United States would, within a relatively short period of time, cast aside their European identities, cultures, and language as they forged or were forced to adopt the loyalties, customs, and language of their new home" (Wilson and Gutierrez 1995, 6). In fact, some factories staged dramatic ceremonies in which immigrants walked onto a stage in their native dress and disappeared behind a huge melting pot, reemerging in the clothing of the American working class. What is clear is that the concept of assimilation and the possibility of the "melting pot" were available only for those who were considered white, primarily European immigrants. It was the immigration and citizenship policies of the United States that made whites the numerical majority. Yet it was the extermination of Native Americans, the enslavement of Africans, the conquering of Mexican land, and the importation of Asian and Latino labor that helped settle this new country in the seventeenth and eighteenth centuries (Wilson and Gutierrez 1995, 7–19).

White Privilege, Internalized White Supremacy, and the Benefits of Being Considered White in the United States

"My schooling gave me no training in seeing myself as an oppressor, as an unfairly advantaged person, or as a participant in a damaged culture. I was taught to see myself as an individual whose moral state depended on individual moral will. At school, we were not taught about slavery in any depth; we were not taught to see slaveholders as damaged people. Slaves were seen as the only group at risk of being dehumanized" (McIntosh 1988, 78). This statement links white privilege with the dehumanization of people of color and the dehumanization of white people who have benefited from racism. Inherent in this logic is the progression that for white people to move beyond their own dehumanization, they must understand white privilege and how they have benefited from racism, and they must be willing to interrupt and change the patterns and power relations that have diminished all races. Many whites are taught that it is rude and racist to even notice racial differences and that it is a badge of our lack of prejudice to say that we do not see color. In fact, since color or race has had such an enormous impact on U.S. history, being aware of how race sits on our collective shoulders is integral to dismantling the dehumanization of racism.

The first task, then, is to understand how white privilege operates. Peggy McIntosh refers to this process as unpacking the invisible knapsack of white privilege. What are some of the items in this invisible knapsack? We have already learned that when we are taught U.S. history we are taught, by and large, European and white history and that the contributions and experiences of people of color are left out or marginalized. So one element of white privilege is that most Americans are taught that people who are considered white made most of the important contributions to U.S. history, literature, and science. The centrality of whites as U.S. presidents, scientist, and authors of "Great American Literature" is so common that its prominence is rarely seen by whites and as a result its legitimacy is rarely questioned. By and large, white parents can be fairly sure that their children will learn white history in school (McIntosh 1988).

Another element of white privilege is position and power. White people can be fairly sure that if they need to speak to the person in charge (e.g., of a store, office, or corporation), in most instances this person will have the same color skin as they. White people can count on their skin color working for them when establishing credit, writing a check, seeking a mortgage, or looking for a job. White people normally do not have to worry about themselves or their children being stopped or harassed by police officers because of the color of their skin. While white parents can choose to teach their children about the effects of racism, they do not have to teach their children how to react and survive in environments in which people may ignore or mistreat them because of the color of their skin. White people are not often asked to speak as representatives of their entire race. White people can go into any drugstore and find bandages, stockings, makeup, and blemish cover-up called "flesh-colored" that closely resembles the color of their skin (McIntosh 1988).

White privilege means not being affected by negative stereotypes that have been ingrained so deeply into the mental models of American society that many people believe them to be fact. It means one can live an entire lifetime without ever being consciously aware of the extent to which one has benefited by being born with a white racial identity (Blackmon 2013). Before we continue, please take a moment and reflect upon your own experiences with and/or observations of white privilege. If you are white, think about the times in your life when your privileged status has been advantageous to you. If you are a person of color think about times when you may have found yourself consciously or unconsciously colluding with the perpetuation of white privilege.

The components of white privilege are particularly difficult to tease into visibility when communities or schools are all or predominantly white. The experience of privilege applies to everyone in this circumstance and seems standard and normal to those in the midst of it. In the absence of the voices of people of color, it becomes the challenge of formal and informal educators to notice and discuss the "presence of absence" (Rosenberg 1997, 82), to point out and include the missing voices of people of color, and to describe and analyze how white privilege operates.

Many white students struggle with this concept of privilege and benefit. If they are working-class or poor, female, disabled, and/or gay or lesbian, they are often most aware of the discrimination they have faced or the hard work they have had to do to get to and stay in college. Often they feel their experiences of discrimination go unnoticed. Sometimes they feel that they are cheated out of jobs by people of color, who they believe receive unfair advantages. There are two important issues to address in this scenario.

First, it is true that there are many forms of discrimination and oppression. Ranking oppression (e.g., mine is worse than yours) is not useful. Individuals can belong to many dominant and targeted identity groups simultaneously. For example, Linda is a white, Jewish, heterosexual woman who is over fifty. She has a mix of benefits from her identities as white and heterosexual; as a second-generation American, her family's assimilation and identification as white give her access to most of the privileges that are listed above. However, as a Jew, a woman, and a person over fifty, she faces some uphill battles. For example, given her age, there are many jobs for which she would not be considered suitable. It is important to acknowledge the ways that class, gender, age, ability, and sexual orientation create privilege and disadvantage and work with and against each other. But they do not erase the benefits of white privilege.

Second, belief in favored treatment for people of color is most often a reflection of a prevailing racial myth. There are no more scholarships designed for African American college students than for white students, and reverse discrimination claims in federal courts are relatively rare in comparison to other kinds of discrimination claims. To illustrate how this myth is typically played out, consider the following incident involving a group of middle school students and one of their parents. Four eighth-grade girls, three white and one black, applied for admission to a selective private high school. All four girls were bright, but the African American girl stood out. She had achieved scores in the ninety-ninth percentile on all the standardized tests she had taken throughout her school career. She had won spelling bees and essay contests and had been invited to speak at public meetings. She was one of the top students in all of her classes, including the advanced and gifted classes she was admitted into because of her test scores and achievement. The private school accepted her and rejected all three white girls. The next day, one of the white girls confronted the black girl and said, "I know the only reason you got in is because you're black." The white girl's mother proceeded to talk in the community about how terrible it was that the school accepted the other girl just because she was black. This grossly inaccurate information spread through parts of the school community of parents and students without much challenge and targeted the girl who was accepted at the private school with the hurt and oppression of racial lies and the not-so-subtle message that whites are more intelligent than blacks. This situation served to perpetuate some of the most egregious ways that young people are socialized by the adults around them to believe the myths of white supremacy. Certainly, the three girls who were rejected by the school they wanted to attend were disappointed and hurt, but at twelve or thirteen, they had not yet formed a rigid, inflexible way to make sense of their experience. Then the outraged adult began to frame the situation as affirmative action run amok and thus sent the following messages to the white girls who were not accepted and to the black girl who was:

- There was no possibility that the black girl was actually a smarter, harder worker and/or a higher achiever than the three white girls.
- The assumption was that the white girls were at least as smart as and at least one of them was likely to be smarter than the black girl who was accepted.
- As a result of this skewed and flawed thinking, the only conclusion was that the black girl must have gotten in because of a requirement for affirmative action or a desire on the school's part to have a racially diverse student body.

The message that this white adult passed on to her daughter and her two white friends is one of presumed white superiority. She was able to redirect the girls' confusion, disappointment, and hurt at being rejected into anger at unfair racial practices. Not understanding much about the history of racism in the United States or in the state, city, or school district they lived in, they saw themselves as the victims of "reverse racism," which theoretically means that the tables are turned and whites are unfairly targeted by preferential treatment in school admissions, scholarships, and so on. At the time, the three white girls had no tools that allowed them to think independently about what had happened, and they found solace in assuming their intellectual equality, if not superiority, to the black girl and blaming the system for its unfairness. They could walk away from that situation disappointed that they would not be able to go to the school of their choice yet still with their sense of the centrality of whiteness and the presumed superiority of whites still intact.

This is a detailed analysis of just one incident in which information is so skewed that the success of an African American girl is viewed as turning the right order of things upside town. In seeking to "right" the decision of the private school, if not to reverse it, the black girl's competitors wanted to at least let everyone know that the proper order had been violated because of unfair advantage given to people of color.

In our lifetimes as children, adolescents, and adults, we receive a multitude of these types of messages in ways that are sometimes subtle enough to be invisible. We are not socialized to think about the fact that the vast majority of the books read in American literature courses are by white authors or that science and history courses are primarily conveyed as the multiple achievements of white men. White privilege and internalized white supremacy are not always based on individual racial hate or bigotry—there does not have to be intent—but if we look at the demographics of indicators such as poverty, education level, and job status and can predict who is most likely to be at the top and who is most likely to be at the bottom with race as a central factor, then the system is based on structural racism and conveys the message of white supremacy. When the lone African American girl was accused of being accepted by a private school only because she was black, her white classmates assumed that her intelligence could not possibly be as high as theirs. When people of color are stopped by the police simply because they are driving or walking through a predominantly white neighborhood, when they are followed by security guards in stores to make sure that they are not stealing—such stories highlight the presumption of white supremacy, internalized white supremacy, and white privilege. According to University of Texas journalism professor and antiracist activist Robert Jensen, who is white, he never has to consider being targeted as a potential thief or presumed to be less intelligent than other races:

> Now, I never have to think about that if I don't want to, because I walk in the world looking "normal," and I use that word normal in quotes of course. But I look like the norm—I look to be the person around whom the world is organized. The world is organized for me, and there is an incredible sort of burden that I don't then have to bear because of that and . . . I'm sorry to go on at length about it, but I think it's one of the things at least I know for me as a white person, one of the things that was hardest just to get a grasp [on]. I really had to listen a long time to the experiences of people of color to get a sense of just what that burden is like. (Wells 2013)

Jensen has focused much of his work on learning about institutional racism and the role of white supremacy and white privilege. Jensen urges whites to pay attention to the stories of the lived experiences of people of color, to refrain from rejecting these experiences simply because they are outside of white experience. According to Jensen and others who have deeply explored the phenomenon of internalized white supremacy, many whites are reluctant to give up pieces of their claim to supremacy. Through the conveyed messages of white supremacy and white privilege, many whites are socialized to see themselves as special and that this specialness is an integral part of who they are and what they deserve in the world. Even those whites who reject the idea of white supremacy fear letting go of the systematic white centrality that supports their own sense of being special. This fear plays out in their insistence on hanging onto the overwhelming dominance of whites in the telling of U.S. history, science, and literature in particular, which serves as another important though less than conscious source of white supremacy (Wells 2013):

> And so you see that white centrality especially in the way that the culture, the dominant white culture, fights for the right to tell the story not only of America but of the world in ways that leave white people at the center and are based on assumptions of the superiority of white people—even if as a culture we've renounced overt segregation and discrimination. Even if as a culture we are post-apartheid in that sense. There's still a struggle going on culturally and you see it most intensely, I think, in education. (Wells 2013)

Where scholars and activists differ is primarily in their analysis of what groups are most likely to have actually internalized white supremacy. In general, activists in antiracism work have slowly begun to combine the notion of internalized white supremacy and white privilege to describe the way these messages have worked their way into the belief systems of even the most dedicated antiracist whites; this process is most insidious for whites who have not examined how and to what extent these racist beliefs have influenced their thoughts and actions. These messages and the resulting beliefs involve the centrality of European Americans in individual achievement and worldwide success in literature, science, and most other fields that matter.

This centrality is based on the same racial myth that is perpetuated in history and social studies textbooks that describe *Brown v. Board of Education* (the Supreme Court decision that struck down the prevailing law and practice of separate but equal schools) and the civil rights movement as having ended all forms of discrimination against blacks. The logical conclusion drawn from this distorted interpretation of historical and contemporary events is that unnecessary compensatory programs for African Americans are still in place and that blacks receive all sorts of unfair advantages (Norton and Sommers 2011). This myth, like all racial myths, is based on misinformation that feeds white privilege, racism, and internalized racism.

White Allies

White students often ask, "If even well-intended white people are socialized to believe some of these myths of superiority and inferiority and we benefit from racism regardless of our beliefs, how is it possible to change things?" This is an important question. The pervasiveness of racism and its dehumanizing effects is staggering and often leads people to feel overwhelmed and sometimes hopeless. But in addition to white people's legacy in perpetuating racism, there is also a legacy of individuals and organizations that are role models of antiracism and offer humanizing possibilities and hope for change. Liberation theory is critical to this understanding in its assertion that we are born without racism and with infinite human possibilities. It is misinformation, in this case about race, that damages both people of color and white people. The hopefulness in liberation theory is that because racism is not innate but learned, it can also be unlearned.

There have been many European Americans throughout U.S. history who have taken it upon themselves to unlearn racism individually and act upon their commitment to end racism. In Chapter 2, we learned about the abolitionist activities of Angelina and Sarah Grimké and the creation of a school for African Americans by Prudence Crandall. These women faced ostracism from their families and communities because they took unpopular, dangerous stands and actions to work against racism. We learned in this chapter that Henry David Thoreau refused to pay taxes and that Horace Greeley used the *New York Tribune* to protest the 1846 declaration of war against Mexico. During the American Indian Movement action at Wounded Knee, many white people stood with the Indians as allies at the Wounded Knee Trading Post and acted as attorneys in subsequent trials. Michael Schwerner and Andrew Goodman lost their lives along with their African Amerian ally

James Cheney as a result of their efforts to register blacks to vote in Mississippi in the 1960s.

The late twentieth-century antiracism movement is populated by white people who continue to examine their own privilege and racism, as well as institutionalized racism, and have taken strong personal and political stands against racism—David Billings of New Orleans, Mab Segrest of North Carolina, Paul Kivel of California, Joan Olsen of Pennsylvania, Tim Wise of Tennessee, and many, many more. These are individuals who have stood as allies with people of color in protests, marches, and courtrooms and have challenged laws, policies, hiring practices, and other forms of discrimination. They are not simply "do-gooders" who want to help other people. These are individuals who are convinced that racism has dehumanized all people and that dismantling racism means a more fully experienced humanity for whites and people of color. These people often see their contributions to ending racism and other forms of oppression as their life work.

There are other ways to be an ally. Not all well-intended whites will decide to dedicate their lives to ending racism. But there are daily reminders of how racism operates that anyone can interrupt. White parents can question and object when advanced classes have a disproportionate number of white children. They can insist that the U.S. history curriculum include the stories of people of color. White allies can also interrupt racist jokes and stories and name calling. Sometimes the people and institutions challenged or interrupted will change, sometimes they will get angry, and sometimes they will do nothing. But the consciousness of white people about the insidiousness of racism, the awareness of white privilege, and the willingness to correct misinformation is a part of the process of liberation, of unlearning racism.

CHAPTER SUMMARY

Students in elementary school and high school in the United States receive limited and often distorted information about our country's racial history. Most of us learned primarily about the immigrant experiences of Europeans in the New World and only bits and pieces about the enslavement of Africans and the conquest of American Indians and Mexicans. We have rarely learned about the immigration experiences of Puerto Ricans, Cubans, Vietnamese, Chinese, or Japanese. Often the information that we get is limited or glossed over to eliminate elements of racial cruelty, violence, or suppression. Sometimes the information that we get is taught to us as African American history or Asian American history—as if it is something completely separate from American history. At best, perhaps we have been taught that while there are unfortunate aspects of racism (slavery) and conquest (American Indians) in our history, there have been many efforts to right these wrongs so that racially the United States now has a level playing field in which people of all races have equal life chances. Rarely is there any analysis of the connection between individual acts of racial hatred and the institutional or structural racism in laws or private businesses that discriminate in housing, health care, education, and employment. And seldom is there any mention of the individuals, groups, and movements that have worked to undo the policies and effects of racism.

There are hard facts in U.S. history. There have been times when dehumanizing a whole group of people has merged with individual acts of hatred and with laws and policies that promote violence and oppression, causing many, many people to die because of racism. While the omission or revision of this part of our history may be intended to keep children from learning such painful parts of our past, the consequences of the distortion of U.S. racial history are far-reaching. "Education as socialization influences students simply to accept the rightness of our society. American history textbooks overtly tell us to be proud of America. The more schooling, the more socialization, and the more likely the individual will conclude that America is good" (Loewen 1995, 307). Education that does not lie is not equivalent to socializing students to believe that America is "bad" rather than "good." Rather it calls for teaching students about the complexities of our stories and how to make inquiries and draw conclusions that allow for critical thinking and autonomous decision making.

The combination of our personal experiences, our formal education, and our exposure to entertainment media constitutes our socialization about race. If this socialization tells us that all is well racially and that everyone has equal life chances regardless of race or ethnicity, we are likely to see any racial problem or failure as strictly the fault of an individual. If we believe that there are no racial barriers to employment, then we will see unemployment among people of color as lazy or slovenly. If we believe that education is equitable for everyone, we will not be open to discuss or vote for remedies to address defects in the educational system that have an adverse impact on students of color. The lump sum of these distortions can be dehumanizing for everyone.

Earlier in the chapter we spoke of building communities based on shared power and mutual respect. Acclaimed writer and activist Audre Lorde wrote, "In our work and in our living, we must recognize that difference is a reason for celebration and growth, rather than a reason for destruction." While our history regarding race may be painful, we must learn it in much the same way that Germans must learn about the Holocaust: to understand our part in it, to understand its impact on the present, to learn how to act on its contemporary implications, and to ensure that it will never happen again. Past history cannot be changed. It can only be rediscovered, reexamined, and revealed. Presenting counternarratives is an essential stage of that revelatory process. But it is only the beginning. We not only have to tell the counterstories, we have to live them. It is only through the liberatory cycle of continuous collective action, personal reflection, honest dialogue, and more action that we can transform our society, purge the toxic racist strains from the American meta-narrative, and put a process in motion that will enable future generations to write it anew.

GLOSSARY OF KEY TERMS

assimilation: Assimilation is the process through which newcomers (children entering a new school, families moving to a new neighborhood, and immigrants arriving in the United States) adjust to a situation by deciding how much of their old culture and habits they want to give up and how much of their new culture they want to absorb. In the context of immigration to the United States, this process includes surface and deep culture: anything from clothing, food, and language to child-rearing, dating and marriage practices, and treatment of elders in the community. Throughout U.S. history, there have been diverse waves of voluntary immigrants and refugees. Other groups have involuntarily become part of the United States through the violent conquest of their land (Mexicans, American Indians) or violent enslavement (African Americans). In order to be considered true Americans, these newcomers were expected to assimilate. The unspoken rules of assimilation were that the closer the immigrants were to existing U.S. citizens of European heritage in terms of skin color and ability to blend in, the more likely they were able to make active choices about the degree to which they wanted to reject their former culture in favor of their new culture. The more they assimilated, and the more their skin color allowed them to assimilate, the more they were entitled to the same privileges as the Europeans who came before them. Most immigrant groups of color, including Africans, Asians, and American Indians, were not entitled to citizenship until decades—sometimes a century—after newer European immigrants because the color of their skin was not considered sufficiently white. Because of this and due to the nature of racial separation in the United States, assimilation was available unequally to whites and people of color, depending on the time of their arrival to the United States.

aversive racism: Aversive racism is a contemporary concept that describes the contradictory beliefs and attitudes of some whites. On the one hand, these individuals have a strong conscious belief in racial equality, individually and institutionally, and are often advocates of policies and programs that enforce racial equity. Ironically, research has shown that individuals who display aversive racism have less than conscious bias against and stereotypes of people of color.

critical race theory: Critical race theory (CRT) is an academic discipline that analyzes race in the United States through the lens of power and law. CRT is based on several core tenets, including the permanence of racism, critique of liberalism, whiteness as property, interest convergence, intersection of racism with other forms of oppression, centrality of personal experience, and use of the counter-narrative as an explanatory and analytical tool. CRT originated in the field of legal research but is a useful framework for social justice activism and scholarship in fields such as education, media studies, history, and the social sciences.

diaspora: A diaspora is the massive spreading of a cohesive group of people with common roots in a particular location to geographic locations far from their long-term accepted homeland. A diaspora is generally involuntary and almost always occurs as a result of violence. The most common uses of the term refer to Jews who were exiled thousands of years ago from the Middle East and to Africans who were transported to North and South America, the Caribbean, and Europe as a part of the transatlantic slave trade.

fictive kinship: Generically, this term describes relationships without any blood ties or marriage that are elevated to the status of family in terms of rights and responsibilities.Fictive kinship had its origin in West Africa, in which some cultures viewed close social relationships as family. Fictive kinship became especially important for African Americans during the time of enslavement in the United States, when husband and wife, children, and siblings could so easily be torn apart through the degrading practice of "selling" slaves. Fictive aunts and uncles, who were regarded the same as blood family, had special bonds with children and would often step in and informally adopt children if their parents died or were "sold" (Chatters, Taylor, and Jayakody 1994).

internalized racism: Internalized racism is the process by which people of color take in negative messages of overt and covert racism, superiority, and inferiority, and apply those messages to themselves and others in ways that are self-destructive rather than self-affirming. Internalized racism, which is always involuntary, is the direct by-product of historical and ongoing racial targeting.

internalized white supremacy: This term has begun to be used more frequently since the late twentieth century. Antiracist activists and scholars have a few different, but highly compatible concepts defining to whom the term is applicable. In general, internalized white supremacy is the assumption of white superiority in intelligence, in achievement, and in the centrality in U.S. culture by individuals who are often aware of its powerful existence. People who internalize this dimension of white supremacy are not generally the same people whose outright racial hatred counts them among the members of the Ku Klux Klan and other racial hate groups. In fact, these people are often shocked and alarmed as they investigate this phenomenon and discover that they have been operating on the assumptions that the tenets of white superiority are "the truth." These messages strongly presume the centrality of European Americans to the individual achievement and success in the United States and to worldwide recognition in literature, science, world peace, and other fields.

meta-narrative: A meta-narrative is a comprehensive "story" of history and knowledge that unifies and simplifies the culture and value of a group or nation. When meta-narratives are applied to nations, they frequently are used to explain and justify the existing power structure.

racial discrimination: An individual act or an institutional pattern that results in the unequal treatment of members of a targeted racial group. Racial discrimination is an *action* or *behavior* that may result from conscious or unconscious *beliefs* (stereotypes) about a racial group or from predetermined *feelings* (prejudices) toward that group.

racialize: To see or describe something from a racial perspective; to emphasize race or to make something seem racial. For example, in the early twentieth century, Jews were racialized in Europe, Russia, and most of the United States. Today, in much of the United

States, Judaism is regarded as a religion rather than a race. Another example occurred in the aftermath of the 9/11 terrorist attacks with the widespread racialization of Muslims and people of Middle Eastern descent.

racism: The content of Chapters 4 and 5 is entirely focused on race and racism, which is a system of institutionalized power that operates through overt or covert policies that favor white people and are biased against people of color. Racism continues to exist today in the hiring practices of some private businesses, government agencies, hospitals, universities, and so on, even where there are policies that clearly state they will not discriminate. Despite such policies, these institutions often devise strategies and engage in practices that result in the virtual elimination of people of color from their pools of potential candidates. Another commonly used approach to understanding racism is based on the comparative analysis of levels of social access—to quality education, jobs, promotions, and other opportunities—between white people and people of color.

schema: A schema is a mental model or pattern of thinking that influences the way we organize and simplify our knowledge of the world around us.

white privilege: White privilege is a set of unearned advantages and opportunities created by racism that are often far more visible to people of color than they are to whites. Despite the pervasiveness of racism in the history and current structures of the United States, many white people believe that racism was eradicated by the late twentieth century and that individual achievement and success are based solely on individual intelligence, motivation, and hard work. As a result of this type of misinformation and socialization, many whites believe that all of their successes are built exclusively on their own talent, skills, merit, and hard work. In fact, in many small and large ways, whites have access to different opportunities and are treated differently than people of color, giving them an often invisible boost to this success to which people of color do not have the same access. For example, white parents rarely need to think about the danger present for their sons at a mall or on the street if they are stopped by a police officer. Ample research and statistics indicate that young African American or Latino men are far more likely to be harassed, abused, and/or arrested by police than young white men. The privilege here is that white parents generally only need to think about this danger if their son will be in an area in which there is high crime. But the danger there is potential criminals, not the police. Whites are rarely asked to speak on behalf of their whole race or justify the criminal activity or failure of other whites, while people of color are frequently asked to do all of these things. White privilege allows whites the luxury and advantage of living in a world where their personal worth, rightness, and personhood are continually validated in ways that do not apply for people of color (Olsson, n.d).

white supremacy: White supremacy is typically thought of as the extremist views and actions of hate groups such as the Ku Klux Klan, White Citizens Council, and Aryan

Brotherhood. This definition of white supremacy is the categorical belief and the actions based on the belief that, in every way, whites are superior to people of color. Often Jews and sometimes Catholics are also included in the category of so-called inferior people. Many of these hate groups are responsible for what we call "hate crimes," in which these "inferior" people are subjected to violence, torture, murder, and destruction of property, which are seen as justified by white supremacist individuals and organizations that believe that these "inferior" groups will destroy America if not eliminated.

There is another type of white supremacy that is more subtle, yet equally insidious in the way it pervades the minds of individuals and permeates the culture. This type assumes the dominance and superiority of white culture as reflected in the academic curricula of U.S. history and literature and science, in which the contributions of white people are more visible and valued more greatly than the contributions of people of color. In this scenario, hate and hate crimes are not central; however, white people are seen as at the center of U.S. culture. "And so you see that white centrality, especially in the way that the culture, the dominant white culture, fights for the right to tell the story, not only of America, but of the world in ways that leave white people at the center and are based on assumptions of the superiority of white people—even if as a culture we've renounced overt segregation and discrimination" (Wells 2013). By this definition, white supremacy is not always based on intent or on individual or even institutional racial hate or bigotry. However, if we look at the demographics of wealth and poverty, educational achievement and level of attainment, and job status, to name a few, we will be able to predict who is most likely to be at the top and who is most likely to be at the bottom, with race as the central factor of these predictions. Then we know that the system is infested with structural racism and the messages involve white supremacy.

REFLECTION, SUMMARY, AND ANALYSIS

Instructions

The chapter questions invite you to engage in an exercise of reflection, summary, and analysis about key terms, topics, and issues discussed in the chapter. The skills involved in responding to the questions are a combination of summary and analysis.

The *summary* component of the questions requires you to demonstrate your understanding of the terms and concepts in the textbook through the use of describing, explaining, and restating. This includes using your own words to paraphrase the materials in the textbook as well as using an occasional direct quote. Any direct quote requires quotation marks and the use of a simple internal citation at the end of the quote in the form of parentheses, the author's last name, the year the quote was published, and the page number, which will look like this: (Sharpe 2014, 38). *Summary* involves primarily answering questions that begin with "what."

The *analysis* component of the questions requires you to use your own independent thinking, your own ideas and arguments. *Analysis* requires breaking something—like a concept, theory, or argument—into parts so you can understand and describe how those parts work together to make the whole. Analytic writing goes beyond the obvious to discuss questions of how and why—so ask yourself those questions as you read. Your responses to these kinds of questions will require that you carefully and clearly state your argument, opinion, or thesis statement and use evidence from the chapter as well as your own experience or observations to support your thesis or view.

The University of North Carolina's Writing Center website has an excellent two-page handout on analysis and summary (http://writingcenter.unc.edu/handouts/summary-using-it-wisely/).

Study Questions

1. What is meant by the shifting definition of race? In what way is race based on biology, politics, economics, and social considerations?
2. Define individual, institutional, overt, and covert racism. What are your views about these different perspectives on racism?
3. What is meant by internalized racism? What are some concrete examples in U.S. history that have contributed to the development of internalized racism? If you are a person of color, give a real example of how you have experienced internalized racism in your own life or that of a friend or family member. If you are white, give an example of what you have observed regarding internalized racism in incidents or experiences involving people of color.
4. What is meant by white privilege? Give one example in U.S. history that has contributed to the development of white privilege. If you are white, give a real example of how you've personally experienced racial privilege in your own life or that of a friend or family member. Comment on how you benefit from historical and current racism, even if you have never acted in openly racist ways. If you are a person of color, give an observed example of how white people or people of European descent continue to benefit from historical and current racism even if they have never acted in blatantly racist ways themselves.
5. What is mean by internalized white superiority? What kind of messages do whites receive from schools, faith groups, and personal experience that convey superiority? How does internalized white superiority appear in the thinking and behaviors of whites?
6. What is assimilation? Give one example from the text and one from your own observation or family experience. Describe some of the ways people have benefited historically by assimilating. Describe some of the costs of assimilation for people who were able to do so.

7. Answer the following questions based on what you know about your family. If you do not know much about that period of your family heritage, use the text-book to find an experience that might be similar to that of your family. Did the racial construct of the time allow your family to assimilate into being considered "white" in the United States? If so, describe the financial and personal benefits and costs of this assimilation. Did the racial construct of the time prohibit your family from assimilating into being considered "white" in the United States? If so, describe the financial and personal benefits and costs of this exclusion from racial assimilation.

8. Select two of the following groups and discuss how each group's history as a target of racism may impact its current access to resources, power, benefits, and the American Dream:
   - American Indians
   - African Americans
   - Asian Americans or Pacific Islanders (if you choose this general group, select a specific group of immigrants, rather than generalizing about all Asian Americans or Pacific Islanders)
   - Latinos or Hispanics (if you choose this general group, select a specific group, such as Colombians, Mexicans, or Puerto Ricans, rather than generalizing about all Latinos or Hispanics)

BIBLIOGRAPHY

Adams, Maurianne, Lee Anne Bell, and Pat Griffin, eds. 1997. *Teaching for Diversity and Social Justice: A Sourcebook*. New York: Routledge.

Adelman, Larry, executive producer. 2003. *Race: The Power of an Illusion*. California Newsreel (originally aired as a three-part series on PBS). http://newsreel.org/video/RACE-THE-POWER -OF-AN-ILLUSION.

Baker, Ray Stannard. 1908. "The Tragedy of the Mulatto." *American Magazine* 65 (April): 582–598.

Baldwin, James. 1955. "Stranger in the Village." In *Notes of a Native Son*. Boston: Beacon Press.

Banaji, Mahzarin R., and Anthony G. Greenwald. 2013. *Blindspot: Hidden Biases of Good People*. New York: Delacorte Press.

Baron, Andrew S., and Mahzarin Banaji. 2006. "The Development of Implicit Attitudes: Evidence of Race Evaluations from Ages 6 and 10 and Adulthood." *Psychological Science* 17, no. 1: 53–58.

Bednarz, Sarah, Catherine Clinton, Michael Hartoonian, Arthur Hernandez, Patricia L. Marshal, and Pat Nickell. 1997. *We the People Discover Our Heritage*. Boston: Houghton Mifflin.

Bigelow, Bill. 2013. "Camouflaging the Vietnam War: How Textbooks Continue to Keep the Pentagon Papers a Secret." *Common Dreams*. June. www.commondreams.org/view/2013/06/18-0.

Blackmon, Michael. 2013. "17 Deplorable Examples of White Privilege: And this isn't even the tip of the iceberg." *BuzzFeed Community*. October. www.buzzfeed.com/michaelblackmon/17-harrowing -examples-of-white-privilege-9hu9.

Blassingame, John W., ed. 1977. *Slave Testimony: Two Centuries of Letters, Speeches, Interviews, and Autobiographies*. Baton Rouge: Louisiana State University Press.

Brave Heart, Maria Yellow Horse. 2000. "Wakiksuyapi: Carrying the Historical Trauma of the Lakota." *Tulane Studies in Social Welfare* 21–22: 245–266.

Brown, Dee. 1970. *Bury My Heart at Wounded Knee: An Indian History of the American West*. New York: Henry Holt.

Cartmill, Matt. 1998. "The Status of Race Concept in Physical Anthropology." *American Anthropologist* (New Series) vol. 100, no. 3: 651–660.

Chao, Julie. 1999. "Census' Complex Multiracial Nightmare." *San Francisco Examiner*, November 28. www.sfgate.com/news/article/Census-complex-multiracial-nightmare-3056527.php.

Chatters, Linda M., Robert J. Taylor, and Rukmalie Jayakody. 1994. "Fictive Kinship Relations in Black Extended Families." *Journal of Comparative Family Studies* 25, no. 3: 297–312.

Crenshaw, Kimberle, Neil T. Gotanda, Gary Peller, and Kendall Thomas, eds. 1995. *Critical Race Theory: The Key Writings that Formed the Movement*. New York: The New Press.

Croteau, David, and William Hoynes. 1997. *Media/Society: Industries, Images, and Audiences*. Thousand Oaks, CA: Pine Forge Press.

Davis, Angela Y. 1981. *Women, Race, and Class*. New York: Random House.

Davis, James E., and Phyllis Maxey Fernlund. 1996. *Civics: Participating in Our Democracy*. Menlo Park, CA: Addison-Wesley.

Delgado, Richard, and Jean Stefancic. 2001. *Critical Race Theory: An Introduction*. New York: New York University Press.

Dill, Bonnie Thornton. 1995. "Our Mothers' Grief: Racial Ethnic Women and the Maintenance of Families." In *Race, Class, and Gender: An Anthology*, ed. Margaret L. Andersen and Patricia Hill Collins, 237–249. Belmont, CA: Wadsworth.

Downing, Karen E., Darlene P. Nichols, and Kelly Webster. 2005. *Multiracial America: A Resource Guide on the History and Literature of Interracial Issues*. Lanham, ME: Scarecrow Press.

Eltis, David. 2001. "The Volume and Structure of the Transatlantic Slave Trade: A Reassessment." *The William and Mary Quarterly*. As cited by the U.S. National Park Service Ethnography Program, U.S. Department of the Interior. www.nps.gov/ethnography/aah/aaheritage/histcontextsd.htm.

Fair Housing Center of Greater Boston. 2013. "1920s–1948: Racially Restrictive Covenants." www.bostonfairhousing.org/timeline/1920s1948-Restrictive-Covenants.html.

Feagin, Joe R. 2009. *The White Racial Frame: Centuries of Racial Framing and Counter-Framing*. New York: Routledge.

Feagin, Joe R., and Melvin P. Sikes. 1994. *Living with Racism: The Black Middle-Class Experience*. Boston: Beacon.

Gould, Stephen Jay. 1981. *The Mismeasure of Man*. New York: W.W. Norton.

Greenwald, Anthony G., and Linda H. Krieger. 2006. "Implicit Bias: Scientific Foundations." *California Law Review* vol. 94, no. 4.

Greenwald, Anthony G., and Mahzarin Banaji. 1995. "Implicit Social Cognition: Attitudes, Self-Esteem, and Stereotypes." *Psychological Review* 1: 4–27.

Guinier, Lani, and Gerald Torres. 2002. *The Miner's Canary: Enlisting Race, Resisting Power, Transforming Democracy*. Cambridge, MA: Harvard University Press.

Guisepi, Robert A., ed. "Destruction of Native American Cultures." *The International History Project*. (Updated 2007.) http://history-world.org/american_indians_or_native_ameri.htm.

Hacker, Andrew. 1992. *Two Nations: Black and White, Separate, Hostile, Unequal*. New York: Charles Scribner.

Hamamoto, Darrell Y. 1994. *Monitored Peril: Asian Americans and the Politics of TV Representation*. Minneapolis: University of Minnesota Press.

Jablonski, Nina G., and George Chaplin. 2000. "The evolution of human skin coloration." *Journal of Human Evolution* 39(1): 57–106.

———. 2003. "Skin Deep." *Scientific American*, 13, no. 2 (August): 72–79.

Jones, Nicholas A., and Jungmiwha Bullock. 2012. "The Two or More Races Population: 2010." *2010 Census Briefs*. The United States Census Bureau. www.census.gov/prod/cen2010/briefs/c2010br-13.pdf.

Kaufman, Cynthia. 2001. "A User's Guide to White Privilege." *Radical Philosophy Review* 4, no. 1/2: 30–38.

Kivel, Paul. 1996. *Uprooting Racism: How White People Can Work for Racial Justice*. Gabriola Island, BC: New Society.

Leary, Joy DeGruy. 2006. *Post-Traumatic Slave Syndrome: America's Legacy of Enduring Injury and Healing*. Milwaukie, OR: Uptone Press.

Lewontin, Richard C. 1970. "Further Remarks on Race and the Genetics of Intelligence." *Bulletin of the Atomic Scientists* 26, no. 5: 23–25.

Lipsitz, George, ed. 1998. *The Possessive Investment in Whiteness: How White People Profit from Identity Politics*. Philadelphia: Temple University Press.

Loewen, James W. 1995. *Lies My Teachers Told Me: Everything Your American History Textbook Got Wrong*. New York: Touchstone.

Lynch, Hollis R. 2007. "Americans of African Ancestry." The International World History Project. http://history-world.org/black_americans.htm.

Madrid, Arturo. 1995. "Missing People and Others: Joining Together to Expand the Circle." In *Race, Class, and Gender: An Anthology*, ed. Margaret L. Andersen and Patricia Hill Collins, 291. Belmont, CA: Wadsworth.

Matthiessen, Peter. 1983. *In the Spirit of Crazy Horse*. New York: Viking.

McIntosh, Peggy. 1988. "White Privilege and Male Privilege: A Personal Account of Coming to See Correspondences Through Work in Women's Studies." In *Race, Class, and Gender: An Anthology*, ed. Margaret L. Andersen and Patricia Hill Collins, 82–83. Belmont, CA: Wadsworth.

Menchaca, Martha. 2001. *Recovering History, Constructing Race: The Indian, Black, and White Roots of Mexican Americans*. Austin: University of Texas Press.

Mickelson, Roslyn Arlin, and Stephen Samuel Smith. 1995. "Education and the Struggle Against Race, Class, and Gender Inequality." In *Race, Class, and Gender: An Anthology*, ed. Margaret L. Andersen and Patricia Hill Collins, 291. Belmont, CA: Wadsworth.

Moore, Joan, and Racquel Pinderhughes. 1995. "The Latino Population: The Importance of Economic Restructuring." In *Race, Class, and Gender: An Anthology*, ed. Margaret L. Andersen and Patricia Hill Collins, 227–230. Belmont, CA: Wadsworth.

Moraga, Cherie. 1995. "La Guerra." In *Race, Class, and Gender: An Anthology*, ed. Margaret L. Andersen and Patricia Hill Collins, 60–61. Belmont, CA: Wadsworth.

Norris, Tina, Paula L. Vines, and Elizabeth M. Hoeffel. 2012. "The American Indian and Alaska Native Population." *2010 Census Briefs*. U.S. Census Bureau www.census.gov/prod/cen2010/briefs /c2010br-10.pdf.

Norton, Michael I. and Samuel R. Sommers. 2011. "Whites See Racism as a Zero-Sum Game That They Are Now Losing." *Perspectives on Psychological Science* 6, no. 3: 215–218. http://ase.tufts .edu/psychology/sommerslab/documents/raceInterNortonSommers2011.pdf.

Ogletree, Charles J. 2004. *All Deliberate Speed: Reflections on the First Half Century of Brown v. Board of Education*. New York: W.W. Norton.

Olson, Joan. (n.d.) "The Four Faces of Racism." Unpublished handout adapted from Cultural Bridges Training. Posted in the compilation, *We're All In It Together*, by North American Students of Co-operation (NASCO). http://kalamazoo.coop/sites/default/files/We're%20all%20in%20it%20together.pdf.

O'Neil, Moira. 2009. *Invisible Structures of Opportunity: How Media Depictions of Race Trivialize Issues of Diversity and Disparity*. Washington, DC: FrameWorks Institute.

Outlaw, Lucius T. 2005. *Critical Social Theory in the Interests of Black Folks*. Lanham, MD: Rowman & Littlefield.

Padilla, Laura M. 2001. "But You're Not a Dirty Mexican": Internalized Oppression, Latinos & Law. *Texas Hispanic Journal of Law & Policy* 7: 1.

Paris, Peter J. 1995. *The Spirituality of African Peoples: The Search for a Common Moral Discourse*. Minneapolis: Fortress Press.

Pew Research Center. 2012. "Hispanics of Cuban Origin in the United States: 2010 Statistical Profile." *Pew Research Hispanic Trends Project*. www.pewhispanic.org/2012/06/27/hispanics-of-cuban -origin-in-the-united-states-2010/.

Reid, Frances, dir. 1995. *Skin Deep: College Students Confront Racism*. Video. San Francisco: Resolution/California Newsreel.

Ritchie, Donald A., and Albert S. Broussard. 1997. *American History: The Early Years to 1877*. New York: McGraw-Hill.

Roediger, David R. 2005. *Working Toward Whiteness: How America's Immigrants Became White: The Strange Journey from Ellis Island to the Suburbs*. Cambridge, MA: Basic Books.

Rosenberg, Pearl M. 1997. "Underground Discourses: Exploring Whiteness in Teacher Education." In *Off White: Readings on Race, Power, and Society*, ed. Michelle Fine, Lois Weis, and Mun L. Wong, 82. New York: Routledge.

Schmidt, Kathleen, and Brian A. Nosek. 2010. "Implicit (and Explicit) Racial Attitudes Barely Changed During the Campaign and Early Presidency of Barack Obama." *Journal of Experimental Social Psychology* 46: 308–314.

Segrest, Mab. 1994. *Memoir of a Race Traitor*. Boston: South End Press.

Son Hing, Leanne S., Greg A. Chun-Yang, Leah K. Hamilton, and Mark P. Zanna. 2008. "A Two-Dimensional Model That Employs Explicit and Implicit Attitudes to Characterize Prejudice." *Journal of Personality and Social Psychology* 94, no. 6: 971–987.

Steele, Claude M. 1997. "A Threat in the Air: How Stereotypes Shape Intellectual Identity and Performance." *American Psychologist* 52: 613–629.

———. 2010. *Whistling Vivaldi: And Other Clues to How Stereotypes Affect Us*. New York: W.W. Norton.

Steele, Claude M., and Joshua Aronson. 1995. "Stereotype Threat and the Intellectual Test Performance of African Americans." *Journal of Personality and Social Psychology* 69, no. 5: 797–811.

Takaki, Ronald. 1979. *Iron Cages: Race and Culture in the 19th Century*. New York: Knopf.

———. 1993. *A Different Mirror: A History of Multicultural America*. Boston: Little, Brown.

Tatum, Beverly Daniel. 1997. *"Why Are All the Black Kids Sitting Together in the Cafeteria?" and Other Conversations About Race*. New York: Basic Books.

Taylor, Edward, David Gilborn, and Gloria Ladson-Billings, eds. 2009. *Foundations of Critical Race Theory in Education*. New York: Routledge.

Templeton, Alan R. 2002. "Out of Africa Again and Again." *Nature* 416: 45–51.

U.S. Census Bureau. 2010. "American Community Survey." www.census.gov/acs/www/about _the_survey/puerto_rico_community_survey/.

Vaughan, Alden T. 1995. *Roots of American Racism: Essays on the Colonial Experience*. New York: Oxford University Press.

Wells, Kathleen. 2013. "Prof. Robert Jensen Discusses Racism, White Supremacy and White Privilege (Part 2)". *The Blog/HuffPost Black Voices*. www.huffingtonpost.com/kathleen-wells/prof-robert -jensen-discus_b_2500184.html.

West, Cornel. 1995. "Race Matters." In *Race, Class, and Gender: An Anthology*, ed. Margaret L. Andersen and Patricia Hill Collins, 557. Belmont, CA: Wadsworth.

Wijeyesinghe, Charmaine L. 1998. "Diversity and Learning: Identity, Community, and Intellectual Development." Presentation at American Association of Colleges and Universities Conference, November.

Wijeyesinghe, Charmaine L., Pat Griffin, and Barbara Love. 1997. "Racism Curriculum Design." In *Teaching for Diversity and Social Justice: A Sourcebook*, ed. Maurianne Adams, Lee Anne Bell, and Pat Griffin, 91. New York: Routledge.

Williams, Heather A. 2005. *Self-taught: African American Education in Slavery and Freedom*. Chapel Hill: University of North Carolina Press.

Wilson, Clint C., and Felix Gutierrez. 1995. *Race, Multiculturalism, and the Media: From Mass to Class Communication*. 2nd ed. Thousand Oaks, CA: Sage.

Woo, Deborah. 1995. "The Gap Between Striving and Achieving: The Case of Asian American Women." In *Race, Class, and Gender: An Anthology*, ed. Margaret L. Andersen and Patricia Hill Collins, 224. Belmont, CA: Wadsworth.

Zinn, Howard. 1995. *A People's History of the United States: 1492–Present*. New York: Harper Perennial.

5

Stories of Race in Popular Culture

Even the most seemingly benign TV programs articulate the relationship between race and power, either explicitly or through implication.

—*Darrell Hamamoto,* Monitored Peril

Historically, the U.S. media have taken "whites" to be the norm against which all other racial groups are measured. The taken-for-granted nature of "whiteness" means that it need not be explicitly identified. For example, we generally do not talk about "white culture," or "the white community" or the "white vote," and so forth. We do, however, often hear reference to "black culture" or "the Latino community," and so on. The absence of a racial signifier in this country usually signifies whiteness. The pervasiveness of white perspectives in media is perhaps its most powerful characteristic.

—*David Croteau and William Hoynes,* Media/Society

ENTERTAINMENT MEDIA AND RACE

The study of entertainment media and race is complex. Scholars, media critics and commentators, passionate media observers, and people who watch a lot of television and/or movies have conducted academic studies and have formed unscientific personal opinions about the images of various racial groups in film and television and music. There are competing theories and perspectives about how to evaluate and understand the impact and meaning of these images and themes. As we discovered in Chapter 4, the historical experiences of various immigrant and racial groups in the United States are profoundly different from each other. Since these varied histories are often inaccessible in our schools and personal lives, their representation in media takes on added significance. There is also a high degree of complexity within each so-called race. For example, images of Asians are often collapsed and homogenized as one in media when, in fact, the experiences and cultures of various immigrant groups (i.e., Chinese, Japanese, Mung, Vietnamese, Filipino) vary widely. And to add one more complicating factor, the work that has been done regarding the representation of various racial groups in popular culture is wildly uneven. Far more information is available about images and themes of African Americans and American Indians in entertainment media than about Asians and Pacific Islanders or Latinas/Latinos. There has been very little research conducted on popular music in relation to Asians and Pacific Islanders, Latinas/Latinos, or American Indians.

Adding to some of this confusion is the use of language to name or describe various races and ethnicities. As we discussed in Chapter 4, there is much evidence that what we know as race or "color" differences do not play out in genetic differences and that, in fact, there are far more genetic differences within one race than there often are between the various races. Race is largely a social, political, and economic construct that has been used to establish hierarchies of power and privilege. So we begin with the dilemma of naming categories of people that have been initiated to establish fictional superiority and inferiority. Not such an appealing proposition.

However, while the origins of these categories are deeply flawed, it is also true that many people feel deeply connected to their racial and ethnic groups and that while "race" may be a fiction, racism is unfortunately light-years away from fictional.

In this book, we have made decisions about what language to use to name racial groups, based on what we have discussed with and observed as the preferences of groups and organizations that advocate for racial equity as well as our own sense of race and gender parity. There are times when we have elected to use some names interchangeably. Some of the names are bulky and do not easily roll off the tongue when speaking or reading. At the risk of interrupting the mellifluous flow for the reader, we have chosen to use some of the cumbersome language to reflect as much accuracy and inclusiveness as possible.

For the rest of this chapter, you will see the terms "African American" and "black" and "African heritage" used interchangeably for individuals and groups whose heritage is originally from Africa.

The terms "Asian and Pacific Islander" and "Asian American" will be used collectively to include individuals and groups with heritage from central Asia, the Pacific islands, and South Asia. These are comprehensive terms that combine very different national origins, traditions, and histories in the United States. Whenever possible, we will use the actual country of origin to describe heritage or identity.

We will use the terms "Latina" and "Latino" together and interchangeably for groups and individuals with heritage that is Mexican, South and Central American, or Spanish. We chose this term over the term "Hispanic" since many advocacy groups object that "Hispanic" more narrowly defines only those individuals with heritage from Spain. We have elected to use the feminine form "Latina" and the masculine form "Latino" interchangeably rather than the more common usage of the male form alone. This choice makes for a slightly more awkward read, but it is a good reminder that language often uses the male form to represent everyone and how accustomed many people in the United States have become to that usage. While various communities and cultures identify their *race* as Latino or Hispanic, the 2010 U.S. Census provides these terms as multiple-choice options for nationality or ethnicity. According to the Census Bureau, an individual may be African American, white, Asian/Pacific Islander, or American Indian in addition to being Latino or Hispanic.

We also will use the terms "American Indian" and "Native American" interchangeably in deference to the various advocacy groups and individuals who use either or both.

The most widely accepted inclusive term for all of the groups that are otherwise referred to as "minorities" is "people of color." We have made a deliberate choice not to use the term "minority" except in a quote or to describe a population that is smaller compared to a larger population. Some of the thesaurus synonyms for "minority" are "underground" and "marginal," while one of the dictionary definitions actually labels it an "offensive term." The term "minority" has historically been used to imply that people of color are somehow less than, inferior to, or actually "minor" in comparison to whites.

And, finally, we will most often use the term "white" and occasionally the term "European American" for groups and individuals with European heritage.

When even the language for racial groups is so contested and often emotional and the research about groups so uneven, how do we sort through what is available, make sense of what is not available, and begin to have some understanding of the construct of race in popular media without oversimplifying or making it so complex that it becomes inaccessible and daunting?

In order to take a close look that is historical, analytical, and experiential, we have framed this section on entertainment media and race around eight questions:

1. What role does entertainment media play in socializing the people in the United States about race?
2. What are the messages and themes about various races in entertainment media?
3. How do these messages and themes differ by race?
4. How have these messages and themes changed over time?
5. How are these messages and themes conveyed in different forms of popular culture—film, television, and music?
6. What are the messages of the **dominant culture** with regard to race, and how do themes and characters in entertainment media reinforce these messages?
7. What are some examples of entertainment media that challenge dominant culture messages about race?
8. What is the impact of entertainment media and race on audiences?

We will use content analysis, media history, economics, and cultural studies as the primary methods to analyze entertainment media and race. Readers are invited and challenged to consciously and deliberately bring their understanding of their personal experiences and their current intellectual understanding of race to this study and to bring forward new information in the form of history and theories and concepts about race from Chapter 4.

That is the context and overview. Here is an extraterrestrial thought that Linda has contemplated over time: if someone from another planet wanted to study the United States and determine what is most important to us and perhaps what we worship, they might come to a surprising conclusion. They would look at U.S. homes, apartments, mobile homes, and dorm rooms and find an object in each of these domiciles. Many of these homes have several; they occupy a central space in living rooms, family rooms, bedrooms, kitchens and, sometimes, even bathrooms. People frequently look at these

Media Activity 5.1
Childhood Television Favorites and Race

Instructions

List your five favorite television programs from your childhood (ages 6 to 12). Limit these programs to those with a narrative story line (either comedy or drama). This requirement eliminates programs such as *Sesame Street, Saturday Night Live*, reality programs, variety programs, and news programs.

1. _____

2. _____

3. _____

4. _____

5. _____

For each of these five programs, answer the following questions:

1. What was the total number of major characters combined in these five programs? (Remember that major characters are those without whom the plot would make no sense.) _____

2. Of these major characters, write in the numbers of each race:
   a. African American (black) _____
   b. Asian American _____
   c. American Indian _____
   d. Latino _____
   e. European American (white) _____
   f. multiracial* _____
   g. other (please specify if possible)

   _____ _____
   h. unknown _____
   Total numbers of characters of color (add a, b, c, and d) _____

*For the purposes of this activity, multiracial is defined as any character that clearly has parents of one or more of the racial groups listed in a through e of this question. This category is not intended for characters that "appear to be" or "might be" multiracial.

3. In general, did the character development and plots commonly revolve around any of the following major themes? Place a check mark (√) by any and all of the themes that are present in this episode.
   a. exploration of various cultures according to race (e.g., music, dress, attitudes, beliefs) _____
   b. exploration of the family relationships of people of color _____

c. exploration of interracial friendships   _____
d. exploration of interracial romance   _____
e. depiction of racial conflict   _____
f. depiction of barriers to racial equality or racial discrimination   _____
g. depiction of racial pride   _____
h. other (please briefly describe any other themes that involve race) _____   _____

Total number of themes related to race   _____

objects in a way that is very concentrated, almost an absorbed or dazed stare. In rooms where people congregate, the sofas and chairs are often gathered around this object and people sit together to watch it with focused attention and absorption. Perhaps the visiting alien from another planet would conclude that Americans have a common religion and the symbol that they worship together is the television. In fact, these visitors from another planet might not be too far off base.

Let us bring this study of entertainment media into the room where you watch TV. Follow the instructions in Media Activity 5.1 to begin your exploration of racial messages in prime-time television.

Depending on when you grew up, you will find different results. Most people age twenty and older discover that there were few, if any, major characters of color and very few major themes that involved race. If you are under twenty years old, you may find a few major African American characters and an isolated theme or two about race, but in general you are likely to find that few major characters were Asian or Pacific Islander, American Indian, or Latina/Latino.

What can we begin to conclude from this rough data? Until very recently, depictions of families and workers and neighborhoods on prime-time television have been predominantly white and middle-class. Most comedies and dramas have reflected the standards, values, customs, lifestyles, family patterns, and physical manifestations of this group. For a variety of reasons that we will explore in this chapter, prime-time television has historically reflected the standards of the dominant culture and portrayed it as "normal." This is not always apparent or visible to the viewing audience. While we may at times be aware of the absence of characters of color, we are often unaware of the invisible repetition of certain sets of experiences and values that sit squarely in the white middle class.

What is challenging about identifying the signs and reflection of dominant culture in popular media is that most of us have been so thoroughly immersed in popular culture that its messages and values seem "normal" to us as well. We are looking to be entertained primarily, not to analyze the way we are being socialized. Yet the constant repetition in popular culture of what is conveyed as "normal" affects all of us regardless of our race and ethnicity. In order to continue our quest for independence in defining what we believe to be true about human diversity, it is important to tease out these invisible messages of dominance in entertainment media, for "images in the mass media are infused with color-coded positive and negative moralistic features. Once these symbols become familiar and accepted, they fuel misperceptions and perpetuate misunderstandings among the races" (Dates and Barlow 1990, 4).

As we explore the portrayals, images, messages, and themes about race in popular music, film, and television, we will examine how the standards of the dominant culture are reflected, reinforced, or challenged. Part of our work together will be to explore the idea that we all have been influenced by the invisible messages of race in entertainment media and to undertake the task to make these illusive messages tangible and accessible. Once we can see and identify these messages, we can then begin to make conscious choices of whether and how we are influenced, persuaded, or socialized by popular culture.

AMERICAN INDIANS IN ENTERTAINMENT MEDIA

In Chapter 4 we explored some of the history of American Indians that was not available to many of us in our earlier years in school. We learned about the vast and violent extermination of much of the American Indian population, land, and culture—measures that were justified by the U.S. government as necessary to the pursuit of Manifest Destiny, the expansion of the United States to its "natural" borders. Biased characterization of American Indians as uncivilized savages fueled these policies. To what extent have entertainment media reinforced or challenged these messages?

Prime-Time Television and American Indians

"During the era when television was dominated by 'westerns' (1950s–1960s), Indians were relegated to their movie image, serving as either foils or backdrops to the stories of how the West was won" (Wilson and Gutierrez 1995, 95–96). Even the common phrase "how the West was won" is synonymous with the selling of **Manifest Destiny** and brutal destruction of Native American culture and lives. In early television, the most familiar representation of American Indians was Tonto in *The Lone Ranger*, who rode a pinto pony, dressed in fringed buckskin, spoke broken English, and served the Lone Ranger as a faithful sidekick.

A new film version of *The Lone Ranger*, with Johnny Depp as Tonto, was released in the summer of 2013. While the film was a box office flop and was panned by most reputable film critics, some American Indian activists commended Depp and Disney for creating a different and better image of Tonto than the old stereotype (Del Barco 2013). In addition, according to National Public Radio, the Walt Disney Studios went out of its way to court Native American groups, giving the proceeds from the film's world premiere to the American Indian College Fund. Hanay Geiogamah, a Kiowa tribe member and University of California, Los Angeles, professor, was offended, however, by two major elements of the film as well as the portrayal of Tonto. First, he criticized Depp as one of a long string of white actors playing Native Americans and said that Disney and Depp would have done a greater service had Depp played the Lone Ranger and hired any one of many talented Native American actors to play Tonto. Second, Geiogamah objected to both the exaggerated, dramatic, and unrealistic visual depiction of Tonto and Depp's version of Tonto's language as a "sort of monosyllabic stuttering, uttering. Hollywood Indian-speak" (Del Barco 2013).

There were essentially three features of American Indian representation in prime-time television throughout the 1960s, 1970s, and 1980s. First, there were very few Indian characters or themes; most of the Indian characters were men. Second, those few characters and themes available were almost always simple and stereotyped. Third, the scarcity of American Indian images combined with the repetition of the same images reinforced two messages: that American Indians were not important and that they served only as secondary companions to white men (and were clearly not as intelligent).

An alternative image of American Indians was presented in the groundbreaking television program *Northern Exposure* (1990–1995). *Northern Exposure* was set in a very small town in Alaska where a young, white, Jewish doctor was doing service in order to pay back his medical school loans. What distinguished this program was that its central theme was the education of Doctor Joel Fleischman rather than his noble service to the Alaskan people. There were many recurring and occasional characters of color that were full and complex. One such character was Native Alaskan (Eskimo) Marilyn Whirlwind, who served as Dr. Fleischman's assistant. She was depicted as wise and spiritual but also with an offbeat sense of humor and a strong and clear set of values. It was largely through Marilyn that Fleishman's lack of understanding and appreciation for Native Alaskans was revealed. Ed Chigliak, another multiracial (white and American Indian) character in this ensemble cast, offered a contrast to Marilyn. Ed single-mindedly pursued a career in filmmaking. While Marilyn was portrayed as intelligent and wise, Ed was portrayed as simple and somewhat limited in his abilities. The fact that the cast contained multiple and diverse American Indian characters and themes meant that there was much less of a chance for stereotypes to occur. The program's offbeat approach to multiracial relationships created many ironic and humorous situations and also challenged some of the biased information that many of us have been socialized to believe about American Indians. *Northern Exposure* was on the air for five years and was quite successful, a good example of how quality programming can entertain, offer alternative images of race, and be profitable as well.

Northern Exposure, however, is the exception to much of the depiction of Native Americans in media. According to Debra Merskin,

> These media portrayals . . . tend to rely on stereotypical images of Natives or to show them as existing only in the past. As a method of actual as well as **symbolic annihilation**, Native Americans have been categorized as one homogeneous group of "Indians" and considered on the basis of overgeneralized physical, emotional, and intellectual characteristics. Inaccurate portrayals impact not only white beliefs about Natives Americans but also how Natives view themselves. (1998, 333)

Television and other media stereotypes not only reinforce misinformation among non-Natives but also can contribute to internalized racism in Native Americans themselves.

Without sufficient positive and diverse media images or intervention from families, teachers, or others who might present narratives that counter the repeated stereotypes, Native Americans take in the same biased messages that non-Native audiences do.

From the 1999 television season through 2002, American Indians were virtually invisible on the small screen (Hunt 2003). From 2003 to 2009, there was one miniseries about American Indians and one significant Indian character. The miniseries, *Dreamkeeper*, is the story of a Native American man taking his grandson to a large American Indian gathering in which the boy has no interest. During their travels, the grandfather keeps the boy's attention by telling him authentic Indian folktales that are depicted in the program. The fact that *Dreamkeeper* won the Best Film Award in the 2003 American Indian film festival had little effect on increasing the presence of Indian characters or themes on television.

During the eighth season of *Law and Order: Special Victims Unit*, American Indian actor Adam Beach became part of the squad as Detective Chester Lake, a character who was outspoken about his pride in his Mohawk ancestry. Detective Lake became a regular character by the ninth season; however, his character was never fully developed and Lake was written out of the program after a two-year stint (Canote 2009). As "captured through the lens of broadcast television, Native-Americans continue to be a faceless, voiceless group within American society, their relevance seemingly reduced to a distant, historical connection" (NAACP 2008, 15).

The impact of the *absence* of Native American images and themes on television is just as powerfully negative and potentially damaging as the *presence* of stereotypes. It sends the same invisible but potent messages to audiences of all races, including American Indians: (1) American Indians are not important, (2) American Indians are not interesting, and (3) groups that are more widely represented on television are far more interesting, attractive, and significant than American Indians. These messages become embedded in the audience psyche and, in the absence of any contradictory information, they pose as the truth.

American Indians and Film

Images of American Indians in film were predated by images in nineteenth-century literature as noble savages, with emphasis on the word "savage." The theme of Manifest Destiny was constantly underscored in the literature of the time, depicting Indians as the less than human "other," who by their very otherness served as the justification for bloody wars and land grabs. Images of Indians typically showed them burning, looting, and scalping the "good" white guys who were either defending themselves and "civilized" America or simply pursuing their right to Manifest Destiny.

In early film, American Indians and other people of color were often portrayed as less intelligent and less moral than whites, thus emphasizing the myth of white superiority. Many images of American Indians in Westerns involved a vicious attack on a wagon train by hostile warriors with face paint and loud, unintelligible war cries. Surprisingly, silent films offered some alternative and complex views of American Indians and the history of western expansion.

Silent films produced by Thomas Ince were mixed in their portrayal of American Indians and the conquest of the West. In Ince's 1912 film *Custer's Last Fight*, he presented a traditionally patriotic view of General George Armstrong Custer as a brave Indian fighter of the stereotypically vicious Sioux, who were depicted as opposing the advance of white civilization. But in the 1912 film *The Indian Massacre*, Ince showed how whites shot and killed Indians for sport in much the same way as they slaughtered buffalo. In this film, Ince portrayed Indians as fully human, grieving over the loss of children (Aleiss 1995, 3).

When sound was first introduced in film, any sympathetic and complex representation of American Indians disappeared from the screen. The depictions of American Indians in the 1930s and 1940s solidified a series of clichés. The first of these was the reinforcement of the myth of their place in the fulfillment of Manifest Destiny. To serve this purpose, Native American characters were the requisite savages in films such as *Drums Along the Mohawk* (1939) and *Northwest Passage* (1940). Second, American Indians were lumped together in film as one, with no distinction among various tribes. Third, until the 1960s, many films depicted the concept of "**Old Custerism**."

"What is this Custerism? The celluloid residuals of Manifest Destiny played out as emotional climax" (Seals 1991, 2). In fact, Ronald Reagan himself played General Custer in the 1940 film *Santa Fe Trail*. The 1940s film *Cheyenne Autumn*, directed by John Ford, focused on a love story between two white characters rather than the deathly trip of the Cheyenne from Oklahoma to Montana in the 1870s (Seals 1991, 3). Old Custerism replayed over and over the classic "cowboy and Indian" trope in which the "good guys," who were whites, the cavalry, and the U.S. Army, triumphed over the "bad guys," who were inevitably the Indians (Wilson and Gutierrez 1995, 75).

The civil rights movement, which focused on discrimination against and the rights of African Americans, finally provided momentum to shift images of Native Americans in film. "White America (in the midst of the Black-inspired Civil Rights Movement) experienced a guilt complex over the historical and persistent mistreatment of Native American Indians" (Wilson and Gutierrez 1995, 87). The late 1960s and 1970s were a decade of pro-Indian films, or "**New Custerism**," which began with the 1970 film *Little Big Man*. Although *Little Big Man* still featured a white man as the central character, it significantly revised the image of Custer from a hero to Custer as a violent perpetrator of atrocities against American Indians. Custer's own violent death is portrayed in this film as well deserved (Seals 1991, 3).

Idealized images of Indians became trendy in 1990s films such as *Dances with Wolves*, in which Indians were romanticized as almost universally spiritual and good. This continued the era of New Custerism by creating a new stereotype that, despite its more positive characterization, was still oversimplified. Even with these new sentimentalized images of American Indians, the plot of *Dances with Wolves* still revolved around white characters. Shifting from images of the oversimplified bad Indian to the oversimplified good Indian may provide temporary relief from negative stereotypes, yet ultimately it continues to dodge the stories of racism, the slaughtering of American Indians, and the human complexity of individuals.

As we learned in Chapter 4, one of the consequences of being a conquered people has been devastating poverty on American Indian reservations and in urban communities. The Old Custerism perpetuated an image of the violent, hostile Indian and revised history in a way that glorified the cavalry and Manifest Destiny. While New Custerism may have had better intentions in its attempt to paint the massacre of the noble, romantic American Indians, it has done little to depict the contemporary consequences of hundreds of years of conquest, land evictions, and bloody wars. This lack can leave an uninformed audience feeling angry or guilty about white violence toward Native Americans, but relieved by the sense that it is all in the past.

A few films in recent decades have had some measure of commercial success in depicting an alternative view of American Indians as characters as well as the impact of history on contemporary Indians. One of these is the 1992 film *Thunderheart*, which is available from Netflix, and other online companies and the few remaining film rental companies.

Thunderheart departs from both the Old Custerism and the New Custerism. It offers a predominantly Indian cast of characters with themes that depict relationships and struggles. The wide range of Indian characters includes the somewhat romanticized character of Sam Reaches, the spiritual wise man; Jack and Richard, who wish to profit from the suffering of their people; and Maggie, Walter, and ultimately Ray, who take great risks to reveal how the government has exploited the Indian reservation and its people.

The use of visions to explore history and the visual devastation of the reservation offers still another alternative to classic Indian stereotypes. The film demonstrates contemporary devastation and poverty and avoids a more common film practice, which holds individuals responsible for their circumstances. Instead, *Thunderheart* more appropriately attributes poverty to a multilayered and complex history, politics, and policies. While the film is not entirely true to the factual information about the American Indian Movement's occupation of Wounded Knee, nevertheless it attempts to show the complexity of the politics and the economics of the situation. The secret strip mining of the reservation in the film is representative of centuries of exploiting Indian land.

While the film's ending, with its requisite chase and modern-day cavalry and American Indian confrontation may be entertaining, it ultimately detracts from the serious and intricate messages in the film. Still, it is a reversal of most traditional Westerns in which the cavalry typically surrounds the American Indians and mounts an impressive, dramatic, and righteous victory.

A discussion of images and themes of American Indians would not be complete without the analysis of two very different films: the Disney production of *Pocahontas* and the independently produced *Smoke Signals*.

Pocahontas, released in 1995, emerged out of a history of racial criticism of Disney animated films of the 1980s and 1990s. The 1992 *Aladdin* was criticized for its stereotypical depiction of Arabs, and *The Lion King* in 1994 was criticized for depicting the hyenas as stereotypical black and Latina/Latino ghetto characters. As a result, Disney executives began the creation of *Pocahontas* with an eye to sensitivity and avoidance of criticism about depiction of American Indians (Edgerton and Jackson 1996, 2).

The results were mixed. Disney hired a number of American Indian consultants and performers to serve as the voices of the Indian characters. One particular coup was the casting of American Indian Movement (AIM) activist Russell Means as Chief Powhatan, Pocahontas's father. Means's involvement and support of the film was an attempt to demonstrate a commitment to authenticity (Edgerton and Jackson 1996, 3).

Pocahontas was a tremendous commercial success, earning $91 million in its first four weeks and promoting and selling a number of tie-ins, including musical tapes, Burger King toys, moccasins, and a doll that looked suspiciously like Barbie. "Pocahontas, the 400-year-old legend, was expertly redesigned to Disney's usual specifications—meaning a full-length animated feature with a host of commodity tie-ins—thus becoming the version of the Pocahontas story that most people recognize today" (Edgerton and Jackson 1996, 4).

The film was never intended to be historically accurate. While Disney's goal was to offer positive and sympathetic Indian characters, it was never the company's intent to convey the history of the time. Disney became part of a long tradition in mythologizing the story of Pocahontas as a symbol of assimilation, showing how the natives could be civilized and made Christian. This myth was certainly not challenged in the 1995 Disney version of *Pocahontas*.

In fact, the real Pocahontas was twelve and the real John Smith was twenty-seven when they met in 1607, and most historians agree that they were never lovers. "In relying so completely on their romantic coupling, however, Disney's animators minimize the many challenging issues that they raise—racism, colonialism, environmentalism, and spiritual alienation" (Edgerton and Jackson 1996, 6). Once again, history is revised in film to show the triumph of the individual and of love, rather than the more complex racial relations and themes of conquest.

Finally, the process of designing the character Pocahontas is revealing of the literal whitewashing of the film. The original order from Disney executives to the artist was to create a fine creature that was not a cookie-cutter replication of white females in past Disney features. The artist's original drawings were based on four real women: paintings of the real Pocahontas, an American Indian woman, a Filipino model, and a white supermodel. The artists and decision makers of the final image of Pocahontas were all white males, and the ultimate drawing, while exotic, remained most true to the image of the white supermodel. In the end, Disney's version of Pocahontas offered a nod of sensitivity to American Indian characters but succumbed to a dominant view that "pushes native perspectives to the margins of society, if not entirely out of view. Disney's Pocahontas is thus another example of the 'white man's Indian'" (Edgerton and Jackson 1996, 8–9).

The 1998 release of *Smoke Signals* was a breakthrough in that it was the first feature film in the United States to be directed and coproduced by American Indians. *Smoke Signals* was not an epic or revision of history such as *Dances with Wolves* nor an idealization and assimilation story as in *Pocahontas*. Rather, it was a character study of Victor and Thomas, two young American Indian men on a journey to rediscover one of their fathers and in the process reclaim their own selves. The use of humor in the film was striking as it highlighted Indian stereotypes and satirized them at the same time. In one classic scene, Victor and Thomas, riding on a bus, begin singing a musical satire which repeats the lyrics "John Wayne's teeth," poking fun at Wayne's classic depiction in Westerns as the great white man who conquers the savage Indians.

Smoke Signals kicked off a small but mighty group of late twentieth-century films in which American Indians had central roles in writing, directing, and/or producing their own films, offering new, fresh themes and characters (Anderson 1998, 139).

Edge of America was written by a white screenwriter, Willy Holtzman, and directed and coproduced by an American Indian director, Chris Eyre. It stars no less than four professional American Indian actors as part of an ensemble cast. The *Edge of America* team also held open auditions on a reservation in the Southwest to cast at least that many parts with nonprofessionals playing high school girls. The film, based on a true story, conveys the hopelessness of life on a reservation where everything from sports to academics for young people looks and feels like failure. The story involves a new teacher who comes to the "res" to teach English and ends up coaching the perpetually losing high school girls' basketball team.

The twist on this story from the classic white-teacher-brings-hope-to-the-students-of-color theme is that the new teacher/coach is African American, and it is the interplay between the coach and the students, as well as Native American adults, that offers some of the most novel complexities of the film in the depiction of cross-race relationships. The primary interactions in the film are between Native Americans and between Native Americans and the African American coach, with interactions with white characters on the sideline. This, in itself, sends a message to audiences about the significance of relationships between American Indians and other people of color.

As a teacher and scholar of media and diversity and as the sister of the screenwriter, Willy Holtzman, Linda had the opportunity to sit in the director's booth with Chris Eyre for a few days of the filming of *Edge of America*. While the actors were clearly working from a script, she also observed a fascinating collaborative process in which the actors became an ad hoc part of a writing team. If actors thought a line was forced or false or inconsistent with their character, Eyre and Willy Holtzman encouraged them to speak up, and often the result was a new line contributed by the actor or a shift in emphasis that strengthened the authenticity of the characters and shed many of the classic stereotypes.

Stereotypes of American Indians as savages and noble savages, princesses and sidekicks still pervade the film industry. In the absence of personal experience with American Indians and the lack of education regarding the complex American history vis-à-vis American Indians, it is these biased images, themes, revisionist histories, and stereotypes that fill a void and often constitute what we come to believe as real. Films such as *Thunderheart*, *Smoke Signals*, and *Edge of America* signal possibilities for offering alternative and complex images that can have critical success, move in the direction of commercial success, and begin to tell authentic Indian stories and history.

ASIANS AND PACIFIC ISLANDERS IN ENTERTAINMENT MEDIA

Throughout the history of film and much of television, there have been several common stereotypes of Asians and Pacific Islanders. The so-called "yellow peril" has been the predominant image, joined by the dragon lady, the delicate lotus blossom, the mild and asexual Asian or Pacific Islander male, and the fierce master of martial arts (Kawai 2005, 2; Shah 2003). The "**model minority**" is the most recent addition to these stereotypes. While it appears to be a positive twist away from negative stereotypes, just below the surface, it is an oddly harmful image.

The "yellow peril" stereotype brands Asians and Pacific Islanders as a great danger to the United States. Some of these images have been blatantly negative, such as World War II film portrayals of Japanese Americans (or the derogatory "Jap") as a threat to American security. Some of these images mark Asians and Pacific Islanders as different, odd, the "other"; as such, they are either a source of mockery and cruel humor or a more serious threat to the "American way." These images of Asians and Pacific Islanders often signal the message that white Americans are the unchallenged keepers of the dominant culture and that Asians and Pacific Islanders are either a menacing challenge to this power and dominance or so ridiculous as not to be worth considering. Either way, if these stereotypes are consistently portrayed in media and remain without contradiction, audiences can be socialized to regard Americans of Asian heritage as quintessentially foreign, different, and ultimately un-American, regardless of how many generations their families have been American citizens.

The "dragon lady" stereotype is one in which Asian American women are depicted as evil and diabolical (Shah 2003) and at times dangerously and exotically sexual. By contrast, the "lotus blossom" image depicts Asian women as meek, subservient, and submissive to men as in the "Geisha girl" image. This same stereotype can morph into an exotic sexuality parallel to the dragon lady's, but instead of being dangerous, the lotus blossom sexuality is aimed to please and serve, rather than to manipulate, a man.

The stereotypes of men of Asian heritage have parallel contrasts and similarities as those of women. The ferocious martial arts stereotype evokes both admiration and fear, depending on whether the particular character is a hero or villain. Either way, this type of character is presented as a threat to the ideology of white men as dominant. The mild and submissive Asian or Pacific Islander male character in film is typically depicted as weak and asexual; and while he is not submissive to white men in the same way as the lotus blossom stereotype, he is nevertheless often portrayed as an object of pity or ridicule and as nonthreatening to white male dominance.

The last and most recent stereotype of the Asian or Pacific Islander seems oddly out of place. The idea of the model minority, which is often used to describe Asian Americans as highly intelligent, professionally successful, and talented, would seem to be a positive depiction conveying messages that are decent and admirable—certainly not the usual ingredients of stereotypes. However, several dynamics combine to make the model minority subtly insidious. "Asian Pacific Islanders have been historically and racially triangulated as 'aliens' or 'outsiders' with regard to White Americans but as 'superior' in relation to African Americans" (Kawai 2005, 2).

Although, on the surface, the concept of a model minority seems complimentary to Asians and Pacific Islanders, it ultimately serves a politically and racially divisive function. The misinformed notion that the civil rights movement corrected all racial discrimination against African Americans, thereby creating a level playing field, is a contemporary myth that resulted from little educational access to the history of race and racism in the United States. This myth then leads to another mistaken idea that it is both possible and desirable to be "color-blind." **Color-blind ideology** suggests that race does not matter in terms of U.S. history, historical or contemporary racial discrimination, pride in the accomplishments of one's race against difficult odds, and ultimately as a part of personal and group identity. As a result of missing, incorrect, or biased information, in our formal education and from popular media, there is often the misguided and ultimately flawed application of color-blind ideology in which the "success" of Asians and Pacific Islanders is "used to deny the existence of institutional racism and to 'prove' that U.S. society is reasonably fair and open for racial minority groups to move up the social ladder" (Kawai 2005, 6).

Often these twin beliefs of the "level playing field" and a "color-blind" U.S. society begin with the benign intent to consider everyone and everything to be equal. The problem is that this benevolent intent does not take into account two important considerations. The first consideration is that many people of color are proud of the personal and group struggles that they and their families have survived and that have contributed to character, integrity, and sheer strength. Ignoring one's "color," race, and ethnicity by virtue of "color-blindness" serves to negate a history of struggle, survival, and accomplishment. The second consideration is that various racial groups have experienced historical instances and patterns of institutionalized racism in very divergent ways. Just one example will illustrate the problems inherent in a color-blind approach. Before the Civil War, it was illegal to teach African Americans, as enslaved people, to read; as a result, throughout 200 years, many generations of blacks were not allowed to go to elementary and high school. Among other fundamental rights (e.g., employment, health care, citizenship, voting), this lack of basic education made it virtually impossible in later years for blacks to compete for college entrance or jobs with others who had the advantage of multiple generations of higher education.

By contrast, many Asians and Pacific Islanders were voluntary immigrants to the United States, and although they faced individual and institutionalized discrimination in employment, legal rights, and the right to citizenship, education was not legally denied. The ability to be the well-educated and professionally successful model minority is a "both/and" phenomenon, which means that this success is in part due to individual drive and motivation and in part very much a result of advantages in education that other people of color did not have.

The term "model minority" suggests that the success of many Asians and Pacific Islanders negates the racial barriers and struggles faced by other groups. These messages convey the misinformation that there is an intergroup competition in which Asians and Pacific Islanders have "won," with the implication that other groups have lost or failed.

As we begin to take a close look at images of Asians and Pacific Islanders in popular media, there are several important concepts to bring forward. First, some European Americans and those in power tend to homogenize Asians and Pacific Islanders into one group rather than recognizing and understanding various countries of origin, cultures, and the differences in immigrant experiences. The second tendency is the myth of the model minority. Do entertainment media reinforce these two misconceptions? Do television, film, and popular music still convey the same stereotypes? Are there examples of more complex and alternative images of Asians and Pacific Islanders? These are some of the questions we will explore in this section.

Asians and Pacific Islanders and Popular Music

Here is an easy yet disturbing exercise in content analysis. Listen to the Top 40, rock, and alternative radio stations in your community for two hours this week or look at the hit charts for these genres. Observe if there are any artists with Asian first names or surnames and if there are any songs with Asian or Pacific Islander themes. I can almost guarantee that your numbers will be zero. In a scan of Top 40 singles in the last thirty years, we found one specifically Asian song from 1963—"Sukiyaki"—written by Japanese composers Rokusuke Ei and Hachidai Nakamura. The lyrics are Japanese and the translation reveals the loneliness of love lost (Wikipedia 2013).

Some forms of musical entertainment that originated in Asia, such as karaoke, are popular in this country. However, with notable exceptions—such as Indian sitar player and composer Ravi Shankar (Robindro Shaunkor Chowdhury), who generated U.S. interest in Hindustani music and instrumentation during the 1960s and 1970s and, more recently, Korean entertainer Park Jaesang (performing as Psy), who, in 2012, briefly drew American attention to Korean popular music (K-Pop) with the satirical song and dance video "Gangnam Style"—few Asian artists or musical genres have gained mainstream popularity in the United States. Rather, music that is popular in Asian and Pacific Islander communities has tended to be an interesting amalgamation of the musical styles of immigrant cultures and those of mainstream American popular music.

> Popular music has frequently been portrayed as a homogenizing influence on minorities, but Asian-Americans frequently appropriate the styles and sounds of popular music to their own culture. The Filipino-American rapper La Quian asserts his multicultural identity within the context of rap music. Many Vietnamese-Americans enjoy Karaoke because it allows them to explore both their Vietnamese heritage and their current concerns. Rather than stifle creativity, these popular music forms are transformed by the Asian communities. (Wong 1994, 1)

These developments in music that were popular in various Asian and Pacific Islander communities have had little impact on the images of Asians and Pacific Islanders in the wider society.

A 2007 article in the *New York Times*, "Missing: Asian-American Pop Stars," explains this absence as the result of a particular type of racism. A talented singer, of Chinese and Filipino heritage, appeared on the music scene in the 2003 reality show *Fame* and was predicted by many to be the performer who would break through the barrier. But at age forty, Harlemm Lee was still working as a secretary (Navarro 2003). "People in the music

Some record executives think that multiracial Asians are more marketable than "monoracial" Asians. What do you think? [Left to right: members of the Grammy award–winning group Black Eyed Peas in 2009: Taboo, Fergie, apl.de.ap, and will.i.am.] *(Source: Wikimedia Commons, Les Black Eyed Peas en concert au VIP Room Paris 3, http://commons.wikimedia.org/wiki/file:Les_Black_Eyed_Peas_en_concert_au_VIP_Room_Paris_3.jpg.)*

industry, including some executives, have no ready explanation, but Asian-American artists and scholars say that racial stereotypes—the image of the studious geek, the perception that someone who looks Asian must be a foreigner—clash with the coolness and born-in-the-USA authenticity required for pop stardom" (Navarro 2003).

According to Asian Nation, record executives tend to think that multiracial Asians are more likely to be "'culturally acceptable' or 'marketable' to American consumers and therefore are more eager to promote them than monoracial Asian artists"; multiracial artists such as apl.de.ap of the Black Eyed Peas (Filipino and African American), Joseph Hahn (Korean and white), and Norah Jones (Asian Indian and white) are examples of this bias (Le 2013). This trend seems parallel in some respects to the way that film and television have historically leaned toward casting light-skinned African Americans. Both of these phenomena may be part of a less blatant, but equally insidious, form of racism that fosters success among performers who look less "other" and thus seem safer and more comfortable to executives who are in a position to hire and promote the careers of popular musicians.

Despite this trend, in 2003, a Chinese American hip-hop artist, Jin, was the first Asian musician to sign with a major label, Ruff Ryder. The CD did not make it big; nevertheless, Jin is still considered a breakthrough artist in hip-hop, providing some inspiration for other Asians who hope that their Asian appearance combined with racial stereotypes will not stand in the way of successful music careers (John 2004).

Asians and Pacific Islanders and Film

Early silent films typically perpetuated the "yellow peril" stereotypes of Asians and Pacific Islanders. In the 1916 film *The Yellow Menace*, Asians (of no identifiable ethnicity) were portrayed as diabolical as they joined with Mexicans to launch a subversive plot against the United States. With the notable exception of Japanese actor Sessile Hayakawa, who played lead Asian roles in early silent films, many Asian film characters were played by white actors (Wilson and Gutierrez 1995, 73–74).

The passage of the 1924 Immigration Act effectively halted the portrayal of Japanese or Japanese Americans in film until they were resurrected once again as the "yellow peril" directly before, during, and after World War II. During the early twentieth century, attention in film focused on China, with the development of the thoroughly evil villain Fu Manchu. In the series of Fu Manchu films that were popular from 1933 to 1936, "the American audience was given the impression that Chinese people are prone to violence, anarchy, corruption, vice and prostitution" (Wilson and Gutierrez 1995, 82). Another interesting Asian character in film in the 1930s was Charlie Chan, the mysterious crime solver whose lines read like the one-liners in a fortune cookie. Once again, none of the actors who played Chan were Asian. Even in the 1937 film *The Good Earth*, in which Chinese workers were portrayed sympathetically, the lead Chinese roles went to European American actors Paul Muni and Luise Rainer (Nga 1995, 2).

The attack on Pearl Harbor reinstated the Japanese as the "yellow peril" in film. While Chinese images of Fu Manchu and Charlie Chan were clearly stereotypical, Japanese images were more directly evil. In films such as *Wake Island* (1942), *Guadalcanal Diary* (1943), and *Objective Burma* (1945), the Japanese were shown attacking Red Cross ships and children and reveling in torture (Wilson and Gutierrez 1995, 84). These negative Japanese images continued for almost ten years after World War II. In most of these films, Chinese and Korean actors played the roles of Japanese. The ruling Hollywood wisdom determined that Asians of one nationality were replaceable by any other Asians (Nga 1995, 3).

There is no direct evidence that these media depictions prompted or justified the internment of Japanese American citizens during World War II. Yet these films repeatedly portrayed a dehumanized, monolithic, and thoroughly evil series of fictional Japanese characters. This may well have contributed to the political hysteria that characterized Japanese American citizens as the "other" and the enemy. This racist construct served as the justification for imprisoning thousands of innocent American citizens of Japanese origin. During this period surrounding World War II, there were no complex, sympathetic Japanese or Japanese American characters in popular U.S. film. Regardless of the intent of the filmmakers, the combination of this film and newspaper coverage of the evil "Japs" constituted U.S. propaganda that influenced the American public's opinion and fear of anything or anyone with Japanese heritage. Once again, in the absence of education or direct contact and relationships with Japanese Americans that would contradict biased media portrayal, popular stereotypical and fear-mongering images often posed falsely as the "truth."

The postwar United States was characterized by the Cold War and an almost obsessive fear of communism. The wars in Korea and later in Vietnam were ostensibly fought to save the free world from the so-called domino effect of communism. This phenomenon was also reflected in postwar film as the focus of the "yellow peril" shifted from Japan, defeated and no longer the enemy, to China as the newest symbol of Asian evil, this time in the guise of communism.

As sympathetic portrayals of Japanese Americans began to appear in films such as *The Bridge on the River Kwai* (1959) and *Sayonara* (1957), the Chinese were portrayed as an evil and devious threat to the United States and its way of life. Two films, *The Manchurian Candidate* and *The Sand Pebbles*, both released in 1962, typify this menacing image. In *The Manchurian Candidate*, GIs are captured and brainwashed by the "evil" North Koreans and Chinese, who were joined by the Soviets in a frightening experiment in political control through mind control (Internet Movie Database 1999). The evil portrayed here was explicitly communism, and two-thirds of the communists represented were Asian.

Interestingly, there was a remake of *The Manchurian Candidate* in 2004. The setting changed from the Korean War to the Gulf War and communist fear-mongering (read as Chinese) shifted to terrorist fear-mongering (read as Middle Eastern). The year and the target of the racial stereotyping changed in the two versions of the film, but evoking contemporary fear is a trigger in both films for the kind of racial misinformation and panic that contributes to individual and institutional racism in the form of racial profiling.

Throughout film history, the lotus blossom stereotype of the beautiful and exotic Asian woman has most frequently involved a tragic love affair with a white man. This thematic and character stereotype was present in the 1960 film *The World of Suzie Wong*, starring William Holden and Nancy Kwan (Internet Movie Database 1999). Holden plays an artist who unknowingly moves into a hotel in Hong Kong populated by prostitutes. When a beautiful prostitute (you guessed it—Suzie Wong) models for him, he falls in love with her.

The 1961 film *Breakfast at Tiffany's* was the perfect vehicle for Audrey Hepburn, who plays a quirky socialite. Critics raved about the film and its star. According to *Variety*, "What makes *Tiffany's* an appealing tale is its heroine, Holly Golightly, a charming, wild and amoral 'free spirit' with a latent romantic streak. . . . In the exciting person of Audrey Hepburn, she comes vividly to life on the screen" (*Variety* 1960). What is barely mentioned is the offensive depiction of the main character's Japanese neighbor, played by white actor Mickey Rooney. The film's depiction of Mr. Yunioshi and the lack of contemporary criticism are a sign of the times. The 1960s civil rights movement did not include racist stereotypes of Japanese in its agenda at that point. Rooney's portrayal of Yunioshi was complete with the most extreme of Asian stereotypes—a caricature of slanted eyes, buckteeth, and an exaggerated accent that relied on the exchange of *l*s for *r*s for cheap laughs. In the midst of the superlatives about the film, the *Variety* review briefly and mildly referred to this blatant stereotype: "Mickey Rooney as a much-harassed upstairs Japanese photographer adds an unnecessarily incongruous note to the proceedings" (*Variety* 1960).

The end of the Vietnam War sparked the production of a large number of films that analyzed, probed, criticized, and exonerated the controversial war. One similarity of both the pro-war and anti-war films of this era was the depiction of Vietnamese soldiers as crafty and devious. Critically acclaimed films such as *The Deerhunter* (1978), *Coming Home* (1978), and *Apocalypse Now* (1979) focused on the devastating impact of the war on white U.S. soldiers, using minor Asian characters and Vietnam itself as backdrop to the central anti-war message. The devastating impact of the war on the country of Vietnam, its people, and Vietnamese immigrants were not forefronted.

Of this genre of films, it was only *The Killing Fields* (1984) that featured a major character who was both Cambodian and complex and that depicted the impact of the war on him and his country. The film detailed the horrors of war through the characters of an American journalist and a Cambodian journalist, their relationship, and the difference in how the war affected each of them and their families. Significantly, the role of the Cambodian journalist, Dith Pran, was played by Cambodian actor Haing S. Ngor (Internet Movie Database 1999). *The Killing Fields* is a strong example of the possibilities of alternative themes and complex characters even in films dealing with highly controversial and politicized subjects such as the Vietnam War. It was nominated for several Academy Awards and grossed $34.6 million. That *The Killing Fields* was both an artistic and economic success is significant. It provided an opportunity for many Americans to see a well-made film that did not glamorize, villainize, or oversimplify the Vietnam War. And it serves as a model of the potential for feature film to portray difficult topics and themes with depth and texture.

The 1980s replaced the evil Asians with two new contrasting stereotypes: the benign, Zenlike master and the martial arts hero. A glut of popular martial arts movies were produced that ranged from Bruce Lee films to *The Karate Kid* (1984). Another new minor Asian character emerged in the 1980s and 1990s—the forensics expert, the systems analyst, or the above-average-intelligence Asian, subtly reinforcing the model-minority image.

The Joy Luck Club (1993), written by Amy Tan, produced by Oliver Stone, and directed by Wayne Wang, is another example of the possibilities of a successful feature film that depicts complex Asian characters, themes, and history. The film, based on Tan's novel, explores the relationships between Chinese women who immigrated to the United States and their American daughters. In a series of flashbacks to the immigrant women's lives in China, the audience learns something of Chinese history and the treatment of women in these particular characters' lives. Their stories intertwine with the difficulty, love, and complexity of the lives of their assimilated daughters to tell a poignant story of immigration, tragedy, and triumph. Yet, despite the depth of both the themes and characters, only one of the actresses cast in the six major roles was clearly Chinese or Chinese American. Of the other five actresses, one's ethnicity was not identified by either film publicity or reviews; one was born in Vietnam, one in France, one in Macao, and one in Japan. Even

Harold and Kumar Go to White Castle (2004). Do the characters of Harold and Kumar untangle some of the "model-minority" myths and stereotypes of Asian Americans? [Left to right: Kai Penn as Kumar and John Cho as Harold] *(Source: Courtesy of Getty Images. Copyright © 2004 WireImage. Used by permission of Getty Images.)*

in this film, anyone who looked Asian could be recruited to play the part of a Chinese or Chinese American woman.

One offbeat 2004 film, *Harold and Kumar Go to White Castle*, offered quirky comedy and the quintessential anti-stereotype of Asian Americans to counter the frequent model-minority label. "The movie about two postcollegiate buddies, Kumar Patel (Kai Penn), who is Indian-American, and Harold Lee (John Cho), who is Korean-American, in all-night, munchies-inspired pursuit of tasty burgers from their favorite fast-food joint, *Harold & Kumar Go to White Castle* has achieved mild cult status since its release in 2004. It is witty and well acted, and it defies stereotypes, persuasively depicting Harold and Kumar as fully American stoners, not do-gooder children of striving immigrants" (Oppenheimer 2008, 1). Neither profound nor Academy Award material, *Harold and Kumar* achieved something refreshing and important: a counter-stereotype that allows audiences to see the main characters as individuals rather than emblematic and representative of all Asians.

This interruption of stereotypes can have a subtle effect on audiences by also interrupting automatic thinking about the "truth" about people of Asian heritage.

The twenty-first century had more than its share of blockbuster box office hits. As of mid-2010, the film *Avatar* topped the list, taking in more than $759 million. The top box office hits for each year from 2000 through 2010 are listed in Table 5.1 (page 330) with a specific eye toward the inclusion and roles of Asian or Pacific Islander characters and actors. These actors did not fare quite as well as the films themselves. Of the eleven films listed, only three of them included characters of Asian descent. These characters were featured in *How the Grinch Stole Christmas* (a voice only), *Star Wars: Revenge of the Sith*, and *The Dark Knight*. The Asian-heritage actors in these films were ranked in the credits in billing order respectively at 15, 12, and 11. Typically, the major characters in a film and the actors with the highest salaries are ranked anywhere from first to third billing, with occasional top salaries at lower rankings. The table conveys at least two messages. The first is a signal that characters of Asian heritage are not very important, and the second is the message that it is rough going for Asian and Pacific Islander actors to consistently earn a good income in the acting profession.

The 2004 film *Crash* won that year's Academy Award for Best Picture and was touted by both critics and activists as a film that unmasked both overt and covert racism and challenged racist stereotypes at every juncture. The depiction of so many characters of so many races as complex—as neither fully good nor evil—kept the heads of audience members perpetually spinning. Just when viewers had the Matt Dillon character pegged as a complete racist, both ignorant and cruel, the film offers a view of his character's compassionate care for his aging father. And if that was not enough redemption for this racist police officer, he later risks his life to gently and tenderly save the life of an African American woman whom he had cruelly sexually abused in an earlier scene.

A scan of the early reviews of *Crash* revealed that some critics loved it and some found it a little "ho-hum" and recycled, but none of the major early reviews seemed to notice how different the treatment of Asian characters was from the treatment of any other characters in the film. None of the main characters were Asians or Pacific Islanders. The few minor characters who were Asians or Pacific Islanders were shrill, biased against African Americans, spoke with exaggerated accents, and were a throwback to the cheap comic mispronunciation of words. The only other Asian or Asian Pacific Islander characters in the film were either one-dimensional bad guys who inhumanly packed other Asians into a truck and planned to "sell" them or the one-dimensional victims packed into the truck.

The largest failure of the *Crash* portrayal of Asians and Pacific Islanders is that of audiences, critics, and ultimately Academy Award judges who failed to notice the marginalization and blatant stereotypes of Asians and Pacific Islanders in the film. The model-minority stereotype includes the portrayal of Asians and Pacific Islanders as quiet, "well-behaved," and easy to get along with, the polar opposite of troublemakers. Perhaps the failure to notice the biased portrayal of Asians in *Crash* is another consequence of the power of the model-minority stereotype to render Asians and Pacific Islanders invisible.

Table 5.1

Asians and Asian Americans in Twenty-First-Century Box Office Film Hits

Film	Year	Number of Asian/ Asian American characters	Gross profit of the film	Name of character	Character's ranking in billing order	Actor's name	Actor's ethnicity
How the Grinch Stole Christmas	2000	1	$260,031,035	Junie	15th	Nadja Pionilla	No information available
Harry Potter and the Sorcerer's Stone	2001	0	$317,557,891				
Spider-Man	2002	0	$403,706,375				
Lord of the Rings: Return of the King	2003	0	$377,019,252				
Shrek 2	2004	0	$436,471,036				
Star Wars: Revenge of the Sith	2005	1	$380,262,555	Captain Typho	12th	Jay Laga'aia	Many members of the cast were of Samoan or Maori descent but were under extensive makeup for their roles and unrecognizable as a result.
Pirates of the Caribbean: Dead Man's Chest	2006	0	$423,032,628				
Spider-Man 3	2007	0	$336,530,303				
The Dark Knight	2008	1	$533,316,061	Lau	11th	Chin Han	Born and lives in Singapore
Avatar	2009	0	$749,202,090				
Alice in Wonderland	2010	0	$336,530,303				

Source: Internet Movie Database (www.IMDb.com).

Asians and Pacific Islanders and Prime-Time Television

Early prime-time television repeated the stereotype of the stock domesticated and emasculated Chinese bachelor. In programs such as *Bachelor Father* (1957–1962) and *Bonanza* (1959–1972), the Chinese cook or "houseboy" was a regular character (Wilson and Gutierrez 1995, 103). In *The Courtship of Eddie's Father* (1969–1972), it was a Japanese woman who took care of Eddie and his father. In other television classics such as *Hawaii Five-O* (1968–1980), Hawaiians were often depicted as childlike speakers of broken English who served as part of the exotic background. By the time another popular program set in Hawaii, *Magnum, P.I.* (1980–1988), came to the small screen, there were no recurring Hawaiian characters in the series at all (Hamamoto 1994, 11–18).

Originally released as a film, the television program *M*A*S*H* (1972–1983) received critical acclaim, substantial television awards, and an enormous and loyal following. It was understood that both the film and TV program, set in a medical unit in the Korean War, were implicitly critical of the Vietnam War. Despite this level of intentionality about the politics of war, there appeared to be little intention about the presence of Asian characters. Although set in Korea, the program had only one minor recurring Korean character, and few Asians or Pacific Islanders appeared, even infrequently, in the series. According to the Internet Movie Database, over the years, M*A*S*H* had over 100 cast members, some of whom appeared in the show's credits and some who did not. Of those 100 cast members, there was only one credited Asian cast member, Kim Atwood, who played the role of Ho Jon, the Korean houseboy for doctors Benjamin Franklin "Hawkeye" Pierce and John Francis Xavier "Trapper" McIntyre. There were eight noncredited characters, six of whom were Japanese and two of whom were Korean. Both of these bit parts for Koreans were doctors, and the Japanese uncredited characters were golf pros, "caddies," nurses, servants, and prostitutes (Internet Movie Database 1999).

Asian and Pacific Islander characters appeared from time to time in TV Westerns. One example was in the *Annie Oakley* (1954–1956) episode titled "Annie and the Chinese Curse." In this program, an evil white man tries to buy or steal property from a good Chinese man who had immigrated to the United States. In the course of the episode, the Chinese man becomes the target of broken windows and racist notes. Annie's kid brother Tagg is very upset by this unjust treatment, and Annie explains to him that some people just do not take the time to get to know those who are different from them (Hamamoto 1994, 57).

On one level, this program provides a message of justice and equality, squarely against hate and discrimination, unusual and commendable for the mid-1950s. Annie and Tagg, clearly the "good guys," are deeply disturbed and take action to interrupt the racism of the "bad guys." Yet on another level, the episode revises history and misinforms. During the time of the episode, California law forbade Asians from owning property. The premise of the land theft begins with the misinformation that it was even possible for Asians to own land. Both the good guys and the bad guys focused on racism and prejudice as acts that individuals perpetuate and that individuals can counteract. While there is always the possibility of hateful acts and the hope of individuals interrupting them, institutional, legal, and policy issues are the underpinnings of racist acts. As described in Chapter 4, there were laws barring Chinese immigration and citizenship; there was blatant institutional and individual discrimination. "One of the tendencies of popular art is for its creators to apply liberally a revisionist gloss on events drawn from the historical past. Nowhere is this more evident than in the art of the television Western. . . . The normative social order is restored mainly through force by either military (cavalry) or police power (sheriff/marshal). On occasion, lone heroic individuals substitute for state power" (Hamamoto 1994, 49).

By contrast, in 1871 fifteen Chinese immigrants were lynched in Los Angeles. In 1877 a Chinese community was burned in Chico, California, and four Chinese immigrants were burned to death. Twenty-eight Chinese miners were massacred in Wyoming in 1886, and in 1850 a high foreign-miners tax was placed on all mining performed by immigrants (Hamamoto 1994, 52).

The message that American audiences have received, if any, about this time in U.S. history is that while there were some instances of anti-Asian racism, it was not the norm. Television characters portraying the lawmakers, sheriffs, marshals, and good men and women were not racist and stood up for racial justice. With little information about this chapter in American history, TV viewers are left with the belief that anti-Asian racism was rare, somewhat mild, and conducted by individuals, and when it existed, the local people usually corrected it.

The series *All American Girl* (1994) featured comedian Margaret Cho as a first-generation Korean American girl whose parents and grandmother were Korean-born. Cho's character was a feisty, assimilated American girl, and the show centered humorously around the conflicts between the values and culture of her old-world family and her own defiant identification with contemporary American culture. The program was simultaneously entertaining and silly, and it featured interesting issues of culture and assimilation, but it lasted for only one season.

Close examination of Asian and Pacific Islander characters and themes in entertainment media reveals several important trends. The first is that characters of Asian heritage have largely been invisible, minor, and extraordinarily simple. The early television stereotypes of Asian characters and themes include the evil "yellow peril," the benign houseboy, the martial arts expert, the male housekeeper, and the exotic female beauty. Later, these characters and themes were joined by the superintelligent but often nerdy scientist, psychiatrist, forensics expert, and other TV incarnations of the model minority. Characters and programs set in historical contexts focus on the good and evil of individuals and the restoring of justice and order, with virtually no revelation regarding the institutionalized anti-Asian racism that prevailed in much of the nineteenth and twentieth centuries. The combination of low exposure of Asians and Pacific Islanders in popular culture and the repetition of certain themes and stereotypes produces a socialization of audiences who unconsciously take in this misinformation as the "truth." This is particularly true of viewers who have little or no contact with Asians or Pacific Islanders in their life beyond television, little education about this part of U.S. history, and therefore no tools to recognize and challenge the messages in film, television, and music.

The Asian Pacific Media Coalition (APMC) issues regular reports on how the major TV networks are faring in terms of what it refers to as Asian Pacific Americans on the screen and behind the scene as writers, producers, directors, and so on. The APMC provided overall network grades for the 2009 prime-time TV season as compared to the overall grades from the past four seasons (Asian Pacific Islander Justice Center 2009, 1).

The highest two grades for the 2009 season were for ABC and CBS, both ranked at B minus, which would be considered just a breath above an average grade for most students. FOX and NBC were just a little behind, each with an overall grade of C plus for the same season. CBS gained a rousing one grade higher than its C minus grade in 2005, while the other networks each squeaked out a half grade higher in the same five-year period.

On the whole, the numbers of recurring Asian heritage characters on prime time television in 2009 were two fewer than 2008, but according to the APMC report, some of the characters themselves were stronger and more complex, and more of these characters transcended classic Asian stereotypes. The report highlighted the following actors:

- Sandra Oh on ABC's *Grey's Anatomy*
- Daniel Dae Kim, Yunjin Kim, and Naveen Andrews on ABC's *Lost*
- Masi Oka, Senhii Ramamurthy, and James Kyson Lee on NBC's *Heroes*
- Several Asian or Pacific Islander characters on FOX's *Glee* (Asian Pacific Islander Justice Center 2009)

Added to this list is the ongoing role of BD Wong as a forensic psychiatrist, Dr. George Huang, on NBC's *Law and Order: Special Victims Unit* and Tim Kang as Agent Kimball Chou in *The Mentalist* (2008–). It is interesting that Kang, a Korean American, actually plays the part of a Korean-American, which is often not the case given TV's frequent practice of casting "interchangeable Asians." In Kang's own career, he has portrayed Chinese and Japanese characters in the past (Lane 2011). In his role as Agent Cho, he mixes a parody of the Asian stereotype of emotionless inscrutability with a counter-stereotyped image as muscular, emotional, sexy, and sexual, the inscrutability regularly mixed with a mischievous smile and warmth and compassion for his colleagues and the victims of violence. Thrown into at least one of the *Mentalist* episodes was a backstory of Agent Chou as a teen member of a Korean American gang, defying any residual stereotype that could possibly conjure up an image of the "nerd" or the thoroughly "model minority."

Sandra Oh's character, Dr. Cristina Yang, is a medical resident on *Grey's Anatomy*. At first glance she seems to fit the description of the model-minority stereotype. She is brilliant, driven, competitive, and highly accomplished. Yet she has other complexities that defy this stereotype. She is quirky, somewhat neurotic, sometimes distant and cold, and other times compassionate without any visible signs of sentimentality. She is also beautiful and sexy and struggles with love and relationships. She is as far as one can get from the lotus blossom stereotype of the submissive woman. In fact, she can at one moment be tender and loving and the next moment quite calculating about the trade-in value of her primary relationship. In one episode, Cristina is so desperate in her drive to be an exceptional cardiothoracic surgeon that she offers to trade her surgeon boyfriend,

Owen Hunt, to another doctor, a woman who loves Owen—if she will mentor Cristina in cardiothoracic surgery.

The production of films such as *The Killing Fields* and *Harold and Kumar Go to White Castle* and TV programs such as *Law and Order: SVU*, *The Mentalist*, and *Grey's Anatomy* demonstrates the possibilities of providing complex Asian characters and themes that reveal solid information while they entertain . . . and make money for the network and their sponsors.

LATINAS/LATINOS IN ENTERTAINMENT MEDIA

According to a 1988 *Time* magazine article,

> In 1974, several years before she turned her attention to the decadent doings of wealthy WASPS, *Dynasty* co-creator Esther Shapiro brought NBC a script for a much different sort of TV show. Called *Maid in America*, it was a bittersweet movie about a Hispanic [sic] girl who goes to work for an upper-middle-class Anglo family. NBC executives praised the script but ultimately turned thumbs down. The reason, Shapiro recalls, was expressed in one blunt comment: "Tacos don't get numbers." (Zoglin 1988, 134)

Apparently this had not changed much by 1977, when a study of prime-time television on the ABC, CBS, NBC, and FOX networks revealed that only 2.6 percent of characters in entertainment television were Latino/Hispanic. This compared to the actual 10.7 percent of Latinos/Hispanics in the U.S. population at that time (Gerbner 1998, 5).

Several key factors have historically characterized images of Latinas/Latinos in film, television, and popular music:

- Latinas/Latinos have been underrepresented in mainstream film, television, and music.
- Those images of Latinas/Latinos that have existed in film and television have often been simple, stereotyped, and/or negative.
- Portrayals of Chicanos, Puerto Ricans, and other Latina/Latino groups emphasize sameness and blur differences between immigrant groups.
- Spanish-speaking television has drawn enormous Latina/Latino audiences.

As early as the 1830s, popular literature began demonizing Mexicans. "In fact, there is much to suggest that American literature of the period was primarily designed to stir up local sentiment for the overthrow of the Mexican government in Texas and New Mexico. . . . Americans were generally persuaded to visualize the Mexican as an inhuman enemy a decade before war with Mexico was officially declared" (Wilson and Gutierrez 1995, 66). Mexicans were depicted in this nineteenth-century literature as lazy, stupid, and cruel.

These stereotypes are similar to the misinformation about American Indians that allowed the U.S. government to justify conquering their land and livelihood. They also run parallel to the characterization of Japanese American citizens as disloyal and evil "Japs," thus providing ammunition to move a whole group of people to internment camps. These Latina/Latino stereotypes in literature remained constant for decades in film and television, to be joined subsequently by the simple images of Latin lover and exotic seductress.

As we explore the popular media images of Latinas/Latinos in the twentieth and twenty-first century, recall your personal and educational experiences. For most of us, Latinos and non-Latinos alike, formal education supplied little information about the histories of Cuban Americans, Mexican Americans, Puerto Ricans, and other Latinas/Latinos. If you are Latina/Latino or lived in a community with many Latinas/Latinos, you have some personal experience to contradict your mediated world. If you are not Latina/Latino and lived in a community where there were few Latinas/Latinos, the entertainment media may have been your primary source of information, which was more likely to be misinformation. According to the American Psychological Association, the less real-world information viewers have about a group, the more likely they are to accept the media "reality." Let us examine that media reality.

Latinas/Latinos and Film

The earliest silent filmmakers in the United States were often European immigrants who did not initially have the same socialized racism as second- and third-generation Americans. Latinas/Latinos participated as actors in and directors of these early films. The first Charlie Chaplin film had a Latino cameraman. "However, when the denigration of people of color became profitable, these same producers developed the same attitudes and participated in either excluding or exploiting the images of people of color. . . . At this point Latinas/Latinos were excluded from the industry, except in front of the camera where they generally played stereotypical roles" (Rodriguez 1997, 2).

Latinas/Latinos in subsequent silent films were primarily Mexican and Mexican American bandits attacking white people. The pejorative word "greaser" was even used in some silent film titles, such as *Tony the Greaser* (1911) and *The Greaser's Revenge* (1914). By 1922, the Mexican government banned the distribution of such films (Wilson and Gutierrez 1995, 75).

Other Central and South American countries eventually joined the Mexican banning, and its economic consequences had an impact on later Latina/Latino film images. Hollywood began to create stories of hot Latin romance, featuring the new stereotype of the Latin lover. While this provided some opportunities for some Latino actors, many Latino parts were still cast with white actors, such as Paul Muni and Noah Beery in the 1928 film *The Dove* and the 1935 film *Bordertown*. *Bordertown* featured the Latin lover as attracting two white women, one who went to jail and another who eventually died. While the Latin lover may have been hot, he was not allowed to succeed in love that defied cultural taboos (Internet Movie Database 1999).

Like American Indians and Asians, Latina/Latino characters were an integral part of the classic American Western genre. Typically male, the stock Latino character in Westerns was the "greasy" bandit (who spoke broken English), the sidekick (who spoke broken English), or the exotic hero such as Zorro. Film was the first of the popular media to develop a separate Spanish-speaking industry, particularly in Latin America. By the 1960s, Latin themes in Hollywood had further diminished and the "greaser" stereotypes reemerged in the form of Puerto Ricans and Puerto Rican gangs, including musical gangs in films such as *West Side Story* (1961). This trend continued through the 1970s. The few Latina/Latino characters were minor, and the rare Latino themes in films in much of the 1980s and 1990s dealt with drug lords and gangs.

Some examples of Latina/Latino themes and characters, however, offered complexity and alternative images and themes. One example is *Stand and Deliver*, a 1988 film based on an actual story, that cast Edward James Olmos as Jaime Escalante, a Bolivian-born math teacher working in a poverty-stricken barrio in East Los Angeles. He eventually is able to academically motivate kids whose response to poverty and racism had been to become tough, hardened, or apathetic. He cajoles and inspires them to succeed in calculus; several students pass the advanced placement test. The film portrays several striking instances of institutionalized racism. The academic testing company believes that it is impossible for so many students from a poor Latino community to achieve high scores on the test. As a result of this bias, the company challenges the high test scores of these young people from the barrio, accuses them of cheating, and insists that they retake the test.

It is the inspiration and toughness of their teacher that spurs the students to higher self-esteem and success. The film's message involves the power of one person to overcome the power of racism. It is an extraordinary film in its depiction of the barrio, the hopelessness of the young, low-income Latinas/Latinos, and the hopefulness that one man can bring. The film exposes the low expectations that the school system had for Latina/Latino students and the racism of the testing organization. Ultimately, however, it begs the question of structural racism and focuses, instead, on individual characters, who are vivid and complex and dispel stereotypes about Latinas/Latinos. So on one level, *Stand and Deliver* is inspirational and leaves the audience with hope; on another level, it reinforces the concept that one individual can undo structural racism and does not convey what it would take to shift the structure of a school system that has failed to teach low-income children of color at a high academic level nor how to reverse the complicity of testing organizations and other institutions who presume there will be close to pervasive failure among this population. Nevertheless, *Stand and Deliver*, with a relatively low $14 million box office gross, had little chance for its messages about racism to be seen by a wide audience (Internet Movie Database 1999).

While such films do not offer filmmakers much hope that they will become rich, *Stand and Deliver* (1988), along with other powerful films about Latinas/Latinos such as *El Norte* (1983) and *La Mission* (2009), received strong and wide critical acclaim. The late twentieth-century and early twenty-first-century trend of success for relatively small and/or independently produced films such as *Smoke Signals*, *Sling Blade*, *Shine*, *Precious*, *Zero Dark Thirty*, and *Amour* raises hopes of the possibilities for complex themes and characters. With the growth rate of the Latina/Latino population projected at 53 percent over the next decade, this will be a movie audience whose economic potential filmmakers will need to consider.

As we examine more recent trends in Latina/Latino films, characters, and themes, we will add a new tool to entertainment assessment, a formula that conceptualizes stereotyping in a way that allows for clear analysis. This method is framed as an equation (Berg 2002, 15):

$$\text{category making} + \text{ethnocentrism} + \text{prejudice} = \text{stereotyping}$$

According to this formula, the process that we all use to sort the vast amount of information we take in is the value-free process of category making. This process recalls the classic segment of *Sesame Street* that teaches children how to sort objects that are alike and identify them as different from others to the tune of the animated song, "One of These Things Is Not Like the Other." In the wise world of *Sesame Street*, categories are not intrinsically good or bad—just different.

Ethnocentrism is the belief that one's own ethnicity, nationality, or "people" embody a system of beliefs and values that is superior to others, often leading people to make false assumptions about cultural differences. Ethnocentrism is based on the assumption that one's own norms, customs, and beliefs are right and everyone else's are wrong, rather than the assumption that differences are not rooted in superiority or inferiority, the more innocent and laudable *Sesame Street* approach.

When category making is combined with ethnocentrism, the mix becomes toxic, with the members of the dominant group claiming, "Our group is quintessentially better than your group."

When prejudice enters the equation, the negative dimension of stereotyping is complete. "Prejudice holds that THEY are inherently not as good (not as clean, civilized, righteous, religious, intelligent, trustworthy, respectful of life, decent, hardworking, honest, etc.) as WE are because THEY are different from US (in the foods they eat, their skin color, values, religion, language, habits, etc.)" (Berg 2002, 15). Simply put, prejudice assumes that whatever group "WE" are is better than whatever group "THEY" are.

One of the primary dangers of stereotypes is that they are normalized by repetition.

The 1994 film *Clear and Present Danger* features a bad guy who is a Colombian drug lord (Joaquim de Almeida) and a good guy who is white (Harrison Ford). If it were only this single film that portrayed this good guy/bad guy scenario in a white/Latino context, audiences would not necessarily be on the category-making-plus-ethnocentrism-plus-prejudice path that leads to stereotyping. Rather, it is the repetition of this dynamic and the absence of a diverse array of other character dynamics of white and Latino men that make this stereotype stick in the minds of audiences and remain there posing as the truth. According to Berg, the antidote to stereotyping and its potentially dangerous results is knowledge: both knowledge about how the process of stereotyping works and, equally important, knowledge about the diversity and complexity of the history and the people that have been constructed as "the other" (Berg 2002, 23).

The study of representation in the media must be more than simple content analysis, a game of "spotting the stereotype," cataloguing it, then bemoaning Hollywood movies

Table 5.2

Popular Latina/Latino Actors in Film and Television

Actors	Ethnicity	Birth name	Selected major film roles	Types of characters
Cameron Diaz	Father—Cuban-American Mother—Anglo American	Cameron Michelle Diaz	*There's Something About Mary* (1998), the voice of Princess Fiona in all the *Shrek* films (2001, 2004, 2007, 2010), *My Best Friend's Wedding* (1997)	No Latina characters in her major films. Mostly plays comedy. Her characters in the two non-animated films are beautiful, frequently funny, very trusting, and often lean toward simplicity.
Andy Garcia	Born in Cuba	Andrés Arturo Garcia Menéndez	*Godfather Part III*, (1990), *When a Man Loves a Woman* (1994), *Ocean's Eleven* (2001)	*In Godfather Part III*, plays an Italian Mafia "don"; *in When a Man Loves a Woman*, plays airline pilot Michael Green, with no explicit ethnic identity; in *Ocean's Eleven*, plays casino owner Terry Benedict with no explicit identity. No Latino characters in the selected films. His characters are often deep thinkers, on the silent side, and, at least in *Godfather Part II* and *When a Man Loves a Woman*, very complex. *Ocean's Eleven* is a comic adventure in which none of the characters had much depth, including Terry Benedict.
Salma Hayek	Born in Mexico	Salma Valgarma Hayek-Jimenez	*Fools Rush In* (1977), *Dogma* (1999), *Frida* (2002), *Lonely Hearts*, (2006), *Bandidas* (2006)	In *Frida*, plays influential Mexican artist and complex character Frida Kahlo. Hayek's Spanish accent and/or inflection often identifies her as Latina, even at times where the character is not specifically defined as Latina. She is one of only three Latinas to be nominated for a Best Actress Academy Award. Hayek has played a wide range of characters, from comedy in *Fools Rush In* and *Dogma* to criminals and bank robbers in *Lonely Hearts* and *Bandidas*.

Jennifer Lopez	Mother and Father both born in Puerto Rico	*Selena* (1997), *Out of Sight* (1998), *Wedding Planner* (2001), *Shall We Dance?* (2004)	In *Selena*, plays famous Tejano singer; in *Out of Sight*, plays a U.S. marshal kidnapped by George Clooney's character, an escaped convict; in *Shall We Dance?*, plays Paulina (with no apparent last name), a beautiful dance instructor who teaches the Richard Gere character (who has a last name) to dance and re-ignites their respective life passions in the process. All three characters have some dimension to them, but in general are fairly simple and similar: beautiful, sexy, smart, strong, and hurt by and suspicious of men.
Edward James Olmos	Father— Born in Mexico Mother— Mexican-American	*Miami Vice* TV series (1984– 1990), *Selena* (1997), *Stand and Deliver* (1998), *Battlestar Galactica* films and TV series (2003–2009)	From 1984–1989, Olmos portrayed Lieutenant Martin Castillo on the TV series *Miami Vice*. In that role, for which he won an Emmy and a Golden Globe award in 1985, Olmos conveyed quiet authority with a touch of menace as a brooding former DEA agent who heads up a squad of undercover vice detectives. He played complex, full, and nonstereotyped Latino characters in *Selena* and *Stand and Deliver*; non-Latino character in the *Battlestar Galactica* films and TV series.
Martin Sheen	Father— Spanish Mother— Irish	*Apocalypse Now* (1979), *The Departed* (2006), *The West Wing* TV series (1999– 2006)	In *Apocalypse Now*, plays Captain Benjamin Willard; in *The Departed*, plays Captain Oliver Queenan, captain of the Special Investigations Unit of the Massachusetts state police. In these roles and others, Sheen plays complex characters, often leaders with integrity embroiled in internal or external conflict. In the two film roles, he was clearly Anglo. In the film series *The West Wing*, he played a principled U.S. president, a white man from New Hampshire who eventually supported his successor, a Latino from Texas played by Jimmy Smits.

for their pernicious imagery. It has to branch out in at least two directions. First, film representation needs to be understood within a social and historical context. The images of Latinas/Latinos in American film exist not in a vacuum but as a part of a larger discourse on Otherness in the United States. Beyond their existence as mental constructs or film images, stereotypes are part of a social conversation that reveals the mainstream's attitudes about Others. (Berg 2002, 4)

Berg sets an important tone and context for examining Latina/Latino characters and themes in film since the late twentieth century.

This inquiry suggests two important questions: (1) Does the film depiction of Latinas/Latinos in the United States reinforce a sense of "otherness" through the use of stereotyped characters and themes or are there examples of significant change? and (2) Is there a relationship between any change in Latina/Latino "otherness" in film and a larger conversation about individual and institutional racism directed at Latinas/Latinos in mainstream society? We will use these questions to frame our investigation of Latina/Latinos in film since the 1990s.

Six Latina/Latino actors prominent in box office appeal, film awards, and/or award nominations are examined in Table 5.2 (pages 338 and 339). The table lists the actors' given names, ethnicity, a few of their most notable performances and hit films, and a summary of the types of characters they have tended to play. Many of the films listed have drawn large and/or diverse audiences, and the characters played by these actors have the potential of influencing audiences' category making and perhaps stereotyping regarding Latinas/Latinos.

It is interesting to note that audiences do not commonly identify two of the most popular and easily recognized actors in Table 5.2 as Latina/Latino. Neither Martin Sheen nor Cameron Diaz is typically cast in Latina/Latino roles. In fact, Diaz is often cast in romantic comedies; if she is in any stereotypical role at all, it leans toward that of the beautiful "dumb blonde," which, in *There's Something About Mary* and *My Best Friend's Wedding*, translates into a comic, naive, and trusting young woman who lacks any Latina identification.

Sheen frequently plays characters who are strong leaders by virtue of their character and/or position. These characters are often men with great and grave responsibilities and decisions to make. Sheen's characters generally have strong principles and a basic integrity that is often challenged in the course of events, propelling the character into a painful state of inner conflict. Most of Sheen's characters are thoughtful and deliberate, with a complexity that is characterized by many layers of depth; most are white and non-Latino.

The roles played by Sheen and Diaz consequently do not contribute to the reinforcement of Latina/Latino stereotypes, the inquiry posed by the first framing question. The second question regarding how their roles might contribute to larger conversations about racism targeting Latinas/Latinos poses a greater challenge. Do Sheen and Diaz deny their Latin heritage and lose opportunities to portray Latina/Latino characters that challenge the classic stereotypes, or have they been given little choice by agents and casting directors? Is the fact that they are not typecast in stereotypical Latin roles a signal that Hollywood is progressing in a trajectory that allows Latina/Latinos to play a wider range of roles that do not pigeonhole them in only those roles that match their ethnic identity? Such questions are endless. Consider one more. Does the fact that neither Diaz nor Sheen looks stereotypically "Latina/Latino" allow them to "pass" and therefore have a shot at playing white characters and enjoying more lucrative careers? By virtue of how each of these actors appears physically, are they eligible for roles that would automatically exclude other Latina/Latino actors?

First, we know that by 2010 the U.S. Census Bureau had defined Latino/Latina or Hispanic as an ethnicity rather than a race and provided Latinos the option to check whatever box fits how they categorize their own race. We also know from Chapter 4 that the categories of race on the census questionnaire have been a moving target since the census began. Before 1848, the Census Bureau assumed that Americans who were part of families that had immigrated from China or Mexico should each be considered a separate race. But because of the population in California, the 1848 discussion became whether Chinese Americans or Mexican Americans would be defined as white. The decision was to categorize Mexican Americans as white, which, at least temporarily, afforded them more privilege than Chinese Americans. These categories changed again in 1890 and were joined by several so-called racial categories that are not a part of today's conversation about race in the United States. The Census Bureau's historical track record is neither consistent nor accurate; knowledge of these apparently arbitrary decisions about which group is which race makes it difficult to trust the Census Bureau as a reliable authority when it comes to defining race and ethnicity or assigning which groups should check which racial boxes on the questionnaire.

Added to this official designation is the confusion of the decision makers in Hollywood in the creation and casting of Latino characters in film. This confusion is passed on to audiences and contributes to the myths, misinformation, missing information, and biased information that many of us have about race in general and about what it means to be Latino/Latina in particular.

In addition to the multiple messages mixed with accuracy and stereotypes and outright bias, filmmakers inevitably pass on to audiences not only their own biases, but also their unexamined confusion about the relationship between skin color, race, and ethnicity. Nowhere is this confusion more evident than when it comes to the Latino/Latina roles that are created and the actors who are chosen to play these roles.

As you consider this information, the questions raised, and your response to them, remember to observe any internal process of cognitive dissonance and how that affects your response to the questions. Do any of these questions challenge any previously held beliefs or assumptions? Do any of these questions create confusion for you as you try to independently think through the acting careers of Cameron Diaz and Martin Sheen? We'll continue to examine these questions as we assess the other four actors in Table 5.2.

Andy Garcia has played Latino characters who are villains and heroes, leaders in well-respected fields and leaders of drug cartels in films such as *The Disappearance of Garcia Lorca* (1996), *The Lost City* (2005), and *La Linea* (2009). Some of Garcia's most well-known roles, however, are in box office hits where he has played characters with generic names that are presumed to be Anglo, such as Michael Green or Terry Benedict, or the Italian "godfather" of a crime family, Michael Corleone, as depicted in Table 5.2.

The quintessential, often stereotypical Italian character Garcia played in the blockbuster epic *The Godfather Part III* (1990) is rich with depth, complexity, strength, and character contradictions, including compassion and tender love for his family contrasted with violence and brutality in his "business." While the role of the head of a mob family may contribute to an Italian stereotype, the multiple dimensions of the character and Garcia's acting include nuances and intricacies and density that defy stereotype. Any way you look at it, however, it is not a Latino role.

In the film *When a Man Loves a Woman* (1994), once again, Garcia's powerful acting, as well as the scripted development of the character, reveals a man with layer upon layer of strength, profound love for his wife and children, and an equally profound helplessness as he tries to help his wife fight her descent into alcoholism.

As an actor, Garcia has been able to transcend the kind of typecasting that would limit him to Latino-only parts or stereotypes. He also has been offered a wide range of parts and has chosen not to limit himself to Anglo-only roles that would deny him access to play meaty characters that are Italian, Anglo, or Latino. Garcia's career adds another level of response to the framing question about stereotypes and "otherness," in a very different way from Diaz and Sheen. Uniquely positioned in his ability to play across ethnicities, Garcia has benefited from the openness of film decision makers to cast him in a variety of roles. This, combined with his acting talent, has put him in a unique position to choose roles that do not contribute to reinforcing the stereotype of the Latino "other"—the so-called Latin lover, criminal, or desperado.

Salma Hayek was born in Mexico and began her acting career there as a soap opera star with an enormous and loyal fan base. She left Mexico for Los Angeles when she was twenty-five years old (Internet Movie Database 2002). A combination of her heritage, her appearance, and a lingering Spanish accent and inflection has virtually guaranteed that Hayek play mostly Latina roles. These roles, however, have been diverse: her characters are almost always beautiful, but they are sometimes comic heroines and other times criminals, artists, and bank robbers. One of Hayek's most highly regarded and multilayered roles was as the influential Mexican artist Frida Kahlo in *Frida* (2002). Hayek was the second of only three Latinas to have been nominated for an Academy Award for Best Actress (Internet Movie Database 2002). Although she has been typecast in strictly Latina roles, Hayek has generally received strong reviews for her skilled and nuanced portrayals and has rarely played the stereotypical roles of Latin bombshell or servant.

By contrast, Jennifer Lopez has frequently played characters who have Anglo or Latina surnames but whose ethnicity remains unstated or ambiguous. A breakout role for Lopez was as the real-life Tejano singer Selena, in the film of the same name. Lopez, not recognized before or since as an especially talented actor, showed a new level of performance in the film, playing Selena with depth and complexity. Lopez's acting in the film, combined with the scripted development of the character and access to real-life footage of Selena, pulled the role out of the danger zone for stereotypes. Like Cameron Diaz, who has never been in danger of playing stereotypical Latina roles but has, in fact, come close to the dumb blonde stereotype, Lopez has played and/or been directed to the edge and over the edge of the stereotype of the beautiful, often uncomplicated, sexy bombshell, which is much closer to generic gender stereotypes than the classic Latina stereotypes. It is interesting to note that despite the Latina looks and widely recognized beauty of both Lopez and Hayek, the types of roles they have been offered, sought, or accepted have been very different. In some ways this is an oblique response to the question of whether the characters and films of Lopez and Hayek advance the conversation about stereotypes and the "other." The kind of beauty and sex appeal that both Lopez and Diaz, as well as Hayek, possess repeats a familiar stereotype in film and character development where the structural biases of race and gender intersect and are such common images that they are simultaneously and ironically invisible to audiences.

Edward James Olmos frequently plays characters with the same kind of epic strength as those played by Martin Sheen. Olmos's extraordinary acting talent and carriage lend dignity and gravitas to his roles. His appearance is perceived as classically Latino; as a result, given his own choices and the roles he has been offered, he has always played characters that were either explicitly or implicitly Latino. The characters he played as the Bolivian-born math teacher in *Stand and Deliver* and the Mexican father in *Selena* have a basic complexity to begin with that gains additional intricacy and depth in Olmos's adept hands.

The combination of the skills of writers and Olmos's powerful performances create characters that demonstrate elements of the generally pigeonholed fiery Latino machismo combined with the leadership, dignity, integrity, and stolid compassion that defy this label. The result almost guarantees that Olmos's roles and talent will challenge stereotypes as posed in the first framing question. Olmos's roles do contribute to the larger question about adding value to the conversation about individual and institutional racism and "otherness." In *Selena*, the audience is drawn to admire and identify with both the main character, Selena (played by Jennifer Lopez), and with Olmos's character, Selena's father. Once that bond between audience and character is established, the audience begins to care about the racist way that Selena is treated in terms of where and what she should sing, and to root for Olmos as he fiercely objects to the bigotry that attempts to pigeonhole his daughter.

Similarly, in *Stand and Deliver*, Olmos's character takes on bigotry in the form of the institutionalized racism of the school system and the testing agency, which assume that poor kids from the barrio cannot succeed academically. In the film, Olmos's role as a teacher/activist and the way the development of the students defies this stereotype create a space for audiences to learn about institutionalized racism in education and the power of one person to make a difference.

These films come close but ultimately pull back from conveying that, in addition to individual prejudice, there is also a structural dimension to racism embedded in policies and practices. This leaves the issue of raising awareness about institutionalized racism and "otherness" with a flawed piece of information and reinforces the misinformation that if individuals cause racism, individuals can therefore wholly solve it. Recall Berg's notion that untangling stereotypes requires knowledge. When the knowledge is partially false, the understanding of stereotypes sits on a shaky foundation.

The careers of these six successful actors raise larger questions that invite us to take a closer look at how structural, institutionalized, and internalized racism operates on the fictional level, in the characters they play and the dilemmas they face, and on the factual level, in the entertainment industry itself. These questions may also provide some insight as to how the policies and practices of the film industry may reinforce or trigger internalized racism on the part of some Latina and Latino actors.

Consider these questions:

- Does the fact that the U.S. Census Bureau identifies Latinos or Hispanics as an ethnicity, offering them an option of how to identify themselves racially on the census form, create options and/or confusion in casting? For example, could Martin Sheen and Cameron Diaz elect to identify their ethnicity as Latino or Hispanic and identify their race as white or multiracial? What effect would this have on their careers and on their own identity and sense of who they are?
- Do these kinds of external choices make things more challenging and confusing in terms of Diaz's and Sheen's identities and/or easier in terms of the range of acting roles that are available to them?
- How does the culture and power structure of the enormously profitable entertainment industry of film and television factor into the range of choices available to Latina/Latino actors? On what combination of factors do filmmakers base their decisions to cast Latina/Latino actors with Latino surnames, looks, accents, and so on versus actors with or without Latino surnames whose appearance and accents do not announce their ethnicity or race?
- Are actors such as Sheen and Diaz beneficiaries of a wider range of roles than other Latinos because they can "pass" as white, or is that an outdated, racist perspective? Do they simply mirror the way that white privilege typically operates? In other words, in the twenty-first century, can Diaz and Sheen be fully accepted, both internally and through the decisions of institutions such as the entertainment industry and the U.S. Census Bureau, as multiethnic or multiracial or both, allowing them to embrace their full identity and make choices based on "both/and" rather than "either/or"?

As you consider these complex questions, there is one more slice of information and a perspective to add to the already challenging and ambiguous mix of information—the Latino awards in the entertainment industry. The American Latino Media Awards (ALMA) were initiated in 1995 by the National Council of La Raza (NCLR), a national research and advocacy organization that works with and on behalf of Latinos. Its concern was that even in the late twentieth century, employment for Latinos behind and in front of film cameras was very low in proportion to their population and in comparison to other communities of color. NCLR also observed that a disturbing number of the film roles that did exist were steeped in stereotypes. As a result of this analysis, NCLR established the ALMA to meet three basic purposes: to raise the level of employment of Latinos in the industry, to honor the achievement of Latino actors and filmmakers, and to counteract Latino stereotypes and increase understanding of Latino culture in the wider community.

The Latino Media Awards faced several different realities simultaneously, both within and outside the Latino communities and the worlds of film, television, and music. As NCLR developed the scope and nature of the awards, there were many things to consider:

- There were far fewer Latino roles in film and television than were proportionate to the nation's Latina/Latino population.
- Many of these roles were either small and inconsequential or loaded with classic as well as new Latino stereotypes.
- Some Latina/Latino actors accepted non-Latino roles because that was all they were offered and/or because such roles allowed them to break away from Latino stereotypes and simultaneously play a wider range of roles that could translate into more money.

By 1995, groups such as the National Council of La Raza had some understanding about individual and institutionalized racism; however, the entertainment industry showed little understanding of how such racism operates. And there was far less understanding of internalized racism. It's important to remember, as noted in Chapter 4, that internalized racism is never the fault of people of color, who receive the same negative and disturbing messages about their own group as do whites. As a result, people of color often internalize the negative messages and operate in the world as if they were true. Without attention to how internalized racism operates or how to untangle and shed its effects, Latino actors, directors, sound engineers, and other film personnel might unknowingly collude with the racist policies and procedures in the industry.

For Latinos and Latinas, this process is further complicated by confusion about race and ethnicity. The same Census Bureau that arbitrarily decided in 1848 to declare Mexican Americans as white and to officially categorize Chinese Americans as black currently defines Latinas/Latinos and/or Hispanics as an ethnicity or nationality defined by country of origin, rather than a race. While theoretically Latinas/Latinos can check two census boxes—one for ethnicity and one for race—many Latinos identify their race as Latino or Hispanic—which is not an option on the census form. Latinos are also typically treated and considered as a race by non-Latinos. It seems inevitable that this would create and perpetuate confusion for audiences when Latino actors, such as Cameron Diaz and Martin Sheen, who appear to be white, have the option of a much wider range of roles than does Salma Hayek or Edward James Olmos. Diaz and Sheen both typically play white characters; Hayek and Olmos almost always play the roles of Latinos; and Andy Garcia, as well as other actors such as Jimmy Smits, often switch seamlessly from white to Latino characters and other characters whose race or ethnicity is unexplained or ambiguous. This same sort of scenario would not be feasible for actors who are clearly African American or of Asian heritage.

A sign of the times was an ALMA award category that was created in 1995 and ended in 1999, perhaps because it seemed oddly inconsistent with ALMA's stated goals. This particular award, given to actors in either a made-for-TV movie, miniseries, or feature film, honored outstanding performances in a "crossover role." There is no explanation or description of this award on the ALMA website. However, the roles for which actors received crossover awards were always those of white characters. There is no explanation why ALMA stopped giving this award after five years, but perhaps NCLR realized that while playing so-called crossover roles may be an achievement in the expansion of Latina/Latino actors' options or a recognition of their acting ability, it was unlikely to contribute to ALMA's goal of counteracting Latino stereotypes and increasing understanding of Latino culture in the wider community.

Latinas/Latinos and Television

The phenomenon of television has two separate implications with regard to the Latina/Latino community. The first involves the television viewing habits of Latinas/Latinos and the boom of Spanish-speaking television. The second issue is the representation of Latinas/Latinos in prime-time network television.

Spanish-speaking cable television has skyrocketed in its viewing audience, audience spending, and advertising. As a group, Latinas/Latinos watch more television than the general population. In the early 1990s, three-fourths of Latina/Latino viewers spent their time watching Spanish-language programming (Braus 1993, 48). A 1993 study revealed that the Latina/Latino audiences watching prime-time television viewed only one show in common with the rest of the U.S. population. At that time, the Latina/Latino population of 25 million spent $190 million annually, and their growth rate was five times that of the rest of the population ("Hispanics: Last Frontier for Marketing" 1993, 54).

Ten years later, in 2003, the top seventy-two TV programs viewed in Latina/Latino homes were in Spanish on Spanish-speaking cable television (Rincon 2004, 1–2). According to the 2000 U.S. Census, 84 percent of all Latinas/Latinos speak some Spanish, and 58 percent of all Latinas/Latinos prefer speaking Spanish at home. This information regarding Spanish language use and preference accounts, in large part, for the continued programming and economic success of Spanish-speaking television. One of the ways that TV and cable networks measure economic success and growth is through what is called the "upfront ad marketplace." This refers to the initial purchasing of network television advertising by firms who want to have the best selection of available ad placement on the most popular programs. The advertising agencies work with the networks to reserve ad time when the schedule for the upcoming season is first announced. This "upfront" advertising strategy generally requires that the ad agency commit to a longer schedule of advertising and higher prices. For the 2010–2011 television season, the two largest Spanish-speaking networks, Univision and Telemundo, took in a record $1.5 billion in upfront ads between them (Consoli 2010, 1).

These are the five top-ranked television networks watched by Latina/Latino audiences:

1. Spanish-speaking Univision
2. Spanish-speaking Telemundo

3. English-speaking FOX
4. Spanish-speaking Futura
5. English-speaking ABC (Nielsen Company 2009)

CBS and NBC did not even make it into the top five. This is both a strong indication of Latina/Latino audience preference for Spanish-speaking programs and a clue to the preferred content of the programs themselves.

As we take a look at the five top-ranked English-language programs, it is important to keep in mind that even the highest-ranking program, *American Idol*, aired on Wednesdays, has an average of 1,336,000 Latina/Latino viewers compared to the top-ranked Spanish-language program, *Mañana Para Siempre*, aired on Tuesday nights, with an average of 5,132,000 Latina/Latino viewers (Nielsen Company 2009).

The Latina/Latino population and its buying power have become a force for television and advertisers to reckon with. As a result of this viewing pattern, advertisers and demographers have chased this audience—first to analyze it and then to sell to it. Interestingly, the analysis of the Latina/Latino population has led advertisers to look more closely at the demographics of Latinas/Latinos and to determine that they are a multifaceted demographic group in terms of income, generations since immigration, and national origin:

> Some firms are helping businesses approach the Hispanic market by dividing it extensively with a sharp knife. Donnelly Marketing Information Services (DMIS) of Stamford, Connecticut, recently introduced a marketing tool that splits U.S. Hispanics in no fewer than 18 ways. Its Hispanic Portraits system ranges from "Puerto Rican, high income, younger, established with single/multifamily homes" (3 percent of US Hispanic households) to "Mexican, lowest income, younger, low mobility, Hispanic neighborhoods" (16 percent of Hispanic households). ("Hispanics: Last Frontier for Marketing" 1993, 56)

Even the study of Latina/Latino immigration and assimilation patterns has become grist for marketing plans. According to *American Demographics Journal*, Latina/Latino immigrants originally buy the products, such as Colgate toothpaste, that they used in their country of origin. But, according to demographers, it is the desire to become more American that provides the opportunity for advertisers to entice first-generation Latinas/Latinos to switch product brands. One marketing consultant found that Latinas/Latinos thought that within fifty years they would lose their culture and language and become like everyone else in the United States. The job of advertising, apparently, is to promote this assimilation by identifying and selling the most American products. However, marketers are equally concerned about attracting U.S.-born Latinas/Latinos: "Perhaps the safest way of attracting U.S.-born Hispanics is by placing references to Latina/Latino culture in English-speaking advertisements. Such advertisements appeal to Hispanics who primarily speak English but still have pride in their culture" ("Hispanics: Last Frontier for Marketing" 1993, 58).

By the late 1990s, these marketing strategies were focused primarily on Spanish-language television, since only one-fourth of the Latina/Latino audience was regularly watching prime-time network television. The catch-22 of this situation is that in addition to the Latina/Latino audience's self-reported preference for Spanish-language television, the lack of Latina/Latino characters and themes also drove this audience to cable and kept them there. As we will see, prime-time television producers continued reproducing that void for a long time.

One of the major questions raised by Latino population growth and accompanying buying power is if, and to what extent, this growth has affected the number of Latino characters and themes on television and the quality and complexity of their depiction. Let us take a stroll back to the earlier days of network TV to begin to answer this question.

Early Latina/Latino characters on television ranged from the Cisco Kid (*The Cisco Kid*, 1950–1956) in a show with a blend of oversimplified heroes and the stereotype of the faithful, broken-English-speaking sidekick, Pancho, to Ricky Ricardo, the hot-tempered but tolerant Latin-lover husband on *I Love Lucy*. From 1955 to 1964, only one character in 100 on television was Latina/Latino (Rodriguez 1997, 59).

In the early history of prime-time television, there were few leading characters that were clearly Latino and even fewer themes that revolved around issues facing Latinos and various Latina/Latino communities. From 1954 to 1963, *Father Knows Best* episodes occasionally included Frank (pronounced "Fraunk") as the Mexican gardener. From 1957 to 1963, *The Real McCoys* featured Pepino García as a farmhand.

From 1960 to 1961, the popular *Steve Allen Show* introduced and featured a new character, José Jiménez, played by Bill Dana. Dana, of Hungarian-Jewish descent, played this character as a simple-minded fellow who spoke broken English. His stock phrase, spoken with an exaggerated Spanish accent and repeated by viewers with roars of laughter across the country, was "My name—José Jiménez" (Internet Movie Database 1999). *The Bill Dana Show* (1963), which capitalized on the popularity of this character, was a one-season situation comedy in which José Jiménez went through life in a daze of simple-minded errors.

Chico and the Man (1974–1979) was one of the few prime-time network television series to feature characters, themes, and a context that were Latina/Latino. Chico Rodríguez, played by Freddie Prinze, teamed up in business with Ed Brown, played by Jack Albertson. The series was set in a Mexican barrio in East Los Angeles. Later in the 1970s and in the early 1980s there were two Latinos in major television roles. The first was Ricardo Montalbán as the aging, no longer active Latin lover in *Fantasy Island* (1978–1983), and the second was Erik Estrada as a California highway patrolman, Francis "Ponch" Poncherello, in *CHiPs* (1977–1983). Montalbán's accent made his Latin heritage clear, while Estrada's character's heritage was unclear, with little Latino context or background in the program aimed at clarification. From 1984 to 1989, Edward James Olmos played the Latino police lieutenant in *Miami Vice*, contrasting with the regularly appearing Latino drug lords (Wilson and Gutierrez 1995, 100–101). This began an interesting pattern in television cop shows that continued through the 1990s. The top-billed recurring characters in more recent crime shows such as *NYPD Blue*, *Law and Order*, and *NCIS* have almost all been white. But in each of these programs, the police lieutenant or, in the case of *NCIS*, the "Director," characters in positions of higher authority, have been people of color. These regularly appearing characters, however, are not the stars of the show whose personal lives are regularly uncovered and revealed in these series. In *NYPD Blue*, the first police lieutenant was an African American, Arthur Fancy (James McDaniel), followed by Esai Morales as Latino Tony Rodriguez. For most of the long life of *Law and Order*, the lieutenant was African American Lt. Anita Van Buren, played by S. Epatha Merkerson, and the current director in *NCIS* is African American Leon Vance, played by Rocky Carroll.

Actors Jimmy Smits and Benjamin Bratt brought a new kind of "Latin lover" to the small screen, both with great crossover appeal. Smits was born in the United States; his father was Surinamese of Dutch descent and his mother was Puerto Rican. Smits, who self-identifies as Puerto Rican, first appeared in *L.A. Law* (1986–1994) as Víctor Sifuentes, a Mexican American lawyer and one of the major characters in an ensemble cast. While the character's ethnic and racial identity was always clear, the women in his life were usually white and there was almost no mention of any racial context or barriers or problems he faced. Later, Smits became one of the two main characters on *NYPD Blue* (1994–2004). As Bobby Simone, he continued to be the hot love and sex interest on the program, but neither his surname nor his character development was specific about his ethnic identity, heritage, or any racial issues or conflict he might face. Once again, his love interest and eventual wife was a white woman (Internet Movie Database).

Once more we look to what critics call one of the most well-written TV series of all time with an extraordinary ensemble of actors, *The West Wing*. Another interesting and somewhat baffling set of questions about race, ethnicity, and identity is raised by the role Jimmy Smits played in the last two years of *The West Wing*, in contrast to Martin Sheen's role throughout the series' six-season run. Sheen's role was as the progressive and likable U.S. president Josiah "Jed" Bartlett, a highly complex character who frequently struggles with the conflict between the value he places on integrity and ethics and the demands of the politics of his party, reelection, and ultimately his job.

Bartlett is decidedly white and his home state in the series is Vermont. As noted in Table 5.2, Sheen's birth name is Ramón Antonio Gerardo Estévez and both of his parents were immigrants, his mother from Ireland and his father from Spain. Given the current way that the U.S. Census categorizes people who are Latina/Latino or Hispanic, Sheen would technically be white, since both of his parents are white and European, so he would have some choices on the census form. There is no little box for Irish, but Sheen could choose to identify his ethnicity as Latino or Hispanic. As we have already seen, Sheen has almost always played roles that are white and non-Latino. At the same time, thanks to his Spanish father, he has also won several awards for acting by ALMA, the Latino organization that recognizes strong achievement in the entertainment industry by Latinos as well as for roles or content that provides educational information about Latinos.

In the last two seasons of *The West Wing*, Jimmy Smits played the role of Matthew Santos, a Latino senator from Texas who eventually runs for U.S. president and wins. Thus, in the fictional world of *The West Wing*, Matt Santos is the first Latino president.

In the last season of *The West Wing* (1999–2006), ironically, Latino actor Martin Sheen plays outgoing white president Jed Bartlett to incoming Latino president Matthew Santos (Jimmy Smits), conveyed by the replacement of Bartlett's photo with Santos's. Did the eras in which Sheen and Smits entered show business impact the openness of their Latino identity and the kind of roles that were available to them? *(Source: Courtesy of Getty Images. Copyright © 2012 NBC Universal, Inc. Used by permission of Getty Images.)*

As a candidate, Santos struggles with the choices he needs to make about how, when, and where to assert his ethnicity: when to use it to attract votes and when to downplay it. He also struggles with critical political issues such as immigration; he feels strongly that Mexican American and other Central and South American immigrants have been treated poorly and differently from their European white counterparts. For Santos, that is a nonnegotiable position. His handlers on the campaign trail, however, see it differently. They try to convince Santos that he can take that position when he is president, but if he takes it as a candidate, he will alienate a substantial number of Democrats and will never be elected president.

The complexities of the lives and choices of these two actors are oddly parallel to those of the roles they each filled so completely and expertly on *The West Wing*. And the complicated questions about race, ethnicity, personal and political choices, and identity have no easy answers. As you begin to think this through, try on one more question.

Would any of these issues be discussed if the parents of one of these actors were both white and one identified most strongly as ethnically Croatian? Would the issue be different for an actor who, just before World War II when much of the world and many U.S. citizens considered Jews as a race, had a father who was white, of French heritage, and a grandmother, also white and of French heritage, who was Jewish? As we discussed in Chapter 4, race is a political and a social construct, as shown simply by reviewing the ever-changing categories for race in the U.S. census forms.

We suggest that you ponder these questions and sit with the issues they raise for you as well as any cognitive dissonance that arises. Try not to seek definitive answers as you mull over these questions. Consider the thoughts and feelings they evoke. As you think about the varying choices that Jimmy Smits and Martin Sheen and their characters in *The West Wing* considered and made, did you judge any of these choices harshly? Did you find yourself strongly supporting other decisions they made? Did you find the whole issue of race, ethnicity, and Latino/Latina identity a confusing puzzle, unnecessary minutiae, or an important issue to consider? Did you find that some of your own prejudices and biases surfaced to surprise you? Given how few of us have actually learned about and discussed these issues in our families, with our friends, or in our schools, any or all of these responses are normal. The questions you ask can help you decide independently where you stand on these issues, whether you need to and want to get better informed, and/or whether you want to work to unravel any biases you find that you have.

Benjamin Bratt played the role of Detective Reynaldo "Rey" Curtis on *Law and Order* (1990–2010) from 1995–1999 and Dr. Jake Reilly on *Private Practice* (2007–2013) from 2011–2013. The audience does not know that "Rey" is short for Reynaldo. The only way to discover that is to search the Internet on sites such as the Internet Movie Database (IMDb.com) or Wikipedia (Wikipedia.org) or to have seen the few episodes where his full name and/or ethnicity were addressed. The spelling of his name, which the audience does not see, is one of the tip-offs to his Latino heritage. Occasionally, we see Curtis speaking in Spanish to witnesses or suspects or being called derogatory names (such as "beaner") by criminals. These are the only real and rare clues to his heritage. In *Private Practice*, Bratt plays the role of Dr. Jake Reilly, a decidedly Irish surname, which is not identified by race or ethnicity in that TV series.

Although Bratt has most frequently played the role of characters who are explicitly or implicitly Latino, with heritage that is indigenous Peruvian Indian on his mother's side and white of German and English descent on his father side, he has wider racial and ethnic options in the roles he selects. The roles he has played have been Latino, Anglo, and ambiguous; in his off-screen life, he has been a strong advocate and activist in organizations and issues affecting Native Americans and has received acting awards from Latino organizations such as ALMA in the United States (IMDb). Perhaps his multiethnic heritage and diverse life experiences position Bratt to play roles that are not necessarily racially ambiguous, but rather reflect the experiences of many multiracial individuals in the United States who are often asked the curious and offensive question, "What are you?"

"With a growth rate of 102 percent from 1990 to 2006, the Hispanic market has the highest growth rate of any other ethnic group in the United States" (Allied Media Corp.

2008). By 2004, Latina/Latino purchasing power had reached nearly $700 billion (*Hispanic Business Magazine* 2004). By 2012, this buying power had grown to $1 trillion with a projected growth to $1.5 trillion in the next five years (Nhan 2012). This rate of growth is almost three times greater than the national rate for the last decade. Latina/Latino disposable income was $699.78 billion in 2004 and is expected to keep growing proportionately. Despite this surge in population and buying power in the Latina/Latino community, network television has been slow in responding to such a significant market. One study of prime-time television of the 1988 season revealed that there were more extraterrestrial characters on television than Asians and Latinas/Latinos combined. In 1997, only 2.9 percent of network prime-time television characters were Latina/Latino (Gerbner 1998, 2). Another study of prime-time television from 1955 to 1986 indicated that 75 percent of Latina/Latino characters were villains as compared to 39 percent of white characters (Rodriguez 1997, 27).

Research conducted in 2010 revealed that prime-time television was still portrayed primarily as a black and white world.

In 2002, Eric Deggans of Hispanic Online.com reported an increasing number of Latino characters on prime-time television. According to Deggans, "This fall, for the first time in years, network TV will have two series featuring mostly Latina/Latino casts—The WB's *Greetings From Tucson* and ABC's *The George López Show*. And when the 2002–03 TV season debuts Sept. 23, about 5 percent of roles will feature Hispanic actors; from Adam Rodríguez in *CSI: Miami* to *Tucson*'s Julio Oscar Mechoso and *NYPD Blue*'s Esai Morales." The Conference on Latin American History (CLAH) explained this burst in roles was a direct result of activism and a "firestorm of criticism over lack of minority roles" during 2000 and 2001. This most likely was combined with a business awakening and a "firestorm" of overdue understanding of the growth potential for the market and buying power of the Latina/Latino community.

While the Latina/Latino percentage of the entire U.S. population was 14.8 percent, Latinas/Latinos on prime-time television appeared as only 5 percent of the prime-time population in 2007 (Advertising Age 2009). This is a significant underrepresentation of Latinos/Latinas in comparison to whites, whose TV representation was very close to their actual presence in the population, and to African Americans, who constituted 16 percent of the population but occupied prime-time television at a whopping 61 percent (Monk-Turner et al. 2010, 106).

What seems particularly odd about the underrepresentation of Latinas/Latinos in the 2007 prime-time television season is that marketing analyses and advertising agencies had already begun to figure out that Latinos watched television more than any other so-called "minority" group and that they had a tremendous collective buying power.

Activists and researchers during that time analyzed a great deal of information regarding this incongruence, arriving at no easy answers. One possibility that has been historically true for other disenfranchised groups that have slowly moved into TV neighborhoods is that for the overwhelmingly white TV writers and producers, Latinos may be virtually invisible in their lives and thus often absent from their programs. Overt and covert discrimination in the parallel universe of prime time may also render the burgeoning

Latino market equally invisible. An economic factor that continues to contribute to the low numbers of Latinos on prime-time TV is that many Latinos have a strong loyalty to Spanish-language TV and that executives in network TV programming, having assessed that loyalty, see no reason to increase the number of Latino characters (Advertising Age 2009; Monk-Turner et al. 2010, 106).

By 2008, Latinas/Latinos were the largest so-called minority in the United States. With the population hovering at 45 million or 15 percent of the 2008 U.S. population, this group only comprised 6.4 percent of the 2008 TV network population (National Latino Media Council 2009; Screen Actors Guild Awards 2009). Given this disparity between the Latino percentage of the U.S. population and the Latino presence on prime-time network television, it was surprising that the National Latino Media Council (NLMC) reported "incremental progress at all four networks in terms of American Latinos" (National Latino Media Council 2009, 1).

The NLMC provides regular reports about each network's progress in providing programs with Latino/Latina characters and themes; in opting for complex Latino characters rather than resorting to simple stereotypes that provide easy laughs, familiarity, and comfort for the TV audience; and in advancing the understanding of the diversity and depth within the Latino community. The NLMC commended ABC for being "more successful than any other network in promoting Latino actors on scripted shows" (National Latino Media Council 2009, 2). Some of the most impressive roles were those of Sara Ramirez as Dr. Callie Torres in *Grey's Anatomy*, Eva Longoria in *Desperate Housewives*, and America Ferrara in the megahit *Ugly Betty*. The NLMC gave high praise to ABC for *Ugly Betty*: "It is these types of roles that make a difference for our children, teens and young adults. This program shines as an example of one that employs a large number of Latinos and addresses issues that speak to and about the American Latino community in a unique and thoughtful way" (National Latino Media Council 2009, 2).

Modern Family (2009–) pokes fun at age, ethnicity, race, sexual identity, and class. A naturally voluptuous woman, Sofia Vergaro as Gloria Delgado-Pritchett is not immune from the satire. The character's exaggerated Spanish accent and equally exaggerated display of cleavage initially qualify her as one of the conventional stereotypes of Latinas as curvaceous, passionate, oversexed, and seductive. Her TV son Manny Delgado (Rico Rodriguez), an unusually smart and sophisticated child, offers an alternative to the Latina bombshell stereotype. In one episode, Manny takes on a business project as part of a school assignment. He becomes so immersed in it that even while his family is at Disneyland, he is in business attire and constantly on a cell phone cutting deals, with big-time businessman talk. There are several strategies to evaluate ethnic and racial stereotypes on prime-time television. Three of these strategies can be applied to *Modern Family* and the character of Sofia Delgado-Pritchett in the form of the following questions:

- Are the physical features and personality of the character intentionally exaggerated not in order to perpetuate stereotypes, but rather to mock and satirize them, permitting the audience to laugh and be entertained while understanding just how absurd these caricatures are?

Ugly Betty (2006–2010): At left is sweet, smart, and hardworking Betty Suarez (America Ferrara), who challenges some of the classic Latin stereotypes in her role as a secretary working at *Mode*, a high-fashion magazine, where Wilhelmina Slater (at right, played by Vanessa Williams) is the norm—thin, beautiful, and glamorous. *(Source: Courtesy of Getty Images. Copyright © 2006 American Broadcasting Companies, Inc. Used by permission of Getty Images. Photographer/© ABC/Getty Images.)*

- Are there a sufficient number of diverse characters in the series evaluated and on prime-time TV in general to allow audiences to observe and understand that people in a particular group, in this case Latina/Latino, have a wide range of personalities, occupations, physical appearances, and so on? If the answer to this question is yes, then the exaggerated portrayal of Gloria Delgado-Pritchett is no more of a problem than the exaggeration of white characters such as Kramer (Michael Richards) on *Seinfeld* or the three white women from Los Angeles in *Hot in Cleveland*.
- If the program creator's intent is to exaggerate characters in order to promote satire, is the sense of irony and both the humor and social criticism embedded in it accessible

enough for most members of the audience to easily detect? In *Modern Family*, there is a broad exaggeration of other characters, including Gloria's gay stepson Mitchell Pritchett (Jesse Tyler Ferguson) and his partner Cameron Tucker (Eric Stonestreet), that emphasizes the ironic humor aimed not at particular groups or stereotypes but at the absurdity of stereotypes. Is the brush of satire visible enough to most viewers so they do not miss the joke and find that they are laughing at what they believe to be the accurate depiction of Latinas and gay men?

The last question is particularly tricky to answer and depends, in large part, on a convergence of factors that is one of the major tenets of this book. Our personal experience with or without Latinos in our communities, combined with what we learned in school about the contribution and accomplishments of Latinos, will converge with exposure to media content involving Latinos, forming the combination of information or misinformation that we take in and believe to be true about Latinos. The wider and deeper our personal experience, formal education, and popular media exposure regarding Latinas/ Latinos, the less likely we are to be taken in by media stereotypes.

Sofia Vergara, who is from Colombia, South America, made a comment at the 2013 Academy Award television program that demonstrates her own tongue-in-cheek awareness of the use of her appearance as part of the satire of her *Modern Family* alter ego, Gloria. When an interviewer asked Vergara how her parents felt about her becoming an actor, she replied that her disapproving father said that being an actor was the same as being a prostitute. Vergara recalls responding to him by saying that since her "big boobs" already made her look like a "hooker," she might as well go into acting.

Organizations that are strong advocates for representative numbers of people of color in prominent on-screen television roles; prominent off-screen roles such as writers, directors, and producers; and meaningful network diversity programs to increase representative employment across the board walk a fine line between criticizing the slow progress of the networks toward these goals and working with them to encourage their partnership in meeting these goals. Ideally, it would be beneficial to educate network executives and other TV decision makers about why it is important that the Latino TV population closely match the Latino population in the United States and how equally important it is to demonstrate the complexity and diversity of Latino characters and to discontinue the tired and destructive old stereotypes. In a perfect TV world, this type of education, awareness, and advocacy would develop strong, credible studies showing how low representation and stereotypes deeply affect Latino adults and children in the audience as well as non-Latinos. And ultimately, in this parallel world, with the brilliant and patient presentation of the advocates, the executives would understand how a steady diet of this biased misinformation in TV can potentially perpetuate bias in the thinking and action of non-Latino audiences and often show up in Latinas and Latinos as involuntary internalized racism. The happy ending to this fictional story would be the enthusiastic willingness of the TV industry to work with members and leaders of the Latino community to determine the types of scripts, themes, and characters that would allow audiences to see the breadth in the Latino community. Rather than create distorted and destructive images, they would opt to find creative and interesting ways to develop plots and story lines and to paint complex portraits of Latinos with a wide range of values, personalities, and jobs. Some Latina/Latino characters would be smart, honest, and well-meaning; others would be dishonest, egotistical, and hurtful to people in their TV story. And just as people do in real life, some of these characters would demonstrate their potential to grow and change, while others would be violent or self-destructive.

Returning to reality, it is clear that up to this point, much of the television industry's response to advocacy, education, activism, and constructive criticism regarding human diversity of all kinds has been far less of an impetus for program change than demographics and dollar signs.

Is it beginning to sound like a broken record? Recall the section in Chapter 4 on reconstructing knowledge. Remember the histories of conquest, destruction, and violence; remember the laws and policies that reduced opportunities for citizenship and full American rights. Juxtapose this information with the entertainment images and themes that are scarce and, when available, just as likely to be minor, stereotyped, and simple as to be major, nonstereotyped, and complex. American Indian characters are most likely to be invisible. While Asian and Pacific Islander and Latina/Latino characters such as *Grey's Anatomy*'s Cristina Yang and Callie Torres are prominent and complex characters, their onscreen life partners and best friends are white, and they rarely, if ever, have to face either individual prejudice or racial barriers to their personal and professional success. These kinds of characters and themes are choreographed to assimilate in such a way that allows the characters to be treated as white and keep audiences in a comfort zone that discourages any observation or analysis of racial tension or discrimination.

Once again, this permits viewing audiences, with little personal experience or educational exposure to groups that are racially or ethnically different from them, to conclude that there are few problems. One of the dangers in this conclusion is that it almost always implies a subtle political message that is drenched in racism. That message is that if these TV Latina/Latino characters can gain financial and career success and can compete with and get along with white people on television, then it must be the fault of the "real" Latina/Latino people out there if they are stuck in poverty and dead-end jobs or unemployment. The trend of blaming poverty and racism on its targets has been a phenomenon since the late 1970s. While entertainment media cannot bear the full brunt of these disturbing messages and misinformation, popular media often perpetuate and reinforce a set of beliefs that denies structural racism in the United States. If a society cannot see the presence of individual and institutional racism and the consequences of racism, it is exceedingly difficult to address it and seek solutions.

AFRICAN AMERICANS IN ENTERTAINMENT MEDIA

African Americans and Film

The 1988 film *Mississippi Burning* was loosely based on the 1964 disappearance and murder of three civil rights workers. The film received one Academy Award for cinematography and was nominated for six others, including Best Actor, Best Supporting Actress, Best Director, and Best Picture; it grossed over $34 million (Internet Movie Database 1999). This film was controversial when it was released because, while it was based on the actual disappearance of local black activist James Chaney and white, Jewish activists Andrew Goodman and Michael Schwerner, it deliberately deviated from important historical elements of the story. Although the film is now twenty-five-plus years old, it provides an excellent opportunity to analyze some of the less than visible ways that popular media can revise the history of race in the United States.

The film powerfully depicts the racial climate in the Deep South during the Freedom Summer of 1964. Visceral, vicious, and violent racism dominates the screen and is relentless and stunning. The feel of racism in this small town is palpable and frightening. For most viewers with little experience or education about the details of this chapter in U.S. history, from the very beginning the film creates a sense of outrage at the depth of racism in the 1960s. Yet by the end, the film tells the uninformed viewer that justice was done and that as a result of what happened in this small town in Mississippi . . . things did get better.

On closer examination, we can see several aspects of the film that are clearly incompatible with historical truth. First, a simple scan of the characters reveals that all of the major characters are white. While a few African American characters in smaller roles show courage, all of the major heroes are white and, in fact, all of the villains are white. There is diversity among the white characters; they are not all the same or similar. The white characters are the primary characters that display any complexity. Mrs. Pell and FBI agents Ward and Anderson exhibit a disdain for discrimination and demonstrate bravery amid violence and considerable danger to themselves. With the exception of one young black man, the black citizens of this small town are portrayed as frightened into passivity. Anderson imports a mysterious African American "special" agent who kidnaps and graphically threatens to castrate the town's white mayor until he provides names and information about Klan members who were there the night that the three civil rights activists disappeared. The use of this special agent works as a dramatic metaphor, a tale of truth-seeking by turning racism upside down. While an African American man holding the power of life or brutal death over a white mayor does provide a satisfying sense of sweet revenge wrapped up neatly as poetic justice, it was a preposterous scenario for the times and simply did not happen. Yet this particular scene is one of several that adds up to developing the film's "truth" that, ultimately, racism was the loser during that horrible time of violence and that, using a variety of tactics, the good guys won and the bad guys were either run out of town or sent to prison.

What is wrong with this picture? The British film director, Alan Parker, claimed that the film could not have been made even in the 1980s if the heroes were not white. He believed that audiences could accept the premise of racism in the film if those who solved the disappearance of the civil rights workers and worked for justice were white (Kempley 1988, 1). It is debatable whether the film would have reached such a wide audience or grossed as much at the box office with African American characters in the lead roles. But the issue of what would make the film more profitable begs the central questions: how did *Mississippi Burning* revise history and what impact did that have on the audiences that viewed this controversial, yet widely popular and critically acclaimed film?

While there may have been individual white FBI agents who were disturbed by racism and driven to overcome racial injustices in the 1960s and beyond, the director of the FBI, J. Edgar Hoover, had a different agenda. Hoover developed a counterintelligence program called COINTELPRO in which he targeted activists in the civil rights movement (as well as other movements for change), including Martin Luther King Jr., to undermine their efforts to transform and eradicate racism. Hoover's strategies included planting agents within activist organizations and spreading rumors of interracial sex, sexual promiscuity, and connections to communism among civil rights leaders in order to create chaos within the organizations and to diminish their credibility in the communities where they worked. This is the same FBI that is portrayed as showing universal and overwhelming zeal for justice in the film.

In addition, black churches and civil rights organizations played an enormous role in the civil rights movement in small southern towns. Black and white students regularly committed acts of great courage as they organized voter registration drives and participated in sit-ins and other demonstrations to end segregation and Jim Crow laws. Black residents knew they were risking their lives through the simple but courageous act of registering to vote and actually voting. Yet in the film, most of the black characters are part of the background and scenery: simple, fearful, and passively allowing the heroic white FBI agents to seek justice on their behalf.

The characters of FBI agents Ward and Anderson and the racist deputy sheriff's wife, Mrs. Pell, are complex and interesting, and the film itself creates a powerful sense of the horrors of racism. But it also creates illusion and misinformation. The uninformed viewer leaves this film with the same feelings that the old Westerns evoked. We are invited to believe that even the worst injustices can be made right by the good guys in authority and that the public authority (this time the FBI instead of the old Westerns' sheriff's office) is dedicated to lawfulness and equality. The film suggests that black people were in need of saving and had been frightened away from the possibility of standing up for themselves and being heroes in their own liberation. "It views the black struggle from an all-white perspective. And there's something of the demon itself in that. It's the right story, but with the wrong heroes. There's this nagging feeling that it begins where it ought to have ended—with the deaths of the three young activists" (Kempley 1988, 3).

The issue of poetic or dramatic license in this film is worth mentioning. Dramatic license is the right of the artist—in this case, the filmmaker—to take liberties with facts in order to create art. Certainly, director Alan Parker had the right to make the decisions to develop the film he wanted. He never claimed that it was a documentary; it was fiction based on a real story. The problem is that most of us have not been taught and do not know the real story of Chaney, Schwerner, and Goodman and other important aspects of the civil rights movement; hence the version of the "truth" in *Mississippi Burning* may very easily make its way into that vacant spot of our education and become what we believe to be real and true.

A closer look at the history of the portrayal of African American characters and themes demonstrates how the kind of misinformation and distortion in *Mississippi Burning* could have evolved. Edward Guerrero identifies five chronological phases of African American images in film. These include the stereotypes of the plantation genre that emerged in films from 1915 to 1965 (*Birth of a Nation, Gone With the Wind, The Littlest Rebel*); contemporary revisionist images of slavery (*The Color Purple*); the civil rights movement, black power, and blaxploitation films from 1969 to 1974 (*Shaft, Superfly, Sweet Sweetback's Baadasssss Song*); Hollywood conservative backlash films from 1975 to 1989 (*Caddyshack, Stir Crazy*); and the resurgent boom of black films in the 1990s (*Boyz 'N the Hood, Do the Right Thing*) (Guerrero 1993).

Examining some of these films makes more sense when placed in a broader economic and social context. It is clear that the film industry responded at various points, such as the 1960s and the 1990s, to calls for social justice and demands for inclusion of African Americans in both the industry and the content of the films themselves. It is equally clear that the film industry is a business that has evolved through its history and has been driven primarily by economics and profit. For example, from 1964 to 1974 there was a boom in the production of cheaply made films with both black casts and black content. On the surface, it may seem that the civil rights and black power movements' call for African American inclusion in film triggered this growth. In 1963, film stars such as Marlon Brando, Burt Lancaster, and Paul Newman joined the NAACP and the ACLU to attack racism in the film industry. In 1969, the Justice Department announced plans to sue six film studios and two television networks for discrimination in hiring (Guerrero 1993, 82). This is a significant but only partial picture.

Concurrent with developments in the civil rights movement and calls for more participation and fewer stereotypes of African Americans in film were other developments in the industry. Hollywood's once united audience was becoming increasingly fragmented. The huge epics that Hollywood had once relied on as a primary source of profit were no longer predictably successful formulas. The average weekly box office draw sank to $15.8 million in 1971 as compared to $90 million in the years immediately after World War II. African Americans comprised 10 to 15 percent of the 1971 population and 30 percent of the film-going audience. White flight to the suburbs left movie theaters in the cities whose audiences were largely African American. As industry executives were trying to figure out how to recoup audiences and profit, a strategy dropped itself into their collective lap.

In 1971, Melvin Van Peebles scraped together $500,000 in funds and cast himself and friends in *Sweet Sweetback's Baadasssss Song*, taking only three weeks to shoot the film. By the end of one year, *Sweet Sweetback's Baadasssss Song* had grossed $10 million and Hollywood had stumbled onto a winning formula that it repeated many times during this period. In Van Peebles's film, the lead character was a violent rapist, but he also challenged white oppression and won (Guerrero 1993, 86).

The images and stereotypes in *Sweet Sweetback's Baadasssss Song* (and other films of this genre, such as *Superfly*) of violent, supercharged sexuality, drugs, and crime were highly controversial in the African American community and were challenged by many civil rights groups during the years in which these films were popular. But the so-called "blaxploitation" era of film only ended when these films were no longer economically viable for the film industry.

According to film scholar Guerrero, "The black image on the commercial screen, principally Hollywood's ideology of racial domination and difference [,] . . . constructs black people as other and subordinate, while it naturalizes white privilege as the invisible but sovereign 'norm'" (1993, 5). But African Americans have not simply been victims of Hollywood. Because of the fluctuating market for film and the dynamics of economics and audience over the years, both mainstream and independent filmmakers have occasionally created complex African American characters and themes that challenge the **dominant ideology** that Guerrero describes. In this section, we'll examine examples of both the "ideology of racial domination and difference" as well as some of the more complex breakthrough roles and films.

But the film *Birth of a Nation* was most certainly not one of those breakthrough films. In D.W. Griffith's *Birth of a Nation* (1915), a pattern of portraying blacks as inferior was established that would last for decades (Wilson and Gutierrez 1995, 74). While this film used techniques that made it a film classic, it also glorified the Ku Klux Klan. The film grossed $18 million and was denounced by the NAACP for its racist portrayal of blacks:

> In its . . . presentation of the KKK as heroes and Southern blacks as villains . . . , it appealed to white Americans who subscribed to the mythic, romantic view . . . of the Old Plantation South. . . . The film also thematically explored two great American issues: interracial sex and marriage, and the empowerment of blacks. Ironically, . . . the film's major black roles . . . were stereotypically played and filled by white actors—in blackface. (Dirks 1999)

While *Birth of a Nation* was a silent film, it was quite loud in its establishment of two basic slave stereotypes. One glorified the "good old days of slavery" when slaves were portrayed as docile and content as compared to the second stereotype, which depicted dangerous and insolent freed slaves. These images on the screen were particularly dangerous in the context of its 1915 release in the middle of a period in which segregation was being solidified and lynching was at its height. While a direct cause-and-effect link between the film and its era's violent racism cannot be conclusively established, it is clear that the public's tolerance of the Klan drove its membership to 5 million, the highest ever, by 1924 (Guerrero 1993, 13).

Other early silent films such as *Wooing and Wedding of a Coon* (1905) and *The Nigger* (1915) continued these hate-filled stereotypes of African Americans (Wilson and Gutierrez 1995, 75). By contemporary standards, even their titles seem preposterous—unabashedly and outrageously racist. But the acceptability of such titles and the images of blacks that were portrayed reflect the widespread acceptance of anti-black racism during the early twentieth century.

African Americans and their allies of other races protested these images and stereotypes with few concrete results. A notable exception to the minstrel-like images of African American characters can be seen in the counter-narrative filmmaking of Oscar

Mischeaux, a black novelist, who became an insightful writer, producer, and director of independent films depicting characters and themes that challenged prevailing stereotypes (Butters 2000). Although Mischeaux was singularly talented and prolific, he was not the only pioneering black person making films in the early twentieth century. William Foster formed a short-lived movie company in 1910 (Burton 2010), and Spencer Williams (later to gain fame as Andy in the 1950s *Amos 'n Andy* television series) also wrote, directed, and starred in a number of films (Altman 1997). Moreover, several African American women were active in early efforts to make films that presented a more accurate portrayal of black life. Among these pioneering female filmmakers were Eloyce King Patrick Gist, Tressie Sounders, and Maria P. Williams (Morgan and Dixon 2013). Nevertheless, it was not until the United States was on the brink of World War II that mainstream white Hollywood began to rethink the images and stereotypes of slavery and race.

The 1930 self-regulation of the film industry through the Hays Code (the same code that governed the depiction of sex and sexual orientation) was explicitly racist. "It prohibited scenes and subjects which, however distantly, suggested miscegenation as desirable, thereby building a color barrier in Hollywood's dream world as rigid as the color line in America's real world. By casting the issue of racial mixing in black and white terms, the Code proclaimed an assimilationist ideal for European ethnic groups and a segregationist ideal for the 'colored folks'" (Guerrero 1993, 17).

During the Hollywood heyday of 1930–1945, the stereotypes of blacks in film began to change from the early images spawned by hate to images of happy slaves and servants. African American actors and musicians such as Lena Horne and Louis Armstrong were cast as musicians in films in which there was little interaction with other characters. Prior to World War II, black characters were cast as people who knew their place and whose "inferiority" was used to make audiences laugh. The character known as Stepin Fetchit was the classic example of this demeaning treatment of black actors and black characters. In the 1920s, black comedian Lincoln Theodore Monroe Andrew Perry joined with comic Ed Lee, creating an act they called "Step and Fetch It." Perry later went solo under the name of Stepin Fetchit. The roles he played in film used some of the most offensive and degrading stereotypes of black people, including laziness, sloth, and slow-wittedness, to create comic effect (Bogle 1989, 4). This character clearly knew his place in society, and the films with Stepin Fetchit underscored the subordination of blacks. Even today, the word "Stepnfetchit" is a term used to name the most insidious black stereotypes.

The young black characters and actors in "Our Gang" also embodied demeaning stereotypes. In *The Little Rascals* (*Our Gang*) films of the 1920s, the African American characters of Buckwheat, Farina, and Stymie were immersed in humor that often depended on rolling their eyes to depict exaggerated surprise, fear, or disdain and the use of a caricature of black dialect. These portrayals regularly crossed the border into stereotypes. Yet positioned side-by-side with these blatant stereotypes were the depiction and normalization of interracial friendships between black and white children that were highly unusual for the times. Like the early Latinos who worked as silent film directors, this was an anomaly, a case of "both/and" in which the most offensive stereotypes coexisted with the most benign and ordinary relationships that defied stereotypes.

The 1935 Shirley Temple films *The Little Colonel* and *The Littlest Rebel* were other examples of both/and. They were both therapeutic Depression-era escapist films, featuring Shirley Temple, who delighted 1930s audiences, but containing dehumanizing racial images as well. In both films, Shirley Temple's character interacted and danced with an African American man, the talented actor, singer, dancer Bill Robinson, who was portrayed as a childlike servant, preserving the early slave stereotype of docility and dependency (Guerrero 1993, 26).

Set during the Civil War, *The Littlest Rebel* story centers around Virgie Cary (Shirley Temple) and her father, a Confederate officer who sneaks back to his rundown plantation to see his family and gets arrested. A compassionate Yankee helps him escape and is captured and sentenced to hang. With the help of terminal cuteness on Virgie's part and some delightful song and dance with "Uncle Billy" (Bill Robinson), the unlikely pair beg President Lincoln to intercede and stop the execution. There is certainly an engaging and inevitable cuteness to the film when Shirley Temple is on the screen, and the singing and dancing of Temple and Robinson display talent and charm. Ultimately, the central and most disquieting message of this film falls under the category of what Guerrero refers to as revisionist history of slavery.

The multiple dimensions of the stereotype of "Uncle Billy" are a large part of this disturbing revision. He is the quintessential happy slave, who is delighted with his "little miss" and will almost always do whatever she, albeit with charm, tells him to do. The big grin never leaves his face unless it is for an occasional equally broad and caricatured frown. Even the name "Uncle Billy" suggests an equal and highly unlikely family relationship that conveniently forgets that the white part of the "family" is free and the black part of the family is enslaved, even to the finest detail in which Vergie calls him "Uncle Billy" and he calls her Miz Vergie or Miz Carey. It is unlikely that any but the youngest of audiences would believe this film to be historically accurate or true. But repeated messages such as these create the strange phenomenon in which audiences take in the information in a way that allows them to hold at least two contradictory thoughts simultaneously. Examples of two contradictory thoughts in relation to *The Littlest Rebel* are the following:

> I know that the period of slavery was harsh and cruel and dehumanizing, since even the kindest masters were nevertheless "masters" and owned other people, black people, exactly as if they were property.

and

> One of the sweet things about the Civil War days was how close some of the white families, and especially the children, were with their black slaves. The slaves were so delightfully childlike that they made wonderful company for the children and could sing and dance and play with them at their own level.

Generally, the insidious lies in the second statement are less than conscious for audience members, and only stray pieces of it are actively accessible. However, these are the very same stray pieces that, conscious or unconscious, can stubbornly stick in our minds and pose as the truth.

A word about Bill Robinson and the other black actors, such as Willie Mae Taylor and Billie Thomas, who played Buckwheat in Hal Roach's *The Little Rascals* (*Our Gang*) film series, and Ed Lee, who played the film character Stepin Fetchit, is in order here. Over the years, these actors and other black actors who played film and television characters, roles that embodied the quintessential and insidious black stereotypes, have received criticism for taking these roles, creating and perpetuating misinformation and lies that infantilized and vilified African Americans. This criticism is misguided. These actors were seeking jobs, acting was their field, and these were the jobs that were available to them They did, however, open doors and were the first African Americans to pave the way for the possibilities of more dignified roles for talented actors such as Lena Horne and Sidney Poitier, and record-breaking Academy Award winners Denzel Washington, Halle Berry, Jamie Fox, Forest Whitaker, Morgan Freeman, Jennifer Hudson, Mo'Nique, and others.

After World War II, there was a transition in the portrayal of blacks. Stereotypes once again shifted and themes of discrimination began to emerge in films such as *Pinky* (1949) and *Blackboard Jungle* (1955). Sidney Poitier emerged as the actor who epitomized Hollywood's portrayal of black men during this time. He was intelligent and handsome, spoke standard and elegant English, was respectful and proud, and was usually depicted as asexual, presumably to prevent him from being threatening to both white women and the white men who might feel the need to protect them. In *Lilies of the Field* (1963), *Guess Who's Coming to Dinner* (1967), and *In the Heat of the Night* (1967), Poitier played characters that were good men who handled prejudice with dignity. His characters could be admired by any race and they posed no threat (Wilson and Gutierrez 1995, 87). The characters played by Poitier were often criticized for being so thoroughly assimilated that there was no trace of connection to the African American community or culture.

Still another shift of black characters occurred in the mid-1960s and early 1970s with the so-called blaxploitation films. These were action films featuring defiant black male heroes victorious over white people and sexually conquering black women. The year 1971 was a big year for these films. As mentioned previously, *Shaft* and *Sweet Sweetback's Baadasss Song* appealed primarily to black audiences and were also financially successful. Sweetback, played by Melvin Van Peebles, who also directed and produced the film, beats two white policemen after they brutalize a black suspect. An incongruous character who serves a both/and function, Sweetback is a dangerous, violent rapist, but also a courageous hero in that he stands up to white people, fearlessly disrupts racist business as usual, and wins.

These both/and scenarios and characters offer a complexity that can have different types of audience impact. For example, audiences can see Sweetback as a character that embodies the violence that may be endemic to the community or situation in which he was raised. Simultaneously, audiences may be able to interpret Sweetback's heroism and fierce and courageous anti-racism as an outcome of the same roots as his dangerous, criminal violence. This complexity requires an audience that is able to actually see structural racism and how it affects an individual in a way that creates negative internal messages and belief that can be translated into externally damaging behaviors. The both/and perspective is that elements of the so-called blaxploitation films also provided models, albeit flawed, of the possibility that African Americans can rise above the destructive images and messages to do good things in the world and contribute to making a better society.

Another of the quintessential blaxploitation films was the 1971 *Shaft*. Richard Roundtree's character, John Shaft, is a suave, handsome, and sexy black detective who according to the soundtrack is "a bad mother—shut yo' mouth." *Shaft* was produced by MGM for $1.2 million and grossed $10.8 million within a year (Guerrero 1993, 86).

The blaxploitation genre of film had ambiguity in both message and production and even in the name itself, a combination that touted African American economic success in film and also acknowledged the exploitation of African American images for profit on the screen. While they were widely publicized as black films, many of them were produced, written, and directed by whites. Some African Americans welcomed any film that portrayed defiant black characters who triumphed over white oppressors; other groups, such as the NAACP, denounced the repeated portrayal of blacks as drug pushers, pimps, and gangsters (Bogle 1994, 242). Despite all these drawbacks and stereotypes, these films were significant for the number of black actors they employed. This was to change once again in the 1980s.

By the early 1980s, roles for black actors and films with black themes once again became scarce. In 1974, at the height of the blaxploitation era, Hollywood produced a total of 295 films, 45 of which included primarily black themes or casts. In 1981, there were 240 Hollywood films and only six of them featured primarily African American characters or themes (Guerrero 1993, 107).

The 1980s featured complex images of African Americans as well as the remaking of old stereotypes. The theme of slavery was reconstituted in films such as *The Toy* (1982) in which Jackie Gleason actually "purchases" a black janitor (played by Richard Pryor) as a toy for his son because the man has made his son laugh (Guerrero 1993, 82). Critics generally panned *The Toy*. Some said it was a waste of the considerable talent of both Gleason and Pryor; others said that despite an attempt at ironic and perhaps twisted humor, the film was blatantly racist in its brazen replica of slavery in the act of a white man "buying" a black man. The *Rotten Tomatoes* cable program named *The Toy* as 1982's number one kids' movie that was inappropriate for children. Despite its poor reviews, tastelessness, and outright racism, the film earned about $14 million and was the fourteenth-highest-grossing film in 1982.

According to a 2005 *New York Times* obituary of Richard Pryor, he "unleashed a galaxy of street characters who traditionally had been embarrassments to most middle-class blacks and mere stereotypes to most whites. And he presented them so truthfully and hilariously that he was able to transcend racial boundaries and capture a huge audience of admirers in virtually every ethnic, economic and cultural group in America." Although Pryor received the Kennedy Center's Mark Twain Prize for humor in 1998, *The Toy* missed the mark of racial satire and lacked Pryor's usual sharp eye and even sharper tongue in slicing and dicing racism.

Films with African American characters shifted from African American themes and casts to the use of isolated superstars. The popularity of Richard Pryor, Eddie Murphy, and Whoopi Goldberg was on the rise. Films that appealed to both black and white audiences, so-called crossover films, became the norm.

These shifts took place in the context of Reaganism and the political backlash aimed at feminism, the civil rights movement, and **affirmative action**. Under Reagan's presidency, there was a political and social movement afoot to restore the United States after what some of the public perceived as a decline due to Watergate, Vietnam, and social change movements. Deregulation also characterized this period, and Hollywood was not immune to this trend. During the 1980s, the film industry steadily became part of larger conglomerates in which movies came to be viewed increasingly as "products" and film studios were owned and operated by people who had little or no expertise or experience in film.

The combination of the political climate and the changes in the corporate structure of the industry swept Hollywood into a conservative political backlash. By using the mix of new film technology and conservative ideology, the industry began to produce films that emphasized the triumph of the white working class, individualism, and the American Dream. Sylvester Stallone's *Rocky* exemplifies this trend. From 1977 to 1990, five *Rocky* films were produced and distributed (Guerrero 1993, 115).

The Color Purple (1985), directed by Steven Spielberg and based on the novel by Alice Walker, demonstrated an interesting mix of the 1980s trends. The film was one of the few during this time period with a predominantly African American cast, based on an original story written by an African American woman. But *The Color Purple* also converted the anti-racist themes of the novel into a mainstream film that in many significant ways reflected the dominant ideology.

In the novel, Walker explored abuse and internalized racism as experienced by Celie, Sophia, Mister, and Harpo. The male characters, Mister and Harpo, were abusive to black women, but were depicted as complex characters who "learned" to hate themselves and abuse women as a result of the emotional, psychological, and physical brutality of racism and the resulting internalized racism of parallel intensity and brutality. In the book, Mister begins to change at the end. Celie also forms a tender sexual relationship with Mister's lover, Shug, and the fullness of the two women's love for each other is expressed on many levels. In the novel, Shug rejects her father, a minister, and his church because they mimic white oppression.

In the film, little of this political consciousness remains. The black male characters are overly simple, and their abuse and cruelty to women, void of the political context, appears to be solely the result of individual character defects or evil. The relationship between Shug and Celie is tender but superficial, and their sexual relationship is reduced to one chaste kiss. At the film's climax, Shug symbolically leaves singing at a juke joint to go to her father's church in a way that symbolizes her return from immorality to the purity of the church. The only remaining image of racism is a confrontation between Sophia and the white mayor and his wife (Guerrero 1993, 51). Aside from this scene, the film erases racism from its center, and the blame for problems that African Americans face seems to be placed or, more accurately, misplaced primarily on the shoulders of African American men.

It is unlikely that the messages conveyed in the film were the result of sinister intentions or even full awareness on the part of Spielberg or others who made the shift from Walker's small but powerful book to the big screen. The original novel was filled with the characters' internal and external experiences, traumas, observations, and transformations, all centered on race and racism and often intertwined with the depiction of sexism. Most likely, the changes were designed to simplify some of the book's most subtle and complex elements in order to create larger-than-life characters and situations that would be visually and financially successful for the big screen. Intentionally or not, *The Color Purple*'s transition to film sacrificed much of the depth, subtlety, complexity, brutality, and persistently insidious manifestations and effects of racism.

The Color Purple grossed $94 million at the box office and almost $50 million in video rental (Internet Movie Database 1999). It starred Whoopi Goldberg and Danny Glover and was the film debut for Oprah Winfrey. Film critics were all over the place with *The Color Purple*. Some critics touted it as an extraordinary film that stayed true to the spirit of the book in reflecting the pain of racism and the triumph of the human spirit. Other critics said that it portrayed a brutal, misogynistic image of black men to the glorification of black women. Still others had political objections to the film because its message was about individualized racism and triumph rather than about systemic racism and organizational change (Bobo 1995, 54).

The careers of Richard Pryor and Whoopi Goldberg exemplify what was available to black stars in the 1980s. Both of their stand-up comedy routines were based on reflections of African American characters and culture and the hard-edged comic criticism of racism. But in film, Pryor's economically successful biracial buddy comedies with Gene Wilder (*Silver Streak* and *Stir Crazy*) featured Pryor teaching Wilder how to act black and scary. Dramatic and more complex roles for Pryor, such as *Blue Collar* (1978), were box office flops, and the lesson was not lost on Hollywood. So-called crossover films, attracting the broadest possible multiracial audience, became the central force of mainstream films with black characters. These biracial buddy films, featuring, for example, Eddie Murphy or Danny Glover in tandem with white actors such as Dan Aykroyd and Mel Gibson, became a genre of their own. These buddy films conveyed a fictional sense of racial equality through partnership while ignoring the more factual state of race relations. Once again, this sent a false message that all is well on the U.S. race front.

Eddie Murphy and Whoopi Goldberg continued to have wide crossover appeal to both black and white audiences through much of the 1990s. While Murphy played largely comedic roles, Goldberg's roles ranged from the comic *Sister Act* and *Sister Act II* in the early 1990s to the dramatic *The Color Purple* (1985), *Sarafina* (1992), and *Boys on the Side* (1995). Often both Murphy and Goldberg played the classic black "buddy," the only person of color in a film.

By the 1990s, several films emerged that examined life in black communities in central cities. In 1990 and 1991 alone, there were more films focused on African Americans than during the entire blaxploitation film period (Guerrero 1993, 159). This boom in African American films was kicked off by director Spike Lee's production of *She's Gotta Have It* (1986). Using what came to be known as "guerrilla cinema," Lee built on the successful formula of the blaxploitation era by making the film with his family and friends in twelve days for $175,000. The film grossed over $7 million (Guerrero 1993, 145). This film and several that followed were produced independently. This independence allowed Lee to create African American characters that were complex characters in their own right and represented a range of different types of individuals and a range of individual and structural manifestations of racism.

During the 1990s, other African American directors emerged, including John Single-ton, Robert Townsend, Charles Burnett, and Julie Dash. Some of the films they produced used Lee's guerrilla cinema tactics and were made and distributed as independents, while others were financed and produced through major studios. Ironically, the ability to use the best technology and financing through a major studio to produce a film that would be seen by a wide audience meant that these directors were under the constraints of the industry to produce a profitable product. The mainstream pressure to sell the product often meant diluting insurgent ideology that challenged stereotypes, the dominant ideology, and structural racism and replacing it with what the studios thought would sell.

Do the Right Thing (1989) and *Boyz 'N the Hood* (1991) were directed by Spike Lee and John Singleton, respectively. *Do the Right Thing* was financed by Universal Studios for $6.5 million and grossed $27.5 million. *Boyz 'N the Hood*, financed by Columbia, grossed $57.5 million. These films demonstrated the artistic and economic possibilities of the collaboration between African American directors or screenwriters and major studios. Both films introduced complex themes and frankly explored racism, using contemporary rap music as background and as political commentary.

Do the Right Thing takes place on one hot summer day in a New York neighborhood in which relationships, racial dynamics, bigotry, and confusion are portrayed among white Italians, Asians, and African Americans in the community. The poverty, heat, and racism create a pressure cooker that ultimately explodes. This was a warning from Lee that if poverty and anti-black racism are not seriously addressed, urban racial tensions could become volatile and even violent. Lee addressed racism in the exchanges between the white Italian pizza shop owners and their black customers and in the ownership of stores in the neighborhood by people of Asian heritage. He also employed a sort of modern-day Greek chorus of older African American men hanging out in the neighborhood and commenting on the action and relationships. The danger of the film losing its political edge rested in the risk that the audience would reduce complex social issues to disputes between individuals. But Lee reduced this risk with his closing image of a handshake between Martin Luther King Jr. and Malcolm X, suggesting that it is the combination of their political approaches that offers the promise of racial justice. Some critics and audiences saw *Do the Right Thing* not as a warning of what could happen if racism and poverty are not addressed, but rather as a threat. These variant interpretations largely rested on whether an audience member walked into the theater with a fear of the consequences of racism or with a fear of African Americans.

Boyz 'N the Hood is set in South Central Los Angeles, where gang and police violence are depicted as regular occurrences. The film follows a young Tré Styles (Cuba Gooding Jr.), his relationship with his father, Furious (Laurence Fishburne), and their effort to fight the violence and damage of racism while living in the midst of it. *Boyz* was also the film debut of rapper Ice Cube as Doughboy, a young man whose violence is portrayed as a complex but inevitable result of the collision of personal and societal factors.

In one powerful scene, the complexity and systemic nature of racism is explained by Furious to Tré and his friends. Furious wants these young men to understand the source of the guns and drugs that have invaded their lives, the neighborhood redevelopment and gentrification, and who benefits and who suffers from it. This portrayal of a wiser and certainly imperfect older man, explaining how institutionalized racism operates, where the power is located, and how it is destroying black neighborhoods and damaging black families, is an extraordinary piece of filmmaking. Furious is respected by Tré and his friends; he is still young enough and hip enough to communicate with them about music and women; but he also has an incisive analysis of racism that he explains to these young men so that they will not forget either his goodness or their own and will be able to make decisions that move away from the sinkhole that structural racism and its unwilling partner, internalized racism, create. As the audience is also educated by Furious, those in the audience who have never heard racism described that way can try it on in the context of the movie and perhaps become open to the possibility of making different choices about beliefs and behavior regarding racism.

Tré, Furious, Doughboy, and his brother Ricky are all complex characters that demonstrate varying degrees of internalized racism and varying methods of fighting the internal and external impact of racism. Despite the complexity of male characters and the sophisticated portrayal of racism in *Do the Right Thing* and *Boys 'N the Hood*, both movies paint one-dimensional portraits of black women. In *Do the Right Thing*, the women are the main character's sister and girlfriend; the first is an archetypical virgin and the second is stereotypically highly sexed and sexy. In *Boyz 'N the Hood*, the women are in the background as mothers and girlfriends. Ricky and Doughboy's mother is shown to favor Ricky and verbally and physically abuse Doughboy—one explanation the film provides for Doughboy's violence. Still another mother in the "hood" is shown as a crackhead, abusing and neglecting her children. Tré's mother and girlfriend are shown as "good women," but one-dimensional. The range and depth of the women in the film are thin and shallow compared to the depth and complexity of the male characters.

The 1990s was an interesting decade for black characters and racial themes in film. Actors Denzel Washington, Morgan Freeman, Wesley Snipes, Samuel L. Jackson, Laurence Fishburne, Eddie Murphy, Whoopi Goldberg, Angela Bassett, and Whitney Houston played a range of characters from Malcolm X to the "nutty professor" and from Tina Turner to a revolutionary teacher in South Africa. Some of these actors and their films have received critical acclaim, such as Denzel Washington in *Glory* and Angela Bassett's portrayal of Tina Turner in *What's Love Got to Do With It*. Some of these films have complex characters and themes that wove in race and racism, and others are simpler stories of love and sex or comic relief. In addition to these mainstream films, there were also independent films, such as Julie Dash's 1992 production of *Daughters of the Dust*, a rich and textured story of black families and black women, critically acclaimed and economically unsuccessful.

For all its flaws, the 1995 film *White Man's Burden* took some interesting risks and twists on the theme of racism and power in black and white relations. Written and directed by Japanese American Desmond Nakano and starring Harry Belafonte and John Travolta, the film invites the audience to suppose what would happen if African Americans were in power in the United States. Some of the image reversals in the film cause viewers' heads to spin as we begin to ponder what we have come to consider as "normal." In one scene, wealthy African Americans sponsor a benefit for inner-city white children who appear in their ragtag clothes as their black benefactors talk about how cute they are. In another scene, a young white boy channel surfs to find that most of the TV characters are black. And when the boy goes with his father to select his birthday present, the only "cool" action figures are black.

As we approached the millennium and beyond, a relative explosion of African Americans in film hit Hollywood and movie theater circuits. A scan of the top box office hits in the years 2000 to 2009 tells only part of the story. A close look at top-billed African American actors during this time reveals another dimension. Top-billed actors are those actors who are listed in the top spots of each film, as they would appear in the credits of the film, ranked not in order of appearance but in order of importance of the character and sometimes according to the fame or box office appeal of the actor. This ranking invariably means that the top-billed actors are also the highest-paid actors in the film. Of the top 100 box office hits during the ten years from 2000 to 2009, African American actors were among the five top-billed actors in thirty-four of these films, a full 34 percent.

There were some actors and actresses who appeared in several of these box office hits, including Will Smith, who starred in four films in the first decade of the twenty-first century. The diversity of film and roles during this decade is noteworthy. Samuel L. Jackson, for example, played a dramatic role in two of the *Star Wars* epic films and also did a voice-only part in the animated film *The Incredibles*. In *Chicago*, Queen Latifah played the role of prison matron Mama Horton in a part that was not designated as "black." Because the film was a musical with scenes that clearly teetered back and forth from "reality" to fantasy, director Rob Marshall's multiracial casting that ignored the racial realities of Chicago in the 1920s was a robust success.

During this same period, Halle Berry had a role in both versions of the comic book–based *X-Men* and the powerful independent drama *Monster's Ball*. Despite its critical acclaim and Berry's Academy Award–winning performance, *Monster's Ball* did not make the list of top box office hits. In the film, "Billy Bob Thornton and Berry star as Hank and Leticia, in two performances that are so powerful because they observe the specific natures of these two characters, and avoid the pitfalls of racial clichés. What a shock to find these two characters freed from the conventions of political correctness, and allowed to be who they are: weak, flawed, needful, with good hearts tested by lifetimes of compromise" (Ebert 2002). The film tells a story of race and racism, of hopeless characters who in small ways discover each other and rediscover their connection to humanity. Not only are the characters complex, but the themes about race are also complex and firmly nudge even the most resistant audiences to ponder the powerful questions about race and humanity that *Monster's Ball* raises. That Berry, previously almost exclusively touted for and cast in deference to her great beauty, became, in this part, the first African American woman to win an Academy Award for Best Actress is a tribute to a talented actor portraying a challenged, challenging, and complex woman.

That same year, 2001, Denzel Washington won his second Academy Award, his first for Best Actor, for his role in the film *Training Day*, making it a double first. This was the first time that African Americans won Academy Awards in the categories of Best Actor and Best Actress in the same year. Washington had previously been most well known for playing characters with great integrity, leadership, and/or heroism in films such as *Glory*, *Hurricane*, and *Malcolm X*. In *Training Day*, Washington plays a veteran narcotics cop: corrupt, cruel, and often violent. Some critics considered it another sign of racism that both Berry and Washington, who had each turned in powerful performances in previous films, won their Oscars for playing characters that represented enduring black stereotypes—a highly sexualized and desperate black woman dependent upon a white man coming to her rescue and a shady black cop who abuses his authority to engage in criminal activity and gets his comeuppance from an honest white police trainee. Others applauded Berry and Washington for having the talent to play—and the Academy for having the courage to recognize—characters who were not easily pegged as solely evil but who conveyed their humanity through the grimness of their life circumstances and choices.

During the first decade of the twenty-first century, black actors and films with themes about race and racism took 16 percent of five of the top Academy Awards: Best Picture, Best Actor and Actress, and Best Supporting Actor and Actress. Remarkably, these roles were characterized by depth, complexity, and a solid range of diversity among them. These award-winners were Morgan Freeman as Eddie Dupris in *Million Dollar Baby*, Jamie Fox as Ray Charles in *Ray*, Jennifer Hudson in *Dreamgirls*, Forest Whitaker as dictator Idi Amin in *The Last King of Scotland*, and Mo'Nique in *Precious*.

When the 2011 film *The Help* was released, it created major buzz in many contradictory ways. In the plus column was the Oscar buzz for the extraordinary performances of Viola Davis and Octavia Spencer. Davis and Spencer were nominated for Academy Awards, respectively, for Best Actress and Best Supporting Actress, and Spencer won in her category. Both women played the role of maids in the homes of southern white families in the early days of the civil rights movement. The characters cleaned their employers' homes and played central roles in raising their children, receiving low pay and no health insurance or any other benefits. In addition to other indignities, Spencer's character, Minny Jackson, was given the humiliating order that she was not to use the bathroom that she cleaned.

Yet Minny Jackson and Aibileen Clark (Davis) were neither caricatures nor stereotypes of African Americans nor of maids of that time period. Each character was complex. They told each other pieces of their life stories at Aibileen's kitchen table, so that the audience was allowed to peek into the tragedies and joys that had shaped these women as well as the complicated relationships they had with the white women for whom they worked. They were both angry at the inhumane treatment they were expected to swallow, but they expressed it in very different ways so that people in the audience who had never spoken

At its best, *The Help* (2011) tells two stories, of the racism, indignity, and invisibility faced by black maids in the homes of many white southern women and the parallel story of the dignity, grace, and gratifying irreverence of their friendships, helping each other to survive the hardships of racism and poverty. Abileen Clark (Viola Davis) [left] and Minnie Jackson (Octavia Spencer) [right] are atypically visible in their love and support of each other. *(Source: Courtesy of Associated Press, Copyright © 2011 by Rex Features. Used by permission of Associated Press.)*

to a black maid in the South could learn about their lives as if they too were sitting at the table in Aibileen's kitchen.

There was also significant criticism about *The Help*. Ann Hornaday of the *Washington Post* said,

> as gratifying as it is to watch Davis and Spencer bring Aibileen and Minny to pal-pable, fully rounded life, their narrative, like "The Blind Side" a few years ago, is structured largely around their white female benefactor. That this is the story we keep telling ourselves is all the more puzzling—if not galling—when viewers consider that, precisely at the time that "The Help" transpires, African Americans across Mississippi were registering to vote and agitating for political change. In other words, they were helping themselves. And, on screen at least, their story remains largely untold. (Hornaday 2011)

Roger Ebert of the *Chicago Sun-Times* echoed one of the most prevalent criticisms of the film, that "*The Help* is a safe film about a volatile subject. Presenting itself as the story of how African American maids in the South viewed their employers during Jim Crow days, it is equally the story of how they empowered a young white woman to write a best seller about them and how that book transformed the author's mother. We are happy for the two white women, and a third, but as the film ends it is still Jackson, Mississippi, and Ross Barnett is still governor" (Ebert 2011).

While stereotypes of African Americans in film have not disappeared, the beginning of what could be an important phenomenon emerged in the 1990s. There were an increasing and consistent number of films with black characters and themes that had a wide range of images and messages. This means that the same primary, consistent, negative messages (blacks as subservient, blacks as ridiculous, blacks as violent) were not always bombarding audiences. There were increasingly more comedies and dramas, extraordinary films and ridiculously awful films, and more Academy Award–nominated films with African American characters and themes than ever before. It is premature to refer to this as a trend, but if this trajectory continues it could mean a wider array of African American characters, themes, and images that explore the nature and impact of racism, as well as drama and comedy featuring other themes, characters, and experiences of African Americans. The more variety there is in the kind of films and characters produced, the less likely it is that even the most insidious stereotypes will stick with audiences in a way that gets inside our heads and convinces us that they are true. "The black filmmaker must struggle to depict the truth about black life in America while being inextricably tied to the commercialized sensibilities of a mass audience that is for the most part struggling to deny or avoid the full meaning of that truth" (Guerrero 1993, 168).

In 2013, the year preceding publication of this edition of *Media Messages*, three films nominated for the Academy Award for Best Picture involved major contemporary and historical themes that addressed race in the United States. These films were *Django Unchained*, *Lincoln*, and *Beasts of the Southern Wild*. In addition, that same year, Denzel Washington was nominated for Best Actor for his role in *Flight* and Quvenzhane Wallis (who was six years old when filming began) for her extraordinary performance in *Beasts of the Southern Wild*. The year 2013 also saw the theatrical release of forty-eight films featuring African American characters and/or themes. Among the top grossing and most critically acclaimed were Lee Daniels's *The Butler*, *42*, *The Best Man Holiday*, *After Earth*, *12 Years a Slave*, and *Fruitvale Station* (Hilton 2013; Obenson 2013). This is indeed a positive development; however, as one critic observes, ". . . honoring the achievements of black filmmakers by declaring it 'their' year does them a disservice. Lumping together heavy dramas with lighthearted romcoms simply because of the skin color of the actors or director prevents these films from being measured against the whiter counterparts that actually share their genre—inadvertently ghettoizing the former and protecting the latter from scrutiny. It's difficult to imagine pulling, say, *Blue Is the Warmest Colour*, *The Great Gatsby*, *The Hangover Part III*, and *The Fifth Estate* into a story declaring 2013 the year of the 'white movie'" (Hilton 2013). It remains to be seen whether this consistent appearance of films with interesting, diverse, and often complex African American themes and characters is a trend or an anomaly or, like the blaxploitation phenomenon before, just another isolated moment in time in which content and economics come together temporarily.

African Americans and Popular Music

The relationship between blacks and whites in the United States and the history of race and racism are intricately woven into popular music written, produced, and recorded by African Americans. One of the ways in which free and enslaved Africans in the Americas preserved and continued to develop their culture was through music. Beginning with the early work songs and spirituals, a multitude of uniquely black musical forms, including blues, gospel, jazz, rhythm and blues, and hip-hop, have evolved. This evolution might be regarded metaphorically as a tapestry of the African American cultural experience—neither fully African nor fully European, but rather a synthesis of both with an infusion of American Indian, Caribbean, and other cultural influences as well. "African-Americans found themselves fusing African and European musical forms while attempting to maintain their neo-African cultures. By the end of slavery, African Americans had blended in survival traits with the newly acquired western lifestyle. Their post-emancipation music developed vocally and instrumentally and transcended what could be considered true folk music" (Lawrence-McIntyre 2011, 35). The music ranges from direct and straightforward to subtle and complex, but the racial context is often multilayered and rarely simple.

A content analysis that provided a quick scan of six decades of music from 1955 to 2005 reveals a different pattern than any other representation of people of color in popular culture. The songs that made the Top 40 charts for the years 1955, 1965, 1975, 1985, 1995, and 2005 were scanned for the presence of African American recording artists. During that period, the African American percentage of the U.S. population never exceeded 12.8 percent. However, in 1955 the percentage of black recording artists to hit the Top 40 charts was 9 percent, in 1965 it was 20 percent, in 1975 it was 9 percent, and in 1985 it was 13 percent. In 1995, the percentage of African American artists in the Top 40 charts was 34 percent (Holtzman 2011; LyricsMode 2013). By 2005, black recording artists in these same charts reached 51 percent, over half of the *Billboard* Hot 100 list.

To begin to make some sense of this unusual occurrence in popular culture, we will examine cover music, the Motown sound, and rap and hip-hop music. This analysis will focus on two important dimensions of black music. The first is the widespread popularity across racial boundaries of music that has a "black sound." The crossover phenomenon that has occurred in film with black actors emerged in a very different way in popular music. The second dimension is the way that race, economics, and politics intersect to influence the business decisions, the financial success, and the political and racial context and messages of black music.

From the ragtime era of Jelly Roll Martin (Ferdinand Joseph LaMothe) and Scott Joplin, through the big band sounds of Edward Kennedy "Duke" Ellington and Louis Armstrong, the vocal expressions of Ella Fitzgerald and Billie Holiday (Eleanora Fagan), the bebop explorations of Charles "Charlie" Parker and John Burks "Dizzy" Gillespie, and the post-bop advances of Miles Davis and John Coltrane, black artists and composers had a profound influence on American popular music in the first half of the twentieth century. However, an overtly exploitative and insidious phenomenon emerged in the post–World War II entertainment industry. Cover music is a term that describes the 1950s strategy to promote white singers who recorded music that imitated or "covered" music created by black recording artists. This racist practice was based on the premise that white singers would sell more records, and the result was that many black singers and songwriters were relegated to the background at the expense of their careers and their bankbooks. White singers such as Pat Boone and Georgia Gibbs were cover artists for many black singers. Gibbs covered the sexually suggestive song "Roll with Me, Henry," which became "Dance with Me, Henry" in her version.

At the same time that even the Beatles and the Rolling Stones covered black songs in the 1950s, white teenagers were exploring black music. "For the popularity of white covers or imitations of black rhythm and blues (R&B) in the 1950s had conferred a mystique on the original black versions, which led many curious white teenagers to seek out the real thing. . . . The cultural and economic consequences were large. These teens, with more expendable money than their parents had when they were teenagers, became a real presence in the mass marketplace by the 1950s" (Early 1991, 13). The hyper-segregation of the 1950s influenced the development of cover music and the financial impact on black artists. When the civil rights movement and activism of the 1960s emerged, both the appealing sound of the music and the inequities for black artists converged in the first major explosion of the "black" sound on the popular music scene.

Part of the declaration of white adolescents' independence from their parents in the United States has always been their choice of music. The music of moderate rebellion of adolescents in the 1930s and 1940s was swing; in the 1950s and 1960s it was rock and roll. Heavy metal, R&B, punk, rap, and hip-hop have all at one time or another been part of popular youth culture, driving parents of every generation to begin sentences with, "These kids today . . . " But it was in the 1950s that large numbers of white teenagers first became taken with black music. Whether they listened to rhythm and blues in the 1950s or rap and hip-hop in the 1980s and 1990s, these white adolescents were not necessarily making a political statement that identified with anti-racism and black liberation. Instead, by and large, they liked the sound, the music, and its sense of hipness or coolness. Rather than serving as a declaration of independence from their parents, black adolescents have tended to regard the music of the times as a cultural extension of what has come before. The emphasis in music making is all about innovation and synthesis with a healthy dose of competition. Even the most current and progressive artists continue to sample and allude to songs, performers, and musical forms from generations before. When it comes to music, the sense of rebellion among African American youth tends to be directed more at existing political and economic power structures.

During the mid- to late twentieth century, black entrepreneurs began to take advantage of the crossover appeal of their music. In 1959, Berry Gordy founded Motown, a black-owned and -operated recording studio and record production company that promoted and recorded black artists. Gordy understood the historical context of the movement toward civil rights, the growth of black identity, and the phenomenon of white youths' fascination with black music. Ultimately, Motown became the most successful independent record company and the most successful black business in the United States for that time period. The tremendous success of Motown was in part due to the strength and appeal of the music and in part due to Gordy's understanding of business, politics, and culture.

Gordy employed a two-tiered marketing strategy. He marketed some R&B songs to be covered by white artists, and he marketed the original black recording artists as well (Early 1991, 13). Artists, songwriters, and superstars associated with Motown in the early years included Smokey Robinson and the Miracles, Diana Ross and the Supremes, the Temptations, Mary Wells, and the early hits of Stevie Wonder and Marvin Gaye.

Motown was a predominantly black business, but from the beginning Gordy also hired white producers, promoters, and sales representatives. Gordy managed to establish an organization that appealed to blacks and whites in its strong black identity, its successful economics, and its interest in racial integration. These organizational characteristics fit well with the 1950s historical context. "These were the years, then, in which America recognized, and cringed before, the social reality that would not hide itself anymore. . . . And the 'new' popular music helped to expose the false separation of America from itself, by revealing the culture's essential fusion all the more inescapably" (Early 1991, 14). The 1950s and 1960s Motown organization and sound and its wide appeal across racial lines gave a sense of hope and promise to blacks and whites who wanted integration. Here was a place where black and white people worked side by side to make and appreciate something together—music. In its organization, its recording artists, and its audiences, the business and sound of Motown was the first major crossover phenomenon.

The Motown of the 1960s was very different from the Motown of the 1970s. The difference is revealed in the numbers of songs by black artists in the *Billboard* 100: a high of 20 percent in 1965 and a drop to 9 percent in 1975. The early Motown sound of the 1950s and 1960s was carefully constructed for crossover appeal and included the universal appeal of love songs by The Supremes, Smokey Robinson and the Miracles, and the early songs of Marvin Gaye, such as "I Heard It Through the Grapevine" (1966). In the 1970s, this same Motown sound continued as a benign soundtrack to the civil rights movement, including nonviolent protest of racism and violent resistance to racism. Berry Gordy and Motown took some musical risks in the 1970s with songs such as Marvin Gaye's political commentary in "What's Going On" (1971) as well as the now mature Stevie Wonder sound in the 1973 "Living for the City," in contrast to his early days as "Little" Stevie Wonder and songs like the 1963 "Fingertips (part 2)." While there is no concrete research one way or the other, it would seem that the deep divisions in the 1970s in the United States over civil rights, the Vietnam War, women's rights, and other movements for human rights and equity may have also influenced the drop in the crossover appeal of black music in the mid-1970s.

Hip-hop originated in New York in the 1970s. It began as a youth movement of sorts, a musical declaration of pride and identity amid urban poverty and alienation. Hip-hop was music, and it was clothing, language, and neighborhood identity and culture. The early days of hip-hop predated its discovery by mass media and a wider audience. Its musical form followed the African tradition of storytelling and oral history of the "griots" or African storytellers. "Rappers have become urban griots, using their lyrics to disperse social commentary about what it means to be young and black in the late twentieth century" (Croteau and Hoynes 1997, 220). Performers such as The Last Poets and Gil Scott-Heron were early purveyors of this approach to social commentary through music and spoken word.

Hip-hop and its most popular form, rap, shifted and expanded their range from the 1970s to the 1990s. In their earliest form and in some of their contemporary incarnations, hip-hop and rap were political protest, socially and politically conscious music (Aldridge 2005, 226). Cultural studies scholars have analyzed political forms of rap as a popular and original form of music that often challenges and resists the dominant culture. "In the face of under- and/or misrepresentation in traditional media, black youths have turned to hip-hop as a means to define themselves. In terms of resistance, hip-hop provided a forum from which black youth can portray what it means to be young and black in America and protest against it" (Croteau and Hoynes 1997, 222).

A strong example of political resistance in rap is Public Enemy's "Fight the Power," which was used as an anthem in Spike Lee's film *Do the Right Thing*. Public Enemy's lead rapper, Chuck D, was very explicit about the group's name and the political purpose of its music: "The sociopolitical meaning of Public Enemy came after we decided the group would be called that, because the meaning and the connection of what we were about fit right in. The Black man and woman were considered three-fifths of a human being in the Constitution of the United States. Since the government and the general public follow the Constitution, then we must be the enemy" (quoted in Croteau and Hoynes 1997, 84). While the political messages, establishment of an alternative culture, and resistance to the dominant culture still exist to some degree in contemporary twenty-first-century rap and hip-hop, another trend emerged in the 1980s that changed hip-hop from an art form that was at its core a challenge to the dominant ideology, particularly regarding the politics and inequity of race in the United States. Hip-hop's political core was strongly impacted by the enormous surge in the white audience for rap. "Although rap is still proportionally more popular among blacks, its primary audience is white and lives in the suburbs" (Early 1991, 24). Rap crossed over to white audiences in 1984 with Run-DMC and King of Rock. The 1970s rappers were immersed in urban street culture, while the rappers in these 1980s crossover groups were middle-class young men dressed according to the urban hip-hop mode (Samuels 1991, 26).

Public Enemy's message was clearly that of political resistance and black nationalism, accompanied by a number of contradictory elements. Public Enemy was formed not on the streets of New York, but in suburban Long Island, where the group's members grew up. Their protest came not from the urban streets but from suburban college students who were standing up to racial inequality. This type of protest was valid, yet removed from the urban street authenticity of early hip-hop. Their song "Fight the Power" (1989) became the biggest college hit to cross racial lines (Samuels 1991, 27). In fact, hip-hop culture, language, and dress rapidly shifted from a phenomenon among young African Americans to include a subculture among young white men and teens.

In some ways, the popularity of rap and hip-hop culture in suburban white communities was the continuation of the popularity of the Motown sound and R&B in general among white audiences, complete with the coming-of-age separation of youth from their parents and from the dominant culture. In this regard, the attraction of some white teens and young adults to rap is not unlike similar attractions to rock or heavy metal or punk music.

What differentiates the attraction of vast white audiences to rap from those audiences drawn to Motown in earlier years are the messages in the music. Early Motown was doo-wop and love songs with simple messages of love lost or love gained, and in the 1970s Motown moved toward a wider array of songs, including some with strong political messages. It is interesting that early hip-hop, with its challenge to the dominant culture, emerged on the New York musical scene in the 1970s, picking up the threads of political protest that Motown tentatively began along with spoken word releases from artists such as Gil Scott-Heron and The Last Poets. The political messages in rap in the 1970s ran the gamut from protest against racism and police brutality to the brazen social messages of sex, violence, and abuse of women in gangsta rap. Why would these messages have such deep and wide appeal to young white men?

Some critics speculate that in addition to a declaration of generational independence and an attraction to the beat of the music, young white men are opposing racial discrimination through their musical tastes as a type of protest. Other critics see rap as a door through which young white people try to see and understand black culture. Still other critics see it as a way for white youth to appropriate black culture without ever being required to have personal contact with black people. "The ways in which rap has been consumed and popularized speak not of cross-cultural understanding, musical or otherwise, but of a voyeurism and tolerance of racism in which black and white are both complicit" (Samuels 1991, 29).

Whichever explanations seem reasonable to you, the fact is that since 1991 most popular music charts identify black music as occupying at least seven of the top ten positions. This phenomenon, with African Americans likely to be involved in the writing and production of the music, the content itself, and in performing the music, is unlike any other in popular forms of media.

Hip-hop and rap music have generated heated discussions and debates among critics, academics, activists for racial equality, and listeners across generations. One of the few things these groups agree on is an aversion to any lyrics that blatantly support abuse of women, **misogyny**, or any type of call to violence. Three of the major perspectives on the role of hip-hop are (1) hip-hop as an art form, (2) the civil rights movement and hip-hop as divergent and incompatible, accompanied by mutual hypercriticism, and (3) hip-hop as a continuation of the civil rights movement in its advocacy of another level of racial justice.

Michael Eric Dyson sees rap as representative of the different aesthetic sensibilities of blacks of different generations, not unlike the different aesthetic sensibilities of generations of whites preferring rock and roll or heavy metal music. Dyson regards hip-hop as a serious cultural art form and as social and political commentary on poverty, racism, and equity.

> Besides being the most powerful form of black musical expression today, rap projects a style of self into the world that generates forms of cultural resistance and transforms

the ugly terrain of ghetto existence into a searing portrait of life as it must be lived by millions of voiceless people. For that reason alone, rap deserves attention and should be taken seriously; and for its productive and healthy moments, it should be promoted as a worthy form of artistic expression and cultural projection and an enabling source of black juvenile and communal solidarity. (Dyson 2004, 68)

The divergence between the generation of the civil rights movement and the hip-hop generation in views, perspectives, artistic sensibility, and even ironic humor is exemplified in a controversy that developed over the 1999 song by Outkast with the title "Rosa Parks." The only mention of Rosa Parks is in the title, and most critics familiar with the genre understood the song's repetitive lyrics of "Everybody move to the back of the bus" as a convention of hip-hop in which groups challenge each other competitively. This interpretation suggests that Outkast is instructing other hip-hop groups to move to the back of the bus because Outkast is taking over, and the title "Rosa Parks" is simply ironic, perhaps with some sideways or mischief-making interest in being provocative. Whether that was the intent or not, the title and lyrics of the song provoked Rosa Parks's attorneys, who did not see the song as benign, to sue Outkast for using Rosa Parks's name without permission in a way that they perceived as both disrespectful and profane.

Other scholars and critics take Dyson's observations about hip-hop to another level in which they regard rap and hip-hop as an important progression of the civil rights movement, albeit in a completely different form, style, and language. Aldridge addresses socially and politically conscious hip-hop in particular and identifies specific ways that hip-hop carries on the goals and ideals of self-determination and the civil rights movement, including the use of hip-hop techniques of sampling and scratching (Aldridge 2005, 226–228).

Sampling inserts digital sounds from different times in music and the spoken word into contemporary hip-hop. In the 1989 recording "Fight the Power," Public Enemy explores the contemporary problems of poverty and discrimination; the music video evokes the long history of the black struggle for rights by visuals of marchers carrying signs with pictures of Harriet Tubman, Frederick Douglass, Paul Robeson, A. Philip Randolph, Martin Luther King Jr., Malcolm X, and others (Aldridge 2005, 332). An older hip-hop technique, scratching, was done by disc jockeys who move a stylus back and forth on a vinyl record to create a literal scratching sound (The Art of Turntablism 2013).

According to this line of thinking, hip-hop is connected to a long line of activists, artists, and scholars who have advocated black dignity and pride through a strong sense of self that is embodied in self-reliance and self-determinism. Like early spirituals and the blues, hip-hop emerged from the debilitating oppression of African Americans and, like its musical forebears, elements of hip-hop cry out and sometimes scream out for self-determination. Aldridge cites the example of lyrics by Grand Puba of Brand Nubian: "Drugs in our country (that ain't right), Can't even get a job (that ain't right), Lyin' who is God (that ain't right)"; the song finishes with both a solution and a message of self-determination: "Knowledge of self, to better ourself, 'cause I know myself, that we can live much better than this" and "Move on black man, move on, you gotta move on black man, move on" (Aldridge 2005, 236).

Those who see the hip-hop culture continuing the important work of the civil rights movement are also aware of the conflict between the generations. Some of those who were active in the movement admired and longed for the dignity of their work together, the leadership of the black church, and the focus on love, peaceful resistance, and strength as an inner resource, as well as the way these qualities were simultaneously a reflection of the goals of the movement and integral in its very actions. These civil rights era admirers often see hip-hop as frivolous, irrelevant, profane, and with no respectable, respectful, or concrete strategy for change, while the hip-hop generation often sees those of the civil rights era as irrelevant, out-of-date, and unaware of the depth of the problems for the current black generation. Aldridge gives advice to both generations to listen to each other, to understand each other, to be open to criticism, and to offer respect to each other for different approaches in different circumstances. "Only when both generations heed these concerns, will we have the collective strength to 'fight the power' of discrimination, racism, and poverty that continues to impede the progress of African American communities" (Aldridge 2005, 248–249).

Robert J. Price describes an oddly fitting analogy between the Dr. Seuss story of *Green Eggs and Ham* and hip-hop culture.

> We are socialized [sic] to like certain cultures and not others. This applies to "green eggs and hip hop culture" and the life experiences or social constructions of reality that shape our cultural biases and worldviews. Eighty-two times "I do not like" or "not" is mentioned in this children's story, but the writer never tried it! The point of the story is: we make "rational" and "objective" decisions that derive from subjective categories regarding difference without first experiencing it. This is what Walter Lippmann . . . meant when he coined the concept of stereotype: we believe first, then see; rather than see first, then believe. Once again, we must transcend cultural bias and take hip-hop seriously. (Price 2005, 57)

African Americans and Prime-Time Television

"In American society, it is argued, the mass media help to legitimate inequalities in class, race, gender, and generational relations for commercial purposes—communication matters only insofar as it encourages consumer consumption" (Dates and Mascaro 2010, 51). Nowhere is that more apparent than in the medium of television, where commercials reign and where critically acclaimed series such as *Frank's Place* and *Under One Roof* can be canceled after one season or even less because they have not brought in the viewers to bring in the advertisers to pay for the commercials that pay for the programming that gets us in the stores to buy things we do not need. In this section, we will investigate shifts, trends, and changes in stereotypes of African Americans and major roles for African American actors independently and in relationship to commercial success in prime-time television.

If you are old enough and/or were allowed to watch the adult prime-time programs in 1999, you may have noticed that some programs had multiracial casts. In 1999, you may have found some dramas such as *The Practice*, *ER*, *Chicago Hope*, and *Law and Order* with a predominantly white cast and a handful of major characters that were African American or Latina/Latino, but very few, if any, Asians, Pacific Islanders, or Native Americans. You may have also noticed a few actors of color as guest stars who played a significant role for an episode or two. This was progress in normalizing multiracial programming with scripts in which professional and personal relationships were developed among coworkers and colleagues, who sometimes discussed race seriously and other times were portrayed as comfortable enough to joke with each other about race.

Homicide: Life on the Street (1993–1999) was in the same genre as the other multiracial dramas, yet stood out from the other programs in its extraordinary writing, directing, and acting and most significantly in its development of an ensemble cast of multiracial characters. What was original and exciting about *Homicide* was both the complexity of the many characters in the ensemble and the diversity among them, particularly among the several African American characters. The black characters in this series differed in the roles they played within the Baltimore Police Department. The man at the top was Colonel George Barnfather (Clayton LeBoeuf), a light-skinned, slender African American man who made it to the top by compromising important values and climbing up the backs of others. The head of the unit was Lieutenant Al Giardello, a large, dark-skinned African American man with Sicilian heritage and a large and fiery passion for justice, successfully closing homicide cases, and Sicilian food. In the first few seasons, the two black detectives on the squad were Meldrick Lewis (Clark Johnson) and Frank Pembleton (Andre Braugher). Pembleton, Lewis, and Giardello were major characters while Barnfather was in a significant recurring role, but was only rarely central to the week's plot. These four characters were very different in the way they dressed, in the extent and quality of their education, in the way they used standard English and/or black vernacular, in skin color, in hairstyles, in values, in personality, and in temperament. Even by current standards of multiracial ensembles, this kind of diversity among African Americans was rare and impressive.

By 2013, the above-mentioned programs had disappeared, but had been replaced by an interesting array of programs with multiracial casts, including *Grey's Anatomy*, *Law and Order SVU*, *Heroes*, *Private Practice*, *Southland*, and some of the various versions of *CSI* and *NCIS*. Many of these programs' ensemble casts featured people of color in major roles and/or significant recurring roles. As *Grey's Anatomy* was ending its eighth season, the African American characters that played major roles in multiple episodes included Dr. Preston Burke, Dr. Miranda Bailey, Chief of Staff Dr. Richard Webber, and more recently Dr. Jackson Avery. *Private Practice*, which ended its five-year run in 2013, often centrally and sequentially featured six of its ensemble cast. Of these six primary characters, African Americans Dr. Sam Bennett (Taye Diggs) and Dr. Naomi Bennett (Audra McDonald) were on the program for 111 episodes and 77 episodes respectively (Internet Movie Database 2013). Audra McDonald left the series to play the role of Bess in the 2008 revival of *Porgy and Bess*.

A more recent ABC hit series which debuted in 2012 is *Scandal*, in which the lead character is an attorney, a major Washington, D.C., insider and "fixer," Olivia Pope, played by African American actor Kerry Washington. The major "scandal," though certainly not the only one, in the program is that the president of the United States, Fitzgerald "Fitz" Grant (Tony Goldwyn), is white, married, and deeply in love with Olivia Pope. Their love is reciprocal, an intelligent, playful, and agonizing connection that has proved to be as irresistible for audiences as it is for Olivia and Fitz (Internet Movie Database 2013). In a spring 2013 Nielsen analysis of one week of TV watching habits of the entire U.S. prime-time viewing audience as compared to African American viewers and Latino viewers, *Scandal* had an unusual position with viewers. In the tradition of *Scandal*, we'll wait until the end of the chapter to reveal the program's position among general audiences and African American audiences and what it could portend.

Multiracial casts are a fairly new trend in entertainment television programming and until very recently have most often consisted of predominantly white actors with one or even two recurring characters who are African American or other races. We will examine this emerging pattern and take a close look at the industry, the racial content and messages of programming, and the impact on audiences.

Understanding the relationship of advertising to entertainment television is key to understanding the evolution of African American images and what it could mean for programs with some of the unique qualities of *Scandal*. Because television in the United States is part of private industry, the success of individual programs has always been based on a particular program's ability to reach a wide audience. This popularity or projected popularity is what generates advertising, profit, and the length of the run of a program. Advertisers' pursuit of larger audiences plays a critical role in shaping prime-time content. Until relatively recently, a widely held belief in the television industry and in the advertising agencies that serve as the de facto advisers of the industry was that since the majority of the audience was white, this was the "mass" to whom the mass media's programming should be directed. "It was the task of the mass media to find commonalities among members of the audience; common themes, ideas, interest areas that would attract and not offend the mass audience. With few exceptions, this meant that the content of the mass media reinforced, rather than challenged, the established norms and attitudes of society. To do otherwise would be to risk offending significant numbers of the mass audience, and in the process, lose the large audience demanded by the advertisers" (Wilson and Gutierrez 1995, 41–42). In the language of cultural studies, this has often meant that television families have reflected the dominant ideology of race and of the "norms" of what it means to be a family.

There have been few prime-time programs with serious African American themes, characters, and messages. These few programs were often critical successes with loyal audiences that ran deep instead of wide. The struggles, conflicts, and choices of the characters in these programs and the issues that they confronted were often incompatible with what advertisers and producers saw as the elements of commercial success. The powers that be in TV therefore colluded with the belief that the ideology of the dominant culture must generally remain prominent by placing these programs in unpopular time slots, moving them from time slot to time slot, and failing to promote them adequately.

Among these unique programs were *Frank's Place* (1987–1988) and *Under One Roof* (1995). Both received extraordinary critical acclaim. *Frank's Place* was a CBS program that made it through just one season and was canceled after it was moved through six different time slots on four different nights. In the show, Frank Parrish (played by Tim Reid) is a newcomer to New Orleans, having inherited a bar from his estranged father. "Rather than offering American viewers a peek into the living room of a family headed by a successful lawyer and doctor [a reference to *The Cosby Show*], *Frank's Place* demanded that a viewer leave behind all presumptions about the South, New Orleans, and the African American community in a particular locale and engage social issues, a new television genre, a beautiful but unfamiliar setting, and a central character on a quest for understanding" (Whitt 2005, 41).

The show, considered a situation comedy, alternated between humor and something else that was not quite drama or comedy. *Frank's Place* regularly introduced uninitiated audiences into very unfamiliar territory on the inside of private internal discussions among African Americans. In one episode, Frank, invited to join an elite black club, is at first honored and delighted. Quickly the audience is given an insider's peek into how racism in the dominant culture gets translated into a kind of internalized racism in the form of skin color preference. In the dominant culture's standards of beauty, white is the preferred skin color. This preference is transferred to the black community as a preference for light-skinned African Americans. Frank is given a skin color orientation by a woman who works for him in the bar. Anna May holds up a brown paper bag to Frank's face, which is clearly darker than the bag, and informs him that the club will never accept him since he does not pass the "paper bag test."

Under One Roof was a CBS midseason replacement for *Rescue 911* and was poorly publicized. It was one of the only television dramas with a predominantly African American cast. The recurring characters demonstrated a range in class, language, dress, and values, with identities that ranged from Afrocentric to assimilated. The short-lived series offered universal themes of family life, love, and conflict, but also focused on plots revolving around interracial friendship, racist business practices, and the intersection of poverty and race. Through these characters and themes, the program not only challenged black stereotypes, but also offered an alternative to the dominant ideology in prime-time TV represented by the omnipresent white, middle-class family consisting of two parents and their children.

Under One Roof was set in Seattle, where three generations of a family live in a two-family house. Neb Langston, played by James Earl Jones, is a black Seattle police officer, the patriarch of the family. Neb lives downstairs with his adult daughter and teenage foster son. Living upstairs are Neb's son, his wife, and their two children. With only six episodes of *Under One Roof* produced and aired, the series examined interracial friendships of both adults and adolescents, racism in the construction industry, the struggles of an African American man coming home from the military, the challenges of an at-home mother shifting back to college and the job market, and the difficulties of an older man, a recently bereft widower, raising a teenage boy who witnessed his drug-addicted mother dying of an overdose. The themes of the episodes were rich with drama and recognizably authentic family banter and arguments, minus the familiar stereotypes or easy answers to the serious problems that were raised.

Under One Roof was the victim of a changing of the guard in CBS's entertainment division with an accompanying change in vision. Leslie Moonves, in 1994 the new president of entertainment at the network, wanted to change the image of CBS from the network for older Americans to one that would include younger, hipper programming. When *Under One Roof*, with an actor of the caliber of James Earl Jones, could not pull a wide audience in its six weeks on the air, it became a casualty of economics and network politics, and CBS pulled it off the air.

Images of African Americans on television changed throughout the decades in part according to the racial climate and culture of the times, but the bulk of these changes can be attributed to shifts in viewing patterns and profitability. Since the 1950s, much of prime-time television has reflected and reinforced the stereotypes, race relations, and prejudices of the dominant culture. "Racial images in the mass media are infused with color-coded positive and negative moralistic features. Once these symbols become familiar and accepted, they fuel misperceptions and perpetuate misunderstandings among the races" (Dates and Barlow 1990, 4). Tracing the history of the images of African Americans on prime-time television will help develop a perspective on how far the entertainment television industry has come in creating complex, authentic characters and stories that contribute to a greater understanding of some elements of black culture, while providing the kind of entertainment that will keep the commercial revenue flowing and keep the program on the air.

In the 1950s, African American characters as servants were the norm on prime time. *Beulah* (1950–1953), played by Louise Beavers, was a wide-eyed, grinning, heavy-set woman who served as a maid to a white family. This was the first television show to star an African American actor. But while Beulah was the title character of the show, her whole life revolved around the white family she served; her own family and independent life were invisible.

In *The Jack Benny Show* (1950–1964), *The Stu Erwin Show: The Trouble with Father* (1950–1955), *My Little Margie* (1952–1955), *Make Room for Daddy* (1953–1964), *The Great Gildersleeve* (1955–1956), and *Father of the Bride* (1961–1962), the only black characters were butlers, maids, or handymen in minor or one-shot roles. "The domestic was a symbol that a White family was successful. Therefore, it was this decoding of the servant role that antagonized the NAACP and Black middle class. While it is true the Black middle class were antagonistic toward the portrayals of Black men and women as maids and butlers in film, radio, and television, their quest for a piece of the American Dream was the critical element to understanding their strategy for censorship in these popular forms" (Nelson 1998, 81).

Like Beulah, *Amos 'n Andy* (1951–1953) was based on an old radio show. While African American actress Hattie McDaniel originated the role of Beulah on radio, it was two white men who played Amos and Andy before it made the jump to TV. The male characters (Andy, Amos, Kingfish, and Lightning) on *Amos 'n Andy* were alternately sly, cunning, and conniving, while the women (Sapphire and Mama) were domineering, loud, big, and shrewish. The stereotypes on *Amos 'n Andy* were so strong that the NAACP made the protest of this program central to its 1951 convention and platform.

The messages about African Americans in the 1950s were abundantly clear. Their overall absence on TV marked their perceived insignificance in the dominant culture. The fact that the few roles available to African Americans were as servants and/or buffoons reinforced stereotypes and reflected the misinformation and belief in their inferiority to whites.

The 1968–1971 series *Julia*, the first to feature a black star since *Amos 'n Andy*, signified a new kind of African American character. Played by Diahann Carroll, Julia was a nurse and single parent. In 1968 Martin Luther King Jr. was assassinated and the Poor People's Campaign occurred in Washington, D.C., but in the world of *Julia* the message was assimilation and the invisibility of race. Race was rarely mentioned. Racism and racial struggle did not exist in this television land (Dines and Humez 1995, 416).

The primary 1970s programs with African American characters were *Room 222* (1969–1974), *Sanford and Son* (1972–1977), *The Jeffersons* (1975–1985), *Good Times* (1974–1979), and *What's Happening* (1976–1978). All of these programs were situation comedies. Three of them (*Good Times*, *Sanford and Son*, and *What's Happening*) were set in low-income black urban areas and foregrounded fun and laughter amid the mostly unaddressed background of poverty and struggle. *The Jeffersons* represented the flip side of these programs—the "hilarious" antics of upward mobility and attempted assimilation of an African American family. Unlike the others, *Room 222* was set in a school and involved African American teachers as the main characters. Overall, the decade of the 1970s conveyed the message of the happy but poor black family and failed to demonstrate much about the structural barriers of racism faced by urban black families. Using entertainment media assessment tools to examine complexity in individual characters and diversity among black characters as a test to determine the extent of stereotypes reveals that most of these characters and programs failed. The same messages were repeated over and over to once again reinforce the fallacy of the inferiority of African Americans.

The miniseries *Roots* (1981) was significant on many levels. It was one of the most watched television programs of all times. Families of all races remained glued to their television sets during that week. This created a second element of significance. Each daily installment of this epic, which followed a black family from Africa to slavery to freedom, was the subject of discussions at work and at school. These discussions, often across racial lines, were for some people the first time they had ever discussed race and racism in U.S. history with someone of another race. *Roots* was significant in visually portraying the horrors of slavery and contradicting and disputing stereotypes and myths of white superiority. In the end, many critics and scholars, who were fans of *Roots*, observed that for all of its unique presentation of the African American story in American history, ultimately the miniseries reinforced the myth of the American Dream: "With *Roots* the popular media discourse about slavery moved from one of almost complete invisibility (never mind structured racial subordination, human degradation, and economic exploitation) to one of ethnicity, immigration, and human triumph. This powerful television epic effectively constructed the story of American slavery from the stage of emotional identifications and attachments to individual characters, family struggles, and the realization of the American dream" (Gray 1995, 78).

Throughout television's history, "televised comedies helped Americans adjust to the social order as the transmitted myths and ideology reinforced society's implicit rules and codes of behavior. In their portrayal of African American images, these comedies picked up threads of the established pattern of white superiority and black servitude and continued to weave them back into the popular culture" (Dates and Barlow 1990, 261). This was the trend in prime-time television until the mid-1980s, when *The Cosby Show* marked a shift in the way African Americans were portrayed in television and presented a more complex set of images . . . and problems.

The Cosby Show (1984–1992) was a phenomenal success among both black and white audiences. It was ranked number one during most of the years it was broadcast. The program was a situation comedy featuring an upper-middle-class African American family, the Huxtables, in which Cliff was a doctor and Clair was a lawyer. The story was set primarily in their home and revolved around the interactions between the parents and their five children. Bill Cosby and African American psychiatrist and program consultant Alvin Poussaint aimed to accomplish two objectives with *The Cosby Show*. The first was to entertain. The second was to create a situation comedy that depicted exceptional African Americans who were financially and socially successful in order to depart from previous black stereotypes of poverty, servitude, and buffoonery.

Ironically, a study that was funded by Bill Cosby and his wife Camille suggested that the extraordinarily successful Cosby characters let white audiences off the hook with respect to any complex understanding of continued racism in the United States. Conducted by cultural studies scholars Sut Jhally and Justin Lewis, this study was eventually published in a book with the intriguing title *Enlightened Racism*. Lewis and Jhally used content analysis to identify messages from the series and conducted small racially separate focus groups to discuss responses to various aspects of the program. Jhally and Lewis concluded the following:

- *The Cosby Show* was successful in generating racial tolerance among white viewers and racial pride among black viewers.
- Racially, the United States remained a deeply divided society in desperate need of major structural changes to rectify its profound racism. *The Cosby Show* joined other programs in promoting the fiction that the civil rights movement had "won." By touting the exceptions rather than the rule of class and race oppression, the program contributed to the myth of the American Dream.
- The debate among viewers regarding whether the Huxtables were "too white" was really a debate about class and resulted in confusing both black and white audiences about both race and class.
- *The Cosby Show* contributed to a strong belief among some whites that there was no need to act on racism in this country because it was no longer a serious problem.

- The term "enlightened racism" refers to the complex concept indirectly fostered by *The Cosby Show*, which left white viewers to believe that black people who do not succeed like the Huxtables are individually to blame for their problems and are lazy and/or stupid. (Jhally and Lewis 1992, 83)

Lewis and Jhally also made it clear that black audiences were getting the same messages from *The Cosby Show* that white audiences were getting about the misinformation and distorted logic that the individual triumph of the Huxtable family's economic success was an indictment of African Americans who did not live their lives by TV scripts. The message was that those black families that were not economically successful and those who depended on government programs for survival had no one to blame but themselves. Despite the strong research, the hiring of a black psychiatrist as consultant to the program, and the delightful nature of the program itself, the message was loud and clear: racism is no longer a structural or institutionalized problem in the United States and that with all the changes that came from the civil rights movement, black people had no reason to continue to blame their economic problems on racism.

Lewis and Jhally's research found that for white audiences who bought into this inaccurate portrayal of race relations and racism in the United States, it often transformed a hunch into a certainty that affirmative action, voting rights provisions, and other anti-racism programs were no longer needed and that, in fact, these programs gave blacks an unfair advantage over whites. For African Americans, these same messages often reinforced internalized racism, the involuntary process of taking in disturbing and negative messages about African American groups and individuals. This meant that for many in the black audiences, while *The Cosby Show* was entertaining and a source of pride, it ironically was also a source of deep distress and the burden of blame about what many adults saw as their own failure to get a good job and support their families well.

The Cosby Show was powerful in its signaling of these messages both because of its popularity and because of the extent to which it weekly visited both white and African American homes. But its power also stemmed from the fact that it was among the scarce prime-time images of African Americans during that time. With a limited range of class representations among African American characters and with few themes regarding the continued structural barriers of race, this one program's characters, themes, and messages became increasingly important and potent.

Politically, the 1980s were dominated by a shift in politics marked by the presidency of Ronald Reagan and what was known as Reaganomics. Central to the ideology of the Reagan years was the return to the Western theme of individualism and the belief in the power of one person or one family to create their own destiny. The intersection of class and race and their impact on a person's ability to acquire education, employment, housing, and so forth were not a consideration in the dominant culture of these times. Rather, the political message was the same as that of the classic American Dream—your success or failure is in your hands and your hands alone.

Racially, this meant that a shift was made from the 1960s ideology of low-income African Americans as "victims" of racism to a new belief that it was middle-class white people who suffered from unfair treatment as a result of social welfare, affirmative action, and other so-called special treatment for blacks. "In short, Reaganism had to take away from blacks the moral authority and claims on political entitlements won in the civil rights movement of the 1960s" (Gray 1995, 17).

While *The Cosby Show* and other 1980s programs such as *Benson, Different Strokes*, and *Room 222* unwittingly bought into this political shift, there were also programs such as the short-lived *Frank's Place* and *A Different World* that created more serious and complex characters and images, raised questions about race and racism, and challenged the dominant ideology that the individual is the only source of racial problems and therefore the only source of their resolution.

Several different historical, economic, technological, and cultural issues in the 1980s set the stage for new trends for African Americans in 1990s prime-time television. First, the decline in network viewing due to cable and video forced the networks to rethink and redefine their audiences. This takes us back to the relationship between programming and advertising. Second, the success of *The Cosby Show* signaled the potential for marketing African American programs and casts to both African American and crossover white audiences. Third, the concept of "narrowcasting" was born amid cable and video. This concept was based on research that demonstrated that black audiences watched prime-time television more than any other group at that time and that low-income black audiences were less likely to have cable. All of these factors contributed to the proliferation of black programming and casts and a renewed segregation on prime time.

In 1998, the top ten TV programs watched by black households were strikingly different than those viewed by white households. African Americans watched programs with predominantly black casts and whites watched programs with predominantly white casts. The number one show for African Americans was *Between Brothers* on FOX. This same program was ranked 117 for white viewers. The remaining nine popular programs for black viewers in 1998 were *Living Single, 413 Hope Street, The Steve Harvey Show, The Wayans Brothers, Good News, Malcolm & Eddie, Sparks, Moesha*, and *Smart Guy*. White households preferred *ER, Seinfeld, Veronica's Closet, Friends, Touched by an Angel, NFL Monday Night Football, Home Improvement, Union Square*, and the *CBS Sunday Night Movie* (Richmond 1998, 1).

There were at least two 1990s examples of contemporary situation comedies that served as models for the possibility of addressing race and racism in ways that stayed within the context of humor of the particular program and also raised important questions that transcended stereotypes and the focus on the individual.

Robert Townsend's *The Parent 'Hood* (1995–1999) paid an interesting tribute to the young actor William Thomas Jr., who played the role of Buckwheat in the original *The Little Rascals (Our Gang)*; (1929–1938). The comedy in *The Parent 'Hood* revolved around an African American family. In one episode, the young son Nicholas was required to choose an African American person that he admired and to portray this person in a student production. To his parents' dismay, Nicholas chose Buckwheat.

Buckwheat was a somewhat androgynous character. Contemporary audiences were never sure if Buckwheat was a boy or a girl. Along with the gender ambiguity went a lot of stereotypes. Buckwheat spoke in exaggerated black vernacular, a caricature of one version of black speech. He said "sho'" rather than "sure" and often dressed in a shapeless shift, with a hairstyle that was a cross between contemporary stylish "twists" and the multiple, unkempt pigtails of a so-called "pickaninny" during the time of enslavement. Nicholas's parents were horrified at their son's choice and tried to dissuade him from selecting a character who exemplified some of the worst of African American stereotypes.

Ultimately, Nicholas was determined to stick with his original choice and proceeded to dress as Buckwheat for the school production. His discussion of the actor William Thomas Jr. turned serious as Nicholas explained to the school audience how few options were available to black actors during the 1930s. To Nicholas, William Thomas Jr. was a hero because of his acting talent, his ability to maintain some dignity amid the racist times, and his groundbreaking work that paved the way for African American actors who came after him—including Curtis Williams, the young African-American actor who played Nicholas and who was free to portray a character who did not have to conform to rigid racial stereotypes.

In the situation comedy *Third Rock from the Sun* (1996–2001), the central premise was that a group of aliens inhabited human forms in order to study Earth and its people. While the Solomons had studied many documented aspects of American people and culture, it was frequently clear that their education had significant gaps. The comedy of this program often revolved around these gaps in the aliens' understanding of informal societal rules.

One episode involved the observations of Dick Solomon, an alien posing as a university professor (played by John Lithgow), about the participation of his African American secretary, Nina Simbi Khali, in an African American pride group. Solomon and his colleagues, unaware of the finer points of racism, puzzle over this notion of black pride and begin to inquire about the existence of what they logically think could be parallel "white pride" groups. Through their inquiry, they discover a white supremacist group meeting, which in their ignorance they believe will be equivalent to Nina's black pride group. When they attend this meeting, to their horror they discover the virulence of racism. When the group burns a cross, the Solomons are once again puzzled and question what this white group has against the "small letter 't.'" The story goes on to simulate and mock white paternalism in a variety of ways, consistently remaining faithful to the program's premise and the source of its humor. In selecting the topic of race and revealing it through the untainted eyes of these "aliens," this episode mocks racism and its absurd ranking of people according to skin color.

Both *The Parent 'Hood* and *Third Rock from the Sun* had decent runs of four and five years, respectively, and are examples of the potential of prime-time television to raise serious questions about race, even within the limited genre of the formulaic thirty-minute sitcom.

Grey's Anatomy is a multilayered one-hour drama introduced by ABC in 2005. Critics have been warm, lukewarm, and ice cold about this medical drama, criticizing the premise of another ho-hum medical program and finding pros and cons with the casting, acting, and writing. While some of these mixed reviews may ring true, there is something that this program does fairly consistently and fairly successfully, which is to demonstrate an extraordinary range of possibilities to challenge the dominant ideology about race (see Table 5.3 on pages 390 and 391).

The creator, executive producer, and lead writer for *Grey's Anatomy* is Shonda Rhimes, an African American woman. The ensemble cast has shifted since its first season, adding new characters and losing existing characters, and has managed to maintain an interesting and unusual racial dynamic.

In the first few seasons, Meredith Grey was the only character that was consistently a major character in each episode. The others cycled through in major or minor roles depending on the episode. There were twelve main characters: seven white, three African American, one Latina, and one whose character was identified as Korean American and Jewish. The character who held the most power was chief of staff Richard Webber, an African American. The next most powerful positions were the attending physicians, Shepherd, Burke, Sloan, and Montgomery-Shepherd—three whites and one African American—followed by the residents, Bailey and Torres, who were African American and Latina, respectively. Despite Bailey's official power ranking in the middle of the pack, her character often wielded the most personal and political power and respect in the competitive world of Seattle Grace Hospital. The interns, in the lowest positions, were all white.

The racial casting in *Grey's Anatomy* turned the usual power-equals-white equation upside down. During the first few seasons, Preston Burke, a brilliant African American cardiothoracic surgeon, was the heir apparent to the chief of staff, and he and Cristina Yang (eventually together as a couple) were arguably the most focused, intense, and extraordinary surgeons on the program. The characters of Bailey and Burke were consistently complex, with Bailey's integrity compass generally on target, and Burke often torn between his honorable intentions and his ambition.

In one episode, Bailey is called upon to perform surgery on a white patient with a large swastika tattoo on his chest. When the patient expresses a preference for a surgeon of another race, Bailey calls in Cristina Yang as a way to meet the patient's request and toy with him by bringing in an Asian doctor, when his preference is clearly for a white doctor. With Yang's assistance and through great will and some prayer, Bailey manages not only to successfully perform the intricate, complicated surgery, but also to divide the swastika on his chest by the incision, making it unrecognizable after the surgery. Yang makes it very clear to Bailey that she does not want to be pulled away from another important surgery simply because of her race, and she reminds Bailey that she is Jewish and has family members who were Holocaust survivors and that the swastika is horrifying to her as well.

The complexity of the racial issues and the power relationships in this episode raises serious ethical and racial questions that are played out between people of color, rather than the TV norm of including a requisite white character as part of the mix. Episodes such as this one also invite and often compel the other characters and the audience to examine their assumptions about a person's racial identity and if it can or should be used for personal or professional gain or advantage.

Table 5.3

Race, Power, and Character Type in *Grey's Anatomy*

Character	Actor	Role	Race of character	Level of professional respect/power/authority at the hospital[1]	Level of personal respect/power/authority among friends and colleagues	Major or minor character[2]	Level of complexity[3]
Preston Burke	Isaiah Washington	Attending physician	African American	High	Mostly high/somewhat mixed due to his demeanor, which suggests personal detachment	Major/minor depending on episode	High
Katherine Heigl	Izzie Stevens	Medical intern	White	Low	Medium	Major/minor depending on episode	Medium/high
Alex Karev	Justin Chambers	Medical intern	White	Low	Low	Major/minor depending on episode	High
Addison Montgomery-Shepherd	Kate Walsh	Attending physician	White	Medium/high—due to length of time in position as compared to other attending physicians	Generally high regard for skills and talent and low to medium regard for the incongruence between her values and her behavior	Major/minor depending on episode	Low to medium
George O'Malley	T. R. Knight	Medical intern	White	Low	High	Major/minor depending on episode	High
Derek Shepherd	Patrick Dempsey	Attending physician	White	High	Mostly high/somewhat mixed due to his treatment of Meredith	Mostly major/occasionally minor depending on episode	Medium/high
Mark Sloan	Eric Dane	Attending physician	White	Medium/high—due to length of time in position as compared to other attending physicians	Mixed with generally high regard for his skills and talent and generally low regard for his field in medicine of cosmetic and plastic surgery	Major/minor depending on episode	Low to medium—of all the characters in the early years of the program, Sloan tends to be a simpler character than others due to the stereotypical portrayal as a devilishly handsome and charming womanizer

Callie Torres	Sara Ramirez	Resident physician	Latina	Medium	High		Major/minor depending on episode	High
Chandra Wilson	Miranda Bailey	Resident physician	African American	Medum/high —her position suggests medium; however, the respect she commands suggests high	High		Major	High
James Pickens Jr.	Richard Webber	Chief of surgery	African American	High	Medium/high—mix of extremely high regard because of position of power and difficulty of many staff to treat him as a whole human being	Medium/high	Major/minor depending on episode	Medium/high
Sandra Oh	Cristina Yang	Medical intern	Korean American	Low	Medium/high—a mix of high regard from peers and minimal social skills		Almost always major	High

Explanations

1. Despite the fact that the interns are all low in power and authority at the hospital, there is a high level of external credibility and regard for any individual's intelligence, commitment to a difficult education and training process, and potential for wealth and power, often based on only one piece of information: that the person is a doctor or is in training to be a doctor.

2. Major characters may be recurring characters or characters in only one or limited episodes. The key feature of major characters is that they are an essential part of the plot(s) and/or theme(s), and without them, the series or episode would make no sense. Minor characters may be recurring characters or characters in a limited number of episodes. The key feature of minor characters is that they are not essential to the central plot(s) or theme(s) of the episode and that their absence would cause no more than a minor distraction for the audience.

3. Complex characters have a certain amount of depth in personality and values and at times demonstrate internal conflict between values and behavior. They have the ability to change and/or grow over time (within an episode or during the series). Their motivation is sometimes difficult for audiences to ascertain because of inner conflict or character assets or flaws that may be extremely appealing or challenging to other characters. Audiences generally regard complex characters as more realistic. Simple (low-complexity) characters tend to be one-dimensional, fairly consistent, and predictable in their personality and behavior, and as a result, they are often conveyed as stereotypes. They rarely have any spoken or observed inner conflict. Simple and complex characters can be likable and admired by other characters or unlikable and disdained by other characters.

In 2008, the NAACP released an update of its report about African Americans behind and in front of the TV camera with a variety of findings, both negative and positive. So-called "reality" TV had mixed results for African Americans. On the negative side, the twenty-first-century boom in reality TV posed a problem for actors and writers. According to Screen Actors Guild president Alan Rosenberg, "The displacement of scripted series by reality programming continues to be a severe obstacle to a working actor's ability to earn a living." By 2004, the increase of network programming of reality TV rose to twenty-two hours a week, resulting in the loss of more than 3,000 scripted roles for that year alone. This has had a powerful impact on actors and writers overall, but according to the NAACP the loss has been even greater for actors and writers of color (NAACP 2008, 5).

One positive result of the growth of reality television is that unscripted programs tend to be more racially diverse than scripted programs. Audiences are thus able to see more diverse roles for African Americans in reality programs, where they appear in their real-life occupations as doctors and laborers, highly skilled surgeons and a wide variety of patients, lawyers and secretaries, and homemakers and scientists (NAACP 2008, 6).

In 2010, four scripted narrative programs starring African Americans made it to the overall top twenty positions in the Nielsen ratings for the week of May 17–24. These are the programs on prime-time TV whose black characters are viewed most often by general audiences:

- *NCIS: Los Angeles* with LL Cool J as a federal agent
- *Criminal Minds* with Shermar Moore as an FBI supervisor
- *CSI: Miami* with Khandi Alexander as a doctor
- *CSI: New York* with Hill Harper as a doctor

All of these programs were aired on CBS and all of the characters worked in high-ranking professional positions (Nielsen Research 2010; Internet Movie Database 2010). It is interesting to note that in 2010, although ABC had the highest number of major characters who were black, none of those programs made it to the list most watched by general audiences.

Generally, the billing order or order of actor credits at the opening of a TV program is the same as in film, with the top-billed actors receiving the highest pay. Table 5.4 lists the top-billed African Americans in prime-time programs in 2010. Not coincidentally, these same programs were those most viewed by black audiences. Only two of these six programs, *CSI Miami* and *Criminal Minds*, were also listed among the top twenty programs watched by general audiences.

In May 2010, 35 percent of the top programs watched by African American audiences also had major characters who were African American; in the same time period, only 20 percent of all U.S. audiences tuned into network TV were watching programs that featured main characters who were black. As Table 5.4 shows, of the nine characters viewed by the black audiences, six were doctors, two were in law enforcement, and one character beat Barack Obama to the White House as the first African-American president in the

Table 5.4

Black Characters on TV Programs Most Viewed by Black Audiences

Ranking	Program/network	Actor/role	Year
2	*Grey's Anatomy*/ABC	Chandra Wilson/doctor James Pickens Jr./doctor	2005
5	*Criminal Minds*/CBS	Shemar Moore/FBI supervisor	2005
7	*Law and Order: SVU*/NBC	Ice-T/detective Tamara Tunie/doctor and medical examiner	1999
7	*CSI Miami*/CBS	Khandi Alexander/doctor	2005
9	*CSI Miami*/CBS	Khandi Alexander/doctor	2002
14	*24*/FOX	Dennis Haysbert/U.S. president	2001
16	*House*/FOX	Omar Epps/doctor	2004

Sources: Nielsen Media Research 2010; Internet Movie Database (www.IMDb.com) 2010.

Table 5.5

Black Characters on TV Programs Most Viewed by General Audiences

Ranking	Program/network	Actor/role	Year
8	*NCIS: Los Angeles*/CBS	LL Cool J/federal agent	2009
9	*Criminal Minds*/CBS	Shemar Moore/FBI supervisor	2005
10	*CSI Miami*/CBS	Khandi Alexander/doctor	2002
11	*CSI New York*/CBS	Hill Harper/doctor	2004

Sources: Nielson Media Research 2010; Internet Movie Database (www.IMDb.com) 2010.

program *24*. During the same time period, the total U.S. audience watching prime-time TV saw four African American major characters, two who were in law enforcement and two who were doctors (Table 5.5).

No wonder the NAACP titled its report about the 2006/2007 year on prime-time television *Out of Focus, Out of Sync: Take 4* (NAACP 2008); it could have easily been less elegantly titled, "You Win Some, You Lose More: Take 61."

However, if we fast-forward from the Nielsen report of what American audiences were watching in May 2010 to what they were watching in April 2013, the ABC program *Scandal* may represent something new in the convergence of audiences of different races watching this program, which was developed, produced, and directed by Shonda Rhimes, the same African American woman who created *Grey's Anatomy* and *Private Practice*. According to various media critics and diehard fans, *Scandal* is either intelligent television with engaging and often complex characters and strange plot twists or a guilty

Scandal (2012–): Political consultant and "fixer" Olivia Pope (Kerry Washington) and sitting and married U.S. President Fitzgerald Grant (Tony Goldwyn) are portrayed as desperately, passionately in love, and that's not the only scandal in the series. *(Source: Courtesy of Getty Images. Copyright © 2012 American Broadcasting Companies, Inc. Used by permission of Getty Images. Photographer/© ABC/ Getty Images.)*

pleasure to which we tune in each week and think we've discovered the ultimate *Scandal* scandal, until the plot makes a sharp turn and some other character and plot arc become suspect. Whether it is intelligent TV, guilty pleasure, or some combination, *Scandal* has the potential to herald new trends in portrayal of race in prime-time television.

At the beginning of the new millennium, narrative television was as racially segregated as most churches are on Sunday morning. But in November 2013, something had changed that involved the phenomenon of the series *Scandal*. In April 2013 toward the end of its second season, *Scandal* was ranked as number eleven among general American audiences and as a hands-down number one for African American viewers and by November 2013, it was ranked number one for Thursday nights (Andreeva 2013). Producers and advertisers of *Scandal* and its home network ABC, as well as producers and advertisers of other networks, will be looking to see if this phenomenon persists and eyeing the buying power of such a large black audience combined with a significant multiracial general audience. If the analysis of the demographics of the African American audience of *Scandal* shows that this loyal audience has significant disposable income, these same analysts will be trying to figure out what it is about the premise, plot, and characters of *Scandal* that attracts both the African American audience and the general audience. As they are figuring that out, we are likely to see *Scandal* clones and look-alikes pop up over the next few years.

The walk we took through some of the history of African Americans on prime-time television and the more recent appearance of racially mixed ensemble casts can help us understand why the phenomenon of *Scandal* is a potentially significant game-changer in the world of race and prime-time television.

CHAPTER SUMMARY

With racially segregated neighborhoods and schools still prevalent in the United States, there are limited ways that we can learn about races that are different from our own, the way racism has operated throughout our history, and the contemporary face of racism. We can learn in school; we can learn through our own independent reading or participation in multiracial cultural, social, and political events; and we can learn from the media. As we discovered in Chapter 4, U.S. schools have been notoriously superficial and misleading in the way curricula and texts explain race and racism. Most people living in the United States do not have the information, inclination, or time to seek independent multiracial readings, ideas, or activities. One of the few sources of information about race that is universally available to Americans is popular media in the form of music, film, and prime-time television.

Stretched across these three popular forms of media and the decades of the twentieth and twenty-first centuries is a widely varying picture of Asians and Pacific Islanders, American Indians, African Americans, Latinas/Latinos, and European Americans, their relationships to one another, and the story of race in America. There are, however, some common features.

The evolution of popular media in the United States has been located exclusively in the private sector and largely dictated by economics. When profitable, such as in films of the blaxploitation era, Motown, or *The Cosby Show*, themes and characters of color have proliferated. But even in times of relative abundance, these characters, themes, and inter-racial relationships tend to reinforce a dominant ideology that promotes the dual myths of white superiority and the American Dream. There have been isolated examples in which complex characters, relationships, and themes about race have presented oppositional ideologies that question the racial status quo. Since the end of the twentieth century, there has been an increase in the number of people of color who were musicians and filmmakers and TV producers offering thoughtful alternatives to standard racial representations.

Nevertheless, a late twentieth-century study revealed that only two out of ten Latina/Latino and Asian children, and four out of ten African American children, say they see people of their race "very often" on TV, compared to seven out of ten white children. The impact of this lack of images of people of color is significant for everyone in that it signals who is important in U.S. society and who is not.

While the relatively recent trend of more participation and representation of people of color and racial themes is significant to the production of more diverse images and stories, the role of the audience or media consumer is equally significant in changing the media's racial terrain. The extent to which consumers are able to detect invisible racial and racist messages in media and to question and challenge them is the extent to which we are able to untangle the web of racial fallacies and misinformation.

GLOSSARY OF KEY TERMS

affirmative action: Affirmative action can be defined in two different ways, one that involves the historical reason for affirmative action and the other that describes the action minus the discriminatory history that the policy was designed to remedy. One standard, simply framed legal definitions of affirmative action is the "process of a business or governmental agency in which it gives special rights of hiring or advancement to ethnic minorities to make up for past discrimination against that minority" (USLegal. com 2013). A more common definition and a more common understanding of affirmative action are found in the credible *Merriam-Webster* dictionary that describes it as "an active effort to improve the employment or educational opportunities of members of minority groups and women; also: a similar effort to promote the rights or progress of other disadvantaged persons" (*Merriam-Webster* 2013). The misinformation that is created about affirmative action by removing this historical perspective can mislead some people into believing that the policy itself is discriminatory against whites and/ or men.

color-blind ideology: Color-blind ideology suggests that race is irrelevant in regard to U.S. history, historical and contemporary racial discrimination, pride in the accomplishments of one's race against difficult odds, and ultimately as a part of personal and group identity. On the surface, this may appear as a lofty perspective in its refusal to place race and color in the center of what both differentiates and ranks people in the United States. Right below the surface, however, the danger of color-blind ideology is twofold: (1) it ignores heritage of people of color, which is a source of great pride to many, particularly when the accomplishments of this group are measured against the tremendous racial barriers; and (2) it ignores the historic place of race in the United States, how much damage it has done, and how its legacy and current configuration continues to advantage some races and disadvantage others.

dominant culture: Dominant culture includes the most powerful or prevailing language, race, sexual orientation, religion, behavior, values, rituals, and social customs of a society that generally serve as the norm for the society as a whole. In the United

States, for example, the dominant culture is generally considered white, heterosexual, middle-class, and Christian. The dominant culture is usually in the majority and achieves its dominance by controlling social institutions such as communication, education, artistic expression, law, politics, and business. The behavior and norms of the dominant culture are reflected in entertainment media, which send messages to media consumers about what is considered "normal." For example, in the first thirty years of television, the standard prime-time family was white and middle- to upper-middle-class, with heterosexual parents, a two-story house, and a comfortable income. The members of the family almost invariably consisted of a father who went to work every day and was the heavy when it came to disciplining the children but clumsy with anything domestic, a mother who stayed at home and cleaned and baked cookies (often in a dress, heels, and pearls), and two or three cute, smart kids, including at least one somewhat mischievous child. The situation or problem in each episode was neatly resolved in each episode, which generally included Dad giving the kids stern, fair punishment along with a loving lecture about why the kids' behavior was wrong; properly contrite children; and a silly incident or comment at the very end that sent the whole cast into roaring laughter.

dominant ideology: The dominant ideology is the set of beliefs and values that are the framework and foundation of the dominant culture and often serve as a silent, invisible set of norms and rules for the rest of society. For example, most young people are socialized from a very young age to think forward in their lives toward marrying and having a family. Although this assumption is considered quite "normal" in the United States, it creates a quandary for people who identify as gay, lesbian, bisexual, transsexual, or transgendered in terms of their sense of worth, their sense of belonging, and their legitimate fears of rejection or violence. The dominant ideology is supported and reinforced, by and large, by entertainment media. It is often so prevalent and subtle that without learning about how this framework and ideology function, many of us internalize these values and beliefs without realizing it.

ethnocentricism: Ethnocentricism is the belief that one's own ethnicity, nationality, or "people" embody a system of beliefs and values that is superior to all others. Ethnocentric beliefs often lead people to make false assumptions about cultural differences, assuming their own norms, customs, and beliefs are right and everyone else's are wrong. One alternative perspective is to see values and beliefs as different but not necessarily good or bad, right or wrong, unless they cross a line into behavior that is violent, abusive, or demeaning to other individuals or groups.

Manifest Destiny: Manifest Destiny is a concept from the 1840s that turned into the policy and practice of the right and obligation of the United States to spread its democratic ideals through westward expansion to the Pacific coast. Critics, then and now, saw this idea applied in reality as a justification for taking land, often through violence, from Mexico and from Native Americans.

misogyny: Misogyny is literally defined as "hatred of women." It often refers to institutional policies and practices that discriminate against women and girls and individual behavior that is violent, discriminatory, or demeaning to women and girls.

model minority: "Model minority" is a term that was coined in 1966 in an article in the *New York Times* titled "Success Story: Japanese-American Style" (Peterson 1966). The definition evolved to refer to so-called minority groups that have achieved a high level of success in contemporary U.S. society, exceeding the success of other so-called minority groups and sometimes exceeding the level of success of those in the majority population (whites) (Kasinitz, Mollenkopf, and Waters 2008, 173).

New Custerism: "New Custerism" began to appear in modern Westerns and other films that depicted American Indians sometime in the 1960s and was influenced by the antidiscriminatory message of the civil rights movement and some understanding of the potential impact of media on human thought and values. In New Custerism (e.g., *Dances with Wolves*, *Little Big Man*) white characters were generally central and Indians peripheral, but the roles of good guys and bad guys were reversed. Instead of being depicted as a brave, heroic Indian fighter, taking on the "savage" Indians to save the U.S. traditions, culture, and land, General Custer was portrayed as a violent perpetrator of atrocities against Native Americans. Some critics applauded New Custerism, while others were less celebratory and saw this extreme view of the wholesale flipping of good guys and bad guys as continuing to tell a story with only partial truths (Seals 1991, 634).

Old Custerism: "Old Custerism" describes the depiction of Native Americans and their relationship to General Custer and the cavalry in most films until the 1960s, an image that persisted in many films beyond that point. Old Custerism translated Manifest Destiny into accessible human terms in which Custer and his cavalry were the heroic fighters who bravely fought Indians, primarily the Sioux, to advance civilization and to expand U.S. territory. By contrast, Native Americans were most frequently depicted in this view as vicious, primitive heathens, unredeemable savages, and "the other." Once an image of a group is consistently and repeatedly conveyed as "the other," it becomes easier to justify discrimination and violence in order to protect the "good guys" of the dominant culture (Seals 1991, 635).

symbolic annihilation: A term used to describe any group that is reduced to the most simple and negative images or made invisible in the media. The late George Gerbner (dean emeritus of the Annenberg School of Communication and founder of the Cultural Indicators Research Project and the Cultural Environment Movement) described this process as a deliberate and systematic portrayal of the "absence," "condemnation," or "trivialization" of any group in the media. Symbolic annihilation of any group in the media establishes a pattern of messages that condemns the group as inferior and/ or inconsequential (Coleman and Yochim 2008).

BIBLIOGRAPHY

Advertising Age. 2009. *Hispanic Fact Pack, 2009 Edition: Annual Guide to Hispanic Marketing and Media*. Digital supplement, July 27. http://adage.com/images/random/datacenter/2009/hispfactpack09.pdf.

Aldridge, Derrick P. 2005. "From Civil Rights to Hip-Hop: Toward a Nexus of Ideas." *Journal of African American History* 90, no. 2: 226–252.

Aleiss, Angela. 1995. "Native Americans: The Surprising Silents." *Cineaste* 21, no. 3 (Summer): 34.

Allied Media Corp. 2008. "Hispanic American Demographics." www.allied-media.com/Hispanic%20Market/hispanic%20demographics.html.

Altman, Susan. 1997. "Spencer Williams, Jr., Actor and Director." Source: *The Encyclopedia of African-American Heritage*. New York: Facts on File. African American Registry. www.aaregistry.org/historic_events/view/spencer-williams-jr-actor-and-director.

Anderson, Eric Gary. 1998. "Driving the Red Road: PowWow Highway." In *Hollywood's Indian*, ed. Peter C. Rollins and John E. O'Connor. Lexington: University Press of Kentucky.

Andreeva, Nellie. 2013. "Ratings Rat Race: 'Scandal' Holds Steady for First No. 1 as CBS Comedies Hit Lows." Deadline Hollywood, November 1. www.deadline.com/2013/11/ratings-rat-race-scandal-holds-steady-for-first-no-1-as-cbs-comedies-hit-lows/.

The Art of Turntablism. 2013. Public Broadcast Service. December 6. www.pbs.org/opb/historydetectives/feature/the-art-of-turntablism/.

Asian Pacific Islander Justice Center/Advancing Equality. 2009. "The 2009 Asian Pacific American Media Coalition Report Card on Television Diversity," December 7.

Berg, Charles Ramirez. 2002. *Latino Images in Film: Stereotypes, Subversion, and Resistance*. Austin: University of Texas Press.

Bobo, Jacqueline. 1995. "*The Color Purple*: Black Women as Cultural Readers." In *Gender, Race, and Class in Media*, ed. Gail Dines and Jean M. Humez, 54. Thousand Oaks, CA: Sage.

Bogle, Donald. 1989. *Toms, Coons, Mulattoes, Mammies, and Bucks: An Interpretive History of Blacks in American Films*. 3rd ed. New York: Continuum.

Braus, Patricia. 1993. "What Does 'Hispanic' Mean?" *American Demographics* 15, no. 6 (June): 46.

Burton, Nsenga. 2010. "Celebrating 100 Years of Black Cinema." *The Root*, February 3. www.theroot.com/articles/culture/2010/02/100_years_of_black_cinema_oscar_micheaux_melvin_van_peebles_spike_lee_kasi_lemmons.html.

Butters, Gerald, R., Jr. 2000. "From Homestead to Lynch Mob: Portrayals of Black Masculinity in Oscar Micheaux's *Within Our Gates*." *The Journal for Multimedia History* 3.

Canote, Terence Towles. 2009. "The Invisible Minority: Native Americans on American Television Part Three." A Shroud of Thoughts (blog), July 28. http://mercurie.blogspot.com/2009/07/invisible-minority-native-americans-on_28.html.

Coleman, Robin R. Means, and Emily Chivers Yochim. 2008. "Symbolic Annihilation." In *The International Encyclopedia of Communication*, ed. Wolfgang Donsbach. Malden, MA: Blackwell.

Consoli, John. 2010. "A Very Good Year for Hispanic TV." *The Wrap*, May 11. www.thewrap.com/ind-column/very-good-year-hispanic-tv-17244.

Croteau, David, and William Hoynes. 1997. *Media/Society: Industries, Images, and Audiences*. Thousand Oaks, CA: Pine Forge Press.

Dates, Jannette L., and William Barlow, eds. 1990. *Split Image: African Americans in the Mass Media*. Washington, DC: Howard University Press.

Dates, Jannette L., and Thomas A. Mascaro. 2010 "African Americans in Film and Television: Twentieth-Century Lessons for a New Millenium." *Journal of Popular Film and Television* 33, no. 2 (Summer): 50–55.

Deggans, Eric. 2002. "More Hispanics on Prime Time." Hispanic Online.com (New America Media), October 15. http://news.newamericamedia.org/news/view_article.html?article_id=08acd99e495a5 7adae47bfdeddebddaf.

Del Barco, Mandalit. 2013. "Does Disney's Tonto Reinforce Stereotypes or Overcome Them?" National Public Radio, July 2.

Dines, Gail, and Jean M. Humez, eds. 1995. *Gender, Race, and Class in Media*. Thousand Oaks, CA: Sage.

Dirks, Tim. 1999. "The Birth of a Nation (1915)." Filmsite Movie Review. www.filmsite.org/birt.html.

Dyson, Michael Eric. 2004. "The Culture of Hip-Hop." In *That's the Joint! The Hip-Hop Studies Reader*, ed. Murray Forman and Mark Anthony Neal. New York: Routledge Press.

Early, Gerald. 1991. "One Nation Under a Groove: The Brief, Shining Moment of Motown—and America." *New Republic* 205, no. 3: 30.

Ebert, Roger. 1988. "*Mississippi Burning*." *Chicago Sun-Times*, December 9.

———. 2002. "Monster's Ball." Rogerebert.com, February 1. www.rogerebert.com.

———. 2011. "*The Help*." *Chicago Sun-Times*, August 8.

Edgerton, Gary, and Kathy Merlock Jackson. 1996. "Redesigning Pocahontas: Disney, the 'White Man's Indian,' and the Marketing of Dreams." *Journal of Popular Film and Television* 24, no. 2: 90–98.

Gerbner, George. 1998. "Casting the American Scene: A Look at the Characters on Prime-time and Daytime Television from 1994–1997." Screen Actors Guild Report, December. www.asc.upenn .edu/gerbner/Asset.aspx?assetID=1614.

Gray, Herman. 1995. *Watching Race*. Minneapolis: University of Minnesota Press.

Guerrero, Edward. 1993. *Framing Blackness: The African American Image in Film*. Philadelphia: Temple University Press.

Hamamoto, Darrell Y. 1994. *Monitored Peril: Asian Pacific Islanders and the Politics of TV Representation*. Minneapolis: University of Minnesota Press.

Hilton, Shani O. 2013. "No, 2013 Was Not the Year of 'The Black Movie.'" *BuzzFeed*, December 3. www.buzzfeed.com/shani/black-directors-best-man-holiday-12-years-slave.

Hispanic Business Magazine. 2008. "US Hispanic Purchasing Power 2003–2010." Santa Barbara, CA: HispanTelligence, Hispanic Business.

"Hispanics: Last Frontier for Marketing. (Television Show Viewer Ratings of Hispanic Americans)." 1993. *Broadcasting and Cable* 123: 54–58.

Holtzman, Linda. 2011. Unpublished content analysis of six decades of African American songs, recording audiences, and themes.

Hornaday, Ann. 2011. "Black and White and Not Enough Help." *Washington Post*, August 10.

Hunt, Darnell. 2003. *Prime Time Television's Black and White World*. Los Angeles: University of California, Los Angeles, Center for Communications and Community. Report, June 24. www.c3.ucla .edu/newsstand/art/prime-time-televisions-black-and-white-world/.

Internet Movie Database. 1999, 2002, 2006, 2010, and 2013. www.IMDb.com.

Jhally, Sut, and Justin Lewis. 1992. *Enlightened Racism: The Cosby Show, Audiences, and the Myth of the American Dream*. Boulder, CO: Westview Press.

John, Derek. 2004. "Asian-American Rapper Jin Makes Hip-Hop History." National Public Radio (NPR), October 24. www.npr.org/templates/story/story.php?storyId=4126877.

Kasinitz, Phillip, John H. Mollenkopf, and Mary Waters. 2008. *Inheriting the City: The Children of Immigrants Come of Age*. Cambridge, MA: Harvard University Press.

Kawai, Yuko. 2005. "Stereotyping Asian Americans: The Dialectic of the Model Minority and the Yellow Peril." *The Howard Journal of Communications* 16: 109–130.

Kempley, Rita. 1988. "Mississippi Burning." *Washington Post*, December 9. www.washingtonpost .com/wp-srv/style/longterm/movies/videos/mississippiburningrkempley_a0c9de.htm.

Koch, John. 1989. "A Simple and Soulless Revenge Film." *Boston Globe*, January 26.

Lane, Thomas. 2011. "The Mentalist Profile: Tim Kang." Yahoo Contributor Network, June 24. http://tv.yahoo.com/news/mentalist-profile-tim-kang-223000856.html.

Lawrence-McIntyre, John C. 2011. "African and African-American Contributions to World Music." Portland Public Schools Geocultural Baseline Essay Series. www.pps.k12.or.us/depts-c/mc-me /be-af-mu.pdf.

Le, C.N. 2013. "Writers, Artists, and Entertainers." Asian Nation: The Landscape of Asian America. www.asian-nation.org/artists.shtml.

LyricsMode. 2013. www.lyricsmode.com.

Media Awareness. 1998. www.media-awareness.ca/eng/issues/STATS/issmin.html.

Merriam-Webster. 2013. "affirmative action." www.merriam-webster.com/dictionary/affirmative%20 action.

Merskin, Debra. 1998. "Sending Up Signals: A Survey of Native American Media Use and Representation in the Mass Media." *Howard Journal of Communications* 9, no. 4: 333–345.

Metacritic. 2011. www.metacritic.com.

Monk-Turner, Elizabeth, Mary Heiserman, Crystle Johnson, Vanity Cotton, and Manny Jackson. 2010. "The Portrayal of Racial Minorities on Prime Time Television: A Replication of the Mastro and Greenberg Study a Decade Later." *Studies in Popular Culture* 32, no. 2: 101–114.

Morgan, Kyrna, and Dixon, Aimee. 2013. "African-American Women in the Silent Film Industry." In *Women Film Pioneers Project*, ed Jane Gaines, Radha Vatsal, and Monica Dall'Asta. Center for Digital Research and Scholarship. New York, NY: Columbia University Libraries. https://wfpp.cdrs .columbia.edu/essay/african-american-women-in-the-silent-film-industry/.

National Association for the Advancement of Colored People (NAACP). 2008. "Out of Focus, Out of Sync: Take 4: A Report on the Television Industry." Report, December 18.

National Latino Media Council (NLMC). 2009. www.nhmc.org/about-us/national-latino-media-council/.

Navarro, Mireya. 2003. "Missing: Asian-American Pop Stars." *New York Times*, March 4. www.nytimes .com/2007/03/04/world/americas/04iht-singer.4787848.html.

Nelson, Angela M.S. 1998. "Black Situation Comedies and the Politics of Television Art." In *Cultural Diversity and the U.S. Media*, ed. Yahya R. Kamalipour and Theresa Crilli, 81. Albany: State University of New York Press.

Nga, Thi Thanh. 1995. "The Long March from Wong to Woo: Asians in Hollywood." *Cineaste* 21, no. 4: 38.

Nhan, Doris. 2012. "Buying Power of Hispanics Worth $1 Trillion, Report Says." *National Journal*, May 8.

Nielsen Company. May 2009. "National People Meter Hispanic Sub Sample." New York. http://adage .com/images/random/0709/HispFP2009.pdf.

Nielsen Research. 2010. "Top 10 and Trends for 2010." www.nielsen.com/us/en/newswire/2010/u-s -top-10s-and-trends-for-2010.html.

Obenson, Tambay, A. 2013. "The Top Grossing Black Films of 2013. Shadow and Act: On the Cinema of the African Diaspora." Indiwire, December 30. http://blogs.indiewire.com/shadowandact/the-top -10-grossing-black-films-of-2013.

Oppenheimer, Mark. 2008. "Harold and Kumar Go to the Ivy League." *Chronicle of Higher Education* 54, no. 49: B10–B11.

Peterson, William. 1966. "Success Story, Japanese-American Style." *New York Times*, January 9.

Price, Robert J., Jr. 2005. "Hegemony, Hope, and the Harlem Renaissance: Taking Hip-Hop Culture Seriously." *Convergence* 38, no. 2: 55–64.

Richmond, Ray. 1998. "TV Sitcoms: The Great Divide—Few Shows Bridge Black, White Audiences." *Variety*, April.

Rincon and Associates Market Research and Demography. 2004. "Latino Television Study." Report prepared for the National Latino Media Coalition, February 1.

Rodriguez, Clara E., ed. 1997. *Latin Looks: Images of Latinas and Latinos in the U.S. Media*. Boulder, CO: Westview Press.

Samuels, David. 1991. "The Rap on Rap: The 'Black Music' That Isn't Either." *The New Republic* 205, no. 20: 24–29.

Schickel, Richard. 1988. "Cinema: The Fire in the South, *Mississippi Burning*." *Time*, December 6.

Screen Actors Guild Awards. 2009. www.sagawards.org.

Seals, David. 1991. "The New Custerism." *Nation* 252, no. 18 (May): 634–635.

Shah, Hemant. 2003. "'Asian Culture' and Asian American Identities in the Television and Film Industries of the United States." *SIMILE: Journal of Studies in Media & Information Literacy Education* 3, no. 3: 1–10.

Thomas, Rebecca. 1996. "There's a Whole Lot o' Color in the 'White Man's' Blues: Country Music's Selective Memory and the Challenge of Identity." *Midwest Quarterly* 38, no. 1: 73–89.

Urban Dictionary. 2013. "sampling." www.urbandictionary.com

U.S. Census Bureau. 2005. "Annual Population Estimates 2000–2005." Tables, July 1. www.census.gov/popest/data/historical/2000s/vintage_2005/index.html.

USLegal.com. 2013. "Affirmative Action Law and Legal Definition." http://definitions.uslegal.com/a/affirmative-action/.

Variety. 1960. "Review: Breakfast at Tiffany's." December 31. http://variety.com/1960/film/reviews/breakfast-at-tiffany-s-1200419987/.

Whitt, Jan. 2005. "Frank's Place." *Journal of Popular Film and Television* 33, no. 2: 80–87.

Wikipedia. 2013. "Sukiyaki" (song). http://en.wikipedia.org/wiki/Sukiyaki.

Wilson, Clint C., II, and Felix Gutierrez. 1995. *Race, Multiculturalism, and the Media: From Mass to Class Communication*. 2nd ed. Thousand Oaks, CA: Sage.

Wong, Deborah. Fall 1994. "I Want the Microphone: Mass Mediation and Agency in Asian-American Popular Music." *The Drama Review* 38, no. 3: 152–167.

Zoglin, Richard. 1988. "Awaiting a Gringo Crumb: Hispanics Have Gained on TV—But Oddly, Not Much." *Time*, July 11.

6

Sexual Orientation and the Fabrication of "Normal"

We are your gay and lesbian children: "You must not seek vengeance, nor bear a grudge against the children of your people" (Lev. 19:18); we are the stranger: "You must not oppress the stranger. You shall love the stranger as yourself for you were strangers in the land of Egypt" (Lev. 19:34); we are your gay and lesbian neighbors: "You must not oppress your neighbor" (Lev. 19:13). "You must judge your neighbor justly" (Lev. 19:15). "You shall love your neighbor as yourself" (Lev. 19:18).

—*Lisa Edwards*

Best advice I ever got was from an old friend of mine, a black friend, who said you have to go the way your blood beats. If you don't live the only life you have, you won't live some other life, you won't live any life at all.

—*James Baldwin (quoted in Goldstein 1984)*

PERSONAL EXPERIENCE

In this chapter we will examine the sources of our information and misinformation and reconstruct what we consider to be true about **sexual orientation**. As you begin to think about, or continue, your journey in understanding sexual orientation and identity, consider the four questions in Personal Inventory 6.1 (page 404). Your answers will help you locate your current beliefs and values and questions about **sexual identity**. Your responses to the questions constitute elements of your current beliefs, attitudes, openness, knowledge, and experience about sexual orientation and identity. Your clarity about your starting perspective will help you observe and analyze your response to what you read in this chapter. As always, you are never required to change your beliefs, but only to remember that they are your beliefs, which are not always the same as the "truth." It is important to understand how what you believe influences your openness to new information and experience.

Many people in the United States find sexual orientation and sexual identity more controversial and confusing than any other topic of cultural diversity. We receive less

Personal Inventory 6.1

Locating My Beliefs

Choose the statement that comes closest to matching your current beliefs.

1. The following statement comes closest to matching what I think about what it means to be gay, lesbian, or bisexual.
   a. I think it is wrong to be gay, lesbian, or bisexual.
   b. I believe it is important to judge the sin and not the sinner.
   c. I am confused and not sure what to think.
   d. I respect other people's choices, but I do not agree with the gay, lesbian, or bisexual lifestyle.
   e. I think that gays, lesbians, and bisexuals are just as natural as heterosexuals and should have all the same rights.
   f. I think that being gay, lesbian, or bisexual is liberating and frees people from the constraints of heterosexuality.
   g. Other (please indicate)
2. The following phrase comes closest to describing my academic or intellectual understanding of sexual orientation and sexual identity.
   a. Very little or none
   b. A moderate amount
   c. Some reading and studying
   d. Extensive reading and studying
   e. Other (please indicate)
3. The following statement comes closest to describing my personal knowledge and understanding of sexual orientation and sexual identity.
   a. I have never known anyone who was openly gay, lesbian, or bisexual.
   b. I have met a few people who are gay, lesbian, or bisexual, but I have not been friends with them.
   c. I have one or more friends or family members who are gay, lesbian, or bisexual.
   d. I am part of a community that has members who are openly gay, lesbian, or bisexual.
   e. I am part of a community that is exclusively lesbian, gay, or bisexual.
   f. Other (please indicate)
4. Choose the sentence that comes closest to your thoughts as you begin studying sexual orientation and sexual identity.
   a. I hate the thought of even reading the chapter. The topic disturbs me.
   b. I am uncomfortable about the topic of sexual orientation and identity and am hesitant to study it.
   c. I am confused and unclear about approaching the subject of sexual orientation and identity.
   d. I am neutral and have no strong thoughts or feelings about sexual orientation and identity.
   e. I am somewhat curious and open to learning more about sexual orientation and identity.
   f. I am very curious and open to learning more about sexual orientation and identity.
   g. I am excited that sexual orientation and identity are included in this book. I am eager to learn more.
   h. Other (please indicate)

information about this issue than about gender or race or even socioeconomic class. Many religions teach that to be gay or lesbian or bisexual is a sin. Some people believe that it is a sickness that can be cured. Many people go through much of their lives without ever knowingly interacting with someone who is gay, lesbian, or bisexual. Gay jokes still abound, as do comedic portrayals of gay stereotypes in the media. The word "gay" itself, in recent times, came into widespread use among young people as a catch-all pejorative for any statement or behavior regarded as stupid or uncool. Fortunately, this usage has gradually drifted out of vogue. The lack of experience and/or information about people who are lesbian, gay, bisexual, or transgender (LGBT), coupled with the tacit cultural acceptance of anti-gay bias, makes sexual orientation an especially challenging topic. That many people's attitudes toward individuals who are LGBT are in some way tied to their religious beliefs creates another layer of challenge.

Some of you who are reading this are LGBT and are interested in learning more about the history, oppression, and liberation of your community. You may be impatient with the careful attention to those who judge or discriminate against you. Some of you reading this are friends, relatives, and allies of people who are gay, lesbian, bisexual, or transgender and want to learn more about what you can do to support the liberation of this community. Some of you reading this may have given little or no thought to this issue. Some of you reading this may have negative feelings toward people who are LGBT. Some of you may not be fully conscious of your true feelings. Whoever you are, this chapter is for you. This chapter is for those people who identify with targeted or marginalized groups, those who are in the privileged groups, and those who may not have thought about how cultural dominance and marginalization involving sexual orientation and identity occurs and affects us all.

Now that you have begun to identify your current beliefs and attitudes about sexual orientation, we will examine what contributed to this perspective. As we explore the experience of socialization, it is important to remember that people who are LGBT are subject to the same information, misinformation, and distortions as people who are heterosexual. Answer the questions and total your score in Personal Inventory 6.2 (beginning on page 406).

If you scored a total of 20–25 points, you have been socialized to understand same-sex attraction as a natural phenomenon and have been told that people who are gay, lesbian, bisexual or transgender can be good family members and friends who deserve all of the privileges and rights of heterosexuals. If you scored 15–19 points, you have been taught that being LGBT is acceptable but with some limitations. For example, your parents may have taught you to respect people who are gay, lesbian, bisexual, or transgender but you overheard them telling gay jokes. Or your religion may have taught you that you should feel sorry for people who are perceived to have a sexual orientation that is anything other than heterosexual, but your parents had good friends who were LGBT who you thought were terrific. If you scored 10–14 points, you were socialized to believe that loving relationships between same-sex partners are wrong. You learned from at least one group (parents, religion, peers) that to be gay, lesbian, or bisexual was unnatural or wrong. You may have had at least one or two groups tell you something positive about gays, lesbians, or bisexuals, but it contradicted other things that

Personal Inventory 6.2

How Do I Know What I Know?

Choose the answer that comes closest to your experience and circle the response. After you complete all the questions, add your total score.

1. When I was a child, my parents told me that people who were gay, lesbian, or bisexual were
    a. ___ sinful (0 points)
    b. ___ sick (1 point)
    c. ___ unfortunate people who deserved our sympathy (2 points)
    d. ___ simply homosexual without attaching value judgments (0 points)
    e. ___ a minority that was subject to unfair discrimination (3 points)
    f. ___ a group of people that deserved the same rights as people who were heterosexual (4 points)
    g. ___ a group of people to be respected for their courage to be who they are (5 points)
    h. ___ My parents never said anything about people who were gay, lesbian, or bisexual. (0 points)

2. Mark the answer that comes closest to what you heard or overheard your parents say or do when you were a child.
    a. ___ I heard my parents say hateful or violent things about people who are gay, lesbian, or bisexual. (0 points)
    b. ___ I heard my parents use derogatory terms to describe people who are gay, lesbian, or bisexual. (0 points)
    c. ___ I heard my parents make gay jokes or mock people who they thought were gay, lesbian, or bisexual. (0 points)
    d. ___ I heard my parents say a mix of positive and negative things about people who are gay, lesbian, or bisexual. (3 points)
    e. ___ I heard my parents talk with or about their gay, lesbian, or bisexual friends and about the challenges and joys they faced in their lives. (5 points)
    f. ___ I never heard my parents say anything about people who were gay, lesbian, or bisexual. (0 points)

3. Considering my parents' friends, my friends' parents, and my neighbors as I was growing up
    a. ___ they were all heterosexual (0 points)
    b. ___ one or two people were gay, lesbian, or bisexual (1 point)
    c. ___ a few people were gay, lesbian, or bisexual (2 points)
    d. ___ many people were gay, lesbian, or bisexual (3 points)

4. When I was a child, my peers said the following things about same-sex attraction, love, and marriage
    a. ___ It's evil. (0 points)
    b. ___ It's nasty. (0 points)
    c. ___ It's stupid. (0 points)
    d. ___ I don't get it. (0 points)
    e. ___ It's okay for them but not for me. (2 points)

f. ___ It's fine. (5 points)

g. ___ It's cool. (5 points)

h. ___ They said nothing about same-sex attraction, love, and marriage. (0 points)

5. When I was a child, my religion taught the following about same-sex attraction, love, and marriage

a. ___ It is a sin and an abomination against God. (0 points)

b. ___ It is a sin, but we should hate the sin and not the sinner. (1 point)

c. ___ It is a sickness that we should try to heal. (1 point)

d. ___ It is a natural part of some people's lives. (3 points)

e. ___ It is a human right that we should support in the interest of social justice. (4 points)

f. ___ It is a part of God's plan that we should embrace. (5 points)

g. ___ My religion said nothing about same-sex attraction, love, and marriage. (0 points)

h. ___ I was not exposed to any religious teachings on this subject as a child. (0 points

Total score _____

you learned. This may have created some confusion for you. If you scored 5–9 points, chances are you were told nothing or very little, and what little you were told was very negative about being gay, lesbian, bisexual, or transgender. If you scored under 5, you were socialized to believe that sexual orientation was either a forbidden topic to discuss or that being LGBT was sinful, evil, and wrong. Your parents, religion, peers, or other groups all reinforced this message, so what you learned was consistent.

Linda's Story

As I was growing up, I received no formal information about sexual orientation. I assumed, without any conscious awareness of the assumption, that I was "normal" and expected that I would grow up and marry a man. The first time I can remember being directly told anything about gays or lesbians was the summer before seventh grade, when my best friend's older sister had a talk with us. She told us that we had to stop holding hands when we got to junior high school because everyone would call us "fairies." I was not sure what a fairy was, but I could tell from the way she said it that it was not something good. From that point until much later in my adulthood, I ceased holding hands or having much physical contact with girls or women. My other early memories consist of adults joking about and mocking hairdressers and interior decorators who they assumed were gay men. The mocking always involved a limp wrist and an exaggerated feminine accent. Other than these two experiences, I had absolutely no other formal or informal information about gays, lesbians, or bisexuals. I am not sure I even knew the words. The words I heard were "queer," "fairy," "fruit," and "sissy." I knew that while it was acceptable for a girl to be a tomboy and do boy-type things such as sports and getting dirty, it was not acceptable for a boy to do girl-type things such as play with dolls, cry, or hang out too much with girls.

I was born in 1949, and it was not until the late 1960s and early 1970s that I became aware of any other information or experience about what it meant to be gay, lesbian, or bisexual. During the 1960s, I became involved in what was then called the women's liberation movement and voraciously read everything about women and feminism that I could get my hands on. Some of the books I read discussed coming out as a lesbian as a natural and evolving phenomenon, and other books addressed being a lesbian as the ultimate feminist political statement. In the 1970s, I knew women who had publicly identified as heterosexual who either experimented with relationships with women or came out as lesbian. I was not close enough to any of these women to share the intimate details of this coming-out process. It was not until the mid-1970s that I became close friends with men and women who were gay and lesbian. One friend disclosed to me that she was lesbian with much trepidation. She feared that I would reject her. She feared telling her parents.

I had one male friend whose religion had taught him that to be gay was a sin. For the first four years of our friendship, I thought he was heterosexual. It was not until we had been good friends for that long that he told me of his struggle to address his sexuality. In the early stages of this struggle, he was convinced that he needed to do everything possible to transform, be "normal," and be accepted by his church. He told no one of his sexual identity. He tried dating women. He had a brief encounter with the priesthood. He had a longer encounter with alcohol. It was a more than ten-year process for him to come to grips with and accept his sexuality and the full range of who he is. He is now in a long-term committed relationship with a man. Being a witness to this painful process moved me. Here was an extremely bright, funny, professionally successful, interesting, and compassionate person whose sexual identity and its rejection by society served to torture him for many, many years. It was during that time that I made a conscious decision to be an ally to people who are gay, lesbian, and bisexual.

Since that time, I have had many friends who are gay, lesbian, and bisexual. They are part of a larger group that I consider my community. I never "taught" my children about sexual orientation when they were very young; it was a fact of their life and experience. My students frequently ask me how I could teach such young children about homosexuality and sex. My answer is that when my children were preschoolers, I never taught them about how heterosexuals have sex and would not teach them about homosexual sex either. Rather, I told them that sometimes boys and girls love each other and become life partners or get married, and that sometimes boys and boys or girls and girls do the same. This was confusing for them sometimes because the rest of their environment gave them such strong messages about heterosexuality and marriage.

One time we were having a barbecue and invited many of our close friends, one of whom was Andy (not his real name), a single gay man. My son, who was then three years old, asked me if Andy's wife was coming. I said, "No, Andy doesn't have a wife. Remember—he's gay." To which my son responded, "Who's he gay with?" That's been a joke between Andy, my son, and me for years now. When I told Andy about my son's question, Andy said, "Be sure and tell him that as soon as I find someone to be gay with, he'll be the first to know."

Another time when my son and daughter were eight and nine years old, they each had a friend spend the night. The next morning the four of them were sitting at the kitchen table having breakfast. In those days, playing house and assigning people familiar family roles was common for them. One of their friends said, "Let's pretend we're two married couples having breakfast together." My son responded, "I know, we can pretend to be two gay couples having breakfast together."

My own socialization kicked in during this conversation. My first reaction was, "Oh, no! What if these kids tell their parents that they came to our house and played gay?" That was the reaction of my own homophobia and fear of what other people would think of me, based on my own children's comfort level and openness about sexual orientation. During my second reaction, my intellect kicked in, and I found myself quite proud of my open-minded children.

As an ally to people who are gay, lesbian, or bisexual, I have made some choices in my adult life—some I feel very good about and some I am not particularly proud of. I am committed to interrupting jokes or comments that discriminate against or mock gays, lesbians, or bisexuals. I have spent much time reading, writing, and teaching about the history of both discrimination against and liberation for LGBT. I support domestic partnership benefits in the workplace as well as other issues that make work a safe environment for gay people. I support hate crime legislation that makes it a criminal and enforceable offense to participate in violent or nonviolent acts of hate against gays, lesbians, and bisexuals. I have attended marriages, commitment ceremonies, and anniversary parties of my gay friends as well as cultural events in the community.

I have worked to understand the advantages that I have by being identified as heterosexual, but I have not always been consistent in addressing these privileges. Several years ago, before same-sex marriage was legal or widespread, I asked some of my gay and lesbian friends about the issue of the illegality of civil marriage for gays and lesbians which meant that if they were a couple, they could not make a choice to get married and have it sanctioned by the government. At that point, I had the advantage of having been married publicly with the approval of the state for more than fifteen years. I asked my friends if they would consider it an act of solidarity for me to begin to refer to my husband as my "partner" rather than my spouse or husband. I felt this was parallel to non-Jews wearing yellow armbands in solidarity against anti-Semitism. My friends liked this idea. But the truth is I never did it with any consistency or regularity. True, it was a bit awkward to change a reference to someone from husband to partner. But deeper than that, I realized that I did not want certain people to think I was a lesbian. I wanted my children's teachers to know I had a husband to make sure they knew they were dealing with a two-parent heterosexual family. I wanted my kids to have every edge possible. When I had a customer service complaint, I wanted the store to know that I had a husband who was mythically in the background to back me up if they did not respond to my complaint. I have realized that in many instances, while I am committed to serving as an ally to people who are gay, lesbian, and bisexual, I have not been willing to relinquish the privileges and advantages of being seen as heterosexual. Yet in order to work toward a more level playing field, some of us may need to relinquish some of our privilege and work to create the same privilege and opportunities for gays, lesbians, and bisexuals.

One more story that was an eye-opener for me: I have a close lesbian friend who has children and is in a long-term committed relationship. We have talked about how heterosexuals often say, "Look, I don't care who you sleep with. Your personal life is your own business, but I don't want to hear about it. Keep it in your own mind and in your own bedroom." My friend's response is that people in heterosexual relationships "out" themselves all the time without talking about sex itself. Once, when she went to pick up her daughter from swim team practice, the session ran thirty minutes late. Within the first five minutes, the other waiting parents all "came out" as heterosexual. One woman said, "Boy, I wish they'd hurry up. I told my husband I'd meet him in ten minutes." A man said, "I'd better call my wife and let her know we'll be late for dinner." While this kind of common, casual conversation went on, my friend wondered what would happen if she said, "I'd better call my partner Jane and tell her we'll be late." She imagined, as did I, that while there may not have been any direct nastiness or discrimination, the conversation would not have continued so fluidly or naturally. There may have been awkwardness or tension because her "outing" would have been perceived as outside the norm.

Leon's Story

Growing up, my friends and I used words like "sissy" and "faggot" and "punk." Those words for us had varied but unspoken shades of meaning. The connotation of "sissy," though by no means affirming, was more descriptive than judgmental. A sissy was simply a boy who acted like a girl or a man who acted like a woman. There were clear behaviors and gestures associated with the word. To walk, talk, or dress in a certain way was to be a sissy. On the other hand, to label someone a "fag" was more cutting, possessing sexual overtones that seemed somehow less juvenile than the word "sissy." In my neighborhood, one of the worst near-expletives you could call another guy was "punk," a word designed to be spit rather than spoken. A punk was not only a boy who liked being with boys in the way that boys are supposed to like being with girls, but he was also a weakling, a wimp, a coward—unwilling to engage in a fistfight, afraid to retaliate when attacked, unable to throw a block in a hardscrabble game of football on an abandoned vacant lot. To call someone a punk was to level the condemning accusation that he was not behaving within what we erroneously believed to be the defining contours of manhood.

With girls it was different. It was more or less okay for a girl to act like a boy. In fact, we thought it was kind of cute. The childhood male response tended to range from mild amusement with the actions of those "tomboys" we found attractive to tacit respect for the ones who could hit, throw, curse, fight, or play the dozens like one of the guys. In retrospect, the extent to which our sexism and heterosexism were intricately woven and intertwined is clear to see. Back then, however, such notions were simply a matter of course. Boyish behavior in a girl was regarded as somewhat out of the ordinary but not necessarily perverse. Nor was it a big deal for girls to dance with each other, whisper in each other's ears, touch, or hold hands—all of which were forbidden behaviors for boys.

Only later did we learn to use words like "bull dagger and "dyke" and begin to understand their cruel, toxic connotations.

Kids in my neighborhood were painfully unsophisticated when it came to matters of sexual orientation. We had few opportunities to engage in healthy dialogue on the subject with anyone who could help us understand what same-sex attraction was all about. We were left to our own devices. There was an old man who sometimes rode up and down our block on a bicycle, collecting discarded soda bottles. We called him the "crazy man." He always had a goofy grin on his face and he never spoke—he just made sounds. Our parents told us to stay away from him because he might be "funny," and one of my friends said that if he got too close to you he would kiss you, regardless of whether you were a boy or a girl. In truth, I never saw him try to kiss anyone. He was probably just some poor guy trying to have a little human contact as best he knew how. But whenever we saw him, we ran and hid.

It was not necessary for someone to be a real person to serve as fodder for our childish hetero-hysteria. One time, we were all terrorized by the rumor that a "half-man/half-woman" had escaped from the carnival and was coming to get us. I actually had nightmares about this. Whenever someone claimed to have seen this freak-show fugitive, we would all take off in genuine horror. So it was that for several days one summer, a fabricated monster with an implied identity of sexual otherness became the foil for an extended game of homophobic hide-and-seek that held hostage an entire neighborhood of children.

One could easily dismiss all this as so much childhood silliness, which, indeed, it was, but on another level there was something more insidious occurring. At a very young age, we were being socialized to accept a set of misleading notions about gender, sexual orientation, and so-called normalcy that had no basis in reality. Not only that, we had already begun to succumb to the dangerously false association of gay/lesbian identity with pedophilia. Of course, I should not speak as though this was true for every single kid. These were the baby boom years and there were a lot of us. I now realize that, even then, there were boys and girls around me who were having deeper thoughts and gaining deeper understandings as they worked through personal puzzles about their own gender identity and sexual orientation.

As for me, during my days in elementary school and even into middle school, I walked around in the blissful state of self-satisfied cluelessness that only an assumed identity of privilege can produce. My school was black, my neighborhood was black, my church was black Protestant, and none of the kids I knew came from families of any net worth to speak of. So the inevitable clash and dissonance of class and racial animus had not yet washed up on the shores of my youthful consciousness. Furthermore, my sense of self as a gendered and sexually oriented being was in perfect alignment with the mainstream messages I had always received about what was normal and right and good. When I gave thought to such matters at all, my only references were the gossip and urban mythologies shared among my equally oblivious friends, the cloaked and coded admonitions of adults, and the majoritarian representations of gays and lesbians that emerged sporadically and confusingly through the media. Television and movie messages insinuated that to be "homosexual" was to be inherently sinister, secretive, predatory, and malicious—something no real man would ever "choose" to be, something no boy should ever desire to become. In my young mind, a homosexual was someone who appeared to be one thing but was, in fact, something else—something nasty, dangerous, and foreboding—a shape-shifter, a werewolf, Dr. Jekyll/Mr. Hyde, a shadow, a secretive and horrifying transmutation.

By the time I reached high school, my understanding of sexual orientation had grown more mature but not much better informed. I liked to hang out with a couple of good friends, Kevin and Skip. We went to parties, sneaked drinks, cut classes, discussed music, argued about sports and politics, and shared our visions of future greatness. One evening, during a long telephone conversation, Kevin informed me that he was gay and asked me not to tell anybody. I did not believe him at first—there was nothing "gay" about him—but the next day when I told Skip what Kevin had said, Skip revealed that Kevin had told him the same thing. Skip and I immediately began to distance ourselves from Kevin. For his part, Kevin did not push the issue. He had taken a chance and confided in his two good friends in hopes, perhaps, that we would take the information in stride and the three of us would continue to be close. That did not happen. Skip and I not only disassociated ourselves from Kevin, but, possibly out of mutual suspicion or mutual guilt, we also gradually drifted away from each other. The fragile male bonds that held our friendship together had been irrevocably severed. I harbored an array of feelings about what had transpired. I was angry with Kevin for operating under false pretenses and deceiving me about his true identity. Yet I also felt a twinge of shame for not being stronger and standing by him. I was suspicious of Skip—wondering if he too was secretly gay—wondering if he wondered the same thing about me. That was the crux of the issue, I suppose. Why would a gay person want to be friends with *me*? I knew I wasn't gay, but was there something about me that made me *seem* to be gay? Did my association with Kevin cause other people to *think* I was gay? Did I need to make sure everybody knew I had a girlfriend? Did I need to change the way I dressed, the way I walked and talked? Did I need to lower my voice another octave?

After a few semesters of college, I was in a different place. I was no longer consciously concerned about other people's perceptions of my masculinity. I harbored deep regret for the way I had treated Kevin. I had been weak and foolish and had lost a good friend as a consequence. In college I became a supporter of gay rights and much more enlightened about issues pertaining to sexual orientation. Or so I thought. There was one other incident, however, that continues to haunt me. A well-known and highly respected individual had been invited to serve as scholar in residence at our small, liberal arts school. One evening, he conducted a special seminar for members of the black student organization to which I belonged. After he finished his presentation, he opened the floor for questions. One student asked him if he was gay. He proudly answered yes and proceeded to tell us about some of his experiences as a black gay man who had risen to a position of considerable stature and prominence in his discipline. Unfortunately, he was interrupted by a group of students who harassed him so mercilessly with taunts and jeers that the entire session was brought abruptly to an end. It bothered me that this was happening at a school reputed to be one of the most socially progressive in the country. It bothered me that the hecklers had regularly participated in the black power demonstrations and antidiscrimination rallies we conducted on campus and elsewhere. What bothered me the most, though, was that I had witnessed this entire spectacle as it unfolded and *had done nothing to interrupt it.*

Not long after, I went home for winter break. My brother arrived, on break as well. Still troubled by my failure to act during the heckling incident at my school, I decided to get his perspective since he, too, had experienced similar situations as a result of being openly gay. I never really got the question out because as soon as I made reference to his sexual orientation, my brother pointed out that it was the first time I had spoken about his sexuality. I am sure it seems ironic, given the story I have been relating, that I only now mention that my brother—barely younger by a year or so—is gay. Before that moment, he and I had never talked openly about that fact, but I had always known it. Yet I had also *not* known it. I had known it back in the days when I was referring to people as sissies and punks, known it when I laughed at homosexual jokes and slurs, known it when I ran from the "crazy man," known it when I shunned and disavowed a friend. Yet I had not known my brother was gay when he preferred to play with dolls instead of a ball and bat, not known it when he wore an apron and pretended it was a dress, not known it as we grew older and he showed no particular interest in girls. I had always known it because "it" was who he was and not knowing it would have been impossible for me. Yet, simultaneously, to have known it at that time was impossible for me because *I was who I was* and, for the better part of my growing-up life, I had no place in my psyche to put that information. We had the same parents, the same kid sister; we grew up in the same neighborhood, lived in the same house, and shared the same room. We attended the same schools, ate from the same box of corn flakes, drank the same Kool-Aid, watched the same cartoons. To the best of my recollection, my brother ran from the "crazy man" too. I just didn't (couldn't, wouldn't) see him as a sissy or a punk. I did not see him as possessing those inferior, effeminate traits I had always attributed to guys who were gay. He was not especially weak or cowardly; rather, he was fiercely independent. Some years later he would survive a brutal stabbing attack, contract HIV, and yet go on to become founding director of the African American Collective Theater in Washington, D.C.—where he continues to live—writing and producing powerful, gritty plays exploring black gay life in urban America. But when we were children, I did not see my brother as gay. I simply saw him as my brother.

But is that good enough? The statement I just wrote reminds me of the way well-meaning white people have sometimes told me they "don't see my color"; they simply see me as this or as that. It is hard for me to get them to understand what is wrong with such a disingenuous concept. To say you see me but do not see my color is to render me visible and invisible at the same time. You see me, but only through a lens that filters out what you do not like or do not understand about me. To take such a stance is to imprison oneself in an illusion of one's own construction. That is precisely what I had done with my brother's sexual orientation.

I vividly recall that midwinter day, many years ago, when I first talked openly with my brother about his identity as a black gay man. Although he was relieved and gratified that I had finally spoken his sexual orientation into our shared existence, it was not something he necessarily needed from me. He had always fearlessly and unabashedly expressed who and what he was. Nonetheless, it was an acknowledgement he welcomed. His celebration that day, however, was mostly in recognition of *my* liberation. After all, it was I who knew but didn't know, saw but didn't see. It was I who had locked a part of myself away in a homophobic closet. Fortunately, I had a loving brother who patiently stood by me and was there, just outside the door, with open arms to greet me when I finally managed to come out.

Now it is your turn. Write or tape-record the answers to the questions in Personal Inventory 6.3 that continue your autobiography and discuss them with others to determine what patterns or distinctions emerge. As you think about your answers to these autobiographical questions, try to articulate your beliefs about sexual orientation and what about your convictions is clear and what is perhaps confusing.

Then try one more exercise. Imagine that we live in a world where it is the norm for people to be LGBT. It is legal to have same-sex marriages and illegal to marry someone who is a different sex from yourself. It is dangerous to be an openly heterosexual couple. If you are heterosexual, you may be subject to discrimination in housing, in education, in your job, and in your community. Imagine that you are in constant danger of being shamed publicly or attacked violently by people who do not necessarily know you but, nevertheless, do not like you. You will need to make constant decisions about where and with whom to be out as a heterosexual. People who are gay, lesbian, and bisexual—or perceived to be so—are typically the ones who are in charge of major businesses, educational institutions, and government. Employee benefits, parties at work and in school, health insurance, and other benefits are designed to serve the needs and interests of individuals who are gay, lesbian, and bisexual. Most books, movies, and television shows that portray families are those with gay, lesbian, or bisexual parents and children. Popular music and music videos are all about romantic love and pain between gays, lesbians, and bisexuals.

Now whether you identify as gay, lesbian, bisexual, heterosexual or trans, imagine going through your day with the rules and norms changed in the manner just described. What would be the same about your day? What would be different? What kinds of decisions would you need to make? What kinds of things would be easier and what kinds of things would be more difficult?

The combinations of the exercises and autobiographical information above are elements of your story about sexual orientation. They will help you find your place in the larger story of oppression and liberation of LGBT people. If, like the authors, your childhood was devoid of any formal information about sexual orientation and the only informal information you had was jokes, mocking, and instructions on how not to be mistaken for someone who is LGBT, you were socialized to assume that heterosexuality was good, right, and normal and that any other sexual orientation was by extension bad, wrong, and abnormal. If you identified as heterosexual, this information and misinformation probably underlay assumptions that you made about dating, relationships, and marriage,

Personal Inventory 6.3
Personal Autobiography on Sexual Orientation

Write or record your answers to these questions to develop a more conscious awareness of how you were socialized and what you were taught about sexual identity. Please answer all of these questions, regardless of your sexual orientation.

1. What are your first memories about being told or overhearing anything about sexual orientation? Were these messages positive, negative, or neutral?
2. As a child and teenager, what messages did you hear your parents use about people who were gay, lesbian, or bisexual? Were these words positive, negative, or neutral?
3. As a child and teenager, what messages did you hear your peers use about people who were gay, lesbian, or bisexual? Were these words positive, negative, or neutral?
4. As a child and teenager, what messages did you use about people who were gay, lesbian, or bisexual? Were these words positive, negative, or neutral?
5. Did you, your friends, or your family ever engage in any conflict about sexual orientation?
6. Did one or both of your parents identify as gay, lesbian, or bisexual? What kinds of experiences did you have as a result?
7. How would you classify your sexual orientation—gay, lesbian, bisexual, heterosexual, uncertain . . . ? How old were you when you became aware of your sexual orientation? How is your sexual orientation accepted among your friends, family, and the larger community?
8. Have your views about sexual orientation changed as you've grown older? What experiences or relationships have you had that confirmed or challenged your early beliefs or experiences?
9. What are you proud about regarding your sexual orientation? Is there anything about your sexual orientation that causes you fear, rage, embarrassment, or shame?
10. Is there anything in your beliefs, attitudes, or behaviors toward people who are gay, lesbian, or bisexual that makes you feel proud? Is there anything in your beliefs, attitudes, or behaviors toward people who are gay, lesbian, or bisexual that causes you to feel embarrassment, fear, or shame?

and in this area of your life you most likely felt acceptance from people around you. If you identified as LGBT, this information and misinformation challenged, criticized, and rejected an important part of your identity. You may have chosen to defy these messages, you may have chosen to keep your identity hidden, you may have tried to transform your sexual orientation, or you may have felt uncomfortable about your gender identity but had difficulty articulating those feelings or finding somebody with whom you felt safe enough to discuss them. In any case, it was fairly likely that some people in your life rejected you or were disappointed in you because of this important part of your identity.

When you reflect on the false, distorted, or incomplete information you received as a young person from an array of sources, then you can begin to reconstruct the influences on your views, attitudes, and behavior about sexual orientation and gender identity. It is this knowledge of what forces have shaped you that you can use as a touch point as you begin to consider new information. The way you were socialized and the way you accepted or challenged that socialization will affect the way you respond to the information, history, and theories below. As you study this chapter, it will be important to notice and pay attention to your personal thoughts and reactions to the material presented and to track them back to your earlier informal learning experiences. In this way you will be able to make conscious and deliberate choices about what to believe, what information to retain, and what information to reject.

RECONSTRUCTING KNOWLEDGE AND SEXUAL ORIENTATION

Sexual orientation can be a sensitive topic. As we explore the issues, it will be important to keep several things in mind. First, be aware of your personal experience and socialization about sexual orientation and human sexuality in general. Second, be mindful of any aspects of religion or sex that you believe are private or that you prefer not to discuss. Third, try to maintain awareness of the extent to which your feelings influence your ability to think deeply about these issues, and vice versa. Fourth, remember that as you consider new information that may contradict what you learned elsewhere, your task is to sort through old and new knowledge, formal and informal learning experiences, and then make conscious, independent decisions about your own values and beliefs. Finally, remain open to the probability that the way you and most other people in contemporary society think about sexual attraction, sexual identity, and sexual orientation is quite different from the way people have regarded these issues across the span of human history and culture. In fact, attitudes, beliefs, and theories about what it means to be heterosexual, gay, lesbian, bisexual, transsexual, or transgendered have continuously changed and evolved over the years and among various civilizations in response to a shifting array of political, cultural, social, scientific, and religious influences. This section will consider some of those influences by examining the following:

- terminology regarding sexual identity and orientation and its evolution
- the history of acceptance, celebration, persecution, oppression, and liberation of LGBT people in the United States
- institutionalized religions and sexual orientation
- the current social and legal status of LGBT people in the United States

TERMINOLOGY AND ITS EVOLUTION

To engage in constructive dialogue about individuals or groups, we need to have language with which to communicate clearly and accurately. Understanding the history and politics of terms used in discussing sexual orientation will help us develop a shared lexicon through which we can sharpen our discussion about how the limitations of the language and naming of sexual identities reflect the various ways discrimination and liberation have occurred. The terms **homosexuality** and **heterosexuality** first appeared publicly in 1869 in pamphlets distributed to challenge Prussian legal sanctions against same-sex erotic behavior (Miller 1995, xv; Tamagne 2004, 7). Coinage of the terms is attributed to Karoly Maria Kertbeny, an Austro-Hungarian journalist and translator (Pickett 2011). Kertbeny had engaged in correspondence with a German theorist, Karl Heinrich Ulrichs, who, using different terminology, had originally proposed the concept of homosexuality as a distinct category of social identity a few years earlier. Before this time, same-sex attractions and relationships existed, but were not named or thought of in the same way as they are today. For instance, many ancient Greeks regarded one's sexual interests—same sex, opposite sex, or some combination of the two—as a matter of personal taste rather than a reflection of morality, character, or even identity (Pickett 2011).

The early sexologists in Germany and England were sympathetic to same-sex relationships and opposed laws that criminalized them. While some used the word "homosexual," eventually they adopted the word "invert" to refer to lesbians and gay men. This new name was based on the sexologists' beliefs that people who were attracted to members of the same sex were part of a third or intermediate sex. Their belief was that men who were inverts took on characteristics that were traditionally feminine and women inverts assumed traditionally masculine characteristics. There were other groups in the mid-nineteenth century, religious leaders for instance, who viewed same-sex relationships as sinful. But while the sexologists had limited information about same-sex attraction, their contribution to its evolution was the belief that it was natural and unchangeable. Thus, since the inverts could not change, most of the sexologists concluded that they should not be punished or penalized (Miller 1995, 13).

The work of the German and British sexologists was known by some scientists and doctors in the United States but was not widely known or accepted by the larger population during the nineteenth century. In fact, the construct of homosexuality was largely underground. Through the early twentieth century, there was virtually no open discussion in the United States of gays, lesbians, bisexuals, homosexuals, or inverts. Some women participated in what were called "romantic friendships," which often had a private sexual dimension. The sensibility in the United States at the time was such that there was virtually no publicly articulated concept of sexual relationships between people of the same sex. Thus, there was neither widespread acceptance nor widespread condemnation. This neutral public stance gradually changed as the work of the European sexologists reached the United States. Rather than the limited but sympathetic view held in Germany and England regarding sexual inverts, in the United States the so-called inverts were considered freaks (Faderman 1991, 45).

"Homosexuality" and "heterosexuality" both entered the American lexicon in the early twentieth century as medical terms. Homosexuality was defined in *Webster's New International Dictionary* as "morbid sexual passion for one of the same sex." *Webster's* defined heterosexuality as "abnormal or perverted appetite toward the opposite sex" (Katz 1995, 83–112). Originally, both terms were used primarily by physicians. Eventually, heterosexuality lost its medical connotations and came to be used as a term for so-called "normal sex" between a man and a woman (Katz 1995, 83–112). Homosexuality, however, continued to be officially regarded as a medical abnormality and/or a psychological disorder. By the mid-1930s, homosexuality and individuals who were involved in same-sex relationships were largely reviled in the United States. U.S. psychiatrists, such as Sandor Rado and Charles Socarides, claimed that same-sex relationships were "sick," a function of mental illness, and as such were doomed to failure. The American Psychiatric Association's first catalog of mental disorders listed homosexuality as a sociopathic personality disturbance (Miller 1995, 248). The emphasis of psychiatry was to attempt to cure this so-called "disease." Parallel to this development were beliefs in many mainstream religious institutions that, according to the Bible, affectionate behavior between people of the same sex was a sin.

In the naming of "homosexuality," a group identity began to be constructed. This is parallel to the naming of race and the construction of a race meta-narrative, as discussed in Chapter 4 (Katz 1995, 83–112). The modern meta-narrative for individuals with same-sex attraction gradually crystallized during the first decades of the twentieth century when the label of "homosexual" took on political and social meaning as its definition evolved over time. Conversely, the evolution of the term "heterosexual" as the defining cultural norm helped to reinforce the contemporary cultural paradigm of opposite-sex attraction as the standard acceptable form of human behavior (Katz 1995, 83–112). In 1991 social critic Michael Warner coined the term **heteronormativity** (Weiss 2008) to describe the devaluing and marginalizing of LGBT people based on prevailing institutional practices and cultural beliefs that represent males as "opposite from and superior to females and heterosexuals as opposite from and superior to people who are lesbian or gay" (Gray 2011). By being labeled "sick" and/or "sinful" while heterosexuality was simultaneously considered the healthy and desirable norm, same-sex attraction and romantic behavior took on extremely negative connotations in the United States. The American social climate gradually came to be alienating and potentially dangerous to people who identified as or were perceived to be gay or lesbian.

The terminology for sexual minorities continues to be contentious. Many people reject the term "homosexual" for two reasons. The first reason is that it was the term used for many years to describe same-sex relationships as pathological and/or sinful. A second reason is that the word "homosexual" suggests that a person's identity is exclusively sexual, rather than suggesting that sexual attraction and behavior exist in the context of a broader culture (Jagose 1996, 31). In this chapter, we have minimized our use of the word, except when speaking in historical terms. The terms "heterosexual" and "straight" are the words most commonly used to refer to men and women who are attracted to and/or have sexual relationships with individuals of the opposite sex. While there are currently no other widely used words to describe this kind of sexuality, both terms are problematic. "Heterosexual," like "homosexual," has the implication that it is descriptive exclusively of sex rather than part of a larger cultural context that is assumed to be regular and normal. The word "straight" implies that heterosexuals are upright and good as well as the obverse: that homosexuals are bent or crooked and bad.

The word **gay** began to be used in the second half of the twentieth century as an alternative to "homosexual." "Gay" originally had a political meaning as well as being a term for denoting an individual's sexual orientation. Gay liberation was a political movement in which various groupings of gay men, lesbians, and their allies engaged in activism to claim their rights. But, politically, many women who identified as gay experienced alienation and exclusion from the gay liberation movement in the 1960s and 1970s. They observed that most gay organizations were largely organized for and run by gay men and dealt with men's issues. Many women began to identify separate women's issues and establish women's organizations to advocate for "gay" women. The **lesbian** feminist movement emerged from the frustration of women activists and theorists who were "fed up with the sexism of gay liberation and the homophobia of mainstream feminism" (Eaklor 2011, 145). The term "lesbian" is derived from references to inhabitants of Lesbos, an island in the Aegean Sea where the poet Sappho lived during the late seventh and early sixth centuries B.C.E. Sappho's lyric poetry celebrated love between women (Blank 2011). Sappho and the term *Sapphic* have also become closely associated with lesbian issues.

Bisexual is a term that refers to men and women who are attracted to individuals from both sexes. Some people who are bisexual are attracted to both sexes equally. Some are more strongly attracted to members of the same sex or the opposite sex. Still others are attracted to a given individual with little regard for whether that person is of the same or opposite sex (Woodhouse and Roberts 2013). In the 1920s in Greenwich Village or in Harlem, bisexuality was regarded as hip (Faderman 1991, 67). Alternatively, some lesbian feminists regard bisexuality as sexual confusion or an unwillingness to make a commitment. In truth, people who identify as bisexual are neither inherently hip, confused, nor promiscuous. Bisexuality is a distinct type of sexual orientation. It has nothing to do with character or morals. It reflects a person's attraction to both males and females and the person's potential to be involved with individuals of either sex.

Just as language can be useful in defining and clarifying human experience, it can also serve to limit our understanding of the vast complexity and diversity of that experience. The moment we begin to label people and assign them to categories (e.g., lesbian, gay, heterosexual) is the moment we begin to distort reality by oversimplifying it. For instance, some people regard the concept of bisexuality as an inadequate representation of their sexual orientation. They reject the binary logic of a homosexual/heterosexual, male/female model of human sexuality as being too rigid and confining. They prefer to think of themselves as pansexual because they are attracted to people all along the gender spectrum. Another example of the complexities that must be considered when investigating issues pertaining to sexual orientation has to do with sexual fluidity. Studies over the past several years suggest that a person's sexual interests, attractions, and behaviors are not necessarily fixed and immutable, but rather have the potential to shift multiple times across the lifespan. This appears to be more common in women, although it has also been found to be true of some men (Diamond 2008, 8–15).

The history of oppression and liberation of **transsexual** and **transgender** people is complex and requires more attention than is possible within the scope of this book. This chapter will only briefly touch upon this subject since neither term is specifically about sexual orientation. The terms "transsexual" and "transgender" are often confused with homosexuality. Transsexual issues, however, are situated more accurately in the category of gender identity rather than sexual orientation. In fact, people who identify as transsexual or transgender can have sexual orientation that is heterosexual, gay, lesbian, bisexual, or asexual. Transgender and transsexual people are distinguished by their biological sex being separate and distinct from their sense of themselves as masculine or feminine. They often have the sense that their biological sex does not match their gender identification. For example, some people who are born with biologically female genitals and hormones may nevertheless feel more of a sense of themselves and their gender identity as male.

Outside of the transgender/transsexual community, the distinction between the two terms is generally thought of as this: transgender people live with the complexities of their mismatched sex and gender identity, perhaps using hormones, but not having surgery. In contrast, transsexual people have undergone sex reassignment surgery. Within the transgender/transsexual community, the line between the two terms is not as distinct; the two groups are rather part of a continuum. The abbreviated term "trans" is often used to identify people who fall within that spectrum. For some people, the main distinction between being transgender and being transsexual is the money needed to pay for surgery. For others, it is a long and complex process of self-discovery and self-representation—finding a way to live in a world that is often dismissive or mocking (Adams, Bell, and Griffin 1997, 162). Moreover, some who have had the surgery reject the term "transsexual" entirely and prefer to be identified by their reassigned gender—male or female (Mitchell and Howarth 2009, 12). Because transgender and transsexual people's identity and appearance sometimes (though not always) differ from people who fully identify with the gender/sex they were assigned at birth (cisgender), they are often targeted for the same kind of persecution that is directed at gays, lesbians, and bisexuals. Studies in both the United States and Great Britain yield evidence that a large percentage of people in the trans community have experienced some form of hate crime or harassment by strangers, including verbal abuse, threatening behavior, physical attack, or sexual assault (Mitchell and Howarth 2009, 37).

Coming out, short for coming out of the closet, refers to the individual process by which people who are LGBT choose to move from secrecy to openness in their sexual identity and expression. The process of coming out is not a simple and singular event. Some people are completely out with everyone and make no secret of their LGBT. Others remain deeply closeted or come out only with sexual partners and trusted friends. For many people, being out is situational. They may not feel safe or comfortable being public about their sexual orientation or gender identity among people or in places that are not open and affirming. They may be out with some individuals and groups with which they interact, such as their families, yet remain in the closet with others, such as their employers and coworkers.

The word **queer** was historically a derogatory term used to deride gays and lesbians. More recently, it has been reclaimed by some gays, lesbians, bisexuals, transgender, and transsexual people to describe and dramatize the fact that biological sex, gender identity, and sexual desire do not always match up neatly (Jagose 1996, 3). "Queer" is used fairly regularly in academic circles. Numerous universities have programs in Queer Studies or LGBTQ Studies. Among the U. S. institutions offering majors in the discipline are Wesleyan, University of Chicago, Brown, Hobart, William Smith College, York University, Miami University (Ohio), Ohio State, and San Diego State. Some gay men and lesbians have also reclaimed other formerly derogatory terms such as "faggot" and "dyke." While these words have been recently recovered from their previous exclusively disparaging context, they retain a bitter sting when used outside of the gay, lesbian, and bisexual community as well as for some individuals within the community.

> If there is one major point to be made . . . it is that perceptions of emotional or social desires and formations of sexual categories are constantly shifting—not necessarily through the discovery of objectively conceived truths, as we generally assume, but rather through social forces that have little to do with the essentiality of emotion or sex or mental health. Affectional preferences, ambitions, and even sexual experiences that are considered to be within the realm of the socially acceptable during one era may be considered sick or dangerous or antisocial during another—and in a brief space of time attitudes may shift once again, and yet again. (Faderman 1991, 119)

In reviewing the terms that have been used about sexual orientation for the last hundred years, it becomes increasingly clear that the language reflects the culture and reality of the time and that reality is constantly shifting. Because the language is imperfect, the words we will use in this chapter will also be imperfect. Generally, we will use the words "gay" and "lesbian" to refer to men and women who have same-sex orientation. We will use "gay" to refer to men who are attracted to other men and "lesbian" to refer to women who are attracted to other women. We will use the term "bisexual" when appropriate to refer to men or women who have sexual affinity for both men and women. The words "transsexual," "transgender," or simply "trans" will be used specifically to refer to people whose biological sex and sense of gender identity are aligned unconventionally, regardless of their sexual orientation. The term "**LGBT**" or "**LGBTQ**" (in this instance, the Q stands for "queer" or "**questioning**") will be used as a broad umbrella to include all of those individuals and groups whose perceived sexual orientation or gender identity causes them to be targeted for discrimination. The term "heterosexual" will be used as a broad umbrella for individuals who are perceived as having a sexual orientation that is consistent with current mainstream conventions of attraction to members of the opposite sex. We will avoid the term "homosexual" unless writing about history or from a historical perspective.

Understanding the changes in the language in this section and the historical shifts described in the next section is important in observing your own evolving thoughts, perspectives, and understanding. The topic of sexual orientation is cluttered with misinformation and distortion. The discovery and analysis of clear factual information and the quest for understanding are critical to making independent decisions about our values and beliefs.

THEORIES AND HISTORY OF SEXUAL
ORIENTATION IN THE UNITED STATES

The theories of cultural diversity and oppression introduced in Chapter 1 are an important foundation to understanding the history of oppression and liberation of individuals who are targeted because of their sexual orientation. You may recall that the cultural competence continuum progresses from cultural destructiveness at the bottom of the scale through cultural neutrality in the middle to cultural competence at the top. In the case of sexual orientation, heterosexual individuals and institutions that are characterized by heterosexual norms need to determine where they begin on the cultural competence continuum and what they must do to progress along that continuum.

Cultural destructiveness suggests a belief that heterosexuality is superior to other sexual orientations. Individuals who are culturally destructive when it comes to human sexuality may make hateful comments or jokes or may resort to violence against people they perceive to be outside the heterosexual "norm." A famous example of individual cultural destructiveness occurred in 1998, when two men tortured and killed Matthew Shepard, a student at the University of Wyoming, simply because he was gay. That incident, along with the 1998 dragging and murder of African American James Byrd in Jasper, Texas, by three white supremacists, served as the catalyst for the eventual passage of the Matthew Shepard and James Byrd Jr. Hate Crimes Prevention Act, which was signed into law by President Barack Obama in 2009. Nevertheless, violent crimes against people because of their sexual orientation continue to be committed with regularity in the United States. LGBT individuals are more likely to be victimized by violent attacks than any other targeted population (Potok 2010). Culturally destructive behavior does not always involve a directly violent act but can nevertheless lead to tragic results. Targeting LGBT individuals with taunts, slurs, slights, pranks, and practical jokes, simply because of their perceived sexual orientation, is culturally destructive and contributes to their oppression. In September 2010, a Rutgers University freshman, Tyler Clement, jumped from the George Washington Bridge to his death after he discovered that his roommate had used a clandestine camera to broadcast a live video feed of Clement having a sexual encounter with another male. Cultural destructiveness does not only occur at the individual level. A culturally destructive institution might refuse to hire someone who is perceived to be gay or lesbian or bisexual. A culturally destructive government would pass laws making sex between two people of the same sex illegal. An example of this occurred after World War II, when the federal government sought to fire anyone it believed to be a "sexual deviate."

Cultural neutrality, sometimes referred to as *cultural blindness*, is the point on the continuum at which an individual or institution believes that sexual orientation is irrelevant. On the face of it, cultural neutrality has a certain innocence to it that adheres to the belief that everyone is equal and that no one needs to know or notice another person's sexual orientation. However, people who operate from this point on the continuum also tend to be neutral, blind, or oblivious to the physical threats, social alienation, and legal challenges gay people have to face regularly. Individuals who are culturally neutral to sexual orientation may disregard the concrete and damaging discrimination that a gay person has endured or may not understand the need for an LGBT community of support. They also may find it unnecessary for people who are gay or lesbian to be open about their sexual orientation and relationships. People who are at the culturally neutral position often make statements such as "I don't care what you do in your bedroom; just keep it in your bedroom." What they are often unaware of is that heterosexual people are constantly "out" about their sexual orientation. Every time a young girl speaks about her boyfriend or a man refers to his wife, they are being open about their sexual orientation without ever mentioning sex.

Culturally neutral institutions may, with good intent, ignore the kind of discrimination and lack of safety that LGBT individuals often encounter in the workplace. Because the institutional assumption is that a company, for example, provides a level playing field with regard to sexual orientation, the company executives may not see the ways that heterosexuals are privileged in the workplace. They may be oblivious and thus neutral to the fact that life partners and children of homosexuals do not have the health insurance benefits that their heterosexual peers have. They may refuse to think of ways to protect members of the targeted group against harassment or job discrimination because they do not see the problems. Governments may decide that specific legislation to protect gays and lesbians from hate crimes is unnecessary because they believe that gays and lesbians are just like everyone else and do not require special protection or laws. Fortunately, some of these institutional forms of discrimination have gradually begun to change, but there is still much to be done.

Cultural competence suggests that an individual or institution has worked hard and continues to work to understand the experience, history, and deep and surface culture of gays, lesbians, and bisexuals. An individual may read extensively, attend cultural or political events in the gay and lesbian community, and serve as an advocate and ally in support of LGBT rights. An individual who is culturally competent does not have the equivalent of certification in understanding sexual orientation, but rather understands that the learning process is ongoing. An institution that is culturally competent may offer workshops or courses on sexual orientation and may have policies that offer benefits to domestic partners that are equivalent to those offered to people whose heterosexual relationships are sanctioned by the state in marriage. Governments that are culturally competent may include the LGBT protection in civil rights legislation or anti–hate crime legislation. Individuals and institutions that are culturally competent will still continue to make mistakes as they work to move past their privilege and socialization to understand and support people with diverse sexual orientations and to serve as allies. Despite the academic research and personal work the authors have done to unlearn homophobia, we must acknowledge that we write from a perspective of privilege. As a result, we can be reasonably sure that somewhere in this chapter we have made errors in judgment or understanding. The mistakes—and more important, their corrections—are part of the learning process we must all go through.

If people are serious about understanding the issues and have a genuine desire to promote progressive change in our society, then it is important that they begin by critically examining themselves and deepening their awareness of how they have been socialized. Part of that learning process involves breaking the cycle of oppression through which many people have been inculcated with beliefs that assume heterosexuality is the only natural and acceptable sexual orientation. Early in life, people begin to be exposed to a great deal of misinformation about people who are LGBT. As they grow older, they gradually internalize that misinformation as truth. They then assume attitudes and engage in behaviors that result in the marginalization and exclusion of people who are *perceived* to be gay, lesbian, bisexual, transgender, or transsexual. The word "perceived" is critical to this discussion because homophobia can target heterosexuals who are believed to be LGBT as well as members of the LGBT community. "Homophobia, like other forms of oppression, serves the dominant group by establishing and maintaining power and mastery over those who are marginalized or disenfranchised. Individuals maintain oppressive behaviors to gain certain rewards or to avoid punishment, to protect their self-esteem against psychological doubts or conflicts, to enhance their value systems, or to categorize others in an attempt to comprehend a complex world" (Blumenfeld 1992, 8). Unless individuals have experiences that interrupt the socialization process that imbues them with homophobic beliefs, they are likely to perpetuate the cycle of oppression by colluding with the targeting of gays and lesbians and transmitting their prejudices to the next generation.

Homophobia operates on a number of different levels. On a personal level, it reflects a belief system that pities or despises gays, lesbians, and bisexuals. On an interpersonal level, this bias turns into name-calling, jokes, harassment, rejection, and even violence. On an institutional level, homophobia is at the root of why some businesses, schools, religions, and government agencies have laws, codes, and policies that discriminate against or ignore the existence of sexual minorities. Culturally, homophobia has a list of invisible rules that restrict "normal" behavior to attitudes and actions that are viewed as appropriately masculine for men and traditionally feminine for women. Traveling outside of these norms makes a person suspect as gay or lesbian and thus potentially a target of discrimination (Blumenfeld 1992, 4). According to the theory known as the fabric of oppression, heterosexual privilege is available to individuals who, once again, are perceived to be sexually attracted to or in primary relationships with someone of the opposite sex. This privilege involves personal safety and protection from discrimination, harassment, and violence directed at gays, lesbians, and bisexuals. Heterosexual privilege also includes government sanction and cultural approval. Assumed heterosexuality means that people never have to go through the day wondering if they should disclose or hide that aspect of their identity or weigh the relative danger and safety of being "out."

Homophobia also has an adverse impact on the lives of people who identify as heterosexual. On a personal level, homophobia restricts the way all people dress, talk, and express themselves. In cultures that are extremely homophobic, any deviation from strict gender roles of masculinity or femininity is regarded as suspicious. A woman who identifies as heterosexual who does not want to be accused of being lesbian may feel the need to wear soft, frilly dresses and refrain from engaging in activities or occupations that have been traditionally perceived as male. On an interpersonal level, homophobia limits expression between friends and families. People who are afraid of being called gay or lesbian may hesitate to be physically warm and affectionate with their same-sex friends. Parents may carefully restrict their children from having access to information about sexual orientation while clearly communicating to them that being gay or lesbian is unacceptable. If any of their children have questions about sexual orientation or appear to be gay or lesbian themselves, the parents' homophobia would limit their ability or willingness to communicate with their own children and limit the children's ability to be open about their own identity and sexuality.

Homophobia can pressure young people, as well as adults, to prove themselves to be heterosexual. This phenomenon often is reflected in the ridicule and mistreatment of people who are gay and lesbian. Any time we deliberately mistreat others, we diminish our own humanity. Young people who question their own sexual orientation or are accused of being gay or lesbian sometimes feel pressured to have heterosexual sex prematurely in an effort to prove themselves to their peers (Blumenfeld 1992, 11). Because of the cultural stigma against LGBT people, as well as the homophobia of many parents, schools, and high school students, the suicide rate of gay and lesbian teens is alarmingly high. Fortunately, over the past few years, many students have formed gay/straight alliances in their schools and have worked actively to counteract the stigma and social alienation that gay teens have historically experienced in school.

"Males in our society are saddled with the heavy burden of masculinity. . . . We must 'keep it all together'; we cannot show vulnerability, awkwardness, doubts. . . . To keep us in line, faggot, pansy, wimp, sissy, girl, and homo are thrown at us like spears to the heart" (Blumenfeld 1992, 37). Men and boys learn very early that certain behavior will subject them to ridicule and harassment. Playing with dolls, displaying vulnerability, and crying because of hurt feelings all transgress the traditional rules of what it means to be male. Whether a boy is heterosexual or homosexual, he is subject to the same discrimination and often makes decisions about his behavior based not on what interests him or what he enjoys, but rather on whether other boys will find it acceptably masculine.

Homophobia and the fear of appearing homosexual also reinforce gender stereotyping for women through lesbian baiting. Many women make choices to reject traditionally masculine (and often more comfortable) clothing because people might think they are lesbian. Some women consider jobs such as the military or construction off-limits because people might think they are lesbian. Some women who challenge male power or sexual advances or demand equal rights as women or identify themselves as feminists are accused of being lesbian and are consequently more cautious as they make these kinds of choices. Homophobia has traditionally been so strong in U.S. culture that the fear of simply *appearing* to be gay or lesbian often dictates and limits our behavior.

In fact, ending homophobia is in the interest of those who identify as heterosexual. The work that gays and lesbians and their allies have done to advocate for gay marriage and to win workplace benefits such as health and life insurance for same-sex domestic partners has also benefited opposite-sex domestic partners. Ending homophobia would benefit heterosexuals in the following ways:

- It would expand options for both men and women to transcend rigid gender boundaries.

- It would permit men and women to have closer and more intimate relationships with friends of the same sex.
- It would increase the sense of safety for those perceived to be gay or lesbian.
- It would allow more range in heterosexual relationships by allowing people to safely transcend traditional assumptions of what it means to be masculine or feminine.
- There would be a greater possibility of connection and love between people without the existence of homophobic fear. This could create the possibility of more love and justice in the world. (Thompson 1992, 241–242)

Liberation theory explains that homophobia, heterosexism, and internalized homophobia are the result of misinformation and distortion and omission of information. The same misinformation that heterosexuals receive is also received by homosexuals, who, as a result, may struggle with understanding and accepting their own sexual orientation and identity. In seeking to address this and other concerns within the gay community, some scholars and activists advocate a more radical paradigm. They make a clear distinction between the pursuit of gay rights such as marriage, child adoption, and military service and the advancement of gay liberation: "Gay liberation understands that the problem with appropriating marriage is that access to marriage in its unaltered heteronormativity does not signal a coming to speech for Gay people; rather it signals a subsuming of the Gay consciousness into a thoroughly heterosexual discourse" (Gilreath 2011, 306).

Proponents of a more radical framework for gay liberation believe that same-sex marriage only serves to perpetuate an existing patriarchal system based on heterosexual male hegemony. From this perspective, members of the LGBT community who simply seek the legal sanction to marry and adopt children with a same-sex domestic partner without also seeking to transform the institution of marriage itself in ways that speak to the LGBT reality are merely conforming to the very system that oppresses them. Beyond bringing about institutional and systemic restructuring to be inclusive of all people regardless of sexual orientation, the movement for gay liberation seeks to profoundly alter the mental models that undergird the culture of our society. The optimism in liberation theory suggests that because patterns of discrimination in our beliefs and actions are learned, they also can be unlearned. The next two sections regarding history and religion are designed to provide accurate information and a variety of theories and beliefs to augment and perhaps challenge information you have received in the past. It will be up to you to decide what you believe and if you have any attitudes or behaviors you wish to change.

SEXUAL ORIENTATION IN U.S. HISTORY

Before World War II

While gay and lesbian relationships have been depicted in art and literature since antiquity, it is difficult to pinpoint the earliest documented accounts of same-sex attraction and relationships in the United States. It is clear that before the early twentieth century in mainstream U.S. society, there was no name for individuals attracted to and romantically involved with persons of the same sex. During this period, there was no publicly acknowledged concept of homosexuality; there was no social or political construct that evaluated same-sex relationships as right or wrong, good or evil, healthy or sick. It is true that certain sexual activities were regarded as sinful or even illegal (Eaklor 2011, 15), but there was simply no widely acknowledged concept of homosexuality and heterosexuality as generalized categories of human identity within the meaning-making structures of mainstream society.

To a certain extent, this conceptual absence was cultural. Examples of culturally sanctioned same-sex pairing, bisexual orientation, and transgender identity can be found across an array of civilizations throughout human history. Among these are the tradition of adult men coupling with adolescent boys in Athens (Holmen 2010), boy-wives among the Azande people of northern Africa (Williams 1986, 264), "soft-men" acting as wives to other men among the Asian Chuckchi (Stone 2003, 54), *hijras* of India dressing and carrying themselves as women (Nanda 1999, 19–23), female couples in nineteenth-century southern China (Fletcher et al. 2012, 239–244), and woman-marriage in parts of Africa (Greene 1998, 365).

The American Indian **berdache** or *winkte* has been noted in 130 tribes from the sixteenth to nineteenth centuries. These individuals defied neat classification into Western identity categories. Most often, the berdache was a biological male whose gender sensibility and behavior was female. "Berdaches represented a special category among many Native American tribes. They were men who wore women's clothing, occupied themselves with 'women's work' such as pottery and basket weaving, and took a sacred role in tribal rituals" (Miller 1995, 31). Berdaches were awarded a holy status and were highly respected in most tribes. Male berdaches were permitted to have sex with and be married to men. While there is less known about female berdaches, there is evidence that they also held a special status in at least thirty tribes (Miller 1995, 35).

When the Europeans arrived in North America, they were determined to obliterate the berdaches and their accompanying holy tribal status. As early as the sixteenth century, Spanish conquerors described Indians in Mexico as sodomites and ordered them killed. Some of this hostility was driven by a clash of worldviews and spiritual beliefs. Much of it had to do with the desire for economic accumulation, territorial control, and political dominance. "The conflict over land and resources spawned many others between cultures. Eventually, any variation from European conceptions might be used to justify exploiting, displacing, and exterminating natives when not causing those actions in the first place. In this light, the natives' sex and gender systems were but one more reason to consider them inferior people, ripe for conquest" (Eaklor 2011, 17).

By the early 1800s, the Spanish had successfully eliminated the berdache from California tribes (Miller 1995, 38). A century later, the forced assimilation of American Indians in boarding schools, coupled with the pressure of Western values, had socialized most tribes into viewing the berdaches as deviant in their sexuality and gender identity. Nevertheless, "the berdache shows how certain premodern societies took people who would probably be considered gay or lesbian today and affirmed them, instead of stigmatizing them, giving them important—even sacred—cultural roles" (Miller 1995, 40).

In the United States up until the time of the Industrial Revolution, most women needed to be married and part of a family in order to survive economically. By the end of the nineteenth century, middle-class and owning-class white women could attend college and pursue careers. For the first time, such women were able to live independently from a father or husband. In these circumstances, romantic friendships between women flourished (Faderman 1991, 14). Romantic friendships were affectionate and often long-term. The women lived together and were often devoted to each other, helping each other through illness and hard times. It was not always clear whether these relationships between women were sexual. Romantic friendships were also known as "Boston marriages," in which college graduates set up households together. These relationships were common on the East Coast. "The list of female contributors to twentieth-century social progress and decency who constructed their personal lives around other women is endless" (Faderman 1991, 24). Both Emily Blackwell, the co-founder of Women's Medical College of the New York Infirmary, and Jane Addams, the founder of Hull House and the settlement movement and recipient of the Nobel Peace Prize, were involved in long-term romantic friendships with women (Faderman 1991, 5). Despite the romantic dimension of at least some of these same-sex female friendships, there was still no construct of homosexuality, nor was there a personal identity as lesbian. "Only when individuals began to make their living through wage labor, instead of as parts of an interdependent family unit, was it possible for homosexual desire to coalesce into a personal identity—an identity based on the ability to remain outside the heterosexual family and to construct a personal life based on attraction to one's own sex" (D'Emilio 1992, 8).

Class played an important part in cultural acceptance or rejection of women's same-sex relationships in the early twentieth century. For women of the middle and owning classes, romantic friendships were accepted and often admired largely because the possibility of the sexual dimension of the relationship was unseen, unacknowledged, or dismissed. For the most part, the women in these relationships appeared traditionally feminine and their behavior was viewed as acceptably "ladylike." Working-class women's relationships with each other were quite different in the late nineteenth and early twentieth centuries. Romantic friendships, which often blossomed and took hold in the relative independence and privacy of college, were not readily available to lower-income women. The Industrial Revolution impacted many working-class women as well but in a different way. Many low-income women took jobs and moved to the cities, often sharing rooms or apartments with other women. Some working-class women dressed as men to get better-paying jobs or join the army. This choice was most often motivated by economics rather than sexual attraction or gender identity. But the phenomenon of cross-dressing, working-class women was seized upon by the sexologists, who described these women as inverts, a third sex, or women acting like men. This was the first time in U.S. history that the concept of homosexuality was applied.

This is an important U.S. example of the construct of homosexuality evolving according to "experts" who evaluated women by their appearance and economic class rather than by their identity or behavior. "The sexologists conflated sex role behavior (in this case, acting in ways that have been termed masculine), gender identity (seeing oneself as male), and sexual object choice (preferring a love relationship with another woman). . . . And conversely, women who were passionately in love with other females but did not appear to be masculine were considered for some years more as romantic friends or devoted companions" (Faderman 1991, 45).

Eventually, romantic friendships became suspect as well. Gradually, the concept of the lesbian was constructed. The sexologists began to warn parents and young women that colleges were breeding grounds for lesbians and that physical affection between young women, earlier considered charming, was now considered dangerous (Faderman 1991, 49). Among the only places where lesbian relations could survive openly was in the New York City areas of Greenwich Village and parts of Harlem in "artistic or bohemian pockets, where social rules were relaxed and unconventionality was prized" (Miller 1995, 63).

Around the turn of the twentieth century, the construct of homosexuality, the naming of same-sex attractions and relations, became more widespread. Sexologists in the United States began to use the term "invert," which they thought of as an intermediate sex. They condemned inverts as "sick," yet they also believed that men and women who were attracted to the same sex were born that way and could not change. This was the first time in the United States that the concept of essentialism was introduced, and a debate about the "causes" of homosexuality began that has continued through the twenty-first century.

Essentialism is the belief that people are born with a given sexuality and that it is unchangeable. Some people believed that this essential part of a person was natural and should be accepted. Others viewed it as a "birth defect." "For many, to claim a birth defect was preferable to admitting to willful perversity" (Faderman 1991, 57). Essentialism stresses the difference between homosexuals and heterosexuals—sometimes with acceptance and sometimes with condemnation. In the early twentieth century and other times of extreme homophobia, many gays and lesbians subscribed to this belief as a political strategy to build their own culture, based on the premise that since they were born different they must find ways to rely on themselves (Faderman 1991, 61).

Another belief about the origin of homosexuality is the theory of *social construction*. According to this theory, while same-sex attraction and relationships may exist, certain social and political conditions are necessary for the identity of gay or lesbian or bisexual to be an option for men and women. These conditions include the conceptualization and naming of homosexuality as an identity, the decrease in pressure to procreate, an atmosphere of sexual freedom, and a shift in society in which the traditional nuclear family is not essential for economic survival. Some gay liberation groups and lesbian feminists in the 1960s and 1970s believed that to be gay or lesbian was a political statement that challenged sexism and patriarchal systems. Some conservative religions that condemn homosexuality also believe that same-sex attraction and relationships are socially constructed; these conservatives believe that homosexuality has been made possible by an inappropriately permissive society. In short, *essentialism* posits that one's sexuality is determined biologically, perhaps at the genetic level, and tends to be fixed at birth. *Social constructivism* maintains that sexual orientation is influenced by a range of social, cultural, and environmental influences and has little or no basis in biology. In fact, the so-called causes of a person's sexual orientation are speculative and largely unknown.

Sigmund Freud believed that homosexuality was a combination of biological origin and socialization. He did not regard homosexuality as an illness, a vice, or a cause for shame or disgrace. Freud saw same-sex attraction as a "variation of the sexual function produced by a certain arrest of sexual development" (Abelove 1986, 59–69; Abelove, Barale, and Halperin 1993, 381–382).

Before and during World War I, interactions in Greenwich Village in New York City reinforced Freud's theory of homosexuality as one path on the road to human development and maturity. The Village was a hub of artistic, bohemian, and unconventional behavior in which there was a climate of openness to diverse sexual orientations. Another of Freud's theories helped fuel this carefree spirit of sexual freedom. It was widely interpreted in popular culture that Freud believed it was harmful to repress sexual urges. For many people, their sexuality was not part of their permanent separate identity. Rather, their same-sex relationships or bisexuality became part of a bohemian chic. In the 1920s, many people valued things that were daring and that flew in the face of the ordinary. Bisexuality fit these values perfectly (Faderman 1991; Miller 1995). During World War I, Greenwich Village was famous for balls attended by gay men in flamboyant evening gowns. Working-class bars for gay men began to emerge in lower Manhattan. In gay institutions throughout most of New York City, there was an unspoken agreement with the police that gays would not be bothered. This changed in the 1930s when the New York State Liquor Authority developed a policy that prohibited bars from serving alcohol to gays and lesbians (Miller 1995, 145).

Harlem in the 1920s was also a center of creativity, artistic output, and openness to a range of sexual identities and forms of expression. Harlem was a center of burgeoning African American culture where a number of well-known figures in literature, entertainment, and the performing arts were gay, lesbian, or bisexual. It was also a community where people were more accepting of interracial relationships as another dimension of embracing the taboos of conventional U.S. society. Some white people who wanted to engage in same-sex relationships went to the entertainment districts of Harlem for anonymity. Others bought into the racial stereotype that somehow African Americans were more sexually uninhibited. While there was great ambivalence in the black community about homosexuality, some 1920s Harlem night-spots were accepting of same-sex dancing and affection. Famous women, both black and white, visited Harlem as an experiment in biracial and/or bisexual relationships. Others maintained heterosexual marriages by day and same-sex relationships by night. Movie stars and singers such as Joan Crawford, Tallulah Bankhead, Bessie Smith, and Ethel Waters were Harlem regulars. "These women, who did not take great pains to pretend to exclusive heterosexuality, must have believed that in their own sophisticated circles of Harlem, bisexuality was seen as interesting and provocative. Although unalloyed homosexuality may still have connoted in 1920s Harlem the abnormality of a 'man trapped in a woman's body,' bisexuality seems to have suggested that a woman was super-sexy" (Faderman 1991, 75).

Despite the perceived chicness of bisexuality in urban enclaves such as Harlem and Greenwich Village, the medical concept of homosexuality became increasingly pervasive in the United States from 1900 to 1930. While some doctors called for "decriminalization of homosexuality because 'the poor creatures' are sick, not criminals," others attempted to develop and implement "treatment" of homosexuals. These treatment practices included castration, clitoridectomy, lobotomy, electric shocks, and commitment to mental institutions (Adams, Bell, and Griffin 1997, 166).

The era of openness for gays and lesbians in New York City and elsewhere drew to a close in the early 1930s as a result of two far-reaching societal changes. First, the repeal of Prohibition, although allowing the sale of alcohol to be legal, placed bars, cabarets, and other popular establishments under strict regulation by the State Liquor Authority. Businesses that sold alcohol to homosexuals operated under the threat of having their licenses revoked. The once open and flourishing gay and lesbian community was driven underground (Eaklor 2011, 59). Second, the Depression of the 1930s interrupted even the isolated liberal trends in attitudes toward homosexuality. Economic independence became less of an option for women as jobs became scarce, and hostility increased toward women who were perceived as "stealing" jobs from men, the breadwinners. Some working-class women became "hoboes," traveling around the countryside like their male counterparts to find odd jobs and income. There is documentation that some of these women traveled together as lesbian couples. Most middle-class lesbians, with few economic options, married and led lives in which their sexual identity or behavior was secret. Lesbians were demonized during the Depression, in part because many people scapegoated economically independent women as the cause of the severe economic downturn. Because of the economic and social conditions of the Depression, which signaled more danger for lesbians and a resulting secrecy, the opportunities for community or solidarity were negligible (Faderman 1991).

Surprisingly, the entry of the United States into World War II provided new opportunities to strengthen both the individual identity and the development of group support for gays and lesbians. Although individuals who were gay or lesbian were officially prohibited from serving in the U.S. Armed Forces, informally, men who were suspected of being gay were steered into jobs as clerks and medics, while women who were perceived to be lesbians were assigned to jobs as mechanics and drivers. This channeling of job placement according to stereotypes ironically provided opportunities for personal connection and solidarity (Miller 1995, 231).

A large number of women in the military during World War II were lesbians, but because women's labor was desperately needed, the military closed its eyes to this fact and ignored their sexual identity and behavior (Miller 1995, 231). Orders were given not to penalize lesbians unless their behavior was disruptive to their work. This is a clear example of how different economic times and needs construct different views, policies, and attitudes toward gays and lesbians. This tolerance of homosexuality during the war was viewed as a practical necessity, much like the need for women in the workforce at home.

After World War II, this tolerance changed. "A society that agreed once again that woman's place was in the home saw feminists as a threat to the public welfare, and lesbians, the most obvious advocates of feminism, once more became the chief villains. The social benefits of curing lesbians, who were all sick anyway and needed curing, were unquestionable" (Faderman 1991, 134).

After World War II

After World War II, attitudes, policies, and responses to same-sex attraction and intimacy took another radical turn. In general, there was a strong national urge after the economic hardships of the Depression and the disruption of war to return to "normalcy." Anything that seemed out of the ordinary was scrutinized, criticized, or condemned. Women, who had been in the workforce at home and in the military, were expected to return to marriage and domestic life. Gays and lesbians were once again regarded as "sick" as the medical profession swung into high gear in assessing homosexuality as an illness that needed to be and perhaps could be "cured." Senator Joseph McCarthy and the House Committee on Un-American Activities were on the rise, and LGBT people, along with communists, were reviled and hunted down.

For eighteen months beginning in 1950, individuals perceived to be gay or lesbian were fired from government jobs at a rate of roughly sixty per month. President Dwight D. Eisenhower, who had been one of the military leaders to encourage lesbian employment in the military during the war, issued an Executive Order that made "sexual perversion" sufficient grounds for exclusion and dismissal from federal employment (Miller 1995, 261). Until 1966, the U.S. Post Office monitored men who received "physique" magazines or were part of gay pen pal clubs and put these individuals under surveillance. Regional FBI offices supplied lists of gay bars and other gathering places to local vice squads. Gays and lesbians had little social recourse to fight employment discrimination or raids of gathering places. In the 1950s, even the American Civil Liberties Union (ACLU) was unwilling to provide legal assistance to gay and lesbian organizations and individuals (Miller 1995).

However, a few trends and organizational issues that had emerged during World War II continued to provide support for the embryonic gay and lesbian communities. Although the American Psychiatric Association listed homosexuality as a psychiatric illness in 1952, Alfred Kinsey's 1948 and 1953 reports on American sexual behavior challenged this categorization. Kinsey's findings established that homosexual behavior was much more widespread than commonly believed. Kinsey hypothesized that there was a continuum of sexuality that ranged from heterosexual to homosexual and seriously challenged the medical community's sickness and pathology paradigm.

Kinsey's study was shocking to the medical establishment as well as to the sensibilities of the contemporary American public. The Rockefeller Foundation withdrew funding from Kinsey's study, and the psychiatric community used his data as additional support for their belief in the threat of homosexuality (Miller 1995). But Kinsey and others, continuing to study homosexual behavior and life, demonstrated that psychological adjustment in gays and lesbians had the same range as in heterosexual men and women. Of particular note was the groundbreaking work of Evelyn Hooker. Hooker was a clinical psychologist who, in 1957, published findings from a series of studies in which she refuted the conventional belief that homosexuality was a medical pathology requiring treatment. Other researchers, who replicated her studies, came to the same conclusions. Hooker's efforts eventually led to the removal of homosexuality from the *Diagnostic and Statistical Manual of Mental Disorders* in 1973.

Despite advances in scientific understanding, post–World War II attitudes and policies made it dangerous for gays and lesbians to organize socially or politically. But the connections made during the war and the beginning sense of solidarity had been so important to many gays and lesbians that turning back to isolation and secrecy was not an option. The need and possibility of developing organizations for support and advocacy for homosexuality was almost inevitable. By the 1950s the first American gay and lesbian groups appeared. Daughters of Bilitis was primarily a social club for middle-class lesbians that served as an alternative to meeting and associating with women in bars. The group's name is a deliberately obscure allusion to the *Songs of Bilitis*, a late nineteenth-century French poem about a fictional friend of Sappho who also lived on the Island of Lesbos (Gallo 2005). The goal of the organization was to educate both the lesbian and heterosexual publics. Although the group was intended to protect women's privacy and anonymity, informants infiltrated the organization and turned names over to the FBI (Faderman 1991, 149).

Most women believed that to reveal their sexual orientation as lesbians would threaten their jobs and their incomes and pose potential physical danger. Despite this risk, bars became the center of social life for working-class lesbians. These bars created strict rules of dress for "femmes," who wore traditionally feminine clothing and behaved in ways that were stereotypically feminine, and "butches," who wore clothing and engaged in behavior that resembled that of working-class men (Miller 1995, 314). Long-lasting stereotypes of tough, masculine lesbians evolved out of this part of the newly emerging lesbian culture. Even inside the lesbian community, criticism of the butch-femme culture hinged on the belief that these relationships mimicked heterosexual relations, copying gender oppression as well.

However, the working-class butch-femme culture served two important purposes. First, with such strict rules of dress and behavior, it made it more difficult for informants to infiltrate and thus protected women from arrest and physical danger. Second, it took another step toward creating a lesbian social identity and sense of group belonging that distinguished lesbians from heterosexual women (Faderman 1991, 174).

Taking its name from a secret masked group of traveling performers and protestors in medieval France (Feinberg 2005), the Mattachine Foundation (later changing its name to the Mattachine Society) was developed primarily by and for gay men. Its leader, Harry Hay, was concerned that McCarthy would target gays in the same way that communists were hunted in the 1950s. In fact, the first leaders and members of this organization were primarily communists. They took the position that as gays they were an oppressed minority and like any other minority were entitled to certain rights. Given the climate in the United States at the time, this was a radical and potentially dangerous position to take.

The Mattachine Society engaged in discussion groups and formed an advocacy group whose aim was to outlaw entrapment of gay men; the society also published and distributed its own magazine. Eventually, concern on the part of the Mattachine membership that its communist leadership would make both the organization and gay men more vulnerable to attack prompted the original leadership to resign. The organization switched from advocacy to public education and assumed a low profile. Its goal was to demonstrate that homosexuals were just like heterosexuals except for their sexual orientation. It was this switch in positions and strategies that formed what came to be known as the homophile movement (Miller 1995).

In 1959, San Francisco and New York authorities began, once again, to crack down on gay and lesbian bars and meetings. In San Francisco, this prompted the organization of the owners of gay bars as well as other organizations to hold fund-raisers for legal defense. By this time, the ACLU began to defend gay and lesbian individuals who were arrested in bars and other social gathering places. By 1965, liberal leaders of faith-based organizations became supporters of the rights of gays and lesbians. By the mid-1960s, homosexuals and their allies in San Francisco had become a serious political force (Miller 1995).

Raids on gay bars in New York City were common. But it was not until June 1969 that a group of gays and their allies forcefully resisted a raid that took place at the Stonewall Inn in Greenwich Village, signaling a new age of gay activism and the end of gay men's tolerance for police harassment. The term "Stonewall" has come to have great literal and symbolic meaning for the movement and organization for gay and lesbian liberation.

Stonewall and Its Aftermath

The police raid at the Stonewall Inn in the Greenwich Village section of New York City occurred in the context of a political atmosphere in which college students were organizing for freedom of speech, African Americans and their allies were organizing for civil rights, and women were organizing for equal rights. Against this political backdrop, on June 28, 1969, police served the Stonewall manager with a warrant for selling liquor without a license and ordered customers to leave. This same scenario had occurred many times before and was usually followed by the arrest of some customers, while other patrons departed quietly. But this night at the Stonewall Inn was completely different from the past.

A crowd of Stonewall patrons as well as other gay and lesbian residents of Greenwich Village gathered outside the bar as the police steered those arrested into a paddy wagon. The crowd began to throw beer cans, bricks, and bottles at the police, all the while taunting, jeering, and shouting slogans of gay power. In the end, the police turned a fire hose on the crowd, and thirteen people were arrested. The police returned the next night and so did the crowd, this time with protest signs and a determination to fight this discrimination. This refusal to be victims any longer inspired the beginning of the modern gay liberation movement and marked the transition from the term "homosexual" to the term "gay" (Cruikshank 1992; Miller 1995). "Homosexuals became gay when they rejected the notion that they were sick or sinful, claimed equality with heterosexuals, banded together to protest second-class citizenship, created a subculture, and came out in large numbers. Pride followed visibility: for lesbians and gay men, shame and invisibility are inseparable" (Cruikshank 1992, 3).

As in the other movements for change in the 1960s and 1970s, the gay rights movement encompassed several different political perspectives and strategies for change that were based on distinct political goals. Liberals or moderates in the gay liberation movement wanted equal rights, the same treatment as and an equal chance along with heterosexuals. This political position demanded minority rights and access, the goal to have a piece of the American pie and dream. Radicals in the movement wanted to transform the American pie itself. They saw homophobia as a reflection of a broader range of deeper oppression that resulted from patriarchal and sexist behavior, policies, and institutions. Their goal was to change or overthrow the sexist and heterosexist culture and institutions that perpetuated this repression. It is important to understand these distinctions and not to assume that the movement for gay and lesbian liberation was monolithic. As in all groups and organizations and individuals, there was diversity on many fronts.

While the old homophile movement had advocated assimilation of gays and lesbians, the gay liberation movement was committed to challenging dominant cultural assumption, societal norms, and traditional notions of what it meant to be masculine or feminine. Part of the movement for gay liberation was to support the personal, sexual, social, and political identity of gays and lesbians and to encourage the act of being publicly gay by "coming out" (Jagose 1996). In 1969, the Gay Activist Alliance (GAA) was formed to raise gay issues in mainstream politics through direct action. The "zap" became its modus operandi. For example, GAA learned that a credit agency in New York called Fidelifacts sold information about people's sex lives to its clients. Euphemistically referring to gays, the president of Fidelifacts was quoted as saying that if it looked like a duck and acted like a duck, it probably was a duck. GAA members dressed in duck costumes, held protest signs, and quacked at the front door of Fidelifacts (Miller 1995, 378).

Different political perspectives and divisions emerged as homophobia and internalized homophobia struck the gay liberation movement and the other movements for change in the 1960s. Bayard Rustin, a gay African American man who was a Quaker and a pacifist, made key strategy contributions to the Montgomery bus boycott and organized the logistics of the 1963 civil rights March on Washington that featured Martin Luther King's "I Have a Dream" speech. Senators, congressmen, and the FBI threatened to publicize Rustin's gay sexuality to discredit him among conservative members of the black community, even suggesting that they would falsely claim that King and Rustin were involved in a sexual affair. Civil rights leaders feared that the homophobia of the times was still sufficiently rampant that this threatened exposure would damage the credibility and support of the civil rights movement. King and his advisers therefore chose to put Rustin in the deep background. As a result, his significance was never publicly acknowledged and he has only recently been recognized for the instrumental role he played in the civil rights movement (Branch 1988; Miller 1995).

Other liberation movements were equally susceptible to such homophobia. The National Organization for Women (NOW), spearheaded by Betty Friedan, opposed the up-front leadership role of lesbians. The leaders of NOW believed that the population of women that they were trying to reach and the society they were trying to change would see feminism as one and the same as lesbianism. Some even referred to lesbians as the "lavender menace": they, too, believed that the credibility of the women's movement would be seriously impaired and that their strategies for change would fail if lesbians were seen in leadership roles. Many women, such as Rita Mae Brown, author of *Rubyfruit Jungle*, resigned from NOW in protest against its anti-lesbian policies (Jagose 1996, 50).

The women who resigned from NOW then attempted to become part of the predominantly male Gay Liberation Front. They concluded, however, that the interests of lesbians and gay men were different. They believed that gay men were still privileged by being male and as a result repeated the patterns of male dominance even in their liberatory organizations and ideology (Miller 1995, 375).

Like other activists whose goal was to make society more just, some lesbian feminists sought to both change oppressive institutions and create their own alternative institutions, culture, and structure. They believed that these alternatives could model a way of making decisions, living, and forming families that would be nonhierarchical and liberatory. In this effort, lesbians created women's music and festivals, businesses, health care, and child care centers. Some of these institutions failed and some thrived.

But the legacy of the radical lesbian feminists was important in many ways. It was successful in reducing internalized homophobia. The radical lesbians

> were able to take messages from both the women's movement and the gay movement and weave them into a coherent theory of lesbian-feminism. They identified the women's movement as homophobic and the gay movement as sexist, and they fought against both. In the process they not only forced those movements to open up to lesbian and feminist ideas, but they also established their own movement that created a unique "women's culture" in music, spirituality, and literature that made at least a small dent in mainstream culture. (Faderman 1991, 244)

The Michigan Women's Festival, for example, has historically been a significant hub of lesbian alternative culture.

By the late 1970s, there were several concrete results of the movements for gay liberation and lesbian feminism:

- The U.S. Civil Service Commission stopped excluding gays and lesbians from federal employment.
- The American Psychiatric Association and the American Psychological Association removed homosexuality from the list of mental illnesses.
- Thirty-six cities and towns enacted gay rights laws, and twenty-five states repealed sodomy laws.
- The first national march on Washington for gay and lesbian rights occurred in October 1979. (Adams, Bell, and Griffin 1997; Miller 1995)

Elaine Noble, who served in the Massachusetts House of Representatives, was the first openly gay state legislator. Air Force Technical Sergeant Leonard Matlovich came out as gay and thus initiated the challenge of the gay ban in the military. When Matlovich died, the epitaph on his tombstone was, "When I was in the military, they gave me a medal for killing two men, and a discharge for loving one" (Miller 1995, 395).

In 1975 George Moscone, a supporter of gay liberation, was elected mayor of San Francisco. Harvey Milk, an openly gay man, was elected to the San Francisco Board of Supervisors. Milk was a forceful and vocal advocate for equality and fairness for all people. Yet his most powerful and enduring legacy could well have been his visibility. He openly and proudly claimed his gay identity, becoming one of the first publicly elected American officials to do so. Unfortunately, his life and career were cut short when he was murdered by fellow board member, Dan White, who also shot and killed Moscone. A conservative, White had taken a strong stand against what he called "social deviates." Despite being convicted of the murders and subsequently committing suicide, White's opposition to gays and lesbians marked the beginning of both a local and national shift to the political right that included opposition to abortion, support of school prayer, opposition to the Equal Rights Amendment, and activism against the legal and social rights of gays and lesbians.

In San Francisco this conservative shift was exemplified in the proposed Briggs Initiative of 1978, which was designed to bar gays from teaching in public schools. Dan White was a leader in the effort to pass the Briggs Initiative, and Harvey Milk was instrumental in its eventual defeat. In the aftermath of an ensuing political squabble, White assassinated both Mayor George Moscone and Harvey Milk. White was convicted of voluntary manslaughter and sentenced to only seven years and eight months in prison. This verdict prompted a mass march on city hall in which protesters burned police cars and police retaliated by raiding the gay community in San Francisco's Castro district. At the end, sixty-one police officers and 100 gay men were hospitalized (Miller 1995).

Another challenge to the hard-won victories of the movement for gay rights occurred in Florida. Anita Bryant, a former Miss Oklahoma, pop singer, and the orange juice industry's commercial spokesperson, launched a campaign to repeal a Dade County ordinance that protected gay rights. She collected the necessary signatures for a countywide referendum and in 1977 the ordinance was repealed. Similar ordinances were voted down in St. Paul, Minnesota, and Eugene, Oregon. Oklahoma passed a law to fire openly gay and lesbian teachers. The overturn of these legal protections of gay and lesbian rights spawned protests by gays and lesbians and their allies all over the country (Cruikshank 1992, 16).

In the midst of this backlash, lesbian feminists continued to seek a more just culture by challenging traditional identities and institutions and creating their own. While some lesbians lived private or secret lives and separated themselves from the politics of transformation and the personal commitment to coming out of the closet, radical lesbians continued to pursue political change.

But the radical gay liberation movement that had been primarily populated by men gave way to a more reformist and in some ways conformist strategy by middle-class gay men. While many gay men were political activists and/or part of long-term gay male couples, large numbers of unattached gay men entered into the broader movement of sexual liberation. An urban gay culture emerged in several cities, characterized by gay bars and discos, multiple sexual partners, and bathhouses that were exclusively patronized by gay men. Disco became such a strong part of this culture that Warner Brothers' dance music department spent 10 to 15 percent of its advertising budget in gay newspapers and magazines (Miller 1995, 429).

By the 1980s, coming out for many lesbians was still a political statement, a criticism of the dominant culture, while coming out for many gay men was a statement of sexual freedom and liberation. In 1981, the first case of acquired immune deficiency syndrome (AIDS) appeared (Adams, Bell, and Griffin 1997, 168), and its health and political consequences seriously affected both the identity of lesbians and gay men and the politics and goals of gay and lesbian organizations.

Part of the New Right's political and fund-raising rhetoric involved demonizing homosexuality as the ultimate consequence of a politically liberal agenda and government. The religious right tied homosexuality to "sin," which it claimed was clearly spelled out in the Bible. By the 1980s, the New Right began to use the spread of AIDS in the gay male community as proof of the right-wing belief in God's condemnation of homosexuality. Syndicated columnist Pat Buchanan wrote, "The poor homosexuals: they have declared war on nature and now nature is exacting an awful retribution" (Shilts 1987, 311). The mainstream news media contributed to this discrimination in subtle ways. First, they often referred to the spread of AIDS in the "homosexual" community, ignoring the fact that lesbians had a very low incidence of AIDS. Second, the news media often referred to children as the "innocent victims of AIDS," with the implication that gay men were somehow, therefore, the "guilty" perpetuators of the disease.

A relatively small radical lesbian subculture survived the 1960s and 1970s. Many lesbians moved into the mainstream in the 1980s, much like their counterparts in other liberation movements. Long-term relationships and families were formed in both urban and suburban areas, and educated, middle-class lesbians pursued careers in the dominant culture. Individual women and lesbian organizations were personally and politically moved by the epidemic of AIDS among gay men, both because of human empathy and because of the way the political right was using AIDS to fuel its conservative agenda. Many lesbian leaders concluded that the Right was as dangerous to lesbians as it was to gay men, and by the mid-1980s personal and political alliances between lesbians and gay men were on the upswing.

In April 1983, there were 1,300 cases of AIDS reported in the United States. By mid-1985 there were 8,897 cases reported; half of those diagnosed had already died. More than 70 percent of these recorded cases of AIDS were gay and bisexual men. In the early days of AIDS, there was panic, fear, and confusion about its proportions and how it was spread. By 1983, the virus that caused AIDS (human immunodeficiency virus, or HIV) had been identified and it became clear that it was transmitted not through casual contact, but rather through the exchange of bodily fluids—most likely through sexual contact or the sharing of intravenous needles by drug users (Miller 1995).

This information and the quick spread of the disease and resulting deaths had a devastating impact on the gay male community. Many gay men were dazed by their own diagnoses and grieving the loss of friends and acquaintances in their communities. Some studies found that 50 to 60 percent of sexually active gay men in New York City and San Francisco and 25 percent in Pittsburgh and Boston had tested positive for HIV by 1985 (Miller 1995, 440). Gay leaders and organizations were also conflicted about strategies to fight this disease. Some were concerned about the political backlash that could be caused by rampant press coverage and advocated for low-profile tactics. Others took strong action to raise funds for AIDS research, to educate gay men about the spread of AIDS and methods of safe sex, and to find ways to care for men who were already sick with the disease.

On a personal level, the earlier gay male culture of the baths, the discos, anonymous sex, and multiple sexual partners was changed dramatically by AIDS. The conservative political backlash in general, coupled with the Right's strategy of using homosexuality as a symbol for all that was wrong with the country, also meant that the government, with Ronald Reagan at the helm, would do little to advocate for AIDS research funding. Many gays and lesbians were outraged at the lack of support to find a cure for such a major threat to public health.

With the leadership of Larry Kramer, the organization ACT UP (AIDS Coalition to Unleash Power) was formed to use direct action to fight for research funds and the use of experimental drugs to treat or cure AIDS. The slogan of ACT UP was "silence equals death" (Miller 1995, 458). The political energy fueled by AIDS, the alliance between gay and lesbian organizations, and the militant activism of groups such as ACT UP spawned major political and cultural changes. The Food and Drug Administration made significant changes in its approach to experimental drugs, making them more accessible to AIDS patients. In 1987, 700,000 people attended the national March on Washington for Lesbian and Gay Rights. At the march, the Names Project Quilt was first displayed, featuring 2,000 enormous quilt panels handmade by friends and loved ones of people who had died of AIDS. In 1990, the Gay (Olympic) Games in Vancouver attracted 7,000 athletes, and in 1994 the Gay Games in New York City attracted 11,000 athletes from all over the world. Many progressive organizations have attributed the origins of their activism to the successful efforts of ACT UP (Hirshman 2012 198).

By the end of the 1980s, the term "queer" began to be reclaimed and used in many political circles of gay and lesbian organizations. Some gays and lesbians who supported the use of "queer" viewed the term itself as a serious challenge to conventional understanding of gender and sexual identity. Some queer theorists suggested that the concept of gender identity itself is false and misleading and were critical of gay liberation and lesbian feminism. "According to the liberationist model, the established social order is fundamentally corrupt, and therefore the success of any political action is to be measured by the extent to which it smashes that system. The ethnic model, by contrast, was committed to establishing gay identity as a legitimate minority group, whose official recognition would secure citizenship rights for lesbian and gay subjects" (Jagose 1996, 61). Queer theorists and activists believed that most gay and lesbian organizations had bought into the ethnic model and had consequently become assimilated, losing their radical edge in their efforts to be acceptable and accepted and to get their piece of the American pie.

By the end of the 1980s, another organization, Queer Nation, had emerged that used street theater and confrontation tactics to aim for gay visibility. Queer Nation held kiss-ins at malls and used humor by singing songs such as "It's a Gay World After All" to make its point. It also challenged a long-term cultural belief and practice in the gay community that every gay and lesbian person was entitled to come out at his or her own pace and in his or her own way. Queer Nation began the practice of "outing" famous gays and lesbians. There was much evidence that some prominent, but closeted, gays and lesbians took strong anti-gay public positions in order to deflect any suspicion of their own sexual identity. Queer Nation's controversial practice of outing was an effort to deflate this kind of discrimination and claim pride in a "queer" identity.

By the close of the decade of the 1990s, many of the same issues that had been present for sexual minorities throughout the century still existed, including employment discrimination; the lack of opportunity for same-sex marriage; the frequent failure of institutions to recognize domestic partnerships, thus depriving gays and lesbians of insurance, legal benefits, and rights that are automatic for heterosexual partners; discrimination in housing; and high suicide rates of gay and lesbian teens. In 1987, the Department of Justice commissioned a study of bias-motivated violence. The report listed crimes against gays and lesbians as the most frequent of any hate crime. In 1988, there were more than 7,000 physical attacks on gays and lesbians, including 70 murders. A year later, this number had increased by 67 percent. By 1992, coalitions on the right had targeted gays and lesbians as the cause of what they called the breakdown in family values. A Colorado initiative to ban gay rights legislation was successful and spawned similar efforts in other states. Despite President Bill Clinton's campaign pledge to lift the military ban on gays and lesbians, the outcome of a controversial struggle over this issue was a 1993 policy referred to as "Don't Ask, Don't Tell, Don't Pursue." Homophobia continued to be one of the most active and intractable forms of overt discrimination and oppression. But despite these political setbacks, some states, such as Missouri, passed anti–hate crime legislation that specifically defined hate crimes against gays, lesbians, bisexuals, and transgender and transsexual people and allowed for legal remedies.

Some studies, as well as personal experiences, have demonstrated that when people who identify as heterosexual have interaction with gays and lesbians, fear and discrimination are reduced (Cruikshank 1992). These studies point to the need for education both in and out of school. The documentary *It's Elementary* (Chasnoff and Cohen 1996) highlights curricular projects in elementary and middle schools throughout the country that teach about discrimination against gays and lesbians and demonstrates the positive response and support of this curriculum by parents and the educational value for children. This documentary was aired nationally by the Public Broadcasting System (PBS), yet some local affiliates chose not to screen it for fear of homophobic backlash in their communities. More recently, organizations such as the Anti-Defamation League (ADL) and the Gay, Lesbian, and Straight Education Network (GLSEN) have offered programs to eliminate bias, raise LGBT awareness, and reduce bullying in schools. These are important resources because schools are often sites of intense homophobia. Paradoxically, schools are uniquely situated in the lives of children to interrupt the cycle of homophobic socialization by introducing counterstories that reframe the anti-gay and anti-lesbian meta-narrative.

Developments in the Twenty-First Century

As discussed in Chapter 4, a *meta-narrative* is a grand, sweeping story that sometimes serves to "legitimize power, authority, and social customs" (Wake and Malpas 2006, 24).

In examining the history of the twentieth century, we have traced the construction of an intricate meta-narrative on human sexuality. In the early years of the century, a major shift in popular thinking occurred when sexual orientation came to be regarded as a core component of people's identity rather than simply an indicator of their erotic interests. The once obscure medical terms "heterosexual" and "homosexual" gradually came into widespread public use as the defining labels for categorizing people according to their sexual desires and practices. People perceived as heterosexual came to be regarded as part of the acceptable sexual norm. Conversely, people perceived as homosexual came to be regarded as abnormal and undesirable. As the century unfolded, three sets of social forces—medical/scientific, legal/political, and moral/religious—contributed to the formation of dehumanizing schemas that gave legitimacy and social sanction to interpersonal and institutional LGBT targeting. People who identified as LGBT lived under the almost constant threat of public shame and ridicule, arrest and incarceration, ill-conceived psychiatric treatment, moral condemnation, social alienation, loss of employment, verbal aggression, violent assault, lynching, and murder. Nevertheless, despite numerous setbacks and periods of intense repression, they relentlessly resisted, refusing to be labeled, mislabeled, ostracized, criminalized, and forced into the margins of society. Moreover, many individuals now proudly embrace the very LGBT identities for which they once were shunned. By the beginning of the twenty-first century, the stage had been set for the gay rights and gay liberation movements to achieve major victories on multiple fronts.

In the medical/scientific realm, researchers are continuing to make inroads in understanding the nature of sexual orientation, especially in the areas of genetic predisposition and heritability, hormonal influence in the mother's womb, the structure and organization of the brain, and the interrelationship between biological, social, and environmental factors (Liberty Education Forum 2008). Although some groups continue to advocate efforts to change sexual orientation—so-called conversion or restorative therapies—overwhelming scientific evidence to the contrary has for the most part discredited the notion that same-sex attraction is a mental illness or some form of medical pathology that needs to be fixed or corrected. As quoted in *Medical News Today*, Dr. Qazi Rahman, a specialist in human sexuality, summed up the position of many experts: "the factors which influence sexual orientation are complex. And we are not simply talking about homosexuality here—heterosexual behaviour is also influenced by a mixture of genetic and environmental factors" (Rahman 2008).

There is also a growing body of research in the area of sexual fluidity and the differences between males and females in how sexual orientation manifests itself across a person's lifespan. In the past, studies of sexual orientation focused on gay men with the findings being generalized to both males and females. There is now closer attention given to the gender distinctions to be found in human sexuality (Diamond 2008, 8–9). It is becoming increasingly clear that, in the interest of scientific accuracy, differences between males and females must be attended to in studying sexual orientation. In discussing his own work, Dr. Rahman cautions against not taking gender differences into account when conducting research in this area. "The study is not without its limitations—we used a behavioural measure of sexual orientation which might be ok to use for men (men's psychological orientation, sexual behaviour, and sexual responses are highly related) but less so for women (who show a clearer separation between these elements of sexuality)" (Rahman 2008). As significant as recent findings have been, they are not the complete solution to the elimination of LGBT targeting. Social scientist Lisa Diamond cautions that even if we gained a full scientific understanding of sexual orientation, both the proponents of gay liberation as well as its detractors would use the information as ammunition to support their respective arguments. "All models of sexuality are dangerous in the present political climate. The only way to guard against the misuse of scientific findings is to present them as accurately and completely as possible, making explicit the conclusions they do and do not make" (Diamond 2008, 19).

The present legal/political climate continues to be highly polarized. In 2011, President Barack Obama issued an executive order to abolish the ban on gays in the military. While the move was applauded in LGBT circles, it was widely criticized by social conservatives. Another example of the nation's divided political environment involves the interpretation of the Constitution as it pertains to gay rights. In a landmark case, *Lawrence v. Kansas* (2003), the U.S. Supreme Court ruled that sodomy laws, often used to arrest and imprison gay people, are unconstitutional. Drawing upon the Fourteenth Amendment and the arguments of historians and other scholars (Hurewitz 2004), the Lawrence ruling overturned an earlier case, *Bowers v. Hardwick* (1986), on the grounds that it violated LGBT's constitutional guarantees of due process and equal protection under the law. This ruling added fuel to the movement for gay marriage, which became legal the following year in the state of Massachusetts. Eleven other states, however, almost immediately passed constitutional amendments banning gay marriage (Eaklor 2011, 240). In June 2013, the Supreme Court handed down two decisions that advanced the cause of those who support marriage between same-sex couples. A majority of the justices agreed on a technicality that the challenge to Proposition 8 (*Hollingsworth v. Perry*), a California referendum passed in 2008 that banned gay marriage in the state, was not brought properly before the court, and therefore they declined to issue a ruling. This paved the way for the state to legally allow same-sex marriage. In the other decision (*United States v. Windsor*), which had even broader implications, the high court struck down a key section of the Defense of Marriage Act (DOMA), a federal law enacted in 1996, that withheld benefits from gay and lesbian married couples. The Supreme Court held that DOMA violated the equal liberty granted to citizens under the Fifth Amendment. As a result of that ruling, the federal government now recognizes same-sex marriages for purposes such as Social Security survivors' benefits, insurance benefits, and tax filings.

By January 2014, same-sex marriage was legal in seventeen states and the District of Columbia, while thirty-three states continued to ban marriages between same-sex couples. In Illinois, a law allowing same-sex marriage was scheduled to go into effect in June 2014. Oklahoma and Utah both passed same-sex marriage laws, with further legal review pending.

The majority of people in this country appear to support same-sex marriage, yet there continues to be significant public resistance. According to a Gallup Poll, approximately

52 percent of Americans would vote in favor of a federal law to make same-sex marriage legal in all fifty states, whereas 43 percent would be opposed to such a measure (Saad 2013). There is some evidence that anti-gay social attitudes in the United States are also beginning to change. Since the beginning of the twenty-first century, there has been a steady increase in the general public's acceptance of gay and lesbian relations (Saad 2010). In the decade between 2000 and 2010, the number of Americans who believed that sexual relations between two adults of the same sex is "always wrong" decreased from 53.7 percent to 43.5 percent. Those who believe it is "not wrong at all" increased from 26.4 percent to 40.6 percent during the same period (T. Smith 2011). Two primary influencers of public attitudes in the United States are religion and popular media. We will now turn our attention to those two institutions.

As we move into the next section, which examines religious perspectives on sexual orientation, this brief history of oppression and liberation of sexual minorities in the United States provides a backdrop. You may agree or disagree with the political Right or Left, the gay and lesbian movements for change, or current legislative and policy initiatives. As you consider the chronology, politics, and dynamics of this history, it is also important to think of the human and personal benefits and costs at various points in the twentieth and twenty-first centuries. "The issue is not only whether certain forms of sexual behavior are natural or moral but whether any form of individual behavior not harmful to others should be regulated by the state" (Cruikshank 1992, 53). Another issue involves the way in which judgment and ostracism of people who are different from the dominant culture have historically led to hate, hate crimes, and even genocide. These are the central questions you will need to ask yourself as we tackle the topic of religion and sexual orientation.

RELIGION AND SEXUAL ORIENTATION

We often think of religious beliefs as sacrosanct and immune to challenge or criticism. The tradition of religious freedom in the United States mandates that we respect a wide variety of beliefs and practices as long as they do not break the law or hurt anyone. But public laws and customs as well as religious doctrines and practices have changed throughout our history. For example, many Protestant and Reform Jewish denominations that once excluded women from the clergy now welcome women in these positions. The Church of Latter-day Saints (the Mormon Church) changed its practice of excluding African Americans from leadership and clergy positions. Many houses of worship still continue to be racially segregated, yet more and more have actively sought racial integration of their membership or have formed partnerships with congregations of different races. While not all religions or denominations have changed according to contemporary secular beliefs, laws, and culture, many have seriously assessed their religious doctrines, policies, and practices to weed out discrimination and to find ways to be inclusive that are compatible with their faith.

The role of religion in thought and belief regarding homosexuality is central and critical to many Americans. Those individuals who are deeply committed to their faith and observant of religious doctrine take quite seriously and generally comply with any explicit theology or religious tenet. Other individuals, also committed to their faith, find that their personal beliefs on homosexuality are divergent from their religion's teachings. This divergence can cause conflict and great anguish for some people. Many LGBT people are also deeply committed to their beliefs but are challenged by religious tenets or scriptural references that interpret same-sex attraction, desire, and intimate relationships as being in violation of the laws of their faith. This is not unlike the difficult situation for Catholics who believe that women should be ordained as priests or have the right to choose abortion. There are agnostics and atheists who base their beliefs about sexual orientation on secular values and traditions. There are also many individuals in the United States who are only minimally involved in their religions. Perhaps they go to church twice a year for Easter or Christmas or to temple or synagogue only for the High Holidays. They may not have studied their religion or even be aware of their religion's position on physical intimacy between members of the same sex. But because religious language is so prevalent in public debates about homosexuality, they too may adopt this language and its accompanying beliefs.

It is also important to note that views regarding gay rights are changing even among individuals who identify themselves as religious. There is evidence from multiple sources, including Gallup, ABC/Washington Post, and CNN, of significant increases in support for gay marriage and civil unions, adoption of children by gay couples, and job equality since 2006. According to a report by the Public Religion Research Institute, 52 percent of Catholics and 51 percent of mainline Protestants now favor marriage equality for gays and lesbians. Opinion also breaks down generationally, with a much larger percentage of people between the ages of eighteen and twenty-nine favoring gay marriage than people over sixty-five (Jones, Cox, and Cook 2011).

Some of us have thoroughly studied these issues and have developed thoughtful beliefs with regard to human sexuality, while others of us have not looked below the surface of what we have been told or have come to believe as the "truth." Some of us have clearly separated our religious beliefs from public policy, while others of us have interwoven the threads of misinformation, religious beliefs, and public policy into an intricate and often inseparable fabric.

To look below the surface of our current beliefs—regardless of whether they are strong and clear, ambiguous, or confused—requires separating, studying, and understanding misinformation, religious beliefs, and public policy about same-sex attraction and intimacy. The information provided below offers some tools for this kind of analysis of four major religions in the United States: Protestantism, Catholicism, Judaism, and Islam. As you read this section, please keep in mind that there are many other organized religions and faiths in the United States, including Buddhism, Hinduism, and Bahai, as well as New Age spiritualism, agnosticism, and atheism.

One image of organized religions' response to same-sex orientation is that of a fish-bone in the throat that can neither be ejected nor swallowed (Nugent and Gramick 1989, 7). Different faiths have diverse beliefs about how it is viewed in the Bible, religious theologies, and traditions, as well as the role gays and lesbians are permitted to play as members or leaders of congregations. Even within certain faiths, Protestant and Jewish, for example, there are widely divergent beliefs and practices. For those Americans who are grounded in their faith, this is a particularly complex and difficult analysis. The explicit and implicit role of religion with regard to sexual orientation, however, is critical to the understanding of homophobia and heterosexism in this country.

If our faith teaches us that God loves all human beings and that it is our religious duty to be inclusive of gay, lesbian, bisexual, and transgender people in every aspect of life, we may see other religious beliefs as discriminatory or even barbaric. But if our faith teaches us that God accepts only that sexuality that has the possibility of procreation and that any other sexuality is sinful, we may see other religious beliefs as misinformed at best and sinful at worst.

Much like the discussion about and controversy over abortion, there are no easy answers nor clear-cut guidelines to civil debate and communication on this issue. For this section, we will continue to use the same guidelines and principles we have used throughout the book. We will provide historical information that is not readily accessible in mainstream education and introduce a framework for analysis as well as a variety of theories. As you read this information, keep in mind liberation theory, the cycle of oppression, and other theories that describe the process of socialization that leads to discrimination and oppression, including homophobia, as well as the possibilities for breaking the cycle. As you sort through this section, consider your own socialization as well as old and emerging beliefs and thoughts.

A Framework for Discussion

Most organized religions have official positions on the following topics:

- same-sex attraction and behavior
- civil rights for gays and lesbians
- antigay violence
- the meaning of same-sex relationships
- criteria for leadership and membership in the faith institution

Most religions also have a faith-based history and foundation upon which their moral stance on gay and lesbian relationships is rooted and conveyed to their members. Despite the clarity of institutional religions' beliefs and practices for their own members, many churches, synagogues, and other faith organizations struggle with their role in the larger secular community. Should they take strong positions on employment laws and anti-hate crime legislation that is consistent with their religious beliefs? Should they advocate or oppose domestic partnerships or same-sex marriage? Should they insist that government and corporations have policies and practices that comply with these beliefs? These are some of the questions that will be raised in this section.

There are four basic positions that organized religion can assume about sexual orientation. These different categories of belief will serve as a framework both for understanding the perspectives of different religions and for understanding individual beliefs that are rooted in faith.

The first position is both *rejecting* and *punitive* toward gays, lesbians, and bisexuals. This view holds that physical intimacy between members of the same sex is a sin explicitly prohibited in the Bible. This position encourages LGBT individuals to renounce their sexuality and seek conversion to heterosexuality through spiritual healing. Some religions that hold this view banish gays and lesbians as members and teach that they will go to hell when they die. An extreme interpretation of this position is that AIDS is God's punishment to homosexuals for their sinful behavior (Nugent and Gramick 1989, 32).

A *rejecting but nonpunitive* perspective is the second position a religion may take. This position separates the act of gay/lesbian sexual intimacy from the person, condemning the "sin" but not the "sinner." The central belief here is that any sexuality that does not have the potential to result in procreation is unnatural. Homosexuals are encouraged to seek reorientation or to remain sexually celibate (Nugent and Gramick 1989, 37).

The third religious position involves *qualified acceptance* of homosexuality. This belief, implicit in much of traditional Western culture, suggests that in the hierarchy of sex, heterosexuality is always superior. But qualified acceptance is grounded in the belief in essentialism that says that gays and lesbians have no choice in their sexual orientation and therefore cannot be condemned for something they were born with or that is involuntary. The central thesis of this position is that people who are gay or lesbian will never be capable of reaching the ideal of human existence (Nugent and Gramick 1989, 39).

A final position that organized religions may take is *full acceptance* of gays and lesbians. This position is based on the belief that there is a rich diversity of creation that includes LGBT people. The central thesis here is that "wholesome sexuality is not to be evaluated in terms of procreation, but by the nature and quality of the relationship of the persons involved, regardless of gender" (Nugent and Gramick 1989, 45).

This framework for understanding religion and sexual orientation and the range of possible positions and beliefs will serve as the foundation for examining several religious approaches to sexual orientation. The positions of three major religious traditions previously mentioned will be considered. This debate among and within religious communities has had and will continue to have an enormous impact on the acceptance of sexual minorities within faith-based organizations and the broader secular society.

Protestant Perspectives on Sexual Orientation

The majority of Protestant denominations and churches rely on theology as the basis of their understanding of religion and sexual orientation. Different denominations, clergy, and members of churches interpret theology in very different ways. A number of biblical passages are commonly cited as referring to physical intimacy between same-sex partners. Among these are: Genesis 19:1–11, Leviticus 18:22, Leviticus 20:13, Judges 19:16–24, Romans 1:26–27, 1 Corinthians 6:9–11, and 1 Timothy 1:8–10 (Shore 2012; Lose 2011). Interpretation of the meaning and significance of these scriptures varies. Some Protestant theologians believe that the Bible condemns same-sex intimacy as a sin regardless of the circumstance. Others view same-sex intimacy from a more nuanced perspective, to be judged depending on the context in the same manner as heterosexual intimacy (Gagnon and Via 2003, 1). It is also important to note that there is no scriptural record of Jesus Christ ever having spoken on the subject. For the purpose of examining Protestant perspectives in a little more detail, some of the beliefs, policies, and practices of varying denominations are described below.

With the exception of the Southern Baptist Convention, most Protestant denominations support decriminalization of gays, lesbians, and bisexuals and the protection of their civil rights. The National and World Council of Churches states that sex should occur only within heterosexual marriages. This same body supports LGBT human rights and clear religious disapproval of same-sex relations and state-approved marriage for LGBT people. In this view, there is somewhat of a separation of the beliefs of the church and the role of the government. The Protestant denominations that subscribe to this point of view believe that the government must protect all of its citizens. In a 2010 statement, the National Council of Churches called on "the Church Universal to join us in working to end the violence and hatred against our lesbian, gay, bisexual and transgender brothers and sisters" (NCC 2010).

The Southern Baptist Convention believes that to be gay or lesbian is a sin, spelled out explicitly in the Bible (Green 1998, 118). Southern Baptists see the central biblical covenant with God as heterosexual marriage with the intention to procreate and create family. Any other kind of sexuality or family is seen by this denomination as an affront to God. Because of these beliefs, the Southern Baptist Convention voted to boycott the Disney Corporation when it adopted benefits for domestic partners. A key element of this religious belief involves the role of the government. Southern Baptists and other Protestants that share their views believe that the state should protect its citizens from "false religion" and the "moral wrongness" of homosexuality and that laws should be passed to prohibit this "immorality" (Green 1998, 114). Depending on the particular church and denomination, these beliefs fall somewhere between rejecting/nonpunitive and rejecting/punitive.

On the other side of the spectrum is the United Church of Christ (UCC), which officially supports ordination of gays and lesbians. The United Church of Christ's position is based on the belief that "In faithfulness to the biblical and historic mandate . . . as a child of God, every person is endowed by God with worth and dignity that human judgment cannot set aside; and deplores the use of scripture to generate hatred and the violation of human rights, including human rights violations in relation to sexual orientation, gender identity, or gender expression" (UCC General Synod 2011). This set of beliefs also sees marriage as a covenant with God—one that is based not exclusively on the possibility of procreation but rather on the development of a committed love and friendship and the possibility of the creation of family. These beliefs most closely adhere to full acceptance of homosexuality. This position also strongly believes that political means must be utilized to fulfill this covenant. Other mainline Protestant denominations that now officially allow gays to be ordained as clergy include the Evangelical Lutheran Church in America, the Presbyterian Church (USA), and the Episcopal Church. These official positions are not universally supported among individual members and congregations of their respective denominations. Another Presbyterian group, the Presbyterian Church in America, "does not ordain women or openly gay clergy" (Kaleem 2012). In 2003, when Gene Robinson, who was gay, was named bishop in New Hampshire, the event created a national and global rift in the Episcopal Church that has yet to be resolved.

Protestant churches that are predominantly African American can fall anywhere on the continuum. Black churches have historically advocated monogamous, heterosexual marriage and the creation of family. Some African American church leaders have deep concerns about what they see as the disintegration of family and parenting structures in the black community. While many see these patterns of family as a direct legacy of slavery and racism, some leaders of black churches are concerned that gay and lesbian relationships are another way to destroy the traditional family in the black community (Sanders 1998, 178). Many African American churches fall somewhere in the rejection of homosexuality category, sometimes with and sometimes without a belief that gays and lesbians should be punished for their sexual orientation. Some black scholars and theologians believe that these religious beliefs are based on an over-reliance on Eurocentric philosophy and theological ideas and that there is a basic contradiction between the tradition of liberation and social justice in black churches and their position on loving relationships between members of the same sex. For some church members and leaders, this presents a conflict between what they understand to be the teachings of the church and their loyalty to the advancement of human rights (Dyson 1997, 86). Others argue that the black church is far too complex to be reduced to any kind of all-defining monolithic analysis (Anderson 2000).

As is true of other institutions, black churches continue to change and evolve. In the past, as was common among Protestant groups, female ministers were a rarity, but today, several black denominations fully embrace women in the pulpit and deeply appreciate the perspective they bring to the scriptures. On the question of gay marriage, the African American population in general is much more evenly divided today than even a few years ago. A recent survey found that 44 percent of black respondents in the general public were in favor of allowing gay marriages and 39 percent opposed. Among the traditionally more conservative Evangelical Christians, 76 percent of whites are opposed to gay marriage whereas only 60 percent of blacks are against the practice (Jones, Cox, and Cook 2011). Moreover, whether they are open about their sexual orientation or not, many black LGBT Christians attend church regularly, are welcome members of their congregations, and are often found in leadership roles. This speaks to several enduring strains of the African American cultural legacy that are integral to black Christian faith. These include a strong belief in justice for all people, widespread practices that reflect a shared sense of cultural communalism and fictive kinship (see Chapter 4), and a collective acknowledgment of the church as sacred ground.

Catholic Perspectives on Sexual Orientation

While most Protestant denominations base their beliefs on an interpretation of the Bible, Catholic beliefs on sexual orientation are centered on the understanding and interpretation of divine natural law. Protestant beliefs vary from denomination to denomination and sometimes even from church to church, but the teachings of the Catholic Church are intended to be the norm for all of its members. In reality, Catholic scholars, church members, and theologians may hold beliefs different from the central position. But what distinguishes Catholicism on sexual orientation is that there *is* a central position.

The dominant theology of Catholicism as applied to human sexuality is consistent with the principle that is applied to birth control and abortion—the belief that procreation and the possibility of the transmission of life is the only kind of sex that is sanctioned by God. But like the issues of birth control and abortion, many Catholic scholars, lay people, and priests disagree about the relationship of the church and the government and the right of the government to make decisions about its citizens' sex lives.

One Catholic perspective is that while every act of sex must be open to the transmission of life, gays and lesbians ought not to be punished by the state and should be treated with human dignity and afforded human rights. According to this belief, the government should intervene for only two reasons. The first is to protect human rights. Anti–hate crime laws targeted for the safety of gays and lesbians are consistent with this approach. The second reason the government may intervene is to protect the common good. According to this perspective, there is no common value in same-sex marriage and therefore it should not be considered appropriate (Twiss 1998, 71–74).

Part of the debate about sexual orientation in the Catholic Church centers around the rights and responsibilities of religion to influence law. The United States was founded on the principle of separation of church and state. But some people in the Catholic Church and other religions believe that certain moral convictions are so strong and that their violation has such dire consequences that it is essential to impose these beliefs on the wider public by making them the law of the land.

For example, one set of beliefs holds that committed gay relationships are morally good and should be judged by the same standards as heterosexual relationships. This perspective interprets Vatican II as emphasizing freedom as essential to the common good and translates this emphasis into an imperative to urge the state to promote that freedom (Curran 1998, 87). If this belief is joined with the conviction that it is acceptable for religion to influence law, then it would be logical to pursue or endorse nondiscrimination laws at a minimum and perhaps even same-sex marriage laws. "The sanctioning of divorce by law negatively affects marriage and the family more than does protecting gays and lesbians against discrimination" (Curran 1998, 92); "the civil law allows divorce and remarriage and does not discriminate against divorced people, but the Catholic Church still maintains its moral teaching on divorce" (Curran 1998, 96).

If, on the other hand, the belief that same-sex intimacy is a sin and an affront to God is combined with the belief that the church has the right and obligation to influence law, a completely separate set of actions would follow. If this belief was so strong as to say that as "sinners" people who are gay, lesbian, and bisexual should not have their rights protected by law, then this perspective would lead its followers to pursue repeal of anti-discrimination laws targeted to gays and lesbians and to fight any proposed law that sanctioned same-sex marriage or other rights.

Generally, the beliefs of individual Catholics range from the rejecting and punitive approach to qualified acceptance. The wide majority of Catholic scholars and the Conference of Bishops see same-sex physical intimacy as a violation of one of their basic understandings of God's natural law and at the same time take a strong stand against violence against gays and for respect for their human dignity and rights.

Jewish Perspectives on Sexual Orientation

Judaism is organized into four branches: Reform, Reconstructionist, Conservative, and Orthodox. These branches are diverse in their perspective and approach to homosexuality. And as with Protestants and Catholics, their particular stances and policies vary by individual synagogues and temples, leaders and members.

The debate among Jewish scholars, rabbis, and congregations centers around the understanding of ancient Jewish law and its relationship to contemporary Western life. The traditional law is interpreted by the Orthodox and some Conservatives as meaning that sexual intimacy between same-sex partners should be condemned because the divine law calls for procreation and that gay and lesbian relationships undermine the family and are anatomically and biologically unnatural (Kahn 1989).

Liberal Jewish thinking in the Reform and Reconstructionist branches as well as some Conservative congregations holds that this divine law itself is debatable and that contemporary thinking, values, and beliefs in human rights should weigh heavily in the consideration of contemporary issues—including LGBT rights. Some compare discrimination against gays and lesbians to anti-Semitism and "call for a response to contemporary oppression of gay people that is informed by the historical Jewish experience of discrimination, and insist[s] that a heightened sensitivity to homosexuals' calls for justice and liberation must take precedence over the traditional Jewish teaching" (Kahn 1989, 59). This perspective conforms to a civil rights approach that sees gays and lesbians as a minority that must be protected and given full rights.

The progressive Jewish position found in some Reform and Reconstructionist congregations calls for two principles to be upheld. The first is the belief that God does not create in vain, and therefore gays and lesbians have a covenantal obligation to be fully themselves. Janet Marder was rabbi of Beth Chayim Chadashim in Los Angeles, founded in 1972 as a haven for gays and lesbians. This congregation was instrumental in changing Reform policies and positions about sexual orientation. Marder says, "The Jewish values and principles I regard as eternal, transcendent and divinely ordained do not condemn homosexuality. The Judaism I cherish and affirm teaches love of humanity, respect for the spark of divinity in every person, and the human right to live with dignity. The God I worship endorses loving, responsible, and committed human relationships, regardless of the sex of the persons involved" (Kahn 1989, 66).

A second principle in the progressive Jewish position on LGBT criticizes the civil rights approach that regards gays and lesbians as a minority, arguing instead that sexual orientation needs to be placed in a larger context of sexual identity and sexual ethics. According to this perspective, broader issues must be questioned, including how the dominant system promotes rigid gender roles, compulsory heterosexuality, and the patriarchal social order. Supporters of this perspective believe that without this fundamental overhaul, gays, lesbians, and bisexuals will continue to exist in the margins of Judaism and the broader society (Plaskow 1998, 30).

Generally, Reform and Reconstructionist Jews have official policies of nondiscrimination toward gays and lesbians in leadership, teaching, membership, and other aspects of congregational life. These branches allow for same-sex marriage ceremonies to be performed at the rabbi's discretion (Olyan and Nussbaum 1998, 5). In 1990, the Central Conference of Rabbis voted to admit sexually active and open gays, lesbians, and bisexuals into rabbinic training. With membership numbering 1.5 million nationwide, Reform Judaism became the largest religious denomination to welcome openly gay clergy. Many of these congregations have also taken strong public positions on laws that call for nondiscrimination and protect the rights of gays and lesbians with respect to hate crimes. Some have advocated laws that call for state-approved same-sex marriage (Olyan and Nussbaum 1998, 6).

The Conservative branch of Judaism generally welcomes gay and lesbian members and prohibits same-sex marriages. It is typically the rabbi's decision concerning the level of membership and leadership that is permitted (Olyan and Nussbaum 1998, 5).

The traditional position is reflected in Orthodox Jewish beliefs that procreation is the central and divine purpose of human sexuality and that is the basis upon which sex between individuals of the same gender should be condemned. People who identify as gay or lesbian have traditionally been encouraged to remain celibate and to seek therapy according to this set of beliefs (Olyan and Nussbaum 1998, 15).

For the most part, beliefs and practices in the various branches of Judaism range from rejecting and nonpunitive to fully accepting. Beliefs about the relationship between religion and government seem to be determined by two things: the convictions of the particular congregation and the relationship of the congregation to politics in general. Often, liberal and progressive Jewish congregations see the Holocaust and the failure of religious organizations to take an active stand to stop the government of Germany from its extermination of Jews as a strong rationale for religion to influence law—particularly in reference to discrimination and hate.

Islamic Perspectives on Sexual Orientation

Millions of people, from a diverse range of nations, cultures, and ethnic groups all over the globe, are faithful Muslims. Islam has two main divisions, Sunni and Shia. Sunni is the largest denomination and is further subdivided into four schools: the Hanafi, the Hanbali, the Maliki, and the Shanbali. Despite the variation within the faith, most mainstream interpretations of the Holy Qur'an regard lesbian, gay, and bisexual behavior as being forbidden. Several predominantly Muslim nations, including Saudi Arabia, Iran, Yemen, Qatar, Sudan, Somalia, Nigeria, and Mauritania, hold that gay and lesbian sexual behavior is a crime punishable by death (Human Rights Campaign 2013).

Interestingly, some Muslim nations are more accepting of people who are transgender.

Sex reassignment surgery has been legal in Iran since 1979. In Malaysia, under some circumstances, trans people can have legal documents reissued to more accurately reflect their gender identities. In 1988, an official decree issued in Egypt named transgender identity as a "natural disposition and sex-reassignment surgery permissible if it had been proven that it was impossible for the patient to live according to his or her biological sex and the patient was not consciously choosing to be transgender" (Human Rights Campaign 2013). None of this should be taken to imply, however, that transgender people are universally accepted by all Muslims. Such is not the case.

There are numerous interpretations of the Islamic religious tradition and sacred texts. They are drawn primarily from four sources, which lend multiple layers of complexity to the Muslim belief system. Those sources are the Holy Qur'an (scripture), *hadith* (oral teachings), *fiqh* (legal rulings), and the *shari'a* (rhetoric of orthodoxy) (Kugle 2010, 14). Referencing passages in the Qur'an and teachings in the Hadith, traditional Islamic scholars state unequivocally that gay and lesbian sexual relations are sinful. More moderate Muslims, although the minority, believe these interpretations are too narrow and find no reason to reject same-sex relationships (Human Rights Campaign 2013). A growing number of LGBT Muslims and their allies seek an interpretation of Islam that is free of patriarchal traditions and speaks in support of all oppressed people, regardless of gender, race, class, or sexual orientation. "The challenge is to separate what is imposed by culture from what is essential to faith, on the one hand, and to sift what is essential to faith from what is enshrined in religious tradition, on the other hand" (Kugle 2010, 14–15).

Muslims who espouse progressive beliefs about sexual orientation base their interpretations on seven principles: (1) the inherent dignity of all human beings, (2) the sacredness of life, (3) the ethic of pluralism, (4) the application of God's message in the interest of justice under ever-changing social circumstances, (5) the right and obligation of all Muslims to interpret and discover God's intention "behind, within, and through scripture's words," (6) understanding the Qur'an in the light of reason, and (7) building societies based on moral order and the love of God (Kugle 2010, 59). These principles are not the official or even the predominant stance of the Islamic faith, but they do indicate that, as with most other religions, there exists a range of social and political perspectives among Muslims pertaining to how LGBT people should be treated and regarded.

SUMMARY OF RECONSTRUCTING KNOWLEDGE

Whether we identify as heterosexual, gay, lesbian, or bisexual, most of us were strongly socialized to see heterosexuality as either the only option or as the norm. Many of us received almost no information about the history, debates, or discrimination regarding sexual orientation. For many of us, people we trusted, including our parents, teachers, and clergy, either told us nothing or told us that same-sex love and intimacy is wrong. Much as the construct of race changed over time in the United States, definitions and beliefs and laws about LGBT people have changed significantly over time and across various cultures. There has been a kind of heavy curtain of misinformation drawn over issues of sexual orientation. Given this history, it is not surprising that many people find themselves resistant to new information that challenges their thinking and beliefs. Only recently has that curtain been pulled slightly open by more accurate information and open debate. With this kind of deep and widespread socialization as background, it becomes increasingly important to consider a wide range of perspectives and reach independent and thoughtful conclusions.

SEXUAL ORIENTATION AND ENTERTAINMENT MEDIA

In this section, we will trace the evolution of LGBT themes and characters in popular media and examine the audience impact those themes and characters have had. To place this exploration in a broader context, it is important to take another look at how the entertainment industry is organized and the forces that influence decisions about format and content when it comes to the subject of sexual orientation.

The Popular Media Industry and Sexual Orientation

The vast majority of the organizations that produce entertainment media in the United States are large corporations that are driven primarily by economic interests. While individuals who work in these corporations may be genuinely concerned about the quality of the media content, its artistic value, and its ability to provoke thought, the corporate culture revolves around profit. "Ownership by major corporations of vast portfolios of mass media gives us reason to believe that a whole range of ideas and images—those that question fundamental social arrangements, under which the media owners are doing quite well—will rarely be visible. This does not mean that all images and information are uniform. It means that some ideas will be widely available, while others will be largely excluded" (Croteau and Hoynes 1997, 43).

The centrality of the profit motive has influenced the available range of content in several ways with respect to gay, lesbian, and bisexual characters and themes. First, the drive for economic success pushes programmers and producers to minimize risk. While risk in some cases can mean economic success, generally risky subjects are thought to be money losers. Second, when a successful formula is discovered, its format is frequently mimicked or spun off in another effort to generate new revenues. Whether it is the reality television phenomenon that was spawned by a few successful originals or the many spin-offs of *CSI* and *Law and Order*, copycat tactics in popular media often work.

Until relatively recently, these fundamental industry rules have meant that images of gays, lesbians, and bisexuals were almost completely missing. As these images and themes began to emerge, they most frequently appeared as stereotypes: gay men with flamboyant clothing, style, and exaggerated feminine mannerisms; evil men or women; carefully coded and barely recognizable LGBT characters and victims. In the 1950s and 1960s, stereotypes of gay men were fair game for prime-time television. A limp hand, an exaggerated lisp, and the occupation of interior decorator, hairdresser, or florist were standard fare and likely to evoke a laugh. It has only been since the late 1990s that lesbian, gay, bisexual, and transgender people were featured as complex characters with identities that went beyond their sexual orientation.

Hegemony, as you may recall, allows those in power to rule by consent rather than force. In democratic countries such as the United States, this is a significant and often invisible way that people are induced to agree to certain world-views or universal ways of thinking. People who are elected or hired into leadership positions also serve informally as cultural leaders and often encourage and reinforce the idea that certain things are just "common sense" and certain kinds of behavior are "natural." Entertainment media, religion, and education are institutions that reinforce our sense of what is considered normal. This "normalcy" typically reflects the beliefs or ideology of the dominant culture.

Most of us think our beliefs about what is natural cannot be controlled socially. We believe that is just the way things are. For example, many people once believed and some still do that it is "natural" for women to stay home and raise children and keep house. Some believe it is just part of human nature for people to feel racially superior to others. If we are convinced that something is natural, we are also more likely to believe it is legitimate, permanent, and unchangeable.

The dominant belief has been that heterosexuality is natural and that homosexuality is therefore "unnatural." The scarcity of gay and lesbian characters and themes and the recurrence of negative images were the popular media's contribution to this set of beliefs or ideology during most of the twentieth century. "The media give us pictures of social interaction and social institutions that, by their sheer repetition on a daily basis, can play important roles in shaping broad social definitions. In essence, the accumulation of media images suggests what is 'normal' and what is 'deviant'"; indeed, popular media "have a tendency to display a remarkably narrow range of behaviors and lifestyles, marginalizing or neglecting people who are 'different' from the mass-mediated norm" (Croteau and Hoynes 1997, 166).

This does not mean that media professionals and industry leaders, then or now, have plotted conspiratorially to brainwash audiences to a particular point of view about sexual orientation. They are not necessarily even thinking about ideology as they make programming and content decisions. Rather, they are thinking about and predicting what will sell. It is the stories, messages, and characters selected by those in control of media messages that often create or reinforce our "common sense" and "natural" notions of sexual orientation.

Prime-Time Television and Sexual Orientation

It is your turn again. Complete the exercise in Media Activity 6.1 to take a closer look at sexual orientation in prime-time television. If you are doing this exercise with a class or a group, select different weekday evenings and different networks and compile your data. What percentage of all the major characters you observed were gay, lesbian, or bisexual? What percentage of minor characters were gay, lesbian, or bisexual? What was the total percentage of both major and minor characters? Of this number, what percentage were isolated and what percentage were part of a larger gay or lesbian community?

Media Activity 6.1
Popular Culture and Sexual Orientation

Think back to the time when you were eight through twelve years old and choose the following:

• a minimum of three of your favorite television programs
• a minimum of three of your favorite movies
• a minimum of three of your favorite popular songs

For each of these three categories, answer the two questions below:

1. How many major or recurring characters were gay, lesbian, bisexual, or transgender?
2. How many themes in your favorite television programs, movies, or popular songs involved people who were gay, lesbian, bisexual, or transgender? These themes might include gays and lesbians married or in loving relationships, coming out, people grappling with their sexual orientation, LGBT discrimination, gay bashing, and so on.

What was the percentage of recurring gay characters in a series? What percentage of the gay or lesbian characters were in a same-sex relationship? What percentage were shown displaying physical or sexual affection?

Without question, the numbers and percentages for all of these questions are much higher than they would have been a decade ago. By the 2012 prime-time television season, the numbers of gay and lesbian characters had increased significantly, as had the complexity of individual characters and the range of characters presented. Before the mid-1990s, the number of LGBT characters on prime-time television was so low that their absence has also meant a notable lack of books and articles chronicling sexual minorities in television. Yet while the few gay characters that slipped through were minor, they often triggered major controversy.

In 1974, *Marcus Welby, M.D.* (1969–1976) was a popular dramatic series that revolved around a doctor (played by Robert Young, the same actor who played the classic 1950s father in *Father Knows Best*). One episode featured a gay man who is a child molester; the program suggests that his tendencies to molest are connected to his homosexuality and that his homosexuality could be cured. These ideas provoked protests by gay activists who subsequently organized media watch activities.

By the 1980s, there were occasional gay characters in prime-time television series. While some isolated characters were depicted as complex and "normal," gay characters were usually external to the "natural" order of these programs and often generated protest. *Thirtysomething*, a dramatic series that aired from 1987 to 1991, chronicled marriage, parenthood, careers, dating, abortion, and the affairs of a tight-knit clan of middle-class whites in their early thirties. In one episode, two men, apparently a gay couple, were shown talking in bed. The outcry was strong and well organized; several advertisers withdrew their commercials. The characters were never seen again and the episode was pulled from the summer rerun lineup (Croteau and Hoynes 1997, 164). This event reinforced the already prevailing industry wisdom of the time that creating gay characters as part of an ensemble or regular cast was far too risky for economic success.

But despite the risk, regular characters began to emerge slowly and tentatively on prime-time in the 1980s and 1990s. In 1989, *Roseanne* took another kind of programmatic risk by depicting Arnie's wife, Nancy, coming out as a lesbian. Later in the series, Roseanne's boss and subsequent business partner is depicted as a gay man. Even Roseanne's mom reveals at a Thanksgiving dinner one year that she is a lesbian. In the same year, Steven Carrington on the evening soap opera *Dynasty* was the first bisexual on a prime-time drama. In 1994, *My So-Called Life* was the first program with a regular character who was a gay teen, but the series lasted for only one season.

Northern Exposure (1990–1995) was one of the first prime-time series that featured gay and lesbian characters and themes from the very beginning. In fact, intermittent episodes depicting the founding and development of the small town of Cicely, Alaska, where the story is set, reveal that a lesbian couple founded the fictitious Cicely. Their sexual orientation and relationship, which are central to the early days of the town, are never questioned, challenged, or made the butt of humor. The relationship between the two women is depicted as loving and caring and complex, quite unusual for prime-time television. In addition, there were occasional gay male couples on *Northern Exposure*; one couple considers buying some property and is later shown dancing a slow dance together at an informal gathering of series regulars.

Throughout the 1980s and 1990s, such images continued to be rare. Viewers could watch weeks of prime-time television and never see a gay or lesbian character. Yet some programs did offer the occasional gay or lesbian character. In *Mad About You*, Paul's sister Debbie is engaged to a gynecologist named Joan. From the very beginning of the popular *Friends* series, it is clear that Ross is getting divorced because his wife, Carol, has discovered that she is a lesbian and has developed a live-in committed relationship with Susan. Susan and Carol appear on the show periodically and eventually get "married." The actor who portrayed the minister at the wedding was none other than Candace Gingrich, conservative politician Newt Gingrich's lesbian half-sister. The characters and humor of the series remained consistent as gay and lesbian characters and themes were explored. At the wedding, series womanizer Joey talks about the frustration of being a single man looking for love at a lesbian wedding, to which the consistent romantic loser Chandler replies, "Now you know how I feel all of the time."

It was not until 1997, with the first coming out of a main character—Ellen Morgan of the program *Ellen*—that significant changes in television and sexual orientation emerged. Comedian Ellen DeGeneres, who played the character Ellen, had once upon a time been dubbed the female Jerry Seinfeld as her series emerged with a group of unmarried Generation Xers sitting around their apartments chatting and cracking wise. The show experienced more than moderate popularity in early 1997. Then the rumors began to stir that the character Ellen and the actor Ellen would be coming out at the same time. The media fanfare was enormous. The episode itself was an hour long and featured, among

In 2012, host Ellen DeGeneres and First Lady Michelle Obama check out each other's dance moves on *The Ellen Show*. This photo represents progress in television on so many levels. Ellen, a woman who is an "out" lesbian, is one of the most popular talk show hosts of the early twenty-first century. Not only is the fact that the First Lady is socially and politically comfortable appearing on *The Ellen Show* something that would not have happened even five years before, but the fact that the First Lady is African American is something that many people did not think would happen in their lifetimes. *(Source: Courtesy of Associated Press, Copyright © 2012 by Rex Features. Used by permission of Associated Press.)*

other celebrity guests, Oprah Winfrey as Ellen's therapist and Laura Dern as the woman to whom Ellen declared her sexuality. Before this episode was aired, the Moral Majority urged sponsors to drop the show, and a few did. But ultimately, it was the viewers' reaction that sounded the death knell for *Ellen* in the following season. The month before the coming-out episode, 63 percent of audiences familiar with *Ellen* had no interest in this episode and 37 percent thought it was a bad idea for a major television character to be gay or lesbian (Pela 1997, 3).

The program stayed consistent with its dry and off-beat humor while exploring sexual orientation. In a dream sequence in one episode, Ellen experiences the world as if the dominant group were gay and lesbian and the minority group heterosexual. Her nongay friends were afraid to be "out" and posed as gay or risked ridicule and discrimination. Despite the decline and eventual demise of the series after the coming-out episode, *Ellen* played a significant role in paving the way for other gay and lesbian characters and themes in prime time. A spokesperson for the Gay and Lesbian Alliance Against Defamation said, "The power of Ellen DeGeneres' coming out on and offscreen cannot be underestimated in the annals of gay and lesbian history. . . . It was a giant step forward" (Epstein 1999, 3).

By the late 1990s, there was an increasing number of regular gay and lesbian characters on prime-time television. There was African American doctor Dennis Hancock on *Chicago Hope* and Dr. Maggie Doyle on *ER*. There was clerical assistant John Irvin (also known on occasion as "Gay John") on *NYPD Blue* and the emerging bisexuality of Detective Tim Bayliss, a major character on *Homicide*. There was *Spin City*'s mayoral staff person Carter Heywood and the sexually ambiguous Josh of *Veronica's Closet*.

For the first time, several programs that featured teens (and had much longer shelf-lives than *My So-Called Life*) began to explore gay and lesbian themes. One of *Dawson Creek*'s six regular characters, Jack McPhee, came out in 1999. And in the same year the popular program *Felicity*, set in a New York college, depicted Felicity offering to marry her gay immigrant boss, Javier, so that he would not be deported. Felicity also encouraged her then boyfriend, Noel, to accept the news that his brother was gay. Other programs with teens, such as *That 70s Show*, *Beverly Hills 90210*, and *Buffy the Vampire Slayer*, explored issues such as coming out to one's family and lesbian parenting.

Conservative organizations such as the Christian Action Network expressed concerns about the impact of these images of teen homosexuality and protested many of these programs, advocating an "HC" rating for homosexual content. Executives of these same programs, however, stated that the audience response had been overwhelmingly positive. Youth advocates from gay and lesbian organizations applauded this trend because it presented positive images of young people who were grappling with their sexuality. Cole Rucker, director of the Los Angeles Gay and Lesbian Center, said, "I can't emphasize enough how important these portrayals are. I have gotten phone calls, met youth in person—dozens and dozens of youth—who come in and say, 'I was thinking about killing myself until I saw Ellen come out,' or, 'until I saw *Dawson's Creek*.' Obviously [these programs] are trying to entertain people but they are truly saving the lives of young people when they present positive images on television" (Epstein 1999, 4).

The groundbreaking program *Will and Grace* was a direct descendant of *Ellen*. The premise of the program, which premiered in 1998 and ran for eight seasons, was that two friends move into an apartment together after breaking off their respective long-term relationships. The twist is that Grace is a straight female designer and Will is a gay male attorney. Will is handsome, often mistaken for straight, and openly gay. In another deviation from the norm of sitcoms, Will's best male friend, Jack, is the third of the four main characters. Jack is flamboyant, effusive, and also openly gay. The humor in *Will and Grace* often centered on the characters tenderly poking fun at each other in a way that seemed authentic. In the pilot episode, Grace says to Jack, "My dog knows you're gay," and Will adds, "Dead people know you're gay" (Natale 1998, 1).

The significance of two major gay characters on *Will and Grace* was multifaceted. First, Will and Jack had as much complexity and depth as a sitcom character can muster. They explored friendship, romantic relationships, work, and personal ethics, among other issues. But even more importantly, Will and Jack demonstrated at least two very different styles and personalities. Both the individual complexity and the range of the characters

Ilene Chaiken, creator of the television dramatic series *The L Word* (2004–2009), arrives at a Gay & Lesbian Alliance Against Defamation (GLAAD) awards ceremony. *The L Word* portrayed the lives of a group of lesbians in an interesting and realistic way. *(Source: Courtesy of Associated Press, Copyright © 2008 by Associated Press. Used by permission of Associated Press.)*

went far to dispel gay stereotypes. "The Will-and-Jack dynamic also offered audiences a chance to see how gays relate to one another. Jack was the more expressive character, but, according to the show's creators, he was probably more comfortable with his sexuality. While Jack's extroverted nature was often the butt of Will's jokes . . . it could also be turned back on Will, the more uptight of the two" (Natale 1998, 3).

But while there had been important gay and lesbian breakthrough programs, characters, and themes on prime-time television by the end of 1999, the numbers were still quite small. Even with the more than twenty-five gay characters in prime time, there were only seven appearing regularly on situation comedies (Epstein 1999, 2).

Since 2001, there has been a steady upward trend in the presence of LGBT characters on prime-time television. In 2007, 1.1 percent of the regular series characters were lesbian or gay; in 2008, the figure was 2.6 percent; in 2009, 3 percent; in 2010, 3.9 percent; in 2011, there was a slight dip to 2.9 percent, but then in the 2012 season the percentage rebounded to 4.4 percent (GLAAD 2012). Though the percentages are improving, the

The Fosters (2013–) became the first TV family drama featuring an interracial lesbian couple and their family, a multi-ethnic group of children (including four teenagers) who are related by biology, adoption, and through foster care. The Fosters' family composition and diversity challenges people around them. Time will tell whether this show will raise mainstream viewer awareness by introducing an expanded paradigm of same-sex loving couples, multi-ethnic households, and the dynamics of modern-day family life. [Left to right: Brandon Foster (David Lambert), Jesus Foster (Jake T. Austin), Stef Foster (Teri Polo), Lena Adams (Sherri Saum), and Mariana Foster (Cierra Ramirez).] (*Source: Courtesy of Getty Images. Copyright © 2013 American Broadcasting Companies, Inc. Used by permission of Getty Images. Photographer/© ABC/Getty Images.*)

story is not just in the numbers. Since the year 2000, there has been an improvement in the depth and complexity of the characters themselves. Among the best examples of this are *Noah's Arc* (2005–2006), featuring five young black males and their experiences in Los Angeles, and *The L Word* (2004–2009), the intertwining stories of a tight-knit group of lesbian women along with their family members and assorted friends. This series was also set in Los Angeles. *Modern Family*, which premiered in 2009, is a mockumentary about a quirky extended family that prominently features a gay married couple. *Scandal*, a hit political drama about behind-the-scenes maneuverings in the White House and around the nation's capital, includes a storyline about a gay White House chief of staff who is adopting a child with his journalist spouse; it premiered in 2012. Each of these programs depicts nonstereotypical gay and/or lesbian characters in everyday situations. The availability of these kinds of programs to mainstream viewers is unprecedented and will have an unimaginable impact on viewers' perceptions and attitudes in the years to come.

Popular Music and Sexual Orientation

The 2000 edition of *Media Messages* lamented the absence of LGBT images in popular music, the failure of the recording industry to market to gay audiences, and the inability or unwillingness of music executives to promote openly gay and lesbian artists to potential fans within the mainstream, music-buying public. Much has changed since then. In May 2012, singer-songwriter Adam Lambert, a former *American Idol* runner-up, released his second studio album, *Trespassing*, to widespread critical acclaim. The release made its debut at the number one spot on the *Billboard* 200 chart, making it the first recording by an openly gay artist to do so. In July of the same year, Frank Ocean, a singer-songwriter who is widely respected in the hip-hop world, came out to his fans in an open letter on Tumblr. This was a risky career step because of hip-hop's reputation for homophobia. Nevertheless, Ocean's willingness to publicly acknowledge his gay identity was well received among hard-core hip-hop luminaries, many of whom responded with congratulatory messages and words of encouragement (Fekadu 2012). Ocean went on to receive a 2013 Grammy Award for his album *Channel Orange*. These two examples indicate the extent to which the popular music business has transformed itself over the past decade. Though there is still much progress yet to be made, gay, lesbian, bisexual, and trans artists are not only more widely accepted by the general public, they are often enthusiastically embraced.

There have been similar trends in the other direction. Jennifer Lopez, Janet Jackson, Mariah Carey, and other well-known popular performers actively seek out and cultivate LGBT audiences because of their demonstrated buying power and the influence they have on the public's taste in entertainment (Hampp 2012). Although challenges still exist and the music business still has a long way to go in its relationship with the LGBT community, over the past few years the landscape has clearly begun to shift. In this section, we will examine the music industry and its interaction with gay and lesbian themes and audiences as well as the role of gay, lesbian, and bisexual musicians. We will also take a brief excursion into less mainstream music aimed primarily at gay and lesbian audiences.

The recording industry's past failure to target and market to this audience by promoting openly gay and lesbian artists and gay and lesbian themes had several dimensions. During the early years of the twenty-first century, the music industry relied on a gay and lesbian marketing strategy that involved minimal risk. The Simmons report indicated that gay and lesbian music consumers were well educated and somewhat affluent and tended to purchase music that "looks into the struggles facing the human condition—and that can be a heavy beat, or a soft, classical violin" (Flick 1994b, 2). Nevertheless, larger labels and small independents were still operating from old stereotypes of gay men at discos who preferred dance music with a driving beat and lesbians at coffee houses who wanted plaintive ballads and folk sounds.

Based on these perceptions, music executives employed another marketing strategy that allowed them to avoid promoting gay and lesbian artists and themes through mainstream music. This strategy utilized the connection of concerts and clubs that promoted gay and lesbian artists with retail record stores. Independent retail stores often featured in-store appearances following a live concert or club engagement and reported that gay consumers came in to buy these CDs (Flick 1994b, 2). From the industry's perspective, this was a profitable strategy that avoided the risk of offending larger audiences.

Epic Records began to further explore the gay and lesbian market following the label's success during the 1994 Gay Games and Stonewall 25 Civil Rights March. More than 1 million people attended this event and the musical performances that accompanied it. Subsequently, Epic began circulating a short questionnaire to independent retail record stores throughout the country to take a closer look at the musical interests of gay and lesbian consumers (Flick 1994a, 2). As of 1996, Atlantic Records was seriously considering promoting same-sex themes through the creation of a gay marketing division (Hultberg 1996, 6).

Yet even these tentative steps toward thinking about the possibilities of marketing music more extensively and specifically to gay and lesbian audiences were limited to the consideration of promoting more openly gay artists who, up to this point, had not necessarily addressed gay themes and relationships in their music. One major label executive who declined to be identified said that the industry is not likely to launch a trend in openly gay music or artists: "It'll never happen. You can be gay and have a hit—if your record is soft and by a platinum seller like Elton John. But we're years and years away from the day when a gay artist can be broken out of the box. I hate to say it, but gay people are just too frightening to too many people in the straight world" (Hultberg 1996, 3).

To appreciate the striking contrast between attitudes then and now, consider the public's reaction to Adam Lambert and Frank Ocean and note the following 2012 statement by a record executive describing marketing strategies for gay audiences, as quoted in *Billboard*:

> "Five or six years ago it was almost uncomfortable. Now I sit in label meetings and someone in the room will say, 'We really have to drill down on this market,'" says Scott Seviour, senior VP of marketing and artist development at Epic Records. "On a business level and an industry level, there's a greater respect for that consumer. You've seen them break an artist and make names. They're passionate and they can move the needle." (Hampp 2012)

It would be difficult to attribute such a discernible shift in attitudes to any single factor. A wide range of influences have converged over the past few years to bring the change about. Among these are the increased visibility of gays and lesbians in the other two focal categories of this book—television and films, the public policy debates centering on gay marriage and military service, a U.S. president who has himself made a transition from ambivalence to advocacy on behalf of LGBT issues, the discovery by media companies that there are genuine profits to be made in the LGBT market, and the increasingly vocal support of large numbers of celebrities, public figures, and opinion makers. Of course, the global explosion of social media use has transformed the way people communicate and has also expanded the range of what they communicate about. The social media have exposed many users to people and ideas that previously seemed foreign and unfamiliar.

This is not unlike the impact of television in the 1950s, which, for the first time, brought the visual world into the living room. The difference today is that people not only view social media, they also interact with it. This change has had an immeasurable impact on our society. So it stands to reason that some perspectives have changed and some cultural barriers—such as the gay/straight divide—have at least been penetrated if not completely shattered. Ultimately, it is important to be mindful that the most significant force in bringing about change has been and will continue to be the relentless effort on the part of LGBT people themselves. In looking at the history, this fact becomes abundantly clear.

After Stonewall (1969) and the igniting of the gay pride movement, both heterosexual and gay men began exploring same-sex subjects in their music in the form of gay characters and themes or in the name of shock. The Kinks sang of a drag queen in "Lola," Elton John sang a love song to "Daniel," and Lou Reed told of an Andy Warhol gay scene in "Walk on the Wild Side." "Early 70s glam rock employed shock tactics to shake rock from its post-Beatles doldrums, but at a cost: Androgyny, flirtations with bisexuality, and flamboyant gay imagery was, in retrospect, most often a means to an end, not the sincere expression of proud identity, even if those tactics helped young gay men comprehend their own" (Walters 1997a, 8). But even this burst of shock posing as gay pride was short-lived.

During roughly the same period, evolving along a parallel, underground track was the club-based dance music of the gay black subculture. This unique and infectious blend of gospel, soul, and R&B combined with West African polyrhythms emerged from gay black clubs in New York City. As has often been the case with targeted groups, the gay club scene and the music to which it gave birth were a response to mainstream rejection. Fed up with the racial exclusivity of white gay dance halls and the homophobia of straight black nightclubs, young black gays and lesbians created spaces where they could party among themselves (Thomas 2008). The music eventually gained widespread crossover appeal and became known as disco. Black and white gays found some common ground in their enjoyment of the uplifting, dance-friendly music that was now sweeping the country. Black artists such as Johnny Taylor, Gloria Gaynor, and Donna Summer contributed to its popularity with numerous hits. Singer-songwriter Gwen Guthrie and singer-model-actress Grace Jones were also part of the gay black club and disco scene. In Chicago, house music emerged from similar origins. On the West Coast, a generation before Frank Ocean came out to the world of hip-hop, an openly gay black singer named Sylvester, traveling and recording with back-up singers Martha Wash and Izora Rhodes (better known as Two Tons of Fun), added to the popularity of disco. Once John Travolta, the Bee Gees, and *Saturday Night Fever* became associated with disco, its black gay roots receded into the background of mainstream consciousness, but club music, disco, and house music put an indelible stamp on American popular culture, breaking down a few barriers in the process (Thomas 2008).

Music with lesbian themes by lesbian musicians was consistent with other forms of lesbian culture and was largely independent, alternative, highly politicized, and directed primarily to the lesbian feminist community via independent recording studios (Walters 1997b, 7). The first strongly gay-identified recorded music was written and sung by Alix

Dobkin in her 1971 album, *Lavender Jane Loves Women*. Dobkin's music, embedded in lesbian-feminist politics, featured songs such as "Talking Lesbian" (Faderman 1991, 223).

The independent Olivia Records was established in 1973. Its musical content, artists, and nonhierarchical structure reflected the burgeoning lesbian-feminist culture. In 1975, Olivia released Cris Williamson's album *The Changer and the Changed*, which became popular with feminist and lesbian audiences. Other lesbian musicians performed at women's music festivals and recorded songs with explicit same-sex themes on Olivia and other budding independent labels. Williamson, Margie Adams, Mary Watkins, and others had a steady following of a concert-going and record-buying crowd that was largely female and feminist. This music never quite made it to the mainstream, however.

In fact, as Olivia Records evolved, it reflected the kind of tension that developed in many alternative institutions created in the lesbian-feminist community. Although Olivia's owners and many of its consumers wanted authenticity of lesbian themes in the music, collective and nonhierarchical decision-making, and economic survival, the company was often hard-pressed to be successful at all three endeavors.

Singer Holly Near pierced the mainstream a bit in the late 1970s and early 1980s with her folk-oriented music and identification with the environmental movement. Near's establishment of an independent label paved the way for other lesbian singers in the 1990s whose popularity was on the rise. Meanwhile, by the 1980s, mainstream rock's brief flirtation with gay themes and androgyny went underground. "After disco hit the glass ceiling of homophobic, racist 'disco sucks' backlash and after the English new wave that generated such gay-leaning pop-dance groups as Bronski Beat, Culture Club, Frankie Goes to Hollywood, Erasure, and Wham! subsided, pop's gender-bender boom of the '80s appeared to be over" (Walters 1997b, 9).

In 1994, Bruce Springsteen recorded "The Streets of Philadelphia," the title track of the film *Philadelphia*. The song became the first popular song by a heterosexual man in the voice of a gay man. In the mid-1990s, the mainstream popularity of out lesbian superstars k.d. lang and Melissa Etheridge paved the way for the phenomenal success of Ani DiFranco. Etheridge came out as a lesbian after she had established mainstream success. Despite being wooed by major labels, DiFranco insisted on maintaining her independent status and control and continued to sing of same-sex relationships on her own label, "righteous babe." DiFranco's success was built on the experience and tradition of Holly Near's economic and musical independence and Melissa Etheridge's continued popularity even after declaring that she was a lesbian and posing for magazine photos with her life partner. Meanwhile, Ani DiFranco

> sings love songs directed explicitly at women, proclaimed herself queer, and regularly sold out her concerts, largely due to her dedicated and highly vocal lesbian following. The mood of her shows was much like the women's music circuit, where DiFranco got her start—sisterly, celebratory, and highly cruisy. The difference was that it was taking place under the eye of the mainstream, with plenty of appreciative straight guys in attendance, and for a performer who has been considered one of the most

vital and of-the-moment musicians in rock. The difference is that DiFranco—and her lesbian-inclusive phenomenon—is not the mainstream. (Walters 1997 b, 24)

DiFranco's mainstream success proved to be something of a trend. Perhaps her music paralleled the popularity of the television series *Will and Grace*. For both, the same-sex themes were ironically central in their appeal to gay and lesbian audiences and incidental in their appeal to mainstream audiences. DiFranco's music and *Will and Grace*'s humor worked because they were successful by the rules of their respective genres: rock music and situation comedy. One was visually and musically edgy and interesting, and the other played the same-sex edge while creating familiar characters, themes, and situations and managing to be very funny. Although hardly mainstream, bisexual vocalist and composer Meshell Ndegeocello is another artist of note who managed to combine her musicianship with social activism throughout her career. She has made recordings and performed concerts on behalf of AIDS relief as well as in support of Congolese women.

As we bring this section to a close, it is important to remember that despite the apparent progress that has been made over the past few years, there are still many challenges and obstacles to the advancement of LGBT performers in the mainstream of American popular music. During a 2006 interview, folk artist Doria Roberts described the pressure and frustration she experienced with the hazards of being open about her sexual orientation while dealing with the mainstream recording industry and attempting to build a music career: "The whole thing was they couldn't figure out how to sell. It was going to [be] hard enough to sell a black woman who just does folk rock music, who doesn't do R&B and that sort of stuff. . . . I was feeling like an endangered species at the time: as an artist, as a black woman, as lesbian, as a poor person, all those things" (Beige 2006). Fans and musical genres vary in their level of acceptance and support for LGBT artists. Even those who are moderately supportive anticipate continued barriers to the growth of openly gay and lesbian success.

Sexual Orientation and Film

According to listings published by the AMC Filmsite of the "Top 100 American films" and the "All-Time Box-Office Hits" (Dirks 2013), only a handful of the most highly rated and/or highest-grossing films produced in the twentieth century made reference to LGBT characters or themes, and most of those references were subtextual. In a sense, gays and lesbians were rendered all but invisible to the film-going public. Communications theorist George Gerbner coined the term "symbolic annihilation" to describe the absence, distortion, or marginalization of targeted groups in the media. "Generally applied to women and racial and sexual minorities, *symbolic annihilation* points to the ways in which poor media treatment can contribute to social disempowerment and in which symbolic absence in the media can erase groups and individuals from public consciousness" (Coleman and Yochim 2008).

Sociologist Gaye Tuchman, in her studies of media portrayals of women, divided symbolic annihilation into three aspects—omission, trivialization, and condemnation. In applying this construct to members of the LGBT community, the terms are more or less self-explanatory: Omission refers to the complete absence of LGBT people in a given story or media presentation. Trivialization reflects the minimization of their role in a story and/or the minimization of the significance of their sexual orientation. Condemnation implies that the character's sexual orientation is identified and acknowledged but is painted in a highly negative or villainous light. A few illustrations of the symbolic annihilation of people who are gay, lesbian, and bisexual in past films are listed in Table 6.1. Note that some of the cues used to signal to the audience that a person is gay are specious and highly stereotypical.

As we continue discussing images of people who are gay, lesbian, bisexual, and transgender in film, we will briefly examine the history of the film industry to identify reasons why the symbolic annihilation of LGBT characters has been so commonplace. As has been true of television and popular music, there have been fundamental shifts in filmmaking in recent years that may signal new and positive trends for the future. Moving to the present day, we will look at some of the films released since the beginning of the twenty-first century to see if we can determine how moviemaking is evolving in its treatment of LGBT characters and themes. To begin, take a few minutes to complete Media Activity 6.2 on page 468.

The few images of gays and lesbians in film have all been governed by a combination of legal rulings, external controls by the Motion Picture Production Code, internal controls by a sometimes timid and risk-phobic (not to mention homophobic) film industry, and the profit motive that drives the production of mainstream films. These controls on the industry with regard to sexual orientation have been more thoroughly documented in film than in either television or music, providing fertile ground for analysis. In this section, we will explore some of the limitations on the industry and the evolution of images and themes of gays, lesbians, and bisexuals in film.

A 1915 Supreme Court ruling opened the way for censorship of film along many fronts, including sexuality. The court ruled that movies were a for-profit business and therefore not protected by the right to freedom of speech spelled out in the First Amendment of the Constitution. Within a few years of this ruling, several states began to pass censorship laws that addressed obscenity and "inappropriate" topics for film (Russo 1987, 30). But it was not until 1931 that the film industry began policing and censoring itself through the Production Code and the Hays Censorship Office. Reference to homosexuality, gay and lesbian characters and themes, and even words like "pansy" were out. Thirty years later, in 1961, the Production Code changed once again and homosexuality was permitted official visibility provided it was portrayed with "care, discretion, and restraint" (Russo 1987, 48). Despite these cautions, derisive gay slurs were freely admitted on the big screen. By 1968, the Production Code was eliminated completely and homosexuality was, for the first time, fair game for filmmakers.

In the early days of film, there were some images that could be interpreted as gay, lesbian, or bisexual. "Briefly, in the early '30s, gays were familiar screen types: 'pansies' for comic relief and, more heroically, bisexual heroines (incarnated by Garbo and Dietrich) who looked thrillingly glamorous in their tuxedos and bachelor togs. That was old Hollywood's highest compliment to a woman—that she acted and thought like a man"

Table 6.1

Examples of Symbolic Annihilation in Mid-Twentieth-Century Films

Date	Title of film	LGBT depiction or reference	Aspect
1941	*The Maltese Falcon*	The film makes veiled allusions suggesting that Joel Cairo (Peter Lorre) is gay.	Trivialization
1945	*Lost Weekend*	In the book version, Ray Milland's alcoholic character struggles with being gay. In the film, he only deals with writer's block. Sexual orientation is never mentioned.	Omission
1946	*Night and Day*	In this quasi-biography, the sexual orientation of popular gay composer Cole Porter (Cary Grant) is completely erased.	Omission
1951	*A Streetcar Named Desire*	Blanche (Vivian Leigh) refers to the suicide of her ex-husband; however, his gay identity, as depicted in the original play, is written out of the script of the film.	Omission
1955	*Rebel Without a Cause*	Various hints (style of dress, mannerism, a locker photo of another male) suggest that Plato (Sal Mineo) is gay, but no explicit reference is ever made to his sexual orientation.	Trivialization
1958	*Cat on a Hot Tin Roof*	Maggie (Elizabeth Taylor) makes a barely discernible accusation that her husband, Brick (Paul Newman), and his friend Skipper had a sexual relationship. Brick responds by attempting to attack Maggie.	Condemnation
1961	*The Children's Hour*	Two women who run a private girls' school are accused of being lesbian lovers. One of them realizes that she is in fact attracted to the other and sobs inconsolably about how she has ruined everything and how "dirty" she is. She eventually commits suicide by hanging herself.	Condemnation
1962	*Advise & Consent*	A closeted gay U.S. senator, apparently convincing himself that he is too "dirty" to live, commits suicide by slitting his throat after being confronted by a former lover.	Condemnation
1967	*Bonnie and Clyde*	During encounters between Bonnie (Faye Dunaway) and Clyde (Warren Beatty), the film obliquely alludes to the possibility that Clyde Barrow may have been gay.	Trivialization
1967	*The Fox*	One of the women in a lesbian relationship is killed when a tree falls on her, and the other woman is then free to pursue her attraction to a man, thus being cured of homosexuality.	Condemnation

---

Media Activity 6.2
LGBT Characters and Themes in Film

1. Select the most recent full calendar year. For example, if it is March 2016, select the year 2015.
2. Identify and make a list of the films nominated for the Academy Award for Best Picture for the year.
3. If you have seen the films or are familiar with them, determine if they contain any gay, lesbian, bisexual, or transgender characters or themes. For those films that are unfamiliar to you, you may locate plot summaries and reviews on the Internet Movie Database (www.IMDb.com). Themes might include gays and lesbians married or in loving relationships, coming out, people grappling with their sexual orientation, LGBT discrimination, gay bashing, and so on.
4. What percentage of these nominated films contains gay, lesbian, bisexual, or transgender characters or themes?

(Corliss 1996, 66). In the 1930 film *Morocco*, Marlene Dietrich's character is dressed in a top hat and tails as she performs in a nightclub. She kisses a woman fully on the lips, takes the flower from her hair, and throws it to her love interest in the film, Gary Cooper. The ambiguity of the sexuality of the character and the actor is designed to titillate the audience (A. Weiss 1992, 32).

Greta Garbo, who had a relationship with Salka Viertel, the screenwriter *of Queen Christina*, was in her real life part of an upper-class European lesbian community. Hollywood studios went to great lengths to create an image of Garbo's heterosexual romances. Still, the subtext of Garbo's offscreen life and the film *Queen Christina* itself leave room for an oppositional lesbian reading as her character, the queen of Sweden, dresses in male attire and kisses Countess Ebba on the lips (A. Weiss 1992, 36).

One of the first stereotypical images of gay men in film, the "pansy," predated the Supreme Court decision by one year. In 1914, Stan Laurel's *The Soilers* established a feminized cowboy for laughs and signaled the kick-off of this image that has appeared throughout film history (Russo 1987, 26). After the Production Code adopted by the Hayes Censorship Office was in operation, these references became more oblique because the mention of homosexuality was forbidden. As demonstrated by the examples in Table 6.1, from the earliest days of film through the early 1960s, most gay and lesbian images and themes were under the surface, available only to those willing to look for them in the subtext of the story or in the books or original scripts on which the films were based.

With few exceptions, gay and lesbian characters and themes in the 1960s and much of the 1970s continued to be simple and to conform to the stereotypes of villain, predator, or victim. There were few characters who were complex and compelling and there was almost no range in type of gay and lesbian characters.

One notable exception was a 1961 film, *Victim*, made in England, which pierced some of these solidifying gay stereotypes and taboos. *Victim* was an unabashed plea for the reform of England's anti-sodomy statutes. It features a married but homosexual lawyer, Melville Farr, who is being blackmailed with sexual pictures of himself with a man. An enlightened police detective, who believes that the only function of the sodomy laws is to aid blackmailers, helps Farr resolve the case and end the blackmail. In this film, Farr, played by popular British actor Dirk Bogarde, is the good guy (Dearden 1961). He was not destroyed by his sexuality, but rather was a complex character seeking justice. *Victim* was the first film to insist on acceptance and decriminalization of homosexuality and to actually use the word itself. The revised 1961 Production Code, which called for "care, discretion, and restraint" in reference to homosexuality, interpreted that phrase as justification to refuse its seal of approval to *Victim* unless it cut the use of the word "homosexual." The updated code had been clarified; reference to homosexuality was acceptable but the use of the word itself was not. The film's director and producer refused to make the cuts, and *Victim* was released in the United States without a seal of approval (Russo 1987, 128–129).

"The hero-villain question persisted throughout the Sixties and well into the Seventies, with movie homosexuals increasingly falling victim to their own inherently villainous sexuality—the flaw that always destroyed them in one way or another. Self-hatred was the standard accessory with every new model" (Russo 1987, 136). In fact, from 1950 to 1983 there were at least thirty-three documented murders or suicides of gay characters in film (Russo 1987, 347–349).

After the Production Code was abolished in 1968, an increasing number of films began to portray gay and lesbian characters and themes. While villains and victims were still alive and well, there were also new kinds of gay and lesbian characters and themes and a slowly building but wider range of characters as well. *The Boys in the Band* was released in 1970 after the Production Code was abolished and after gay liberation was heralded by the protest at the Stonewall Inn. It was the first film to feature characters who all are gay. Although there are eight gay characters and the film was written by Mart Crowley, a gay man, the stereotypes of self-hatred persisted. Crowley later said, "I knew a lot of people like those people. The self-deprecating humor was born out of a low self-esteem, from a sense of what the times told you about yourself" (Epstein and Friedman 1995). While mainstream media praised the film, it was criticized in the gay community. "When the Stonewall riots of June 1969 triggered the movement toward gay self-esteem, *Boys in the Band* rapidly became dated. With gays redefining themselves as strong and proud, a play about acid-tongued, self-pitying fairies was bound to resemble the gay equivalent to a minstrel show" (Guthmann 1999). At the time, however, the film was a breakthrough in its direct portrayal of gay characters and themes. Perhaps even in its limitations, the film reflected the internalized homophobia of the time experienced by the writer as well. Internalized oppression is always involuntary, and *The Boys in the Band* is a strong example of how gays and lesbians can receive and internalize the same negative misinformation as heterosexuals.

In the 1972 film *Cabaret*, set in Nazi Germany, Liza Minnelli plays the heterosexual and sexually liberated Sally, and Michael York plays the openly bisexual Brian, both of whom become sexually involved with the same man. While the interpretation of Brian's goodness as a character may be contested, his complexity and sympathetic nature as a character are not. This is still another kind of breakthrough for gay characters.

The decade of the 1980s was the first time that gay and lesbian films emerged with characters that are both good and bad, victims and perpetrators, simple and complex, men and women. Nine films released in the '80s had major homosexual themes, and nineteen major characters were gay or lesbian. Twelve films had at least one gay or lesbian character who was complex. *The World According to Garp* and *Torch Song Trilogy* featured transsexual or cross-dressing characters, Roberta Muldoon and Arnold, respectively, both of whom were complex and likable characters who survived intact in the context of the film. Arnold (Harvey Fierstein) is the major character in *Torch Song*, and while he struggles with love, self-acceptance, and homophobia in his life, in the end he is in a committed relationship with a man, has adopted a son, and has a successful career. Gay or lesbian relationships were depicted in eight of the films. Some of the characters and themes were superficial (*Lianna, Personal Best, Making Love*), but many of the characters in these 1980s films demonstrated more range and complexity than ever before in film history.

The themes in these films were predominantly positive or complex. Love and romance, friendship, coming out, and self-acceptance were explored in eight of the films. The homophobia, violence, and gay-bashing that occur in *Cruising* were treated very differently from the same themes in *Torch Song Trilogy*. In *Cruising*, a heterosexual police officer (Al Pacino) poses as gay to search for a mass murderer who is targeting gay men in New York's S&M (sadomasochistic) clubs. The film is replete with graphic images of the murders and features no major characters who are gay—only one-dimensional victims and one villainous murderer. There was an enormous outcry from the gay community protesting the stereotypes and the violence of this film. By contrast, *Torch Song Trilogy* follows the inner life of Arnold as he grapples with and succeeds in accepting himself and insists on love and acceptance from everyone in his life, including his mother. His family's homophobia is woven in and out of the story line. Ultimately, it climaxes when Arnold's life partner, Alan (Matthew Broderick), is murdered in a horrifying scene of mass gay-bashing. While the scene and Alan's death are depicted as tragic, the violence is not exploited. Rather, it is depicted as the horrible but logical consequence of hate and homophobia and is used as an admonition to both Arnold's mother and the audience.

Once again, no films with major gay or lesbian characters or themes made it to the top ten box office hits in the 1990s, but Tom Hanks won the Best Actor Academy Award in 1993 for his portrayal in the film *Philadelphia* of a gay lawyer with AIDS. The burgeoning trend of LGBT themes and characters that began in the 1980s continued in the 1990s with the depiction of homosexuality in mainstream films and an increase of images in independent films. Three of the more economically successful films made in major studios were *Philadelphia* (1994), *In & Out* (1997), and *The Object of My Affection* (1998). The independently made films included *Go Fish* (1994), *The Incredibly True Adventures of Two Girls in Love* (1995), and *Chasing Amy* (1998).

Philadelphia, starring Tom Hanks and Denzel Washington, is the story of a successful gay lawyer with AIDS and his battle with the disease and with discrimination in his law firm. *In & Out* tells of a high school teacher (Kevin Kline) who is outed while engaged to a woman and apparently before he has figured out that he is gay. *The Object of My Affection* puts a single pregnant woman with a gay male roommate, and as their relationship blossoms, she believes he would make a better life partner and father than her baby's biological father. *Go Fish* is a romantic comedy about a group of lesbian friends, their community, and their intimate relationships. *The Incredibly True Adventures of Two Girls in Love* is a comedy about first love between two high school girls, one white and one black. *Chasing Amy* is the story of a threesome of comic-book-creating Generation Xers in which one of the men falls in love with the woman, who is a lesbian.

On an obvious level, the mainstream films were about gay men and the independents were about lesbians or bisexual women. The independents often allowed for soulful kisses and explicit sex between the women. Of the mainstream films, *Philadelphia* portrayed a body-to-body slow dance between straight actors (cast as gay men) Tom Hanks and Antonio Banderas, and *In & Out* has one whopper of a kiss between two straight actors, Kevin Kline and Tom Selleck. The mainstream films took a safer course in characters, actors, and themes to appeal to wider resources and a broader audience; the independents, on a lower budget, were aimed at a narrower audience and took greater risks in character, themes, and actors.

Another way to analyze the depiction of gay and lesbian characters and themes in film is to examine how they are perceived in the wider culture. Some of this can be determined by exploring reviews, box office success, and ratings and to what degree the meaning and significance of the films are contested. The questions of stereotyping, authenticity, and validity of the messages vary in various publications and perspectives and begin to paint a picture of the changing cultural landscape in the United States. A more in-depth examination of ratings, box office success, and reviews of two of these films, *Philadelphia* and *Go Fish*, reveals some of the contested meaning and cultural terrain.

Roger Ebert, a mainstream reviewer, said *Philadelphia* was groundbreaking because it "marks the first time Hollywood has risked a big-budget film on the subject" of AIDS. He compared it to *Guess Who's Coming to Dinner*, a relatively superficial film but the first widely distributed one to address interracial romance. Like *Guess Who's Coming to Dinner*'s use of stars Spencer Tracy, Katharine Hepburn, and Sidney Poitier to make the film and subject palatable for larger audiences, Ebert believed *Philadelphia* used the same strategy with likable (not to mention heterosexual) stars Tom Hanks and Denzel Washington. Ebert seemed to think that *Philadelphia* had taken about as much risk as it could and still reach a wide audience (Ebert 1994b).

Rita Kempley of the *Washington Post* (also a mainstream publication) disagreed with Ebert. She compared the film with Frank Capra classics that center around traditional American values and noble characters but challenge hypocrisy in the American people. Kempley said that *Philadelphia* asks the important question: "Is not this a land where *all* men are created equal—or must they be *straight* men?" (Kempley 1994b; italics show author's emphasis). Another perspective was presented by reviewer Michael D. Klemm who observed that "compromises were made to make *Philadelphia* accessible to a mass audience, severely weakening what could have been a much more powerful film" (Klemm 1999).

These various interpretations of the film's meaning and impact mark a range of viewpoints among the audiences as well as the reviewers. Significantly, none of the reviewers found the film or the topic offensive, as reviewers did when discussing films such as *Suddenly Last Summer*. The main criticism seemed to be that *Philadelphia* did not go far enough or take enough risks to convey the complexity and dimensions of AIDS and homophobia. Nevertheless, *Philadelphia* grossed more than $200 million worldwide and its message, limited though it may have been, reached the largest audience that any film about homosexuality had ever reached (Demme 1993).

By contrast, *Go Fish* grossed just under $2.5 million. The viewing audience for *Philadelphia* was roughly 200 times larger than the viewing audience for *Go Fish*. As the reviews and contested messages of each film are analyzed, much of the significance of the content is in the context. How many people saw each film and what impact could relative audience size have on cultural views of homosexuality?

The reviews for *Go Fish* were largely positive in both gay and lesbian publications as well as in the mainstream press. Roger Ebert said the film was charming, warm, "honest, forthright and affectionate, and it portrays the everyday worlds of these ordinary gay women with what I sense is accuracy" (Ebert 1994a). Ebert said the weakness was that the film was so matter-of-fact in its recording of everyday life that nothing ever happened and it dimmed in interest.

Rita Kempley of the *Washington Post* liked *Go Fish* too and pointed out the universality of the themes: "An explicit, low-budget tale of lesbians in love, this inventive first film may be aimed at gay audiences, but it turns on a premise familiar to all persuasions: when it comes to relationships, opposites attract" (Kempley 1994a). But it was only in explicitly gay publications that reviewers commented on the significance of *Go Fish*, its characters, and its themes.

A number of films produced since 2000 represent a new wave of filmmaking that seeks to depict LGBT experiences with a level of depth and insight in marked contrast to the omission, trivialization, and condemnation discussed at the beginning of this section. Some people regard the 2005 release of *Brokeback Mountain* as a turning point in mainstream cinema. It is a bittersweet romance that tells the story of two ranch hands who are hired to tend a flock of sheep in the summer of 1963 and end up falling in love. Ennis Del Mar (Heath Ledger) is engaged to be married and dreams of owning a ranch of his own. Jack Twist (Jake Gyllenhaal) is a rodeo cowboy who aspires to greater success. This film was notable for the natural manner in which the characters are depicted, for the deliberate pace at which their relationship unfolds, and for the multidimensional portrayal of the key characters and the situations they face. The film, based on a short story by Annie Proulx and directed by Ang Lee, deconstructs the cowboy archetype, a quintessential symbol of American male masculinity, and in so doing, pushes the audience to see the potential beauty in a loving relationship between two men as well as the residual violence—physical and emotional—brought on by society's mindless rejection of such love. According to one critic, "Indeed, everything about the relationship between

In *Brokeback Mountain* (2005), two ranch hands, Jack Twist (Jake Gyllenhaal) and Ennis Del Mar (Heath Ledger), discover each other while herding sheep in Wyoming. Becoming best friends and lovers, their relationship deconstructs the quintessential American male archetype. [Here, costars Gyllenhaal (left) and Ledger appear at the 2006 Screen Actors Guild (SAG) awards ceremony.] (*Source: Courtesy of Associated Press, Copyright © 2006 by Associated Press. Used by permission of Associated Press.*)

Ennis and Jack is both idealized and utterly true to life. Passion is very much here—a passion that will make the sex obsession many gay men settle for seem so much less. But what's unsettling is the context. What's threatening to some about the movie is the way it blurs friendship and Eros. Jack and Ennis are both best friends and lovers, fishing buddies who bring home no fish" (Holleran 2006).

Another important film released in 2005 was *Transamerica*. It is the story of a pre-operative male-to-female transsexual who, on the eve of her reassignment surgery, discovers she has a teenage son from a prior relationship, who is alone, in trouble, and in need of her help. The film tells the story of these two individuals' discovery of each other and of themselves on a road trip from New York to California. For many critics, the most compelling thing about *Transamerica* was veteran actress Felicity Huffman's stunning and intricate performance. "That the film succeeds without slipping too far into sentimentality or didacticism is in no small measure the result of Ms. Huffman's wit and grace" (Scott 2005). The movie has also been criticized by some for casting a female who is not transsexual in the lead role as well as for colluding with stereotypes about transsexuals and framing the story in a manner that conforms with somewhat distorted mainstream perceptions of what it means to be transsexual (Ira 2012). Other critics disagree: "*Transamerica* is a powerful movie for transsexual-identified people, specifically the trans woman communities, as it provides a three-dimensional character whom individuals can relate to through their lived experiences" (Pettitt and Marciano 2006). Beyond that, it opens a small window, for mainstream audiences, into some aspects of being transsexual. In some ways, the films serves to affirm the life of a transgender person as being neither normal nor abnormal but simply another representation of what it means to be human. Given the reaction to *Transamerica* and the general lack of public awareness, it is clear that our society needs to move beyond its narrow depictions of gendered norms and do a better job of educating people about the full range of human gender and sexual experiences. Entertainment media, and film in particular, have the potential to make a powerful contribution to that glaring need.

The 2008 release *Milk* tells the story of gay activist Harvey Milk (Sean Penn), who became the first openly gay elected official in U.S. history when he took a seat on the San Francisco Board of Supervisors in 1977. The following year, he and Mayor George Moscone were assassinated by former supervisor Dan White. *Milk* was heralded critically for its evocative depiction of the politics of the times as well as its honest, straightforward portrayal of the title character. It is not a gay film, per se; it is rather a film about a civic leader who assumes an active role in the American democratic process and ultimately becomes a national martyr. According to Roger Ebert, *Milk* "tells Harvey Milk's story as one of a transformed life, a victory for individual freedom over state persecution, and a political and social cause" (Ebert 2008).

The 2010 release *The Kids Are All Right* tells the story of Nic (Annette Benning) and Jules (Julianne Moore), a comfortably middle-class lesbian couple whose two teenage children take it upon themselves to track down their anonymous sperm-donor father (Mark Ruffalo) and bring him into their lives, leading to unexpected complications. The film was well received by reviewers. "*The Kids Are All Right* would have been a highly regarded, stinging family drama in the tradition of *American Beauty* and *Ordinary People* even if the subject family was not so proudly unorthodox. What once defined 'American' and 'Ordinary' in terms of the family constitution no longer holds" (Hiller 2010). The significance of the film is that it questions conventional notions of what is "orthodox" and "normal" regarding what a family should look like and what kind of parents should raise kids.

The independent film *Pariah*, released in 2011, is a fascinating coming-of-age movie about a bright teenage girl, Alike (Adepero Aduye), who is trying to come to grips with her lesbian identity while also attempting to navigate and make sense of friendships, relationships, the urban lesbian social scene, and the seething household dynamics of her family. In the process, she experiences infatuation and heartbreak but, as a result, manages to connect with her own gifts and discover the power of self-love and self-awareness. *Pariah*, which was showcased at the Sundance Film Festival and opened in theaters to widespread critical praise, succeeds on many levels. The characters and situations are

The film *Milk* (2008) provides an evocative depiction of the politics of the times and a frank portrayal of the life and tragic death of gay activist/politician Harvey Milk (Sean Penn). [Penn is pictured here after being presented the 2009 Academy Award for Best Actor; in his acceptance speech, he stated, "We've got to have equal rights for everyone."] *(Source: Courtesy of Associated Press, Copyright © 2009 by Associated Press. Used by permission of Associated Press.)*

portrayed realistically. The scene depicting Alike coming out to her parents (Kim Wayans and Charles Parnell) is riveting. What is most profound is that the movie provides a glimpse into the life experiences of a very young lesbian woman at the moment of self-discovery and self-definition.

Some of the recent films described above may be criticized for being too intent on presenting the LGBTQ experience in a manner that conforms to mainstream, heteronormative models of families, couples, and relationships; however, their significance for the advancement of gay rights and gay liberation has more to do with their contribution to the large-scale shifts in public perceptions over the past decade. Each of these films, in its own way, has been successful in contesting the dehumanizing schemas and symbolic annihilation that had been all too common in representations of LGBTQ characters in mainstream cinema during the twentieth century.

As you consider these films, their images, and their popularity, think about which of them you have seen. Have the images and messages about gays, lesbians, and bisexuals been simple or complex? Have there been a variety of characters and themes in the films you have seen, or are character types and topics fairly narrow and repeated? Take a closer look at how these films have reinforced or challenged the information you have taken in about sexual orientation through personal experience, formal education, and other forms of media to determine how you have been socialized on this issue.

CHAPTER SUMMARY

The late twentieth and early twenty-first centuries have been a time of change in the construct of sexual orientation; in the oppression and liberation of gays, lesbians, and bisexuals; and in entertainment media portrayals. Shifts in laws and policies affecting LGBT people include the removal of anti-sodomy statutes and creation of anti-hate legislation in some states, the provision of domestic partner benefits in some businesses, and the lifting of the ban on gay and lesbians engaging in military service. Marriage between partners of the same sex is now legally recognized in seventeen states. In April 2013, NBA center Jason Collins identified himself as gay, becoming the first active player in any of the four major American professional team sports to come out to the general public. Like other public figures who have recently decided to reveal their sexual orientation (professional soccer player Robbie Rogers also revealed himself to be gay recently, as did NFL draft prospect and University of Missouri standout Michael Sam), Collins received widespread support from players, fans, and the general public. All this bodes well for our society and deserves to be celebrated.

Nevertheless, the largest number of hate crimes continue to be directed at people who are perceived to be gay or lesbian, and the highest proportion of teen suicides continue to be those of gay and lesbian teens struggling with their sexual identity. More than any of the issues we have explored, information about sexual orientation is the least available through formal education, personal experience, and popular media. What little information we do receive is often distorted or biased. The fact that many religious denominations interpret homosexuality negatively and infuse same-sex attraction, love, marriage, and intercourse with religious explanations often tends to close discussion before it even begins. As you examine your personal experiences, formal knowledge, and media exposure to homosexuality, it will be important to determine if the facts and messages you acquired from all three sources line up consistently or if they challenge or contradict one another. The more extensive and consistent the information you received, the more likely you were to have been thoroughly socialized about sexual orientation. Unobstructed discussion, accurate information, dispelling of myths, and open airing of disagreements are critically important as we reflect on the extent of our socialization and develop our own independent thinking.

GLOSSARY OF KEY TERMS

berdache or *winkte*: The American Indian berdache or *winkte* has been noted in 130 tribes from the sixteenth to the nineteenth centuries. These individuals did not fit neatly into Western cultural standards of sexual orientation or identity. Most frequently a berdache was a biological male whose sense of self and some combination of clothing, work, and behavior were more traditionally female. Not only were male berdaches permitted to be married to and/or have sex with other males, but they were also awarded a holy and respected status in the tribe. Although less is known about female berdaches, there is also evidence of their special status in at least thirty tribes.

bisexual: While culturally the sexual orientation known as bisexual has been viewed from widely different perspectives, the generally agreed-upon definition is that someone who identifies as bisexual has some degree of physical attraction to both men and women and may or may not choose to act upon either or both attractions, depending on the physical and emotional safety of the environment and the sense of external and internalized stigma. There have been historical times in the United States in which bisexuals have been regarded as hip, free from standard cultural restraints, and other times when they have been judged harshly in the LGBTQ community as unwilling to take the risk necessary to claim their "true" gay or lesbian identity. In the twenty-first-century United States, both of these views exist in various groups and subcultures and are joined by another perspective—that any form of same-sex sexual behavior is wrong or sinful.

coming out: "Coming out" is short for "coming out of the closet" and refers to the individual process by which gays, lesbians, and bisexuals choose to move from secrecy to openness in their sexual identity and expression. Coming out is a ". . . life-long process of self-acceptance. People forge a lesbian, gay, bisexual, or transgender identity first for themselves, and then they may reveal it to others. Publicly identifying one's orientation may or may not be part of coming out" (GLAAD 2013). Because of the extent to which LGBT people are targeted in our society, deciding whether or not to come out in any given situation is a difficult and complex decision.

gay: The term "gay" was first used to describe both men and women whose sexual orientation is generally understood and expressed as same-sex attraction. Eventually, the term "gay" came to be used to refer primarily to men, whose culture and sexual behavior were often very different from that of women, and women eventually chose primarily to be identified separately as lesbians. People inside and outside the LGBTQ community have had a wide range of reactions to the words "gay," "heterosexual," and "homosexual" as neutral, offensive, acceptable, insulting, or reductive. When in doubt, the safest thing to do is to ask people which term they prefer without assuming this will then permanently apply to all people.

heteronormativity: The term "heteronormativity" is the presumption that opposite-sex attraction, dating, relationships, marriage, having children, and all of their accompanying cultural standards are "normal" and the right way to be in the world. It also presumes that individuals who express their sexual orientation and/or identity as different from these norms are therefore abnormal, sick, sinful, or misfits.

heterosexuality: The term "heterosexuality" is explicitly defined as sexual attraction and/or sexual interaction between men and women. The implicit meaning of the term has generally implied privilege: those who are perceived as heterosexual are thought of as normal and superior to those who are perceived as homosexual and are far more likely to have access to the resources and power that allows them to meet their goals in life.

homosexuality: The term "homosexuality" is explicitly defined as sexual attraction and/or sexual interaction between individuals of the same sex. The implicit meaning of the term has often in the past and present been associated with sin, mental illness, and deviance: in contrast to heterosexuality, which is considered "natural" in the dominant culture, homosexuality has been considered "unnatural." Those who are perceived as homosexual are often the target of violence, bullying, ridicule, or rejection by their family and on a concrete level have often been denied the right to marry a same-sex partner, to attend an ill or dying partner in the hospital, or to serve in the military. One of the actions taken by many LGBTQ people has been to reject the negative connotation of the term "homosexuality," in much the same way as American blacks sough to reject the terms "Negro" or "colored" in favor of "black" or "African American." The terms chosen to replace "homosexuality" are intended to reclaim a positive and inclusive identity.

lesbian: A woman who is primarily attracted, physically and emotionally, to other women and engages in same-sex romantic relationships.

LGBT/LGBTQ: This is one of the most commonly used all-inclusive terms for sexual identities and orientations that are "other" in the context of heteronormativity. The letters stand for lesbian, gay, bisexual, transgender/transsexual, or simply trans. The Q is sometimes used to designate queer or questioning. The reclaiming of all of these terms into one larger term is somewhat unwieldy, but among the LGBTQ community and its allies, the need for inclusiveness far outweighs the need for simplicity.

queer: The word "queer" was historically a derogatory and sometimes violent term used to show extreme disdain and disgust toward gays and lesbians. In the late twentieth century, the term "queer" was reclaimed by some gays, lesbians, bisexuals, transgender, and transsexual people to describe and dramatize the fact that biological sex, gender identity, and sexual desire do not always match up neatly. The term "queer" is used in academic circles in which programs formerly known as Gay and Lesbian Studies were renamed Queer Studies. Q is one of the terms used in the acronym LGBTQ.

questioning: The term "questioning" refers to those individuals who are uncertain about their sexual orientation and/or identity. It is one of the other meanings of the letter Q in the acronym LGBTQ. The term "questioning" often refers to adolescents who are wondering if they are gay or lesbian or bisexual or trans. Many youth LGBTQ support groups welcome young people who are questioning as a way of giving them plenty of room to explore their identity without pressure to make up their minds or to be "normal."

sexual identity: The term "sexual identity" has been used in at least two different ways, which overlap yet are different enough to be confusing. "Sexual identity" is often used in the same way as "sexual orientation" to define an individual's same-sex or bisexual attraction as well as his or her sexual behavior. More recently, this term has taken on a more specific definition, which refers to people's felt experience of their gender and whether their internal feelings, thoughts, desires, interests, language expression, and so on are in line with or in contradiction to their biological sex as a man or a woman. Understanding sexual and gender identity and how it matches or does not match the body is an important foundation to understanding the meaning of the terms "transsexual" and "transgender."

sexual orientation: The term "sexual orientation" has evolved over time. It was originally used to describe an individual's so-called sexual "preference" for someone of the same sex or someone of the other sex. The concept of sexual preference was eventually discarded because it assumed that individuals have a choice of whether they "preferred" men or women as sexual partners as they would select whether they preferred the color green or the color orange. While there is still some scientific disagreement on this issue, many scientists agree that our sexual orientation is not something we choose, but rather something we are, such as blue-eyed or brown-eyed. In more recent times, sexual orientation has been understood more frequently as sexual behavior and/or attraction to men or women or both, as well as other, less physical, deep and surface cultural behaviors and norms such as dating and courting. It is important that sexual orientation is used to describe one's sexual attraction and behavior, but does not automatically include the person's gender expression as traditionally or untraditionally male or female.

the T in LGBTQ: The T stands for the terms "transgender" and "transsexual," which are often confused with "homosexual." While there are complexities and analysis beyond the scope of this book, one important thing to remember is that the terms "transgender" and "transsexual" define people's gender identity and whether and to what degree they see themselves as traditionally male or female and whether that gender identity matches their physical body. People who are transgender or transsexual may be attracted to people of the same sex, the opposite sex, or both sexes. The abbreviated expression "trans" has become commonplace as an inclusive word for either or both terms.

transgender: The term "transgender" begins with the same description as the term "transsexual." These individuals' biological sex and genitalia are distinct and separate from their identity as masculine or feminine; transgender people feel as if they have somehow been placed in the wrong body. Individuals who identify as transgender live with the complicated mismatch between their sexual identity and their body. They often use hormones to develop stronger secondary gender characteristics to match their identity, but whether by personal choice or because of personal finances, they do not have sex reassignment surgery.

transsexual: The term "transsexual" begins with the same description as the term "transgender." These individuals' biological sex and genitalia are distinct and separate from their identity as masculine or feminine; transsexual people feel as if they have somehow been placed in the wrong body. Simply put, those who identify as transsexual have made the choice and have figured out how to pay the cost of sex reassignment surgery, which, in addition to changing secondary sexual characteristics (i.e., breasts, voice, muscular structure) through the use of hormones, changes their genitalia to physically match the gender they experience.

REFLECTION, SUMMARY, AND ANALYSIS

Instructions

The chapter questions invite you to engage in an exercise of reflection, summary, and analysis about key terms, topics, and issues discussed in the chapter. The skills involved in responding to the questions are a combination of summary and analysis. The *summary* component of the questions requires you to demonstrate your understanding of the terms and concepts in the chapter through the use of describing, explaining, and restating. Summary involves primarily answering questions that begin with "what."

The *analysis* component of the questions requires you to use your own independent thinking, your own ideas and arguments. Analysis requires breaking something— like a concept, theory, or argument—into parts so you can understand and describe how those parts work together to make the whole. Analytic writing goes beyond the obvious to discuss questions of how and why—so ask yourself those questions as you read. Your responses to these kinds of questions will require that you carefully and clearly state your argument, opinion, or thesis statement and use evidence from the chapter as well as your own experience or observations to support your view. You may also include your own personal experiences in the analysis insofar as they are relevant and support your thesis statement and are not generalized in such a way as to suggest that your experiences are universal.

The University of North Carolina's Writing Center website has an excellent two-page handout on analysis and summary (http://writingcenter.unc.edu/handouts/summary-using-it-wisely/).

Study Questions

1. What is homophobia? What is heterosexual privilege?
2. What are some examples throughout history of discrimination in laws and policies against people who are or are perceived to be gay, lesbian, bisexual, or transgendered?
3. What happened at Stonewall and why is it considered important to gay liberation?
4. What are some of the ways that gays, lesbians, bisexual, and transgendered people experience bias, discrimination, and rejection?
5. What are some of the problems for heterosexuals that emerge because of homophobia? In what ways do some heterosexuals feel they have to monitor their appearance, behavior, and job choices to make sure they aren't perceived as gay or lesbian?
6. Choose one of the religions described in Chapter 6 (yours if it is there) and describe the range of perspectives in that religion about sexual orientation.
7. As you were growing up, what did you learn about what it meant to be gay or lesbian from your family, peers, media, and religion? How is that the same as or different from what you think and believe now?

BIBLIOGRAPHY

Abelove, Henry. 1986. "Freud, Male Homosexuality, and the Americans." *Dissent* (Winter): 59–69.

Abelove, Henry, Michele A. Barale, and David M. Halperin, eds. 1993. *The Lesbian and Gay Studies Reader*. New York: Routledge.

Adams, Maurianne, Lee Anne Bell, and Pat Griffin, eds. 1997. *Teaching for Diversity and Social Justice: A Sourcebook*. New York: Routledge.

Anderson, Victor. 2000. "The Black Church and Sexual Ethics." Presented at the Society on Christian Ethics. www.clgs.org/black-church-and-sexual-ethics.

Beige, Kathy. 2006. "Interview with Doria Roberts: Woman Dangerous—Doria Roberts— Lesbian Music." About.com Lesbian Life. http://lesbianlife.about.com/od/lesbianmusicians/a/DoriaRoberts.htm.

Blank, Paula. 2011. "The Proverbial 'Lesbian': Queering Etymology in Contemporary Critical Practice." *Modern Philosophy* 109, no. 1: 108–134.

Blumenfeld, Warren J., ed. 1992. *Homophobia: How We All Pay the Price*. Boston: Beacon.

Branch, Taylor. 1988. *Parting the Waters: America in the King Years 1954–1963*. New York: Simon and Schuster (Kindle Edition).

Chasnoff, Debra, and Helen Cohen, dirs. 1996. *It's Elementary: Talking About Gay Issues in School*. San Francisco: Groundspark Film.

Coleman, Robin R. Means, and Emily Chivers Yochim. 2008. "Symbolic Annihilation." In *International Encyclopedia of Communications*, ed. Erik Barnouw. Malden, MA: Blackwell.

Corliss, Richard. 1996. "The Final Frontier: Two New Movies Pose the Question, 'Can't Hollywood Treat Gays Like Normal People?'" *Time*, March 11, 66.

Croteau, David, and William Hoynes. 1997. *Media/Society: Industries, Images, and Audiences*. Thousand Oaks, CA: Pine Forge Press.

Cruikshank, Margaret. 1992. *The Gay and Lesbian Liberation Movement*. New York: Routledge.

Curran, Charles E. 1998. "Sexual Orientation and Human Rights in American Religious Discourse: A Roman Catholic Perspective." In *Sexual Orientation and Human Rights in American Religious Discourse*, ed. Saul M. Olyan and Martha C. Nussbaum, 87–96. New York: Oxford University Press.

Dearden, Basil, dir. 1961. *Victim*. 1961. London, UK: Allied Filmakers. Film.

D'Emilio, John. 1992. *Making Trouble: Essays on Gay History, Politics, and the University*. New York: Routledge.

Demme, Jonathan, dir. 1993. *Philadelphia*. 1993. Culver City, CA: TriStar Pictures. Film.

Diamond, Lisa M. 2008. "Sexual Fluidity: Understanding Women's Love and Desire." Cambridge, MA: Harvard University Press.

Dirks, Tim. 1999. "Cat on a Hot Tin Roof (1958)." Filmsite Movie Review, AMC Filmsite. www.filmsite.org/cato.html.

———. 2013. "All-Time Box Office Top 100." AMC Filmsite. www.filmsite.org/boxoffice.html.

Dyson, Michael Eric. 1997. *Race Rules: Navigating the Color Line*. New York, NY: Vintage Books.

Eaklor, Vicki L. 2011. *Queer America: A People's GLBT History of the United States*. New York: New Press.

Ebert, Roger. 1994a. "Go Fish." *Chicago Sun-Times*, July 1.

———. 1994b. "Philadelphia." *Chicago Sun-Times*, January 14.

———. 2008. "Milk." *Chicago Sun Times*, November 24.

Edwards, Lisa. 1998. "A Simple Matter of Justice." Quoted in "Judaism," by Saul M. Olyan, in *Sexual Orientation and Human Rights in American Religious Discourse*, ed. Saul M. Olyan and Martha C. Nussbaum, 36. New York: Oxford University Press.

Epstein, Jeffrey. 1999. "Prime Time for Gay Youth (Gay Characters on Television)." *Advocate*, April 27, 4–6.

Epstein, Robert, and Jeffrey Friedman, dirs. 1995. *The Celluloid Closet*. New York: Sony Pictures Classics. Film.

Faderman, Lillian. 1991. *Odd Girls and Twilight Lovers: A History of Lesbian Life in Twentieth-Century America*. New York: Columbia University Press.

Fekadu, Mesfin. 2012. "Hip-Hop's Anti-Gay Tone Shifting After Frank Ocean's Coming Out." *Huffington Post*, July 24. www.huffingtonpost.com/2012/08/23/hip-hops-anti-gay-tone-frank-ocean_n_1824494.html.

Feinberg, Leslie. 2005. "Mattachine: Unmasking a 'Masked People.'" *Workers World*, June 13. www.workers.org/2005/us/lavender-red-38/.

Fletcher, Garth, Jeffry A. Simpson, Lorne Campbell, and Nickola Overall. 2013. *The Science of Intimate Relationships*. West Sussex, UK: Wiley-Blackwell.

Flick, Larry. 1994a. "Labels Broaden Social Perspectives: Stonewall 25 and Gay Games Major Factors." *Billboard*, June 18.

———. 1994b. "Major Labels Courting Gay, Lesbian Market." *Billboard*, July 30.

Gallo, Marcia M. 2005. "Winds of Change: The Daughters of Bilitis and Lesbian Organizing." Gerber/Hart Library: News and Events. www.gerberhart.org/dob.html.

Gagnon, Robert A. J., and Dan O. Via. 2003. *Homosexuality and the Bible: Two Views*. Minneapolis, MN: Augsburg Fortress.

Gates, Gary J. 2011. "Family Formation and Raising Children Among Same-Sex Couples." *Family Focus* FF51 (Winter).

Gilreath, Shannon. 2011. *The End of Straight Supremacy: Realizing Gay Liberation*. New York: Cambridge University Press.

GLAAD. 2012. "Where We Are on TV: 2012–2013 Season." Los Angeles: GLAAD. www.glaad.org/files/whereweareontv12.pdf.

———. 2013. "GLAAD Media Reference Guide—Lesbian, Gay, Bisexual Glossary of Terms." Los Angeles: GLAAD. www.glaad.org/reference/lgb.

Goldstein, Richard. 1984. "Go the Way Your Blood Beats: An Interview with James Baldwin." *Village Voice*, June 26.

Gray, Emily. 2011. "What Is Heteronormativity?" Gender and Education Association, March 26. www
.genderandeducation.com/issues/what-is-heteronormativity/.

Greene, Beth. 1998. "The Institution of Woman-Marriage in Africa: A Cross-Cultural Analysis." *Eth-nology* 37, no. 4 (Autumn): 395–412.

Guthmann, Edward. 1999. "'70s Gay Film Has Low Esteem/'Boys' Attitude Seems Dated." *San Francisco Chronicle*, January 15, 7.

Hampp, Andrew. 2012. "Why The Wanted Play Gay Clubs: Marketing, Music and the LGBT Community's Mainstream Music Clout." Billboardbiz.com, June 12. www.billboard.com/biz/articles/news/touring/1093688/why-the-wanted-play-gay-clubs-marketing-music-and-the-lgbt.

Hiller, Jordan. 2010. "2010 Year-End Movie Blow-Out—Part I." Bangitout.com, December 30.

Hirshman, Linda. 2012. *Victory: The Triumphant Gay Revolution*. New York: Harper.

Holleran, Andrew. 2006. "The Magic Mountain." *Gay and Lesbian Review Worldwide* 13, no. 2: 12, 15.

Holmen, Nicole. 2010. "Examining Greek Pederastic Relationships." *Student Pulse—The International Student Journal* 2, no. 2. www.studentpulse.com/articles/175/examining-greek-pederastic-relationships.

Hultberg, Jesse. 1996. "'Out' Music's Slow Mainstream Inroads." *Billboard*, May 4, 3–6.

Human Rights Campaign. 2013. "Stances of Faiths on LGBT Issues: Islam." www.hrc.org/resources/entry/stances-of-faiths-on-lgbt-issues-islam.

Hurewitz, Daniel. 2004. "Sexuality Scholarship as a Foundation for Change: *Lawrence v. Texas* and the Impact of the Historians' Brief." *Health and Human Rights* 7, no. 2: 205–216.

Ira, Stephen. 2012. "LGBTQI Week: Transamerica." Bitch Flicks, June 27. www.btchflcks.com/2012/06/lgbtqi-week-transamerica.html.

Jagose, Annamarie Rustom. 1996. *Queer Theory*. Carlton South, Victoria, Australia: Melbourne University Press.

Jones, Robert P., Daniel Cox, and Elizabeth Cook. 2011. *Generations at Odds: The Millennial Generation and the Future of Gay and Lesbian Rights*. Washington, DC: Public Religion Research Institute.

Kahn, Yoel H. 1989. "Judaism and Homosexuality: The Traditionalist/Progressive Debate." In *Homosexuality and Religion*, ed. Richard Hasbany, 59–66. New York: Harrington Park.

Kaleem, Jaweed. 2012. "Presbyterian Church Will Start Ordaining Gay Clergy." *Huffington Post*, July 8. www.huffingtonpost.com/2011/07/08/presbyterian-church-ordain-gay-clergy_n_893210.html.

Katz, Joseph Ned. 1995. *The Invention of Heterosexuality*. New York: Dutton.

Kempley, Rita. 1994a. "*Go Fish* (NR)." *Washington Post*, July 2. www.washingtonpost.com/wp-srv/style/longterm/movies/videos/gofishnrkempley_a0a472.htm.

———. 1994b. "*Philadelphia* (R)." *Washington Post*, January 14. www.washingtonpost.com/wp-srv/style/longterm/movies/videos/philadelphiarkempley_a0a3ff.htm.

Klemm, Michael, D. 1999. "Death Be Not Proud." CinemaQueer.com. http://cinemaqueer.com/review%20pages/longtime.html.

Kugle, Scott Siraj al-Haqq. 2010. *Homosexuality in Islam: Critical Reflection on Gay, Lesbian, and Transgender Muslims*. London: Oneworld Publications.

Liberty Education Forum. 2008. *Is It a Choice? The Science of Sexual Orientation*. Washington, DC: Liberty Education Forum. http://libertyeducationforum.org/docs/whitepapers/is_it_a_choice_white_paper.pdf.

Lose, David. 2011. "What Does the Bible Really Say About Homosexuality?" *HuffPost Religion*, October 10. www.huffingtonpost.com/david-lose/what-does-the-bible-reall_b_990444.html.

Miller, Neil. 1995. *Out of the Past: Gay and Lesbian History from 1869 to the Present*. New York: Vintage Books.

Mitchell, Martin, and Charlie Howarth. 2009. *Trans Research Review*. Research Report 27 (Autumn). Manchester, UK: Equality and Human Rights Commission Research. www.equalityhumanrights.com/uploaded_files/research/trans_research_review_rep27.pdf.

Mustanski, Brian S., Michael G. DuPree, Caroline M. Nievergelt, Sven Bocklandt, Nicholas J. Schork, and Dean H. Hamer. 2005. "A Genomewide Scan of Male Sexual Orientation." *Human Genetics* 116: 272–278.

Nanda, Serena. 1999. *Neither Man nor Woman: The Hijras of India*. 2nd ed. Belmont, CA: Wadsworth Press.

Natale, Richard. 1998. "Will Power." *Advocate*, September 15, 1–3.

National Council of Churches (NCC). 2010. "Clergy and Faith Leaders Say, 'No More Bullying!'" News release, October 19. www.ncccusa.org/news/101019nomorebullying.html.

Nugent, Robert, and Jeannine Gramick. 1989. "Homosexuality: Protestant, Catholic, and Jewish Issues: A Fishbone Tale." In *Homosexuality and Religion*, ed. Richard Hasbany, 19–28. New York: Harrington Park.

Olyan, Saul M. 1998. "Judaism." In *Sexual Orientation and Human Rights in American Religious Discourse*, ed. Saul M. Olyan and Martha C. Nussbaum. New York: Oxford University Press.

Olyan, Saul M., and Martha C. Nussbaum, eds. 1998. *Sexual Orientation and Human Rights in American Religious Discourse*. New York: Oxford University Press.

Pela, Robert L. 1997. "Disney Steps Out." *Advocate*, April 29, 3.

Pettitt, Jessica, and Owen Marciano. 2006. "Transamerica: A Journey Worth Taking?" *GLBT Campus Matters* 2, no. 1 (January). www.jessicapettitt.com/images/TransAmerica_A_Journey.pdf.

Pew Research Center for People and the Press. 2012. "Behind Gay Marriage Momentum, Regional Gaps Persist." Pew Research Center, November 9. www.people-press.org/2012/11/09/behind-gay -marriage-momentum-regional-gaps-persist/.

Pickett, Brent. 2011. "Homosexuality." In *The Stanford Encyclopedia of Philosophy*, ed. Edward N. Zalla. Stanford: Stanford University. http://plato.stanford.edu/archives/spr2011/entries/homosexuality/.

Plaskow, Judith. 1998. "Sexual Orientation and Human Rights: A Progressive Jewish Perspective." In *Sexual Orientation and Human Rights in American Religious Discourse*, ed. Saul M. Olyan and Martha C. Nussbaum, 29–45. New York: Oxford University Press.

Potok, Mark. 2010. "Anti-Gay Hate Crimes: Doing the Math." *Intelligence Report* (Southern Poverty Law Center), no. 140 (Winter).

Rahman, Qazi. 2008. "Sexual Orientation, Genetics and Environmental Factors." *Medical News Today*, June 30. www.medicalnewstoday.com/releases/113259.php.

Reuters. 2013. "Supreme Court Concludes Arguments on Marriage Law." *Chicago Tribune*, March 27.

Russo, Vito. 1987. *The Celluloid Closet: Homosexuality in the Movies*. Rev. ed. New York: Harper & Row.

Saad, Lydia. 2010. "Americans Acceptance of Gay Relations Crosses 50% Threshold." Gallup Politics, May 25. www.gallup.com/poll/135764/americans-acceptance-gay-relations-crosses-threshold .aspx.

———. 2013. "In U.S., 52% Back Law to Legalize Gay Marriage in 50 States." Gallup Politics, July 29. www.gallup.com/poll/163730/back-law-legalize-gay-marriage-states.aspx.

Sanders, Cheryl J. 1998. "Sexual Orientation and Human Rights Discourse in the African American Churches." In *Sexual Orientation and Human Rights in American Religious Discourse*, ed. Saul M. Olyan and Martha C. Nussbaum, 178–184. New York: Oxford University Press.

Scott, A.O. 2005. "A Complex Metamorphosis of the Most Fundamental Sort." *New York Times*. December 2. http://nytimes.com/2005/12/02/movies/02trans.html?_r=0.

Shilts, Randy. 1987. *And the Band Played On*. New York: St. Martin's Press.

Shore, John. 2012. "The Best Case for the Bible Not Condemning Homosexuality." *HuffPost Religion*, April 3. www.huffingtonpost.com/john-shore/the-best-case-for-the-bible-not-condemning -homosexuality_b_1396345.html.

Smith, Barbara. 1993. "Homophobia: Why Bring It Up?" In *The Lesbian and Gay Studies Reader*, ed. Henry Abelove, Michele A. Barale, and David M. Halperin. New York: Routledge.

Smith, Tom W. 2011. *Public Attitudes Toward Homosexuality*. Report, September. Chicago: National Opinion Research Center (NORC) at the University of Chicago.

Stackhouse, Max L. 1998. "The Prophetic Stand of the Ecumenical Churches on Homosexuality." In *Sexual Orientation and Human Rights in American Religious Discourse*, ed. Saul M. Olyan and Martha C. Nussbaum, 119–133. New York: Oxford University Press.

Stone, Alby. 2003. *Explore Shamanism*. Avebury, UK: Explore Books.

Tamagne, Florence. 2004. *A History of Homosexuality in Europe Volume I: Berlin, London, Paris, 1919–1939*. New York: Algora.

Thomas, Anthony. 2008. "The House the Kids Built: The Gay Black Imprint on American Dance Music." History Is Made at Night: The Politics of Dancing and Musicking, April 21. http://history-is-made -at-night.blogspot.com/2008/04/expect-to-read-lot-this-year-about-20th.html.

Thompson, Cooper. 1992. "Heterosexual in a Homophobic World." In *Homophobia: How We All Pay the Price*, ed. Warren J. Blumenfeld, 241–258. Boston: Beacon.

Tuchman, Gaye. 1978. "The Symbolic Annihilation of Women by the Mass Media." In *Hearth and Home: Images of Women in the Mass Media*, ed. Gaye Tuchman, Arlene Kaplan Daniels, and James Benet. New York: Oxford University Press.

Twiss, Sumner B. 1998. "Introduction to Roman Catholic Perspectives on Sexual Orientation, Human Rights, and Public Policy." In *Sexual Orientation and Human Rights in American Religious Discourse*, ed. Saul M. Olyan and Martha C. Nussbaum, 57–62. New York: Oxford University Press.

UCC General Synod. 2011. "Supporting International Human Rights Related to Sexual Orientation and Gender Identity." A Resolution of Witness; Adopted by the 28th General Synod of the United Church of Christ, July 2011, Tampa, Florida.

Wake, Paul, and Simon Malpas, eds. 2006. *The Routledge Companion to Critical Theory*. New York: Taylor and Francis,.

Walters, Barry. 1997a. "Rocking the Gay Bandwagon." *Advocate*, November 25, 62.

———. 1997b. "Rock's Queer Evolution." *Advocate*, December 9, 24.

Weiss, Andrea. 1992. *Vampires and Violets: Lesbians in Film*. New York: Penguin.

Weiss, Jillian T. 2008. "Heteronormativity." In *International Encyclopedia of the Social Sciences*, 2nd ed., ed. W.A. Darity Jr. Detroit: Macmillan Reference.

Williams, Walter L. 1986. *The Spirit and the Flesh: Sexual Diversity in American Indian Culture*. Boston: Beacon Press.

Woodhouse, Joe, and Karina Roberts. 2013. "Bisexuality: Some Questions Answered." Gay Lesbian Bisexual & Transgender Resource Center; http://glbtss.colostate.edu/bisexuality-questions -answered.

Acknowledgments

Linda

I completed the first version of *Media Messages* in 1999, and it was published in 2000. So many things about media have changed since that time. In the first edition, there was no mention of reality television programs, social media, or "screen time." Imagine, if you can, a world without Twitter or *American Idol* or smartphones that serve as media platforms; a world where, if you mentioned Facebook, most people would say, "What?" So much change.

Sometime around 2004 or 2005, colleagues began to gently nudge me toward writing a second edition. The media I used as examples in the first edition were just starting to be outdated, and instructors who used *Media Messages* as a textbook were beginning to have to supplement the media and even the demographic information. So, in 2005, I started to get serious about a new edition and contacted M.E. Sharpe. As I recall, I thought that writing a second edition would be a slam dunk and cavalierly told my editor at the time that I would get the manuscript to her within a year. I am forever grateful to Lynn Taylor for her support in the early development of the second edition and her flexibility with deadlines when I experienced multiple crises in my life over the next several years.

I met two close friends, Mike Savage and Aliah Mubarak Tharpe, through our collective activism and community organizing. We worked alongside low-income folks and people of color, trying to create the kind of institutional changes that we believed could empower them to make their lives better—and it actually worked sometimes. Along the way, my life was made better by getting to know so many of the people I met through that work and through my extraordinary friendships with both Mike and Aliah.

On the surface, we couldn't have been more different. Mike was a white, Catholic, out gay man who grew up in a small town in rural Illinois, lived in a lay Catholic community when I first met him, and studied to be a Jesuit priest for a brief time. Aliah was an African American woman who grew up in the central city of St. Louis in a neighborhood that was primarily black. Aliah was deeply committed to a faith community in the Muslim tradition and to figuring out how to exert her leadership to make the world a better place. Mike and Aliah taught me so much about human diversity in the way that they lived their lives and in our deep, intimate, and irreverent conversations about everything from racism and homophobia to movies and sex. They both died way too early, each barely fifty. I am grateful that they were both in my life, even for a short time, because

487

I learned so much from each of them about racism and heterosexism and the way these concepts are internalized, as well as about cross-cultural love of all sorts, and because Aliah and Mike were among the few people in my life who could make me laugh that kind of laugh where your stomach hurts and you become worried about the involuntary release of bodily fluids.

In 2008, my beautiful twenty-two-year-old daughter, Dora Magrath, died suddenly. As young as she was, Dora had a firm and deep emotional understanding and commitment to diversity in her personal relationships, in her work as a singer and songwriter, and in her college studies. She had the most extraordinary way of being fully present with literally hundreds of people from all over the world of different races and cultures and ages. When she died, close to 1,000 people came to her funeral from all over the country, many of whom were friends from faraway places. People who were unable to travel to the funeral sent notes and cards and wrote poems and songs and designed dance choreography and dance concerts they had written for and dedicated to Dora. Months and even years later, they came to visit me because they knew how close Dora and I were, and they wanted to share their love for Dora with me. They were from Massachusetts, Nevada, California, Rhode Island, and Missouri. They were from the elite, private high school with extraordinary riches and resources that she attended for two years and from the urban, multiracial, economically strapped high school that she also attended for two years. There were friends she met in high school and college who were from Israel, Nigeria, Sri Lanka, Bangladesh, Palestine, and Pakistan. Dora lived and understood human diversity from a deep place inside her. Even as a young girl, she often cried bitterly about how unfair life was to some people who didn't have the money or support they needed or enough love and resources to feel good enough about themselves to do well in the world. Thank you, Dora. Your life was too short, but you were and continue to be one of my greatest teachers and inspirations.

I offer much gratitude and love to my dear friends Rachel Sierra and Laurie Smith. Deep thanks to both Rachel and Laurie for hanging in there with me, literally and figuratively through thick and thin, loving me through the toughest times when my absorption in my own life must have been, and still is at times, exasperating. Thanks to Laurie for traveling with me on my most recent visit to Israel and Palestine, participating fully in my work there, and understanding and sharing my friendship and deep love for human rights activists, on both sides of the wall, who have the brilliant audacity to have hope, vision, and strategies that they act upon, seeking a way to live together peacefully. Thanks to Rachel for talking with me (or should I say listening to me talk?) endlessly about my life and *Media Messages* and for sharing my excitement about the new edition, auditioning half-formed ideas, and as always, giving me her unabridged, uncensored response. I also thank Rachel for vetting the first draft of the section "Latinas/Latinos in Entertainment Media," giving me useful feedback and confirming that we were on target about race and ethnicity. Thanks to both Laurie and Rachel for living their lives with authenticity, integrity, ability, and an instinctive commitment to equity and fairness, and for their unique styles, which are quite different from each other but nevertheless naturally infuse kindness and community in so much of what they do.

I give thanks to my son, Alex Magrath, who, throughout multiple setbacks to my health and stamina, periodic medical leaves, and the challenges of teaching full-time while researching and writing the second edition of *Media Messages*, reminded me to take care of myself and to remember that I have to sleep. Alex's courage and tenacity in the face of grave difficulties touches my heart and inspires me when my own tenacity wears thin.

I also give deep thanks to my mom and dad, both the children of Russian Jewish immigrants. I thank my late mother, Evelyn Holtzman, for passing on the recipes and secrets to making some of the cultural marvels of traditional Jewish cooking; she could make a tender brisket, good solid matzo balls, and camish (also known as Mandel) bread like no one else. Although my parents were not particularly observant along traditional religious lines, we always celebrated Jewish holidays with our extended family with great vigor and volume, especially when the event included food. (Come to think of it, other than the fast on Yom Kippur, most Jewish events come with food, and even on Yom Kippur, there are celebrations with food before and after the fast.) I thank my father, Donald "Poppy" Holtzman, who is still kicking strong, albeit from his wheelchair, at eighty-seven. I am grateful that he went first with me and later Dora, at ten, when she was interested and old enough to join us, to temple for the Kol Nidre service of Yom Kippur that the three of us loved. And I thank him for special times, such as the late afternoon that we left memorial services to say Kaddish for my mom and broke the fast at Seamus McDaniels, a restaurant with an Irish name owned by Italian friends that serves classic American food. Talk about diversity.

I offer tender appreciation and love for my paternal grandmother, Dora Holtzman, a Russian Jewish immigrant with a heavy Yiddish accent and a goodness that you could sense a mile away. She never learned to drive but was at home in taxicabs and would often take me to lunch at the restaurant of one of the local department stores. Everything she cooked and baked was from scratch and had a strong Eastern European and/or Jewish tradition. She prepared homemade gefilte fish—elongated patties of chilled ground buffalo fish and carp—to be eaten with horseradish on Rosh Hashanah and Passover. She baked homemade pies and cakes and Jewish delicacies of camish bread, poppy seed cookies, and strudel. Her tradition of baking and cooking, as well as enjoying eating, was passed on to me. I am hopeful that I also inherited just a small part of her shining goodness and kindness to so many people.

I want to thank two of my most brilliant and gracious mentors: Ernest Calloway and George Gerbner. I met the late Ernest Calloway shortly after I became the director of a community organization in the central city of St. Louis. Founded and funded by the Campaign for Human Development to develop jobs, housing, and other resources in the African American community, the organization was committed to providing training and technical assistance to empower low-income people and community groups to develop the skills to access government resources that were intended for low- and moderate-income people but often unethically and, most likely, illegally diverted to wealthier neighborhoods and projects. Calloway (everyone called him by his last name) would introduce me to the movers and shakers in the black community by saying "Here's an organization with Catholic money working in the black community, and they go and hire a nice

Jewish girl as their director." Calloway was seventy-eight years old when I met him, an extraordinary intellectual with a history as a socialist and a researcher for the Teamsters Union. As a young man, he had been a conscientious objector in World War II. His strong objection was to the official and de facto Jim Crow rules in the military that totally isolated, segregated, and failed to appreciate the dedication and sacrifice of black soldiers. Despite our age difference, I think I was half in love with Calloway for his extraordinary commitment to the black community, his belief in me, and his seal of approval for the integrity and credibility of my work in the community, and for managing somehow to combine an Old World chivalry with a fierce support of feminism.

I also am grateful to the late George Gerbner, dean emeritus of the Annenberg School of Communication at the University of Pennsylvania. I first met George on paper as I read his research about the distorted media images of race, gender, class, and age; the homogeneous messages they conveyed; and the impact these messages had on heavy media users. In my mid-thirties, with two toddlers and a job as an adjunct professor in St. Louis, I sent George an audacious letter telling him how much I admired his work and wanted to be him when I grew up, but that, for now, I wanted to learn from him. I mentioned that my job and my family responsibilities made it impossible for me to move to Philadelphia. This was in the very early days of e-mail. Most universities did not yet have e-mail and the main commercial service available was AOL. George told me to get AOL set up right away. He came to St. Louis and stayed with my family as we met with the president and vice president of Webster University to plan the first international convention of his new organization, the Cultural Environment Movement. I co-coordinated this conference, which was George's dream. In turn, he worked with Webster administrators to figure out a way that he could teach me two individualized courses long-distance and online, and he eventually mentored my master's thesis. Like Calloway, George was in his late seventies when I met him and an icon in the field of communication. My life and my work in media and diversity were made richer and more exciting through my work with George. I was delighted when he offered to write a rave review for the back cover of the first edition of *Media Messages*.

My gratitude, admiration, and respect go to the people I have met who are involved in human rights work in Israel and Palestine. These folks are strong advocates of peaceful coexistence and cooperation among Israelis and Palestinians, an end to Israel's occupation of the West Bank, and curtailing the development of Israeli settlements. They are committed to letting the Western press know about repressive and oppressive events, actions, and policies that many of us in the Western Hemisphere never hear about if we are only exposed to U.S. media. Many of these individuals and families have been involved in the movement for fundamental change: equity for Palestinians who are Israeli citizens and for those who have lived in the occupied territory for forty-plus years. They are role models for embracing difference and not turning each other into the personified enemy or the "other."

My friends in Neve Shalom Wahat Salam, about halfway between Jerusalem and Tel Aviv, a thirty-year-old community made up of 50 percent Jewish Israeli citizens and 50 percent Arab and Palestinian citizens, are struggling with the challenges of creating a bicultural, multiethnic, and multireligious community. I wish to express my gratitude to Mikal and Bob and to Rita, and my deep sadness at the sudden accidental death of Ahmad Hijazi (director of the Adult School for Peace at Wahat Salam) and his young son Adam. My gratitude, affection, and highest respect also go out to Hannah and Dalia for their many decades of work for peace and for the rights of Israeli and Palestinian women. And on the other side of the wall, I send Kadra Zreneh my gratitude, respect, admiration, and love. She has an extraordinary ability to teach her own children, as well as tourists visiting Bethlehem in the West Bank, what it has been like to live in an occupied land under siege and war for so long. Kadra's oldest son, Johnny, has learned well from his mother and at age thirty refers to me as his Jewish mother. I am grateful for Johnny's friendship and how much we have learned from each other about human diversity. Although I have formally been his teacher, informally he has taught me as much as or more than I have taught him. I have so much gratitude for the work that many individuals have done in the West Bank to end the occupation and in the meantime to make life livable.

Since I began this seemingly endless stop/start project to complete the second edition of *Media Messages*, I have had the support and guidance of four editors. Each of them has understood and valued the content of the second edition and provided useful feedback on my approach to the book as well as encouragement for the new features and content of the second edition. In their own individual ways, each of them has been extraordinarily kind and patient with the personal loss in my life and the periodic health challenges I have experienced that have often interfered with my ability to complete the manuscript. Many thanks to Lynn Taylor and Gwen Cullen for their belief in *Media Messages*, their confidence that I would finish the manuscript, and their unwavering support. A special thanks to Patricia Kolb, vice president and editorial director of M.E. Sharpe, who stepped in to fill a gap between editors and was especially helpful in working out some complicated details on the business end of the project. During the final stages of writing the second edition, Suzanne Phelps Chambers has been editor and an integral part of the team. Suzanne entered the project with a keen understanding and appreciation for *Media Messag*es and has been Leon's and my guide to the creative and business side of the endeavor; a source of endless knowledge, information, and ideas; and a partner in her passionate support for our goals to teach and learn about media and diversity in a way that combines challenges and encouragement in both intellectual rigor and personal reflection and growth.

Thanks to Dana Petrechko. A former student, while waiting impatiently to begin graduate school, she volunteered her time to gather some excellent research in the early stages of the reworking of Chapter 6.

My gratitude to J. Farand, whom I know as Joseph, who began as a student in my Media Research class and ended up with a research and writing credit for *Media Messages* soon after graduation. Joseph's work in the development of the second edition was invaluable, as were the frequent long talks we had about diversity, particularly about issues related to racism and heterosexism. While we didn't always see things the same way, we respected our very different backgrounds and how they influenced the different perspectives we had on some of the manifestations of oppression. And Joseph's talent as a graphic artist helped to update and modernize some of the figures you will see in Chapter 1.

Finally, my deepest gratitude goes to coauthor and friend Leon Sharpe. Leon and I have worked together for many years as facilitators in antiracism work, most frequently with school administrators and teachers. I have been in awe of his brilliance as a thinker and writer; his thoughtfulness about the concepts, theories, and practical manifestation of human diversity; and the depth of his authenticity, thoughtfulness, intelligence, and warmth that helps students, participants in antiracism training, and colleagues remain open to hearing his affirmation of their ideas, as well as his well-considered and respectful disagreement and challenges. Without Leon's intense involvement in finishing the second edition, I seriously wonder if *Media Messages* would have been like the children's song, "This is a song that never ends . . ."

I am grateful for the many conversations that Leon and I have had about our approach to various topics of human diversity and the ease with which we give and take review, feedback, and constructive suggestions for revisions on the research and writing for which we have each had primary responsibility. I know that with Leon's keen intelligence and wisdom, *Media Messages* has become a far better book. Both literally and figuratively, I doubt that I could have done this important work without him.

Leon

It has been an honor and a pleasure to work with my friend and colleague, Linda Holtzman, on the second edition of *Media Messages*. In addition to her immeasurable gifts as a teacher, trainer, and writer, I continue to be amazed by her analytical insight, her attention to detail, and her indefatigable energy. Linda's capacity for joy in the face of adversity is boundless, and her easy sense of humor, both profound and profane, has kept this project moving forward through its most challenging times.

I also join Linda in acknowledging the wonderful folks at M.E. Sharpe. Thanks to Patricia Kolb for welcoming me aboard and for making me feel like a part of the team right away. Many thanks as well to our editor, Suzanne Phelps Chambers, for her expertise, experience, and skillful guiding hand.

I am appreciative of the support of my colleagues on the faculty and staff of the School of Communications at Webster University, and most especially my students—future filmmakers, scriptwriters, producers, performers, audio engineers, video game designers, journalists, photographers, broadcasters, advertisers—shapers of images, sounds, and ideas. Their many questions, arguments, disagreements, challenges, and discoveries helped to write this book.

I also wish to thank the dedicated cadre of faculty, staff, students, and alums at the University of Missouri–St. Louis College of Education, who are engaged in some incredible scholarship and practice in the interest of advancing the public's understanding of issues pertaining to social justice, educational equity, and global human rights. I offer a special word of appreciation to my dissertation advisor, Dr. Matthew Davis, who has been an invaluable mentor and guide to me and countless others in that work.

Beyond that, I would simply like to express the deepest love and gratitude for my family: My father, Leon Sharpe Sr., who always encouraged me to pursue my dreams and stand up for my ideals, and my mother, Florence Elizabeth Sharpe, who taught me the meaning of unconditional love by demonstrating it every day. Though my parents are both now deceased, they continue to be a part of me and of everything I do.

My partner, Traci, has been there with me and for me, embracing me with her loving spirit and reminding me, always, to keep the faith. Also, Kortni, HB, and Tyler, give me hope for a bright tomorrow. My brother, Alan Sharpe, an insightful and prolific playwright with a fierce, creative mind, and my sister, Cheryl Sharpe, a brilliant, versatile, and inventive business leader with an abundance of warmth, wisdom, and personal power—the two of them have always been my role models.

Then, there are my children: my son, Orlando Sharpe, my daughter-in-law, Gail Rogers Sharpe, and my oldest grandson, Sincere Sharpe; my daughter, Kai Morrow, my son-in-law, James Morrow, my granddaughters, Aislyn Jai Morrow and London Page Morrow, and my youngest grandson, J.T. Morrow. All of you fill me with inexpressible pride. Whenever I falter or get stuck, I can close my eyes and think of my children, their spouses, my four amazing grandkids, and all the things they have accomplished and are accomplishing with their lives, and I immediately grow inspired.

I have also benefited from being a member of an extraordinary extended family of aunts, uncles, cousins, nieces, nephews, and an array of loving kin. Individually and collectively, they have blessed me with the comfort of knowing that my roots go deep, my legacy is strong, and I am forever connected to something far greater than myself.

Index

Note: Page numbers with *f* indicate figures; *mp* indicates media photographs; *t* indicates tables.

About the Authors

Linda Holtzman, professor emeritus at Webster University in St. Louis and a teacher for twenty-five years, is a leader in media and diversity analysis and program development. As a weekly guest on the St. Louis NBC affiliate, she reviewed diversity messages in film and television and received grants for her work in the United States, Israel, and Palestine, analyzing media misinformation, stereotypes, and human rights activism. She serves as an antiracism facilitator for local and national organizations and school districts and has received numerous awards for her work, including the Martin Luther King Award presented personally by Coretta Scott King.

Leon Sharpe is an adjunct professor at the Webster University School of Communications, where he teaches courses that examine the influence of cinema in reinforcing patterns of social power. His research interests include Africana history and literature, critical race theory, transformational learning, and the structural role of mass media in upholding systemic inequities. He is also founder and principal of The Praxis Group, a strategic consulting firm that specializes in building organizational capacity, facilitating leadership development, managing institutional change, and leveraging workforce diversity. He has conducted executive training sessions and implemented performance improvement programs for corporations, foundations, universities, and school districts throughout the United States.

Joseph Farand Gardner, also known as J. Owl Farand, is a writer and black media analyst for Owl's Asylum (www.owlasylum.net), a collection of essays and personal writings regarding U.S. black media, social, and political experiences. He also operates the design agency J. Farand LLC. Gardner earned an associate's degree in website development at Ranken Technical College in St. Louis and graduated from Webster University, where he earned a bachelor of arts degree in media communications and served as a research assistant to Professor Linda Holtzman.